The Church Effeminate

THE CHURCH Effeminate

AND

OTHER ESSAYS

John W. Robbins
Editor

The Trinity Foundation

Cover: Master of the Saint Lucy Legend
(Bruges, active *c.* 1480-1510)
Mary, Queen of Heaven.
National Gallery of Art, Washington, D.C.
Samuel H. Kress Collection.
Used by permission.

The Church Effeminate and Other Essays
Copyright © 2001 John W. Robbins
Published by The Trinity Foundation
www.trinityfoundation.org
Printed in the United States of America
ISBN: 0-940931-54-0

To our friends at
Hobbs Presbyterian Church and
Midway Presbyterian Church,
members together of the
eternal and indestructible
church of Jesus Christ

Contents

7

CONTENTS

Introduction

ONE OF THE achievements of the Reformation in the sixteenth century was the renovation of existing churches and the institution of new churches to make them conform more closely to the Scriptural model. This was done through the preaching of the Gospel, which had been suppressed for a millennium by the Roman Church-State. The recovery of the Gospel, Luther explained, restored the Christian church:

> The Gospel is before bread and baptism the unique, most certain, and noblest symbol of the church because through the Gospel alone the church is conceived, formed, nourished, generated, instructed, fed, clothed, adorned, strengthened, armed, and preserved – in short, the whole life and substance of the church is in the Word of God.... As Christ says, "Man lives by every word that proceeds from the mouth of God...." [1]
>
> These are the true marks whereby one can really recognize the kingdom of the Lord Christ and the Christian church: Namely, wherever this sceptre is, that is, the office of the preaching of the Gospel, borne by the apostles into the world and received from them by us. Where it is present and maintained, there the Christian church and the kingdom of Christ surely exists, no matter how small or negligible the number of the flock. [2]

With the Gospel, a church can be minuscule, and still be a church. Without the Gospel, there can be no church at all, no matter how large.

> People call that the Christian church which is not the Christian church, and that which is the Christian church is often not acknowledged as such.... [3] Whenever you hear or see this Word preached, believed, professed, and lived, do not doubt that the true *ecclesia sancta catholica*, a

---

1. *D. Martin Luthers Werke*, Weimar, 1883-, 7, 721.
2. *Luther's Works*, St. Louis and Philadelphia, 1955, 13, 272.
3. *Luther's Works*, 23, 285.

Christian holy people, must be there, even though their number is very small.

[W]here the Gospel is absent and human teachings rule, there no Christians live but only pagans, no matter how numerous they are and how holy and upright their life may be.[4] [T]he church is not a people that should be judged on the basis of large numbers, of size, of wisdom, of power, of wealth, of prestige, of succession, of office, etc.[5]

Calvin expanded on Luther's doctrine. In the "Prefatory Address to King Francis I of France" in his *Institutes of the Christian Religion*, Calvin wrote:

Surely the church of Christ has lived and will live so long as Christ reigns at the right hand of his Father. It is sustained by his hand; defended by his protection; and is kept safe through his power. For he will surely accomplish what he once promised: that he will be present with his own even to the end of the world. Against this church we now have no quarrel. For, of one accord with all believing folk, we worship and adore one God, and Christ the Lord, as he has always been adored by all godly men. But they stray very far from the truth when they do not recognize the church unless they see it with their very eyes, and try to keep it within limits to which it cannot at all be confined.

Our controversy turns on these hinges: First, they [the opponents of the Reformers, the Roman Catholics] contend that the form of the church is always apparent and observable. Secondly, they set this form in the see of the Roman Church and its hierarchy. We, on the contrary, affirm that the church can exist without any visible appearance, and that its appearance is not contained within that outward magnificence which they foolishly admire. Rather, it has quite another mark: namely, the pure preaching of God's Word and the lawful administration of the sacraments. They rage if the church cannot always be pointed to with the finger. But among the Jewish people how often was it so deformed that no semblance of it remained? What form do we think it displayed when Elijah complained that he alone was left? How long after Christ's coming was it hidden without form? How often has it since that time been so oppressed by wars, seditions, and heresies that it did not shine forth at all? If they lived at that time, would they have believed that any church existed? But Elijah heard that there still remained seven thousand men who had not bowed the knee before Ba'al. And we must not doubt that

4. *Luther's Works*, 39, 305.
5. *Luther's Works*, 4, 53.

Christ has reigned on Earth ever since he ascended into Heaven. But if believers had then required some visible form, would they not have straightway lost courage? Indeed, Hilary considered it a great vice in his day that, being occupied with foolish reverence for the episcopal dignity, men did not realize what a deadly hydra lurked under such a mask. For he speaks in this way: "One thing I admonish you, beware of Antichrist. It is wrong that a love of walls has seized you; wrong that you venerate the church of God in roofs and buildings; wrong that beneath these you introduce the name of peace. Is there any doubt that Antichrist will have his seat in them? To my mind, mountains, woods, lakes, prisons, and chasms are safer. For either abiding in or cast into them, the prophets prophesied."

Yet what does the world today venerate in its horned bishops but to imagine those whom it sees presiding over renowned cities to be holy prelates of religion? Away, therefore, with such a foolish appraisement! Rather, since the Lord alone "knows who are his," let us leave to him the fact that he sometimes removes from men's sight the external signs by which the church is known. That is, I confess, a dreadful visitation of God upon the Earth. But if men's impiety deserves it, why do we strive to oppose God's just vengeance? In such a way the Lord of old punished men's ingratitude. For, because they had refused to obey his truth and had extinguished his light, he allowed their blinded senses to be both deluded by foolish lies and plunged into profound darkness, so that no form of the true church remained. Meanwhile, he preserved his own children from extinction, though they are scattered and hidden in the midst of these errors and darkness. And this is no marvel; for he knew how to preserve them in the confusion of Babylon, and in the flame of the fiery furnace.[6]

In those ages and regions when and where the Word of God is suppressed, the church has disappeared from view. But when the Holy Spirit once again sent forth preachers of the Word, the church was made visible, called forth by the power of the Word of God. In that Word, that is, in the Scriptures, which conceived, created, and constituted the church, there are directives given for the government of the churches. Those directives include the purpose and function of the church, its officers and constitution, warnings to both officers and members about false doctrines and false teachers, the proper administration of baptism

6. John Calvin, *Institutes of the Christian Religion*, John T. McNeill, editor. Philadelphia: The Westminster Press, 24-26.

and the Lord's Supper, and church discipline. As the Reformation flourished, the counsel of God in these matters was preached and applied in the churches, and the churches were transformed into societies comparable to those described by the apostles.

Now nearly 500 years after the Reformation, the Gospel has all but disappeared again; the Word of God is obscured, suppressed, and attacked by religious and secular organizations, and many organizations claiming to be churches at the beginning of the third millennium after Christ are not, because they do not preach the Gospel. The Roman Church-State, of course, was never reformed; in fact, it is doctrinally worse in 2001 than it was in 1517, having multiplied its errors and superstitions by many subsequent actions of its councils and popes. Since Luther wrote, the Council of Trent expressed Rome's hardened heart on justification, and later conciliar and papal decrees added (to name but a few) the infallibility of the pope, the immaculate conception of Mary, and the assumption of Mary to its abundant errors. But the Protestant churches, the heirs of the Reformation, are no longer Reformed either. They have apostatized from the Gospel, and the consequence is that their organizations are looking less and less like Christian churches, and more and more like entertainment and social clubs, social or political action organizations, business enterprises, or temples in which display, demonstration, liturgy, ritual, and ceremony are the focus of activity. The purity and simplicity of the Gospel and the Word of God have been displaced by the smells and bells, the rattle and prattle of "Protestant" priests and priestesses, imitating, wittingly and unwittingly, the false religions of the Orthodox and the Romanists.

One purpose of this book is to remind Christians what the church is, and what churches ought to be. By including excerpts from the writing of men such as Luther, Calvin, Burroughs, and à Lasco, we hope to present the idea of the church as proclaimed by the Reformers. By including essays from later centuries, we hope to emphasize the warnings that have been given from their day to ours about the decline of the church, which begins, always and everywhere, with ignorance of the Word of God. It is our prayer that God will use these essays to restore his churches again, to build his church by sending forth fearless men who will teach the Gospel and the Word.

PART I

THE CHURCH BELONGING TO JESUS CHRIST

"Glorify your Son, that your Son also
may glorify you, as you have given
him authority over all flesh, that he
should give eternal life to as many
as you have given him. And this is
eternal life, that they may know you,
and Jesus Christ whom you have sent."
John 17:1-3

I

The Church

John W. Robbins[1]

The reader is asked to study these passages of Scripture while reading this essay: 2 Timothy 3:14-17; 1 Corinthians 14:26-37; 1 Timothy 2:8-3:13; Titus 1:5-2:8; Acts 6:1-7, and Ephesians 4:1-24.

C ONTEMPORARY popular theology and practice, including the doctrine and practice of the church, is a confused and un-Biblical mess. To quote Augustine and Calvin, many sheep are without and many wolves are within the churches. The confusion can only be eliminated by studying the Scriptures. It is the Bible and the Bible alone that furnishes us with the information we need for a correct understanding of the church. Tradition, history, the needs of men and women, and the ideas of men are simply irrelevant to the doctrine of the church. The Bible alone is the source of our information about the purpose and the organization of the church. A reading of what the New Testament has to say about the purpose and organization of the church quickly leads one to the conclusion that most of those societies that pass for churches today are not churches at all.

At the end of the twentieth century and the beginning of the twenty-first, there are all sorts of ideas being published about the church, its reformation and its reconstruction. Some want the church to be a place of worship, whatever "worship" means. Others claim that their church already is a place of worship. Some want the clergy to wear vestments and crowns, and infants to drink wine and eat bread. In other churches the clergy already wear gowns and crowns, and the infants already drink wine and eat bread. Some advocate a return to iconography; others

---

1. Dr. Robbins is president of The Trinity Foundation. His most recent book is *Ecclesiastical Megalomania: The Economic and Political Thought of the Roman Catholic Church*. This essay is reprinted from *The Trinity Review*.

practice it. Some advocate a return to Rome; others run ahead of the ecclesiastical herd. Some believe women should be ordained; others ordain both women and homosexuals. Still others don't believe in ordination at all. But in this babble of voices there seems to be some agreement: Nearly everyone wants the church to be something other than what God says it should be.

The Purpose of the Church

What is the purpose of the church? What is the purpose of worship? Is it to induce a feeling of awe and dependence in worshipers? A warm glow of fellowship? Is it to re-enact the Gospel or the sacrifice of Calvary? Is it to appeal to the whole person? Is it to do good works? Is a church supposed to be a social action, anti-abortion, anti-war, and anti-poverty organizing center? If once we understand what the purpose of the church is, all the rest of the doctrine of the church falls neatly into place. But if we do not know what the purpose of the church is, then we cannot understand how the church is to be organized and operated.

The purpose of the church is really quite simple: education in the truth. All its activities are to be educational activities, and all its education is to be education in the truth. In his first letter to Timothy (3:15), Paul stated his purpose in writing: "I write so that you may know how you ought to conduct yourself in the house of God, which is the church of the living God, the pillar and ground of the truth." In his commentary on this passage, Calvin wrote: "The reason why the church is called the pillar of truth is that she defends and spreads it by her agency.... The church maintains the truth, because by preaching the church proclaims it, because she keeps it pure and entire, because she transmits it to posterity." Calvin warns pastors: "How dreadful is the vengeance that awaits them if, through their fault, that truth which is the image of the divine glory, the light of the world, and the salvation of men, shall be allowed to fall! This consideration ought undoubtedly to lead pastors to tremble continually, not to deprive them of all energy, but to excite them to greater vigilance." Calvin concludes by arguing that "if the church is the pillar of the truth, it follows that the church is not with them [clergymen] when the truth not only lies buried, but is shockingly torn and thrown down and trampled underfoot.... Paul does not wish that any society in which the truth of God does not hold a lofty and conspicuous place shall be acknowledged to be a church."

In his letter to Timothy, Paul stated his purpose as being to instruct Timothy how to conduct himself in the church. Here are a few of those instructions:

> Remain in Ephesus that you may charge some that they teach no other doctrine, nor give heed to fables and endless genealogies.... Instruct the brethren in these things. These things command and teach. Give attention to reading, to exhortation, to doctrine.... Meditate on these things; take heed to yourself and to the doctrine.... Teach and exhort these things....

In the pastoral epistles and in the rest of the New Testament epistles there is very little mention of baptism and the Lord's Supper, and no mention of those things that modern churchmen take to be so important in worship. Paul is concerned almost entirely with the preaching and preservation of sound doctrine.

In his letter to the Ephesians (4:11-14) Paul wrote:

> And he himself gave some to be apostles, some prophets, some evangelists, and some pastors and teachers, for the equipping of the saints for the work of ministry, for the edifying of the body of Christ, till we all come to the unity of the faith and the knowledge of the Son of God, to a perfect man, to the measure of the stature of the fullness of Christ; that we should no longer be children tossed to and fro and carried about with every wind of doctrine, by the trickery of men, in the cunning craftiness by which they lie in wait to deceive....

In this passage Paul says that the purpose of the church is education: the edifying of the body of Christ until we all come to the unity of the faith and the knowledge of the Son of God. For this purpose, God has established several sorts of teachers: apostles, prophets, evangelists, pastors and teachers. All of these men are teachers, and all are supposed to equip the saints. Paul does not mention worship leaders, music ministers, psychologists, counselors, priests, acolytes, confessors, or popes. The apostles, prophets, and evangelists equipped the saints, that is, the ordinary Christians, not only by speaking, but more importantly by writing the Scriptures, and Christian pastors and teachers teach from these documents today.

Another Scripture that is relevant to this question of the purpose of the church is *John* 21:15-17:

> So when they had eaten breakfast, Jesus said to Simon Peter, "Simon, son of Jonah, do you love me more than these?"

He said to him, "Yes, Lord, you know that I love you."

He said to him, "Feed my lambs."

He said to him again a second time, "Simon, son of Jonah, do you love me?"

He said to him, "Yes, Lord, you know that I love you."

He said to him, "Tend my sheep."

He said to him the third time, "Simon, son of Jonah, do you love me?"

Peter was grieved because he said to him the third time, "Do you love me?" And he said to him, "Lord, you know all things, you know that I love you."

Jesus said to him, "Feed my sheep."

Some trendy holistic gospel people will no doubt think that Christ was talking about literal sheep and food, but Christians know better. He was talking about his chosen ones and the truth. Feeding them is figurative language for educating them in the truth. There is nothing that feeds Christ's sheep and lambs except the Word of Christ, the Scriptures.

Matthew 28:19-20 say: "Go and make disciples of all the nations, baptizing them in the name of the Father and of the Son and of the Holy Spirit, teaching them to observe all things that I have commanded you." Christ's command to the church is to make disciples, to baptize, and to teach all the things he had taught. Even baptism is done in the name of the Trinity; without the doctrine preached, taught, and understood, the ritual is Antichristian. The purpose of the church is education in the truth. Here Christ speaks literally, while to Peter he spoke figuratively.

Now in this benighted twentieth century, many people, including many who claim to be Christians, do not know what the truth is or how it is communicated. Some think that truth is personal, not propositional; when one has a religious experience, one encounters persons, not believes propositions. One trusts in Christ, not believes that Christ died according to the Scriptures, and was buried and rose again the third day according to the Scriptures. Believing propositions, believing doctrines, is belittled as "historical faith" or "intellectual assent." Even the devils have that kind of faith, we are told. One needs a living, vibrant, personal relationship with Christ. Some people think that truth is emotional, not intellectual: The truth stirs one's heart, not enlightens one's understanding. Some think that truth is practical, not theoretical:

One does the truth, not believes it. After all, doesn't *James* say that faith without works is dead?

These modern views of truth, all of which are rejections of the Biblical view, pervert both the doctrine and the practice of the church. Many of the worst practices of those societies professing to be churches stem from their false views of truth and how it is communicated: idolatry, ritual, images, frenzy, emotions, dance, drama, and music.

Granted that truth is propositional and therefore must be communicated by language; granted that truth is the propositions of the 66 books of the Bible and their logical implications; and granted that the purpose of the church is the propagation of the truth, several things follow: All non-educational functions, whether they be charitable,[2] political, social, ceremonial, ritual, aesthetic, or economic are not primary functions of the church, and they are permissible only if they are ancillary to and supportive of the ministry of the Word. The church's principal and essential job is education in the truth, and the only source of truth is the Bible.

Several years ago I taught a class in the doctrine of God at a large and allegedly conservative Presbyterian church near Washington, D. C. There were two or three people in the class, none of whom was a member of the large Presbyterian church in which the class was being held. On the same evening, in the same church, a man and a woman were leading an aerobics class of 25 or 30. That church enjoys a reputation of being alive. And the aerobics class was certainly lively enough. But its reputation is misleading.

The Teachers of the Church

If teaching the Bible is the function of the church, then there ought to be a lot of teaching going on in the church. In the apostolic churches that was so: There was so much teaching going on that one man could not do it all, even though that man was an apostle or a prophet. In the accounts given in the book of *Acts*, the traveling bands of apostles and evangelists were always just that: traveling groups of men. The apostles would no more have thought of sending one man alone out to start a

2. To keep charitable activities from interfering with the purpose of the church, Paul wrote *1 Timothy* 5:4-16. In verse 11 he commands that some widows be denied charity; in verse 17 he commands that competent teachers be paid well. That alone illustrates the primacy of teaching in the church.

church or to be a missionary than they would have thought of sending a woman alone. Yet that is precisely what many denominations, including those that pride themselves on their orthodoxy, do today. When Christ sent out the seventy disciples two by two in *Luke* 10:1, he followed the same practice. Better, he established the example that the apostles and churches later imitated. Perhaps this practice of Christ and the apostles has something to do with the Biblical doctrine that the testimony of two or three witnesses is necessary to establish and confirm the truth.

In *Acts* 13 we are given a list of five men who were prophets and teachers of the church at Antioch. There was no one teaching elder, no one priest, no one pastor, no one minister. There were five. Moreover, they were equal. There were not a pastor, an associate pastor, and a youth minister. There was no hierarchy. There was none of the various offices that modern churches have invented in their foolish attempts to manage the church efficiently. The early Christians took the educational function of the church very seriously. And when the five teachers sent men – or rather when the Holy Spirit sent men – to Cyprus, he sent two, Saul and Barnabas, and they took John with them. By verse 14, the reference is to "Paul and his party." Apparently the party had become so large that John could return to Jerusalem.

This plurality of teachers was the common practice of the apostolic church. *Acts* 14:23 says that Paul and Barnabas appointed elders in every church. Plural, not singular. One kind of officer, not two, three, four, or five. There were no bishops in the episcopal sense, no right reverends, no cardinals, no archbishops, no leaders. Elders, we are told in 1 *Timothy* 3 and *Titus* 1, are to be teachers. There was no such thing as a ruling elder who did not teach in the apostolic church order. There is only one set of requirements for the office of elder, and an elder is to be able to teach. Paul did not require college and seminary training of some elders and not for others. Nor was there a teacher who was not ordained. This is because the only way of ruling in the church is by teaching.

In 1 *Thessalonians* 5:12 Paul exhorts the Christians to "recognize those" (please notice the plural) "who labor among you ... and admonish you." *Hebrews* 13:7 and 17 also contain the plural. In *Acts* 20 there are several elders of the church at Ephesus. *James* 5:14 refers to the elders of the church. *Titus* 1:5 says that Paul commanded Timothy to ordain elders, plural, in every city. *1 Timothy* 5:17 refers to elders in the plural. And *1 Corinthians* 14 specifically instructs the Corinthians to limit the number of men speaking in church meetings to six!

In failing to recognize the importance of teaching and therefore the need for several teachers in each church, virtually all modern churches part company with the apostolic churches. From the Roman Church-State, led by the pope, with each local parish led by a priest, to the local Baptist church led by a pastor, the institution of one-man rule has been with us since the days of Diotrephes. Diotrephes was the church leader described in *3 John* "who loves to have the pre-eminence among them" and who did not receive John or the brethren. He and his church were the prototypical one-minister-one-church institution. It is his example, and not the apostles', that most churches have followed from that day to this.

The Election of Teachers

There are several other important lessons to be learned from the Scriptures if we will be willing and teachable.

First, teachers in the church are to be elected by the congregations from among their own number. Perhaps the most familiar example of this is *Acts* 6, in which we are told that the congregation at Jerusalem elected seven men on the specific instruction of the apostles to hold an election. Apparently we are given a complete account of the election of officers in *Acts* 6 because this is the first time it had happened in the history of the church. Here, in part, is what the apostles said: "Seek out from among you seven men of good reputation, full of the Holy Spirit and wisdom, whom we may appoint over this business."

In this example, written for our learning, the apostles overthrow some of the most cherished practices of ecclesiastical societies today. First, their appointing of officers, including teachers like Stephen and Philip, was not done without the consent of the congregation. From this we learn that ordinary Christians have the right to choose their own officers and teachers. Teachers, much less priests, are not to be imposed on congregations. Furthermore, the apostles did not even presume to propose men for the approval of the congregation; the congregations were to seek out men themselves, for ordination by the apostles. The apostles neither imposed nor chose congregational officers. Second, the apostles specified that the church officers are to be men. Please note that no women were elected or ordained, yet if this were permissible, it should have been done here, for the problem concerned the distribution of food to widows. This would seem to be (according to modern thinking) a perfect illustration of why women deacons and elders are needed. But the apostles commanded that seven men be chosen, and they were. Third, the apostles specified a plurality of men. Fourth, they specified men of good reputation, full of the Holy Ghost and wisdom. Paul makes the qualifications for officers more explicit in 1 *Timothy* 3, where the phrase "full of the Holy Ghost and of wisdom" is defined in detail. The congregation is presumed to have the right and ability to discern which men are full of the Holy Ghost and of wisdom. The apostles, by divine inspiration, state the qualifications for office, but ordinary Christians are regarded as competent to judge who meets those qualifications. When we read later in *Acts* that the traveling apostles ordained elders in every city, we ought to assume that they used the same method in all the churches as they did in *Acts* 6: congregational election followed by apostolic appointment or ordination. Indeed, the Greek word that is used in *Acts* 14:23, as Calvin argues, means elected by show of hands. Once the procedure was described in *Acts* 6 there was no need to repeat the description every time it happened. The apostles regarded ordinary Christians as competent judges of who was filled with the Holy Ghost and with wisdom.

This means, of course, that those modern societies that do not elect their congregational officers but have leaders imposed are not following the apostolic pattern. It means that those societies that elect or are taught by women are not following the apostolic pattern. It means that those churches that do not elect their officers from among their own number are not following the apostolic pattern. It means that those churches that elect officers who are not filled with the Holy Ghost and with wisdom are not following the Biblical pattern. If the congregation is expected to judge, then the congregation must be informed about the men on whom they are to vote. This cannot be done, as modern churches seem to think, by listening to ministerial candidates preach trial sermons. The men whom the apostles appointed officers in every city were local men, not immigrants. They were familiar with the congregation, the town, and the Gospel.

The Equality of Teachers

In the Christian church, there is no hierarchy, nor even a first among equals. God is a democrat.

> But you, do not be called "Rabbi," for one is your Teacher – the Christ, and you are all brethren. Do not call anyone on Earth your Father; for one is your Father, he who is in Heaven. And do not be called Teachers, for one is your Teacher, the Christ. But he who is greatest among you shall be your servant. And whoever exalts himself will be abased, and he who humbles himself will be exalted (*Matthew* 23:8-12).

By these words Christ outlawed all titles and marks of distinction or nobility in the church. No one is to be called Rabbi, nor Father, and, what seems most harmless of all, not even Teacher. All such titles are both inaccurate and signs of pride. Yet societies claiming to be churches call their clergy Fathers, Reverends, Right Reverends, and Rabbis. Worse, they reserve these titles for elite groups within their leadership: Not all elders are called Reverend; not all leaders are called Fathers; not all teachers are called Rabbis. Not only has the clear command of Christ been ignored, but also a new group, not found in the New Testament, called the clergy, has emerged.

In *Matthew* 20 Christ expands on this prohibition:

> You know that the rulers of the Gentiles lord it over them, and those who are great exercise authority over them. Yet it shall not be so among you; but whoever desires to become great among you, let him be your servant. And whoever desires to be first among you, let him be your slave – just as the Son of Man did not come to be served, but to serve, and to give his life a ransom for many.

The only authority elected officers of the church have is both given and limited by the Bible. It is delegated authority, limited by the terms of the delegation. It is ministerial authority, not magisterial authority. There are no leaders, no Führers, no masters, no one with magisterial authority – in the churches. The officers' duty is to teach the truth. The power of excommunication is vested, not solely in the officers, but in the congregation. Paul gives a good example of the proper exercise of the power of excommunication in his letters to the Corinthians. In the first letter, he wrote to them – and notice the involvement of the whole congregation, not simply the elders –

In the name of our Lord Jesus Christ, when you are gathered together, along with my spirit, with the power of our Lord Jesus Christ, deliver such a one to Satan for the destruction of the flesh, that his spirit may be saved in the day of the Lord Jesus.

In his second letter, Paul wrote: "The punishment which was inflicted by the majority [note well] is sufficient for such a man, so that on the contrary you ought rather to forgive and comfort him." Paul refers to the punishment of excommunication as being inflicted by a majority of the congregation, not a minority.

The commands which Christ gave in *Matthew* 18 similarly involve discipline by the majority: Go to your brother first. If he will not hear you, take a witness. If he still does not listen, tell it to the church. If he will not listen to the church, let him be to you like a heathen and a tax collector. The church, it must be said, is not merely the church officers: It means the entire assembly, the *ecclesia*. Just as the congregation is presumed competent to choose its own officers, it is presumed competent to excommunicate its own members.

Moreover, this procedure of church discipline and excommunication applies to all Christians, not just to laymen. The apostles established no special courts for judging the "clergy." All Christians are brothers, and to establish separate judicial procedures for officers and for laity is un-Biblical. The Bible regards ordinary Christians, assuming the teachers have been doing their job correctly, as entirely competent to judge, as well as to counsel, one another.

The Remuneration of Teachers

All teachers in the church are to be paid: You shall not muzzle the ox that treads out the corn. Paul did not ordinarily receive compensation from the churches he helped establish, but he was quite clear in asserting the propriety and the duty of paying teachers according to their competence and diligence, and not according to seniority, years of experience, or number of degrees. To such things the world looks, but not the church. While Paul did not take any money, his words about the duty of paying teachers must not be misunderstood to mean that the teachers in a church should receive all their income from the church. Today many churches pay only one teacher, the minister or priest or pastor, and if they are large enough, his associate, his secretary, the janitor, the choir director, and maybe the organist. But that is not what Paul commands: All the oxen, all the teachers, especially those who do their job well and eagerly, are to be paid. That does not mean that they must live solely from the fruits of their labor in the church, but it does mean that their work is to be recognized as valuable by the congregation.

If men are to be elected from the congregation as teachers, they will already have another job by which they can support themselves should the congregation fire them. This would have several beneficial side-effects. If teachers are not completely dependent upon the congregation for their livelihood, they might be less apt to suppress truths that the congregation does not want to hear. Second, if the teachers can partially support themselves, the congregation will be able to support all the teachers according to their competence and diligence. Rather than paying one large salary to one man, the congregation will be able to pay smaller salaries to several men.

This division of labor would have several additional benefits: First, it would tend to reduce burnout. No one man would be expected to carry the load for the church. He would not become the Atlas carrying the church on his shoulders. Second, it would ensure that the church would continue its purpose uninterruptedly should one teacher resign, die, or become involved in a scandal. Third, it would reduce the personality cult and conflict that sometimes cause people to attend and to leave a church because they like or do not like the pastor or the way he preaches. There would be no central figure to like or dislike. There are many more additional benefits from having a plurality of teachers, some of which may not become obvious until it is tried. It is difficult to imagine all the ramifications of a system of church organization that has not been seriously tried in modern times.

The Structure of Church Meetings

1 *Corinthians* 14 contains a wealth of information about the meetings, as does 1 *Timothy* 2. Some of this information is angrily rejected today by those who think they know better than God, but this is what God commands.

First, he commands the men to pray: "I desire that the men pray everywhere" (1 *Timothy* 2:8). The women are to adorn themselves with modest apparel and with good works. In contrast to the men, who are commanded to pray, the women are to keep quiet: "Let a woman learn in silence."

Second, Paul makes provision for several men to speak, as many as six in one meeting. They are to speak, and the rest are to judge. Here again is the appeal to the congregation to judge. Moreover, after the men have spoken, there is to be a period of discussion and questions. This seems to be implied by the fact that the women are prohibited from asking questions in church meetings, but the men are not. Such a prohibition makes sense only if there is a discussion period following each sermon. This prohibition has several good effects: First, it maintains order in the church; second, it ensures the continuation of teaching at home in the family; third, it teaches Christians how to answer questions, how to defend the faith.

While 1 Corinthians 14 refers to prophets and those who speak in a foreign language, the principles stated in that chapter apply to modern church meetings even though there are no prophets today. The elected elders today would oversee congregational worship. They are the elected teachers of the people. Moreover, the assembly for worship would be an assembly of all the people; there would be no division into Sunday School classes with their programs of planned retardation for the youngsters. All the women and children would learn in silence during the assembly; any questions that arose in their minds would be asked at home.

The Ideal Church

I would like to suggest several characteristics of the church as it might be and ought to be. The church as it might be and ought to be would consist of a well-informed congregation taught by several elected, ordained, and paid married male teachers. There would be a great deal of teaching going on at the church, all for the purpose of building the people up in the knowledge of Christ, so that they might grow in faith and knowledge, and spread that knowledge throughout the community.

The plurality of teachers would mean that teaching would be plentiful, that one teacher's errors could be corrected by the rest, even before the error is propagated. The teachers could meet regularly to discuss their teaching, to offer each other criticism and guidance, to suggest appropriate books to read, to prepare for the meetings on the Lord's Day or at other times during the week, and to encourage each other in the faith. Mutual constructive and friendly criticism would tend to keep the teachers humble. Burnout, which has become more and more common among one-man churches, could be virtually eliminated. The church was never intended to function with one teacher, and a plurality of teachers would get a much larger job done better.

A church so arranged would also eliminate some of the squelching of local talent that the present unscriptural system of church government encourages. Many parachurch organizations, to the extent that they are performing jobs that the church ought to be doing, are doing so because the local churches could not find, or would not find, any way to use the abilities and energies of local Christians. In a one-man church, there is room for only one man. All others are spectators.

The institution of the Sunday School, which is only 200 years old, would be eliminated. Families would worship together as families, rather than being segregated by age. In the order of worship a sermon or lecture might occur after some singing and prayer, followed by questions from the congregation and a general discussion to make sure that the sermon has been understood. During this discussion, all the men of the congregation might participate. In the *Institutes* Calvin says, "It is clear that every member of the church is charged with the responsibility of public edification according to the measure of his grace, provided he perform it decently and in order."

This discussion in turn would be followed by more prayer and singing, which is also to be educational. Many have drawn a false dichotomy between learning and worship – a dichotomy that flows from the more fundamentally false dichotomy between the mind and the spirit, or between the head and the heart – so that what is worship cannot be educational or intellectual, and what is educational or intellectual cannot be worshipful. But such people are far from the Bible. *Colossians* 3:16 says, "Let the Word of Christ dwell in you richly in all wisdom, teaching and admonishing one another in psalms and hymns and spiritual songs, singing with grace in your heart to the Lord." *Ephesians* 5:18 and 19 say, "And do not be drunk with wine, in which is dissipation; but be filled with the Spirit, speaking to one another in psalms and hymns and spiritual songs, singing and making melody in your heart to the Lord."

Notice how neatly the two activities, teaching one another and praising God, fit together. If we sing with grace in our hearts to God, we are teaching and admonishing one another also. There is no incompatibility between worship and learning; because God is truth, they are inseparable. Indeed, the highest worship we can pay to a God who has given us a thousand-page book to read is to study that book and believe what it teaches; and the most insulting thing we can do to an author, whether human or divine, is to refuse or neglect to learn what he has written. Nothing is more suspicious than people who claim to know Jesus, or to have a religious experience or a personal relationship with God, but who show little interest in a serious study of the Bible. Christ said, If you love me, obey my commands. Of course, one must know the commands before one can obey them; but knowledge, according to some people, has nothing to do with religion. Perhaps knowledge has nothing to do with their religion, but then their religion is not Christianity.

In the order of worship after the first cycle of sermon, discussion, prayer, and singing, the cycle might begin again. Or perhaps two of the elders could speak on the same topic or passage of Scripture. The important thing is to end the monologue that characterizes most churches today, the sermon following which no discussion or asking of questions is permitted. That simply is not a procedure conducive to learning. Christ himself entertained questions from his listeners. He even responded to the questions of the lawyers and Pharisees who were trying to trick him.

But to return to the church: A group of elected teachers, all of whom earn part of their salaries from the church and part from secular pursuits, would be more likely to preach the whole counsel of God than a single man who is totally dependent on the congregation for his support or on the denomination for his pension and health insurance. The apostolic church model would increase both the quantity and quality of teaching.

When one reads the book of *Acts* and discovers just how well the apostolic model worked, an additional though inconclusive reason is added to the argument for reforming the church. Of course, one can also point to the obvious success of the Roman Church-State, which is about as far removed from the Biblical church pattern as one can get. Obviously, success *per se* is not a sound argument. But my argument is that only the apostolic model of the church is consistent with the system of truth revealed to us in Scripture. The Diotrephesian model followed by the Roman Church-State is not compatible with the truth, and the Roman Church-State has not succeeded in propagating the truth. A false church and false doctrine go together; the apostolic church and the apostolic doctrine go together as well. Not only have we been given a system of truth in the Bible, but also as part of that system of truth we have been given information about a form of organization designed to propagate the truth. The medium and the message go together because God has given us a message about the medium. As Christians we are sinning by failing to teach the truth in the way that God commands.

2

The Apostolic Church

Thomas Witherow[1]

Statement of the Question

IT IS VERY common for professing Christians to draw a distinction between *essentials* and *non-essentials* in religion, and to infer that, if any
fact or doctrine rightly belongs to the latter class, it must be a matter of
very little importance, and may in practice be safely set at nought. The
great bulk of men take their opinions on trust; they will not undergo
the toil of thinking, searching, and reasoning about anything, and one
of the most usual expedients adopted to save them the trouble of inquiry, and to turn aside the force of any disagreeable fact, is to meet it
by saying, "The matter is not essential to salvation; therefore, we need
give ourselves little concern on the subject."

If the distinction here specified is safe, the inference drawn from it is
certainly dangerous. To say that because a fact of Divine revelation is
not essential to salvation, it must of necessity be unimportant, and may
or may not be received by us, is to assert a principle, the application of
which would make havoc of our Christianity. For what are the truths
essential to salvation? Are they not these: That there is a God; that all
men are sinners; that the Son of God died upon the cross to make atonement for the guilty; and that whosoever believes on the Lord Jesus Christ
shall be saved? There is good reason for believing that not a few souls
are now in happiness, who in life knew little more than these – the first
principles of the oracles of God – the very alphabet of the Christian
system; and if so, no other Divine truths can be counted absolutely

1. Thomas Witherow (1824-1890) was a pastor in Northern Ireland and Professor of
Church History in Londonderry. Witherow wrote more at length on this subject in
The Form of the Christian Temple. The Apostolic Church first appeared in 1856.

essential to salvation. But if all the other truths of revelation are unimportant, because they happen to be non-essentials, it follows that the Word of God itself is in the main unimportant; for by far the greatest portion of it is occupied with matters, the knowledge of which, in the case supposed, is not absolutely indispensable to the everlasting happiness of men. Nor does it alter the case, if we regard the number of fundamental truths to be much greater. Let a man once persuade himself that importance attaches only to what he is pleased to call essentials, whatever their number, and he will, no doubt, shorten his creed and cut away the foundation of many controversies; but he will practically set aside all except a very small part of the Scriptures. If such a principle does not mutilate the Bible, it stigmatizes much of it as trivial. Revelation is all gold for preciousness and purity, but the very touch of such a principle would transmute the most of it into dross.[2]

Though every statement in the Scripture cannot be regarded as absolutely essential to salvation, yet everything there is essential to some otherwise and important end, else it would not find a place in the good Word of God. Human wisdom may be baffled in attempting to specify the design of every truth that forms a component part of Divine revelation, but eternity will show us that no portion of it is useless. All Scripture is profitable. A fact written therein may not be essential to human salvation, and yet it may be highly conducive to some other great and gracious purpose in the economy of God – it may be necessary for our personal comfort, for our guidance in life, or for our growth in holiness, and most certainly it is essential to the completeness of the system of Divine truth. The law of the Lord is perfect. Strike out of the Bible the truth that seems the most insignificant of all, and the law of the Lord would not be perfect any more. In architecture, the pinning that fills a crevice in the wall occupies a subordinate position, in comparison with the quoin [cornerstone or keystone]; but the builder lets us know that the one has an important purpose to serve as well as the other, and does its part to promote the stability and completeness of the house. In shipbuilding, the screws and bolts that gird the ship together are insignificant, as compared with the beams of oak and masts of pine, but they contribute their full share to the safety of the vessel and the security of

2. This argument also implies, of course, that most of the Word is not only unimportant, but non-essential, an impious and blasphemous conclusion. – *Editor.*

the passenger. So in the Christian system, every fact, great or small, that God has been pleased to insert in the Bible is, by its very position, invested with importance, answers its end, and, though perhaps justly considered as non-essential to salvation, does not deserve to be accounted worthless.

Every Divine truth is important, though it may be that all Divine truths are not of equal importance. The simplest statement of the Bible is a matter of more concern to an immortal being than the most sublime sentiment of mere human genius. The one carries with it what the other cannot show – the stamp of the approval of God. The one comes to us from Heaven, the other savors of the Earth. The one has for us a special interest, as forming a constituent portion of that Word which is a message from God to each individual man; the other is the production of a mind merely human, to which we and all our interests were alike unknown. Any truth merely human should weigh with us light as a feather in comparison with the most insignificant of the truths of God. The faith of a Christian should strive to reach and grasp everything that God has honored with a place in that Word, the design of which is to be a light to our feet as we thread our way through this dark world. Besides, this, unlike every other book, is not doomed to perish. Heaven and Earth may pass away, but the words of Christ shall not pass away. The seal of eternity is stamped on every verse of the Bible. This fact is enough of itself to make every line of it important.

With these observations we deem it right to introduce our exposition of ecclesiastical polity. Few would go so far as to assert that correct views on church government are essential to salvation, and yet it is a subject whose importance it were folly to attempt to depreciate. The Holy Spirit, speaking in the Scriptures, treats of this theme. The Christian world has been divided in opinion about it ever since the Reformation.[3] We cannot attach ourselves to any denomination of Christians without giving our influence either to truth or error on this very point; and the views we adopt upon this subject go far to color our opinions on matters of Christian faith and practice. With such facts before us, though we may not regard the polity of the New Testament church as

---

3. Of course, the Christian world was divided on the question before Rome succeeded in imposing its hegemony on the Western churches. During Rome's domination, those who dissented on the matter of church government were excommunicated, exiled, or executed. – Editor.

essential to human salvation, we do not feel at liberty to undervalue its importance.

The various forms of church government that we find existing at present in the Christian world may be classed under some one or other of these three heads: *Prelacy, Independency*, and *Presbytery*. We do not employ these terms in an offensive sense, but as being the best calculated to denote their respective systems. *Prelacy* is that form of church government which is administered by archbishops, bishops, deans, archdeacons, and other ecclesiastical office-bearers depending on that hierarchy; and is such as we see exemplified in the Greek Church, the Church of Rome, and the Church of England. *Independency* is that form of church government whose distinctive principle is that each separate congregation is under Christ, subject to no external jurisdiction whatever, but has within itself – in its office-bearers and members – all the materials of government; and is such as is at present in practical operation among Congregationalists and Baptists. *Presbytery* is that form of church government that is dispensed by presbyters or elders, met in Session, Presbytery, Synod, or General Assembly; and is such as is presented in the several Presbyterian Churches of Ireland, Scotland, England, and America. These three forms of ecclesiastical polity are at this moment extensively prevalent in Christendom. Indeed, every other organization that any considerable body of Christians has adopted, is only a modification or a mixture of some of the systems we have named.

A very brief examination enables us to see that these three systems differ very widely in their characteristic features. Not only so, but Prelacy, in all its main principles, is opposed to Presbytery; and Independency, in its main principles, is opposed to both. It follows that three forms, differing so very much, cannot all be right, and cannot of course have equal claims on the attachment and support of enlightened and conscientious men. It is self-evident, moreover, that the Word of God, the only rule of faith and practice, cannot approve of all; for, as the Word of God never contradicts itself, it cannot sanction contradictory systems. Some one of these three must be more in accordance with the will of God, as expressed in the Scriptures, than either of the others; and to know which of them is so, should be a subject of deep interest to every child of God. A Christian, of all men, is bound to be a lover of truth; and we are warranted in supposing that, if a Christian could only see to which of these competing systems the Word of Truth bears witness, he would support it with all his might, and would lend no encouragement to the others. If a man, after he sees the difference, can hold what he knows to be merely human in the same estimation with what he knows to be Divine, let him bid farewell to his Christianity, and cease to pretend that he cherishes any attachment to the truth. The religion of the Lord Jesus, except we mistake its spirit far, binds all who receive it to prefer the true to the false, the right to the wrong, the good to the evil; and for us to be tempted by any consideration to hold them in equal reverence and render them equal support, is to fling one of the first requirements of Christianity away from us. The influence of a Christian is often very little in this world, but whatever it is, it is a talent, for which, like his time, his money, or his intellectual power, he is accountable to God, and that influence ought ever to be on the side of the truth, never against the truth.

Which, then, of the three forms of church government prevalent throughout the world is it the duty of a Christian to select and to support?

This is a question of great importance. It is, besides, forced upon our consideration in every locality where a dissenting chapel lifts its front, and a church steeple tapers into air. And yet it must be admitted that the majority of Christians contrive to pass through life without ever giving an hour's thought to this most interesting theme. Most people are content to let their ancestors choose a church for them, and every Sabbath walk to Divine worship in the footsteps of their great-grandfathers – they know not why, and care not wherefore. Some shrink from inquiry, lest it should turn out that the church to which they are bound by ties of family, education, and habit, is destitute of all Scriptural authority, and lest they feel uncomfortable by having their convictions and their interests set at war. But the great reason why the spirit of inquiry is almost dead on this subject is that the pulpit is silent, or nearly so, on ecclesiastical government. On this topic the trumpet gives not an uncertain sound, but commonly no sound whatever. There are, we are persuaded, few ministers in any denomination who could say to their people that, on this subject, "we have not shunned to declare to you the whole counsel of God." The people never having had their attention specially directed to those passages of Scripture where the principles of church government are embodied, give no time or thought to the consideration of the subject. The result is, that vast masses of men and women live in utter ignorance, not only of the Scriptural facts bearing on the case, but even of their own denominational peculiarities; they are Prelatists, Independents, or Presbyterians by birth, not by conviction; they view all forms of church government as equally true, which is the same thing as to count them equally worthless; they have no definite ideas on the subject; and thus, in absence of public instruction, they are, by the education of circumstances, prepared to fall in with any system or no system, as may best suit their private convenience or promote their worldly ambition. So it is that many who, in the judgment of charity, are Christians, regard the denomination with which birth or accident has connected them, either with a blind attachment or a sinful indifference; and, though rival systems of church polity have their representatives in every village, they plod the weary way of life in happy unconcern about all such matters and are never troubled with the question that the very sight of a church spire suggests to other men – *Which of these is true?*

Most people who withdraw from the communion of one church to connect themselves with another, and thus exercise their right of choice between the various forms of ecclesiastical government, are induced to give their preference from motives such as should never influence an intelligent Christian. They are guided by feeling rather than by judgment. They do not first ascertain the principles of the denomination from its acknowledged standards, and then examine these principles in the light of the Word of God. The bulk of mankind are not intellectual enough to search for principles and weigh them. At least, they do not take the trouble, but are influenced in their choice, either by the authority of some great man, or the moral worth of some particular persons, or the piety and eloquence of some local minister – or perhaps by paltry pique, or petty gain, or love of the rank, or fashion of the world, or by some other equally low and vulgar consideration. But to decide the rival claims of Prelacy, Independency, and Presbytery by any such tests as these is absurd in the extreme. Try them by the authority of great men! There is not one of the three systems that could not present a long catalogue of distinguished men who were its warm supporters till the last hour of life. Test them by moral worth! There is not one of them that could not present a goodly number of the excellent of the Earth, waiting on its ministrations and reposing beneath its shadow. If we ask which of these systems provides able and pious ministers to instruct the people, we find a large number of such persons filling the pulpits of each of them; and if we examine further, we will find that not infrequently there may be in the same town a minister who is an eloquent man and mighty in the Scriptures, who, all the week in the garden of the Lord, is active as the busy bee, and who, when Sabbath comes, dispenses the sweets of the Divine Word to admiring multitudes; while, in connection with the same denomination, there may be on the other side of the street some poor pitiful drone, who is doomed to hum to vacancy all the year round. Any such modes of testing ecclesiastical systems, however common, are unsure and unsafe.

To us it seems there is a much more satisfactory way of deciding upon the claims of those forms of church government which obtain at present in the world – that is, to test their peculiar principles by the standard of the Word of God. That book is quite sufficient to point out the path of duty to the Christian in this as well as in all matters, for it was intended by its Divine Author to be our guide in matters of practice as well as of faith. The Bible furnishes us with peculiar facilities for forming an opinion on this very point. It tells us of a church that was organized in the world eighteen hundred years ago. The founders of that church were Apostles and Prophets, acting by the authority of God. Every fact known with certainty about the original constitution of the church is preserved in the Bible; everything preserved elsewhere is only hearsay and tradition. We read in Scripture very many facts that enable us to know with tolerable accuracy the history, doctrine, worship, and government of that church which existed in apostolic days. The principles of government set up in a church that was founded by inspired men must have had, we are sure, the approbation of God. Corruptions in government, as well as in doctrine, sprang up at a very early period, but the church in apostolic days was purer than it ever has been in subsequent times. The most obvious method, therefore, of arriving at the truth is to compare our modern systems of ecclesiastical government with the model presented in the Holy Scriptures. That which bears the closest resemblance to the Divine original is most likely itself to be Divine.

The warmest friends of existing ecclesiastical systems cannot fairly object to such a test. There is scarcely a church on Earth that is not loud in its pretensions to apostolicity. The Prelatic churches claim to be apostolic. The Independent churches claim to be apostolic. The Presbyterian churches claim to be apostolic. Each of these denominations professes to maintain the same doctrine, worship, and government that distinguished the church which was planted by the Apostles of the Lord. On one of these points – that of ecclesiastical government – we propose to examine these claims by the very test that they themselves have chosen. Divesting ourselves of all prejudice, we come to the law and to the testimony, desirous to know what God says on the topic in question, and determined to follow where the Scripture points, let that be where it may. Let us search the Bible, to see what it teaches on this great theme. If, on a thorough examination, we fail to discover there any clear and definite principles of church government, the conclusion of necessity follows, that Prelacy, Independency, and Presbytery are upon a level – none of them is based upon Divine authority – and it becomes a matter of mere expediency or convenience which form we support. If we find, on the other hand, that certain great principles of church government are embodied in the Scriptures, then, when we have ascertained accurately what these principles are, we have reached the mind of God upon the matter, and we have discovered a touch-stone wherewith we can try the value of existing systems and determine how much is human and how much is Divine in every one of them.

Meaning of the Word "Church"

The word *church* in our common discourse is used in a variety of senses. Sometimes it signifies the material building erected for Divine worship; sometimes it means the people usually assembling in such a building; sometimes the aggregate body of the clergy as distinguished from the laity; sometimes the collective body of professing Christians. As general use is the law of language, it does not become us to take exception to the variety of significations that are given to the term by our best writers; nor can we even say that much practical inconvenience arises from them, inasmuch as the accompanying circumstances usually determine the specific sense in which the word is to be understood. But it is never to be forgotten that, when we come to the interpretation of the Word of God, the variety of senses commonly attached to the term is altogether inadmissible, and would, if adopted, darken and corrupt the meaning of Divine revelation. The word *church* in Scripture has always one meaning, and one only – *an assembly of the people of God – a society of Christians.* The Greek word *ecclesia*, in its primary and civil sense, means any assembly called together for any purpose

(*Acts* 19:32); but in its appropriated and religious sense, it means *a society of Christians*, and is invariably translated by the word *church*. Examine the Scriptures from the commencement to the close, and you find that the word *church* never has any other meaning but that which we have stated. Let any man who feels disposed to dispute this statement, produce, if he can, any passage from the Word of God where the sense would be impaired, if the phrase *society of Christians*, or *Christian assembly* were substituted for the word *church*. This, we are persuaded, would be impossible.

Though the meaning of the word *church* is in Scripture always the same, let it be observed that its applications are various. It is applied, at the pleasure of the writer, to any society of Christians, however great, or however small. Examples of this fact will not fail to suggest themselves to all who are familiar with the Word of God. We give a few passages as specimens:

Colossians 4:15: "Salute the brethren which are in Laodicea, and Nymphas, and the church which is in his house." There the term is applied to a *society of Christians* so small as to be able to find accommodation in a private dwelling-house.

Acts 11:22: "Then tidings of these things came unto the ears of the church which was in Jerusalem." There it means a *society of Christians* residing in the same city, and including, as we know on excellent authority, several thousand persons.

Acts 7:38: "This is he [Moses] that was in the church in the wilderness with the angel who spoke to him in the Mount Sinai, and with our fathers: who received the lively oracles to give unto us." Here the word signifies a *society of Christians* – an assembly of God's people so large as to include a whole nation, consisting at the time of at least two millions in number. The term is also applied to the people of God in the days of David, when residing in Canaan, spread over a great extent of territory, and amounting to many millions. (*Hebrews* 2:12, compared with *Psalm* 22:22-25.)

1 Corinthians 12:28: "And God hath set some in the church, first, apostles; secondarily, prophets; thirdly, teachers; after that miracles; then gifts of healings, helps, governments, diversities of tongues." Here the term means the *society of Christians* residing on Earth; for it was among them, not among the saints in glory, that God raised up men endowed with apostolic and prophetical gifts.

Ephesians 5:25: "Husbands, love your wives, even as Christ also loved the church, and gave Himself for it." The word is here used to signify the *society of Christians* in the largest sense – all for whom Christ died – the whole family of God – all saints in Heaven and all believers on Earth, viewed as one great company.

Let it be observed, however, that amid all this variety of application, the word *church* never alters its sense. Its meaning in every occurrence is the same. However applied, it never ceases to signify a *society of Christians*, but whether the society that the inspired writer has in view is great or small, general or particular, is to be learned, not from the term, but from the circumstances in which the term is used. In every instance it is from the context, never from the word itself, that we are to gather whether the society of Christians, intended by the writer, is to be understood of the collective company of God's people in Heaven and Earth, or only of those on the Earth, in a nation, in a city, or in a private house. The practice – into which the best expositors of Scripture are occasionally betrayed – of taking up some idea conveyed by the context only, and regarding that idea as entering into the meaning of some particular word, has been shown by a late eminent critic to be the origin of those numerous significations – perplexing by their very multitude – appended almost to every word in our classical dictionaries, and the prolific source of errors in the interpretation of the Word of God. This is obviously what has led many to suppose that the word *church* has two meanings – signifying something different when referring to the universal body of believers, from what it does when denoting the body of believers connected with a particular locality. The truth is that the word *church* has only one meaning, but it has a variety of applications. The term of itself never conveys any idea but a society of Christians; it is the context that invariably determines its general or particular application: It is manifestly inaccurate, therefore, to maintain that an idea, invariably conveyed by the context, enters into the meaning of the term; when, as all must admit, the term, apart from the context, does not suggest either a limited or universal application.

Had we occasion to speak of the several Christian congregations of a province or nation in their separate capacity, it would be quite in accordance with the Scriptural idiom to designate them the *churches* of that region. None can forget how frequently the apostle speaks of the churches of Syria and Achaia, Galatia and Asia. So, if we were required to speak of the individual congregations of Christians in Ireland – the separate Christian societies scattered over the country – we might denominate them the churches of Ireland, there being nothing in existing ecclesiastical usages to make such language either unintelligible or liable to be misunderstood. But it deserves to be noticed that, when we use such phrases as the "Established Church of Scotland," the "Episcopal Church of America," or the "Presbyterian Church of Ireland," there is no departure whatever from the Scriptural sense of the word. The meaning of the word in Scripture, as we have seen, invariably is a society of Christians, and this is precisely its meaning in any of the above phrases; the context, at the same time limiting the Christians in question to those professing certain principles, and belonging to a particular country. When we employ, for instance, such a designation as the *Presbyterian Church of Ireland*, the word *church* is used precisely in the Scriptural sense to denote a society of Christians, which we learn from the context professes Presbyterian principles and resides in Ireland.

The propriety of applying the term to signify the Christian people of a country does not arise from the fact that they are ever assembled in one congregation, either personally or by representatives, but from the fact that the mind contemplates them as a collective body. All saints in Heaven and believers on Earth are styled the *church*, not because they are assembled either literally or figuratively, but because, in the view of the mind, they are regarded as a great society, separated from the world, and united by common principles into one great brotherhood. And so the Christians of any denomination, though composing a multitude of congregations, may, in their aggregate capacity, be properly styled a church, not because they are either figuratively or literally assembled, but because, in the view of the mind, they are regarded as a collective body, distinguished from others, and united among themselves, by the profession of a common creed.

It was once doubted whether the Scriptures contain an example of the word *church* being applied to the Christians of a *country*. The science of Biblical criticism has now set that question at rest in all time coming. The true reading of *Acts* 9:31, is, "Then had the *church* rest throughout all Judea, and Galilee, and Samaria; and walking in the fear of the Lord, and in the comfort of the Holy Ghost, *was* multiplied." No man, with the slightest pretensions to scholarship, can now hesitate about receiving this as the original form of the text, when it is known that the lately discovered *MS* – the *Codex Sinaiticus* – is in its favor, no less than *A B C*; these four being at once the most ancient and valuable manuscripts of the New Testament now extant.[4] Not to speak of the evidence derivable from versions and Fathers, the united voice of these four *MSS* is enough to settle the correct form of any text; their testimony as to the original reading of *Acts* 9:31 none can question; and to that passage we confidently point as a clear word *church* being applied to the Christians of a country, viewed as one collective society, though in reality divided into many separate congregations.

Some writers, indeed, give a different account of the matter. They tell us that the universal community of Christians in Heaven and on Earth is called in Scripture the *church* not because they are viewed as one great brotherhood, united by common principles, but because they "are at all times truly and properly assembled in Jesus." It is a mere fancy to suppose that the mind ever takes such a fact into account, when employing the term in its universal application; but, if so, it does not alter the case. The Christians of a particular district, or of a province, or of a nation, may be properly designated a church for the same reasons; because they also "are at all times truly and properly assembled in Jesus." There is no sense in which all the Christians on Earth and in Heaven are "assembled in Jesus," that the Christians of any particular country are not thus assembled. If the whole is assembled, so also are the parts. Take the matter either way, the Christians of a district, or a province, or a kingdom, holding certain principles in common, if viewed as a collective community, are a church, exactly in the sense of the Scriptures. They are a *society of Christians*.

Government of the Church

The Christian society on Earth, or, as it is usually called, the church, is represented in the Scriptures as a *kingdom*. It was of his church that the Lord Jesus spoke when he said to Pilate, "My kingdom is not of this world" (*John* 18:36). The fact of its being a kingdom necessarily implies at least three things – a *king* or governor; secondly, *subjects*; thirdly, *laws*. In the church or kingdom of God, the king is *Christ*; the subjects are *believers*; the laws are the *Scriptures* of truth.

---

4. Witherow seems too much impressed by textual criticism. See Gordon Clark's *Logical Criticisms of Textual Criticism* and Wilbur Pickering's *The Identity of the New Testament Text. – Editor.*

Every king has officers under him, who are charged with the execution of his laws, and who have authority from the crown to do justice and judgment. Judges and magistrates are the office-bearers of a kingdom, deriving their power from the monarch under whom they serve, and putting the laws in force among all ranks and classes of the people. Hence a very palpable division of a kingdom is into *rulers* and *ruled* – those whose duty is to administer the law, and those who are bound to obey it.

The same distinction holds in the kingdom of Christ. It also consists of rulers and ruled – the office-bearers entrusted with the dispensation of the laws, and the people who are commanded to yield them submission. This is very plain, from *Hebrews* 13:17: "Obey them that have the rule over you, and submit yourselves: for they watch for your souls, as they that must give account." It is clear from this passage that there are some in the church whose duty is to rule; office-bearers of the church. It is no less clear that there are others in the church, whose duty is to obey; they are the private members – the subjects of the kingdom – the people.

But in every society where it is the acknowledged duty of some parties to exercise authority, and of others to practice submission, there must be what is called *government*; for in such authority exercised on the one hand, and in such submission rendered on the other, the essence of all government consists. Even were there no passage in the Scriptures but that last quoted bearing upon the subject, it is undeniable that government was established in the apostolic church. If government existed, some *form* of government must have been adopted; for to say that there was established in the kingdom of Christ government without a form of government is absurd. History tells us of many ecclesiastical and political wonders, but of all the strange things that have been witnessed in the world or in the church since the beginning of time, there has never yet appeared government without a form of government. The thing is impossible. Government in itself is an abstraction. The moment it puts forth power, it becomes a reality – it stands before the world as a visible thing– it assumes a form.

That there was government in the apostolic church, and that this government existed under a certain form, seems clear to demonstration. To determine with precision what this form was, is a matter of great consequence; for it must be evident to all that a plan of church government, instituted by the Apostles of the Lord, acting under the guidance of the Holy Spirit, must carry with it a degree of lawfulness and authority that no human system, though in itself a masterpiece of wisdom – made venerable by age, or recommended by expediency – ever can exhibit; and that every existing form of church government is deserving of respect only so far as it conforms in its principles to that Divine original. But there are obvious reasons that make it a matter of some difficulty to ascertain with accuracy the system of ecclesiastical polity that was established in the New Testament church.

(1) The Apostles, writing to Christians who were themselves members of the apostolic church, and of course well acquainted with its organization, did not judge it necessary to enter into detailed descriptions of the Christian society. To do so would have been unnatural. They do occasionally state facts bearing on church government, and hint indirectly at prevailing practices. These hints and facts were sufficiently suggestive and intelligible to the persons originally addressed, but by us, who live in a distant age, in a foreign country, and among associations widely different, they are not so easily understood.

(2) They do not even arrange such facts as bear upon the question in systematic order. If man had had the making of the Bible, it would have been a very different book; but as that circumstance was not left to our option, we must take it as we find it. On examination, we see that it teaches nothing in scientific order. Even morality and doctrine are not there arranged in regular system, but are conveyed in detached portions, and our industry is stimulated by having to gather the scattered fragments, to compare them with each other, and to work them up into order for ourselves. So ecclesiastical polity is not taught in Scripture methodically; but away over the wide field of revelation facts and hints and circumstances lie scattered, which we are to search for, and examine, and combine, and classify. Now, all do not agree in the arrangement of these facts, nor in the inferences that legitimately flow from them, nor in the mode of constructing a system from the detached material.

These things make it difficult to ascertain with accuracy, and still more so with unanimity, the form of church government that existed in apostolic days. But difficult as it seems, it is proved quite possible by a thorough and unprejudiced examination of the Scriptures, to discover the main principles that entered into the constitution of the primitive

church. We say the *main principles*; more than these we need not expect to find. The Word of God, except in some rare instances, never
enters into details – it states principles. This is a very noticeable peculiarity of the Divine legislation that deserves a passing remark. In every
civilized country, it may be observed how those entrusted with the duty
of government aim to provide a law for every specific case. The human legislator descends to details. The result of this in our own country is that the common and statute laws of England are so bulky that
the books in which they are written would make of themselves a
magnificent library; Parliament meets every year for the express purpose of constructing new, and amending old laws, to suit the ever varying circumstances of the country and the times; and notwithstanding
all, cases occur daily in the public courts, wherein the most accomplished jurists have to acknowledge that the existing laws determine
nothing. But observe how the Divine law proceeds on a method quite
different. It rarely enters into specific details, but lays down general
principles, any one of which is quite sufficient to decide a whole multitude of cases. Instead, for instance, of attempting to prescribe every
form of good that it is right for a man to perform to his neighbor, it lays
down a principle quite sufficient to meet every case – Thou shalt love
thy neighbor as thyself. Instead of enumerating the different ways by
which children are to discharge the duties that they owe their parents,
Scripture enacts this general law, holding good in every case – Honor
thy father and thy mother. Declining to specify every semblance of sin
that it were well for Christians to avoid, the statutes of the Lord direct
us to abstain from all appearance of evil. Human legislation enters into
minute details, but Divine legislation enacts general principles. The
result is that, while there is perhaps more room left for difference of
opinion in the interpretation and application of the enactments of a
code of law constructed on the latter system, yet this disadvantage is
more than counterbalanced by the fact that the laws of God are in themselves perfect; that they do not change with the ever varying circumstances of countries and of times; that they meet every case which can
possibly occur; and that they are compressed into a reasonable size,
being all written in a book so small that it can be lifted in the hand, or
carried in the pocket. Now, the Scripture teaches us church government, as it teaches morality. It does not furnish minute details, but it
supplies *the great leading principles* that entered into the polity of the

apostolic church. What these main principles were, it is now our purpose to ascertain.[5]

It is the common practice of writers, in discussing the important subject of ecclesiastical government, to select some one of our modern churches which happens to be a favorite, delineate its characteristic features, and then proceed to show that they are a reflection of the pattern presented in the Word of God. That this plan has some recommendations, we can readily believe, but it is no less obvious that it is liable to grave objections. It seems to assume at the commencement the conclusion to which the reasoner can only hope to conduct us after a sound process of logic. It somehow produces the fatal impression that the writer has determined in the first place that his view of the subject is right, and then goes to Scripture to search for proof of it. The author may be the most impartial and truth-loving of men, but his very plan betrays a preference for some particular system, and thus, at the outset, awakens the prejudices of many readers. Besides, it affords opportunities for viewing passages of Scripture apart from their connection, and tempts writers to quote in their favorite texts, the sound of which only is upon their side. For these reasons we do not choose to adopt this method on the present occasion.

The plan of procedure we propose is more unusual, though, we trust, not less satisfactory. We will examine the Holy Scriptures with a view of ascertaining from them the various facts that bear on the government of the apostolic church. We will produce the passages, contemplate them in their immediate connection, unfold their meaning, and try if, by their aid, we can arrive at *great principles*. We will then turn to our modern churches, view the different forms of ecclesiastical polity that exist in the world at present, and see which of them it is that embodies all or most of these principles. When this is done, we shall have found the denomination that, in point of government, is best entitled to be regarded as the *apostolic church*.

This process of reasoning is so very clear and simple that there is no room for practicing deception either on ourselves or our readers. The very humblest intellect may follow our logic to the close. There are but two steps till we arrive at the conclusion. *First*, we are to ascertain from the unerring Word of God what were the main principles in the govern-

5. This paragraph was suggested by reading Dr. [William] Paley's sermon on *Romans* 14:7.

ment of the churches founded by the Apostles of the Lord; and, *secondly*, we are to ascertain in which of our modern churches these main principles are most fully acknowledged and carried out. We will then apply to the settlement of the matter an axiom, radiant in the light of its own self-evidence. That axiom is, *The modern church which embodies in its government most apostolic principles comes nearest in its government to the apostolic church.*

Apostolic Principles

From a careful examination of the Scripture, we find at least four different kinds of office-bearers in the apostolic church: (1) apostles; (2) evangelists; (3) bishops (also called pastors and teachers); (4) deacons. Each one of these had a right to exercise all the offices inferior to his own; but one filling an inferior had no right to discharge the duties of a superior office. Thus, the apostolic office included all the others; and a bishop or elder had the right to act as a deacon, so long as his doing so did not impede the due discharge of duties peculiarly his own. A deacon, on the other hand, had no right to exercise the office of a bishop; nor had a bishop any authority to take on him the duties of an apostle. Each superior office included all below it.

Two of these offices – those of apostle and evangelist – were temporary, necessary at the first establishment of Christianity, but not necessary to be perpetuated. The *apostles* were witnesses of the resurrection of the Lord Jesus, endowed with the power of working miracles and of conferring the Holy Ghost by the laying on of their hands, the infallible expounders of the Divine will, and the founders of the Christian church; and, having served the purpose for which they were sent, they disappeared out of the world, and, as apostles, have left no successors. *Evangelists* were missionaries – men who traveled from place to place preaching the Gospel, and who acted as the assistants and delegates of the apostles in organizing churches. Of these, Philip and Timothy and Titus were the most eminent examples. It deserves to be remarked, with regard to these temporary, or, as they are usually called, extraordinary office-bearers, that their sphere of duty was not limited to a congregation, but extended to the church at large. They were members of any Christian Society within whose bounds they resided for a time, but their mission was to the world, and their authority extended to the church universal.

The offices of *bishop* and *deacon* were, on the other hand, designed to be perpetual in the church. The bishops, or, as they are more usually called, elders,[6] and pastors, and teachers, were office-bearers, whose duty it was to instruct and govern the church. The deacons had charge of temporal concerns, and were entrusted with the special duty of ministering to the necessities of the poor. The church can never cease to have need of these two offices, so long as its members have spiritual and temporal wants to be supplied. But it is to be observed, with regard to the bishops and deacons, that they were mainly congregational officers. The sphere of their duty was not so general as that of apostles, prophets, and evangelists, but lay for the most part within the bounds of that particular church or district for which they were appointed to act.

Dr. Campbell thus expounds the special necessity that existed in the primitive church, both for the temporary and perpetual office-bearers:

> To take a similitude from temporal things: It is one thing to conquer a kingdom and become master of it, and another thing to govern it when conquered, so as to retain the possession which has been acquired. The same agents and the same expedients are not properly adapted to both. For the first of these purposes, there was a set of extraordinary ministers or officers in the church, who, like the military forces intended for conquest, could not be fixed to a particular spot whilst there remained any provinces to conquer. Their charge was, in a manner, universal, and their functions ambulatory. For the second, there was a set of ordinary ministers or pastors, corresponding to civil governors, to whom it was necessary to allot distinct charges or precincts, to which their services were chiefly to be confined, in order to instruct the people, to preside in the public worship and religious ordinances, and to give them the necessary assistance for the regulation of their conduct. Without this second arrangement, the acquisitions made could not have been long retained. There must have ensued an universal relapse into idolatry and infidelity. This distinction of ministers into extraordinary and ordinary, has been admitted by controvertists on both sides, and therefore cannot justly be considered as introduced (which sometimes happens to distinctions) to serve an hypothesis.[7]

With these preliminary observations, we proceed in search of –

---

6. This is assumed for the present: It will be proved afterwards.

7. *Lectures on Ecclesiastical History*, Lecture 4, Third edition, London, 1824.

The First Principle

All offices in the Christian church take origin from the Lord Jesus. He himself is the author and embodiment of them all; he is the Apostle of our profession; he is an Evangelist, preaching peace to them that are afar off, and to them that are nigh; he is the great Pastor or shepherd of the sheep – the Bishop of souls; and he is the Deacon or servant who came not to be ministered to, but to minister. All offices in the church are embodied in the person of Christ.

The apostles were the only office-bearers chosen during the lifetime of the Lord. They held their appointments immediately from himself. They were called to the work of the ministry by his voice, and they received their commission at his hands. Simon and Andrew were casting their nets into the Lake of Galilee, as Jesus walked upon the beach, but at his call they left their nets to follow him through the world. The sons of Zebedee heard his voice, and forthwith they forgot both father and mother in their ambition to become fishers of men. When Christ said, Follow me, Levi forsook the receipt of custom, and was a publican no more. The personal call of the Lord Jesus was then, and is still, the first and best of all authority to hold office in the church of God. Let a man only satisfy us that he holds his appointment directly from the Lord, as the apostles did, and we require no more to induce us to submit to him.

But after the Lord had ascended to Heaven, the personal call, except in case of Paul, who was one born out of due time, was not the passport of any man either to the ministry or apostleship. Men were no more put into office by the voice of the living Lord Jesus. The departure of the Master, and the vacancy left in the list of apostles by the death of Judas, gave opportunity for bringing into operation a new principle. The first chapter of the *Acts of the Apostles* brings the whole case before us. Let us specially examine the passage – *Acts* 1:13-26 – that we may have full possession of the facts. It appears that, in the interval between the Ascension and the Day of Pentecost, the disciples met for prayer and supplication in the upper room of the city of Jerusalem. The mother and brethren of Jesus were present, as were also the eleven apostles. Taken together, they numbered one hundred and twenty in all. Peter rose and addressed the company. He reminded them of the vacancy in the apostleship. Judas, who betrayed the Master, was dead, and the office that he forfeited by his transgression must be conferred upon another. Peter states the necessary qualifications of him who was to be the successor of Judas. He must be one who had intercourse with the eleven from the commencement of Christ's ministry to the close. He states the duties of the new apostle; he was to be with the others a witness of Christ's resurrection. Such was the case that Peter put before the men and brethren, met together in that upper room of Jerusalem. We then read in verse 23, "*They appointed two*, Joseph called Barsabas, who was surnamed Justus, and Matthias." In consequence of this double choice, it became necessary to decide which should be regarded as the true apostle; which, after prayer, was done by casting lots. But let it be particularly observed that, while Peter explained the necessary qualifications, and the peculiar duties of the office, the appointment of the person did not rest with Peter, but with the men and brethren to whom the address of Peter was directed. Farther, it is not to be forgotten that the office to which Matthias succeeded is, in the 20th verse, termed a *bishopric*, and how it is said in the 25th verse, he had "to take part of this *ministry* and apostleship." The men and brethren, at the instigation of Peter, exercised the right of appointing a man to a bishopric – that is, to the office of a bishop, and to take part in the ministry. In the apostolic church, the people appointed Matthias to be a minister – a bishop – an apostle.[8] The case recorded in *Acts* 14:23 is to the same effect, though, from a mistranslation, the force of it is lost upon the English reader. The *Authorized Version* represents the two apostles, Barnabas and Paul, as *ordaining* elders in every church; whereas the true meaning of the word in the original is "to elect by a show of hands" – a fact now admitted by the best expositors.[9] We must not allow a faulty translation to rob us of the testimony of Scripture to an important fact – namely, that the elders of the New Testament church were appointed to office by the popular vote.

The sixth chapter of *Acts* comes next under consideration. At the period to which the narrative there recorded refers, the disciples at Jerusalem had grown numerous. The Grecians began to complain against the Hebrews, how that their widows were neglected in the daily ministrations. Hitherto the twelve had attended to the wants of the poor; but their hands were at the same time full of other work, and, among such

8. Actually, the people chose two, and the Holy Spirit ordained one to be an apostle. – *Editor.*

9. See Dean Alford on the passage.

a multitude, it is not surprising that some were neglected, nor is it very wonderful, considering what human nature is, that some were found to murmur, even when apostles managed the business. What was now to be done? A division of offices was clearly a necessity. But were the apostles to take it on themselves to select persons on whom should devolve the duty of attending to the temporal wants of the community? Had they done so, few would dispute their right, or venture to charge inspired men with the exercise of a despotic or unwarranted authority. But, instead of this, they adopted a course of procedure unaccountable to us on any other principle, than that they purposely managed the matter in such a way as would guide the church in the appointment of office-bearers when they themselves would be removed, and thus form a precedent for future ages. The apostles summoned the multitude together and explained the case. They said their appropriate business as ministers was with the Word of God. They said it was unreasonable for them to have to neglect the spiritual province, in order to attend to temporal concerns; and they called upon the brethren to look out among themselves for seven men, of good character, gifted with wisdom and the Spirit of God, who might be appointed to take charge of this secular business, and who would leave the apostles free to attend to duties peculiarly their own – namely, prayer and the ministry of the Word. "And the saying pleased the whole multitude; and *they chose* Stephen, a man full of faith and of the Holy Ghost, and Philip, and Prochorus, and Nicanor, and Timon, and Parmenas, and Nicolas, a proselyte of Antioch; whom they set before the apostles; and when they had prayed, they laid their hands on them" (*Acts* 6:5-6). The seven men whom the multitude chose on this occasion were the first *deacons*. Though not expressly called so in the Scriptures, yet they are admitted to have been such, by almost universal consent. The lowest office-bearers, therefore, in the apostolic church, were chosen by the people.

Here, then, are three clear facts, fully sufficient to be the basis of a principle. The first chapter of *Acts* supplies us with an instance of the assembled men and brethren appointing to office one who was both an apostle and a minister. The fourteenth chapter shows that the elders of the congregation were chosen by popular suffrage. The sixth chapter furnishes an example of the whole multitude of the disciples choosing seven men to be deacons. On these three facts, clear and irresistible, we found the principle of *popular election*. The conclusion that follows from this evidence, we find it absolutely impossible to evade, namely – that in the apostolic church the *office-bearers were chosen by the people*.

The Second Principle

There is a class of office-bearers very frequently mentioned as existing in the early church, and to which, as yet, we have only made a slight allusion. We mean the *elder*, or *presbyter*, as he is frequently called. This church officer is often mentioned in the *Acts* and *Epistles*; but an attentive reader will not fail to remark that no passage of Scripture ever speaks of him as holding an office distinct from the *bishop*. The same verse never speaks of bishops and elders. When Paul, for example, writes to the Philippian church (1:1), he mentions the bishops and deacons, but says nothing of elders. When James directs the sick to call for the elders of the church (5:14), he says nothing of bishops. If the offices of bishop and elder were quite distinct – if a bishop were an office-bearer bearing rule over a number of elders, it does seem strange that no passage of Scripture speaks at the same time of bishops and elders. There is one supposition, and only one, that would furnish a satisfactory reason for this fact. If the two terms be only different names for the same office, then to speak of *bishops* and *elders* would be a violation of the laws of language – it would be tautology – it would be the same thing as to speak of presbyters and elders, or of bishops and bishops. To suppose that the two offices were identical accounts sufficiently for the significant fact that they are never mentioned together in the same passage of the Word of God; for it is plain that one of the terms being adequate to indicate the office-bearer intended, there was no need to introduce the other at the same time.

Still there must be something stronger than a presumption to warrant us in saying that the two terms were only different names for the same person. However improbable it may appear, it is still possible that these two, bishop and elder, were distinct office-bearers even though the same passage never speaks of them together. This obliges us to consult the Scriptures further on this question.

The first passage that comes before us is *Titus* 1:5-7: "For this cause I left you in Crete, that you should set in order the things that are wanting, and ordain elders in every city, as I had appointed you: If any be blameless, the husband of one wife, having faithful children, not accused of riot or unruly. For a bishop must be blameless, as the steward of God; not self-willed, not soon angry, not given to wine, no striker, not given to filthy lucre." This passage strongly confirms the truth of the supposition already made, that the two offices were identical. It appears that Paul left Titus behind him in Crete to ordain elders in every city. To guide him in the discharge of this duty, the apostle proceeds to state the qualifications of an elder. No private member of the church was eligible to that office except he was a man of blameless life, the husband of one wife, and had obedient children; "for," says he, "a bishop must be blameless, as the steward of God." Dr. King well observes on this passage,

> that the term *elder*, used at the commencement, is exchanged for the term *bishop* in the conclusion, while the same office-bearer is spoken of. An *elder* must have such and such qualifications. Why? Because a *bishop* must be blameless, as the steward of God. Does not this identify the elder and the bishop? If not, identification is impossible. Were it said, the Lord Mayor of London must devote himself to his duties, for the chief magistrate of such a city has great responsibilities, would not the language bear, that the Lord Mayor and the chief magistrate were the same office-bearer? Otherwise, the representation would be absurd; for why should the mayor devote himself to his duties because some other person had great responsibilities? Yet the mayor and chief magistrate are not more identified in this comparison than are the elder and bishop in Paul's instructions to Titus.[10]

It must be evident to every unprejudiced man that the apostle would never state as a reason for ordaining none but men of good moral character to the office of *eldership*, that a *bishop* must be blameless, if he did not understand that elder and bishop were only different designations for the same office. On any other supposition, the language of the apostle would be without coherence and without sense.

Again, we turn to 2 *John* 1, and we find how the Apostle John styles himself an *elder* – "The elder unto the elect lady and her children, whom I love in the truth." Next comes up 1 *Peter* 5:1, and we find there that the Apostle Peter calls himself an *elder* – "The elders which are among you I exhort, who am also an elder, and a witness of the sufferings of Christ." That John and Peter were both bishops all admit; but these passages show that they were elders also. This however, brings us but a step to

10. *Exposition and Defence of the Presbyterian Form of Church Government*, Edinburgh, 1853, 176-177.

the conclusion. It may be true that every general is an officer, but it does not follow from this that every officer is a general. A bishop may, like John and Peter, be an elder, but it does not necessarily follow that an elder is a bishop. This may be true, but we require more proof before we can reach a conclusion. This we have as fully as can be desired in *Acts* 20:17-28. We read there how Paul sent for the elders of the church at Ephesus to meet him at Miletus. He spoke of his ministry in their city, the great theme of his preaching being repentance toward God, and faith toward the Lord Jesus Christ. He foretold the afflictions awaiting him at Jerusalem and elsewhere, and he saddened their hearts by saying to them that they would see his face no more. And he warned them to take heed to themselves and to the flock over which the Holy Ghost had made them *overseers* – that is, *bishops*, as the word is elsewhere rendered. Every reader acquainted with the original is aware that the word translated *overseers* in *Acts* 20:28 is the very same as that translated *bishops* in *Philippians* 1:1, so that we have here the evidence of inspiration, that the elders of Ephesus were bishops by appointment of the Holy Ghost. This makes the chain of reasoning strong and conclusive. Bishops, as we have seen, were elders, and elders, as we now see, were bishops. This conducts us to a principle – namely, that *in the apostolic church, the offices of bishops and elders were identical*. An elder was not inferior to a bishop, nor was a bishop superior to an elder. It was the same office-bearer who was known by these different names.

We are not disposed to attach much value to the opinion of such a man as Edward Gibbon, on any question of doctrine or morality, but that distinguished historian was competent to grapple with a matter of fact, and may be heard as one who, from being unprejudiced in favor of any religious system whatever, was in a position to judge impartially in a case of this kind. Speaking of the government and administration of the church prior to the Council of Nicæa he says,

> The public functions of religion were solely entrusted to the established ministers of the church, bishops and the presbyters; two appellations which, in their first origin, appear to have distinguished the same office, and the same order of persons. The name of presbyter was expressive of their age, or rather of their gravity and wisdom. The title of bishop denoted their inspection over the faith and manners of the Christians who were committed to their pastoral care.[11]

11. *History of the Decline and Fall of the Roman Empire*, chapter 15.

The Third Principle

Let it not be forgotten that we have now ascertained that *presbyter* and *bishop* were, in their first origin, only different names for the same ecclesiastical office-bearer. Enough has been found in the Scriptures to satisfy us that bishops were elders, and that elders were bishops, in the apostolic church. We are warranted, therefore, to regard this fact as fully substantiated, while we proceed to the discovery of a third principle.

The fourteenth chapter of *Acts* describes a missionary journey of Paul and Barnabas. There was an attempt made to stone them at Iconium, but they fled to Lystra and Derbe. When Paul made a cripple at Lycaonia leap and walk, the priest of Jupiter brought oxen and garlands to the gates, and it was with some difficulty the people in their pagan ignorance were restrained from paying divine honors to the two preachers. But so fickle are the sentiments of the multitude that, shortly afterwards, the great apostle was stoned nearly to death at the very place where he had been almost worshiped as a god. Barely escaping with his life, Paul and his companion revisited Derbe, and Lystra, and Iconium, and Antioch, preaching the Gospel, confirming the souls of the disciples, and exhorting them to continue in the faith. And the sacred historian, in the narrative of this evangelistic tour, informs us of this important fact, that *they appointed elders in every church*. His words are – "And when they had chosen for them, by suffrage, elders in every church, and had prayed with fasting, they commended them to the Lord, on whom they believed" (*Acts* 14:23). We have seen already that a church in Scripture signifies any assembly of Christians, however great or small. It was the primitive practice to call the believers residing in any town, however large, or in any village, however small, the church of that place. Many of these societies, collected from among the heathen by these pioneers of Christianity, organized in the face of difficulty, and thinned by intimidation, must have been weak in point of numbers. Still, the two apostles were not satisfied with appointing one elder or bishop in each society, however small in numbers; but as we are taught by the Holy Spirit, they appointed *elders in every church*. If, then, the evangelist Luke, speaking as he was moved by the Holy Ghost, is a true witness, there were more elders than one in each congregation of the apostolic church. How many, whether two, three, or more, we are not informed, but that in each church there was a plurality of elders is clear.

We proceed once more to the twentieth chapter of *Acts*. Here Paul is represented as travelling from Greece on his way to Jerusalem. Having stopped a week at Troas, he went upon his onward way, sometimes by sea and sometimes by land, striving to reach the Jewish capital before Pentecost. Having touched at Miletus, a seaport of Ionia, thirty-six miles south of Ephesus, he sent a message to that city for the elders of the church. The words of inspiration are – "And from Miletus he sent to Ephesus, and called the elders of the church" (*Acts* 20:17). From this, it appears the church of Ephesus had not only one elder, but more, and we have already seen that, in verse 28, its elders are called bishops. Unless language mean nothing, and the statements of Scripture be as unintelligible as the leaves of the Sybil, there was *a plurality of elders or bishops* at Ephesus.

Still farther, Philippi was a city in the confines of ancient Thrace. To the classic reader it is known as the place where Augustus and Antony wrested from Brutus and Cassius, in a pitched battle, the empire of the world; to the Christian it is remarkable as being the first spot in Europe where the banner of the Cross was unfurled, and sinners listened to the Gospel of Jesus. There the heart of the seller of purple was opened to attend to the things that were spoken by Paul. It was there that, for casting the spirit of divination out of a soothsayer, Paul and Silas were beaten by the magistrates, and had their feet made fast in the stocks. It was there at the dead hour of the night, when the foundations of the prison shook, and every door in the jail flew open, and every man's chains fell from his arms, that the keeper of the prison asked two of his prisoners the most important question that was ever put by a sinner to a minister of God – "Sirs, what must I do to be saved?" In this town of Philippi a church was organized, though in face of determined opposition; and, some ten or twelve years after Paul's first visit, he thought it right to address to this church a letter. This letter has been preserved. It finds a place in the Word of God. It is that known to us as the *Epistle to the Philippians*. One has some curiosity to read what an apostle thought it good to write to a church, at the head of whose roll of members stood the names of Lydia and the jailer. As might be expected, it is full to the brim of precious and consoling truths; but, what is more to our purpose at present, we find these words in the first verse of the first chapter: "Paul and Timotheus, the servants of Jesus Christ, to all the saints in Christ Jesus which are at Philippi, with *the bishops* and deacons" Philippi was, no doubt, a considerable town; but, in point of population and importance, it was no more to such a city as Dublin or Liverpool than a parish is to a diocese. Yet, in modern times, one bishop is thought sufficient even for London, where professing Christians are numbered by millions, whereas a single Christian congregation gathered out of a heathen population, possessing ecclesiastical existence only for ten or twelve years and suffering for Christ's sake, and located in a outskirts of Macedonia, had a *pluraliy of bishops*. Paul, in writing to that church, addresses his epistle to the *bishops* and deacons

Let the candid reader glance again at the ground over which we have passed. He sees that Paul, in writing his *Epistle* to the church at Philippi, addressed it to the *bishops*. He sees there were *elders* in the church at Ephesus when Paul sent for them to Miletus. He finds it stated that Barnabas and Paul ordained *elders in every church*. How is it possible for him to resist the conclusion that, in apostolic days, there was in each congregation a plurality of elders, or what we have seen amounts to the same thing, a plurality of bishops? This leads us to the third principle of apostolic government – that *in each church there was a plurality of elders*.

The Fourth Principle

Ordination is the solemn designation of a person to ecclesiastical office with the laying on of hands. Every permanent office-bearer in the church, whether bishop or deacon, was set apart solemnly to his office by the act of ordination. In its outward form it consisted of three things – fasting, prayer, and imposition of hands. The imposition of hands was used when spiritual gifts were conferred (*Acts* 8:17; 19:6); and it was also practiced when the sick were miraculously healed (*Mark* 16:18; *Acts* 9:17; 28:8). But, distinct from all such cases, the laying on of hands was used at the ordination of church office-bearers, and when no extraordinary or miraculous gift was bestowed (*Acts* 6:6; 13:1-3; and 1 *Timothy* 4:14; 5:22). The withdrawment of miraculous powers cannot therefore be any valid reason why, at ordinations, the practice should be set aside; the imposition of hands in such cases never was the medium of imparting the Holy Ghost, but only the form of investing with ecclesiastical office.

The great question regarding ordination is whether it is the act of one individual or more, of one elder or many elders, of a bishop or a presbytery? That the Lord Jesus may give a special call to any laborer, and send him to work in his vineyard, none disputes. There can be very little doubt also that, if an inspired apostle were still upon the Earth, he would have the right to ordain alone, if he thought it right to do so. Nay, if some modern evangelist could show, as Titus could, that an apostle had left him behind for this special duty in virtue of the right conferred upon him by a higher power, he would have the privilege of ordaining (*Titus* 1:5). Anyone, therefore, claiming the right of doing all that an evangelist did, would require to show that, if not an apostle, he possesses, like Titus, the authority delegated to him by an apostle. But here every ruler in every church must fail. It remains, therefore, that we examine the Scriptures to discover who it was that, in the absence of apostles, or those delegated by apostles, had the privilege of solemnly setting apart others to ecclesiastical office, and especially to ascertain if this power was lodged in one individual or in more.

First, we turn to 1 *Timothy* 4:14. We have there the ordination of Timothy. The apostle exhorts his son in the faith to employ to good purpose the gift of the ministry that had been conferred upon him. He intimates that this gift had been given by prophecy – that is, in consequence of certain intimations of the prophets, who were numerous in that age of spiritual gifts, marking him out as one who would be an eminent minister. He adds that the gift was conferred *with the laying on of hands of the presbytery* – that is, by the presbyters or elders in their collective capacity. The words of the apostles are – "Neglect not the gift that is in thee, which was given thee by prophecy, *with the laying on of the hands of the presbytery.*" These words are decisive as to the parties with whom the power of ordination is lodged.

Again, we turn to *Acts* 13:1-3. It appears that, in the church of Antioch, there were certain prophets and teachers whose names are there recorded. They ministered to the Lord and fasted; and, while thus employed, it was intimated to them by the Holy Ghost that they should separate Barnabas and Saul for missionary work among the Gentiles. Both had been preachers of the Gospel previously; but now they were to enter on a new sphere, and engage in a new department of the work. It was right, therefore, that the prophets and teachers should solemnly set apart the two brethren to the missionary work by the act of ordination. We read, accordingly, in verse 3, that "when *they* had fasted and prayed, and *laid their hands on them*, they sent them away." The act of ordination was here evidently not the work of one teacher, but of several. A plurality took part in it.

Another instance of a plurality of church rulers taking part in this rite is recorded in *Acts* 6:6. We have there the ordination of the deacons. The church at Jerusalem chose seven men to attend to the necessities of the poor, "whom they set before the apostles: and when they had prayed, *they laid their hands* on them." This is particularly valuable, as it proves that, when it was convenient or practicable for a plurality of rulers to take part in the act of ordination, the apostles themselves preferred that course.

Glance again at the ground over which we have now passed. It was the practice of an apostle, or one directly appointed by an apostle for this specific purpose, to perform alone the act of ordination. But they did not ordain singly where it was possible for them to associate. Where a plurality could be had conveniently, as in the case of the deacons, it was common for more than one to take part in the ceremony. In the absence of apostles we have seen, in the case of Saul and Barnabas, ordination was the act of certain prophets and teachers; and, in the case of Timothy, it was the act of the presbytery. This conducts us to our fourth principle, namely, that, *in the apostolic church, ordination was the act of the presbytery* – of a plurality of elders.

The Fifth Principle

The fifteenth chapter of *Acts* is much too long to be here transcribed. But before the reader proceeds farther, let him open the Bible and read that chapter carefully from the commencement to the close. If he is really in search of truth, and disposed to receive it in its simplicity, the perusal of that chapter will satisfy him that the following facts are there embodied:

It appears that certain men came down from Judea to Antioch, and taught the church there that circumcision is necessary to salvation. Paul and Barnabas set themselves to oppose these teachers, but in vain. It was then agreed that certain of the church of Antioch, including in their number Barnabas and Paul, should go up to Jerusalem and lay the case before the apostles and elders. When they reached Jerusalem – at that time the metropolis of Christianity – the apostles and elders came together to consider the question. At first there was in the assembly considerable difference of opinion. Peter at last rose to speak. He reminded them how God had honored him in making him the instrument of first preaching the Gospel to the Gentiles, and how it had pleased God, without respect of persons, to bestow the Holy Ghost upon them as well as upon Jewish believers. He argues, therefore, that to make circumcision necessary to salvation – to bind a yoke upon the Gentiles which even the Jews were not able to bear – would be to tempt God; and he closes by enunciating the great truth that Jews and Gentiles, both alike, obtain salvation through the grace of our Lord Jesus Christ. Barnabas and Paul followed, declaring that by them, too, God had wrought among the Gentiles miracles and wonders. James next delivered his opinion. He showed that the truth declared by Peter, namely, that God had taken out of the Gentiles a people for his name, was the subject of ancient prophecy. He quotes from the prophet Amos to show how God had promised to build the tabernacle of David which had fallen into ruins, that the residue of men and the Gentiles called by his name should seek after the Lord. He ends by declaring his judgment to be that the Gentiles already turned to the Lord should not be troubled with any unnecessary burden, but that they should be directed to abstain from pollutions of idols, and from fornication, and from things strangled, and from blood. The opinion of James was approved by the assembly. The apostles and elders, with the whole church, agreed to send Judas and Silas down to Antioch, with Barnabas and Paul to announce the result. The decision of the meeting was embodied in letters, which ran in the name of the apostles, elders, and brethren, and were addressed to the Gentile Christians in Antioch, Syria, and Cilicia. The epistle charged those who taught that circumcision was necessary to salvation with troubling the brethren, and subverting their souls; denied that they had authority from the apostles and elders so to teach; mentioned that Judas and Silas were empowered, along with Barnabas and Paul – men who hazarded their lives for the name of the Lord Jesus – to declare verbally the decision of the assembly; and stated that it seemed good to the Holy Ghost and to them to impose upon the Gentile converts no burden except abstinence from meats offered to idols, from blood, from things strangled, and from fornication. Such was the substance of the letter that was carried down to Antioch by the deputies from the assembly at Jerusalem. The multitude gathered to hear it; it was delivered and read, and the people rejoiced for the consolation. Judas and Silas added their exhortations, and the brethren were confirmed in the faith. Shortly afterward, Paul, having had some difference with Barnabas, chose Silas as his fellow-traveler, and set out on another missionary journey, the object of which was to visit the converts in every city where he had preached the Word of God, and see how they did. Commended by the brethren to the grace of God, Paul and Silas departed from Antioch, and went through Syria and Cilicia confirming the churches. Derbe and Lystra and other cities of Asia Minor were visited on this occasion, and, as they went through the cities, they delivered to them the decrees for to keep which were ordained of the apostles and elders that were at Jerusalem (*Acts* 16:4).

Every candid man must admit that this is a fair representation of all facts bearing on the subject, as put before us in the fifteenth and sixteenth chapters of *Acts*. Let it be remarked that, in the simple narrative, the following facts stand noticeably out:

(1) That Barnabas and Paul had a dispute about circumcision with certain false teachers who came down from Judea;

(2) This dispute was not settled in the church of Antioch where it originated;

(3) The matter was referred to an external ecclesiastical assembly consisting of the apostles and elders at Jerusalem;

(4) This assembly met publicly to deliberate on the question;

(5) They pronounced a decision;

(6) To this decision the church of Antioch and the churches of Syria and Cilicia yielded submission.

These facts are on the face of the narrative, and cannot be denied. That they were permitted to take place, and that a record of them is inserted in the Holy Scriptures, seems strange if these things did not happen for an example to us. Were it enough for the church of Antioch to be made certain of the mind of God upon the point in dispute, Paul, who was present, could have declared this with infallible accuracy; for he was one who not only spoke as he was moved by the Holy Ghost, but who often decided matters equally important by a word from his lips or a stroke of his pen. A single sentence from the very apostle who was then at Antioch is admitted by the church of God to be decisive on any point of Christian faith or Christian duty; so that, if an infallible decision was the only thing required, one does not see why the matter was ever carried further. When the case did come up to Jerusalem, had the appeal been to inspiration only, one does not see what business the elders had to meet with the apostles to consider the matter; surely the apostles were competent to declare the mind of God without the aid of uninspired men. If nothing was necessary but for the apostles to pronounce an infallible deliverance, why was there such a thing as disputing in the assembly, or even the semblance of deliberation, or why should one apostle after another state his opinion? We would suppose the deliverance of a single inspired man quite sufficient. If the disputing that occurred in the assembly was only among the elders, the elders must have been very silly to dispute about a matter that inspiration was to settle, and with which they, as uninspired men, could have nothing to do, but to listen to the voice of God; and why did the apostles permit them to dispute, when a word from the infallible expounders of the Divine will could have decided the question? And when the decree went forth, why was it in the name of the apostles and *elders* that were at Jerusalem? There is one way of accounting for this satisfactorily, and only one so far as we can see. These events were permitted to take place, and are recorded for our guidance under all similar circumstances. Should any difference arise, which cannot be settled within the limits of the congregation where it occurs, it is to be referred for settlement to the rulers of the church in their assembled capacity. If the apostles were alive upon the Earth to meet with the elders, and by aid of their inspiration, to guide them to an unerring decision, and were we to refer our differences to such an assembly, this would be literal obedience to the example put before us in the Divine Word. But when, in their personal absence, we refer our differences to the assembly of the elders, and when the elders, guided by the inspired writings of the apostles as contained in the Scriptures, pronounce a deliverance on the question, and when to such deliverance we yield submission in the Lord, this is more than acting up to the spirit, it is acting up to everything but the letter, of apostolic example.

We are thus conducted to this twofold fact that, in the apostolic church, there existed the privilege of referring disputed matters to the decision of an assembly of living men, external to the congregation where such dispute originated, and composed of the rulers of the church; and that this ecclesiastical assembly, in the absence of the apostles, consisting simply of the rulers of the church, has a right to meet, to deliberate, to decide, and to demand obedience to its decisions in the Lord. This twofold principle we designate *the privilege of appeal to the assembly of elders, and the right of government exercised by them in their associate capacity.*

It would scarcely be necessary to say a word on the presence of the *brethren* in the assembly at Jerusalem, were it not that some parties have made this fact the foundation for special cavil. As they are mentioned separately from the apostles seems to us clear that the "brethren" must have been the non-official members of the church, or, as in modern times they would be called, the laity. That they were present at the meeting; that they concurred in the decision; and that the letter sent down to Antioch was written in their name, as well as in that of the apostles and elders, are, in our opinion, undeniable facts – patent on the face of the narrative. But we have not all the facts of the case before us, except we observe –

(1) That the original reference from Antioch was not to the brethren, but to the apostles and elders (verse 2);

(2) That it is not said that the brethren assembled to deliberate on the question, but that "the apostles and elders came together for to consider of this matter" (verse 6)

(3) That we do not read of any of the brethren speaking on the subject submitted, but that they "kept silence" while others spoke (verse 12);

(4) That the decrees are not said to be ordained of the brethren, but "of the apostles and elders which were at Jerusalem" (*Acts* 16:4).

The unprejudiced inquirer will observe that the private members of the church, here designated the "brethren," did not ordain the decrees, nor speak in the meeting, nor assemble to deliberate, nor was it to them that the appeal from Antioch was brought. He will, on the other hand, remark that they were present in the assembly, that they concurred in the finding, and that, as it was important to show that all the Christians of Jerusalem were unanimous on the subject, the letter embodying the decision was written in their name as well as in that of the apostles and elders. From motives of courtesy, and for the purpose of Christian salutation, Silvanus and Timotheus are represented as uniting with Paul, in his *First Epistle to the Thessalonians*, but this does not imply that Silvanus and Timotheus were inspired men, much less that they were conjoined in the authorship of the letter. And, in the same way, the letter addressed to the Gentiles of Antioch, Syria, and Cilicia was the letter of the apostles and elders – the name of the brethren being added to show, not that they took part in the composition, but that they concurred in the sentiments. Persons, therefore, who desire to convince us that private Christians in the apostolic church were not only present as auditors at assemblies of church rulers, but also shared in the deliberations, and acted as constituent members of ecclesiastical courts, would require to produce something much more explicit on the subject than the fifteenth chapter of *Acts*. To us it seems clear that the apostles and elders assembled, deliberated, and decreed; the brethren were present, listened, and concurred. The apostles and elders were, as we would say, members of court; the brethren were only auditors, who gave their assent to the decision of the rulers.

Our fifth principle, therefore, may be summed up in these terms: *the privilege of appeal to the assembly of elders, and the right of government exercised by them in their corporate character.*

The Sixth Principle

It is a distinctive feature of the apostolic government that church rulers did not render spiritual obedience to any temporal potentate, or to any ecclesiastical chief. Paul seldom commences any of his epistles without reminding his readers that he held his apostleship by the will of God, not by the favor of man. Take, as an example, *Galatians* 1:1: "Paul, an apostle (not of men, neither by man, but by Jesus Christ, and God the Father who raised Him from the dead)," etc. In the picture of apostolic times presented in the New Testament, we can detect no instance of the church acknowledging the spiritual dominion of any earthly monarch, or consenting to surrender a portion of its religious liberty for any temporal advantage whatever. We find no provision made in the Gospel for the supremacy of a Christian, much less of a heathen, king in the things of God. The law of Scripture is express: "Render to Caesar the things that are Caesar's, and to God the things that are God's" (*Mark* 12:17). In all temporal matters the members of the apostolic church regarded it their duty to yield obedience to the civil rulers of the country in which they lived; in all spiritual matters they did homage to a higher power. In temporal matters an apostle bowed to the laws of the land as administered by the magistrate of a village; in spiritual matters he would not bow to Caesar on his throne.

It does not alter the case to say that we look in vain for such an example to the Scriptures, owing to the fact that, in the primitive age, no temporal prince was made a convert to Christianity, and therefore none was in circumstances to dispense ecclesiastical patronage and serve as the depository of spiritual power. But God is not limited by want of instruments. The same grace that subdued Saul of Tarsus, at a time when he was breathing out slaughter against the saints of the Lord, could have converted Pilate, or Agrippa, or Caesar at Rome. Had the example been useful, the necessary means of supplying the example would not have been lacking to God. The very fact that, in apostolic days, God did not take some heathen prince and make a Christian of him, in order that he might fill the office of temporal head of the church on Earth, is in itself an instructive fact – fraught with a moral. And let it be remarked that the Scriptures make no provision for such an occurrence in after times. They contain no principle authorizing the prince either to claim or exercise authority in ecclesiastical matters, when in the course of ages a Christian potentate would appear. If there be such a principle it is unknown to us; and it is certainly incumbent on those who approve of such an arrangement to produce from the Scriptures, if they can, their warrant for maintaining that a Christian king has a right to exercise supremacy over the church in spiritual matters. Till this is done we must be excused for believing that no temporal prince has a right to act as a lord over the heritage of God.

Nor was supreme spiritual power lodged in the hands of any office-bearer of the church, however distinguished by his gifts, his sufferings, or his abundant labors. The private members, indeed, had it in command to obey the rulers or elders of the church; but the elders, on their part, were enjoined not to act as lords over God's heritage, but to be examples to the flock (1 Peter 5:3). Even the apostles did not claim to have dominion over the people's faith, but only to be helpers of their joy (2 Corinthians 1:24). And among these apostles it does not appear that pre-eminence was vested in any. Peter is the only one for whom, in later times, official supremacy is ever claimed; but he never claimed it for himself; he always acted with his fellow apostles as a simple preacher of the cross of Christ; he is never presented in the Scriptures as nominating to ecclesiastical office, or as exercising any peculiar control over the inferior officers in the church. On one noted occasion, when he exhibited some tergiversation, we are told of another apostle who withstood him to the face, because he was to be blamed (*Galatians* 2:11). The Scripture, therefore, furnishes no ground whatever for believing that supreme spiritual power is deposited in any ecclesiastical officer any more than in any temporal prince.

The Scriptures are to be our guide on this as well as on all other religious matters. We turn to the following passages, and find where the source of all spiritual power exists:

Ephesians 1:20-23: "Which he [God] wrought in Christ, when he raised him from the dead, and set him at his own right hand in the heavenly places, far above all principality and power, and might, and dominion, and every name that is named, not only in this world, but also in that which is to come, and hath put all things under his feet, and gave *him to be the head over all things to the church*, which is his body, the fullness of him that fills all in all."

Ephesians 5:23: "For the husband is the head of the wife, even *as Christ is the head of the church*, and he is the Saviour of the body."

Colossians 1:18: "And he [Christ] *is the head of the body, the church*: who is the beginning, the firstborn from the dead; that in all things he might have the pre-eminence."

The passages now quoted are taken from the Holy Scriptures – the only rule of Christian faith and practice. We have given them our attentive consideration, and they have led us to the conclusion that the sole headship of Christ over the church was the doctrine of apostolic days. What the head is to the human body Christ is to the church, and as the body cannot have two heads, so the church cannot have two heads – neither Christ and the pope, nor Christ and the monarch. To us there seems no middle way in this matter. We must either reject the authority of the Bible, or believe what it teaches – namely, that *Christ is head over all things to the church*. We choose the latter. The *headship of Christ* is the sixth principle of government that we find in operation in apostolic days. Let us observe the consequence of this principle; for as Christ is the head of the church, the members of the church are to be subject to him; and, as we have no way of ascertaining the mind of Christ except through the Scriptures, it follows that the affairs of the church are to be managed by those officers whom the Lord Jesus has entrusted with that power, and are, without the interference of any external authority, to be regulated according to the mind of God as expressed in his Word.

Application of the Test

Let the reader seriously consider the evidence submitted in the previous chapter, and we think he will be satisfied that there is Divine authority for saying that the principles, of which the following facts are the realization, were in practical operation in the apostolic church:

(1) The office-bearers were chosen by the people.

(2) The office of bishop and elder was identical.

(3) There was a plurality of elders in each church.

(4) Ordination was the act of a presbytery – that is, of a plurality of elders.

(5) There was the privilege of appeal to the assembly of elders; and the power of government was exercised by them in their associate capacity.

(6) The only head of the church was the Lord Jesus Christ.

The principles embodied in these six facts cover the whole platform of church government, each rising in importance above that which precedes it, in an ascending series, from popular election up to the headship of the Lord. We have been conducted to them, not by any process of wiredrawn logic, but by receiving the Scriptures, as we think every child of God should receive them, except there be manifest and good reasons to the contrary, in the plain, simple, and natural sense. The most unlettered reader, if he be only unprejudiced, cannot examine the passages of Scripture we have specified, and fail to see that these six great principles were all embodied in the government of the apostolic church. But whether they are embodied in those forms of ecclesiastical government at present existing in the world is another and a very important question – a question which it is now our business to answer. We proceed, therefore, to bring the existing systems in succession to the test of the apostolic standard.

Prelacy

As already explained, Prelacy is that system of church government which is dispensed by archbishops, bishops, priests, deans, deacons, and other office-bearers. It is exemplified in the Church of Rome and in the Church of England, both of which are prelatic in their government; the difference being, that the prelacy of Rome vests the ecclesiastical supremacy in the pope, while the prelacy of England vests it in the reigning monarch. With this exception, the two churches, however widely they may differ in doctrine, are, in every important point of government, the same. As many may be disposed to consider the prelacy of a Protestant church much less objectionable than the prelacy of Rome, and as we have neither necessity nor desire to take any unfair advantage in argument, we prefer to bring the prelacy of Protestantism into comparison with the apostolic standard.

The fountain of jurisdiction in the Church of England is the monarch for the time being, who inherits the throne by hereditary descent, and who, irrespective of all character, is, by Act of Parliament, the only supreme head of the Church of England and Ireland (37 Henry VIII, chapter 17). No person can be received into the ministry of that Church till he subscribe this article: "That the king's majesty, under God, is the only supreme governor of this realm, and of all other his highness' dominions and countries, *as well in all spiritual, or ecclesiastical things* or causes, as temporal" (Canon 36). The appointment of all the archbishops and bishops is vested in the Crown, which is guided in the selection by the political administration of the day – a body composed of persons of every hue of religious profession, and only kept in its place by the majority of votes it can command in Parliament. The highest ecclesiastical office-bearers under the Crown are the archbishops, of whom there are two in England – the archbishops of Canterbury and York, and two in Ireland – the archbishops of Armagh and Dublin. Each of these has under him a number of suffragan bishops, and each bishop has under his care the inferior clergy of his diocese, who preach and dispense the ordinances of religion to such inhabitants of their parishes as are pleased to receive them. The parish clergy are, in some instances, appointed by the Crown, in others by the bishop, in others by a lay patron, and sometimes in a mode still more objectionable.

Such is Prelacy in its most favorable form, as presented in the Protestant Establishment of England. Let us compare it with the system of government which we have already ascertained to exist in the apostolic church.

In the apostolic church, the office-bearers were chosen by the people; but, in the Church of England, archbishops and bishops are chosen by the Crown, and the subordinate clergy are appointed to their charges either by the diocesan, or by some landed proprietor, or by some civil corporation. The people of the apostolic church exercised the privilege of electing an apostle; the people in the Church of England have not power to elect a curate.

In the apostolic church, the office of bishop and elder was identical; the elders of Ephesus were the bishops of the flock; but in the Church Establishment it is very different. The apostolic elder, being a teacher and ruler of a congregation, resembles more closely the parish clergyman than any other office-bearer in the Church of England. But it is very evident that, in that Church, a parish clergyman holds a position widely different from a bishop. The rector wields the jurisdiction of a parish; but the bishop governs a diocese that usually includes a whole multitude of parishes. The one presides over a single congregation; the other, over many congregations. The one exercises authority over the laity, but a Church of England bishop is the ruler of a band of clergy. If, then, the parish clergyman corresponds to the presbyter or elder of apostolic times, it is very clear that, in the Establishment, the bishop and elder are not identical in office. In the Established Church every elder is subject to his bishop but, in the apostolic church, every elder was a bishop himself.

In the Church of England each congregation is under the care of one presbyter. When a second is called in, he is a mere curate in the employment of another, and void of all ecclesiastical jurisdiction. It is not very common, and certainly not essential to the system, to have more than one presbyter or elder in each church; whereas, we have seen that, in each church of apostolic times, there was a plurality of elders.

In the Church of England ordination is an act exclusively performed by a prelate; he may ask others to unite with him, but it is his presence, not theirs, that is essential to the act: Whereas, in the apostolic church, it was the practice to ordain men to the office of the ministry with the laying on of the hands of the presbytery.

In the Church of England, no matter what ecclesiastical grievance may exist, there is no power of appeal except to the courts of law, or the Queen's Privy Council, or some such tribunal. The practice is unknown in the denomination of bringing any matter for consideration before the assembly of elders for them to decide upon, in accordance with the apostles' word. But this, as we have seen, was the mode in which affairs were managed in the apostolic church.

In our Protestant Establishment the monarch is, by act of Parliament, head of the Church, and to the king or queen, as the case may be, the 37th Article informs us that "the chief government of all estates of the realm, whether they be ecclesiastical or civil, in all causes, doth appertain"; whereas, in apostolic times, the church had no head but Jesus Christ.

We have thus examined and compared the two churches as closely and candidly as it is possible for us to do, and we feel ourselves forced to the conclusion that, of the six great principles of ecclesiastical government that met in the apostolic church, there is not one embodied in the Prelacy of the Church of England. We infer, therefore, that, while that Church may be entitled to great respect as a human system, maintained by Act of Parliament, and numbering in its ranks many estimable people, there is no ground whatever for regarding it, in point of government, as an apostolic church. At the peril of excommunication we feel bound to declare our conviction that the government of the Church of England is repugnant to the Word of God.[12]

Independency

It is difficult to ascertain the particulars of ecclesiastical order approved by Independents, inasmuch as we are not aware that they have embodied their views of what the Scriptures teach on the subject in any common formula, and as every congregation, standing apart from every other, may differ sometimes widely on important points. We are, therefore, left to discover their views of church polity from the general practices known to exist among them, and from the principles advocated by their most eminent writers. These, however, are sufficiently known to enable us to compare the Independent system of church government with the apostolic standard.

The principle of popular election existed, as we have seen, in the primitive church, and had the sanction of the apostles of the Lord. Among the Independents this principle is preserved in its integrity. With them every ecclesiastical office-bearer is chosen by the people.

---

12. No. VII of the *Constitutions and Canons Ecclesiastical*, agreed upon with the king's license in 1603, and republished by the Prayer-Book and Homily Society (1852) is as follows: "Whosoever shall hereafter affirm, That the government of the Church of England under his majesty by archbishops, bishops, deans, archdeacons, and the rest that bear office in the same, is anti-Christian or repugnant to the Word of God; let him be excommunicated *ipso facto*, and so continue till he repent, and publicly revoke such his wicked errors."

In the apostolic church the office of bishop and elder was identical; the bishop did not exercise any authority over the elder; on the contrary, every bishop was an elder, and every elder a bishop. So it is with Independents. Every one of their pastors fills the office of bishop and elder, and none of them claims authority over others. With them a bishop and elder are only different names for the same office-bearers, as it was in apostolic days.

We have seen how, in apostolic times, there was a plurality of elders in each church. Here the Independent system fails. On the principles of that theory of church government, it is scarcely possible to have a plurality of elders, and in practice it rarely, if ever, occurs. Among them there is only one minister, or bishop, or elder, in each congregation. Practically, their system admits only of one elder to each church. If an apostle were writing an epistle to an Independent church, he would never think of addressing it to the *bishops*, as well as to the deacons, for the simple reason that, with them, there is usually but *one* bishop to one church: Nor could an apostle ever send for the *elders* of an Independent church, as Paul sent for the elders of Ephesus, for the plain reason that, in an Independent church, there is usually but one elder. A single pastor, with deacons under him, governing a church, is the prominent feature that the Independent system everywhere presents – an arrangement than which none can be more opposed to the plurality of elders that existed in each congregation in primitive times. Some Independents attempt to palliate their departure from apostolic precedent, by saying that a plurality of elders is desirable, but their churches are not able to support them. Does it never strike our esteemed brethren that there must be some remarkable disparity between the apostolic system and theirs, when the richest of their churches now cannot afford to possess what was possessed by the very poorest churches in the days of the apostles? It is the Word of God that says of Paul and Barnabas: "They ordained elders in *every* church."

The office-bearers of the apostolic church were set apart to the discharge of their peculiar duties with the laying on of the hands of the presbytery. Among Independents, however, ordination of any sort is not essential; frequently it is counted unnecessary. Instances are known of persons acting as pastors of churches for a lifetime who were never inducted to office with the imposition of hands and prayer. Ordination is not required by the system. With them it is a mere matter of taste, left in each case to the individual choice. If the newly elected pastor choose to have himself ordained, it can only be done in a way inconsistent with Independent principles. The congregation, being destitute of a plurality of elders, his ordination can only come from the people, who have no Scriptural right to confer it, or from the neighboring pastor. But who does not see that the latter practice is entirely at variance with the foundation principle of Independency, namely, that each congregation has *within* itself complete materials for government? So much is this felt to be the case, that while some ask of the pastors of the district on such occasions, those who choose to carry out their Congregationalist principle with a little more consistency make light of ordination, think it unnecessary, and prefer to go without it.

In the apostolic church there was the privilege of appeal to the assembly of elders. Among the Independents nothing of this kind can exist. The distinctive principle of their system precludes all appeal. The decision of the pastor, and deacons, and people, assembled in a church meeting, is final in every case. No matter how partial or unjust their decision is felt to be, there is no power of bringing the sentence under review of a less prejudiced and more enlightened tribunal. The judgment of the church may be in strict accordance with justice, or it may be the offspring of prejudice or malevolence in a few of the leaders of the meeting, masked, of course, under zeal for purity of communion, and for the cause of religion; but, no matter how superficial the investigation, or how deep the wrong, the system deprives the injured man of the privilege of appeal, and clothes the perpetrators with irresponsible power. By denying and repudiating all association, it enables the rulers to be, if they please, the tyrants of the church, and strips the injured of the possibility of redress. "Independency," says Dr. Wardlaw, "is the *competency* of every distinct church to manage, *without appeal*, its own affairs."[13] This is an ingenious mode of disguising the most repulsive feature of the system. Very few would deny that a church is competent to manage its own affairs in such a way as to obviate the necessity of appeal; but what we assert is, that when the church lacks the necessary wisdom and discretion to do so, appeal among Independents is not permitted, the injured is deprived of redress, and power, for which the possessor is irresponsible to man, degenerates into tyranny when it

13. *Congregational Independency*, Glasgow, 1848, 232.

is unwisely exercised, and there is nothing to keep it in check. The case of Antioch shows that, when a difference arose in the primitive church, there was a right of referring the matter to the assembly of elders, who, under the guidance of the apostles, settled the business. Elders might still meet, and the written word of the apostles is accessible to all, and a decision pronounced by parties removed from the scene of controversy, untainted by local prejudices, and standing far away from the partisanship of the leaders, might go far now, as in ancient days, to calm dissentions, should they unfortunately arise. But Independents, in this respect, repudiate the apostolic example. Their principle is to refuse all recognition of external authority, to make the decision of the church meeting final in every case, and to deny to them who are aggrieved the privilege of appeal.

The headship of Christ was a principle of apostolic times. Independents, we are happy to say, acknowledge this principle in all its integrity.

The result of our comparison is, that there are three principles of the apostolic church that we find fully acknowledged and acted upon among our Independent brethren, namely, popular election, the identity of presbyter and bishop, and the headship of Christ over the church. But there are three apostolic principles that we fail to find in their system, namely, the plurality of elders in each church, ordination with the laying on of the hands of the presbytery, and the privilege of appeal. We conclude, therefore, that, while the Independent system of government advances to the pattern of primitive times much more closely than that which exists in the Churches of England and Rome, still it is not the system entitled to plead the precedent of the apostolic church.

Presbyterianism

It now only remains that we compare the Presbyterian system with the standard of the Law and of the Testimony. The term *Presbyterian* is derived from the word *presbytery,* because the leading characteristic of this form of church government is that it entrusts the duty of ruling the church to the presbytery–that is, to the presbyters or elders of the church in their assembled capacity. But let us bring it, as well as the others, to the Scriptural standard.

In the apostolic church, we have mentioned frequently already that popular election was an admitted principle. It is so with Presbyterians. In all Presbyterian churches throughout Britain and America, with the single exception of the Established Church of Scotland, the members of each congregation invariably elect their own office-bearers. The privilege has been sometimes abused, as what good thing has not been abused by the sin and infatuation of man? But it is a Scriptural privilege that the apostolic church bequeaths us, and Presbyterians have often shown that they count it more precious than gold.

In the primitive age, the office of bishop and elder was identical. An elder was not inferior, in point of official standing, to a bishop, nor a bishop to an elder. It is so in the Presbyterian church. Every elder is a bishop, or overseer of the flock; and every bishop is an elder, one whose office is to rule in the house of God. There are two departments in the office of the elder – that of teaching, and that of ruling; but the office itself is one.

There was a plurality of elders or bishops in each congregation of the apostolic church. Such is the practice in every Presbyterian church at the present day. There is in each of their congregations a number of persons ordained to the office of the eldership, one of whom at least gives himself to the work of the ministry in its various departments, particularly that of public instruction, while the others give their principal attention to ruling in the church of God. Teaching and ruling, as we have already stated, are different departments of the same office; and, while there can be no doubt that those appointed to the office have, in the abstract, a right to fill both departments, yet, in practice, it is found more convenient and beneficial for the people that each elder give most of his attention to that department whose duties he is best qualified to discharge. All elders, being bishops, have an equal right, according to the Scriptures, to preach, baptize, administer the Lord's Supper, and ordain,[14] but these duties it is arranged to devolve on one of the elders, called by distinction the *minister*, who is specially trained to his work, and is, by general consent, admitted to possess most gifts and attainments, and who, in consequence, is the best qualified to make these ordinances edifying to the church; while the majority of the elders only rule, visit the sick, superintend Sabbath Schools, conduct prayer meetings, and make themselves useful in other ways. Presbyterians,

14. It is to be understood that in the Presbyterian church it is only those licensed and ordained by the Presbytery to the office of the Ministry who may administer the Sacraments. (This seems to be a departure from the practice of the apostolic church. – *Editor.*)

therefore, maintain a plurality of elders in every church; and, as it was in apostolic days, it is customary among them for elders to rule who do not labor in Word and doctrine. Any unprejudiced person may see from 1 *Timothy* 5:17 that the office of the eldership divided itself into two great departments of duty in primitive times, even as at present. "Let the elders that rule well be counted worthy of double honor, especially they who labor in the Word and doctrine." Dr. King's comment on this text must, for sense and truthfulness, commend itself to every intelligent man:

> These words could suggest to an unbiased reader only one meaning, that all elders who rule well are worthy of abundant honor, but especially those of their number who, besides ruling well, also labor in word and doctrine. Of course, the passage so interpreted, bears that, of the elders who rule well, only some labor in word and doctrine – that is, there are ruling elders, and among these teaching elders, as we have at the present day.[15]

We are tempted thus to insert the true exposition of this celebrated passage, of which we have been often charged by our opponents as giving interpretations the most grotesque and extravagant. But the reader is requested to observe that the point which we have particularly in view at present is that the Presbyterian, like the apostolic church, has, in every congregation, a plurality of elders.

Office-bearers were set apart to their distinct spheres of duty in the apostolic church with the laying on of the hands of the presbytery. The Presbyterian church, in its several branches, is the only one known to us that carries this Scriptural principle invariably into practice.

In the apostolic church there was recognized the privilege of appeal and the right of government. This privilege is not only admitted, but it is one of the most distinguishing principles of Presbyterianism. Should any difference arise in a congregation, the members are competent to settle the matter without appeal, if they please; but, should this fail, it is equally competent for them to refer the whole matter, either for advice or decision, to the assembly of elders met in presbytery. The highest ecclesiastical court known to the system is the *Presbytery*; the *Synod* being the name usually given to the presbytery of a province,

---

15. *Exposition and Defence of the Presbyterian Form of Church Government*, 115.

and the *General Assembly* being the name that convenience has attached to the presbytery of a nation. The General Assembly has jurisdiction over a Synod only because it is a larger presbytery. Hence, that *subordination of church courts*, which some injudicious friends of Presbyterianism speak of as being a main feature of the system, is a mere accidental arrangement, which experience has proved conducive to union and strength, but which is by no means essential to the existence of the system. This is proved by the fact that a denomination, without either synod or assembly, and possessing no church court whatever except a district presbytery, is, nevertheless, a complete Presbyterian body. Let there be only one assembly of elders to which a congregation can submit an appeal, and the apostolic principle is preserved. It is not even certain that *representation* is a main feature of the system, although a virtual representation is the result of existing arrangements. There is representation so far as that a few office-bearers, chosen by the people on their first admission to office, transact business for the many. Nor are all office-bearers privileged to find admission to the higher courts; for, although all elders are, in the abstract, equal in point of official power, and have, of course, equal right to sit in presbytery, yet, for convenience sake, it has been agreed upon that only a part of them shall at the same time exercise this right. In the Presbyterian Church of Ireland, it has been the immemorial custom, and long experience has only served to confirm its advantages, for two elders, the teaching elder or minister, and a ruling elder, to take their seats in presbytery. The result of these arrangements is, that a virtual representation occurs, and the system enjoys all its advantages; but to say it is a main pillar of Presbyterianism is contrary, in our opinion, to the facts of the case. Were the platform of the presbytery so widened as to give every elder a seat in our church courts, this would, in a great measure, do away with representation, and would be unwise for many reasons, but would not shake a pillar of the system. In the meantime, whatever may be thought of the principle of representation and the subordination of church courts, there can be no doubt that the Presbyterian form of government, in common with that of the apostolic church, secures to the people *the right of appeal to the assembly of elders, and grants to the assembly of elders the right of government* – a privilege which, so far as known to us, is enjoyed by no denomination that is not, in point of government, Presbyterian.

In the apostolic church, the Lord Jesus alone was king and head. This is a truth acknowledged by all Presbyterians, and practically acted upon by all, except a very few, who, owing to their connection with the state, have been charged with a virtual departure from the principle. All Presbyterian churches rank among their most cherished, as well as distinctive principles, that *Christ alone is King and Head of his Church*. As a denomination, Presbyterians have ever held that the church, independent of the civil rulers, has supreme jurisdiction in all spiritual matters, and that its office-bearers are bound to exercise that jurisdiction in conformity to the mind of Christ, as expressed in his Word. The doctrine of the Supreme Headship of Jesus Christ over his church is one to which Presbyterians have always been warm in their attachment.

We find, then, on minute and patient examination, that the six main principles of government that were, by inspired men established in the apostolic church, are all recognized and practically carried out among Presbyterians. We know no other denomination in the world, of whose form of ecclesiastical government the same statement could be made without departure from the truth.

The Result

Here, then, is the result of our investigations and comparisons. The Word of God contains six great, well-defined principles of government that were embodied in that church which was planted and organized by the inspired apostles of the Lord. All existing modern churches claim to be apostolic, and, with the exception of the Greek and Roman Churches, profess to adopt the Scriptures as the sole rule of faith and practice. But, on comparing the prelacy of the Church of England with the standard of the Divine Word, it is found that in that Church not one of the apostolic principles of government is recognized or embodied. Among the Independents, three of the apostolic principles are exemplified in practice; the remaining three are nowhere to be found. Among Presbyterians, these six principles are all acknowledged, and every one of them is a main feature of the Presbyterian system. We now remind the reader of the axiom with which we entered on the investigation: *The modern church which embodies in its government most apostolic principles, comes nearest in its government to the apostolic church.* We apply this axiom to the settlement of the case. Our conclusion is, that, while the prelacy of Rome and England is in direct opposition to the form of ecclesiastical government that was sanctioned by inspired men; and while Independency approaches much more nearly, but still falls short of the primitive model, *the Presbyterian is, in point of government, the only apostolic church.*

We are, indeed, very far from maintaining that any church on Earth is *in everything* a model of the pattern presented in the primitive age. It requires very little thought to see that the apostolic church of the Scriptures is altogether unique – one that in *all its parts* is never to be realized in this world again. There were in it apostles, prophets, and apostolic delegates – all vested with extraordinary powers, which have been handed down to no successors. It was quite common for the early preachers to work miracles in confirmation of their doctrine, and confer the Holy Ghost by the laying on of their hands. Sometimes in the same congregation there were several gifted brethren, who could look into the future with prophetic eye and declare infallibly the mind of God. In the church of Jerusalem, organized by the whole college of apostles, and the mother of all other churches, there was a community of goods established; and it was quite a common thing for the people of those days, when their hearts were warm with the first glow of love to the Lord Jesus, to sell their property, and lay the price of it at the apostles' feet. There were no public buildings erected for the celebration of Christian worship during all the apostolic age; and public teachers, instead of confining the labors of a life to one little district in the country, went everywhere preaching the Word. These are matters as to which no sect that we know of has been able yet to copy the apostolic church, or is ever very likely to do so.

Again, there are some arrangements, some of them very unimportant, interwoven with the Presbyterian system, for which it would be difficult to find precedent in the Scriptures. We have already adverted to *representation* – the practice of one or two elders representing their brother elders in our meetings of presbytery – an arrangement founded more on common sense than Scripture, and adopted to prevent any individual congregation from exercising a preponderance of influence, and to secure, as far as possible, calm deliberation and impartial sentences. Could we command in the assembly of elders the personal presence of inspired apostles to guide the brethren to a right decision, we are sure all would go well, and we might not be so solicitous as to representation; but, so long as humanity falls short of perfection, it is right to guard against abuses, and to impose upon the exercise of arbitrary power a salutary check. There is no plan better adapted to accomplish this, and to secure at the same time the confidence of the people, than that of representation. We have also spoken of the subordination of church courts, an arrangement entered into for giving effect to the principle of appeal, and which not only gives to the denomination unity and strength, but is obviously attended with many other advantages. The utility of both these principles is undoubted, but it were vain to say that they are essentials of Presbyterianism.

It is not uncommon to hear people speak of the advantages that accrue to the Presbyterian system from the admittance of the *lay* element into church courts. This must be a misunderstanding altogether. None but elders – teaching and ruling elders – are competent [authorized] to sit in any Presbyterian church court, from the session of a congregation up to the General Assembly, and, as we have already seen, all elders are equal in point of official standing, for though their departments of duty are in some respects different, yet the office is one and the same. No elder of any kind is a *layman*, but an ecclesiastical officebearer, ordained with the laying on of the hands of the presbytery and appointed to the oversight of the flock and to the discharge of spiritual duties. Nor does an elder sit in our church courts to represent the laity. He represents the laity in no sense different from that in which the minister represents them; both are chosen by the people, and both fill the one office in the church, the only difference between them being one of education, of labor, and of reward. The notion is only plausible from the fact that most elders are engaged in secular pursuits. But it should be remembered that all ministers were so engaged at the first. Even an apostle lived by his trade, as he repeatedly informs us (*Acts* 20:34; *1 Corinthians* 4:12; *1 Thessalonians* 2:9; *2 Thessalonians* 3:8); and it was part of Paul's charge to the bishops of Ephesus, "that *so laboring* they ought to support the weak" (*Acts* 20:35). If the pursuit of secular employments proves our elders to be laymen – then the bishops of Ephesus were laymen, and the apostle of the Gentiles was a layman too. It is equally in vain to argue that, as the brethren were present in the apostolic council (*Acts* 15:23), the laity are entitled to be represented, and are represented by the elders in our church courts; for, as every one knows, elders and brethren were both present in that council, and therefore the one could not represent the other – each class had a place and a function of its own. Elders sit in their own right as spiritual rulers in the house of God. There are in our church courts no *lay* representatives and no *lay* elders – a name which ignorance invented and malevolence has preserved, in order to bring the office into contempt and disrepute.

It is, however, only candid to say that such grotesque notions of ecclesiastical order, as these terms betray, have received countenance from the disparity that in the course of time has risen between the elders who teach and the elders who rule. This disparity is not the result of any ecclesiastical enactment, but was at the beginning, and still is, the effect mainly of a difference of gifts. The most gifted of the elders was in the beginning set to preach, and what at first was only a difference of gifts has grown in the progress of time to wear the appearance of a difference of rank. One is here reminded of the truthful remark of Dr. Campbell: "Power has a sort of attractive force, which gives it a tendency to accumulate, insomuch that what in the beginning is a distinction barely perceptible, grows in process of time a most remarkable disparity."

The disparity existing among teaching and ruling elders among Presbyterians, instead of being defended, is very much to be lamented, and ought as much as possible to be removed. This is to be done, however, not by lowering the teaching elder, but by elevating the ruling elder, and appointing to office those only who are distinguished from the people by more than a common measure of graces and gifts, who are aware of the responsibilities of the eldership, and who are determined, for the Lord's sake, to the best of their ability to discharge its duties. Besides, the office of deacon, existing at present only in some congregations, should be revived in every church, where elders can manage temporal matters only by neglecting the spiritual concerns peculiarly their own. These and other defects can be remedied, when once they are seen to be defects; for it is one among the many recommendations of the Presbyterian church polity, that it possesses within itself a purifying and reforming power, by which, while always preserving the Scriptural and essential principles of the system, it can alter any arrangement that experience has proved in its practical operation not to be productive of good.

We do not, then, assert that the Presbyterian church is in everything an exact copy of the apostolic church. There are some things found in the one that must be forever wanting in the other; and conversely, there are some things wanting in the one that are found in the other. But in doctrine, they are exactly the same: In worship they are exactly the same: In government, all the main principles of the one are found in the other. There is no other church on Earth of which the same statements can be made in truth. We regard it, therefore, as put beyond all reasonable doubt, *that of all the Churches now existing in the world, the Presbyterian church comes nearest to the model of apostolic times.* That such is the fact, every man, who gives to the evidence here submitted that careful and unprejudiced consideration to which it is entitled, must, as we think, be convinced.

Practical Lessons

The apostolic principles of church government are the peculiarities of the Presbyterian system. That other churches neither practice nor acknowledge these principles is the main ground why Presbyterians remain separate from them.

I know of no good reason for my being a Presbyterian rather than an Independent, except that I believe Presbyterianism has done what the rival system has failed to do – preserved the principles of apostolic government; and, for this reason, possesses an amount of Scriptural warrant (not to speak of unity, coherence, and vigor), that Independency can never have. The absence of these apostolic principles in the Prelatic Establishment must always keep enlightened and conscientious Presbyterians out of its pale, no matter what be the modifications introduced into its articles, or what change be wrought upon its ritual.

If our distinctive principles are not apostolic and important, Presbyterianism is not only folly, but also very great folly; and, by standing apart from other denominations upon such a ground, we only perpetuate needless divisions in the church of God. If we discover that the peculiarities of the system are either not true, or truths of minor consequence, we should take speedy steps to heal the schism that exists, and exemplify Christian union on a large scale by uniting with some sister sect, whose principles are more Scriptural and important than our own. But if, on the other hand, our distinctive principles are very important as well as true, then duty to God and the church demands that we avow, illustrate, and defend them, and press them on the notice of the world.

In discharging either of these duties, Presbyterians at present seem rather remiss. As a denomination we show no desire to renounce our distinctive principles, and merge into Prelacy or Independency; nor, on

82

the other hand, do we make such efforts to teach and propagate them as the truth has a right to expect at our hands. By deriving the name and character of our ecclesiastical system from these principles, we seem to tell the world that they are of very great importance; by our habitual reserve on this topic in our pulpit ministrations, we seem to say that they are of very little. Our conduct is in this respect ambiguous and vacillating. We construct with the one hand, and demolish with the other. On the ground of certain principles we keep apart from other sects; and yet to teach these principles from the pulpit is usually viewed as an intrusion inconsistent with the Gospel. Our separate existence as a church clothes our peculiarities with consequence; our habitual forgetfulness of impressing them upon the people, deepens, if it does not produce, the popular notion that they are of no consequence whatever.

That expositions of our principles are very rarely delivered from the pulpit is a fact that few acquainted with the circumstances of the case will venture to deny. I sat myself for years in various Presbyterian churches of town and country. I never failed to hear the Gospel of Christ, and the great precepts of Christian morality preached by our ministers, and enforced always with great faithfulness, and sometimes with considerable power, but I do not remember to have ever heard on any occasion, except at the settlement of a minister, any attempt made to teach the people why they should be Presbyterians and not Prelatists – and yet I never worshiped where there was not a parish church within a distance of two miles. I have met with not a few others, who tell me they have sat all their lives in Presbyterian churches, and do not remember to have heard on any Sabbath a single principle of Presbyterian church polity stated and explained. The *Plea of Presbytery*, one of the very ablest defenses of apostolic church government and worship that the present century has produced, testifies to the singular fact of the silence of the pulpit on our distinctive principles. In the preface to their volume, the authors of that work make the following observations: "Can he [Mr. Boyd] point to a single Presbyterian minister *in Ulster*, who had previously addressed a congregation for four successive Sabbaths on the peculiarities of Presbyterianism? Can he name a Presbyterian minister who had previously employed a single Sabbath in the discussion of the subject? *We are satisfied that he cannot plead even one such case* as an apology for his agitation of the controversy." To all this there may be some honorable exceptions; but still it cannot be fairly denied that the exposition of our church polity has, in general, become unfashionable and unusual. Even at ordinations, the explanation of our principles is beginning to be felt as a periodical encumbrance – inconsistent with the liberality of modern times – which immemorial custom has entailed upon us; and good easy people, who wish, at any price, to stand well with their neighbors, and fear to give offence by telling honest truth, desire to have the discourse on Presbyterianism, customary on such occasions, either entirely abolished, or, what amounts to the same thing, so softened down as to please everybody. And from the press an exposition of Presbyterian principles rarely issues, except when some champion of another sect, animated by our apathy, is brave enough to attack our system; and then some Presbyterian warrior, clad in the panoply of battle, descends into the field of controversy; but before he strikes a blow, he takes care to apologize for his intrusion upon the public, by alleging that he appears in self-defense which is much the same as saying that he would not have troubled the world by telling it the truth had he not been provoked by the occasion. This candid avowal prepares the reader, at the very commencement, to regard the warmth of the writer's zeal as only an ebullition of personal resentment, and the keenest thrusts of his logic as only the envenomed stings of sectarian retaliation.

The causes of this guilty silence are manifold. I do not believe that we are ashamed of our Presbyterianism, and yet it seems very much as if it were so. The fact, however, is that some ministers never have had their attention particularly directed to the vast importance of making their people familiar with the grounds on which Presbyterians stand separate from other Christians; and a knowledge of which every reflecting mind must see is so necessary to produce consistency of conduct, and to perpetuate our denominational existence. Others keep silent, because to betray strong attachment to Presbyterian principles seems bigoted and uncharitable, and interferes too rudely with the evangelical heresy so popular in our day – that all forms of the Protestant religion are equally true and equally deserving the support and encouragement of Christians. But the main cause of the silence of the pulpit on the subject is the impression so prevalent among the ministry, that our distinctive principles are so clearly written in the Scriptures as to be evident to all, and that, therefore, the public advocacy of Presbyterianism is unnecessary. This, I am persuaded, is a clerical delusion, gross and gigantic. Presbyterian principles are, indeed, clearly embodied in the

Bible, but we are not to forget that what is very clear to one man may be very dark to another. The popular mind, so acute in the business of everyday life, is but a dull learner in the things of God, and at every step needs help and guidance, in order that it may reach right views on spiritual matters. Clearly as Presbyterianism is written in the Scriptures, I consider the Gospel to be written there still more clearly; and yet it is no uncommon thing to meet people familiar with the sound of the Bible from childhood, and clergymen whose business is to preach it, and authors who have attempted to instruct the world on religion, who are all alike ignorant of the main principles of the Gospel of Christ. As it would not be wise for the preacher of the Cross to leave the multitude to discover in the Bible the Gospel for themselves, so it is not wise to leave them without assistance in their search for Presbyterianism. One a very little more advanced in knowledge than ourselves can, in a few minutes, show us meaning in a passage of Scripture that we never saw in it before, and can leave us wondering why we read it so often, and never viewed it till that moment in a light so beautiful and true. Besides, it seems clear that, if church government is a portion of the revealed will of God, duty demands that from every faithful minister it should receive, in the prelections of the pulpit, a place proportioned to its importance. There is peculiar need, moreover, that, in this department, the people should receive the assistance of the minister; for, in dealing with the apostolic system, there is an amount of labor in the collection of passages, in the comparison of facts, and in the deduction of inferences, that few minds, left to their own unaided efforts, are zealous enough to engage, and vigorous enough to accomplish. And whose duty is it to supply help, if not his, who is called by the Holy Ghost, and chosen by the voice of the people, to labor in word and doctrine? "The priest's lips should keep knowledge, and they should seek the law at his mouth."

Whatever be the cause of the silence of the pulpit on the distinctive principles of the Presbyterian system, the sad results of it are manifest every day. The intelligent few who have attained to some acquaintance with our principles have derived their knowledge from the Bible and from books, very seldom from the pulpit; while the many, being uninformed on such subjects, act sometimes in open violation of them. Multitudes frequent the meeting-house, because they have been accustomed to do so from childhood, not because they have ever thought of the peculiar principles of the Presbyterian system, and from an examination of the Word of God are satisfied of their truth. They are Presbyterians by birth and habit only, very seldom by conviction. Not being systematically taught that the principles of government operating in their own church are exclusively apostolic, many of the Presbyterian people appear to regard all Protestant churches as standing upon the same level of truth; they do not trouble themselves with forms of faith; in their view the *Westminster Confession* and the *Thirty-nine Articles* are only facsimiles of each other; Prelacy, Independency, and Presbytery are all alike to them – it is only bigotry that pretends to see a difference. Opinions of this sort are now so common that no odium attaches to their profession, and are vastly popular, especially with rich Presbyterians, who ape at fashion and meditate at some early-day renegadism to the Establishment. Nor is it very wonderful that many others, untaught to consider Presbyterian principles as a portion of Divine revelation, and surrounded by many circumstances tending to deepen the impression that all forms of the Protestant faith are equally Scriptural, are kept in the church only by the force of habit, or personal attachment to some worthy minister, and are ready to fling the nominal profession of apostolic principles away from them, so soon as the time comes that a secession from the Presbyterian church can advance their worldly interests, please their superiors, feed their revenge, or gratify a whim.

There can be little doubt that ignorance of the Scriptural truth and practical value of our principles has made the Presbyterian community much colder to their own church than otherwise they would be. I have often remarked how a Roman Catholic, a Methodist, a Baptist – each thinks his own church the purest and best in the world; while a Presbyterian is usually a man who regards any other Protestant church as being at the very least as good as his own. It is this popular persuasion that in Ulster lends proselytism all its power. Some of the smaller sects endeavor to diffuse the impression that the differences between Protestant churches are of no consequence, and it is their interest to do so; they have little to lose and much to gain by such an impression being abroad. Every minister among them who knows his business is, of course, a vigorous and doubtless a conscientious supporter of the Evangelical Alliance. The prelatic clergy also, except in some rare case, do their best to diffuse the same feeling among Dissenters, because it gives them freer access to convey their Puseyism into Presbyterian families;

and because, being wise in their generation, they have the sagacity to see that, when the Presbyterian mind becomes saturated with the feeling that there is no difference between the two churches, the question will soon follow – Why tax ourselves for nothing; why be at the expense of supporting a separate church; why not join the Establishment? If proselytism gives us any annoyance, we have none but ourselves to blame. Were we faithful to our own principles, the people would be faithful to us. The prevalent indifference to Presbyterianism that our defective instruction has produced has left us open to the incursions of every sect that chooses to give us opposition, and which, in so doing, may always safely reckon on the countenance and co-operation of some of ourselves. It has turned the Presbyterian Church of Ireland into a sort of ecclesiastical preserve, where foot of papist dare not trespass, but where every marksman who wears the mask of Protestantism is free to sport at pleasure and to bag his game. Let the blame be all our own, if the thoughtless among our people are, from time to time, taken in the snare of the fowler.

Instead, however, of pouring forth unavailing regrets over past deficiencies, perhaps it were well for all of us to consider the most likely expedient for communicating a new and better tone to the Presbyterian mind. This the ministry have it in their power to do the very moment that they *will* it. The clergy of no other denomination are able to wield over intelligent society an influence equal to ours. The General Assembly comprises the assembled ministers of the kingdom, and a great master mind, taking advantage of his position in the house to write some great truths on the hearts of his audience, can give an impulse to a principle that is felt to the very extremities of the nation. Like the sons of youth, each auditor there is an arrow in the hands of a mighty man. The sentiments and principles there enunciated are conveyed by each minister to his respective sphere of labor; and in his hands sentiment becomes embodied in action. Scattered at due intervals over all parts of the kingdom, our ministers are each the center of a circle peculiarly his own; they come into contact with society at all points, from the highest to the lowest in the scale of intelligence; they address the people publicly at least once or twice a week the whole year round, and they go forth to hold private intercourse with every family at its own fireside; they take part in public meetings, preside over the education of youth, contribute to newspapers and magazines, and have access, in many other different ways, to the intellects and hearts of the people. It is needless to add that this gives us vast influence for good or for evil. We have it in our power to mould the opinions of our own community, and to make deep impression on society beyond. We have only to be unanimous for a principle, and advocate it with enthusiasm, in order to fasten that principle very deeply in the intellect of the kingdom. There is as much mind in the Presbyterian ministry at this moment as, if wisely directed, could revolutionize the religious sentiment of the nation.

Premising these things, it is obvious we have only to enter vigorously on a new line of action, in order to turn the tide of popular feeling completely in favor of Presbyterianism. It is never to be forgotten that, as ministers of the Gospel, there is deposited in our hands a very important trust. The duties of this trust are best discharged by each man striving to cultivate, to the utmost extent possible, that portion of the vineyard committed to his individual care. Zeal in other matters never can make up for deficiency in this. Let our ministers continue, as at present, to preach the Gospel faithfully, and to maintain that soundness in the faith, without which there can be no religious prosperity. Let them continue to exemplify in their own life and character that pure morality which they inculcate upon others. Let them redouble, if it be possible to redouble, their attention to the people, and spare no pains to carry the message of life to every fireside. Let them visit the sick, comfort them that mourn, instruct the ignorant, sympathize with the poor and oppressed, encourage missions, and lend a helping hand to every scheme that has for its object the promotion of benevolence and virtue. Let them, in everything, study to show themselves approved unto God workmen that need not to be ashamed. But let them be assured that they neither serve the church nor serve themselves, if they do not, by pulpit exposition and private instruction, use their efforts to engrave deeply on the minds of the people the distinctive principles of the Presbyterian system. I am far from saying that these things should be substituted for the Gospel of Christ; but as we believe they form an integral portion of Divine revelation, it is our duty, as faithful ministers of Christ, to teach them to the people. I do not mean that any denomination should be systematically assailed in a bitter and an unchristian spirit; but it seems to me that, if a preacher only prophesy smooth things, preach only what he considers palatable to his audience, spare errors that are abroad in the community working much evil, and purposely keep back any portion of the truth for fear of being pronounced sectarian and uncharitable, he ceases to be the minister of God and becomes the servant of man. So long as we stand separate from the Establishment, it is no less our interest than our duty to make the Presbyterian people thoroughly acquainted with our reasons for maintaining and perpetuating a distinct ecclesiastical existence. Let our dissent rest upon the intelligence, not upon the ignorance, of the people; and instantly it becomes rational and consistent, and of course more formidable than ever. Personal attachment to a minister is a tie too weak to bind a people to the church; for death or a removal may snap it asunder any day. The bonds of custom, kindred, and early association, though in some instances powerful enough, are not too strong to be broken, as experience often shows. It remains that we teach our congregations that our principles, forming, as they do, a portion of the Word of God, should be to all God's people, precious as gold. We should instruct them periodically as to what Presbyterianism is. Let each minister do this as mildly as he pleases, but let it be done faithfully and firmly. Let him not be turned from his purpose by the murmurs of disaffected parties within, or the clamors of enemies without, remembering that the patient cries most loudly when the physician probes the sore. Let him leave no man in doubt that he himself believes the principles of which he is the public representative, and that they are very dear to his heart. Let him take no steps tending to spread the popular error that our distinctive principles are trifles. While careful not to oppose other Christians who aim to advance the glory of God in their own way, he should neither aid nor encourage persons who systematically repudiate what we regard as great and important truths. And let him not fear to be called a bigot, for what is a bigot but the bad name which the world gives a man who ventures to have principles, and is firm enough to show through life a consistent attachment to them? In a word, the aim of all of us should be to make every man who is a Presbyterian by name a Presbyterian by conviction.

The lukewarm and odious indifference to Presbyterian principles that in this day meets one everywhere calls loudly for a remedy of some kind. The best I know is from the textbook of the Divine Word to teach the people publicly and privately what Presbyterianism really is. Had we entered into one vast conspiracy to let our principles die out of the memory of the world, we could not adopt any course more likely to accomplish our end than never to breathe them from the pulpit. But if we wish the people to know and value them, it is very plain we must show that we know and value them ourselves. If we would drive any principles into the popular mind, and make them as "nails fastened by the master of assemblies," we must never cease to hammer at them. Sentiments perpetually failing from the pulpit, the platform, and the press cannot, in the course of nature, forever fall pointless to the Earth; they may at first be disliked by not a few, but they will modify the views even of persons whose judgments have already attained maturity – they will fasten with the greatest tenacity on young minds opening to thought – they will spread abroad in ever-enlarging circles – they will grow to be public opinion at the last. The pulpit is the proper sphere for the promulgation of religious truth. Error needs no effort to spread it through the world, even as the seeds of nature, carried by the autumn wind, are sown broadcast over the land, and germinate in the soil without the culture of the husbandman; but truth rarely goes forth alone – the human heart has no natural affection for it – ignorance and prejudice obstruct its progress at every step – it requires an impulsive force to carry it though the world. Weeds grow of themselves, but the flower requires all the skill and care that the gardener can give it. Error sprouts rankly in human bosoms without any help of ours; but truth needs some kind hand to plant and water it, and keep it in the sunshine. Religious truth, of all others, presents least charms to the natural mind – and how truth of this nature can be expected to make its way through such a world as ours, without receiving an impetus from the pulpit, I do not know – I cannot even imagine. It is certain that a man who, at the proper time and place, states and illustrates his principles, and satisfies others that he believes and prizes them himself, is sure, sooner or later, to make converts to his views; but a man who is known to profess opinions, and is always silent on them, raises doubts as to his own sincerity, and never makes one.

If we wish to have Presbyterianism the religion of the church universal, we must let the world know that we cherish a warm and devoted attachment to its principles. We should not halt between two opinions, clinging to one sect and giving our influence to another. We should cease to be a lukewarm and hybrid generation – Presbyterians only in name. This is not a time for inconsistency and doubt – but for decision, for energy, for action. Presbyterianism should be on the move. Every hour we delay to enter on some vigorous course of policy, our interests, as a denomination, suffer. In our circumstances, hesitation and inaction are fraught with danger, if not denominational death. Every pulpit we can command in the kingdom should strike instantly to a high Presbyterian key. If, as a denomination, we would be faithful to the truth of God; if we would have the people to understand and to love our system; if we would marshal public opinion against renegadism, and hold it up to contumely and scorn; if we would push our Presbyterianism, and call the attention of our fellow Christians to its scripturality and its vigor; if we would have our friends to follow, and our enemies to fear us – then we should learn to regard our distinctive principles as our pride and glory, and preach and teach them, till the people know them like the alphabet, and an unwilling world be compelled to listen. The church that forgets to assert and teach her peculiar principles lives in such a world as this only by sufferance; her own children are cold to her; and when she sinks to dust, she shall have few to lament her fall. But the church that thunders its opinions in the ears of mankind, and which neither force nor flattery can silence, is a church that will have many bitter enemies, but many warm friends – it will have many to hate, but it will have some to love, and some to die for it – it may be everywhere spoken against, but faithful to the truth of God, it will have saints and martyrs, and, in due time, bring the world to its feet.

A word, in conclusion, to the Presbyterian people. This little book is sent to the world principally on your account, that you may know the Scriptural grounds on which the Presbyterian form of church government rests, and how its claims to apostolicity are so far superior to those of any rival system. I, at first, engaged in the study of the subject for my own personal profit and satisfaction, it afterwards occurred to me that a line of argument, which to me seems so clear and convincing, might be serviceable to others who are anxious, as I was, to know the mind of Christ on this much controverted subject. I entered on the investigation with considerable misgivings, lest it should turn out that the system of ecclesiastical government with which I am connected is not divine in its origin. These misgivings were mainly produced by the plausible representations and confident assertions of Independent writers; and I do acknowledge that, had I given ear to their bravadoes, without consulting the Scriptures for myself, I must have ceased to be a Presbyterian. But with me it has ever been a principle to call no man master, and to take my opinions on religious matters from the Word of God alone. I sought light from the Fountain of Light. I asked the guidance of the Divine Spirit. I went directly to the Word of God, compared one passage with another, and endeavored to arrive at apostolic principles. I brought the existing systems of church government into juxtaposition with the Bible, and examined them in the light that shines from the Lamp of God. Lest any important passage of Scripture or any weighty argument might escape my notice, I read some of the most plausible attacks ever made on Presbytery, and I have studied Prelacy and Independency as presented in the pages of the very ablest of their advocates. The result is that I am persuaded Prelacy is a human system altogether – from top to bottom a fabric constructed by men. I am satisfied that Independency, insofar as it differs from Presbyterianism, is not so erroneous as it is defective; and that it stands in need of someone "to set in order the things that are wanting." I am also fully convinced that the Presbyterian form of church government approaches more closely than any other to that which existed in the apostolic church. To do full justice to all arguments that might be advanced in favor of this system of ecclesiastical polity, would require a large book; but, as large books are often written but seldom read, I thought it better to go directly to the root of the matter, present you with the Scriptural view of the subject, and enable you to judge for yourselves. I have throughout studied to be brief, that you may have time to read, and plain, that the very humblest of you may understand. I have purposely shunned all elaborate discussion and intricate argumentation, and have tried to present you with facts from the Word of God bearing on the case – leading the reader by the hand to that pure fountain, and permitting him to draw water for himself. I now invite you to view in all its parts the evidence here submitted; examine if I have misquoted a text, falsified a fact, distorted a testimony, or taken the Scriptures in any other than their plain and natural sense; put the reasoning here presented to the very severest test that in fairness and honesty you can apply; give the statements of the Divine Word the weight to which they are justly entitled, and I am confident you will come to think with me that all the apostolic principles of ecclesiastical government are found in the Presbyterian church alone. It is something to you, surely, to have good reasons for knowing that that church, with whose ordinances the thoughts of your childhood are entwined – within whose temples beloved friends, now in Heaven, learned the way of salvation, and were taught the lessons of life – and whose psalms and services are fragrant with the memory of martyrs, is, in its government, no less than its doctrine and worship, founded on, and agreeable to, the Word of God. Satisfied of this, it is your duty through life to give it a cordial and consistent support, to attend upon its sanctuaries, receive its lessons, and take your part in the various departments of usefulness which it presents. There is such a thing as being a Presbyterian without being a Christian, as it is possible to be a Christian without being a Presbyterian. Depend upon it, it is best to be both. Make the atonement of Christ the refuge of your souls; hold fast by every truth of God's Word, small and great; lend no encouragement to opposing errors; take no pains to conceal your attachment to Presbyterian principles; and strive to do honor to the system with which you claim connection, by your love to Christ, by an upright and consistent life, and by earnest endeavors on your part to deserve the character which distinguished the saints of God in other and better days – "a peculiar people, zealous of good works."

3

The True Church[1]

J. C. Ryle[2]

Upon this rock I will build my church, and the gates of Hell shall not prevail against it (Matthew 16:18).

WE LIVE IN a world in which all things are passing away. Kingdoms, empires, cities, ancient institutions, families, all are liable to change and corruption. One universal law seems to prevail everywhere. In all created things there is a tendency to decay.

There is something saddening and depressing in this. What profit hath a man in the labor of his hands? Is there nothing that shall stand? Is there nothing that shall last? Is there nothing that shall endure? Is there nothing of which we can say – This shall continue forevermore? You have the answer to these questions in the words of our text. Our Lord Jesus Christ speaks of something which shall continue and not pass away. There is one created thing which is an exception to the universal rule to which I have referred. There is one thing which shall never perish and pass away. That thing is the building founded upon the rock – the church of our Lord Jesus Christ. He declares, in the words you have heard tonight, "Upon this rock I will build my church, and the gates of Hell shall not prevail against it."

There are five things in these words which demand your attention:

I.   *You have a Building:* "My church."

1. The Bible uses the word *church* in several different senses. Ryle here discusses the most fundamental sense – not the local church, nor an association or denomination of local churches, but the church universal, the bride of Christ. This sermon was first preached in 1858. It is reprinted from J. C. Ryle, *Warnings to the Churches*. The Banner of Truth Trust [1967] 1992, 9-28.

2. John Charles Ryle (1816-1900), educated at Eton and Oxford, served as an Anglican minister for nearly 60 years, spending his last 20 years as Bishop of Liverpool.

II. *A Builder*: Christ says, "I will build my church."

III. *A Foundation*: "Upon this rock I will build my church."

IV. *Perils Implied*: "The gates of Hell."

V. *Security Asserted*: "The gates of Hell shall not prevail against it."

. . .

I. You have, firstly, a *Building* mentioned in the text. The Lord Jesus Christ speaks of "my church."

Now what is this church? Few inquiries can be made of more importance than this. For want of due attention to this subject, the errors that have crept into the church, and into the world, are neither few nor small.

The church of our text is no material building. It is no temple made with hands, of wood, or brick, or stone, or marble. It is a company of men and women. It is no particular visible church on Earth. It is not the Eastern Church or the Western Church. It is not the Church of England or the Church of Scotland – much less is it the Church of Rome. The church of our text is one that makes far less show in the eyes of man, but is of far more importance in the eyes of God.

The church of our text is made up of all true believers in the Lord Jesus Christ. It comprehends all who have repented of sin, and fled to Christ by faith, and been made new creatures in him. It comprises all God's elect, all who have received God's grace, all who have been washed in Christ's blood, all who have been clothed in Christ's righteousness, all who have been born again and sanctified by Christ's Spirit. All such, of every nation, and people, and tongue, compose the church of our text. This is the body of Christ. This is the flock of Christ. This is the bride. This is the Lamb's wife. This is "the holy catholic church" of the Apostles' Creed. This is the "Blessed company of all faithful people" spoken of in the communion service of our *Prayer Book*. This is the church on the rock. . . .

This is that church to which all visible churches on Earth are servants and handmaidens. Whether they are Episcopalian, Independent, or Presbyterian, they all serve the interests of the one true church. They are the scaffolding, behind which the great building is carried on. They are the husk, under which the living kernel grows. They have their varying degrees of usefulness. The best and worthiest of them is that which trains up most members for Christ's true church. But no visible church has any right to say, "We are the only true church. We are the men, and wisdom shall die with us." No visible church should ever dare to say, "We shall stand forever. The gates of Hell shall not prevail against me."

This is that church to which belong the Lord's precious promises of preservation, continuance, protection, and final glory. "Whatsoever," says Hooker, "we read in Scripture concerning the endless love and saving mercy which God showeth toward his churches, the only proper subject thereof is this church, which we properly term the mystical body of Christ." Small and despised as the true church may be in this world, it is precious and honorable in the sight of God. The temple of Solomon in all its glory was mean and contemptible in comparison with that church which is built upon a rock....

II. I pass on to the second point, to which I proposed to call your attention. Our text contains not merely a building, but a *Builder*. The Lord Jesus Christ declares, *"I will build my church."*

The true church of Christ is tenderly cared for by all the three Persons of the blessed Trinity. In the economy of redemption, beyond all doubt, God the Father chooses, and God the Holy Ghost sanctifies, every member of Christ's mystical body. God the Father, God the Son, and God the Holy Ghost, three Persons and one God, cooperate for the salvation of every saved soul. This is truth which ought never to be forgotten. Nevertheless, there is a peculiar sense in which the help of the church is laid on the Lord Jesus Christ. He is peculiarly and pre-eminently the Redeemer and the Saviour. Therefore it is, that we find him saying in our text, "I will build: The work of building is my special work."

It is Christ who calls the members of the church in due time: They are "the called of Jesus Christ" (*Romans* 1:6). It is Christ who quickens them: "The Son quickens whom he will" (*John* 5:21). It is Christ who washes away their sins: He "has loved us, and washed us from our sins in his own blood" (*Revelation* 1:5). It is Christ who gives them peace: "Peace I leave with you; my peace I give unto you" (*John* 14:27). It is Christ who gives them eternal life: "I give unto them eternal life, and they shall never perish" (*John* 10:28). It is Christ who grants them repentance: "Him hath God exalted to be a Prince and a Saviour to give repentance" (*Acts* 5:31). It is Christ who enables them to become God's children: "To as many as received him, to them gave he power to become the sons of God" (*John* 1:12). It is Christ who carries on the work within them when it is begun: "Because I live, you shall live also" (*John* 14:19). In short, it has "pleased the Father that in Christ should all fulness dwell" (*Colossians* 1:19). He is the author and finisher of faith. From him every joint and member of the mystical body of Christ is supplied.

Through him they are strengthened for duty. By him they are kept from falling. He shall preserve them to the end, and present them faultless before the Father's throne with exceeding great joy. He is all things, all in all to believers.

The mighty agent by whom the Lord Jesus Christ carries out this work in the number of his churches is, without doubt, the Holy Ghost. He it is who applies Christ and his benefits to the soul. He it is who is ever renewing, awakening, convincing, leading to the cross, transforming, taking out of the world, stone after stone, and adding it to the mystical building.

But the great Chief Builder, who has undertaken to execute the work of redemption and bring it to completion, is the Son of God: the Word who was made flesh. It is Jesus Christ who "builds."

In building the true church, the Lord Jesus condescends to use many subordinate instruments. The ministry of the Gospel, the circulation of the Scriptures, the friendly rebuke, the word spoken in season, the drawing influence of afflictions – all are means and appliances by which the work is carried on. But Christ is the great superintending architect, ordering, guiding, directing all that is done. What the Sun is to the whole solar system, that Christ is to all the members of the true church. "Paul may plant, and Apollos water, but God gives the increase." Ministers may preach, and writers may write, but the Lord Jesus Christ alone can build. And except he builds, the work stands still.

Great is the wisdom wherewith the Lord Jesus Christ builds his church. All is done at the right time, and in the right way. Each stone in its turn is put in the right place. Sometimes he chooses great stones, and sometimes he chooses small stones. Sometimes the work goes on fast, and sometimes it goes on slowly. Man is frequently impatient, and thinks that nothing is doing. But man's time is not God's time. A thousand years in his sight are but as a single day. The great Builder makes no mistakes. He knows what he is doing. He sees the end from the beginning. He works by a perfect, unalterable, and certain plan. The mightiest conceptions of architects like Michelangelo and Wren are mere trifling child's play in comparison with Christ's wise counsels respecting his church.

Great is the condescension and mercy which Christ exhibits in building his church. He often chooses the most unlikely and roughest stones and fits them into a most excellent work. He despises none, and rejects none, on account of former sins and past transgressions. He delights to show mercy. He often takes the most thoughtless and ungodly and transforms them into polished corners of his spiritual temple.

Great is the power which Christ displays in building his church. He carries on his work in spite of opposition from the world, the flesh, and the devil. In storm, in tempest, through troublous times, silently, quietly, without noise, without stir, without excitement, the building progresses, like Solomon's temple, "I will work," he declares, "and none shall let it."

Brethren, the children of this world take little or no interest in the building of this church. They care little for the conversion of souls. What are broken spirits and penitent hearts to them? It is all foolishness in their eyes. But while the children of this world care nothing, there is joy in the presence of the angels of God. For the preserving of that church, the laws of nature have oftentimes been suspended. For the good of that church, all the providential dealings of God in this world are ordered and arranged. For the elect's sake, wars are brought to an end, and peace is given to a nation. Statesmen, rulers, emperors, kings, presidents, heads of governments, have their schemes and plans, and think them of vast importance. But there is another work going on of infinitely greater moment, for which they are all but as the axes and saws in God's hands. That work is the gathering in of living stones into the one true church. How little are we told in God's Word about unconverted men compared with what we are told about believers! The history of Nimrod, the mighty hunter, is dismissed in a few words. The history of Abraham, the father of the faithful, occupies several chapters. Nothing in Scripture is so important as the concerns of the true church. The world takes up little of God's Word. The church and its story take up much.

Forever let us thank God, my beloved brethren, that the building of the one true church is laid on the shoulders of One that is mighty. Let us bless God that it does not rest upon man. Let us bless God that it does not depend on missionaries, ministers, or committees. Christ is the almighty Builder. He will carry on his work, though nations and visible churches do not know their duty. Christ will never fail. That which he has undertaken he will certainly accomplish.

III. I pass on to the third point, which I proposed to consider: The *Foundation* upon which this church is built. The Lord Jesus Christ tells us, "Upon this rock will I build my church."

What did the Lord Jesus Christ mean when he spoke of this foundation? Did he mean the Apostle Peter, to whom he was speaking? I think assuredly not. I can see no reason, if he meant Peter, why he did not say, "Upon thee" will I build my church. If he had meant Peter, he would have said, I will build my church on thee, as plainly as he said, "to thee will I give the keys." No! It was not the person of the Apostle Peter, but the good confession which the Apostle had just made. It was not Peter, the erring, unstable man; but the mighty truth which the Father had revealed to Peter. It was the truth concerning Jesus Christ himself which was the Rock. It was Christ's Mediatorship, and Christ's Messiahship. It was the blessed truth that Jesus was the promised Saviour, the true Surety, the real Intercessor between God and man. This was the Rock, and this the foundation upon which the church of Christ was to be built.

My brethren, this foundation was laid at a mighty cost. It needed that the Son of God should take our nature upon him, and in that nature live, suffer, and die, not for his own sins, but for ours. It needed that in that nature Christ should go to the grave, and rise again. It needed that in that nature Christ should go up to Heaven to sit at the right hand of God, having obtained eternal redemption for all his people. No other foundation but this could have borne the weight of that church of which our text speaks. No other foundation could have met the necessities of a world of sinners....

To this one foundation every member of Christ's true church is joined. In many things believers are disunited and disagreed. In the matter of their soul's foundation they are all of one mind. They are all built on the Rock. Ask where they get their peace and hope and joyful expectation of good things to come. You would find that all flows from that one mighty truth – Christ the mediator between God and man, and the office that Christ holds as High Priest and Surety of sinners....

Look to your foundation, my beloved brethren, if you would know whether or not you are members of the one true church. It is a point that may be known to yourselves. Your public worship we can see, but we cannot see whether you are personally built upon the Rock. Your attendance at the Lord's table we can see, but we cannot see whether you are joined to Christ, and one with Christ, and Christ in you. But all shall come to light one day. The secrets of all hearts shall be exposed. Perhaps you go to church regularly, you love your *Prayer Book*, you are constant in attending on every means of grace your church supplies. All this is right and good, so far as it goes. But all this time, see that you make no mistake about your own personal salvation. See that your own soul is upon the Rock. Without this, all else is nothing. Without this, you will never stand in the Day of Judgment. Better a thousand times in that day to be found in a cottage upon the Rock, than in a palace upon the sand!

IV. I proceed, in the fourth place, to speak of the *Implied Trials* of the church, to which our text refers. There is mention made of "the gates of Hell." By that expression we are meant to understand the power of the devil!

The history of Christ's true church has always been one of conflict and war. It has been constantly assailed by a deadly enemy, Satan, the prince of this world. The devil hates the true church of Christ with an undying hatred. He is ever stirring up opposition against all its members. He is ever urging the children of this world to do his will, and injure and harass the people of God. If he cannot bruise the head, he will bruise the heel. If he cannot rob believers of Heaven, he will vex them by the way.

For six thousand years this enmity has gone on. Millions of the ungodly have been the devil's agents, and done the devil's work, though they knew it not. The Pharaohs, the Herods, the Neros, the Julians, the Diocletians, the bloody Marys – what were they all but Satan's tools, when they persecuted the disciples of Jesus Christ.

Warfare with the powers of Hell has been the experience of the whole body of Christ. It has always been a bush burning, though not consumed – a woman fleeing into wilderness, but not swallowed up. The visible churches have their times of prosperity and seasons of peace, but never has there been a time of peace for the true church. Its conflict is perpetual. Its battle never ends.

Warfare with the powers of Hell is the experience of every individual member of the true church. Each has to fight. What are the lives of all the saints, but records of battles? What were such men as Paul and James and Peter and John and Polycarp and Ignatius and Augustine and Luther and Calvin and Latimer and Baxter but soldiers engaged in a constant warfare? Sometimes their persons have been assailed, and sometimes their property. Sometimes they have been harassed by calumnies and slanders, and sometimes by open persecution. But in one way or another the devil has been continually warring against the church. The "gates of Hell" have been continually assaulting the people of Christ.

Men and brethren, we who preach the Gospel can hold out to all who come to Christ exceeding great and precious promises. We can offer boldly to you in our Master's name the peace of God which passes all understanding. Mercy, free grace, and full salvation are offered to everyone who will come to Christ and believe on him. But we promise you no peace with the world, or with the devil. We warn you, on the contrary, that there must be warfare, so long as you are in the body. We would not keep you back or deter you from Christ's service. But we would have you "count the cost" and fully understand what Christ's service entails. Hell is behind you. Heaven is before you. Home lies on the other side of a troubled sea. Thousands, tens of thousands have crossed these stormy waters, and in spite of all opposition, have reached the haven where they would be safe. Hell has assailed them, but has not prevailed. Go forward, brethren, and fear not the adversary. Only abide in Christ, and the victory is sure.

Marvel not at the enmity of the gates of Hell. "If you were of the world, the world would love his own." So long as the world is the world, and the devil the devil, so long there must be warfare, and believers in Christ must be soldiers. The world hated Christ, and the world will hate true Christians as long as the Earth stands. As the great Reformer Luther said, "Cain will go on murdering Abel so long as the church is on Earth."

Be prepared for the enmity of the gates of Hell. Put on the whole armor of God. The tower of David contains a thousand bucklers, all ready for the use of God's people. The weapons of our warfare have been tried by millions of poor sinners like ourselves, and have never been found to fail.

Be patient under the enmity of the gates of Hell. It is all working together for your good. It tends to sanctify. It keeps you awake. It makes you humble. It drives you nearer to the Lord Jesus Christ. It warns you from the world. It helps to make you pray more. Above all, it makes you long for Heaven, and say with heart as well as lips, "Come, Lord Jesus."

Be not cast down by the enmity of Hell. The warfare of the true child of God is as much a mark of grace as the inward peace which he enjoys. No cross, no crown! No conflict, no saving Christianity! "Blessed are you," said our Lord Jesus Christ, "when men shall revile you and persecute you and say all manner of evil against you falsely, for my sake."

V. There remains one thing more to be considered: the *Security* of the true church of Christ. There is a glorious promise given by the mighty

Builder, "The gates of Hell shall not prevail against it." He who cannot lie has pledged his royal Word that all the powers of Hell shall never overthrow his church. It shall continue, and stand, in spite of every assault. It shall never be overcome. All other created things perish and pass away, but not the church of Christ. The hand of outward violence, or the moth of inward decay prevail over everything else, but not over the temple that Christ builds.

Empires have risen and fallen in rapid succession: Egypt, Assyria, Babylon, Persia, Tyre, Carthage, Rome, Greece, Venice – where are all these now? They were all the creations of man's hand, and have passed away. But the church of Christ lives on.

The mightiest cities have become heaps of ruins. The broad walls of Babylon are sunk to the ground. The palaces of Nineveh are mounds of dust. The hundred gates of Thebes are only matters of history. Tyre is a place where fishermen hang their nets. Carthage is a desolation. Yet all this time the true church stands. The gates of Hell do not prevail against it.

The earliest visible churches have in many cases decayed and perished. Where are the Church of Ephesus and the Church of Antioch? Where are the Church of Alexandria and the Church of Constantinople? Where are the Corinthian and Philippian and Thessalonian Churches? Where, indeed, are they all? They departed from the Word of God. They were proud of their bishops, and synods and ceremonies and learning and antiquity. They did not glory in the true cross of Christ. They did not hold fast the Gospel. They did not give Jesus his rightful office or faith its rightful place. They are now among the things that have been. Their candlestick has been taken away. But all this time the true church has lived on.

Has the true church been oppressed in one country? It has fled to another. Has it been trampled on and oppressed in one soil? It has taken root and flourished in some other climate. Fire, sword, prisons, fines, penalties, have never been able to destroy its vitality. Its persecutors have died and gone to their own place, but the Word of God has lived and grown and multiplied. Weak as this true church may appear to the eye of man, it is an anvil which has broken many a hammer in times past, and perhaps will break many more before the end. He that lays hands on it is touching the apple of God's eye.

The promise of our text is true of the whole body of the true church.

Christ will never be without a witness in the world. He has had a people in the worst of times. He had seven thousand in Israel even in the days of Ahab. There are some now, I believe, in the dark places of the Roman and Greek churches, who, in spite of much weakness, are serving Christ. The devil may rage horribly. The church may in some countries be brought exceedingly low. But the gates of Hell shall never entirely prevail.

The promise of our text is true of every individual member of the church. Some of God's people have been brought very low, so that they despaired of their safety. Some have fallen sadly, as David and Peter did. Some have departed from the faith for a time, like Cranmer and Jewel. Many have been tried by cruel doubts and fears. But all have got safe home at last, the youngest as well as the oldest, the weakest as well as the strongest. And so it will be to the end. Can you prevent tomorrow's Sun from rising? Can you prevent the tide in the Bristol Channel from ebbing and flowing? Can you prevent the planets moving in their respective orbits? Then, and then alone, can you prevent the salvation of any believer, however feeble – of any living stone in that church which is built upon the Rock, however small or insignificant that stone may appear.

The true church is Christ's body. Not one bone in that mystical body shall ever be broken. The true church is Christ's bride. They whom God has joined in everlasting covenant shall never be put asunder. The true church is Christ's flock. When the lion came and took a lamb out of David's flock, David arose and delivered the lamb from his mouth. Christ will do the same. He is David's greater son. Not a single sick lamb in Christ's flock shall perish. He will say to his Father in the last day, "Of those whom you gave me I have lost none." The true church is the wheat of the Earth. It may be sifted, winnowed, buffeted, tossed to and fro. But not one grain shall be lost. The tares and chaff shall be burned. The wheat shall be gathered into the barn. The true church is Christ's army. The Captain of our salvation loses none of his soldiers. His plans are never defeated. His supplies never fail. His muster roll is the same at the end as it was at the beginning. Of the men that marched gallantly out of England a few years ago in the Crimean War, how many never came back! Regiments that went forth, strong and cheerful, with bands playing and banners flying, laid their bones on a foreign land, and never returned to their native country. But it is not so with Christ's army. Not one of his soldiers shall be missing at last. He himself declares "They shall never perish."

The devil may cast some of the members of the true church into prison. He may kill, and burn, and torture, and hang. But after he has killed the body, there is nothing more that he can do. He cannot hurt the soul. When the French troops took Rome a few years ago, they found on the walls of a prison cell, under the Inquisition, the words of a prisoner. Who he was, we know not. But his words are worthy of remembrance.... He had written on the walls, very likely after an unjust trial, and a still more unjust excommunication, the following striking words: "Blessed Jesus, they cannot cast me out of thy true church." That record is true. Not all the power of Satan can cast out of Christ's true church one single believer.

The children of this world may wage fierce warfare against the church, but they cannot stop the work of conversion. What said the sneering Emperor Julian, in the early ages of the church – "What is the carpenter's son doing now?" An aged Christian made answer, "He is making a coffin for Julian himself." But a few months passed away, when Julian with all his pomp and power, died in battle. Where was Christ when the fires of Smithfield were lighted and when Latimer and Ridley were burnt at the stake? What was Christ doing then? He was still carrying on his work of building. That work will ever go on, even in troublous times.

Fear not, beloved brethren, to begin serving Christ. He to whom you commit your souls has all power in Heaven and Earth, and he will keep you. He will never let you be cast away. Relatives may oppose; neighbors may mock. The world may slander and sneer. Fear not! Fear not! The powers of Hell shall never prevail against your soul. Greater is he that is for you, than all they that are against you.

Fear not for the church of Christ, my brethren, when ministers die, and saints are taken away. Christ can ever maintain his own cause; he will raise up better and brighter stars. The stars are all in his right hand. Leave off all anxious thought about the future. Cease to be cast down by measures of statesmen, or the plots of wolves in sheep's clothing. Christ will ever provide for his own church. Christ will take care that the gates of Hell shall not prevail against it. All is going on well, though our eyes may not see it. The kingdoms of this world shall yet become the kingdoms of our God and of his Christ....

PART 2

The Purpose of the Church

...to the intent that now the manifold wisdom of God
might be made known by the church to the
principalities and powers in the heavenly places,
according to the eternal purpose which
he accomplished in Christ Jesus our Lord....
Ephesians 3:10-11

Christ loved the church and gave himself for it,
that he might sanctify and cleanse it
with the washing of water by the Word,
that he might present it to himself a glorious church,
not having spot or wrinkle or any such thing,
but that it should be holy and without blemish.
Ephesians 5:25-27

4

The Primacy of Preaching

Martyn Lloyd-Jones[1]

WHY AM I prepared to speak and to lecture on preaching? There are a number of reasons. It has been my life's work. I have been forty-two years in the ministry, and the main part of my work has been preaching; not exclusively, but the main part of it has been preaching. In addition it is something that I have been constantly studying. I am conscious of my inadequacies and my failures as I have been trying to preach for all these years; and that has led inevitably to a good deal of study and of discussion and of general interest in the whole matter. But, ultimately, my reason for being very ready to give these lectures is that to me the work of preaching is the highest and the greatest and the most glorious calling to which anyone can ever be called. If you want something in addition to that I would say without any hesitation that the most urgent need in the Christian church today is true preaching; and as it is the greatest and the most urgent need in the church, it is obviously the greatest need of the world also.

The statement about its being the most urgent need leads to the first matter that we must discuss together – Is there any need of preaching? Is there any place for preaching in the modern church and in the modern world, or has preaching become quite outmoded? The very fact that one has to pose such a question, and to consider it, is, it seems to me, the most illuminating commentary on the state of the church at the present time. I feel that that is the chief explanation of the present more or less parlous condition and ineffectiveness of the Christian church in the world today. This whole question of the need of preach-

1. D. Martyn Lloyd-Jones, M.D., was pastor of Westminster Chapel in London. This lecture is reprinted from his book *Preaching and Preachers*, Zondervan, 1972. Copyright 1971, Lady Elizabeth Catherwood.

ing, and the place of preaching in the ministry of the church, is in question at the present time, so we have to start with that. So often when people are asked to lecture or to speak on preaching they rush immediately to consider methods and ways and means and the mechanics. I believe that is quite wrong. We must start with the presuppositions and with the background, and with general principles; for, unless I am very greatly mistaken, the main trouble arises from the fact that people are not clear in their minds as to what preaching really is. So I am going to deal with the matter in general before I come down to particulars of any type.

Here is the great question, therefore: Can we justify preaching? Is there need of preaching at all in the modem world? This, as you know, is a part of a larger question. We are living in an age when not only preaching but the very church herself is being questioned. You are familiar with the talk of "religionless Christianity," with the idea that many have that the church herself is perhaps the greatest hindrance to the Christian faith, and that if we really want to see people becoming Christians, and the world being "Christianized," as they put it, we have to get rid of the church, because the church has become an obstacle standing between people and the truth that is in Christ Jesus.

With much of this criticism of the church one has, of course, to agree. There is so much that is wrong with the church – traditionalism, formality and lifelessness and so on – and it would be idle and utterly foolish to deny this. Often one really has to ask about certain gatherings and communities of people whether they are entitled to the name *church* at all. The church so easily can degenerate into an organization, or even, perhaps, into a social club or something of that kind; so that it is often necessary to raise the whole question of the church herself. However, that is not our object in these lectures, and we are not going to deal with the nature of the church as such; but, as part of the general attitude to the church, this matter of preaching must obviously arise acutely; and that is the theme with which I have to deal.

What is the cause of the present reaction against preaching? Why has preaching fallen from the position it once occupied in the life of the church and in the esteem of people? You cannot read the history of the church, even in a cursory manner, without seeing that preaching has always occupied a central and a predominating position in the life of the church, particularly in Protestantism. Why then this decline in the place and power of preaching; and why this questioning of the necessity for any preaching at all?

I would divide my answer to that question under two general headings. First of all, there are certain general reasons which account for this, and then there are certain particular reasons in the church herself. When I say "general" I mean certain common ideas current in the world outside the church. Let me illustrate what I mean. When making this point, for instance, in Great Britain I generally refer to it as Baldwinism. For those not familiar with that term let me explain what it means. There was a Prime Minister in Britain in the twenties and in the thirties named Stanley Baldwin. This man, who was of such little significance that his name means nothing even today, had a considerable effect upon people's thinking concerning the value of speaking and oratory in the life of peoples. He came into power and into office after the era of a coalition government in England led and dominated by men such as Lloyd George, Winston Churchill, Lord Birkenhead and others of that type. Now these men were orators, great speakers. Stanley Baldwin did not have that gift, so he saw that if he was to succeed it was essential that he should discount the value and the importance of speech and oratory. He was competing with brilliant men who were at the same time great orators; so he posed as the simple, honest, ordinary Englishman. He said that he was not a great speaker, and conveyed the suggestion that if a man is a great speaker he is a man whom you cannot trust, and is not quite honest. He put up these things as antitheses; and his line was to adopt the pose of the plain Englishman who could not indulge in great flights of oratory and imagination, but who made simple and plain and honest statements.

This attitude to oratory and the power of speech has quite definitely become a vogue, especially amongst the politicians, in Britain. But, alas, I maintain that it has had an influence also upon the church. There has been a new attitude toward oratory and eloquence and speaking worthy of the name. It is one of distrust of the orator. And, of course, accompanying this, and enforcing this whole attitude, there has been a new emphasis on the place of reading. The argument is that nowadays we are a more cultured and educated people; that in the past people did not read for themselves and were dependent upon great speakers, great orators; but that that is no longer necessary because we have books and libraries and so on. Then in addition, we now have the radio and the television with knowledge and information concerning truth coming directly into the home. All these, I believe, in a general way have influenced the church, and the outlook of the church and of Christian people, upon the spoken word, and upon preaching as such.

Now I do not want to take too much time in refuting this general atmosphere which is inimical to preaching; I would simply content myself by saying this – that it is a very interesting thing to note that some of the greatest men of action that the world has ever known have also been great speakers and great orators. It is not an accident, I think, that in Great Britain for instance, during the two World Wars in this present century, the two great leaders that were thrown up happened to be great orators; and these other men who tend to give the impression that if a man can speak he is a mere talker who does nothing, have been refuted by the sheer facts of history. The greatest men of action have been great speakers; and, of course, it is a part of the function of, and an essential desideratum in, a leader that he can enthuse people, and rouse them, and get them to take action. One thinks of Pericles and Demosthenes and others. The general history of the world surely demonstrates quite plainly that the men who truly made history have been men who could speak, who could deliver a message, and who could get people to act as the result of the effect they produced upon them.

There it is then, in general. But we are more concerned about certain attitudes in the church herself, or certain reasons in the church herself which account for the decline in the place of preaching. I suggest that here are some of the main and the leading factors under this heading. I would not hesitate to put in the first position: the loss of belief in the authority of the Scriptures, and a diminution in the belief of the truth. I put this first because I am sure it is the main factor. If you have not got authority, you cannot speak well, you cannot preach. Great preaching always depends upon great themes. Great themes always produce great speaking in any realm, and this is particularly true, of course, in the realm of the church. While men believed in the Scriptures as the authoritative Word of God and spoke on the basis of that authority, you had great preaching. But once that went, and men began to speculate, and to theorize, and to put up hypotheses and so on, the eloquence and the greatness of the spoken word inevitably declined and began to wane. You cannot really deal with speculations and conjectures in the same way as preaching had formerly dealt with the great themes of the Scriptures. But as belief in the great doctrines of the Bible began to go out, and sermons were replaced by ethical addresses and homilies, and moral uplift and socio-political talk, it is not surprising that preaching declined. I suggest that that is the first and the greatest cause of this decline.

But there is a second; and we have got to be fair in these matters. I believe that there has been a reaction against what were called "the great pulpiteers," especially of the second half of the last century. They were to be found in great numbers in England and also in the U.S.A. I always feel that the man who was most typical in this respect in the U.S.A. was Henry Ward Beecher. He illustrates perfectly the chief characteristics of the pulpiteer. The term itself is very interesting, and I believe it is a very accurate one. These men were pulpiteers rather than preachers. I mean that they were men who could occupy a pulpit and dominate it, and dominate the people. They were professionals. There was a good deal of the element of showmanship in them, and they were experts at handling congregations and playing on their emotions. In the end they could do almost what they liked with them.

Now this, I am sure, has produced a reaction; and that is a very good thing. These pulpiteers were to me – with my view of preaching – an abomination; and it is they who are in many ways largely responsible for this present reaction. It is very interesting to notice that this has happened in times past, not only with regard to the preaching of the Gospel, the Word of God, but in other realms also. There is an interesting statement in a book by Edwin Hatch on the influence of Greek ideas upon the Christian church which seems to me to put this very well. He says that it is a fact that philosophy fell into disrepute and waned in the life of Greece as "the result of rhetoric and the increasing use of rhetoric." Let me quote the words of Hatch. He says:

> If you look more closely into history you will find that rhetoric killed philosophy. Philosophy died because for all but a small minority it ceased to be real, it passed from the sphere of thought and conduct to that of exposition and literature. Its preachers preached not because they were bursting with truths which could not help finding expression, but because they were masters of fine phrases and lived in an age in which fine phrases had a value. It died, in short, because it had become sophistry, but sophistry is of no special age or country, it is indigenous to all soils upon which literature grows. No sooner is any special form of literature created by the genius of a great writer than there arises a class of men

who cultivate the style of it for the style's sake. No sooner is any new impulse given either to philosophy or to religion than there arises a class of men who copy the form without the substance, and try to make the echo of the past sound like the voice of the present. So it has been with Christianity.

That is a most important point, and I think it has very real relevance to this point I am making about the pernicious influence of pulpiteerism upon true preaching. You see, the form became more important than the substance, the oratory and the eloquence became things in and of themselves, and ultimately preaching became a form of entertainment. The Truth was noticed; they paid a passing respect to it; but the great thing was the form. I believe we are living in an age which is experiencing a reaction against that. And this has been continued in the present century when there has often been a form of popular preaching, in evangelism particularly, that has brought true preaching into disrepute because of a lack of substance and too much attention being paid to the form and to the presentation. It degenerates ultimately into what I have described as professionalism, not to say showmanship.

Finally, I would suggest that another factor has been the wrong conception of what a sermon really is, and therefore of what preaching really is. It is that same point concerning the form again, not in the crude way to which I have been referring, but I believe that the printing and publication of sermons has had a bad effect upon preaching. I refer particularly to the publication of sermons, speaking roughly, since somewhere about 1890, and – dare I say it? – I have a feeling that the Scottish school of preachers have been the greatest offenders in this respect. I believe it happened in this way. These men were endowed with a real literary gift, and the emphasis passed, unconsciously again, from the truth of the message to the literary expression. They paid great attention to literary and historical allusions and quotations and so on. In other words, these men, as I shall suggest in a later lecture, were essayists rather than preachers; but as they published these essays as sermons, they were accepted as sermons. That has undoubtedly had a controlling effect upon the thinking of many in the church as to what a sermon should be, and also as to what preaching really is. So I would attribute a good deal of the decline in preaching at the present time to those literary effusions which have passed under the name of sermons and of preaching.

The result of all these things has been that a new idea has crept in with regard to preaching, and it has taken various forms. A most significant one was that people began to talk about the "address" in the service instead of the sermon. That in itself was indicative of a subtle change. An "address," no longer the sermon, but an "address" or perhaps even a lecture. I shall be dealing with these distinctions later. There was a man in the U.S.A. who published a series of books under the significant title of *Quiet Talks*. *Quiet Talks*, you see, as against the "ranting" of the preachers! *Quiet Talks on Prayer*, *Quiet Talks on Power*, etc. In other words the very title announces that the man is not going to preach. Preaching, of course, is something carnal, lacking in spirituality; what is needed is a chat, a fireside chat, quiet talks, and so on! That idea came in.

Then on top of this, a new emphasis was placed upon "the service," what is often called "the element of worship." Now these terms are very misleading. I remember a man once in a conference saying, "Of course, we in the Episcopal churches pay greater attention to worship than you do in the Free Churches." I was able to point out that what he really meant was that they had a liturgical form of service and we did not. But he equated the reading of the Liturgy with worship. So the confusion grows.

However, there has been this tendency; as preaching has waned, there has been an increase in the formal element in the service. It is interesting to observe how Free-Church men, non-Episcopalians, whatever you may call them, have been increasingly borrowing these ideas from the Episcopal type of service as preaching has waned. They have argued that the people should have a greater part in the service and so they have introduced "responsive reading" and more and more music and singing and chanting. The manner of receiving the people's offerings has been elaborated, and the minister and the choir often enter the building as a procession. It has been illuminating to observe these things; as preaching has declined, these other things have been emphasized; and it has all been done quite deliberately. It is a part of this reaction against preaching; and people have felt that it is more dignified to pay this greater attention to ceremonial, and form, and ritual.

Still worse has been the increase in the element of entertainment in public worship – the use of films and the introduction of more and more singing; the reading of the Word and prayer shortened drastically, but more and more time given to singing. You have a "song leader" as a new kind of official in the church, and he conducts the singing and is supposed to produce the atmosphere. But he often takes so much time in producing the atmosphere that there is no time for preaching in the atmosphere! This is a part of this whole depreciation of the message.

Then on top of this, there is the giving of testimonies. It has been interesting to observe that as preaching as such has been on the decline, preachers have more and more used people to give their testimonies; and particularly if they are important people in any realm. This is said to attract people to the Gospel and to persuade them to listen to it. If you can find an admiral or a general or anyone who has some special title, or a baseball player, or an actor or actress or film-star, or pop-singer, or somebody well-known to the public, get them to give their testimony. This is deemed to be of much greater value than the preaching and the exposition of the Gospel. Have you noticed that I have put all this under the term "entertainment"? That is where I believe it truly belongs. But this is what the church has been turning to as she has turned her back upon preaching.

Another whole section in this connection has been the increasing emphasis upon "personal work," as it is called, or "counseling." Again it would be very interesting to draw a graph here as with those other things. You would find exactly the same thing – as preaching goes down, personal counseling goes up. This has had a great vogue in this present century, particularly since the end of the First World War. The argument has been that owing to the new stresses and strains, and difficulties in living life in the modern world, that people need much more personal attention, that you have got to get to know their particular difficulty, and that you must deal with this in private. We are told that it is only as you deal with them one at a time that you can give people the needed psychological help and so enable them to resolve these problems, to get over their difficulties, and so live their life in an effective and efficient manner. I hope to take up some of these things more in detail later on, but I am giving a general picture now of the things that are responsible for the decline of, and the subordinate place given to, preaching in the Christian church.

To make the list complete I must add tape-recording – as I see it, the peculiar and special abomination at this present time.

There, then, are certain general changes which have happened in the church herself. So far I have been speaking about people who believe in the church, and who attend the church. Among them there has been this shift in the place and the position of preaching. Sometimes it has been expressed even in a purely physical manner. I have noticed that most of the new chapels that have been built in our country no longer have a central pulpit; it is pushed to one side. The pulpit used to be central, but that is so no longer, and you now find yourself looking at something that corresponds to an altar instead of looking at the pulpit which generally dominated the entire building. All this is most significant.

But now, turning from what has happened in that way amongst those who still believe in the church, let us look at those who are more or less suggesting that the church herself may be the hindrance, and that we have got to abandon the church if we really are to propagate the Gospel. I am thinking here of those who say that we must, in a sense, make a clean break with all this tradition which we have inherited, and that if we really want to make people Christians, the way to do so is to mix with them, to live amongst them, to share our lives with them, to show the love of God to them by just bearing one another's burdens and being one of them.

I have heard this put in this way even by preachers. They have faced the fact of the decline in church attendance, particularly in Britain. They say that this is not surprising, that while the preachers preach the Bible and Christian doctrines they have no right to expect any other result. The people, they say, are not interested; the people are interested in politics, they are interested in social conditions, they are interested in the various injustices from which people suffer in various parts of the world, and in war and peace. So, they argue, if you really want to influence people in the Christian direction you must not only talk politics and deal with social conditions in speech, you must take an active part in them. If only these men who have been set aside as preachers, and others who are prominent in the church, were to go out and take part in politics and in social activities and philanthropic works, they would do much more good than by standing in pulpits and preaching according to the traditional manner. A very well-known preacher in Britain actually put it like this some ten years ago. He said that the idea of sending out foreign missionaries to North Africa – he was dealing with that area in particular on that occasion – and training them to preach to these people was quite ridiculous, and it was time we stopped it. He suggested that instead we should send Christian people out to those places, and they should take on ordinary jobs, mix among the people, and more especially, enter into their political and social affairs. If you did that as Christians, he said, then there would be some hope perhaps that the grandchildren of this present generation might become Christian. But that was the way, you see, to do it. Not preaching, not the old method, but getting among the people, showing an interest, showing your sympathy, being one of them, sitting down among them, and discussing their affairs and problems.

This is being advocated a great deal in many countries at the present time, either as a means of bringing people to places of worship to listen to the Gospel, or else as not only a substitute for that, but as a very much better method of propagating the Christian faith.

Well now the great question is – what is our answer to all this? I am going to suggest, and this will be the burden of what I hope to say, that all this at best is secondary, very often not even secondary, often not worthy of a place at all, but at best, secondary, and that the primary task of the church and of the Christian minister is the preaching of the Word of God.

I must substantiate that statement, and I do so in the following way and for these reasons. First of all, what is the answer of the Bible itself? Here, and confining ourselves only to the New Testament – though we could give evidence also from the Old Testament in the prophets – we start with our Lord himself. Surely nothing is more interesting in his story than to notice these two sides, or these two parts, to his ministry. Our Lord performed miracles, but the interesting thing is that the miracles were not his primary work, they were secondary. John, as you know, refers to them always as "signs," and that is what they were. He did not come into the world to heal the sick, and the lame, and the blind, or to quell storms on the sea. He could do such things and did so frequently; but these are all secondary; they are not primary. What was his primary object? The very terms he uses answer the question. He says he is "The light of the world." He says, "Seek ye first the kingdom of God and his righteousness, and all these things shall be added unto you." Those things are legitimate but they are not primary: They are secondary; they are consequences; they are effects; they are results. Or take his famous reply to the people who came to him putting the question whether they should pay tribute money to Caesar or not? "Render unto Caesar the things that are Caesar's, and [or, but] unto God the things that are God's." This was his special emphasis. Most people are concerned about the first thing, "rendering unto Caesar"; the thing that is forgotten, he suggests, is that you "render unto God the things that are God's."

Then there are some very interesting sidelights on this whole matter, it seems to me, in what he did. You remember how after the miracle of the feeding of the five thousand we are told that the people were so impressed that they came and they tried to take him by force to make him a king (*John* 6:15). They felt, "Now this is just what we want. He is dealing with a practical problem, hunger, the need of food. This is the one to be made king. He has got the power. He can do this." But what we are told is that he pushed them away, as it were, "and went up into a mountain himself alone." He regarded that as a temptation, as something that would sidetrack him. It was precisely the same in the case of the temptations in the wilderness that we read of in *Luke* 4. The devil offered him all the kingdoms of this world and so on. He rejects this deliberately, specifically. These are all secondary, they are not the primary function, not the primary task.

Or take another very interesting example of this found in *Luke* 12:14, where we are told that on one occasion our Lord had been speaking as he was sending out the disciples to preach and to teach, and telling them about their relationship to God and how they were to deal with opposition. He seems to have paused for a moment and immediately a man blurted out a question, saying, "Speak to my brother that he divide the inheritance with me." Our Lord's reply to that man surely gives us a great insight into this whole matter. He turned to him and said, "Man, who made me a judge or a divider over you?" In other words he made it clear that he had not come into the world to do such things. It is not that these things do not need to be done; they do need to be done; justice and fair play and righteousness have their place; but he had not come to do these things. He said in effect, "I have not left Heaven and come on Earth in order to do something like that; that is not my primary task." So he rebuked this man. Indeed we find that many times when he had worked some striking and notable miracle and the people were trying to hold him, hoping he would work still more, he deliberately left them and would go on to another place; and there he would proceed to teach and to preach. He is "The light of the world" – this is the primary thing.

"I am the way, the truth, and the life: No man comes unto the Father but by me." *All* these other things *are* secondary. And you notice that when he sent out his disciples, he sent them out "to teach, and to cast out devils." The teaching is the first thing, and he reminded them that the Christian is the light of the world. As he is the light of the world, so the Christian becomes the light of the world. "A city that is set upon a hill cannot be hid," and so on. I suggest that in the *Gospels*, and in the life and ministry of our Lord himself, you have this clear indication of the primacy of preaching and of teaching.

Then after the Resurrection, and in the remainder of the New Testament, you get exactly the same thing. He tells these chosen men that they are primarily to be "witnesses unto Me." That is to be their first great task. He is going to give them other powers, but their main business is to be witnesses unto him. And it is therefore interesting to observe that immediately these men are filled with the Holy Spirit on the Day of Pentecost, they begin to preach. Peter preaches and expounds and explains the Truth to the people at Jerusalem. What is this phenomenon that had just happened and had produced such a change in the disciples? That question can only be answered by preaching; so you get the sermon recorded in the latter portion of the second chapter of the *Acts of the Apostles*.

And when you go to the third chapter of *Acts* you find the same thing again. Peter and John heal this man at the Beautiful Gate of the Temple, and that creates excitement and interest. The people think these are miracle workers and that they are going to get great benefits out of them; but Peter again preaches and corrects them, and immediately draws their attention, as it were, from the miracle that he and John had just worked to the great truth concerning Christ and his salvation, which is so infinitely more important. The apostles always bring out this emphasis.

And again in the fourth chapter of *Acts* – I am taking this in detail because this is the origin of the church; this was what she actually did at the beginning. She was commissioned, sent out to preach and teach, and this is the thing that she proceeded to do. "They spoke with boldness." What the authorities were anxious to do above everything else was to stop these men teaching and preaching. They always criticize that much more than they do the miracles: It was the preaching and the teaching in this "Name" that annoyed them. And the reply of the apostles is, "We cannot but speak of the things which we have seen and heard." This was the thing that made them speak; they could not help themselves; they were conscious of the great constraint that was upon them.

But, and in many ways the most interesting statement of all, I sometimes think in this connection, is one that is found in the sixth chapter of the book of the *Acts of the Apostles* where we are told that a great crisis arose in the life of the early church. I know of nothing that speaks more directly upon the present state and condition of the church, and what is her primary task, than this sixth chapter of the book of the *Acts of the Apostles*. The essential message is in the first two verses: "And in those days, when the number of the disciples was multiplied, there arose a murmuring of the Grecians against the Hebrews, because their widows were neglected in the daily ministration. Then the twelve called the multitude of the disciples unto them, and said, It is not reason that we should leave the Word of God, and serve tables."

This is surely a most interesting and important statement, a crucial one. What was the church to do? Here is a problem; here are these widows of the Grecians, and they are not only widows but they are in need and in need of food. It was a social problem, perhaps partly a political problem, but certainly a very acute and urgent social problem. Surely the business of the Christian church, and the leaders particularly, is to deal with this crying need? Why go on preaching when people are starving and in need and are suffering? That was the great temptation that came to the church immediately; but the apostles under the leading and the guidance of the Holy Spirit, and the teaching they had already received, and the commission they had had from their Master, saw the danger and they said, "It is not reason we should leave the Word of God, and serve tables." This is wrong. We shall be failing in our commission if we do this. We are here to preach this Word; this is the first thing, "We will give ourselves continually to prayer and the ministry of the Word."

Now there the priorities are laid down, once and forever. This is the primary task of the church, the primary task of the leaders of the church, the people who are set in this position of authority; and we must not allow anything to deflect us from this, however good the cause, however great the need. This is surely the direct answer to much of the false thinking and reasoning concerning these matters at the present time.

And as you go through the book of the *Acts of the Apostles* you find the same thing everywhere. I could take you through almost chapter by chapter and show you the same thing. Let me content myself with just one more example. In chapter 8 we are told of a great persecution that arose in Jerusalem, and how all the members of the church were scattered abroad except the apostles. What did they do? We are told in verses 4 and 5: "Therefore they that were scattered abroad went everywhere preaching the Word." That does not mean preaching from a pulpit. Someone has suggested that it should be translated "gossiping" the Word. Their chief desire and concern was to tell people about this Word. "Then Philip went down to the city of Samaria, and preached Christ unto them." There, in verse 5 a different word is used. This means heralding, it is more a picture of a preacher in the pulpit or at any rate standing in a public place and addressing people. And so it goes on right through that book.

In the *Epistles,* in the same way, the Apostle Paul reminds Timothy that the church is "the pillar and ground of the truth." She is not a social organization or institution, not a political society, not a cultural society, but "the pillar and ground of the truth."

Paul in writing to Timothy in the *Second Epistle* in the second chapter and the second verse puts it like this: "The things that you have heard of me among many witnesses, the same commit to faithful men, who shall be able to teach others also." His last word to him in a sense is this: "Preach the Word; be instant in season, out of season; reprove, rebuke, exhort with all longsuffering and doctrine." There it is, surely, quite plainly.

I have simply skimmed the argument, the statement of it, in the New Testament. All this is fully confirmed in church history. Is it not clear, as you take a bird's-eye view of church history, that the decadent periods and eras in the history of the church have always been those periods when preaching had declined? What is it that always heralds the dawn of a Reformation or of a revival? It is renewed preaching. Not only a new interest in preaching, but a new kind of preaching. A revival of true preaching has always heralded these great movements in the history of the church. And, of course, when the Reformation and the revival come, they have always led to great and notable periods of the greatest preaching that the church has ever known. As that was true in the beginning as described in the book of *Acts*, it was also after the

Protestant Reformation. Luther, Calvin, Knox, Latimer, Ridley – all these men were great preachers. In the seventeenth century you had exactly the same thing – the great Puritan preachers and others. And in the eighteenth century, Jonathan Edwards, Whitefield, the Wesleys, Rowlands, and Harris were all great preachers. It was an era of great preaching. Whenever you get Reformation and revival this is always and inevitably the result.

So my answer so far, my justification of my statement that preaching is the primary task of the church, is based in that way on the evidence of the Scriptures, and the supporting and confirming evidence of the history of the church. We shall go on to reason and to argue it out yet further.

5

Preaching to the Heart

Jay E. Adams[1]

FOR YEARS homileticians have been exhorting preachers to "preach to the heart." But what are they talking about? Do you know? Do *they?* Is the concept Biblical, and if so, how does one do it?

The blame for confusion about what it means to "preach to the heart" does not lie solely with homileticians, while preachers go off scot-free. Homileticians should make themselves clear. But if they don't, it is the responsibility of the preachers to pound on their doors until they do. So neither is guiltless. There has been a conspiracy of ignorance in which words and phrases have been uttered again and again as though the speakers and the listeners knew perfectly well what they were talking about, when all the while they did not. As a homiletician who has been at fault in this matter, I believe something must be done. It is time the whole matter were cleared up. That is the point of this book.

The first Christian sermon, preached on the day of Pentecost by the apostle Peter, was preached to the heart. Luke wrote: "Now when they heard this, they were stung to the heart and said to Peter and the rest of the apostles, 'Brothers, what should we do?' " (*Acts* 2:37). That crowd's response was the fruit of effective preaching, empowered by the Holy Spirit. But effective, heart-penetrating preaching can also lead to the opposite response: "Now when they heard these things, they were pierced through to their heart and gnashed their teeth at him" (*Acts* 7:54).

When Peter preached, great numbers repented and believed the Gospel; when Stephen preached, his listeners killed him. Yet both were filled with the Spirit and preached to the heart. This double and opposite response makes one thing clear at the outset: While preaching to

---

1. Dr. Jay E. Adams is a prolific author and speaker. This essay is an excerpt from a book of the same title, copyright 1983, Jay E. Adams.

the heart is a desirable effect brought about by the power of the Spirit, the exact nature of that effect on the listener may vary greatly and cannot be predicted beforehand.

In either case, Spirit empowered, Biblical preaching strikes squarely at the heart. It elicits a response. No hearer can remain apathetic: *He must respond.* To speak of preaching to the heart, then, is to speak of preaching that brings a definitive response; it is preaching that evokes words and action from the listener.

What Is the Heart?

A clear idea of what the Bible means by *heart* is foundational to all else that we shall consider in this little book. Indeed, the widespread, careless use of that word is responsible for the confusion and vagueness that surround exhortations to preach to the heart.

"But," you object, "everyone knows what *heart* means. I don't see why you are making such a fuss over it. Surely it doesn't take an entire chapter to define something so obvious, does it?" Yes. You see, that's exactly what is wrong: Everyone thinks he understands the term, but very few do. Ask yourself, "Exactly what does the word *heart* mean in the *Scriptures?*" Can you give a precise definition? "Well, maybe not an exact one, but I know what it means, nevertheless."

Do you?

Let's test your understanding a bit, okay? What do you think of the often-quoted sentiment, "What we need is more heart knowledge and not just head knowledge"? Do you think it does or does not convey an acceptable idea of *heart* as the word is used in the Bible?

"Well, I guess so, but I'm not sure; anyhow, I know what the sentence is getting at."

What?

"It is saying that it isn't enough to merely know truth, that truth must grip you – it has to affect your emotions as well."

You are probably correct about the way that sentence is used; but the fact is, it suggests an incorrect interpretation of the Biblical word *heart*. If *heart* is used to refer to feelings or emotions as over against thought or intellect, that use is discordant with Scripture. Never in the Bible is the word *heart* set over against the head or the intellectual processes. That is a modern, Western idea of heart, introduced into the Bible from the outside. One would never get that idea from the Bible itself. Indeed, that is a Roman rather that a Biblical view of the heart. The Valentine's Day cupid, shooting arrows through little red or pink hearts, is the culprit behind this modern, un-Biblical view. To Western origins may be attributed all of our romantic notions, which include the idea of heart-as-feeling. No such conception can be found in the Scriptures.

Consider instead what *is* contrasted with the word *heart* in the Bible. In *Matthew* 15:8, for instance, we read that the people honor God "with their lips, but their heart is far from" him. That sort of contrast is regularly made in the Scriptures. You find the same thing in the well-known passage in *Romans* 10 in which we are told that it is not enough to confess Christ with the mouth; the one making the profession also must believe in his heart. Notice the contrast: heart/lips, heart/mouth. In the important passage 1 *Samuel* 16:7, we are assured that "man looks on the outward appearances, but [in contrast] God looks on the heart." Plainly, in all of these pivotal passages there is a contrast between the heart as something inner and the lips, mouth, and appearance as something outer. That is the true Biblical contrast, not a contrast between intellect and emotion.

The word *heart* has become a devalued currency in our culture. Preachers too often read the modem Western view of heart-as-emotional-commitment back into Scripture and thus mistake and distort what the Holy Spirit moved the writers of the Bible to say. It is time to restore the true Biblical content of the word so that we may profit from an understanding of those many passages in which it occurs.

If the heart of man in the Bible refers to the inner life, from which all else flows, what is the point of preaching to the heart? In the light of this meaning, we may say that preaching that goes to the heart genuinely affects the person. He has been hit at the very source of his whole life (*Proverbs* 4:23). He has been pierced by the preached Word where it counts. This does not necessarily mean that he is converted or, in the case of a believer, that he will repent of his sin, but it does mean that the sermon has truly hit home. That is why, whether the response is favorable or unfavorable, preaching that pierces the heart is preaching that elicits a response. It could not do otherwise because, as we have just seen, the heart is the source of every response. It also may be said that preaching that penetrates or cuts through to the heart is preaching that elicits a *genuine* response – whether it be faith or fury. Preaching that gets through to the heart does not leave the listener apathetic.

In contrast, preaching that does not go to the heart of a man is preaching without any genuine effect. While the listener may express gratitude for the help he has received, the words on his lips do not flow from heartfelt conviction. In time, his speech and actions will reflect the true condition of his heart. "By their fruits shall you know them." When the inner man is truly affected by the Word for good, that will lead to a positive, lasting change in his outward behavior. The outer and inner man will come into closer sync through discernible patterns of growth.

So, you can see how desirable it is to preach to the heart. Indeed, a strong Biblical case could be made that unless preaching penetrates deeply enough to affect the inner life, it is not preaching at all. True Biblical preaching changes people. It did in Bible times, and there is no reason why it will not do so today.

Boldness of Heart

If there is one characteristic that typifies modern preaching, it is its insipid, obsequious approach to speaking the truth. So unlike the early preachers, the Reformers, and the great preachers of all time, many modern Bible-believing preachers seem afraid to tell it like it is. And yet, that modern phrase, "tell it like it is," indicates that people generally appreciate hearing truth for what it is, even when what they hear isn't altogether pleasant. But it seems that in Christian circles, in particular, there is a pseudo-pious reserve or over-sophistication in which hypersensitive listeners are horrified by anything frank in preaching. There is, therefore, something wrong with modern preaching and in many of those who have been brought up on it that must be corrected. It is basically a willingness to compromise – even God's truth – which stems from a lack of boldness.

I am not commending rudeness or crudeness. These unnecessary characteristics are often assumed to be synonymous with boldness. But there is nothing rude or crude about the preaching in the book of *Acts*. The preaching found there is straightforward, clear, explicit, hard-hitting, and – in short – bold. In fact, the only feature of apostolic preaching described in *Acts* is its boldness.

It was said that when they saw the boldness of Peter and John, they recognized that "they had been with Jesus." The way some prissy Christians today look aghast at any boldness in preaching, you would think instead that a bold preacher had been with the devil! Most people, however, recognize a truly bold preacher as an unusual man and are interested in him and often in what he has to say. One reason why much contemporary preaching not only fails to reach the heart, but also is so uninteresting, is that it is timid and pale. Bold preaching is never dull.

What is boldness? The Greek word *parresia* means freedom in speaking, openness, willingness to be frank; it is plain speech that is unencumbered by fear. A bold preacher is one who has no fear of speaking the truth – even when it hurts. Many ministries are hampered today simply because of the fear of men. "Will Mrs. Jones take offense if I preach this?" "What will happen if I teach this to the congregation?" and similar thoughts go through the minds of far too many preachers, even when what they ought to be asking themselves is, "What will God think of me if I don't teach his truth?"

There is far too little teaching about judgment, Hell, and the other doctrines on the dark side of the Scriptural spectrum. There is too little reproving of sin. There is too little church discipline and confronting error, even when it is seriously affecting the membership of the church. There is a fear of controversy.

In some circles, the fear of controversy is so great that preachers and congregations following after them will settle for peace at any cost – even at the cost of truth, God's truth. The idea is that peace is all-important. Peace is a Biblical ideal (*Romans* 12:18 makes that clear: "If possible, so far as it depends on you, be at peace with everybody"), but so is purity. The peace of the church may never be bought at the cost of the purity of the church. That price is too dear. But why do we think that we can get along in this world – or for that matter, even in the church – without conflict and controversy? Jesus didn't. Paul didn't. None of the preachers of the apostolic age who faithfully served their Lord were spared controversy. Who are we to escape controversy when they did not? The story of the advance of the church across the Mediterranean world from Jerusalem to Rome is a story of controversy. When the Gospel is preached boldly, there will be controversy. Most of the *Epistles* themselves were called forth to counter error of doctrine and sinfulness of life. In them there is controversy. The life of Paul is a life of controversy. Tradition tells us that every apostle except John, who was exiled for his faith, died a violent death.

What is this hypersensitivity that is so often found among a particular brand of evangelicals today? Children around us grow up on television and movies that feature not only conflict, but also violence and crudity. Who in our age is so allergic to frankness that the open preaching of God's Word will cause him to break out in horror? Pale, insipid preaching is what drives people from Christ and the church, not bold preaching. It seems to me that the problem with hypersensitive evangelicals is not really the one stated up front – offending those to whom we preach – but, more often than not, simply a lack of boldness. And that lack of boldness boils down to a simple fear of men – fear of the consequences of telling it like it is.

Boldness characterized the preaching of the apostles and other early preachers, Luke says. Let's take just a brief glimpse at a bit of their preaching. When the 3,000 were stung in their hearts, what sort of preaching was it that led to that? First of all, we see that it was preaching that did not hesitate to contradict the expressed ideas of men. Some said that the 120 who were speaking in foreign languages were drunk. But when Peter got up to preach, the very first words out of his mouth contradicted this foolish accusation: "Certainly these people aren't drunk, as you imagine; it's only nine o'clock in the morning!" (*Acts* 2:15). Well-meaning and fearful preachers will tell you that to openly contradict the audience is a poor preaching tactic – especially at the beginning of a sermon! But Peter had not read the experts; he simply relied on the Holy Spirit and went ahead speaking the truth. To win friends and influence people, you are supposed to begin by gaining agreement. But Peter was more interested in the truth than in manipulating people by selling techniques.

Not only did Peter begin all wrong, according to the experts, but also he was far too frank when he discussed his congregation's behavior. After all, Peter, it isn't polite to say such things as "this Man, delivered up by God's predetermined plan and foreknowledge, you killed by crucifixion!" (*Acts* 2:23). That sounds like a direct accusation, if not an attack on the audience. You'll never get anywhere that way, Peter. But Peter isn't finished. Listen to the conclusion: "So then, let the whole house of Israel know for certain that God has made this Jesus whom you crucified both Lord and Christ." Now there you've done it, Peter! Just when it looked as if you might have pulled your sermon out of the fire after that opening blunder, you went ahead and spoiled everything by adding that last dig, "whom you crucified." And, while I'm at it, let me tell you something else, Peter. You will never get anywhere using the second person in preaching; it's too personal. It is possible that you might have gotten away with saying everything you said – even those all-too-frank accusations – if you had only phrased then in the third person, in a more abstract way.

Preaching from God's Heart

The preachers God uses are men who are *after* (literally, "as") his heart. That is to say, they understand God's purposes and his ways; they are in harmony with them; and they are anxious to tell others about them. The concerns they have were first God's concerns. Such shepherds feed God's flock what he wants them to: "knowledge and understanding." Where do they get it? From his Word. Men who preach to the heart, then, are men who know God's Word, who personally accept and are molded by God's Word, and who, as a result, are capable of feeding others on that life-giving and nourishing Word. So, the preacher must be capable of understanding God's Word and feeding others on it.

The source of heart-reaching messages is the Bible. "Faith" comes from hearing the Word (*Romans* 10:17). Prophets and apostles had direct revelation from God; today we have that same revelation in an inscripturated form. The idea of the written Word of God is not recent; it is Biblical. The Bible calls itself God's Word (compare especially *Psalm* 119), despite what liberals confidently say to the contrary. So, if preachers wish not only to preach to the heart, but to preach in ways that are pleasing to God, they must preach "after [as] his heart." To do that, they must learn his thoughts and intents (heart) and become attuned to them in their own lives. They may learn from the Bible all that is necessary to preach (compare 2 *Timothy* 3:16, 17). Indeed, there is only one way to preach to hearts: to preach from God's heart; but God has revealed his heart only in his written Word.

How tragic, therefore, that men in the pulpit prattle on about the ideas of other men, share their own opinions, and feed God's sheep on diets of everything else. All the while, food provided by God – available, nourishing, life-giving – is almost totally neglected. Preacher, you will preach to the heart only when you preach from God's heart. You will preach from God's heart only when you know what is in his heart. And you will know what is in his heart only when you know his Word. You must dedicate yourself, therefore, to a thorough study of that Word so that you will truly become a workman in the Word who does not need to be ashamed, because you have accurately handled the Word of Truth (2 *Timothy* 2:15) in your preaching.

A Heart-adapted Form

In *Colossians* 4:3-4, Paul wrote: "... praying at the same time also about us, that God may open for us a door for the Word, to speak about the secret of Christ, because of which I am in bonds, so that I may proclaim it clearly, as I ought to." To "proclaim it clearly, as I ought to" – those words have to do with form.

Paul's one goal was to avoid anything that might obscure God's truth and to do everything that he could to present it as clearly as possible. There is no contradiction between that desire and an unwillingness to have his listeners' faith depend upon something other than the Gospel of Christ. In fact, the two concerns dovetail: If anything obscures the Gospel, it isn't possible for people to understand and believe it. Preacher, that means that you must not seek to become a Demosthenes, calling attention to your rhetorical powers, but you must do whatever is necessary to be sure that your proclamation of the convicting, nourishing Word is clear. You must aim not at the applause of men, but at reaching their hearts.

Clarity is one prerequisite pertaining to form that is essential to preaching to the heart. How sad it is that preachers do not work more on this matter of clarity. How important it must be if the apostle Paul himself was concerned enough about it to ask for prayer. Have you ever asked your congregation to pray for clarity in your preaching? Have you ever asked them to pray about your preaching at all? Clarity is the thing. Paul was right – that is how he was to speak; preacher, it is also how you ought to speak.

6

The Fallibility of Ministers[1]

J. C. Ryle

But when Peter came to Antioch, I withstood him to the face, because he was to be blamed. For before certain Jews came from James, he did eat with the Gentiles: but when they were come, he withdrew and separated himself, fearing them which were of the circumcision. And the other Jews dissembled likewise with him; insomuch that Barnabas also was carried away with their dissimulation.

But when I saw that they walked not uprightly according to the truth of the Gospel, I said unto Peter before them all, "If you, being a Jew, live after the manner of Gentiles, and not as do the Jews, why do you compel the Gentiles to live as do the Jews?" We who are Jews by nature, and not sinners of the Gentiles, knowing that a man is not justified by the works of the law, but by the faith of Jesus Christ, even we have believed in Jesus Christ that we might be justified by the faith of Christ, and not by the works of the law: for by the works of the law shall no flesh be justified (Galatians 2:11-16).

Have we ever considered what the Apostle Peter once did at Antioch? It is a question that deserves serious consideration.

What the Apostle Peter did at *Rome* we are often told, although we have hardly a jot of authentic information about it. Roman Catholic writers furnish us with many stories about this. Legends, traditions, and fables abound on the subject. But unhappily for these writers, Scripture is utterly silent upon the point. There is nothing in Scripture to show that the Apostle Peter ever was at Rome at all!

But what did the Apostle Peter do at *Antioch?* This is the point to which I want to direct attention. This is the subject from the passage

1. Reprinted from J. C. Ryle, *Warnings to the Churches*. The Banner of Truth Trust [1967] 1992, 93-121.

from the *Epistle to the Galatians*, which heads this paper. On this point, at any rate, the Scripture speaks clearly and unmistakably.

The six verses of the passages before us are striking on many accounts. They are striking, if we consider the *event* which they describe: Here is one apostle rebuking another! They are striking, when we consider who the two men are: Paul the younger rebukes Peter the elder! They are striking, when we remark the *occasion:* This was no glaring fault, no flagrant sin, at first sight, that Peter had committed! Yet the Apostle Paul says, "I withstood him to the face, because he was to be blamed." He does more than this: He reproves Peter publicly for his error before all the Church at Antioch. He goes even further: He writes an account of the matter, which is now read in two hundred languages all over the world. It is my firm conviction that the Holy Ghost means us to take particular notice of this passage of Scripture. If Christianity had been an invention of man, these things would never have been recorded. An imposter, like Mahomet, would have hushed up the difference between two apostles. The Spirit of Truth has caused these verses to be written for our learning, and we shall do well to take heed to their contents.

There are three great lessons from Antioch which I think we ought to learn from this passage:

1. The first lesson is that *great ministers may make great mistakes.*

2. The second is that *to keep the truth of Christ in his church is even more important than to keep peace.*

3. The third is that *there is no doctrine about which we ought to be so jealous as justification by faith without the deeds of the law.*

The first great lesson we learn from Antioch is that *great ministers may make great mistakes.*

What clearer proof can we have than that which is set before us in this place? Peter, without doubt, was one of the greatest in the company of the apostles. He was an old disciple. He was a disciple who had had peculiar advantages and privileges. He had been a constant companion of the Lord Jesus. He had heard the Lord preach, seen the Lord work miracles, enjoyed the benefit of the Lord's private teaching, been numbered among the Lord's intimate friends, and gone out and come in with him all the time he ministered upon Earth. He was the apostle to whom the keys of the kingdom were given, and by whose hand those keys were first used. He was the first who opened the door of faith to the Jews by preaching to them on the day of Pentecost. He was the first who opened the door of faith to the Gentiles by going to the house of Cornelius and receiving him into the church. He was the first to rise up in the Council of the fifteenth of *Acts* and say, "Why do you tempt God by putting a yoke upon the neck of the disciples, which neither our fathers nor we were able to bear?" And yet here this very Peter, this same apostle, plainly falls into a great mistake. The Apostle Paul tells us, "I withstood him to the face." He tells us that "he was to be blamed." He says, "he feared them of the circumcision." He says of him and his companions that "they walked not uprightly according to the truth of the Gospel." He speaks of their "dissimulation." He tells us that by this dissimulation even Barnabas, his old companion in missionary labors, "was carried away."

What a striking fact this is. This is Simon Peter! This is the third great error of his which the Holy Ghost has thought fit to record! Once we find him trying to keep back our Lord, as far as he could, from the great work of the cross, and severely rebuked. Then we find him denying the Lord three times, and with an oath. Here again we find him endangering the leading truth of Christ's Gospel. Surely we may say, "Lord, what is man?" The Church of Rome boasts that the Apostle Peter is her founder and first Bishop. Be it so: Grant it for a moment. Let us only remember that of all the apostles there is not one, excepting, of course Judas Iscariot, of whom we have so many proofs that he was a *fallible* man. Upon her own showing the Church of Rome was founded by the most fallible of the apostles.[2]

But it is all meant to teach us that even the apostles themselves, when not writing under the inspiration of the Holy Ghost, were at times liable to err. It is meant to teach us that the best men are weak and fallible so long as they are in the body. Unless the grace of God holds them up, any one of them may go astray at any time. It is very humbling, but it is very true. True Christians are converted, justified, and sanctified.

---

2. It is curious to observe the shifts to which some writers have been reduced in order to explain away the plain meaning of the verses which head this paper. Some have maintained that Paul did not really rebuke Peter, but only feignedly, for show and appearance' sake! Others have maintained that it was not Peter the Apostle who was rebuked, but another Peter, one of the seventy! Such interpretations need no remark. They are simply absurd. The truth is that the plain, honest meaning of the verses strikes a heavy blow at the favorite Roman Catholic doctrine of the primacy and superiority of Peter over the rest of the apostles.

They are living members of Christ, beloved children of God, and heirs of eternal life. They are elect, chosen, called, and kept unto salvation. They have the Spirit. But they are *not infallible.*

Will not rank and dignity confer infallibility? No, they will not! It matters nothing what a man is called. He may be a Czar, an Emperor, a King, a Prince. He may be a Pope or a Cardinal, an Archbishop or a Bishop, a Dean or an Archdeacon, a Priest or Deacon. He is still a *fallible man.* Neither the crown, nor the diadem, nor the anointing oil, nor the mitre, nor the imposition of hands can prevent a man making mistakes.

Will not numbers confer infallibility? No, they will not! You may gather together princes by the score, and bishops by the hundred; but, when gathered together, they are still liable to err. You may call them a council or a synod or an assembly or a conference, or what you please. It matters nothing. Their conclusions are still the conclusions of *fallible men.* Their collective wisdom is still capable of making enormous mistakes. Well says the twenty-first Article of the Church of England, "General councils may err, and sometimes have erred, even in things pertaining unto God."

The example of the Apostle Peter at Antioch is one that does not stand alone. It is only a parallel of many a case that we find written for our learning in holy Scripture. Do we not remember Abraham, the father of the faithful, following the advice of Sarah, and taking Hagar for a wife? Do we not remember Aaron, the first high priest, listening to the children of Israel, and making a golden calf? Do we not remember Nathan the prophet telling David to build a temple? Do we not remember Solomon, the wisest of men, allowing his wives to build their high places? Do we not remember Asa, the good king of Judah, seeking not the Lord, but the physicians? Do we not remember Jehoshaphat, the good king, going down to help wicked Ahab? Do we not remember Hezekiah, the good king, receiving the ambassadors of Babylon? Do we not remember Josiah, the last of Judah's good kings, going forth to fight with Pharaoh? Do we not remember James and John, wanting fire to come down from Heaven? These things deserve to be remembered. They were not written without cause. They cry aloud, *No infallibility!*

And who does not see, when he reads the history of the church of Christ, repeated proofs that the best of men can err? The early fathers were zealous according to their knowledge and ready to die for Christ. But many of them countenanced monkery, and nearly all sowed the seeds of many superstitions. The Reformers were honored instruments in the hand of God for reviving the cause of truth on Earth. Yet hardly one of them can be named who did not make some great mistake. Martin Luther held pertinaciously the doctrine of consubstantiation. Melanchthon was often timid and undecided. Calvin permitted Servetus to be burned.[3] Cranmer recanted and fell away for a time from his first faith. Jewel subscribed to popish doctrines for fear of death. Hooper disturbed the Church of England by over scrupulosity about vestments. The Puritans, in after times, denounced toleration as Abaddon and Apollyon. Wesley and Toplady, last century, abused each other in most shameful language. Irving, in our own day, gave way to the delusion of speaking in unknown tongues. All these things speak with a loud voice. They lift up a beacon to the church of Christ. They all say, "Cease from man"; – "Call no man master"; – "Call no man father upon Earth"; – "Let no man glory in man"; – "He that glories, let him glory in the Lord." They all cry, *No infallibility!*

The lesson is one that we all need. We are all naturally inclined to lean upon man whom we can see, rather than upon God whom we cannot see. We naturally love to lean upon the ministers of the visible church, rather than upon the Lord Jesus Christ, the great Shepherd and Bishop and High Priest, who is invisible. We need to be continually warned and set upon our guard.

I see this tendency to lean on man everywhere. I know no branch of the Protestant church of Christ which does not require to be cautioned upon the point. It is a snare, for example, to the English Episcopalian to make idols of Bishop Pearson and "the Judicious Hooker." It is a snare to the Scotch Presbyterian to pin his faith on John Knox, the Covenanters, and Dr. Chalmers. It is a snare to the Methodists in our day to worship the memory of John Wesley. It is a snare to the Independent to see no fault in any opinion of Owen and Doddridge. It is a snare to the Baptist to exaggerate the wisdom of Gill and Fuller and Robert Hall. All these are snares, and into these snares how many fall!

We all naturally love to have a pope of our own. We are far too ready to think that because some great minister or some learned man says a thing – or because our own minister, whom we love, says a thing – it

---

3. Calvin appealed to Servetus' judges as witnesses that he had opposed the burning of Servetus. – *Editor.*

must be right, without examining whether it is in Scripture or not. Most men dislike the trouble of thinking for themselves. They like following a leader. They are like sheep – when one goes over the gap all the rest follow. Here at Antioch even Barnabas was carried away. We can well fancy that good man saying, "An old apostle, like Peter, surely cannot be wrong. Following him, I cannot err."

And now let us see what practical lessons we may learn from this part of our subject:

(a) For one thing, let us learn not to put implicit confidence in any man's opinion, merely *because he lived many hundred years ago*. Peter was a man who lived in the time of Christ himself, and yet he could err.

There are many who talk much in the present day about "the voice of the primitive church." They would have us believe that those who lived nearest the time of the apostles must of course know more about truth than we can. There is no foundation for any such opinion. It is a fact that the most ancient writers in the church of Christ are often at variance with one another. It is a fact that they often changed their own minds and retracted their own former opinions. It is a fact that they often wrote foolish and weak things and often showed great ignorance in their explanations of Scripture. It is vain to expect to find them free from mistakes. *Infallibility is not to be found in the early fathers, but in the Bible.*

(b) For another thing, let us learn not to put implicit confidence in any man's opinion, *merely because of his office as a minister.* Peter was one of the very chiefest apostles, and yet he could err.

This is a point on which men have continually gone astray. It is the rock on which the early church struck. Men soon took up the saying, "Do nothing contrary to the mind of the Bishop." But what are bishops, priests, and deacons? What are the best of ministers but men – dust, ashes, and clay – men of like passions with ourselves, men exposed to temptations, men liable to weaknesses and infirmities? What says the Scripture, "Who is Paul and who is Apollos, but ministers by whom you believed, even as the Lord gave to every man?" (1 Corinthians 3:5). Bishops have often driven the truth into the wilderness, and decreed that to be true which was false. The greatest errors have been begun by ministers. Hophni and Phinehas, the sons of the high priest, made religion to be abhorred by the children of Israel. Annas and Caiaphas, though in the direct line of descent from Aaron, crucified the Lord. Arius, that great heresiarch, was a minister. It is absurd to suppose that ordained men cannot go wrong. We should follow them so far as they teach according to the Bible, but no further. We should believe them so long as they can say, "Thus it is written," "thus says the Lord;" but further than this we are not to go. *Infallibility is not to be found in ordained men, but in the Bible.*

(c) For another thing, let us learn not to place implicit confidence in any man's opinion, *merely because of his learning.* Peter was a man who had miraculous gifts and could speak with tongues, and yet he could err.

This is a point again on which many go wrong. This is the rock on which men struck in the Middle Ages. Men looked on Thomas Aquinas and Duns Scotus and Peter Lombard and many of their companions as almost inspired. They gave epithets to some of them in token of their admiration. They talked of "the irrefragable" doctor, "the seraphic" doctor, "the incomparable" doctor, – and seemed to think that whatever these doctors said must be true! But what is the most learned of men, if he be not taught by the Holy Ghost? What is the most learned of all divines but a mere fallible child of Adam at his very best? Vast knowledge of books and great ignorance of God's truth may go side by side. They have done so, they may do so and they will do so in all times. I will engage to say that the two volumes of Robert M'Cheyne's *Memoirs* and *Sermons* have done more positive good to the souls of men than any one folio that Origen or Cyprian ever wrote. I doubt not that the one volume of *Pilgrim's Progress,* written by a man who knew hardly any book but his Bible and was ignorant of Greek and Latin, will prove in the last day to have done more for the benefit of the world than all the works of the schoolmen put together.

Learning is a gift that ought not to be despised. It is an evil day when books are not valued in the church. But it is amazing to observe how vast a man's intellectual attainments may be, and yet how little he may know of the grace of God. I have no doubt the authorities of Oxford in the last century knew more of Hebrew, Greek, and Latin, than Wesley, Whitefield, Berridge, or Venn. But they knew little of the Gospel of Christ. *Infallibility is not to be found among learned men, but in the Bible.*

(d) For another thing, let us take care that we do not place implicit confidence *on our own minister's opinion,* however godly he may be. Peter was a man of mighty grace, and yet he could err.

Your minister may be a man of God indeed, and worthy of all honor for his preaching and practice; but do not make a pope of him. Do not place his word side by side with the Word of God. Do not spoil him by flattery. Do not let him suppose he can make no mistakes. Do not lean your whole weight on his opinion, or you may find to your cost that he can err.

It is written of Joash, King of Judah, that he "did that which was right in the sight of the Lord all the days of Jehoiada the priest" (2 *Chronicles* 24:2). Jehoiada died, and then died the religion of Joash. Just so your minister may die, and then your religion may die too – may change, and your religion may change, may go away, and your religion may go. Oh, be not satisfied with a religion built upon man! Be not content with saying, "I have hope, because my own minister has told me such and such things." Seek to be able to say, "I have hope, because I find it thus and thus written in the Word of God." If your peace is to be solid, you must go yourself to the fountain of all truth. If your comforts are to be lasting, you must visit the well of life yourself, and draw fresh water for your own soul. Ministers may depart from the faith. The visible church may be broken up. But he who has the Word of God written in his heart has a foundation beneath his feet which will never fail him. Honor your minister as a faithful ambassador of Christ. Esteem him very highly in love for his work's sake. But never forget that *infallibility is not to be found in godly ministers, but in the Bible.*

The things I have mentioned are worth remembering. Let us bear them in mind, and we shall have learned one lesson from Antioch.

2. I now pass on to the second lesson that we learn front Antioch. That lesson is that *to keep Gospel truth in the church is of even greater importance than to keep peace.*

I suppose no man knew better the value of peace and unity than the Apostle Paul. He was the apostle who wrote to the Corinthians about charity. He was the apostle who said, "Be of the same mind one toward another"; "be at peace among yourselves"; "mind the same things"; "the servant of God must not strive." "There is one body and there is one Spirit, even as you are called in one hope of your calling, one Lord, one faith, one baptism." He was the apostle who said, "I become all things to all men, that by all means I may save some" (*Romans* 12:16; *1 Thessalonians* 5:13; *Philippians* 3:16; *Ephesians* 4:5; *1 Corinthians* 9:22). Yet see how he acts here! He withstands Peter to the face. He publicly rebukes him. He runs the risk of all the consequences that might follow. He takes the chance of everything that might be said by the enemies of the Church of Antioch. Above all, he writes it down for a perpetual memorial, that it never might be forgotten; that wherever the Gospel is preached throughout the world, this public rebuke of an erring apostle might be known and read of all men.

Now why did he do this? Because he dreaded false doctrine; because he knew that a little leaven leavens the whole lump; because he would teach us that we ought to contend for the truth jealously, and to fear the loss of truth more than the loss of peace.

St. Paul's example is one we shall do well to remember in the present day. Many people will put up with anything in religion, if they may only have a quiet life. They have a morbid dread of what they call "controversy." They are filled with a morbid fear of what they style, in a vague way, "party spirit," though they never define clearly what party spirit is. They are possessed with a morbid desire to keep the peace and make all things smooth and pleasant, even though it be at the expense of truth. So long as they have outward calm, smoothness, stillness, and order, they seem content to give up everything else. I believe they would have thought with Ahab that Elijah was a troubler of Israel and would have helped the princes of Judah when they put Jeremiah in prison to stop his mouth. I have no doubt that many of these men of whom I speak would have thought that Paul at Antioch was a very imprudent man and that he went too far!

I believe this is all wrong. We have no right to expect anything but the pure Gospel of Christ, unmixed and unadulterated – the same Gospel that was taught by the apostles – to do good to the souls of men. I believe that to maintain this pure truth in the church men should be ready to make any sacrifice, to hazard peace, to risk dissension, to run the chance of division. *They should no more tolerate false doctrine than they should tolerate sin.* They should withstand any adding to or taking away from the simple message of the Gospel of Christ. For the truth's sake our Lord Jesus Christ denounced the Pharisees, though they sat in Moses' seat and were the appointed and authorized teachers of men. "Woe unto you, Scribes and Pharisees, hypocrites," he says, eight times over, in the twenty-third chapter of *Matthew*. And who shall dare to breathe a suspicion that our Lord was wrong?

For the truth's sake Paul withstood and blamed Peter, though a brother. Where was the use of unity when pure doctrine was gone? And who shall dare to say he was wrong?

For the truth's sake Athanasius stood out against the world to maintain the pure doctrine about the divinity of Christ and waged a controversy with the great majority of the professing church. And who shall dare to say he was wrong?

For the truth's sake Cranmer, Ridley, and Latimer, the English Reformers, counseled Henry VIII and Edward VI to separate from Rome, and to risk the consequences of division. And who shall dare to say that they were wrong?

For the truth's sake Whitefield and Wesley a hundred years ago denounced the mere barren moral preaching of the clergy of their day and went out into the highways and byways to save souls, knowing well that they would be cast out from the church's communion. And who shall dare to say that they were wrong?

Yes! peace without truth is a false peace; it is the very peace of the devil. Unity without the Gospel is a worthless unity; it is the very unity of Hell. Let us never be ensnared by those who speak kindly of it. Let us remember the words of our Lord Jesus Christ: "Think not that I came to send peace upon Earth. I came not to send peace, but a sword" (*Matthew* 10:34). Let us remember the praise he gives to one of the churches in the *Revelation*: "You cannot bear them who are evil. You have tried them which say they are apostles, and are not, and have found them liars" (*Revelation* 2:2). Let us remember the blame he casts upon another; "You allow that woman Jezebel to teach" (*Revelation* 2:20). Never let us be guilty of sacrificing any portion of truth upon the altar of peace. Let us rather be like the Jews, who, if they found any manuscript copy of the Old Testament Scriptures incorrect in a single letter, burned the whole copy, rather than run the risk of losing one jot or tittle of the Word of God. Let us be content with nothing short of the whole Gospel of Christ.

In what way are we to make practical use of the general principles which I have just laid down? I will give my readers one simple piece of advice. I believe it is advice which deserves serious consideration.

I warn then every one who loves his soul *to be very jealous as to the preaching he regularly hears and the place of worship he regularly attends.* He who deliberately settles down under any ministry which is positively unsound is a very unwise man. I will never hesitate to speak my mind on this point. I know well that many think it a shocking thing for a man to forsake his parish church. I cannot see with the eyes of such people.

I draw a wide distinction between teaching which is *defective* and teaching which is thoroughly *false* – between teaching which errs on the negative side and teaching which is positively unscriptural. But I do believe, if false doctrine is unmistakably preached in a parish church, a parishioner who loves his soul is quite right in not going to that parish church. To hear unscriptural teaching fifty-two Sundays in every year is a serious thing. It is a continual dropping of slow poison into the mind. I think it almost impossible for a man willfully to submit himself to it and not take harm. I see in the New Testament we are plainly told to "prove all things," and "hold fast that which is good" (1 *Thessalonians* 5:21). I see in the *Book of Proverbs* that we are commanded to "cease to hear instruction which causes to err from the paths of knowledge" (*Proverbs* 19:27). If these words do not justify a man in ceasing to worship at a church, if positively false doctrine is preached in it, I know not what words can.

Does any man mean to tell us that to attend the parish church is absolutely needful to an Englishman's salvation? If there is such an one, let him speak out and give us his name. Does anyone mean to tell us that going to the parish church will save any man's soul, if he dies unconverted and ignorant of Christ? If there is such an one, let him speak out and give us his name. Does anyone mean to tell us that going to the parish church will teach a man anything about Christ, or conversion, or faith, or repentance, if these subjects are hardly ever named in the parish church and never properly explained? If there is such an one, let him speak out and give us his name. Does anyone mean to say that a man who repents, believes in Christ, is converted and holy will lose his soul, because he has forsaken his parish church and learned his religion elsewhere? If there is such an one, let him speak out and give us his name. For my part I abhor such monstrous and extravagant ideas. I see not a jot of foundation for them in the Word of God. I trust that the number of those who deliberately hold them is exceedingly small.

There are not a few parishes in England where the religious teaching is little better than popery. Ought the laity of such parishes to sit still, be content, and take it quietly? They ought not. And why? Because, like Paul, they ought to prefer truth to peace.

There are not a few parishes in England where the religious teaching is little better than morality. The distinctive doctrines of Christianity are never clearly proclaimed. Plato, or Seneca, or Confucius, or Socinus could have taught almost as much. Ought the laity in such parishes to sit still, be content, and take it quietly? They ought not. And why? Because, like Paul, they ought to prefer truth to peace.

I am using strong language in dealing with this part of my subject; I know it. I am trenching on delicate ground; I know it. I am handling matters which are generally let alone, and passed over in silence; I know it. I say what I say from a sense of duty to the Church of which I am a minister. I believe the state of the times, and the position of the laity in some parts of England, require plain speaking. Souls are perishing in many parishes in ignorance. Honest members of the Church of England in many districts are disgusted and perplexed. This is no time for smooth words. I am not ignorant of those magic expressions, "the parochial system, order, division, schism, unity, controversy," and the like. I know the cramping, silencing influence which they seem to exercise on some minds. I too have considered those expressions calmly and deliberately, and on each of them I am prepared to speak my mind:

(a) The *parochial system* of England is an admirable thing in theory. Let it only be well administered and worked by truly spiritual ministers, and it is calculated to confer the greatest blessings on the nation. But it is useless to expect attachment to the parish church when the minister of the parish is ignorant of the Gospel or a lover of the world. In such a case we must never be surprised if men forsake their parish church and seek truth wherever truth is to be found. If the parochial minister does not preach the Gospel and live the Gospel, the conditions on which he claims the attention of his parishioners are *virtually violated,* and his claim to be heard is at an end. It is absurd to expect the head of a family to endanger the souls of his children as well as his own for the sake of "parochial order." There is no mention of parishes in the Bible, and we have no right to require men to live and die in ignorance in order that they may be able to say at last, "I always attended my parish church."

(b) *Divisions and separations* are most objectionable in religion. They weaken the cause of true Christianity. They give occasion to the enemies of all godliness to blaspheme. But before we blame people for them, we must be careful that we lay the blame *where it is deserved.* False doctrine and heresy are even worse than schism. If people separate themselves from teaching which is positively false and unscriptural, they ought to be praised rather than reproved. In such cases separation is a virtue and not a sin. It is easy to make sneering remarks about "itching ears," and "love of excitement," but it is not so easy to convince a plain reader of the Bible that it is his duty to hear false doctrine every Sunday, when by a little exertion he can hear truth. The old saying must never be forgotten, "He is the schismatic who causes the schism."

(c) *Unity, quiet, and order* among professing Christians are mighty blessings. They give strength, beauty, and efficiency to the cause of Christ. But even gold may be bought too dear. Unity which is obtained by the sacrifice of truth is worth nothing. It is not the unity which pleases God. The Church of Rome boasts loudly of a unity which does not deserve the name. It is unity which is obtained by taking away the Bible from the people, by gagging private judgment, by encouraging ignorance, by forbidding men to think for themselves. Like the exterminating warriors of old, the Church of Rome "makes a solitude and calls it peace." There is quiet and stillness enough in the grave, but it is not the quiet of health, but of death. It was the false prophets who cried "Peace," when there was no peace.

(d) *Controversy* in religion is a hateful thing. It is hard enough to fight the devil, the world, and flesh without private difference in our own camp. But there is one thing which is even worse than controversy, and that is false doctrine tolerated, allowed, and permitted without protest or molestation. It was controversy that won the battle of Protestant Reformation. If the views that some men hold were correct, it is plain we never ought to have had any Reformation at all! For the sake of peace, we ought to have gone on worshiping the Virgin and bowing down to images and relics to this very day! Away with such trifling! There are times when controversy is not only a duty but also a benefit. Give me the mighty thunderstorm rather than the pestilential malaria. The one walks in darkness and poisons us in silence, and we are never safe. The other frightens and alarms for a little season. But it is soon over, and it clears the air. It is a plain Scriptural duty to "contend earnestly for the faith once delivered to the saints" (*Jude* 3).

I am quite aware that the things I have said are exceedingly distasteful to many minds. I believe many are content with teaching which is not the whole truth and fancy it will be "all the same" in the end. I am sorry for them. I am convinced that nothing but *the whole truth* is likely, as a general rule, to do good to souls. I am satisfied that those who willfully put up with anything short of the whole truth will find at last that their souls have received much damage. Three things there are which men never ought to trifle with – a little poison, a little false doctrine, and a little sin.

I am quite aware that when a man expresses such opinions as those I have just brought forward there are many ready to say, "He is no Churchman." I hear such accusations unmoved. The Day of Judgment will show who were the true friends of the Church of England and who were not. I have learned in the last thirty-two years that if a clergyman leads a quiet life, lets alone the unconverted part of the world, and preaches so as to offend none and edify none, he will be called by many "a good Churchman." And I have also learned that if a man studies the *Articles* and *Homilies,* labors continually for the conversion of souls, adheres closely to the great principles of the Reformation, bears a faithful testimony against popery, and preaches as Jewel and Latimer used to preach, he will probably be thought a firebrand and "troubler of Israel," and called no Churchman at all! But I can see plainly that they are not the best Churchmen who talk most loudly about Churchmanship. I remember that none cried "Treason" so loudly as Athaliah (2 *Kings* 11:14). Yet she was a traitor herself. I have observed that many who once talked most about Churchmanship have ended by forsaking the Church of England and going over to Rome. Let men say what they will. *They are the truest friends of the Church of England who labor most for the preservation of truth.*

I lay these things before the readers of this paper and invite their serious attention to them. I charge them never to forget that truth is of more importance to a church than peace. I ask them to be ready to carry out the principles I have laid down, and to contend zealously, if needs be, for the truth. If we do this we shall have learned something from Antioch.

3. But I pass on to the third lesson from Antioch. That lesson is that *there is no doctrine about which we ought to be so jealous as justification by faith without the deeds of the law.*

The proof of this lesson stands out most prominently in the passage of Scripture which heads this paper. What one article of faith had the Apostle Peter denied at Antioch? None. What doctrine had he publicly preached that was false? None. What, then had he done? He had done this: After once keeping company with the believing Gentiles as "fellow-heirs and partakers of the promise of Christ in the Gospel" (*Ephesians* 3:6), he suddenly became shy of them and withdrew himself. He seemed to think they were less holy and acceptable to God than the circumcised Jews. He seemed to imply that the believing Gentiles were in a lower state than they who had kept the ceremonies of the Law of Moses. He seemed, in a word, to add something to simple *faith* as needful to give man an interest in Jesus Christ. He seemed to reply to the questions, "What shall I do to be saved?" not merely, "Believe on the Lord Jesus Christ," but "Believe on the Lord Jesus Christ, *and be circumcised*, and keep the ceremonies of the law."

Such conduct as this the Apostle Paul would not endure for a moment. Nothing so moved him as the idea of adding anything to the Gospel of Christ. "I withstood him," he says, "to the face." He not only rebuked him, but he recorded the whole transaction fully, when by inspiration of the Spirit he wrote the *Epistle to the Galatians*.

I invite special attention to this point. I ask men to observe the remarkable jealousy which the Apostle Paul shows about this doctrine, and to consider the point about which such a stir was made. Let us mark in this passage of Scripture the immense importance of justification by faith without the deeds of the law. Let us learn here what mighty reasons the Reformers of the Church of England had for calling it, in our eleventh Article, "a most wholesome doctrine and very full of comfort."

(a) This is the doctrine which is *essentially necessary to our own personal comfort*. No man on Earth is a real child of God and a saved soul till he sees and receives salvation by faith in Christ Jesus. No man will ever have solid peace and true assurance until he embraces with heart the doctrine that "we are accounted righteous before God for the merit of our Lord Jesus Christ, by faith, and not for our own works and deservings." One reason, I believe, why so many professors in this day are tossed to and fro, enjoy little comfort, and feel little peace is their ignorance on this point. They do not see clearly justification by faith without the deeds of the law.

(b) This is the doctrine which *the great enemy of souls hates, and labors to overthrow*. He knows that it turned the world upside down at the first beginning of the Gospel in the days of the apostles. He knows that it turned the world upside down again at the time of the Reformation. He is therefore always tempting men to reject it. He is always trying to seduce churches and ministers to deny or obscure its truth. No wonder that the Council of Trent directed its chief attack against this doctrine

144

and pronounced it accursed and heretical. No wonder that many who think themselves learned in these days denounce the doctrine as theological jargon and say that all "earnest-minded people" are justified by Christ, whether they have faith or not! The plain truth is that the doctrine is all gall and wormwood to unconverted hearts. It just meets the wants of the awakened soul. But the proud, unhumbled man who knows not his own sin and sees not his own weakness cannot receive its truth.

(c) This is the doctrine, the *absence of which accounts for half the errors of the Roman Catholic Church.* The beginning of half the unscriptural doctrines of popery may be traced up to rejection of justification by faith. No Romish teacher, if he is faithful to his church, can say to an anxious sinner, "Believe on the Lord Jesus Christ and you shall be saved." He cannot do it without additions and explanations which completely destroy the good news. He dare not give the Gospel medicine without adding something which destroys its efficacy and neutralizes its power. Purgatory, penance, priestly absolution, the intercession of saints, the worship of the Virgin, and many other man-made services of popery all spring from this source. They are all rotten props to support weary consciences. But they are rendered necessary by the denial of justification by faith.

(d) This is the doctrine which is *absolutely essential to a minister's success among his people.* Obscurity on this point spoils all. Absence of clear statements about justification will prevent the utmost zeal doing good. There may be much that is pleasing and nice in a minister's sermons, much about Christ and sacramental union with him, much about self-denial, much about humility, much about charity. But all this will profit little if his trumpet gives an uncertain sound about justification by faith without the deeds of the law.

(e) This is the doctrine which is *absolutely essential to the prosperity of a church.* No church is really in a healthy state in which this doctrine is not prominently brought forward. A church may have good forms and regularly ordained ministers, and the sacraments properly administered, but a church will not see conversion of souls going on under its pulpits when this doctrine is not plainly preached. Its schools may be found in every parish. Its ecclesiastical buildings may strike the eye all over the land. But there will be no blessing from God on that church unless justification by faith is proclaimed from its pulpits. Sooner or later its candlestick will be taken away.

Why have the churches of Africa and the East fallen to their present state? Had they not bishops? They had. Had they not forms and liturgies? They had. Had they not synods and councils? They had. But they cast away the doctrine of justification by faith. They lost sight of that mighty truth, and so fell.

Why did our own church do so little in the last century, and why did the Independents and Methodists and Baptists do so much more? Was it that their system was better than ours? No. Was it that our church was not so well adapted to meet the wants of lost souls? No. But their ministers preached justification by faith, and our ministers, in too many cases, did not preach the doctrine at all.

Why do so many English people go to dissenting chapels in the present day? Why do we so often see a splendid Gothic parish church as empty of worshipers as a barn in July, and a little plain brick building, called a Meeting House, filled to suffocation? Is it that people in general have any abstract dislike to episcopacy, the *Prayer Book*, the surplice, and the establishment? Not at all! The simple reason is, in the vast majority of cases, that people do not like preaching in which justification by faith is not fully proclaimed. When they cannot hear it in the parish church they will seek it elsewhere. No doubt there are exceptions. No doubt there are places where a long course of neglect has thoroughly disgusted people with the Church of England, so that they will not even hear truth from its ministers. But I believe, as a general rule, when the parish church is empty and the meetinghouse full, it will be found on inquiry that *there is a cause.*

If these things be so, the Apostle Paul might well be jealous for the truth and withstand Peter to the face. He might well maintain that anything ought to be sacrificed rather than endanger the doctrine of justification in the church of Christ. He saw with a prophetical eye coming things. He left us all an example that we should do well to follow. Whatever we tolerate, let us never allow any injury to be done to that blessed doctrine – that we are justified by faith without the deeds of the law.

Let us always beware of any teaching which either directly or indirectly obscures justification by faith. All religious systems which put anything between the heavy-laden sinner and Jesus Christ the Savior, except simple faith, are dangerous and unscriptural. All systems which make out faith to be anything complicated, anything but a simple, childlike dependence – the hand which receives the soul's medicine from the physician – are unsafe and poisonous systems. All systems which cast discredit on the simple Protestant doctrine which broke the power of Rome carry about with them a plague-spot and are dangerous to souls.

Baptism is a sacrament ordained by Christ himself, and to be used with reverence and respect by all professing Christians. When it is used rightly, worthily, and with faith, it is capable of being the instrument of mighty blessings to the soul. But when people are taught that all who are baptized are as a matter of course born again, and that all baptized persons should be addressed as "children of God," I believe their souls are in great danger. Such teaching about baptism appears to me to overthrow the doctrine of justification by faith. They only are children of God who have faith in Christ Jesus. And all men have not faith.

The Lord's Supper is a sacrament ordained by Christ himself, and intended for the edification and refreshment of true believers. But when the people are taught that all persons ought to come to the Lord's table, whether they have faith or not; and that all alike receive Christ's body and blood who receive the bread and wine, I believe their souls are in great danger. Such teaching appears to me to darken the doctrine of justification by faith. No man eats Christ's body and drinks Christ's blood except the justified man. And none is justified until he believes.

Membership of the Church of England is a great privilege. No visible church on Earth, in my opinion, offers so many advantages to its members, when rightly administered. But when people are taught that because they are members of the church they are as a matter of course members of Christ, I believe their souls are in great danger. Such teaching appears to me to overthrow the doctrine of justification by faith. They only are joined to Christ who believe. And all men do not believe.

Whenever we hear teaching which obscures or contradicts justification by faith, we may be sure there is a screw loose somewhere. We should watch against such teaching, and be upon our guard. Once let a man get wrong about justification, and he will bid a long farewell to comfort, to peace, to lively hope, to anything like assurance in his Christianity. An error here is a worm at the root.

In conclusion, let me first of all ask everyone who reads this paper to arm himself with a *thorough knowledge of the written Word of God*. Unless we do this we are at the mercy of any false teacher. We shall not see through the mistakes of an erring Peter. We shall not be able to imitate the faithfulness of a courageous Paul. An ignorant laity will always be the bane of a church. A Bible reading laity may save a church from ruin. Let us read the Bible regularly, daily, and with fervent prayer, and become familiar with its contents. Let us receive nothing, believe nothing, follow nothing, which is not in the Bible, nor can be proved by the Bible. Let our rule of faith – our touchstone of all teaching – be the written Word of God.

In the next place, let me recommend every member of the Church of England to make himself acquainted with the *Thirty-nine Articles of his own Church*. They are to be found at the end of most prayerbooks. They will abundantly repay an attentive reading. They are the true standard by which Churchmanship is to be tried, next to the Bible. They are the test by which Churchmen should prove the teaching of their ministers, if they want to know whether it is "Church teaching" or not. I deeply lament the ignorance of systematic Christianity which prevails among many who attend the services of the Church of England. It would be well if such books as Archbishop Ussher's *Body of Divinity* were more known and studied than they are. If Dean Nowell's *Catechism* had ever been formally accredited as a formulary of the Church of England, many of the heresies of the last twenty years could never have lived for a day.[4] But unhappily many persons really know no more about the true doctrines of their own communion than the heathen or Mahometans. It is useless to expect the laity of the Church of England to be zealous for the maintenance of true doctrine, unless they know what their own Church has defined true doctrine to be.

In the next place, let me entreat all who read this paper to be *always ready to contend for the faith of Christ,* if needful. I recommend no one to foster a controversial spirit. I want no man to be like Goliath, going up and down, saying, "Give me a man to fight with." Always feeding upon controversy is poor work indeed. It is like feeding upon bones. But I do say that no love of false peace should prevent us striving jealously against false doctrine and seeking to promote true doctrine wherever we possibly can. True Gospel in the pulpit, true Gospel in every Religious Society we support, true Gospel in the books we read, true Gospel in the

---

4. Dean Nowell was Prolocutor of the Convocation which drew up the *Thirty-nine Articles* in the form in which we now have them, in the year 1562. His *Catechism* was approved and allowed by Convocation.

friends we keep company with – let this be our aim, and never let us be ashamed to let men see that it is so.

In the next place, let me entreat all who read this paper *to keep a jealous watch over their own hearts* in these controversial times. There is much need of this caution. In the heat of the battle we are apt to forget our own inner man. Victory in argument is not always victory over the world or victory over the devil. Let the meekness of Peter in taking a reproof be as much our example as the boldness of Paul in reproving. Happy is the Christian who can call the person who rebukes him faithfully a "beloved brother" (2 *Peter* 3:15). Let us strive to be holy in all manner of conversation, and not least in our tempers. Let us labor to maintain an uninterrupted communion with the Father and with the Son, and to keep up constant habits of private prayer and Bible-reading. Thus we shall be armed for the battle of life and have the sword of the Spirit well fitted to our hand when the day of temptation comes.

In the last place, let me entreat all members of the Church of England who know what real praying is *to pray daily for the Church to which they belong.* Let us pray that the Holy Spirit may be poured out upon it, and that its candlestick may not be taken away. Let us pray for those parishes in which the Gospel is now not preached, that the darkness may pass away and the true light shine in them. Let us pray for those ministers who now neither know nor preach the truth, that God may take away the veil from their hearts and show them a more excellent way. Nothing is impossible. The Apostle Paul was once a persecuting Pharisee; Luther was once an unenlightened monk; Bishop Latimer was once a bigoted papist; Thomas Scott was once thoroughly opposed to evangelical truth. Nothing, I repeat, is impossible. The Spirit can make clergymen preach that Gospel which they now labor to destroy. Let us therefore be instant in prayer.

I commend the matters contained in this paper to serious attention. Let us ponder them well in our hearts. Let us carry them out in our daily practice. Let us do this, and we shall have learned something from the story of Peter at Antioch.

7

Exclusive Psalmody

W. Gary Crampton[1]

CHAPTER 21 of the *Westminster Confession of Faith*, "Religious Worship and the Sabbath Day," describes how we are to worship God:
"[T]he acceptable way of worshiping the true God is instituted by himself, and so limited by his own revealed will, that he may not be worshiped according to the imaginations and devices of men, or the suggestions of Satan, under any visible representation, or any other way
not prescribed in the Holy Scripture." This rule of worship is called the
regulative principle. It has always been the principle governing public
worship within Reformed churches.

What are the parts of worship, according to the Westminster Assembly, commanded and approved by God? In section 5 of Chapter 21 they
conclude that along with prayer (which is mentioned in sections 3, 4,
and 6):

> The reading of the Scriptures with godly fear, the sound preaching
> and conscionable hearing of the Word, in obedience unto God, with
> understanding, faith, and reverence, singing of psalms with grace in the
> heart; as also, the due administration and worthy receiving of the sacra-
> ments instituted by Christ, are all parts of the ordinary religious wor-
> ship of God: beside religious oaths, vows, solemn fastings, and thanks-
> givings upon special occasions, which are in their several times and sea-
> sons, to be used in an holy and religious manner.

For the purpose of our study, we shall focus on the phrase "singing
of psalms with grace in the heart." Did the Westminster Assembly restrict the church to the exclusive use of *Psalms* in public worship? Are

---

1. Dr. W. Gary Crampton is a free-lance writer living in Virginia. This essay is reprinted from *The Trinity Review*.

those churches which practice the singing of hymns and spiritual songs with melody (or grace) in their hearts (*Ephesians* 5:19; *Colossians* 3:16), whether of the inspired[2] or uninspired (*e. g., Amazing Grace, Holy, Holy, Holy*) varieties, along with the *Psalms*, violating either the *Confession* or the *Scriptures*? That is the question before us.

Exclusive Psalmody

The exclusive Psalmodists reply in the affirmative. For example, G. I. Williamson, after admitting that "It cannot be argued that the exclusive use of the *Psalms*, in worship, was ever entirely universal in the Reformed churches. Some, including Calvin's church in Geneva, sang at least a few other songs," goes on to say: "This is a subject [exclusive Psalmody] that I began to study many years ago, and from my research two things have greatly impressed me: (1) I have never seen any exegetical proof that God wants us to produce our own hymns in order to sing them in worship instead of the inspired *Psalms* He has provided.... (2) In the second place it is simply an historical fact that the great change, in substituting uninspired hymns for the inspired *Psalms*, was not the result of new discoveries in the content of Scripture. It was not a reluctant change compelled by careful exegesis (at least this is true in the several instances of this innovation in the history of the Reformed churches known to the writer). No, the change came, rather, by way of giving in to increasing popular demand; it was a change made to please the people."[3]

2. Some have argued that these verses contain portions of early hymns: 1 *Corinthians* 13:1-8a; *Philippians* 2:6-11; *Colossians* 1:15-18; 1 *Timothy* 3:16; *Hebrews* 1:3; 1 *Peter* 3:18-20; and *Revelation* 4:8, 11; 5:9, 10, 12, 13. For the argument that at least some of the inspired New Testament hymns were composed by the early church and incorporated into formal worship, see Donald Guthrie, *New Testament Theology* (InterVarsity, 1981), 343-365. Exclusive Psalmodists frequently deny that there are any "hymnic fragments" of the early church found within the New Testament, but this is obscurantism. Robert L. Reymond, for instance, in his *Jesus, Divine Messiah: The New Testament Witness* (Presbyterian and Reformed, 1990) confirms that it is the consentient report among New Testament scholars that such hymns did exist in the early church, and that we possess fragments of them in the New Testament. Regarding the *Philippians* 2:6-11 pericope, for example, he writes, "It is safe to say...that on at least one issue all the scholarly literature...agrees: that in *Philippians* 2:6-11 we have (at least a fragment of?) an early Christian hymn.... I repeat, they [the scholars] all agree that the *Philippians* 2:6-11 is of 'hymnic' literary genre" (251, 252).

3. G. I. Williamson, *The Scriptural Regulative Principle of Worship* (Bonclarken Assembly, 1990), 17. The second part of Williamson's argument is virtually irrelevant.

Another exclusive Psalmodist, Raymond P. Joseph, says:

> I hope that the church soon will reawaken to what her Lord gave her in His *Psalms*; to the realization that He gave them to be the very center of her practical theology, so that regular congregational *Psalm* singing would be a weekly (and daily) review and reminder of how great our Lord is in His majesty and glory and holiness of judgment.... We can safely entrust our souls to God's infallible Word, a Word free from the shackles of man's subjective preferences and limited vision. Let us sing man's writings in other places. But let us worship our God with His *Psalms*.[4]

Rowland Ward, speaking with regard to the English Puritans, such as those who wrote the *Westminster Confession of Faith*, says, "all Puritans... favored the metrical use of *Psalms* [in public worship].... In this they had a fair measure of agreement with many Anglicans."[5]

The Reply

How should we reply to such comments as these? First, it should be stated that even if the majority of the Westminster Assembly were exclusive Psalmodists, it does not follow that one is non-confessional if he is not an exclusive Psalmodist. Chapter 21 of the *Confession* does not denounce the use of inspired or uninspired hymns and songs; it merely refers to the "singing of psalms."

Gordon Clark points out that the word "psalm" originally referred to a tune played on a harp. Thus, when the word is used, it need not be considered as only referring to the inspired *Psalms* of Scripture.[6] Stephen Pribble agrees. In his *A Defense of Hymn-Singing in Worship,* he says that Westminster claims that religious worship should include the "singing of psalms," not *"the Psalms."*[7] The term "psalms" is here used by Westminster in the general sense of the word, which, according to the *Oxford English Dictionary,* means "any sacred song...sung in religious

---

Whether or not "the change" came about "to please the people" says nothing with regard to the legitimacy of uninspired hymns. What Williamson believes is historical fact is really historical opinion.

4. *Psalms for Singing,* 1988, 4.

5. *Psalm-Singing in Scripture and History* (Australia: R .S. Ward, 1985), 36.

6. *Ephesians* (The Trinity Foundation, 1986), 181; *What Do Presbyterians Believe?* (Presbyterian and Reformed Publishing Company, 1985), 198.

7. *A Defense of Hymn Singing in Worship* (1990), 9.

worship." Perhaps this is why A. A. Hodge, in commenting on this section of the *Confession*, suggested that we can summarize the statement "singing of psalms," with the phrase "singing of praise."[8]

A Little Church History

There is little question that through centuries of church history exclusive Psalmody has been endorsed by a number of scholars within the Reformed community, but it has not been uniformly so. For example, R. G. Rayburn writes that the most basic form of worship in the early church included, not only the reading and exposition of Holy Scripture, prayer, and the proper administration of the sacraments, but also the use of the *Psalms* for singing, as well as singing both inspired and uninspired hymns.[9]

H. M. Best and D. Huttar aver that the early church did not in any way restrict itself to the singing of the *Psalms*, even though the Christian community was very careful as to how it conducted itself in public worship. Paul's admonition to the Ephesians (5:19) and Colossians (3:16) to sing "psalms, hymns, and spiritual songs" was understood to mean that the church should worship the Triune God by means of both inspired and uninspired songs of praise. These two passages were not intended to restrict the church to "exclusive Psalmody."[10]

Church historian C. Gregg Singer further confirms this. In his "Lectures on Church History," Singer maintains that exclusive Psalmody was never the majority report within Christendom until the time of the Puritans, *i.e.*, the 17th century. In the post-Apostolic church, the Psalter was used in public worship, along with other "hymns and spiritual songs."

The Canons of Laodicea (A.D. 360, canon 59) forbade the singing of uninspired hymns in the worship service, but did not enjoin the exclusive use of *Psalms*. The Council of Chalcedon (A.D. 451) followed suit, as did the Second Council of Braga (*c*. A.D. 563, canon 12). None of these outlawed the singing of inspired hymns and spiritual songs in addition to the *Psalms*.

8. A. A. Hodge, *The Confession of Faith* (The Banner of Truth Trust, 1983), 279.

9. *Evangelical Dictionary of Theology*, Walter A. Elwell, editor (Baker, 1984), 1193.

10. *The Zondervan Pictorial Encyclopedia of the Bible* [ZPEB] (Zondervan, 1975-1976), IV, 316-318. Augustine notes that the church in Milan under Ambrose had instituted "after the manner of the Eastern Church, hymns and psalms...[to be] sung...which custom, retained from then to now, is imitated by many, yea, by almost all of Thy congregations throughout the rest of the world" (*Confessions* 9.7.15).

The Second Council of Tours (A.D 567, canon 23), and the Fourth Council of Toledo (A.D 633) defended the use of non-canonical hymns. The early church had such fourth century hymn writers as Ephraem, Gregory Nazianzen, and Ambrose, who wrote in Syriac, Greek, and Latin, respectively; and the seventh century boasted the hymn writer Caedmon.[11]

Some of the Reformers held to the view that the only proper songs to be used in formal worship are those found within Scripture, but they did not adopt exclusive Psalmody. John Calvin preferred the congregational singing of the *Psalms*, without musical accompaniment, yet he also used a metrical version of the Ten Commandments and the Lord's Prayer in public worship, along with the recitation of the Apostles' Creed.[12]

The Westminster Assembly sponsored a metrical translation of the 150 *Psalms*. The American Puritans also prepared a metrical version of the Psalter to be used in public worship. Leland Ryken agrees with Singer that the majority report among the Puritan theologians was that of exclusive Psalmody. Noteworthy, however, is the fact that the Apostles' Creed was frequently recited in Puritan worship services, an act that many exclusive Psalmodists consider a violation of the regulative principle.[13] Yet Puritan writers such as John Bunyan did compose hymns which may have occasionally been used in public worship.[14]

With the coming of the eighteenth century, the church in general returned to the use of inspired and uninspired hymns along with the Psalter. Hymn writers such as Benjamin Keach, Isaac Watts, John Newton, and William Cowper were instrumental in this movement. Since that time, except for a part of the Scottish church (the Free Church of Scotland), the majority of Reformed churches have followed suit.[15]

11. Rowland Ward, *Psalm-Singing in Scripture and History*, 25, 26.

12. Ward, *Psalm-Singing in Scripture and History*, 27-30; J. W. Keddie, *Why Psalms Only?* (Edinburgh: Burlington, 1978), 10.

13. Leland Ryken, *Worldly Saints* (Zondervan, 1986), 119-124; compare Ward, *Psalm-Singing in Scripture and History*, 35-40.

14. Keddie, *Why Psalms Only?* 10, 11.

15. Exclusive Psalmodists have argued that the return of the church to inspired and uninspired hymnody during the eighteenth century brought about church splits over the issue. Further, they maintain that Watts had to "sell" his hymnody by calling the hymns "imitation *Psalms*." But these are hardly refutations of the use of Biblically based hymnody in public worship. In the first place, Paul tells us that not all church

Jonathan Edwards

Jonathan Edwards is an example of an eighteenth century Puritan who, although he roundly endorsed the use of the Psalter, did not restrict himself to it in public worship. In *Some Thoughts Concerning the Present Revival of Religion in New England,* he wrote:

> I am far from thinking that the book of *Psalms* should be thrown by in our public worship, but that it should always be used in the Christian church until the end of the world: but I know of no obligation we are under to confine ourselves to it. I can find no command or rule of God's Word, that does any more confine us to the words of Scripture in our singing, than it does in our praying; we speak to God in both. And I can see no words that we find in the Bible, in speaking to him by way of praise, in meter, and with music than when we speak to him in prose, by way of prayer and supplication. And it is really needful that we should have some other songs besides the *Psalms* of David. It is unreasonable to suppose that the Christian church should forever and even in times of her greatest light, in her praises of God and the Lamb, be confined only to the words of the Old Testament, wherein all the greatest and most glorious things of the Gospel, that are infinitely the greatest subjects of her praise, are spoken of under a veil, and not so much as the name of our glorious Redeemer ever mentioned, but in some dark figure, or as hid under the name of some type. And as to our making use of the words of others, and not those that are conceived by ourselves, it is no more than we do in all our public prayers; the whole worshiping assembly, excepting one only, makes use of the words that are conceived by him who speaks for the rest.[16]

The Witness of Scripture

The witness of church history, of course, is not our standard for determining such matters. Scripture alone is to be our standard. It is here that the present writer finds no support for the exclusive use of the *Psalms* in public worship.

"splits" or strong differences of opinion are bad. Rather they help to hone the church in matters of doctrine (1 *Corinthians* 11:19). And in the second place, the church, under such stalwarts as Jonathan Edwards, recognized these so-called "imitation *Psalms*" as Biblically proper and a proper means by which to worship the Triune God.

16. Jonathan Edwards, *Works* (Edinburgh: The Banner of Truth Trust, 1984), I, 396.

Leonard Coppes, in his unpublished essay, "Exclusive Psalmody and Progressive Revelation – A Response," argues that the numerous songs that existed in Old Testament Israel prior to the formation of the Psalter militate against exclusive Psalmody. He contends that other songs were obviously used in the Jews' worship of God. For example, in *Exodus* 15 we have the song of Moses (verses 1-18), which is repeated in heavenly worship (compare *Revelation* 15:3), and the song of Miriam (verses 20, 21). In *Judges* 5, we have the song of Deborah (see also *Numbers* 10:35, 36; 21:17, 18).[17] Even the inspired Psalmist (*Psalm* 119:54) speaks of the Mosaic statutes, and not simply the Psalter, as being his songs.[18]

Dr. Coppes maintains that the songs found in the book of *Revelation* (*e.g.*, chapters 4, 5, 7, 11) support the use of more than the 150 *Psalms* in formal worship. After all, we in the New Testament church have, through our Mediator Jesus Christ, already entered into heavenly worship (*Hebrews* 2:12, 13; 9:24; 10:19-22; 12:22).[19] He writes, "the Biblical standard for song in worship is faithfulness to what has been revealed and not inspiration.... Therefore, the regulative principle does not obviate the use of uninspired songs in worship whether private or public."[20] As long as an uninspired hymn is Biblically correct and appropriate for worship, it should be allowed in the public worship of God.

There are several more Biblical obstacles that exclusive Psalmody must overcome. First, it would seem that the various uses of the New Testament word "hymns," such as *Colossians* 1:15-18 and *Philippians* 2:6-11, would give us reason to use such songs in the public worship of God.

Second, in the *Philippians* 2:6-11 hymn, the first century church has properly taken the most sacred name of Jesus and incorporated it into

17. J. Barton Payne is in complete agreement with Coppes (*ZPEB*, IV, 924-947).

18. One exclusive Psalmodist recently stated that many exclusive Psalmodists *might* consider singing some of the inspired Old and New Testament songs, such as are found in *Exodus* 15 and *Luke* 1:46-55, in public worship. I would respectfully remind exclusive Psalmodists that there are 65 other books in the Word of God which are as God-breathed as the book of *Psalms*.

19. The fact that the New Testament church is already involved in heavenly worship, a form of worship that uses musical instruments (*Revelation* 5:8; 15:2, 3), would seemingly permit the use of such instruments in public worship. Gordon Clark notes that since the word "*psalm* originally meant the tune played on a harp, and since even the Covenanters admit that the Old Testament approves of the use of musical instruments, it is hard to accept their view that the New Testament has abolished instrumental worship" (*Ephesians*, 181).

20. Coppes, "Exclusive Psalmody and Progressive Revelation – A Response," 1-2.

a "spiritual song" (verses 9-11). It is a hymn of praise to the Lord Jesus, who as the divine *Kurios,* is the fulfillment of the Yahweh enthronement *Psalms* (93, 97, 99). The church gladly confesses in song that "Jesus Christ is Lord (*Kurios*)." As Jonathan Edwards pointed out, an exclusive Psalmodist can never take the Savior's name upon his lips in public singing, for the name "Jesus" is not found in the Psalter.

Some exclusive Psalmodists maintain that they take the name Jesus upon their lips when they sing the name Jehovah (found some 13 times in the *Scottish Psalter*). But this is fallacious reasoning. To sing the name *Jehovah* is obviously not the same as singing the name *Jesus.* The name *Iesous* (Jesus) is a transliteration of the Hebrew *Yehoshua* (Joshua), which means "Jehovah is salvation." So if one says the name *Jesus,* it is plausible to argue that one means *Jehovah* by implication. But *Jehovah* means neither *Joshua* nor *Jesus.* The Psalmodists' argument is backward. For their argument to even seem plausible, *Jehovah* would have to mean *Jesus* or *Joshua.* It means neither. The name Joshua (*Iesous* in the *Septuagint*) is found nowhere in the Psalter.

Furthermore, exclusive Psalmodists cannot appeal to meanings and implications. When they advocate exclusive Psalmody and object to the use of uninspired hymns, even though they be theologically correct, they have limited themselves to the exact words in the *Psalms.* If meanings were acceptable, they could not object to Biblically sound but uninspired hymns.

Further, Jehovah is not the name of only the Second Person of the Godhead; it is also the name of the Father and of the Holy Spirit. All three Persons are properly worshiped when the name Jehovah is sung. But according to the New Testament, it is the incarnate Son alone who bears the name Jesus. It is he "who saves his people from their sins" (*Matthew* 1:21). It is he whose name we take upon our lips when we sing of our Savior. It is he alone who purchased his people with his blood. The exclusive use of the *Psalms* would prevent us from singing the praise of Jesus Christ in worship.

Third, for their argument to be valid, the exclusive Psalmodists must distinguish between teaching by preaching, singing, and reciting Biblical truth. In *Ephesians* 5:19 we are told to "speak" *(laleo)* to one another, and in *Colossians* 3:16 to "teach" *(didasko)* one another, "by means of psalms, hymns, and spiritual songs." Yet, Paul also instructed Timothy to "teach" *(didasko)* (*1 Timothy* 4:11; 6:2) and to "preach" *(kerusso)* (*2 Timo-*

thy 4:2) to his congregation in public worship. Now is it rational to suppose that it is Biblically proper to preach the truths found in the Apostles' Creed and not be able to sing or recite the same truths because they are nowhere found in the *Psalms*? This is far from likely; indeed, it is nonsensical. The church has every Biblical warrant to formulate scripturally accurate uninspired hymns, songs, creedal statements, and so forth, and incorporate them into the public worship of God as a means of praising him and teaching one another.

Fourth, another question that must be posed to the exclusive Psalmodists is this: "What constitutes a metrical *Psalm*?" How faithful must the *Psalms* sung be to the Scriptures? Some of the metrical *Psalms* are at best rough paraphrases of the Hebrew text. Exclusive Psalmodists would not tolerate such looseness in their Bibles. Singing these *Psalms* is far from singing "inspired Scripture." Does the exclusive Psalmodist violate the regulative principle when he does not sing the *Psalms* in the exact language of the Hebrew?

Fifth, *Ephesians* 5:19 and *Colossians* 3:16 strongly support, not only the use of *Psalms*, but also the use of other Biblically based hymns and songs in public, as well as in private, worship.[21] Exclusive Psalmodists contend that these verses refer exclusively to the Psalter. That is, they correctly note that the Greek translation of the Hebrew Old Testament, the *Septuagint* (*LXX*), uses these three words as titles in its version of the Psalter. The word psalm (*psalmos*) is found 67 times, hymn (*humnos*) occurs 13 times, and song (*ode*) is found 36 times. In the superscription of *Psalm* 76, all three occur. As Gordon Clark points out, however, "these three titles seem to be insertions in the *Septuagint* without Hebrew evidence."[22] But even if Clark's contention were not true, to maintain that because these three terms are used in the Greek version of the Psalter Paul is thereby restricting the church to exclusive Psalmody in public worship is as clear a case of question-begging as one could ask for.

Furthermore, the *Septuagint* also uses these three words in places other than the *Psalms*. The word *ode*, for example, is found in numerous

21. For the argument that these two passages refer to public worship, see Albert Barnes, *Barnes' Notes* on Ephesians 5:19; Jonathan Edwards, *A History of the Work of Redemption* (Yale University Press, 1989), sermon seven; and Gordon Clark, *Colossians*, 121. The reflexive pronoun *heautois* (dative plural) is used here in the reciprocal sense, i.e., as *allelois* ("to one another"), in *Ephesians* 4:32 (William Hendriksen, *N. T. C.: Galatians and Ephesians* (Baker, 1979), on Ephesians 5:19).

22. *Colossians*, 121.

Old Testament passages (*e.g., Exodus* 15:1; *Deuteronomy* 31:19, 21, 22; 32:44; *Judges* 5:12; 2 *Samuel* 22:1; *Habakkuk* 3:1, 19). Isaiah exhorts the saints to sing a new hymn *(humnos)* (42:10). And in the New Testament we read of odes being sung in *Revelation* 5:9; 14:3; and 15:3. Clark is correct when he maintains that this argument from titles "is very flimsy support for exclusive Psalmody."[23]

William Hendriksen, in his *New Testament Commentary: Galatians and Ephesians*, commenting on *Ephesians* 5:19, writes:

> The term *psalms* in all probability has reference, at least mainly, to the Old Testament Psalter; *hymns,* mainly to New Testament songs of praise to God and to Christ...and finally, *spiritual songs,* mainly to sacred lyrics dwelling on themes other than direct praise to God and Christ. There may, however, be some overlapping in the meaning of these three terms as used here by Paul.

Hendricksen finds not even a hint that Paul is speaking solely of the use of the Psalter.

F. F. Bruce, in his *New International Commentary on the New Testament: The Epistles to the Colossians, to Philemon, and to the Ephesians,* says, regarding the Pauline usage of psalms, hymns, and spiritual songs in *Colossians* 3:16:

> It is unlikely that any sharply demarcated division is intended, although the "psalms" might be drawn from the OT Psalter (which has supplied a chief [N.B.: not "the only"– WGC] vehicle for praise from primitive times), the "hymns" might be Christian canticles, some of which are reproduced, in whole or in part, in the NT text, and the "spiritual songs" might be unpremeditated words sung "in the Spirit," voicing holy aspirations.

Further, in a footnote concerning *Colossians* 3:16, Bruce claims that "it is unlikely that the *psalmoi* [psalms] and *humnoi* [hymns] and *odai pnuematikai* [spiritual songs] should be confined to three types of composition specified in the Hebrew titles to the OT Psalter."

Finally, John Calvin, the prince of exegetes, says:

> They [the three words under study] are commonly distinguished in this way – that a psalm is that, in the singing of which some musical instrument besides the tongue is made use of; a hymn is properly a song of praise, whether it be sung simply with the voice or otherwise; while

23. *Ephesians,* 181.

an ode contains not merely praises, but exhortations and other matters. He [Paul] would have the songs of Christians, however, to be spiritual, not made up of frivolities and worthless trifles.[24]

Again, there is no indication that Paul is even alluding to exclusive Psalmody. Calvin's last sentence seems to indicate an acceptance of uninspired songs, so long as they are theologically sound.

Some exclusive Psalmodists argue that the three nouns found in *Ephesians* 5:19 – psalms, hymns, and songs – are in "the same grammatical category," united by the conjunction "and" (*kai*). Thus, say these exegetes, "hymns" and "songs" are to be considered as equal to the "psalms." Therefore, if the psalms are Scripture, so also are the hymns and songs. Similar usages of *kai* can be found in *Matthew* 28:19 and *2 Corinthians* 13:14, where the three persons of the Trinity are spoken of in "the same grammatical category."

This, of course, is one possible interpretation. However, just because *kai* is used in this manner in *Matthew* 28:19 and *2 Corinthians* 13:14 does not mean that this is the Pauline usage in *Ephesians* 5:19. In fact, in *Colossians* 3:16, the only other New Testament verse where Paul uses these three nouns together, the conjunction *kai* is not used at all with regard to psalms, hymns, and songs. Hendriksen, Bruce, and Calvin see no such "categorizing." Furthermore, this argument may equally well lead to the conclusion that Paul does not mean inspired *Psalms*. That interpretation also would keep the terms equal.

Some of the same exegetes claim that the adjective "spiritual" (*pneumatikais*), as used in *Ephesians* 5:19, modifies all three of the nouns. The verse would then read, "in psalms and hymns and songs spiritual." Not only, they say, are the *Psalms* "Spirit-breathed," so also are the hymns and songs; they are all equally Scripture. (Actually, since *pneumatikais* is feminine, it modifies *odai*, which is also feminine; *psalmois* and *hymnois* are both masculine.) If one follows this theory of the exclusive Psalmodists, the syntax of the verse would require the psalms and hymns to be specific kinds of "spiritual odes." This is highly unlikely. New Testament scholars such as Hendriksen, Bruce, Calvin, and Lenski maintain (with the translators of the *King James*, the *New King James*, the *New American Standard*, the *New International Version*, and the *Revised Standard Version*) that the most natural reading of the verse is that "spiri-

24. John Calvin, *Commentary on Colossians* (Baker, 1981), 3:16.

160

tual" modifies only the noun *songs* (*odais*). The burden of proof here is on those adopting exclusive Psalmody; they must conclusively show that in Paul's use of these three terms he limits the church to the use of the Psalter in formal worship. If this cannot be accomplished, then *Ephesians* 5:19 and *Colossians* 3:16 stand as refutations of exclusive Psalmody. I suggest that their exegetical burden is too great to bear. The evidence, at best, is "flimsy."

The present writer is very much in favor of the singing of the metrical *Psalms* in public (as well as private) worship. The church needs to return to this practice, as a part of the regulative principle. It is a rich privilege, yielding spiritual blessings, to be able to sing the inspired songs of Zion as found in the Psalter. If we wish to learn how to sing – and how to pray – well, we need to study the *Psalms*. Gordon Clark is correct when he says that "a hymn book without a good proportion of *Psalms* is not fit for a church service."[25] Yet, there seems to be no Biblical warrant for us to eliminate altogether the use of other hymns and songs, so long as they are theologically sound. The witness of church history is far from convincing us of exclusive Psalmody, and the Biblical evidence overwhelmingly supports the use of "hymns and spiritual songs," both inspired and otherwise, along with the singing of *Psalms*.

25. *Colossians*, 121.

8

Scripture and the Ordering of Worship

The Geneva Service Book of 1556[1]

ECAUSE there is no way more ready or sure to come to him than by framing ourselves altogether to his blessed will, revealed unto us in his Word; we, to whom though God hath given more liberty, yet no less lamenting your bondage than rejoicing in our own deliverance from that Babylonian slavery and Antichristian yoke, have earnestly endeavored, amongst other things which might bring us to the worthy consideration of God's Word, to frame our lives, and reform our state of religion in such sort, that neither doubt of the certainty thereof should make us fear, nor yet man's judgment discourage us, and cause us to shrink from this enterprise most acceptable to God, comfortable to his church, and necessarily appertaining to every Christian man's duty.

1. The Vestment Controversy of 1550 had not settled differences among the English Protestant leaders. Disagreement over the second *Book of Common Prayer*, which was completed in 1552, quickly surfaced. One of King Edward's chaplains, John Knox, now became the chief spokesman of those who could not agree to the official claim that the latest revision (the first Edwardian *Prayer Book* had appeared in 1549) had made the book "fully perfect." Knox's influence secured a few alterations before the *Prayer Book* was enforced by law, but only eight months were to pass before this settlement was overthrown by the death of Edward on July 6, 1553.

In the persecution which ensued after the accession of Mary, later known as Bloody Mary, the Protestant leaders who remained in England bore witness to their common faith in the Gospel by their martyrdoms, while others who escaped to the Continent formed congregations of English refugees. One of the first of these congregations gathered in Frankfort in 1554, and as its prevailing outlook was in sympathy with that of Knox, whom they called to be one of their ministers, the full use of the 1552 *Prayer Book* was discontinued and in place of the English liturgy a new order of service was drawn up by Knox, Whittingham, Gilby, Foxe, and Cole. This was not, however, brought into immediate use due to the lack of full agreement in the congregation, and when a new party of refugees arrived in March 1555 who were representatives of the "official" reformation policy of Cranmer and Ridley, harmony became impossible and it was necessary for Knox and those who shared in a concern for further reformation to

We, therefore, not as the greatest clerks of all, but as the least able of many, do present unto you which desire the increase of God's glory, and the pure simplicity of his Word, a form and order of a reformed church, limited within the compass of God's Word, which our Saviour hath left unto us as only sufficient to govern all our actions by; so that whatsoever is added to this Word by man's device, seem it never so good, holy, or beautiful, yet before our God, which is jealous and cannot admit any companion or counselor, it is evil, wicked, and abominable. For he that is the wisdom of the Father, the brightness of his glory, the true light, the word of life, yea truth and life itself, can he give unto his church (for the which he paid the ransom of his blood) that which should not be a sufficient assurance for the same? Can the Word of Truth deceive us? The Way of Life misguide us? The Word of salvation damn us? God keep us from such blasphemies, and so direct our hearts with his Holy Spirit, that we may not only content ourselves with his wisdom, but so rejoice in the same, that we may abhor all things which are contrary.

The which considerations, dear brethren, when we weighed with reverent fear and humbleness; and also knowing, that negligence in reforming that religion which was begun in England, was not the least cause of God's rods laid upon us, having now obtained by the merciful providence of our heavenly Father a free church for all our nation in this most worthy city of Geneva, we presented to the judgment of the fa-

---

withdraw to Geneva where a new English congregation was formed in November 1555. This became the strongest and most influential English congregation in the exile period and it has often been spoken of as the cradle of English Puritanism.

The order of service drawn up in Frankfort was now brought into use and it was published early in 1556 under the title: *The Form of Prayers and Ministration of the Sacraments, etc., used in the English Congregation at Geneva*. The Preface to this *Book of Geneva*, as it became known, gives the first statement by an English church that the regulative principle of Scripture is foundational to the church's government and worship. It was probably written by William Whittingham, who was to become one of the leaders of Elizabethan Puritanism, and a man who was more than once in trouble with the ecclesiastical authorities before his death at Durham in 1579. The *Geneva Book* became the Service Book of the Church of Scotland, was secretly used by English Puritans, and was being reprinted as late as 1644. This extract is taken from the Preface. This essay is taken from *The Reformation of the Church*, edited by Iain H. Murray, and published by The Banner of Truth Trust, 1965.

The section on the *Interpretation of the Scriptures* appears later in the book, in a portion of the order describing the meetings of the church. The text is based upon its published form in *The Works of John Knox*, edited by David Laing (Edinburgh, 1895), volume 4; spelling and punctuation have been modernized.

mous man John Calvin, and others learned in these parts, the order which we minded to use in our church: who approving it, as sufficient for a Christian congregation, we put the same in execution, nothing doubting but all godly men shall be much edified thereby. And as for the Papists, or malicious men and ungodly, we have not labored to satisfy them, because we knew no sovereign medicine for their cankered sore, except it may please God, by our prayers, to be merciful to them, and call them home, if they be not already forsaken.

But yet, for as much as there are some, which through continuance in their evil, rather delighting in custom than knowledge, cannot suffer that men should once open their mouths against certain old and received ceremonies, we thought good in this place somewhat to touch that scrupulosity. For as ceremonies grounded upon God's Word, and approved in the New Testament, are commendable (as the circumstance thereof does support), so those that man has invented, though he had never so good occasion thereunto, if they be once abused, import a necessity, hinder God's Word, or be drawn into a superstition, without respect ought to be abolished.

For if Hezekiah was commended by the Holy Ghost for breaking in pieces the brazen serpent, which Moses had erected by God's commandment, and now had continued above 800 years, which thing of itself was not evil, but rather put men in remembrance of God's benefit; yet because it began to minister occasion to the people to commit idolatry, was not to be borne withal: How much more ought we to take heed, that through our occasion men commit not idolatry with their own imaginations and fantasies? It was not without great cause, commanded by Almighty God, that the places, and other appurtenances, which had served to idolatry should be utterly consumed, lest babes and children, through occasion remembering the same, should fall into like inconvenience. And think you that we ought to be wiser? and not rather take heed, that those things which the Papists and other idolaters have invented, or else observe as invented by man, may not enter into Christ's church, as well to the end that the weak may not be confirmed in their error, as that we may altogether separate ourselves from that idolatrous Babylon and temple of Belial, wherewith Christ hath no concord nor agreement?

There was no one ceremony more ancient, nor yet of better authority, than the washing of the disciples' feet, which was observed a long time in the church, and instituted by Christ himself, yet when some were persuaded that it was a portion of the Lord's Supper, and others thought it served instead of Baptism, the godly churches in Augustine's time thought it better to leave that which was ordained for a good use, than by retaining the same, confirm an error or superstition. The Corinthians, for the relief of the poor, and to increase brotherly amity together, did institute a feast, immediately after the Lord's Supper. But how sharply Paul did reprehend the same, condemning in comparison, that men should add anything to the Lord's institution, it appears by what he says, "I have received of the Lord that which I gave you."

We read also, that Hezekiah and his nephew Josiah restored the use of the Passover, which had been a very long time discontinued; but in the ministration thereof, they observed no other ceremonies than God had left to Moses from the beginning. Circumcision, likewise a sacrament, was evermore after one sort ministered, even as the Lord commanded it. But such is the nature of flesh, it will be wise, and have a stroke in God's doings; yea, and how willfully it causes man to maintain his own fantasies, it is manifest to them which have perused the ancient records of the church. For beginning at Jerusalem, and so coming to the rest of the churches, as Constantinople, Antioch, Alexandria, and Rome, he shall see plainly that their greatest disturbance and overthrow chanced through ceremonies. What conflict was at all times betwixt the Latin and Greek churches for the same, no Christian can consider without tears. And was there anything more objected against Paul, both of the Galatians and also of others, than that he would not observe the ceremonies as the chief apostles did? And yet he kept them whilst any hope was to gain the weak brethren, and therefore circumcised Timothy; but when he perceived that men would retain them as necessary things in the church, he called that which before he made indifferent, wicked and impious, saying that whosoever was circumcised, Christ could nothing profit them. Fearing also, lest he had taken pains among them in vain, which joined Christ with beggarly ceremonies. Therefore, dear brethren, being hereby persuaded, and with many more reasons confirmed (which opportunity permits not here to write), we have contented ourselves with that wisdom which we have learned in God's Book, where we be taught to preach the Word of God purely, minister the Sacraments sincerely, and use prayers and other orders thereby approved, to the increase of God's glory, and edification of His holy people.

Interpretation of the Scriptures

Once every week, the congregation assembles to hear some place of the Scriptures orderly expounded.[2] At which time, it is lawful for every man to speak or enquire, as God shall move his heart, and the text minister occasion; so it be without pertinacity or disdain, as one that rather seeks to profit than to contend. And if [it] so be any contention arise, then such as are appointed moderators, either satisfy the party, or else if he seems to evil, exhort him to keep silence, referring the judgment thereof to the ministers and elders, to be determined in their assembly or consistory before mentioned.

2. *1 Corinthians* 14:1ff.; *1 Thessalonians* 5:20; *Ephesians* 4:29; *1 Corinthians* 12:28-31.

9

The Christian Education of the Children and Youth in the Presbyterian Church[1]

Samuel Miller

THE LONGER and more seriously the committee has deliberated on the adoption of measures "for securing to the children and young people of our church more full advantages of Christian education than they have hitherto enjoyed,"[2] the deeper has become their impression, at once, of its transcendent importance, and of the exceedingly great difficulty – in the present state of our country and of the church – of doing it justice, even in theory, and much more of proposing such plans as will admit of general and convenient execution.

There can be no doubt that one great end for which the church was established by her infinitely wise and gracious Head was that she might train up a godly seed, enlightened in the truth, and imbued with the sentiments and habits adapted to the maintenance and spread of our holy religion in all its purity and power.

1. *The Christian Education of the Children and Youth in the Presbyterian Church* was published as a small book in 1840, by direction of the General Assembly, bearing the imprint of the Presbyterian Board of Publication. The text has been edited to reflect greater conformity to contemporary spelling, punctuation, and grammar. Copyright 1984, 1997 by Kevin Reed.

2. The committee's charge reads as follows: "Resolved, that the Rev. Samuel Miller, Archibald Alexander, Charles Hodge, J. Addison Alexander, and James Carnahan, be a committee to inquire whether any, and, if any, what measures ought to be adopted for securing to the children and young people of our church more full advantages of Christian education than they have hitherto enjoyed" (Minutes of the 1839 General Assembly in the "Advertisement" of the published edition of the committee's report). Although this report reflects the consensus of the committee, it bears Miller's name as the author.

This great principle is not merely left to be inferred from the general nature and character of the church, but is essentially included in the ordinances appointed by her Divine Head, and in the direct and solemn commands with which her statute-book abounds. Hence, in the ancient church, her children, while yet infants, were recognized and sealed as members; were carried up at an early age to the great feasts at Jerusalem; and that they might be taught to take an interest in all that pertained to the people of God, the command of Jehovah was, "These words, which I command you this day, shall be in your heart: and you shall teach them diligently unto your children, and shall talk of them when you sit in your house, and when you walk by the way, and when you lie down, and when you rise up" [*Deuteronomy* 6:6-7]. Nay more, it was not only enjoined on parents under that economy to teach their children all the commands of God (and continually to inculcate obedience to them), but also to make them familiar with the history of the church – continually reminding them of all Jehovah's dealing with his covenant people, his heavy judgments, and the various ways by which he led them on and accomplished his purposes toward them.

When the New Testament economy was introduced, the same great principles of duty toward the children of the church were not only retained, but with the increasing light and spirituality of the new dispensation were extended in their application, and urged with new force. Still, while in their infancy, the church (by a solemn rite) was commanded to recognize her children as the members of her body, to regard herself as their moral parent, and to make their early instruction and discipline an object of unceasing care and labor. Some of the examples of this care, and of the happy results of it, recorded in the early history of the church, are at once memorable and instructive.

The pious "witnesses for the truth" in the dark ages were, perhaps, more remarkable for nothing than for their faithfulness in the instruction and discipline of their children. In particular, the devoted and exemplary Waldenses were probably indebted, under God, to their peculiar diligence in the discharge of this duty for their remarkable success in keeping their body together, in transmitting their testimony from generation to generation, and in remaining so long as they did a beacon for the admiration and guidance of the church in after times. Historians tell us that these pious people were in the habit of employing every hour that they could rescue from labor and sleep in gaining religious knowledge themselves, and in imparting it to the children and young people of their community; that they were careful to prepare excellent catechisms and other formularies for their youth; and that their pastors made the religious instruction of youth a leading and unceasing object of their labors.

In imitation of their example, the most pure and enlightened of the Reformed churches have ever directed their attention to the education of their children as an object of primary importance in promoting the great interests of religion. Among these churches, that of Scotland is (on several accounts) most instructive and most interesting to us, as bearing to us, more than any other, the relation of parent. This church, from the earliest period of her establishment, has made careful provision for the early instruction and discipline of her children. By different acts of her General Assembly, from time to time, she has declared their education to be under the supervision and government of her judicatories, and directed the course of their studies accordingly. The General Assembly, soon after its first formation in 1560 (and at different times afterwards), directed the several presbyteries to settle a church school in every parish, and to see that the teacher employed in each was a pious, orthodox, well-qualified man – adapted to instruct youth in the Scriptures, in the catechism, and in all the most important things, as well as in the elements of literature. By an act of the General Assembly of 1642, a grammar school was erected in every presbytery. The Assembly of 1700 enjoined on all presbyteries to "take special, particular, and exact notice" of all schoolmasters, governors, and instructors of youth within their respective bounds, and oblige them to subscribe the *Confession of Faith*; and, in case of continued negligence (after admonition), error, or immorality – or not being careful to educate those committed to their charge in the Protestant Reformed religion – pointed out the mode in which they were to be punished. By the Assembly of 1706, it was enjoined that presbyteries visit the grammar schools within their respective bounds twice a year, by some of their number. And, finally, in 1738, the General Assembly revived and ratified the acts of preceding Assemblies, by which visitations of colleges were directed to be kept up by committees of the Assembly; and the principal regents, professors, masters, and doctors within the same were required to be tried concerning their piety, their soundness in the faith, their ability to discharge the duties of their calling, and the honesty of their conversation.

Several other Reformed churches might be cited, as furnishing eminent and instructive examples of fidelity in discharging the great duty which it is the object of this report to recommend. The church of Holland will alone be noticed at present. By the synodical assemblies of that church it is directed that the consistories in every congregation shall provide good schoolmasters, who shall be able not only to instruct children in reading, writing, grammar and the liberal sciences, but also to teach them the catechism, and the first principles of religion.

Every schoolmaster was to be obliged to subscribe the *Confession of Faith* of the Belgic churches, or the *Heidelberg Catechism*. With regard to instructing children in the catechism, a threefold attention to it is solemnly enjoined in that church, *viz.*, first, *domestic*, by *parents;* second, *scholastic*, by *schoolmasters;* and third, *ecclesiastic*, by *pastors*, assisted by other members of their consistories; and all whose duty it is to inspect schools are "admonished to make this an object of their very first care." It is further provided that no person shall be appointed to the charge of any school who is not a member in full communion with the Reformed Belgic church, and who shall not previously have subscribed the *Confession of Faith* and *Catechism* of the church, and solemnly promised to instruct the children committed to his care in the principles contained in the standards of the church. More than this, it is enjoined that every schoolmaster shall employ two half days in every week, not only in hearing the children repeat, but in assisting them to understand the catechism. And to ensure fidelity in these teachers, it is made the duty of the pastors and elders of each church frequently to visit the schools; to encourage and direct the teachers in the proper method of catechizing; to examine the children "with mild severity"; and to excite them to industry and piety by holy exhortations, by seasonable commendations, and by little appropriate rewards.

Nor is this zealous and persevering labor in the religious training of youth confined to Protestant churches. It is well known that among some of the Roman Catholic congregations of Europe, the children are imbued with a knowledge of their erroneous system with an indefatigable diligence and patience which may well put to shame the professors of a more scriptural creed. The consequence is that so large a number of that denomination of professing Christians have an attachment to their sect, and an expertness in defending their superstitious peculiarities, rarely found among the mass of Protestants.

When your committee contrast these facts with the state of things now existing – and which has for a long time existed and been manifestly growing – in the Presbyterian Church (in regard to the religious training of her children), they experience a degree of mortification which it is not easy to express. For a number of years, indeed, after the planting of our church in this country, that portion of our members which had migrated from Scotland, or the north of Ireland, and their immediate successors, retained much of their European habit in regard to this matter. Their children were, to a considerable extent, trained as was customary in the land of their fathers, and made perfectly familiar with the catechisms of the church, and the elementary principles of religion. But even this remnant of European fidelity has, in a great measure, disappeared. The catechisms of our church have nothing like the currency, even among this class of our young people, that they had fifty years ago. From many parts of the church in which they were then habitually taught, they are now, in a great measure, banished. The religious instruction of our youth, instead of becoming more ample and faithful (as the facilities for its accomplishment have multiplied), has undoubtedly declined, both as to extent and fidelity. The children of church members are, in a multitude of cases, totally neglected and left to ignorance and heathenism. In other instances, they are committed to the tuition of the intemperate, the profane, and the profligate. Not infrequently they are sent to institutions taught by Papists, or other errorists, who are known to make every effort to instill their erroneous opinions into the minds of the youth committed to their care. It may be doubted whether there is a body of people at this time on Earth so orthodox in their creed, and at the same time so deplorably delinquent in the religious education of their children as the Presbyterian Church in the United States.

In this state of things, no wonder that so many of the children of our beloved church grow up in ignorance, and regardless of the religion of their fathers; some becoming profane and impious; others turning aside to various forms of fatal error; and a large majority feeling little attachment to the good old way, in which they ought to have been faithfully and prayerfully trained. And it is painful to recollect that, amidst this unhappy delinquency, the judicatories of our church have in a great measure slumbered over the evil, and have taken no systematic or efficient order for the removal of it.

The mischiefs flowing from this neglect of early religious instruction are numberless and deplorable.

The first and most serious of these mischiefs is *its tendency to destroy the souls of children.*

On the one hand, when the early youth of children is passed without proper instruction in divine things, it is difficult to measure or conceive the thick darkness which generally covers their minds, and appears to defy all ordinary endeavors to impart to them the knowledge of evangelical truth. When men grow old in ignorance as well as in sin, they are surrounded with a double barrier against the entrance of heavenly light. It becomes almost necessary to teach them a new language before the instructor, in such cases, can be understood. Accordingly, the probability of such persons being ever brought to a saving acquaintance with the Gospel is greatly diminished, and, in many cases, rendered in a great measure hopeless. On the other hand, when the seeds of truth and duty are early and faithfully sown in the minds of youth, though they may long lie buried, there is strong ground of hope that they will eventually spring up and bring forth a rich harvest. Who can estimate, then, the cruelty, the awful guilt, of those (whether parents or pastors) who neglect that which is so closely connected not only with the present happiness, but with the everlasting welfare of every youth committed to their care?

Closely allied with that which was last stated is another evil resulting from the neglect of a religious education of the children of the church: and that is the frequency with which our young people may be expected, in such case, to depart from the church of their fathers and either stray into communions of the most corrupt character, or become totally regardless of religion in any form. The fact is, even if the preaching of a pastor is ever so sound and able, yet if he neglects the appropriate training of the young people of his charge, and leaves them to the small gleanings of instruction which they will be likely to catch by the ear from the pulpit, they may be expected to grow up little better than heathen in fact, though Christian in name. The consequence must inevitably be the decay and final ruin of those flocks which have not some other means by which to supply the places of their dying members, than the seed of the church.

Further, the pastor who neglects the religious training of the young people of his charge will find them altogether unprepared to profit by his public ministry. If a pastor desires to render his discourses from the pulpit as profitable as possible to the youth of his flock, he cannot take a more direct course for the attainment of his object than to attend to them with parental diligence and affection; to become personally acquainted with them; to meet them frequently in private as a body; to catechize them; to render them familiar with his person, his modes of thinking and speaking, and to imbue their minds with those elementary principles of divine knowledge which will prepare them to hear him in the pulpit with intelligence, with respect, and with profit. If a preacher wished for the most favorable opportunity conceivable for preparing the youth of his charge to listen to his sermons to the greatest advantage, it would not be easy to devise one more admirably suited to his purpose than to meet them, by themselves, once a week, in a paternal and affectionate manner; to teach them the elementary principles of that system which his discourses from the pulpit are intended to explain and inculcate; thus to accustom them to his topics, his phraseology, his manner, his whole course of instruction, and prepare them to receive the richest benefit from his public discourses. There can be no doubt that one great reason why many young people receive so little profit from the pulpit discourses of their minister is that he has taken so little pains to open their minds by previous instruction, to prepare the soil for the seed, to prepossess them in favor of the substance and mode of his teaching. That minister who desires that his preaching may make the deepest and most favorable impression on the minds of the children and young people of his charge is an infatuated man – regardless of all the dictates of reason, experience, and the Word of God – if he does not employ himself diligently in laboring to pave the way for their reception of his more formal and public instruction. Young people thus prepared to attend on his preaching will, of course, understand it better; receive it more readily and respectfully; and be more likely, by the grace of God, to lay it up in their hearts, and practice it in their lives.

Again, the pastor who neglects the religious instruction of the children of his flock neglects one of the most direct and powerful means of winning the parents themselves to the knowledge and love of the Gospel. It cannot have escaped the notice of any attentive observer of human affairs that there is no avenue to the hearts of parents more direct and certain than diligent and affectionate attention to their children. On the one hand, it would seem as if they could often bear to be themselves neglected, if their beloved children are followed with manifestations of interest and good will. And, on the other hand, if they see their children overlooked and neglected, scarcely anything in their view can atone for this negligence. Instances of the most striking character have occurred, in which parents appeared to receive the strongest impressions in favor of particular ministers, and in favor of the cause in which they were engaged, chiefly because those ministers had given their children affectionate paternal counsel and instruction, and appeared to manifest a peculiar interest in their temporal and eternal welfare. Nor is this all. It is undoubtedly a fact that, in some cases, one of the best methods of addressing parents on the great subject of religion is through the medium of their children. The catechizing, instructing, and exhorting of children in the presence of their parents has frequently proved the means of the conversion of those parents. And it has often happened that the manifest improvement, and especially the hopeful conversion of children in catechetical and Bible classes, has been signally blessed to the spiritual benefit of their parents, and indeed, of the whole families to which they belonged. What must be thought, then, of the indolence or blindness of that pastor who can willingly forego all these blessings, and incur all the opposite evils, by habitually neglecting the children of the flock committed to his care?

It follows, of course, that the pastor who does not diligently attend to the religious instruction of the young people of his charge is blind to the comfort, the acceptance, and the popularity of his own ministry. Why is it that so many ministers, before reaching an infirm old age, grow out of date with their people, and lose their influence with them? Especially, why is it that the younger part of their flocks feels so little attraction to them, dislikes their preaching, and sighs for a change of pastors? There is reason to believe that this has seldom occurred, except in cases in which pastors have been eminently negligent of the religious training of their young people; in which, however respectable they may have been for their talents, their learning, and their worth, in other respects they have utterly failed to bind the affections of the children to their persons; to make every one of them revere and love them as affectionate fathers; and, by faithful attentions, to inspire them with the strongest sentiments of veneration and filial attachment. Those whose range of observation has been considerable, have, no doubt, seen examples of ministers whose preaching was by no means very striking or attractive, yet retaining to the latest period of their lives the affections of all committed to their care, and especially being the favorites of the young people, who have rallied round them in their old age, and contributed not a little to render their last days both useful and happy. It may be doubted whether such a case ever occurred excepting where the pastor had bestowed much attention on the young people of his charge.[3]

Such are some of the evils which flow from neglect on the part of the church to train up her children in the knowledge of her doctrines and order. She may expect to see a majority of those children – even children of professors of religion growing up in ignorance and profligacy; of course forsaking the church of their fathers; leaving her either to sink, or to be filled up by converts from without; turning away from those pastors who neglected them; and causing such pastors to experience, in their old age, the merited reward of unfaithful servants.

The truth is, if there is any one part of the pastor's duty which, more than almost any other, deserves to be considered as vital and fundamental, it is that which bears immediately on the seed of the church – the nursery of Christ's family: that branch of his labor which has for its object the extending and perpetuating of the church by raising up a godly seed to take the place of their parents when they shall be laid in the dust.

In this view of the subject, shall nothing be done by the supreme judicatory of our church to rouse the attention, and direct the efforts, of our churches to this most important, but long neglected concern? That something ought to be done is manifest. It is surely high time to awake out of sleep, and inquire what we can do, and ought to do, as a Christian denomination.

The committee is not unmindful of the difficulties which beset this great subject; and which will render a prompt and thorough return to

---

3. It is important that the church educate the children, but such education is not the function of the pastor alone. Presbyterianism teaches the plurality of elders in each local congregation, not a one-priest-one-parish structure, and the office of deacon as well. To assume, as Miller seems to do, that all teaching in the church is to be done by the "pastor" or "minister" or "teaching elder" is not only unrealistic, but also unbiblical. Note his last paragraph, page 183, where he realizes that the burden will be overwhelming, yet imposes it anyway. This position seems to stem from his implicit three-office view of church government – minister, elder, deacon – an errant view among Presbyterians. – *Editor.*

our duty in regard to it an arduous, if not an almost impracticable task, filled with difficulties arising from our long continued habits of delinquency; from the scattered state of the population in many parts of our church; from the sentiments in favor of a spurious liberality, which prevails so peculiarly and extensively among many denominations of Christians in the United States, and among none more than Presbyterians; and from the constant and indefatigable labor required for a faithful discharge of the duty recommended. But great as these difficulties are, they may be surmounted by faith, patience, labor, and prayer. And it is evident that even if the difficulties attending the faithful discharge of the duty in question were far more numerous and formidable than they are, the rewards would, more than an hundred fold, counterbalance all the care and toil bestowed on the object. At any rate, if our delinquency is ever to be repaired, and any real improvement in this great field of Christian effort attained, the sooner we begin, the better. The souls of our children are precious; the exigencies of the church are pressing; and every hour we lose in commencing the work of reform is a loss to all the best interests of the church, and the world – a loss stretching into eternity.

After these preliminary remarks, the committee would beg leave to present a sketch of what they think may and ought to be attempted in reference to this important subject. They are aware that what they are about to propose has nothing of novelty in it, but, if adopted, would be only returning, in substance, to the forgotten and neglected usages of our venerated fathers, both in Europe and in our own country. And although they are sensible that some of their suggestions may not equally apply (and may not be capable of being carried into execution with equal convenience), in all the churches of our denomination, yet they would fain hope that a plan be suggested which, if carried into effect, may be productive of some benefit to the rising generation. They would, therefore, most respectfully propose to the Assembly the adoption of the following recommendations, to be sent down to all the subordinate judicatories and churches under our care.

I. It is recommended that the subject of the Christian education of children be frequently brought before the people in the instructions and devotional exercises of the pulpit, in a manner so pointed and solemn, as may be adapted to inform the minds, and impress the consciences of parents and church officers, in regard to a matter so little understood, and so little laid to heart even by many who profess to be truly pious.

II. It is recommended that when pastors visit families, whether the visitation be performed formally or otherwise, all the children of every family be attended to with particular care; that their names be taken down, that every important circumstance concerning each be recorded, that each be affectionately noticed and addressed, that God's claim to them be presented and urged, and that every practicable method be adopted to render such interviews interesting and instructive. For this purpose, there may be a little tract given to one, an appropriate striking anecdote related to another, and some expression of interest and regard suited to win the confidence of a third, and so of the whole youthful circle. This would require no expense – nothing, at least, but thought and prayer, as tracts (and other little publications suitable to be thus employed) may be had if not gratuitously, at least on very easy terms, and to almost any extent.

III. It is recommended, that every congregation shall establish one or more *church schools,* adapted to the instruction of children between six and ten years of age. These primary schools had better, usually, be taught by females, decidedly pious, intelligent, and of known attachment to the doctrines and order of our church. These teachers ought to be selected by the church Session, and governed by rules formed by that body. Females would be preferable as teachers in such schools because they may, for the most part, be had on more economical terms than teachers of the other sex; and because, if of a suitable character, they will apt to train up their pupils with more soft and gentle manners. As children of this tender age cannot travel far to school, there ought to be several of this class of schools in every congregation of any size, as not more than twenty-five, or, at most, thirty scholars of this age ought ever to be placed under one teacher. In these schools the Bible ought to be used every day, and the *Shorter Catechism* of the church recited at least once every week; and the pastor and elders ought frequently to visit them and see that the teachers are faithful, that all the methods of instruction employed are of the best kind, and that the manners and habits of the children are such as become those who are training up for usefulness here and for the family of Christ hereafter. In these lower schools it may be proper that the females are sometimes employed, at the discretion of the teachers, in sewing, and in other occupations adapted to their sex. The exercises, every day, should be opened and closed with prayer.

IV. It is recommended that, in populous towns, *infant schools* be established as far as circumstances will admit. These, of course, should be placed under the direction of pious, enlightened females; and it is important that all the religious exercises which take place in them be in conformity with the usages of our own church, and that nothing be admitted which will have a tendency to introduce forms which distinguish other denominations. In these infant schools, the simpler portions of the Holy Scriptures, the *Catechism for Young Children* (furnished by the Assembly's Board for Publication), and such oral instruction as may be adapted to the weakest capacities, ought to be constantly employed.

V. It is recommended that there be established in every presbytery at least one grammar school or academy, and in the larger and more opulent presbyteries more than one, adapted for training youth in the more advanced branches of knowledge, and preparing such of them as may desire it for an introduction into college. These academies ought to be under the immediate instruction of ripe and accomplished scholars – men in full communion with the Presbyterian church, of pious and exemplary deportment, and of known attachment to the faith and order of our church. These institutions ought to be under the supervision of the respective presbyteries in which they are placed, and a committee of ministers and elders appointed by each presbytery to visit them, and to watch over the whole course of instruction and discipline in them. It is by no means, indeed, intended to advise that no pupils be received into such academies but such as are connected with the Presbyterian church; but it is intended to be earnestly recommended that all the religious exercises in the same be strictly Presbyterian in their character, and that no youth be allowed to enter them (or to continue a day in them) who is not perfectly correct and unexceptionable in his moral character, and disposed to treat the ordinances of religion with entire respect. In these academies it is recommended that the *Larger Catechism* of our church be made a *class book;* and if not wholly committed to memory, at least made the subject of recitation and commentary, and accompanied with such other reading and oral instruction as may be adapted to make the pupils familiar with the faith and order of the Presbyterian Church, and with the considerations which explain and vindicate the same.

VI. It is recommended that when many of our youth are destined to enjoy the privileges of a college or university, there be the utmost care exercised in selecting for them those institutions in which their moral and religious training will receive the most faithful attention – institutions in which, as far as they can be found, the professors are orthodox and pious, and in which the whole weight of their instruction and influence will be thrown into the scale of pure and undefiled religion, as well as sound learning. No child of the church ought ever to be sent to any seminary of learning, however high its literary character, in which sound religious instruction is not made a constant and governing object of attention. That person who selects for his son a college in which his moral and religious interests will run the risk of being sacrificed, or even jeopardized, for the sake of indulging some petty taste or prejudice, is chargeable with an unfaithfulness and cruelty of the most inexcusable kind. In several parts of our church, academies and colleges have been founded by presbyteries and synods, and placed entirely under the direction of the judicatories which founded them. This, where it can be done, is a wise plan, and adapted more effectually to secure to our youth the advantages of thorough and unshackled religious training than is possible upon any other plan.

VII. It is recommended that all parents and heads of families be in the constant habit of assembling the children and youth of their families in the evening of every Lord's Day, and spending at least an hour in attending to the recitation of the catechism, and such other modes of oral instruction in divine things as the capacity and character of each may require. Let the head of the family, whether male or female (as the case may be), take this opportunity of speaking seriously to each of the young persons present, and administering an affectionate but solemn rebuke for any disorderly conduct on that day (or the preceding week), closing with exhortation and a comprehensive prayer. And that this domestic service may not interfere with attendance on public services which, in some churches, are statedly held on that evening; in such churches, let the hour devoted to this family interview be the one immediately preceding the evening meal. In all cases in which the catechism is recited, let one or two proof texts be carefully quoted and committed to memory for the support of each answer; and let the children be always reminded that the Bible is the only infallible rule of faith and practice, and that the catechism owes all its authority and value to the fact that it contains the system of doctrine taught in the Holy Scriptures.

VIII. It is recommended that pastors and church Sessions be diligently attentive to the catechizing and religious instruction of all the children and young people under their care, through the whole course of their childhood and youth. No recitation of the catechism in any other school or place ought to supersede this. However constantly and faithfully it may be attended to by the parents, or by Sabbath school teachers, still the pastor and the elders ought to deem it a privilege (as well as a duty) to convene the children of the church, and to endeavor to establish that acquaintance with them, and that influence over them, which will be likely to result in rich advantages to both. Even if a wise and faithful pastor were certain that the religious instruction of the children committed to his care would be adequately discharged without his aid, still he ought (as we have seen) for his own sake, as well as theirs, to desire to bring his personal instruction into contact with their minds; and thus to prepare *them* to love his person, and profit by his ministry; and to prepare *himself* to understand, in some measure, the character and wants of each, and the best means of doing them good.

Nor ought these meetings with the children of the church to be so rare as they too commonly are. Some pastors assemble their children to be catechized and addressed once or twice a year, and others, at most, once in two or three months. It is deliberately believed by the committee that such infrequent meetings are of little or no real value. As a source of instruction to the children, they are of very small advantage, if of any at all; and as a means of making the pastor personally acquainted with the children, and enabling him to judge of the temper, capacity, and disposition of each; to adapt himself to their respective characters; to mark the progress or retrocession of each; and to gain the confidence and affection of all, they might almost as well be omitted. These interviews ought to take place *every week* – to be attended with as much punctuality as the public exercises of the Sabbath; and to be engaged in with pencil and memorandum-book in hand, so that the appearance and outmaking of each may be kept in mind from week to week; and to be conducted throughout with the indefatigable diligence, patience, and affection which are adapted to reach and win the hearts of the children. In large congregations, the members of which are widely scattered, it may not be easy (or even practicable) to meet all the children of the same church, in a single body, once in every week. In this case, it may be expedient to have two or three little assemblies of children convened in different parts of the congregation every week; and once in each month the whole of the children and young people of the congregation may be assembled in the afternoon of the Lord's Day, in the church; and there, instead of the usual afternoon service, a service intended especially for their benefit may be conducted in the presence of their parents and others, in such a manner as to be even more instructive, solemn, and touching to all. But this matter may be conducted, where circumstances render it expedient, somewhat differently.

Suppose that there are three catechizing stations in different parts of the congregation. These may be all punctually attended in the same week, and even on the same day of the week: one by the pastor, and the other two by two of the elders. On the succeeding two weeks the pastor may change places with his elders; so that he may, in turn, attend every class once a month, and, at the end of the month, meet and address them all in a body, as before suggested. These exercises on the catechism will be of little value, if the children are merely called upon to repeat by memory the words of the formulary. Every answer ought to be analyzed and explained in the most simple and patient manner – condescending to the weakness of the youthful mind, and endeavoring to communicate truth in the most practical and affectionate form. In any and every case it is important that the elders take a part in this work, that they may become personally acquainted with the children of the church, and also that the work may not be neglected when the pastor is unwell or absent.

IX. It is recommended that one or more *Bible classes* be established in every congregation. The best methods of conducting these will readily occur to every enlightened pastor, and although they are (and ought to be) primarily intended and adapted for the instruction of the young, they may (and ought to) include as many of both sexes and of all ages as can be prevailed upon to engage in the study of the Bible.

X. It is recommended that all the Sabbath schools in every congregation be under the constant supervision and direction of the pastor and eldership. Sabbath schools are too often surrendered to the guidance of irresponsible persons, and sometimes to persons making no profession, and manifesting no practical sense of religion – and whose teaching, of course, must be of a very equivocal character. And sometimes books are introduced from well-meaning donors (and regulations formed) by no means adapted to promote the spiritual interests of the children. Everything of this kind ought to be avoided. All the teachers employed, all the books used, and all the regulations adopted ought to be such as the pastor and Session approve. The pastor, as often as his engagements allow, ought to step in – if it is but a few minutes – to the various schools, and manifest his interest in them by a word of counsel or of prayer, as the case may be, and thus put himself in the way of knowing personally how everything is conducted, and how everything prospers, and thus qualify himself to preside over the whole with intelligence and fidelity.

XI. It is recommended that the *baptized children* of the church be assembled three or four times in each year, and be affectionately addressed and prayed with by the pastor. At these interviews it will be generally advisable to have the parents present, and also the elders, and to accompany the exercises with such tender appeals to *parents,* as peculiarly charged with the religious training of their offspring; and to the *elders,* as being the spiritual *overseers* of the youth of the church – as may tend at once to remind both of their duty, and to impress on their minds a sense of their solemn obligations. As almost every church may be supposed, of course, to have one or two social services, in the secular evenings of each week, these interviews with baptized children may be made (once in three months) to take the place of one of these meetings, so as to avoid the undue multiplication of public services, which might prove oppressive both to the pastor and to the people of his charge.

XII. It is earnestly recommended that all our church Sessions, presbyteries, and synods direct particular attention to this important subject. It will be expedient for them once a year, at least, to ascertain how this great concern stands in their bounds. And if they duly appreciate its importance, it will often engage their attention. They will feel that it is impossible too early to enter on the work of forming a large and digested system of religious training which shall, in some good degree, carry us back to the habits of our venerated fathers, on this subject, with such improvements as the advantages and facilities furnished by modern times may enable us to apply.

XIII. It is recommended that the foregoing system, as far as applicable, be enjoined by the General Assembly to be adopted at all our missionary stations among the heathen. If it is important among the regular and established churches of Christendom, it is in some respects still more vitally important in evangelizing the pagan world. It is believed that the advantages of directing special attention to heathen youth have never yet been either sufficiently appreciated or pursued. When the time shall come in which, as the Scriptures declare, "nations shall be born in a day" [*Isaiah* 66:8], perhaps nothing will be more likely to prepare the way for such wonders, than having previously scattered amongst youth the seeds of Gospel truth.

It may, perhaps, be remarked by some, on a survey of the foregoing recommendations, that they present an amount of attention, and of unceasing labor, which cannot fail of pressing heavily on the mind, the heart, and strength of every pastor. This is not denied. To accomplish, from year to year, the aggregate of what has been recommended, must indeed make large drafts on the time, the thoughts, and the efforts of every spiritual overseer. But surely no faithful minister will complain of this. Can he wear out in any branch of labor more likely to turn to great account? Can he devote himself to any object more worthy of his care; more adapted to reward his work of faith and labor of love; or more fitted to build up the church, and promote his own acceptance and happiness as an ambassador of Christ, than to train up a generation to serve God when he shall have gone to his eternal reward?

PART 3

THE OFFICERS OF THE CHURCH

He himself gave some apostles, some prophets, some evangelists,
and some pastors and teachers,
for the equipping of the saints for the work of ministry,
for the edifying of the body of Christ,
till we all come to the unity of the faith
and the knowledge of the Son of God,
to a perfect man,
to the measure of the stature of the fullness of Christ;
that we should be no longer children,
tossed to and fro and carried about with every wind of doctrine,
by the trickery of men,
in the cunning craftiness
by which they lie in wait to deceive.
Ephesians 4:11-15

10

The Teachers of the Church[1]

John Calvin

THOSE WHO preside over the government of the church, according to the institution of Christ, are named by Paul, first *Apostles*; secondly, *Prophets*; thirdly, *Evangelists*; fourthly, *Pastors*; and, lastly, *Teachers* (*Ephesians* 4:11). Of these, only the two last have an ordinary office in the church.... The nature of the apostolic function is clear from the command, "Go ye into all the world, and preach the Gospel to every creature" (*Mark* 16:15). No fixed limits are given them, but the whole world is assigned to be reduced under the obedience of Christ, that by spreading the Gospel as widely as they could, they might everywhere erect his kingdom. Accordingly, Paul, when he would approve his apostleship, does not say that he had acquired some one city for Christ, but had propagated the Gospel far and wide – had not built on another man's foundation, but planted churches where the name of his Lord was unheard. The apostles, therefore, were sent forth to bring back the world from its revolt to the true obedience of God, and everywhere establish his kingdom by the preaching of the Gospel; or, if you choose, they were like the first architects of the church, to lay its foundations throughout the world. By *Prophets*, he means not all interpreters of the divine will, but those who excelled by special revelation; none such now exist, or they are less manifest. By *Evangelists*, I mean those who, while inferior in rank to the apostles, were next them in office, and even acted as their substitutes. Such were Luke, Timothy, Titus, and the like; perhaps, also, the seventy disciples whom our Savior appointed in the second place to the apostles (*Luke* 10:1). According to this interpretation, which appears to me consonant both to the words and the meaning of

1. John Calvin, *Institutes of the Christian Religion*, Henry Beveridge, translator. Eerdmans, 1970, 318-322.

Paul, those three functions were not instituted in the church to be perpetual, but only to endure so long as churches were to be formed where none previously existed, or at least where churches were to be transferred from Moses to Christ; although I deny not, that afterwards God occasionally raised up apostles, or at least evangelists, in their stead, as has been done in our time for such were needed to bring back the church from the revolt of Antichrist. The office I nevertheless call extraordinary, because it has no place in churches duly constituted. Next come *Pastors* and *Teachers,* with whom the church never can dispense, and between whom, I think, there is this difference, that teachers preside not over discipline or the administration of the sacraments, or admonitions or exhortations, but the interpretation of Scripture only, in order that pure and sound doctrine may be maintained among believers. But all these are embraced in the pastoral office.

We now understand what offices in the government of the church were temporary, and what offices were instituted to be of perpetual duration. But if we class evangelists with apostles, we shall have two like offices in a manner corresponding to each other. For the same resemblance which our teachers have to the ancient prophets, pastors have to the apostles. The prophetical office was more excellent in respect of the special gift of revelation that accompanied it, but the office of teachers was almost of the same nature, and had altogether the same end. In like manner, the twelve, whom the Lord chose to publish the new preaching of the Gospel to the world (*Luke* 6:13), excelled others in rank and dignity. For although, from the nature of the case, and etymology of the word, all ecclesiastical officers may be properly called apostles, because they are all sent by the Lord and are his messengers, yet as it was of great importance that a sure attestation should be given to the mission of those who delivered a new and extraordinary message, it was right that the twelve (to the number of whom Paul was afterwards added) should be distinguished from others by a peculiar title. The same name, indeed, is given by Paul to Andronicus and Junia, who, he says, were "of note among the apostles" (*Romans* 16:7); but when he would speak properly, he confines the term to that primary order. And this is the common use of Scripture. Still pastors (except that each has the government of a particular church assigned to him) have the same function as apostles. The nature of this function let us now see more clearly.

When our Lord sent forth the apostles, he gave them a commission (as has been lately said) to preach the Gospel, and baptize those who believed for the remission of sins. He had previously commanded that they should distribute the sacred symbols of his body and blood after his example (*Matthew* 28:19; *Luke* 22:19). Such is the sacred, inviolable, and perpetual law enjoined on those who succeed to the place of the apostles – they receive a commission to preach the Gospel and administer the sacraments. Whence we infer that those who neglect both of these falsely pretend to the office of apostles. But what shall we say of pastors? Paul speaks not of himself only but of all pastors, when he says, "Let a man so account of us, as of the ministers of Christ, and stewards of the mysteries of God" (*1 Corinthians* 4:1). Again, in another passage, he describes a bishop as one "holding fast the faithful Word as he hath been taught, that he may be able by sound doctrine both to exhort and convince the gainsayers" (*Titus* 1:9). From these and similar passages which everywhere occur, we may infer that the two principal parts of the office of pastors are to preach the Gospel and administer the sacraments. But the method of teaching consists not merely in public addresses, it extends also to private admonitions. Thus Paul takes the Ephesians to witness, "I kept back nothing that was profitable to you, but have showed you, and have taught you publicly, and from house to house, testifying both to the Jews, and also to the Greeks, repentance toward God, and faith toward our Lord Jesus Christ." A little after he says, "Remember, that, for the space of three years, I ceased not to warn everyone night and day with tears" (*Acts* 20:31). Our present purpose, however, is not to enumerate the separate qualities of a good pastor, but only to indicate what those profess who call themselves pastors – *viz.*, that in presiding over the church they have not an indolent dignity, but must train the people to true piety by the doctrine of Christ, administer the sacred mysteries, preserve and exercise right discipline. To those who are set as watchmen in the church the Lord declares, "When I say unto the wicked, Thou shalt surely die; and thou givest him not warning, nor speakest to warn the wicked from his wicked way, to save his life; the same wicked man shall die in his iniquity; but his blood will I require at thine hand" (*Ezekiel* 3:18). What Paul says of himself is applicable to all pastors: "For though I preach the Gospel, I have nothing to glory of: for necessity is laid upon me; yea, woe is unto me if I preach not the Gospel" (*1 Corinthians* 9:16). In short, what the apostles did to the whole world, every pastor should do to the flock over which he is appointed.

While we assign a church to each pastor, we deny not that he who is fixed to one church may assist other churches, whether any disturbance has occurred which requires his presence, or his advice is asked on some doubtful matter. But because that policy is necessary to maintain the peace of the church, each has his proper duty assigned, lest all should become disorderly, run up and down without any certain vocation, flock together promiscuously to one spot, and capriciously leave the churches vacant, being more solicitous for their own convenience than for the edification of the church. This arrangement ought, as far as possible, to be commonly observed, that everyone, content with his own limits, may not encroach on another's province. Nor is this a human invention. It is an ordinance of God. For we read that Paul and Barnabas appointed presbyters over each of the churches of Lystra, Antioch, and Iconium (*Acts* 14:23); and Paul himself enjoins Titus to ordain presbyters in every town (*Titus* 1:5). In like manner, he mentions the bishops of the Philippians, and Archippus, the bishop of the Colossians (*Philippians* 1:1; *Colossians* 4:17). And in the *Acts* we have his celebrated address to the presbyters of the Church of Ephesus (*Acts* 20:28). Let everyone, then, who undertakes the government and care of one church, know that he is bound by this law of divine vocation, not that he is astricted to the soil (as lawyers speak), that is, enslaved, and, as it were, fixed, as to be unable to move a foot if public utility so require, and the thing is done duly and in order; but he who has been called to one place ought not to think of removing, nor seek to be set free when he deems it for his own advantage. Again, if it is expedient for anyone to be transferred to another place, he ought not to attempt it of his own private motive, but to wait for public authority.

In giving the name of bishops, presbyters, and pastors, indiscriminately to those who govern churches, I have done it on the authority of Scripture, which uses the words as synonymous. To all who discharge the ministry of the Word it gives the name of bishops. Thus Paul, after enjoining Titus to ordain elders in every city, immediately adds, "A bishop must be blameless," etc. (*Titus* 1:5,7). So in another place he salutes several bishops in one church (*Philippians* 1:1). And in the *Acts*, the elders of Ephesus, whom he is said to have called together, he, in the course of his address, designates as bishops (*Acts* 20:17). Here it is to be observed, that we have hitherto enumerated those offices only which consist in the ministry of the Word; nor does Paul make mention of any others in the passage which we have quoted from the fourth chapter of the *Epistle to the Ephesians*. But in the *Epistle to the Romans*, and the *First Epistle to the Corinthians*, he enumerates other offices, as powers, gifts of healing, interpretation, government, care of the poor (*Romans* 12:7; 1 *Corinthians* 12:28). As to those that were temporary, I say nothing, for it is not worthwhile to dwell upon them. But there are two of perpetual duration – *viz.* government and care of the poor. By these governors I understand seniors selected from the people to unite with the bishops in pronouncing censures and exercising discipline. For this is the only meaning which can be given to the passage, "He that ruleth with diligence" (*Romans* 12:8). From the beginning, therefore, each church had its senate,[2] composed of pious, grave, and venerable men in whom was lodged the power of correcting faults. Of this power we shall afterwards speak. Moreover, experience shows that this arrangement was not confined to one age, and therefore we are to regard the office of government as necessary for all ages.

---

2. Latin, "senatum." French, "conseil ou consistoire;" council or consistory.

II

The Presbyterian Doctrine of Ordination[1]

Gordon H. Clark

In 1976 a *Report* to the Reformed Presbyterian Church, Evangelical Synod advocated the ordination of women to the diaconate. It failed, however, to consider the meaning of ordination. This strange omission should be remedied, for it would be most unfortunate, were the synod to decide to ordain women without considering what ordination is. A previous paper[2] contested the view of the diaconate which the above mentioned *Report* held forth. Here the subject is ordination. The following material is roughly divided into three sections. The first section takes up the Scriptural teaching and includes arguments from the works of George Gillespie. The second and shortest section of the three briefly disposes of the liberal ecumenical movement. Third, because it comes from a sister church, a *Report* to the Synod of the Christian Reformed Church will be examined.

1

The Scriptural material can well begin with some Old Testament anticipations. Frequently in the Old Testament an anointing with oil was the method of inducting someone into a particular office. Anyone not so anointed was guilty of a grave offense, if he dared to execute that office. Saul and Uzziah are two examples. If, now, the New Testament provides some means for inducting a person into an office, the Old Testament ceremony must be regarded as an anticipation of the New Testament requirements. Hence it is profitable to glance at the Old Testament method and its significance.

---

1. This essay is reprinted from Gordon H. Clark, *The Pastoral Epistles*, published by The Trinity Foundation, [1983] 1998.
2. This paper is titled "The Ordination of Women" and appears on pages 217-233.

The examples of Saul and Uzziah, as well as the directions for anointing partially explained in *Exodus* 30:30-33, show that something was conferred on the recipient that he had not possessed before. This something was in one case the authority to act as a priest, and in another case the authority to act as a king. God prohibited anyone from so acting without being anointed.

In the New Testament, anointing has no place. To be sure, the Messiah is the Lord's anointed, but Jesus never had holy oil poured on his head. Paul in *2 Corinthians* 1:21 also refers to a figurative non-literal anointing. In this verse Paul may have had only the apostles in mind; but it is possible, because of the following verse, that he meant an anointing of every believer. That such a figurative development of the idea of anointing should have occurred is not surprising. In fact, the figurative use is quite clear in *1 John* 2:27.

Nevertheless, since the New Testament also speaks of inducting elders into their office, it would be perverse to limit the anticipation of the Old Testament to Jesus as Messiah plus a general anointing of all believers. Since there are distinct offices both in the Old Testament and in the New Testament, the anointing in the Old Testament is best understood as anticipating New Testament ordination. This would help to support the idea that ordination confers authority upon the ordained.

The Old Testament also provides for induction into office by the laying on of hands. In the case of Jacob and the two sons of Joseph, the laying on of hands is not an induction into office, but the bestowal of a blessing. *Numbers* 8:10, however, inducts the Levites into office by this rite. Similarly, in *Numbers* 27:18-23 Moses appointed Joshua as his successor by the laying on of hands. By so doing, Moses "put some of [his] honor upon him...and gave him a charge." That God may have given the Holy Spirit to Joshua before Moses ordained him is irrelevant to the point at issue. The point is that there was a public ceremony of induction, without which Joshua could not have officiated. The induction may not have given him the Spirit, but it surely gave him the authority to act. Someone may boggle at the anointing with oil, but who can fail to see here an anticipation of the ordination of New Testament elders?

It is the New Testament that most concerns us. The one man who most fully worked out the New Testament doctrine of ordination was the Scottish commissioner to the Westminster Assembly, George

Gillespie. The argument will now show considerable dependence on *Aaron's Rod Blossoming, Dispute Against the English Popish Ceremonies,* and *Miscellany Questions.* The pagination comes from the 1844 Edinburgh edition of Gillespie's works.

At the climax of the Reformation, the age of the Westminster Assembly, this young man exhaustively examined the Scriptures and applied them to refute Romanism, Erastianism, and Socinianism alike. It is to be feared that Gillespie's scriptural analysis is not well known in this present decadent century.

Since it is the Socinian view of ordination, rather than the Romish or Erastian view, that troubles us today, only short references to the latter two will be made. For example, against the Erastianism of a certain Mr. Hussey, Gillespie writes, "Civil governors cannot be the elders mentioned by the apostle Paul, except Mr. Hussey make them bishops and invest them with the power of ordination" *(Aaron's Rod Blossoming,* II, ix, 124/2). Aside from the application to Erastianism, the sentence quoted refers to a certain power of ordination, that is, a power conferred by ordination. What this power is must be ascertained if one is to understand the Presbyterian doctrine of ordination.

On the following page Gillespie denies that elders are "without any power or authority of government." The source of that authority and its conferral are matters that must be determined. Gillespie at the place indicated continues for a column or so to show that elders have authority to rule. He adduces *Hebrews* 13:7, "Remember them that have the rule over you, men that spoke unto you the Word of God." The idea of ruling can be supported by other verses, such as 1 *Timothy* 3:4-6, 12, and 5:17. But as these will be more carefully examined later, there is no need to quote them here. Prior to the assertion that elders have authority to rule, it is logically necessary to show that the New Testament identifies something for the elders to rule over. That something is the visible, organized church. "The Scripture is plain that a visible, ministerial church is the body of Christ" (136/2). Scriptures supporting this are: *Romans* 12:4-5, "Even as we have many members in one body,... so we who are many are one body in Christ"; 1 *Corinthians* 10:17, "Seeing that we, who are many, are one bread, one body"; and similarly 1 *Corinthians* 12:12-28. To which may be added *Luke* 19:14, 27, "His citizens hated him...saying, We will not have this man reign over us.... But these mine enemies, which would not that I should reign over them, bring hither and slay them before me." This passage, which may at first puzzle a person studying ordination and church government, Gillespie uses as the answer to the rhetorical question, "Dare any say that the Lord Jesus shall not govern the Church of England and reign over the same?"

More obvious in their reference to an organized church over which Christ reigns through his stewards are *Acts* 2:36; *1 Corinthians* 15:24; *2 Corinthians* 10:4-6; and *Ephesians* 1:21-23; all of which assert Christ's lordship over his church and kingdom. A kingdom requires laws, officers, and courts. Since this is true of earthly kingdoms, how much more so of Christ's kingdom! Christ's kingdom is not of this world; nor is justice administered by swords and staves and torches. But it is a kingdom nonetheless. To deny laws and officers is to deny the kingdom, and to deny the kingdom is to deny the King. Mr. Hussey, on the contrary, had said that the visible church is not the body of Christ, nor is Christ its head, nor does the kingdom have any officers except the Holy Spirit. Against Mr. Hussey, Gillespie appeals to *Romans* 12:4-5; *2 Corinthians* 10:16-17; and *1 Corinthians* 12:12-28. But since the kingship of Christ is not questioned in the present controversy, it is hardly necessary to quote these additional verses. If now it be admitted that elders are rulers in the organized church, one of *The Sins of the Ministry of Scotland* is "Entering the ministry without trials and receiving ordination...sometimes without or against the mind of presbytery." Since exercising the office without ordination is a sin, it is important to understand the significance and proper method of ordination. With his view of an established religion, Gillespie wants "Princes...to provide that men of those ecclesiastical orders, and those only which are instituted in the New Testament by divine authority, have vocation and office in the church." This includes deacons, as is clear in the context, for on the next page he says, "Deacons were instituted by the apostles [to help the poor], besides which employments the Scripture hath assigned neither preaching nor baptizing nor any other ecclesiastical function" (*Dispute Against the Ceremonies,* Chapter VII, Digression 1, pages 160/1, and 161/2).

Some exception may be taken to Gillespie's denial that deacons should neither preach nor baptize, for although the activities of five of the original seven are not described, the other two did in fact preach and baptize. However, with respect to ordination, Gillespie on these pages says, "Now, beside the apostles, prophets, and evangelists, which were not ordained to be ordinary and perpetual offices in the church, there are but two ecclesiastical orders or degrees instituted by Christ in the New Testament, *viz.*, elders and deacons."

Again, speaking of the prince (162/1) Gillespie says that the prince "should cause, not one disdainful prelate [to examine and ordain], but a whole Presbytery or company of elders to take trial of" the candidate. That is to say, an election of a candidate by the congregation, which Gillespie is strong to enforce, is nonetheless insufficient. There must also be Presbyterial action; and this seems to apply to deacons as well.

With the threat of Rome on his mind, and with the episcopal policy of Charles I before his eyes, Gillespie is anxious to maintain the Presbyterian principle of congregational election. For this reason he sometimes seems to lessen the emphasis on ordination, or at least on the imposition of hands. Because of this anti-prelatical concern, which might have induced him to abandon ordination altogether, as was the result in the Reformation's left-wing, Gillespie's insistence on ordination, as in the preceding quotation, is all the more important to us today.

Thus, in spite of his Reformation opposition to Romish ordination, Gillespie asserts its necessity as well as the necessity of election. The *Ceremonies* (162/2) states, "The outward calling is made up of election and ordination.... Let the *Acts of the Apostles* and the epistles of Paul be read, how ministers were elected and ordained...." *Acts* 1:15, 23 show election by the congregation; and *Acts* 6:2-3 show the same in the case of deacons.

Whether Presbytery's doing something with its hands refers to ordination or to raising their hands in a voting procedure has occasioned some confusion. The participle in *2 Corinthians* 8:19 is almost surely an election; yet the same verb in *Acts* 14:23 rather clearly refers to ordination, for its subject is Paul and Barnabas, who certainly would not have elected local elders. But this confusion does not arise in some other verses because they use a different verb.

To explain: Neither *leinein* nor *anateinein* occurs in the New Testament. In classical Greek these verbs mean *stretch* or *strain*. There is no hint of *raising* hands, though *anateinein* can sometimes mean to vote. Hence *cheirotonetheis* in *2 Corinthians* 8:19 can mean a show of hands in voting. But *Acts* 6:6, 8:17, and 13:3 have a completely different verb: The phrase is *epithentes tas cheiras*. Clearly this is not hands *raised* in voting, but hands *laid upon* the candidate for ordination. Ordination therefore was not election by the congregation, but an act of the apostles. Gillespie is right in supporting election and prohibiting patronage, prelatic assignment, and any ignoring of the desires of the congregation. While so arguing he may seem to cast a shadow on ordination itself. Nevertheless he says clearly,

> The act of ordination stands in the mission to the deputation of a man to an ecclesiastical function with power and authority to perform the same; and thus are pastors ordained when they are *sent* to a people with power to preach the Word, minister the sacraments, and exercise ecclesiastical discipline among them. For "How shall they preach except they be *sent?*" (*Ceremonies*, 165/1).

Note well that ordination confers authority to preach, administer the sacraments, and exercise discipline. A presbyterial or congregational rite that does not convey this authority is not an ordination service, and should not be so called. Or, conversely, persons chosen for non-authoritative functions are not to be ordained.

Presumably in an over-reaction against Romish superstitions, Gillespie shows little enthusiasm for the Presbyterian act of the laying on of hands. After the preceding quotation he adds, "Unto which mission or ordination neither *prayer nor the imposition of hands,* nor any other of the church's rites is essential." Today few Reformed presbyters would approve of omitting prayer. But perhaps in a time of insurrection or riot, an ordination by presbyterial vote only would be considered valid. But the omission of the laying on of hands could be excused only by reason of some great disaster that would also excuse the omission of prayer. In this light one may accept his statement, "The essential act of ordination [is] a simple deputation and application of a minister to his ministerial function with power to perform it. This may be done...by word alone, without any other ceremony...." The example of Christ sending out the seventy is given as evidence.

While one may guess, from silence, that Christ did not ordain the seventy by laying his hands on them, the instance is irrelevant because it occurred before the resurrection. Christ and the original twelve observed the Mosaic rituals, which are not binding upon us; and negatively they were not baptized with the Trinitarian formula, nor did they observe the Lord's Supper before its institution, both of which of course oblige us today. The normative example for this age, with respect to ordination, is the apostolic action of the laying on of hands. Gillespie says this rite is "permissible," but not necessary. "This rite," he says, "shall with our leave be yet retained in the church." Unfortunately, he adds that although the rite may be retained "with our leave," the church "hath full liberty either to use any other decent rite...or else to use no rite at all."

Surely this is not the Reformed view or the Puritan principle. The Bible teaches that we should do all that God requires and no more: We should neither add to nor subtract from the prescribed elements of worship. Surely a Reformed theologian must deny that the church can do anything or omit anything by its own leave. If the laying on of hands is to be omitted, it would have to be during riot or insurrection, or other circumstance when the Lord's Supper also would have to be omitted.

In admitting that the laying on of hands is proper, decent, and permissible, Gillespie refers to 1 *Timothy* 4:14 – a passage that says more than he desires to say. Paul's instructions here, which, if not wholly concerned with the organization of churches, are at least the apostolic norm for ministerial conduct, not only mention the laying on of hands, but assert further that the grace of preaching authority, by the prophetic act of election, was given to Timothy with the presbytery's laying its hands on him. There may be some doubt whether or not the prophecy mentioned was the presbyterial election, but there can be no doubt about the presbyterial ordination with the laying on of hands. The verb does not mean a raising of hands in voting, but the laying of hands upon (*epi*) Timothy.

If Gillespie, in our judgment, does not sufficiently esteem the laying on of hands, he most emphatically supports ordination. The *Miscellany Questions* (III, 16/1) says,

> If it were an intolerable usurpation, in a man's own family, if any man should take on him the steward's place to dispense meat to the household, not being thereunto appointed, how much more were it an intolerable usurpation in the church.... Suppose they be well gifted, yet they may not preach except they be sent.... This sending needs be ordination, not the church's election; a people may choose to themselves, but they cannot send to themselves.

In the next column he continues,

> There are five necessary means and ways which must be had and used by those who look to be saved: (1) calling on the name of the Lord; (2) believing on him; (3) hearing his Word; (4) a preaching ministry; (5) mis-

sion or ordination. If the first four be perpetually necessary to the end of the world, so must the fifth be; for the apostle lays almost as great necessity on this last as on the rest.... There can be no ministerial office without a mission or ordination.

One of Gillespie's opponents had argued that no ministerial or ecclesiastical sending was in view in the New Testament, "for then none could be an instrument to convert another but a minister or preacher sent...; therefore...the apostle speaks of a providential sending, by giving men gifts, and working with them in their use and exercise." To which Gillespie answers,

> In Christ himself...his having the Spirit of the Lord upon him was not his mission, but is plainly distinguished from his mission and ordination to his office which he had from God; *Luke* 4:18, "The Spirit of the Lord is upon me because he hath anointed me to preach the Gospel to the poor; he hath sent me...."

The *dunamis* or ability of gifts to the office is one thing; the *exousia* or authority to it is another thing (page 17, and the argument continues for another column on page 18).

Ordination, therefore, is not simply an apostolic function to cease with the first century. Preaching is ordinary and regular. Therefore, mission or sending is too. The Great Commission of *Matthew* 28:19-20 shows that mission is perpetual, and thus sending likewise. To the same effect is *Luke* 12:42. Since the illustration describes the work of a steward, its lesson is not applicable to all Christians. The immediate application is to the disciples or apostles themselves. The extended application is to future stewards. They are to be held more responsible than lesser servants. Verse 43 shows that the warning remains in effect until Christ returns. The steward of the parable and the minister of a church have therefore been appointed with authority. The connection between a steward and a bishop is made in *Titus* 1:7.

To this someone objects that since probationers preach, ordination is not necessary. The reply is that they do not preach regularly, ordinarily, or *ex officio*. They preach occasionally, without ministerial office. And even so, they must have been licensed. Note, too, that the seven deacons, after they were elected, were ordained by the apostles; and though we do not know much about their activities, those mentioned in *Acts* included evangelism.

That ordination is requisite to the preaching of the Gospel and that it confers authority may be inferred from *Hebrews* 5:1-4: "For every high priest taken from among men is ordained...that he may offer both gifts and sacrifices for sin.... And no man takes this honor unto himself...." The Socinians, who took a low view of ordination, restricted the application of this passage to the apostles. But this low view, or, rather, denial of ordination, fails to note that the priesthood was ordinary and continuing. Therefore, the passage applies to the ordinary and continuing Christian ministry, an inference reinforced by the completely general statement of verse 4. When this verse says that no man takes this honor unto himself, it need not, it hardly can mean, "this Aaronic honor." There is no demonstrative pronoun here – just the article; and hence the meaning can be and likely is honor as an abstract noun, any ecclesiastical honor. Even if someone contentiously insists that the article serves as a demonstrative, and thus refers to the Aaronic honor, nevertheless, the whole passage applies to the New Testament ministry. Not only is the epistle addressed to Christians, but one may also argue that if the lesser Aaronic honor required ordination, then *a fortiori* the greater honor of the New Testament ministry cannot be had without ordination. Scriptural analogy also is given in *Romans* 13:7, *1 Timothy* 3:1, and more pointedly in *1 Timothy* 5:17, "Let the elders that rule well be counted worthy of double honor."

Another passage in *Hebrews* also advances the argument. Chapter 6:1-2 list some elementary teachings, such as might be required of catechumens before baptism or even before a church was organized. One of these elementary points is ordination, clearly necessary to the organization of a church. Thus in addition to repentance and faith, ordination ranks as an elementary doctrine.

Ordination should be distinguished from the bestowal of the Holy Ghost as described in *Acts* 8:17-19. The deacons in *Acts* 6:3, 6 were first perceived to be full of the Holy Ghost, second elected, and third ordained. Later *1 Timothy* 4:14 shows that ordination is an act of presbytery. *1 Timothy* 5:22 warns against laying hands suddenly on some attractive neophyte. And *Titus* 1:5, by the words "in every city," shows that ordination is regular and ordinary. Such was not the case when Simon Magus wanted to buy apostolic power with money.

That ministers are the regular and ordinary officers of the church bears emphasis. Ministers of the Gospel are called shepherds, entering by the door and not breaking in; they are called angels, ambassadors, and rulers. But men do not give themselves the position of ambassador or even of shepherd. They must be appointed and sent. *Luke* 12:42 has already made this point with reference to stewards. Paul calls himself a steward in *1 Corinthians* 4:1, and calls all bishops so in *Titus* 1:7. Ministers are therefore servants; they invite guests to the wedding feast. But clearly no one can properly invite guests to a lord's wedding feast, unless the lord had previously appointed him. Paul was so appointed: "Whereunto I am ordained a preacher and an apostle" (*1 Timothy* 2:7), in which phrase we note that Paul was ordained a preacher as well as an apostle. He repeats this in *2 Timothy* 1:11. Preachers, therefore, are to be given authority to preach by ordination.

Preachers are permanent and regular officers of the church. Paul and the New Testament refute the position of the Socinians and Anabaptists because *2 Timothy* 2:2 commands generation after generation to appoint faithful teachers. Paul does not refer to any and all Christians; he does not even have all gifted Christians in mind. Aptitude is one thing; calling and authority are something else. There is more to the calling of pastors than the church's electing them, for, as Gillespie says, "Those unto whom the power of ordination belongs do also *commit* unto them that which they are entrusted with: 'the same commit you' " (*Luke* 12:48).

Ordination, authority, and the submission of the congregation go hand in hand. The latter, the submission of the congregation, presupposes an authority in the pastors. That the Scripture requires submission is clear in *1 Thessalonians* 5:12-13: "And we beseech you, brethren, to know them which labor among you, and are over you in the Lord, and admonish you; and to esteem them very highly in love for their work's sake. And be at peace among yourselves"; and in *Hebrews* 13:17, "Obey them that have the rule among you and submit yourselves...." The same submission is implied in the ministers' right to receive remuneration (*1 Corinthians* 9:7, 9, 11, 13). What will the Socinians and Anabaptists do? If ordination is not necessary, will they pay salaries to all who preach; or, to avoid such Scripturally enjoined expense, will they prohibit preaching altogether?

There are other passages which reinforce these main lessons; but these are sufficient to conclude this Scriptural section by asserting that ordination confers authority to teach, and that therefore the New Testament is violated if women are ordained.

2

The second section of this paper may be made very brief because the ecumenical movement does not acknowledge the Bible as the infallible norm for either theological doctrine or ecclesiastical practice. Its procedures, however, may serve as a warning to any who may wish to disregard Scriptural restrictions.

Two periodicals only need be consulted: *The Churchman* (Volume 88, October-December 1974), and *The Journal of Ecumenical Studies* (Volume 10, 1973). Whatever authority *The Churchman* accords to the Bible in its defense of ordaining women, it also appeals to "the promptings of the Spirit" especially when a solemn synod is assembled, of which its first example is Vatican II. "Catholic bishops, under the guidance of the Spirit, could change this triadic order" and are today "in the process of recognizing other orders...of non-Roman and even non-episcopal ministers as apostolic..." (262). The articles in their entirety place authority in the church, rather than in the Bible. The church changes itself. Thus, though *The Churchman* spends many pages advocating the ordination of women, I hope Reformed Presbyterians will remain unimpressed.

The Journal of Ecumenical Studies is more interesting. J. Massyngberde Ford guesses that "*Luke* 8:1-3, 10:38-42...may reflect the role of deaconesses within the early church," and "whereas the twelve all appear to be male Jews...one cannot make the same assumption about the seventy or seventy-two disciples whom Jesus commissioned" (672-673). The role of Mary at the wedding in Cana "may be of symbolic and theological importance and may represent such behavior of Mary as typical." In fact, "it may well be that Jewish women converts [from paganism] rose to influential positions in the synagogue." And it may well be that J. M. Ford is highly imaginative.

She assures us that Phoebe was "a minister, *diakonos,* of the church at Cenchrea.... Most importantly, however, is the word *prostatis....* Our conclusion would be that the deacon Phoebe is in a position of authority and responsibility" (674-677). (On this point see the companion paper on "The Ordination of Women.")

Those who argue for the ordination of women give themselves the liberal benefit of any doubt. After discussing Priscilla, Dr. Ford writes, "it is *possible* that...the word *diakonos* alludes to both men and women deacons. One cannot *dogmatically* argue that only males are addressed."

And, "*Romans* 16:1 very strongly suggests an active and *authoritative* position of women ministers" (678). Why not say, Romans 16:1 hardly even suggests authority and one cannot *dogmatically* argue that *diakonos* refers to ordained women deacons?

More frequently, however, not even this much authority is accorded to Scripture. On *1 Corinthians* 11 Dr. Ford says, "Firstly, one notes that the teaching contained in *1 Cor.* 11 is the personal opinion of Paul, not dominical teaching; *e.g. thelo* (I wish, v. 3)." In opposition to such lax exegesis, consider the very verse she mentions: "I would have you know," or "I want you to know that the head of every man is Christ." Is the headship of Christ nothing more than a culturally conditioned personal opinion of Paul? Is it not rather authoritative theology?

Again, "*1 Cor.* 11 must be based on a literal interpretation of *Gen.* 3, which exegetes could not accept nowadays.... Paul gives no indication whatsoever that women are precluded from any of these [gifts in *1 Cor.* 12-14], even apostleship or administration" (680). No indication whatsoever? How about *1 Corinthians* 14:34, "Let your women keep silence in the churches, for it is not permitted unto them to speak; but they are commanded to be under obedience, as also saith the law"?

This verse, which should settle the whole matter, causes Dr. Ford no difficulty whatsoever: "These verses are placed after verse 40 in D, G.... There is therefore some justification for arguing that they are an interpolation" (681). Some justification? How much? For arguing? Where is the argument? Dr. Ford seems to think that a transposition of verses in two uncials, against p^{46}, *Aleph, A, B, K, Psi,* and plenty of cursives, so conclusively proves this to be spurious that the church is authorized to abandon its age-long practice of ordaining men only. Could it not better be argued, that if Christ had wanted women to be ordained, he would have chosen at least one woman as a disciple? Or, after the resurrection, one woman as an apostle? Or even one woman as a deacon?

On a passage that corroborates *1 Corinthians* 14:34, Dr. Ford writes, "With regard to *1 Tim.* 2:9-15, one may note again...the fact that Paul expresses his own wish *(boulomai,* v. 8, and 'I do not permit,' *epitrepo,* in v. 12), *not* that of the Lord" (682).

Must we then say that "I wish men to pray" is merely a personal wish? And when Paul says "I do not permit a woman to teach," does he lack apostolic authority?

To make this poor argument a bit more palatable, Dr. Ford mistranslates the verse, as "I do not permit a woman to teach or to have supreme authority but to be modest." The verse actually says, "I do not permit a woman to teach nor have authority over a man, but to keep quiet."

Dr. Ford, by inserting the word *supreme,* wants to allow women an authority, though less than supreme. But if, as has been shown, she allows for women *apostles,* how can she deny them supreme authority? Then she tries to make the word *teach* mean *formulate doctrine.* The women can teach, but only the bishops can make creedal decisions.

But let us say sharply against all this baseless imagination that the verses contain no such ideas. Finally in her Summary Dr. Ford delivers this astounding assertion: "Even if Jesus were a male by his incarnation ...the Spirit of God is thought of as the feminine principle in the Deity" (691).

The conclusion of this second section may well be that the demand for women's ordination is just one more element in the apostasy of the large denominations and the decline of our civilization. It was certainly not initiated by any reverent and scholarly study of the Biblical text. No one would even have thought it up apart from the liberal women's movement.

Wherever this new idea occurs in relatively conservative churches, it must be explained by the influence around us, most viciously exemplified in drug addiction and the murder of babies, seriously enough exemplified in crimes of violence, sexual abominations, and disregard of property rights, and least disturbingly but more profoundly exemplified in the rejection of Biblical inerrancy by hitherto conservative scholars and seminaries: This moral collapse engulfs all church members and infects their opinions, however slightly and unwittingly. The demand for the ordination of women is one result.

3

The third section of this paper now considers an example of this deleterious influence in a denomination that has boasted loudly of its Reformed theology. It is *Report 44* to the 1969 Synod of the Christian Reformed Church. On page 643 the *Report* gives a curious argument relative to the ordination of deacons in *Acts 6:1-6.* Quoting verse 6 the *Report* says, "The way the passage reads in the original makes it appear that the entire congregation did the laying on of hands, though there are interpreters who hold that only the apostles did the laying on of hands. We shall not try to settle this question."

But it is of some use to settle this question; nor is it hard to do so. The *Report* quoted only verse 6. In this verse the praying and the laying on of hands are immediately dependent on the word *apostles*. It is grammatically possible, though rather forced, to take the participle *praying* and the verb *laid* as referring to the congregation. What settles the matter, however, is verse 3, which the *Report* failed to mention. The verse says, "Then the Twelve...said...you select seven men...whom we may appoint over this business." The multitude of disciples was to choose seven men; but the multitude could not ordain them; it was "we" the apostles who delegated authority to the seven.

Acts 13:3 is something else again. Here certain prophets and teachers, explicitly inclusive of Barnabas in verse 1, obviously inclusive of Saul in verse 2, are commanded by the Holy Ghost to lay hands on Barnabas and Saul. Since all of these, especially Saul, had already been ordained, the passage describes, not an ordination service, but a commissioning to a particular task. It is repeated today whenever a mission board prays and lays hands on an already ordained man as they send him out to Africa or Asia. This passage is therefore irrelevant for establishing the doctrine of ordination.

The passages in 1 *Timothy* 4:14 and 2 *Timothy* 1:6 have occasioned debates that are more ingenious than instructive. That the presbytery laid hands on Timothy is not inconsistent with Paul's being present and having done so with them. Whether it was the presbytery of Lystra or of Ephesus, and in particular what deep theological difference it makes, is all a matter of guesswork. The important point is that this presbyterial ceremony conferred a gift on Timothy, which Paul now exhorts Timothy to exercise. This gift can be no other than the authority "to rule well...especially...in the Word and doctrine" (1 *Timothy* 6:17). Nothing in these two epistles permits reduction of this event to a mere commissioning for a limited missionary tour.

The *Report* to the Christian Reformed Synod (647-648) urges that God gave Timothy gifts of wisdom, eloquence, or whatever characteristics are useful in the ministry, before he was ordained, and that the ceremony did not confer these gifts. So be it. But why suppose that ordination confers wisdom and eloquence? And if it does not, why suppose that it confers nothing? The *Report's* argument is defective, for ordination confers the gift of authority to use the gifts of wisdom and eloquence in the preaching of the Gospel. The *Report* misses the issue. Therefore one must disagree with at least one of the *Report's* conclusions, namely, "The gift must not be understood as some indelible character conveyed to Timothy by the imposition of hands, since Timothy is told too that he must use and cultivate his gift." The logic of the since-clause is doubly faulty.

First, an exhortation to use a gift does not imply that it cannot have been given by the imposition of hands. Indeed, the opposite is the case: "Now that you have received the gift at my hands, Timothy, make use of it." Then second, giving a gift by the laying on of hands does not preclude it from being "indelible." If anyone dislikes the historical origin of the term *indelible*, we can more literally call it a permanent possession, no doubt withdrawable on account of great sin, but otherwise a life-long authority to preach. Contrary to the position of the *Report* that "There is no indication in Scripture that an authorization or appointment symbolized and confirmed by the laying on of hands was necessarily to be for the life-time of the person appointed" (649), one must ask, was Paul's gift of apostleship and Timothy's ordination to preach intended to be valid for only eighteen months or two years?

The *Report* contains other peculiar assertions. For example, in arguing that Christian ministers are not an exclusive priesthood, and that the kingship in Israel does not convey political authority on contemporary elders – all of which is true – the *Report* states, "If the Lord found it necessary to warn against a coercive authority on the part of Old Testament kings, how much more sensitive ought we not to be concerning coercive authority today?" (652). There is considerable confusion here. For one thing, although God charged the Israelites with sin for rejecting the system of judges and desiring a king, he nonetheless gave the kings coercive authority; and this was reaffirmed in the New Testament. But any application of such material to elders, whether to support or deny authority, is mistaken, for elders are not civil rulers. Nor does the priesthood of all believers militate against the prerogatives of the ministry. What seems to be operative several times in this *Report* is an over-reaction against Romanism. The papacy may be the Antichrist, as the *Westminster Confession* says; but nonetheless, most of what Romanism says about the Trinity, the two natures of Christ, and even some things about ordination are true.

The apparent intent of the Christian Reformed *Report*, not exactly to abolish, but at least to minimize orderly church administration, depends here and there on obviously bad logic. Consider: "Does the fact that a 'disciple' in the broader sense was permitted to baptize, according to *Acts 9*, imply that all the 'disciples' in the broader sense could likewise administer baptism?... There is nothing in the book of *Acts* which would rule out an affirmative answer to these questions." The reference to *Acts* 9 indicates that the *Report* has Ananias in mind. Although the text does not explicitly say that Ananias baptized Paul, it is so likely that it may be taken for granted. But was Ananias a "disciple in the broader sense"? To be sure, all Christians could be called disciples, but it by no means follows that Ananias was not an elder or deacon. The fact that God spoke directly to him is enough to conclude that nothing in the chapter "would rule out a *negative* answer to these questions." The *Report's* arguments from silence do not support its assumptions and conclusions. Yet there are two more arguments from silence on the same page (666).

Even the conclusion on the following page attacks a straw man. It says, "We may well agree with G. R. Beasley-Murray when he says, 'To insist that the apostles personally conducted every baptism in the primitive church is an absurdity that no one, so far as I am aware, has asked us to believe!' " Beasley-Murray is quite right; and for that very reason the *Report* is quite wrong. No one asserts that the Apostles personally baptized every first century convert. Our contention is that baptism is to be administered by ordained officers.

A further silence the *Report* brings up is in *1 Timothy* 4:13 and *2 Timothy* 4:1-2. The *Report* notices that among the duties Paul enjoins, baptism "is conspicuous by [its] absence." True enough, baptism is not mentioned in these verses. But should the absence be called "conspicuous" or significant? Note that the Lord's Supper is absent too. The Lord's Supper is conspicuous by its presence in *1 Corinthians* 10:16-17, 11:20ff, and one would think that baptism is sufficiently conspicuous in *Matthew* 28:19, not to mention *Acts* 2:38 *et passim*.

It must be conceded that the *Report* uses something better than silence when it appeals to Jewish customs. A priest was not the only person who circumcised infants, nor did every family need a priest to celebrate the Passover. It is another matter, however, whether this implies that unordained laymen should baptize and administer the Lord's Supper. The *Report* itself under the subhead, "The Fluid New Testament Situation with Regard to Office," acknowledges that 1 *Thessalonians* 5:12-13 and 1 *Corinthians* 16:15-16 speak of men who had some degree of prominence, to whom, Paul says, the church members should submit. Submission certainly gives the impression that such men, and others who labored with Paul, had received authority.

The New Testament period may have been "fluid," in the sense that the many congregations established developed at different speeds, and to different degrees of organization. It is certainly true that the evidence and even the instruction relative to administration in the New Testament is "scanty" (674) in comparison with the theological content of *Romans,* or even with the moral problems in Corinth. But we totally reject the *Report's* poorly disguised suggestion that the New Testament "includes such a variety of obscure, ambiguous, and even contradictory statements." We particularly object to the accusation that Scripture contradicts itself. One need not, however, hesitate to say that the "tunnel period," that is, the formative period in the first century, exhibits diversity and the "the later epistles reflect some changes in emphasis as compared with the early ones" (674). This would be normal, as Paul's early successes in evangelization led to a subsequent amount of instruction in organizing particular congregations. One can even acknowledge that "up to the year 100 A.D. the organization of the local church was not a matter of paramount concern." Several times the *Report* uses the word *necessarily,* or here *paramount,* to obtain a degree of plausibility while evading the main question. Ordination may not have been a matter of "paramount" concern; but it was a matter of concern, even at the date of the epistle to the *Romans,* for the idea, if not the word, occurred in *Romans* 10:15. Because of a verse like this, and a certain number of others, elsewhere exegeted, one can hardly approve the *Report's* assertion that "the changes in the concept of office which occurred during the ancient period were often subtle and obscure. What is beyond dispute is that a major change did take place during that period" (647). That there were changes in the actual organizations of local congregations is indeed beyond dispute; but that there was any *major* change in the *concept* of ordination must be repudiated. Paul may have added details to his earlier instruction on ordination, but he never contradicted himself. An inspired writer, through whom God breathes out his words on the written page, does not assert falsehoods. But if two assertives contradict, one must be false. For the rest, a paragraph on the fifth century (675) is irrelevant to the matter now under discussion.

More to the point are the remarks concerning the Reformation's opposition to sacerdotalism. The *Report* correctly stresses and condemns the popish claim that ordination confers the power of performing the miracle of transubstantiation. Rejection of this claim, however, does not entail rejection of an indelible character conferred by ordination, nor even of a "second class citizenship in the Church of Christ," no matter how repulsive this phraseology is; for no one can deny that the laity lack ministerial authority. The *Report* also correctly notes that the Reformers were preoccupied with the doctrine of grace, and not with the nature of ordination. "Yet in spite of these difficulties, it is possible, by way of implication, to draw...some conclusions" (679). Indeed, though the *Report* is not overly optimistic at this point, it is possible to draw some implications relative to the office of deacon. At any rate, it is possible to contradict the *Report's* assertion that "all believers are 'ordained' priests, prophets, and kings" (681). Clearly not all believers have been elected by the congregation and installed in office by laying on of hands.

The *Report* is once more correct in stating that the Reformers aimed to avoid both the Romish view and that of the Anabaptists and Socinians. But it seems to dismiss Luther's and Calvin's later more conservative position as chiefly an historical reaction against leftwing chaos. True, the *Report* acknowledges that the two Reformers appealed to Scripture, but its emphasis is on "fear of the Anabaptists as disturbers of civil and ecclesiastical peace." It would be better to say that these disturbers forced Calvin to study material in the Scriptures to which previously, and because of the major concern with Romanism, he had paid little attention. Action in an historical context (681) does not imply non-scriptural norms of action.

The authors of the *Report* may reject these criticisms on the ground that they explicitly recognize the assertions of Zwingli and the *Second Helvetic Confession*. Granted, granted; but some of the phraseology seems to minimize the "conservative" thrust of the "later" Luther and Calvin.

This minimizing is again found in the words "functional or instrumental" (682). One could say that the Romish priesthood also was functional and instrumental. The two words have an extensive application.

But if the *Report* means that ordination is merely a pragmatic happenstance, rather than a divine command, a New Testament student must disagree. The wording of the *Report* is disturbing: "Although such division of labor is necessary for good order and efficiency, it does not create an essentially different order or hierarchy in the church that may be regarded as an end in itself" (682). But even the Romish priesthood is not "an end in itself." And Protestant or Biblical ordination does indeed create an "order" on which the laity must not encroach. Laymen may bring charges against an elder, but the Session is the judicatory. Whether this authority is called "status" or "function" or "office" is merely semantics. By any name it is a divine ordinance, reserved to those only who are so elected. The language of the *Report* and of R. G. Johnson, whom it quotes, raises a false disjunction: "Although Calvin views the ministry as an institution of God, he still speaks of it in strongly functional terms." How else could anyone describe the office of King, President, or Senator except in "functional" terms, strongly or not? To use such terms does not deny the honor of the position. The *Report* embarrasses us by quoting Calvin's *Institutes,* IV, iii, 4, where he seems to say that the offices of apostle and prophet continue sporadically to the present day, even though "Paul gives the appellation of 'prophets,' not to all interpreters of the Divine will, but only to those who were honored with some special revelation." In view of Calvin's and all the Reformers' stress on *sola Scriptura,* one cannot believe that Calvin, when he said, "the Lord...still raises up [apostles and prophets] on particular occasions, when required by the necessity of the times," meant what the words seem to say.[3]

Because of the great doctrines of grace, for which the Protestants were being martyred and massacred, Calvin did not produce too detailed a doctrine of ordination. In his *Ecclesiastical Ordinances* he recommends that the ordaining presbytery should abstain from laying on of hands "because of the infirmity [*i.e.* the superstitions] of the times." Yet in the *Institutes,* IV, iii, 16, he alleges that the example of the apostles should not be abandoned for "their very observance ought to serve in lieu of a precept." This latter consideration surely outweighs the dangers of superstition. The Reformers did not abolish baptism, even though several superstitious rites had been attached to it; and none of

3. See pages 187-191 above. – *Editor.*

them ever dreamed of abolishing the Lord's Supper, though the mass was an idolatrous abomination. Considerations of normal routine, pragmatic usefulness, or something so vague as to be called functionalism, are inadmissible. (Compare the *Report*, page 686, Summary, the first paragraph.)

In conclusion, therefore, we assert, that ordination is a Scriptural ceremony by which the presbytery confers authority to preach the Gospel and to rule the church. The offices involved are those of elder and deacon. Since Scripture explicitly forbids women to teach or exercise authority, it is a violation of divine law to ordain a woman.

12

Paul on Women Speaking in Church

Benjamin B. Warfield [1]

I HAVE RECENTLY received a letter from a valued friend asking me to send him a "discussion of the Greek words *laleo* and *lego* in such passages as 1 *Corinthians* 14:33-39, with special reference to the question: Does the thirty-fourth verse forbid all women everywhere to speak or preach publicly in Christian churches?" The matter is of universal interest, and I take the liberty of communicating my reply to the readers of *The Presbyterian*.

It requires to be said at once that there is no problem with reference to the relations of *laleo* and *lego*. Apart from niceties of merely philological interest, these words stand related to one another just as the English words *speak* and *say* do; that is to say, *laleo* expresses the *act of talking*, while *lego* refers to *what is said*. Wherever, then, the act of speaking, without reference to the content of what is said, is to be indicated, *laleo* is used, and must be used. There is nothing disparaging in the intimation of the word, any more than there is in our word *talk*, although, of course, it can on occasion be used disparagingly as our word *talk* can also – as when some of the newspapers intimate that the Senate is given over to mere talk. This disparaging application of *laleo*, however, never occurs in the New Testament, although the word is used very frequently.

The word is in its right place in 1 *Corinthians* 14:33*ff*, therefore, and necessarily bears there its simple and natural meaning. If we needed anything to fix its meaning, however, it would be supplied by its fre-

---

1. Benjamin Breckinridge Warfield (1851-1921) was a graduate of both Princeton University and Princeton Seminary. He taught theology at Western Seminary in Allegheny, Pennsylvania (1878-1887) and later at Princeton Seminary (1887-1921). This essay is reprinted from *The Presbyterian*, October 30, 1919.

quent use in the preceding part of the chapter, where it refers not only to speaking with tongues (which was divine manifestation and unintelligible only because of the limitations of the hearers), but also to the prophetic speech, which is directly declared to be to edification and exhortation and comforting (verses 3-6). It would be supplied more pungently, however, by its contrasting term here – "let them be silent" (verse 34). Here we have *laleo* directly defined for us: "Let the women *keep silent,* for it is not permitted to them to *speak.*" Keep silent – speak: These are the two opposites; and the one defines the other.

It is important to observe, now, that the pivot on which the injunction of these verses turns is not the prohibition of speaking so much as the command of silence. That is the main injunction. The prohibition of speech is introduced only to explain the meaning more fully. What Paul says is in brief: "Let the women keep silent in the churches." That surely is direct and specific enough for all needs. He then adds explanatorily: "For it is not permitted to them to speak." "It is not permitted" is an appeal to a general law, valid apart from Paul's personal command, and looks back to the opening phrase – "as in all the churches of the saints." He is only requiring the Corinthian women to conform to the general law of the churches. And that is the meaning of the almost bitter words that he adds in verse 36, in which – reproaching them for the innovation of permitting women to speak in the churches – he reminds them that they are not the authors of the Gospel, nor are they its sole possessors: Let them keep to the law that binds the whole body of churches and not be seeking some newfangled way of their own.

The intermediate verses only make it plain that precisely what the apostle is doing is forbidding women to speak at all in the church. His injunction of silence he pushes so far that he forbids them even to ask questions; and adds with special reference to that, but through that to the general matter, the crisp declaration that "it is indecent" – for that is the meaning of the word – "for a woman to speak in church."

It would be impossible for the apostle to speak more directly or more emphatically than he has done here. He requires women to be silent at the church meetings; for that is what "in the churches" means; there were no church buildings then. And he has not left us in doubt as to the nature of these church meetings. He had just described them in verses 26ff. They were of the general character of our prayer meetings. Note the words "let him be silent in the church" in verse 30, and compare them with "let them be silent in the churches" in verse 34. The prohibition of women speaking covers thus all public church meetings – it is the publicity, not the formality of it, which is the point. And he tells us repeatedly that this is the universal law of the church. He does more than that. He tells us that it is the commandment of the Lord, and emphasizes the word "Lord" (verse 37).

The passage in *1 Timothy* 2:11ff. is just as strong, although it is more particularly directed to the specific case of public teaching or ruling in the church. The apostle had already in this context (verse 8, "the men," in contrast with "women" of verse 9) pointedly confined public praying to men, and now continues: "Let a woman learn in silence in all subjection; but I do not permit the woman to teach, neither to rule over the man, but to be in silence." Neither the teaching nor the ruling function is permitted to woman. The apostle says here, "I do not permit," instead of as in *1 Corinthians* 14:33ff., "it is not permitted," because he is here giving his personal instructions to Timothy, his subordinate, while there he was announcing to the Corinthians the general law of the church. What he instructs Timothy, however, is the general law of the church. And so he goes on and grounds his prohibition in a universal reason that affects the entire race equally.

In the face of these two absolutely plain and emphatic passages, what is said in *1 Corinthians* 11:5 cannot be appealed to in mitigation or modification. Precisely what is meant in *1 Corinthians* 11:5, nobody quite knows. What is said there is that every woman praying or prophesying unveiled dishonors her head. It seems fair to infer that if she prays or prophesies veiled she does not dishonor her head.[2] And it seems fair still further to infer that she may properly pray or prophesy if only she does it veiled.[3] We are piling up a chain of inferences. And they have not carried us very far. We cannot infer that it would be proper for her to pray or prophesy *in church* if only she were veiled. There is nothing said about church in the passage or in the context. The word "church" does not occur until the 16th verse, and then not as ruling the reference of the passage, but only as supplying support for the injunction of the passage. There is no reason whatever for believing that "praying and prophesying" in church is meant. Neither was an exercise confined to the church. If, as in *1*

2. Warfield seems to nod here, for this inference is a logical fallacy. If *a*, then *b* does not imply if not *a* then not *b*. – *Editor.*

3. This also is an invalid inference.

Corinthians 14:14, the "praying" spoken of was an ecstatic exercise – as its place by "prophesying" may suggest – then there would be the divine inspiration superceding all ordinary laws to be reckoned with. And there has already been occasion to observe that prayer in public is forbidden to women in 1 *Timothy* 2:8-9 – unless mere *attendance* at prayer is meant, in which case this passage is a close parallel of 1 *Timothy* 2:9.

What must be noted in conclusion is:

(1) That the prohibition of speaking in the church to women is precise, absolute, and all-inclusive. They are to keep silent in the churches – and that means in all the public meetings for worship; they are not even to ask questions;

(2) that this prohibition is given especial point precisely for the two matters of teaching and ruling covering specifically the functions of preaching and ruling elders;

(3) that the grounds on which the prohibition is put are universal and turn on the difference in sex, and particularly on the relative places given to the sexes in creation and in the fundamental history of the race (the fall).

Perhaps it ought to be added in elucidation of the last point just made that the difference in conclusions between Paul and the feminist movement of today [1919] is rooted in a fundamental difference in their points of view relative to the constitution of the human race. To Paul, the human race is made up of families, and every social organism – the church included – is composed of families, united together by this or that bond. The relation of the sexes in the family follows it therefore into the church. To the feminist movement the human race is made up of individuals; a woman is just another individual by the side of the man, and it can see no reason for any differences in dealing with the two. And, indeed, if we can ignore the great fundamental natural difference of sex and destroy the great fundamental social unit of the family in the interest of individualism, there does not seem any reason why we should not wipe out the differences established by Paul between the sexes in the church – except, of course, the authority of Paul. It all, in the end, comes back to the authority of the apostles, as founders of the church. We may like what Paul says, or we may not like it. We may be willing to do what he commands, or we may not be willing to do it. But there is no room for doubt of what he says. And he certainly would say to us what he said to the Corinthians: "What? Was it from you that the

Word of God went forth? Or came it to you alone?" Is this Christianity ours – to do with as we like? Or is it God's religion, receiving its laws from him through the apostles?

13

The Ordination of Women[1]

Gordon H. Clark

THE 154th SYNOD of the Reformed Presbyterian Church, Evangelical Synod (RPCES) (May 1976) received and included in its minutes the *Report* of a Study Committee on the Role of Women in the Church. The *Report* recommended the ordination of women as deacons. The matter at hand is not a matter of deaconesses. For years the Presbyterian Church in the U.S.A. (now the U.P.C.U.S.A., United Presbyterian Church in the U.S.A.) and the Reformed Church of America cooperated in supporting a Deaconess School in Philadelphia, and its graduates served in those denominations. The matter now at hand, however, is not to acknowledge Presbyterian practice, but the quite different and novel proposal to ordain women as deacons.

Although the Study Committee does not advocate the ordination of women as elders, it advocates the ordination of women. Because of our contemporary situation, most recently the actions of the Episcopal Church, it is unrealistic to think that a church that begins with ordaining women as deacons can long deny them ordination as elders. This paper will indeed consider the office of deacon, but the underlying question is the ordination of women, as the title of this paper indicates.

Since this is a modern proposal, the burden of proof falls on the innovators. A short note on history will clarify this point. *Hebrews* 5:1-4 show that the Jewish high priests were ordained: They were all men. A companion paper on "The Presbyterian Doctrine of Ordination" will also mention the ordination, usually by anointing with oil, of lesser Old Testament officials. The Jewish restriction of such ordination to

1. This essay is reprinted from Gordon H. Clark, *The Pastoral Epistles*, published by The Trinity Foundation, [1983] 1998.

men has only recently been questioned by liberal Judaism. The Roman Catholic Church ordains men only. One of the arguments of the high churchmen in the Episcopal Church, relative to its alteration of its government this year, was that the ordination of women would hinder ecumenical reunion with Rome. The Protestant Reformation, for all its opposition to Romanism, never questioned the practice of ordaining men only. Now, if this practice has continued from the time of Abraham down to 1960 or thereabouts, those who are innovators surely must bear the burden of proof. The *Westminster Confession* indeed says, "All Synods...may err, and many have erred." Therefore it is theoretically possible that the Reformed Presbyterian Church is in error. But when the agreement is worldwide over 4,000 years, it is, I repeat, extremely improbable.

Therefore a mountainous burden of proof rests on those who advocate the ordination of women. Suppositions of possible meanings of *gunaikas,* for example, even if "likely," are not enough. What the denomination needs, before it can have the authority to discard the historical concept of ordination, is compelling proof.

The present paper, in contrast with the *Report,* maintains that Scripture requires the historical Presbyterian procedure. In conformity with the third ordination vow of the Reformed Presbyterian Church, Evangelical Synod, our ministers "accept the Presbyterian form of Church Government as derived from the Holy Scriptures" *(Form of Government* V, 1). Therefore, the conclusion here will be that Scripture definitely forbids the ordination of women.

To this end it would be possible to examine the *Report* paragraph by paragraph. But there may be a more orderly way. Of course, the readers of this paper should have the *Report* before them; and references to it will be frequent enough. But the outline, after these introductory lines, will be:

I. The Question at Issue
II. The Basis of the Debate
III. Peripheral Material
IV. The Main Passages.

I. The Question at Issue

As the introductory remarks have already said, and as the *Report* makes clear, the issue is not that of unordained deaconesses. The issue is the ordination of women as deacons. Now, whether such is permissible depends on the doctrine of ordination. Is the Reformed Presbyterian doctrine of ordination Scriptural, or is it not and should it therefore be changed?

It is strange that the *Report,* lengthy as it is, pays so little attention to the doctrine of ordination. Since the ordination of women depends on some view of ordination – a view in conflict with Reformed principles – the *Report* should have included a massive defense of its underlying premise. This it did not do.

Section F (132) is about the most the *Report* has to say. It begins with a statement relative to the official position of the Reformed Presbyterian Church, Evangelical Synod. However, it does not state that position correctly; and insofar as the *Report's* conclusions depend on this inaccuracy, they are to be rejected. The *Report's* statement is: "This denomination...has seen one of the distinctive elements of the elder's role *as distinguished from that of deacon* to be the possession of ecclesiastically binding authority." This statement contradicts the *Form of Government.* Since the immediate aim of the *Report* is to defend the *ordination of women as deacons,* three subject-matters need attention. Ordination is the inclusive one. It is the question at issue. The subordinate points are *deacons* and *women.* What does the *Form of Government,* in its authoritative definition of Reformed Presbyterian policy, say on these two points?

To quote, the *Form of Government,* V, 5 says, "The formal steps by which a young man becomes an ordained minister...." It does not say "a young person," and it does not say "a young man or woman." Since even a few years ago, no one advocated the ordination of women, this reference to a man rather than a woman was neither emphasized nor repeated. At V, 8, the *Form of Government* simply says, "The qualifications of both teaching elders and ruling elders...." "Laymen, ordained to the eldership" is another phrase. It is also said that these elders have "a certain ruling or governing authority." The section on deacons is not so explicit. Had women been envisioned as possible candidates it would have had to be explicit. The *Report* takes the position that Scripture allows the ordination of women as deacons but prohibits their ordination as elders. If this were the Reformed Presbyterian position, the *Form of Government* would have had to state the difference explicitly, clearly, and emphatically. It does not do so. What is explicitly said is,

"The minister shall then propound to the elder- or *deacon*-elect the following questions: See Section 3 of this chapter."

Thus, pastors, elders, and deacons all take the same vows, with the one exception that pastors assent to question 8; while other ministers – not pastors, elders, and deacons – assent to question 9. None of these nine vows explicitly mentions authority to teach. But if this authority is assumed for an elder, it is also assumed for a deacon, because ruling elders, deacons, and non-pastoral ministers are treated as a single class. Then further, in V, 9, c, upon the ordination of a deacon, the minister says, "We give you the right hand of fellowship to *take part of this office with us.*" Note that this is not an ordination of deacons-elect by previously ordained deacons, with the idea that elders are ordained by elders. Such might indeed greatly distinguish elders from deacons. It is the *minister* who says to the deacon-elect, "We *give you* the right hand of fellowship to *take part of this office with us.*"

But the clinching formula is that which the *Form of Government* imposes on the congregation: "Do you, the members of this church, acknowledge and receive this *brother* as a ruling elder (or *deacon*) and do you promise to yield him all that honor, encouragement, and *obedience* in the Lord to which...the Constitution of this Church *entitles* him?"

At this point it seems proper to conclude that the *Report* bases its thesis on a mistaken view of Reformed Presbyterian government. The Reformed Presbyterian Church, Evangelical Synod does not distinguish between an elder and a deacon by the latter's lack of ecclesiastical authority. On the contrary, it explicitly asserts this authority. The application to women – in the light of Scripture yet to be discussed – is automatic. Ignoring our constitution the *Report* continues, "If this distinction is maintained, there need be no question of setting women in authority over men by ordaining them as deacons." But if this unconstitutional distinction were maintained, there would be no need or reason to *ordain* either men or women deacons. Ordination is induction into an authoritative order. This now returns the discussion from the ordination of *women as deacons* to the fundamental question of *ordination*.

There are several views as to the nature of ordination. The one acknowledged by the largest group of people is that of Romanism. At the Reformation, Luther clearly, Calvin more clearly, and a great section of the European populace perceived that the elaborate Roman hierarchy with its awesome claims contrasted sharply with the simplicity of the church as the apostles had organized it. The Romish claims depended largely, perhaps almost entirely, on the premise that ordination confers a special rank of *priesthood* for the purpose of repeating Christ's sacrifice in the mass. In their opposition to the mass, all the Reformers abominated the papal hierarchy and vigorously defended the equal priesthood of all believers. Yet they did not for that reason abolish the ordained ministry.

There were some who did. The radical Anabaptists denounced all church government and civil government, too. Later, and continuing to the present, the Quakers and Plymouth Brethren rejected an official ministry. Even more recently, in opposition to organized religion, some groups would shut down the seminaries, close the church doors, sell the real estate, and – unlike the anarchism of the Anabaptists – spend the proceeds to establish socialism.

Since the *Report* does not discuss these movements, since indeed it makes no effort to explain its new view of ordination, it is not possible to be sure of what direction this movement in our denomination may later take. It is clear, however, that the modern temper among religious people is rather inimical to "organized religion" and favors some form of pietism rather than the Presbyterian position.

Neither Luther nor Calvin accepted this left-wing position. Calvin (*Institutes*, IV, iii, 2) says, "By the ministers to whom [Christ] has committed this office, and given grace to discharge it, he disperses and distributes his grace to the church.... Whosoever therefore studies to abolish this *order* and kind of government,... or disparages it as a minor importance, plots the devastation, or rather the ruin and destruction of the churches." These words show how highly Calvin esteemed ministerial order. That this includes the deacons also a later paragraph (IV, iii) makes clear: "The qualifications of...bishops are stated at large by Paul in two passages.... The same rule is laid down for the deacons and governors."

There are other historical documents. The *French Confession* of 1559 says, "We detest all fantastic people who greatly desire ... to abolish the ministry" (Art. xxv).

The *Second Book of Discipline of the Scottish Kirk* says, "There are four ordinary functions or offices in the Kirk of God, the office of pastor, minister, or bishop; the doctor; the presbyter or elder; and the deacon." In Reformation days the main object was to reject the papal theory of hierarchy, and to insist on the priesthood of all believers. Our Scottish forebears also refused to acknowledge the Anglican ordination of deacons because this was part of the hierarchical scheme. But they ordained deacons, and they had strict views of the significance of ordination. They rejected the "indelible character" imposed by ordination as the Romanists understood it, but they did not object to an "indelible character," a life-long authority, as they themselves defined it.

It is strange, and perhaps one may be so bold as to say significant, that the *Report* in advocating the ordination of women has so little to say about ordination. Since the *Report,* in order to allow women to be ordained as deacons, excludes from ordination the conferring of authority, no one can be sure what theory of ordination the *Report* wishes to introduce into our denomination. One can be sure, however, that its view of ordination is destructive of Presbyterian polity.

During the Reformation, the controversy centered chiefly on the ministry, less on the elders, and least on deacons. Yet the Reformers did not pass over the latter in complete silence. Luther in his *Address to the Nobility,* June 1520, said, "He [the minister] should have as assistants several priests [the term *priest* continued to be used for a time] and *deacons* who should help him to *govern* the people and congregations with sermons and the administration of the sacraments." The *French Confession* of 1559 (previously alluded to) also says, "It [the true church] ought to be governed according to the policy which our Savior Jesus Christ has established, that is, that there be pastors, supervisors, and deacons." Note that deacons form a part of the governing body. The *Genevan Ordinances* of 1541 state something similar: "...let the minister distribute the bread in good order and with reverence; and let no others give the cup except the ones appointed or the *deacons* with the ministers." The *Ordinances* of 1576 make the same statement about the deacons. Again, what Calvin says about women who perform baptism is surely applicable to women who might act as deacons. In his *Tracts* he says, "Even in the minutest matters, as meat and drink, whatever we attempt and dare with a doubtful conscience, Paul plainly denounces as sin. Now, in baptism by women, what certainty can there be, while a rule delivered by Christ is violated? For that office of the Gospel which he assigned to ministers, women seize for themselves." Further, Calvin's reply to the Synod of Lyons in 1563 (compare Quick, *Synodicon* I, 53) says, "*Deacons* and elders, being the arms and hands of the Pastor...may also distribute [the bread and cup] to those who are remote from [the pastor]."

In these passages the mention of deacons is noteworthy because there was a widespread disinclination to allow deacons and even elders to assist in the communion service. Calvin obviously regards deacons as having authority by virtue of their ordination. They are no doubt sub ordinate to the minister. Ordination confers on the minister the authority to preach the Word, and since the sacraments require the Word, ordination confers the authority to administer the sacraments, and also, in conjunction with other ordained men, the authority of the keys. But though the deacons are subordinate to the minister, they participate in that authority. The ordination questions are the same; the minister receives the deacon as taking "part of this office with us"; and the congregation promises obedience to the deacon.

II. The Basis of the Debate

The issue has now been clearly stated. It is the Reformed doctrine of ordination. This doctrine is not the prelatic and hierarchical theory of Rome, nor is it the anarchical chaos of the Anabaptists. But which of the three views is correct? Obviously the Reformed Presbyterian Church forbids the ordination of women. Since, however, "All Synods and councils since the apostles' time...may err, and many have erred," it is theoretically possible that Reformed Presbyterian government is in error. But it is highly unlikely that Presbyterianism is in error on this particular point. The believing Jews before the coming of Christ, as well as the unbelieving Jews afterward, had no women as priests. Neither does Romanism. Neither does Lutheranism. Among these groups there are differences regarding the nature of ordination, its validity, its authority, and more, but all agree that it is wrong to ordain women. Now, where Rabbis Eliezer and Agiba; Popes Leo and Gregory; and Luther, Calvin, and Knox agree on a particular point, it requires overwhelming argument to prove them wrong. On what basis could anyone construct such an argument? There is only one such basis, the Bible.

The Report, be it not only cheerfully but also gratefully acknowledged, appeals to Scripture alone. Were it otherwise they and we would have no common basis of argument. However much the present paper regards the Report's exegesis poor and its argument invalid, the Report is to be highly commended for its repeated rejection of the idea that parts of Scripture are not binding today because they were culturally conditioned. Since this rejection is not the contemporary stance of the religious community, a short paragraph or two stressing the contrast is pertinent.

Dr. Paul King Jewett is a particularly good example, for he has recently argued for the ordination of women. He has no trouble with the Scriptural material; he even agrees substantially that the view defended in this paper is Scriptural; but he simply rejects the Apostle Paul's mistakes as culturally conditioned. The seminary, too, in which Dr. Jewett teaches, is also a good example. Several of its members have publicly engaged in controversy against Scriptural inerrancy. The more conservative faculty members resigned and left the seminary some years ago, yet the seminary claims to be evangelical. They should call themselves modernists, for their position is very much the same as that of the modernists early in this century. Their tactics are also similar, for in debasing the language so as to empty the term *evangelical* of its historic meaning, they repeat the earlier modernists' debasing of the term "the *divinity* of Christ" to accommodate Homer and Shakespeare, if not the divine Sarah. This pervasive influence of liberalism is most clearly seen in the large apostate denominations. In them a minister can be ejected or a candidate can be refused ordination because he disapproves of women's ordination. But liberalism's influence can also be seen, though it may be in modified form, in more conservative churches. Even in our church we must regard it as shortsighted to discuss an issue such as ordination without taking into consideration the conditions that press upon us from every side. Since liberal ideas pervade the entire religious community, Reformed Presbyterians will do well to combat them even in their incipient forms. Too many seminaries and denominations slip into apostasy almost imperceptibly. Let not the heirs of Covenanters meet this fate.

One recent, small, but encouraging sign on the horizon was the 135 to 74 vote against women's ordination in the 1976 General Synod of the Associate Reformed Presbyterian Church. They even voted down a motion to distribute the advocates' *Report* to the session "for prayerful consideration."

The successful introduction of the ordination of women into modern churches is one with the general outlook of women's liberation. Apart from the excesses of left-wing philosophy, the permissiveness of parents and society, and the stress on women's alleged rights even to permitting a teenage girl to get an abortion in defiance of her parents – apart from this sort of thing, it is doubtful that anyone would have agitated for the ordination of women. The mention of Women's Lib and the exceeding great immorality of our times is not intended to cast aspersions on the authors of the *Report*. No one accuses them of sitting enthralled at the feet of Bella Abzug. On the contrary, the procedure of the *Report* explicitly and throughout appeals to Scripture. In this it differs completely from the usual procedures. Is there any instance, in any denomination, of this sort of agitation on strictly Scriptural grounds? The present *Report* seems unique. For its reliance on Scripture, we are grateful. Nevertheless the present sociological propensities tend to produce a more favorable reception of this proposal than the Scriptures warrant. With the *Report's* explicit basis, this paper fully agrees and urges all readers to consult the Scripture alone.

III. Peripheral Material

Some Scriptural material, however, bears on the main topic only to a small degree. Other passages relate more directly, and a few may be decisive. The first class cannot be completely omitted, for the *Report* contains a considerable amount of it, but perhaps in this reply brevity will be acceptable.

One such peripheral point is the matter of women praying in the public church service. The *Report* discusses this at some length. The reason is clear. If Paul has actually forbidden women to pray in public, he certainly would not have permitted them to be ordained. Hence the *Report* must combat this interpretation. On the other hand, if Paul permitted women to pray in public, it by no means follows that he would have ordained them.

This point of logic is sufficient to show the futility of several pages of the *Report*. However, a word in favor of the more obvious interpretation will count against ordination. The verses read, "Let your women keep silence in the churches, for it is not permitted unto them to speak.... It is a shame for women to speak in church" (1 *Corinthians* 14:34-35). The *Report* (116) notes an "apparent conflict" between the prayer of women in chapter 11 and their silencing in chapter 14.

Can ordination solve this apparent conflict? Is it not possible, and much easier, to use another method? Since the later *Corinthian* reference commands silence, and hence rules out ordination, the only problem is that of contradiction. On this point two things may be said. First, as the *Report* itself acknowledges, the prayers of women that Paul permits may have taken place in informal prayer meetings. Or, what the *Report* does not consider, the prayers may have been made in women's own homes. Of course, as the *Report* says at the bottom of page 115, "These texts clearly presume that women did pray and prophesy." But the point at issue is where and when? The text does not say "in the church." Therefore, these words should not be inserted. Then when another text says explicitly, Let women keep silence in the church, it follows that 1 *Corinthians* 11 *cannot* mean "in the church." It must refer to some informal gatherings, such as one of our women's missionary societies. The *Report* acknowledges that this solves the problem of alleged contradiction. But it rejects the solution because "it is doubtful that the case can be sustained exegetically"(116).

Doubtful? Not very. The clarity of chapter 14 and the absence from chapter 11 of the words "in the church," seem to be exegetically sufficient. Furthermore, so far as the main question of ordination goes, it is not necessary to sustain this interpretation exegetically. The immediate point is the solution of an apparent contradiction, and even the *Report* agrees that the interpretation given here is satisfactory. On the other hand, the *Report's* interpretation cannot be sustained exegetically. How can one extract from the verse the words that are not there? Yet the *Report* should provide exegetical certainty because it bears the burden of proof.

But that there were – actually and historically – occasions of prayer and prophecy other than the regular church service, and that therefore the present interpretation does not depend on unsupported assumptions, is clear, if not from *Acts* 11:28, at least from *Acts* 21:9-11. What Agabus did hardly fits into a worship service; and exegesis cannot deny that Philip's daughters prophesied, like Agabus, when no church service was in progress.

The result of this analysis is (1) that pages 115-117 of the *Report* hardly bear on the question at all; (2) that the solution rejected on page 116 remains satisfactory; and (3) that the *Report's* "Conclusion: 1 *Corinthians* 11:5 probably refers to public worship services" is not more than *probable,* and probably less compelling than what the *Report* rejects as a "weak possibility." It must be insisted that the advocates of women's ordination, not those who defend the official Reformed Presbyterian principles, must produce the "compelling external evidence." The burden of proof rests on the innovators, not on those who maintain the actual standards.

Another peripheral matter concerns Paul's stylistic abilities. In order to substitute its interpretation for the more obvious one, the *Report* argues in several places that there cannot be a "violent break" in subject matter between the two verses in question. There must be a smooth transition. Now, admittedly, most verses connect logically with their preceding and succeeding verses. Otherwise there could be no continuous discussion. Nonetheless, paragraph breaks occur; and sometimes there are two or more sudden shifts within a very few lines.

A major example is the well-known passage, *Romans* 5:12-19. There, the passage has a single theme, but Paul mixes together many strands of a complex subject. There are parentheses within parentheses, and the sentence becomes so complicated that Paul breaks it off and begins over again in verse 18.

Active minds, like Paul's, are apt to write intricate sentences, including parenthetical remarks. And they jump back and forwards as their thoughts come in profusion. Note therefore another example: *1 Timothy* 5:17ff., an epistle if not a chapter that occupies many pages in the *Report*. After discussing the plight of widows in the first half of the chapter, Paul turns to the Old Testament admonition that congregations should support their pastors; then come directions concerning judicial cases; then a warning against ordaining young men, or newly converted Christians; then some medicinal advice to Timothy. Finally, two verses – which do not connect with the medicinal advice – are vague enough to make any connection uncertain. In view of such examples as these, and there are others, this paper will not relinquish its interpretation when the argument for its alternate depends so heavily on the assumption that Paul must write as smoothly as the *Report* expects. In fact the *Report* itself (83) has to adjust itself to an "abrupt transition."

The Question of Phoebe

Under the rubric of "Peripheral Matters" there are distinctions in degree. A not-so-peripheral matter is the use of the term *deacon* in the New Testament.

If the New Testament contained even a single instance of the election and apostolic ordination of a woman as a deacon, the fact would be conclusive. Without an example, however, the argument can never be conclusive. The best that can be done is to refer to *Romans* 16:1, where Phoebe is called *diakonon,* and from this infer that the church members had elected her and that the apostles thereupon ordained her.

Such an inference is invalid. Note that in *Acts* 6:1 there was a daily *diakonia* before "deacons" were elected and ordained. The word originally was not the name of an ordained officer, but designated anyone who served the needs of others. In *John* 2:5, 9 it refers to those who were serving the marriage banquet. Compare *Matthew* 22:13. In *John* 12:26 it refers to any faithful servant of Christ. Thence the term can be applied to Phoebe, or to any other Christian, without implying ordination. In fact, so far as the term itself goes, it even refers to servants of Satan (2 *Corinthians* 11:15).

In 1 *Timothy* 4:6, Timothy is called a servant, a *diakonos;* though he was an elder or bishop and not a "deacon." So too the apostles themselves are called servants: *Acts* 6:2 says that the apostles had been serving *(diakonein)* tables, but henceforth they must drop this task and give themselves to the ministry of the Word *(diakoinia toulogou).* When it is noted that the seven chosen were not called "deacons" in this passage, and that the verb *diakonein* applies to the apostles, must we conclude that Phoebe was an apostle?

Quite the contrary; the term *diakonos* was a name given to any servant. Its application to Phoebe in *Romans* 16:1 carries no implication of ordination.

The *Report* tries to dispose of this contention on page 134:

> Because the word *diakonos* can be translated either "deacon" or "servant" it is important to note that Paul did *not choose to use the feminine form of the word but rather broke gender to identify Phoebe with the masculine form of the noun* [italics in *Report*]. This very strongly suggests that he was not simply calling her a servant...but was rather using a formal term identifying her as a deacon.

But where in Greek literature does such a feminine form of the word occur? Neither *Liddell and Scott* nor *Arndt and Gingrich* lists any feminine form. On the contrary, they both cite passages in which the masculine form applies to women.

With respect to the masculine and feminine forms of Greek nouns, another point deserves mention. The *Report* is unique in that it recommends women for deacons but forbids their ordination as elders. Proposals and their adoption in other denominations include and indeed stress ordination as ministers. This is because these other denominations have little regard for Scripture, while the *Report* desires to follow the Bible. The *Report* has no inclination to argue that the Bible allows women to be ordained as pastors. Nevertheless, one can wonder whether or not the ordination of women as pastors can be prevented once the momentum has begun in their ordination as deacons. Indeed it is possible to guess a part of the future argument. It will be pointed out that if we now ordain women as deacons, although there is no such form as *diakone* in the New Testament (or elsewhere?), we ought all the more to ordain woman as pastors because 1 *Timothy* 5:1, 2 explicitly mentioned *presbuterai* (women elders) as well as *presbuteroi* (men elders).

The words *diakonos* and *presbuteros* are not the only examples of words used colloquially, which we almost without exception use technically. The word *church (ecclesia)* is another example. In *Acts* 2:47 the Lord added converts to the "church" daily; and the context shows what church was meant. But the tumultuous assembly of heathen in Ephesus is thrice called the *ecclesia* (*Acts* 19:32, 39, 40). Hence the term *diakonos,* applied to Phoebe, is no evidence that she was ordained.

But it is said that Phoebe was not merely a servant of the Lord, she was also a *prostatis* of many. The argument is that *prostates* (masculine) and therefore *prostatis* (feminine) meant ruler, authority, defender, guardian, presiding officer, patron, etc. Thus Phoebe was a regularly ordained officer with authority over many people.

Unfortunately the masculine form does not occur in the New Testament and the feminine form only this once. The verb, however, occurs about seven times and certainly indicates authority and command. To those who advocate the ordination of women, this one word seems to be strong evidence, and perhaps conclusive. But surely one ought to have more than a *hapax legomenon* to overturn thousands of years of ecclesiastical procedure. Nor is this all that can be said. For the verse itself says that Phoebe was a *prostatis* to Paul himself. Thus Paul must have been an inferior member of the order over which Phoebe was president and ruler. Contrary to these unacceptable inferences, this paper concludes that Phoebe was a faithful servant who had been of great help to many people and to Paul himself, as Peter's mother-in-law served *(diakonei)* Christ in *Matthew* 8:15.

This section on peripheral material has now canvassed the topic of women praying in church, Paul's stylistic peculiarities, and the usage of the term *deacon*. But as the discussion now continues, the material bears more and more directly on the main issue.

IV. The Main Passages

1 *Timothy* 2 is surely one of major importance. Upon first reading it seems definitely to rule out the ordination of women. Indeed a second and a third reading confirm this impression. In fact the chapter goes further than forbidding such ordinations: It even forbids women to pray in the public services.

Against this clear statement the *Report* struggles at some length (79-90). It first notes that the subject of the chapter is "prayer in the church." This of course is true, but it can lead to a misunderstanding. Chapter 2 is a subdivision of the epistle as a whole, the subject of which is broader than prayer. 1 *Timothy* covers the general subject of worship, and hence Paul can pass from prayer to other phases of worship. By narrowing the subject to prayer, the *Report* wishes to avoid an alleged violent break supposedly required by the usual interpretation. The *Report* is extremely detailed and should be consulted. It would be unreasonably burdensome here to examine every line. But in general the *Report* argues that on the usual interpretation, there would be an impossible break "because it does not actually present Paul's intended contrasts but treats v. 8 (men praying with holy hands) as if it stood next to vv. 11*ff*...."(80). The *Report's* argument seems to depend on the assumption that Paul could not have considered, in the same verse, two related subjects – here, in fact, one main subject and a subordinate part.

The argument of the *Report* is defective at several points. Paragraph (1) on page 80 says, "If the intended comparison is the sex roles, the comment on holy hands...seriously obscures Paul's central but *unspoken* point that women should not pray." To this, one can reply that there is not just one "central" point in the passage, unless it be the general topic of orderly worship. Many verses in Scripture contain several distinguishable points. Here, in addition to *holy hands and modest apparel,* the "sex roles" can hardly escape notice. Far from being "unspoken," as the *Report* strangely repeats three times over, verse 12 says, "she must be silent." This silence is consonant with the progression of thought in verses 8 and 9. Men are to pray (in the church), women are to dress modestly, and learn in silence and subjection. Verse 10, not verse 9, may be a parenthetical aside, for such are not absent from Paul's style, but there is no violent break or "parenthetical aside which seriously obscures Paul's central...point."

The *Report* makes much of the word *hosautos* in verse nine. The *Report* admits that it would be wrong to translate the verse as, "Similarly also I want the women to pray"(80). This is a welcome admission, but the *Report* apparently fails to see how it undercuts its own contentions. First, it must be insisted upon that the prohibition of public prayer of women is not "unspoken." The *Report* at least three times asserts that it is unspoken, and upon this erroneous assertion builds part of its argument. Second, *hosautos kai* admittedly draws some kind of parallel. But the *Report* has already admitted that the parallel is not, I want men to pray...I also want women to pray. For this reason the parallel can as little be, I want men to pray with holy hands and I want women to pray in modest dress. And for this reason the argument of pages 80-82 ought to be adjudged a failure.

Someone now is sure to ask, But then what is the parallel? This is a legitimate question, but it is permissible to decide that the *Report's* view is impossible without being able to answer this question. The *Report's* view is impossible because of the *spoken* (written) command of silence. However, a plausible answer to the question is at hand, and the *Report* itself vaguely hints at it (page 82, last paragraph of the section). Briefly it is this: Paul's ideas came to him in profusion; the general subject here is public worship and not prayer alone; therefore, one may accept the words, if not the intention, of the *Report* (page 82 end), "a continuation of Paul's discussion of prayer...understood as discussing...worship." If so, Paul has said, "Men are to worship by lifting holy hands in prayer, *likewise also* women are to worship by dressing modestly and remaining silent."

Such is the conclusion proposed here. But a further point is that the wording of the *Report* is most misleading when it says, "we must question whether it is at all a tenable inference that women were silent at all times in the Pauline assemblies" (page 82). Of course it is not a tenable inference. The inference is exactly the opposite: Women were not always silent in the Pauline assemblies; that is why Paul wrote to correct the disorder. A similar peculiarity occurs on the next page also: "Why did the problems of prayer, prophecy, and teaching arise, if he never permitted women to speak in the churches?" (page 83, last line). One might as well ask about 1 *Corinthians* 7, Why did the problem of incest arise, if Paul had never permitted incest in his churches?

Since the remainder of Part I (pages 84-90) is interesting, instructive, and substantially acceptable – in fact, since this material agrees more with the Reformed Presbyterian position and less with the *Report's* conclusions; and again since its firm rejection of "cultural limitations" is so gratifying – it may not be altogether improper to skip to pages 132*ff*. on 1 *Timothy* 3:8-13. That the *Report* on this page does not accurately state the Reformed Presbyterian position has already been made clear. But the "exegetical debate over 1 *Timothy* 3:11," on which "hangs the demonstration of biblical warrant" for the ordination of women, "centers on the meaning of the word *gunaikas*." Therefore, the *Report* must *demonstrate,* by strictly valid implication – or as the *Confession* says, "by good and *necessary* consequence" – that *gunaikas* must mean "women deacons," and cannot possibly mean wives of deacons or elders.

Far from being a necessary deduction, the *Report's* argument is deficient both in premises and procedure. Note its starting point on page 133: "We may *confidently* dismiss [the view that *gunaikas* means either women in general or it means wives of elders and deacons]." This confidence, however, is based on the assertion that "it would not be *probable* that Paul would break his train of thought." But, first, probability is not demonstration. Second, we have already seen how frequently Paul "breaks his train of thought." And third, he does not really break his train of thought, though he may put a coach or dining car between two Pullmans. Hence the *Report's* "probable" and "unlikely" (page 133) have no force in proving its conclusion.

It is here true that if Paul had inserted a *tas* (article) or an *auton* (pronoun), there could have been no doubt as to the translation *wives.* But then Paul frequently enough omits the article where English requires it. The *Report* asserts that the *King James* translation "gratuitously" supplies the word *their.* But if neither Paul nor the congregation had any idea of ordaining women, the article or pronoun was unnecessary. The *Report's* argument tends to circularity: *Their* is gratuitous because Paul meant women deacons; and he meant women deacons because *gunaikas* does not mean wives; and *gunaikas* does not mean wives because the *King James their* is gratuitous. Hence Paul approved the ordination of women.

The *Report* next reverts to what is "unlikely": "It is unlikely that he would carefully comment on deacons' wives and neglect those of the elders." But this, too, is rather circular. How does the *Report* prove that Paul neglected to speak of elders' wives, if he actually spoke of deacons' wives? Only on the ground stated above that "it would not be *probable* that Paul would break his train of thought concerning deacons." On the contrary, it is quite possible – and by the text quite probable that – after Paul had spoken of elders (3:1) and deacons (3:8), he inserted a parenthetical remark (3:11) concerning their wives, elders' wives as well as deacons' wives.

The *Report* takes notice of this latter interpretation, but it claims that its own view is "more likely." Now aside from the fact that the present article does not think the *Report's* interpretation is more likely – in fact considers it less likely and even quite improbable – one must insist that the *Report's* conclusion requires necessary consequence and valid argument. A doubtful likelihood about a single verse is not sufficient to overturn the Presbyterian view of ordination.

The *Report* continues with an argument about Phoebe, but this was disposed of a few pages ago. Phoebe was never "Madame President" (page 134) to Paul.

This is the end of the *Report's* argument. "Conclusions and Recommendations" follow. This is also the end of this paper's argument. Its conclusion can easily be anticipated. Using the wording of the *Report* (*Diakonate,* page 135), but contradicting its sense by switching positives and negatives, the conclusion is: "The office of deacon is an office which involves the exercise of ecclesiastical authority. In the Pauline churches it was closed to women. It therefore must be closed to women in our churches."

And furthermore – with the pope, John Knox, the Scottish Kirk, and all Christendom – we believe that the position of the Reformed Presbyterian Church in refusing to ordain women is solidly Biblical, against which likelihoods have no logical force.

Subsequent to the circulation of the *Report* and of this essay, the Reformed Presbyterian Church, Evangelical Synod did not adopt the *Report's* recommendation that it ordain women as deacons, but it did allow women to be appointed – but not ordained – to boards of deacons. – *Editor.*

14

The Church Effeminate

John W. Robbins

C HRISTIANITY is for women. That seems to be the consensus in the
United States, whose nominally Christian churches are filled with
women, and whose pulpits are becoming filled with women. Men – at
least masculine men – do not go to church.[1] Effeminate men do, however, go to nominally Christian churches, and in most churches the doctrines of feminism and sodomy prevail. The homosexuality – the effeminacy – which formerly was largely confined to Anglican and Roman Catholic boys' schools, seminaries, monasteries, and pulpits has
entered and is increasingly influential in mainline Protestant denominations. The Roman Church-State still receives some headlines – despite its best efforts at covering up the extent of its official sexual perversion – about priests, bishops, and cardinals who have molested children
and/or carried on homosexual affairs with each other. In the future,
those headlines will be shared by Protestants, as effeminacy grows in
the mainline churches. Rome has shown the way.

In February 1987 John Paul II, the current Emperor of Rome, declared 1988 a Marian year – a year specially devoted to Mary. The year
2000 was also a year devoted to Mary. John Paul II has frequently displayed his constant devotion to Mary, calling her the "heavenly mother
of the church" and invoking her intercession in public prayers. In his
December 1987 encyclical letter, *Sollicitudo Rei Socialis, On Social Concern*, the pope declared that

> I have called the current Marian year in order that the Catholic faith-
> ful may look more and more to Mary, who goes before us on the pil-
> grimage of faith and with maternal care intercedes for us before her

1. If they do, they go to a synagogue or a mosque.

Son, our Redeemer. I wish to entrust to her and to her intercession this difficult moment of the modern world.... [W]e present to the Blessed Virgin difficult situations, so that she may place them before her Son.... But we also present to her social situations and the international crisis itself.... In a filial spirit we wish to place all this before her "eyes of mercy," repeating once more with faith and hope the ancient antiphon: "Holy Mother of God, despise not our petitions in our necessities, but deliver us always from all dangers, O glorious and blessed Virgin. Mary most holy, our Mother and Queen...." [2]

The Roman Church-State has venerated and adored Mary for centuries, elevating the "Mother of God" to near equality with God in one of the first and most enduring movements to feminize both God and Christianity. Various popes have referred to Mary as Mediatrix, co-Redemptrix, and Queen of Heaven. It is significant that the stated cause for proclaiming another Marian year was anti-intellectualism within the Roman Church-State. According to Monsignor Diarmuid Martin of the Pontifical Commission for Justice and Peace: "The [Roman] Church has become extremely intellectual after the Second Vatican Council, and the Holy Father wants to bring back some of the traditional warmth that has gone out of fashion." Another Vatican official lamented, "Today, many people, especially the young, think that being a Catholic means to be part of an unending debate over church doctrines or the church's stand on global issues of peace and justice." The Marian year, the official said, is designed to recover the "warmth and simplicity associated with traditional religious life." [3]

The study of the feminization of the Roman Church-State is a major study in itself. It would include such things as the Latin liturgy, which refers to the Trinity as feminine: "sancta Trinitas." It would involve not only the growth of devotion to Mary and the naming and worship of female saints, but also to the growth of convents, nunneries, and religious orders. This feminization of the Roman Church-State began centuries ago. Humbert of Romans (d. 1277) Master-General of the Dominicans, wrote of women:

2. Encyclical Letter Sollicitudo Rei Socialis of the Supreme Pontiff John Paul II to the Bishops, Priests, Religious Families, Sons and Daughters of the Church, and All People of Good Will for the Twentieth Anniversary of Populorum Progressio (Boston: St. Paul Books and Media, 1988), 94-95.

3. Sam Koo, "Marian Year Called Return to Tradition," The Washington Post, February 21, 1987, G10.

Note that God gave women many prerogatives, not only over other living things, but even over man himself, and this (i) by nature; (ii) by grace; and (iii) by glory.

(i) In the world of nature she excelled man by her origin, for man he made of the vile earth, but woman he made in Paradise. Man he formed of the slime, but woman of man's rib. She was not made of a lower limb of man – as for example of his foot – lest man should esteem her his servant, but from his midmost part, that he should hold her to be his fellow, as Adam himself said, "The woman thou gavest me as my helpmate."

(ii) In the world of grace she excelled man.... We do not read of any man trying to prevent the Passion of our Lord, but we do read of a woman who tried – namely, Pilate's wife, who sought to dissuade her husband from so great a crime.... Again at his resurrection, it was to a woman that he first appeared – namely, to Mary Magdalene.

(iii) In the world of glory, for the king in that country is no mere man, but a mere woman is its queen; nor is anyone who is merely man as powerful there as a mere woman. Thus is woman's nature in Our Lady ranked. It is not a mere man who is set above the angels and all the rest of the heavenly country in worth, and dignity, and power; and this should lead woman to love God and hate evil.[4]

In effeminate medieval Romanist devotions, Jesus is referred to as Mother. In the Eucharist, Jesus nurses his children. These effeminate and sometimes pornographic devotions were adopted, toned down, and incorporated into Protestantism by the pietists and some Puritans. The importance of Christmas, in which Jesus is regarded as a baby and not a man, beginning in medieval female religious orders, to the feminization movement in both Protestant and Roman churches should not be overlooked. (Male religious orders fixated on Mary.) Most noticeably, this feminization movement proceeds in partnership with spirituality or mysticism in both Protestant churches and the Roman Church-State.

Bernard of Clairvaux, the great mystic, pope-maker, and instigator of holy wars in the twelfth century, was also a leader in the feminization movement in the Roman Church-State. He referred to himself as a woman, and urged his Cistercians to be Mothers as well. More recently, in the United States the Catholic bishops have appointed nuns

4. Quoted in Bede Jarrett, *Social Theories of the Middle Ages, 1200-1500*, 1966, 70-72.

and (divorced) laywomen to preside over parishes. In many Catholic seminaries, even today, the men give themselves the names of women.

The Reformation ended this sickly Antichristian piety, at least for a time. "The Reformation substantially purged Christianity of its feminine elements, leaving men and women alike faced with a starkly masculine religion."[5]

> The overwhelming image of both God and the believer in Luther's writings is a masculine one.... True faith is energetic, active, steadfast, mighty, industrious, powerful – all archetypally masculine qualities in the sixteenth (or the twentieth) centuries. God is Father, Son, Sovereign, King, Lord, Victor, Begetter, "the slayer of sin and the devourer of death" – all aggressive, martial, and totally male images. With the home now the center of women's religious vocation, even the imagery of the church becomes masculine, or at least paternal and fraternal.[6]

But the masculine Christianity of the Reformers has long been displaced by the effeminate Christianity of the moderns. However interesting and revealing the study of the feminization of the Roman Church-State may be, in this essay I intend to focus my attention on developments within Protestant churches. But it is instructive to note that in both churches, Protestant and Roman Catholic, the feminization of theology and the church is a consequence of mysticism and anti-intellectualism.

It is not simply the contemporary obsession with the leadership and ordination of women to which I refer; that controversy is simply the latest episode in a process of feminizing the Protestant churches that has been going on for about two centuries. The problem we face, as well as its solution, is far more serious than merely rebutting the vociferous demands for women preachers, teachers, elders, and deacons. What is needed is a thorough understanding of how far the church has fallen, and how much must be recovered before we can once again seriously speak of the church as a Christian church.

There are two aspects of the Church Effeminate that I would like to discuss: Her leadership and her theology. During the past two centuries Protestant theology has become first sentimentalized and then effemi-

5. Peter Stearns, *Be a Man! Males in Modern Society*, 1990, 39.
6. Merry Weisner, "Luther and Women: The Death of Two Marys" *Disciplines of Faith: Studies in Religion, Politics, and Patriarchy*, Obelkevich, editor, 1987, 103.

nate, and leadership in the churches has passed more and more into the hands of women and epicene men. To a large extent the two have proceeded simultaneously, but the change in theology both preceded and caused the change in personnel. Though the feminization of theology caused the feminization of the church, and is therefore more important, I shall discuss the feminization of church leadership first. I do this for two reasons: First, by displaying the effect before the cause, I hope to draw greater attention to the cause. Second, as a result of the very theological development we are discussing, people are more interested in practical affairs than in theology and philosophy; therefore, I will speak of the more interesting subject first, and hope, by that means, to lead the reader's attention to the perhaps less interesting but certainly more important material.

Three Modern Movements

During the nineteenth century, there were three major movements in American Protestant churches that began the process of feminizing their leadership. The first of these was the Sunday School movement; the second was the foreign missions movement; and the third was the deaconess movement. Before the last quarter of the eighteenth century, Sunday Schools did not exist, missionaries were men, and there was no such office as deaconess. During the nineteenth century the feminists, many of whom were not women and most of whom were moderate by today's standards, began their drive to control the churches. The drive began first with the Sunday School movement.

The Sunday School Movement

Clergymen who opposed women in the pulpit welcomed them into the newly invented Sunday School. There the women could teach children other than their own with the blessing of the churches, and, as women, they were believed to be more emotionally suited for doing so than men. Joanna Graham Bethune, a Presbyterian who has been called the "mother of Sabbath schools in America," was quite influential in the American Sunday School movement. She founded the Female Union Society for the Promotion of Sabbath Schools in 1816. In 1824 the American Sunday School Union was organized. By the end of the century there were more than 8,000 Presbyterian Sunday Schools with over one million students in the United States alone.

The Presbyterian Sunday Schools were merely a fraction of the total movement. In 1889 E. Payson Porter reported that "It would be perfectly safe to say that in the United States of America we have 10,000,000 connected with our Sunday schools. We claim in the United States, 60,000,000 of population, and this would give us about 15 percent of the population attending the Sunday schools."[7] The percentage in Great Britain, where Sunday Schools had originated in the late eighteenth century, was even higher. While the Presbyterians were only a part of the Sunday School movement, they did boast the largest Sunday School in the United States and reportedly the second largest in the world at the end of the nineteenth century and the beginning of the twentieth. John Wanamaker, the Pennsylvania retailer, was its superintendent.

The invention of the Sunday School was a major factor in feminizing the church for several reasons. Not only did the Sunday School permit women to teach in church meetings, it reinforced the idea that there were two sorts of church meetings: formal and informal, worship meetings and educational, social, or prayer meetings.[8] This convenient but unscriptural distinction between types of church meetings permitted the clergy to enforce God's prohibitions against women speaking in church meetings in "formal" or "worship" services, but not in informal, social, prayer, or educational meetings. They seemed to have forgotten that God had commanded, "as in *all* Christian assemblies, let your women keep silence in the assembly." "Church," now meaning only the "worship service," and today generally restricted to the hour between 11 a.m. and 12 noon on the Lord's Day, was distinguished from Sunday School, and the rules that applied in one did not apply in the other.[9]

---

7. E. Payson Porter, *First World Convention* (London, 1889), 76; as quoted in Gerald E. Knoff, *The World Sunday School Movement* (New York: Seabury Press, 1979), 3.

8. Like Sunday Schools, prayer meetings seem to be a recent invention. Prayer meetings in which both men and women pray aloud were not common in the Protestant churches before the nineteenth century. Before then Christians generally believed and obeyed the Biblical command that women not pray in public. Certain anabaptist groups, of course, had disobeyed that command, just as they had disobeyed other Biblical commands about order in the church meetings.

9. The Sunday School movement in the nineteenth century with its uniform lessons, superficial doctrine, national, international, and world conventions, had another major impact on the church: It fueled the ecumenical movement, leading to the organization of the Federal Council of Churches (later the National Council of Churches) in 1908.

Foreign Missions

The Sunday Schools were the first major domain of women in the churches; the foreign mission fields were second.

The Boston Female Society for Missionary Purposes was organized in October 1800. In the first half of the nineteenth century there was only one society organized on a denominational basis for missions: the women's society of the Freewill Baptist Church. It is not without significance that that church stood for "freedom of thought, freedom of the will, free grace and free communion,"[10] for the growing rejection of Calvinism during the eighteenth and nineteenth centuries is a major factor in the feminization of American theology.

Women's missionary societies became common during the middle and late nineteenth century. At first, such societies were organized only within the local congregations and only for the purpose of raising money to support the male missionaries sent by the churches. But soon the structure of the women's societies changed. They organized themselves into presbyterial, synodical, denominational, and interdenominational groups and began sending women missionaries abroad. In 1860 the first interdenominational women's missionary organization was formed, the Women's Union Missionary Society, by women from six denominations. In 1868 and 1869 the Congregationalists and the Methodists withdrew to form their own denominational organizations.

The Presbyterian noted that by the late 1870s there were fifty more Presbyterian women than men on the mission field. Although such women missionaries were supposed to perform only those functions permitted to women at home, that is, teaching women and children, in actual practice even this restriction disappeared and women became full-fledged, though unordained, missionaries. A. J. Gordon, writing in 1894 in the *Missionary Review of the World*, pointed out that

> For while it is true that many Christians believe that women are enjoined from publicly preaching the Gospel, either at home or abroad, it is certainly true that scores of missionary women are at present doing this very thing. They are telling the good news of salvation to heathen men and women publicly from house to house, to little groups gathered

10. R. Pierce Beaver, *American Protestant Women in World Mission* (Grand Rapids, Michigan: Eerdmans, 1980), 43.

by the wayside, or to larger groups assembled in the zayats [religious meeting houses]. It is not affirmed that a majority of women missionaries are engaged in this kind of work, but that scores are doing it with the approval of the board under which they are serving. If any one should raise the technical objection that because of its informal and colloquial character this is not preaching, we are ready to affirm that it comes much nearer the preaching enjoined in the great commission than does the reading of a theological disquisition from the pulpit on Sunday morning, or the discussion of some ethical or sociological question before a popular audience on Sunday evening.[11]

As early as 1840, the Presbyterian Board of Foreign Missions had solicited "unmarried female teachers" for its work. But the great surge in women missionaries did not occur until the 1870s, coinciding with the rapid development of women's missionary societies. D. L. Leonard, associate editor of the *Missionary Review of the World*, reported that in the 1870s ordained missionaries numbered 4,300, and unordained, unmarried women serving as missionaries totaled 3,400. By the 1880s most Presbyterian denominations had national women's boards of home and foreign missions. In 1896 the PCUSA General Assembly reported that 1,000 women were employed as missionaries by the boards of the church and 60,000 were employed as teachers in the Sunday Schools. In 1936 Arthur Judson Brown, who served as secretary of the Board of Foreign Missions of the PCUSA for 34 years, reported that "a majority of the foreign missionaries of the Church are women. Wives, and single women evangelists, teachers, physicians and nurses have for many years formed approximately two-thirds of the total missionary force." [12]

In 1933 William G. Lennox published a study entitled *The Health and Turnover of Missionaries*, a study of missionaries serving under the boards of six United States denominations until 1929. He drew the following conclusions:

11. A. J. Gordon, "The Ministry of Women," *Missionary Review of the World* (December 1894), 910; as quoted in Rosemary Radford Ruether and Rosemary Skinner Keller, *Women and Religion in America, Volume 1: The Nineteenth Century* (San Francisco: Harper and Row, 1981), 196-197.

12. Arthur Judson Brown, *One Hundred Years: A History of the Foreign Missionary Work of the Presbyterian Church in the U.S.A., With Some Accounts of Countries, Peoples and the Problems of Modern Missions* (New York, 1936), 114; as quoted in Lois A. Boyd and R. Douglas Brackenridge, *Presbyterian Women in America: Two Centuries of a Quest for Status* (Westport, Connecticut: Greenwood Press, 1983), 165.

Of the total years which missionaries of these six boards have served, three-fifths belonged to women, two-fifths to men. In the course of the century there has been a remarkable increase in the number of women workers as compared with the increase of men. In 1830, like animals entering the Ark, missionaries went to the field in pairs: for each man there was nearly one woman. In 1880, for each man there were one and one-third women; in 1929, for each man there were 2.02 women. Expressed in percentages, the missionary personnel was female to the extent of 49 percent in 1830, 57 percent in 1880, and 67 percent in 1929. [13]

The table below indicates the degree to which foreign missions were feminized during the early twentieth century. [14]

Year	Missionaries	Men	Single Women	Wives
1900	18,782	10,214	4,228	4,340
1910	21,307	9,788	5,585	5,934
1923	29,188	11,444	9,125	8,619

In 1910 Mrs. Helen B. Montgomery published a book surveying the role of women in foreign missions during the preceding half century. Mrs. Montgomery wrote:

We began in weakness, we stand in power. In 1861 there was a single missionary in the field, Miss Marston, in Burma; in 1909, there were 4,710 unmarried women in the field, 1,948 of them from the United States. In 1861 there was one organized women's society in our country; in 1910 there were forty-four. Then the supporters numbered a few hundreds; today there are at least two millions. Then the amount contributed was $2,000; last year four million dollars was raised. The development on the field has been as remarkable as that at home. Beginning with a single teacher, there are at the opening of the Jubilee year [1910] 800 teachers, 140 physicians, 380 evangelists, 79 trained nurses, 5,783 Bible women and native helpers..... [T]he women's missionary organizations have built colleges, hospitals, dispensaries, nurses' homes, orphanages, leper asylums, homes for missionaries' children, training schools, and industrial plants.[15]

13. William G. Lennox, *The Health and Turnover of Missionaries* (New York: Foreign Missions Conference of North America, 1933), 28; as quoted in R. Pierce Beaver, 111.
14. Adapted from Beaver, 110.
15. Helen B. Montgomery, *Western Women in Eastern Lands* (New York: MacMillan, 1910), 243; as quoted in Beaver, 139.

As the activities of the women grew during the nineteenth century, so did their money. By 1890 the General Assembly of the Presbyterian Church noted that women, through their own organizations, contributed $40,000 more than all the Presbyterian churches put together for foreign and home missions. By the 1920s, there were more than 6,000 local women's missionary societies in the Presbyterian church that controlled more than three million dollars per year. [16] Then, and only then, when the women's societies had grown to such a size that they threatened the control of foreign missions by the clergy themselves, did any serious opposition to them arise.

Robert Speer, senior secretary of the Presbyterian Board of Foreign Missions, contributor to the series of books called *The Fundamentals*, and one of J. Gresham Machen's adversaries in the Presbyterian controversy in the 1920s and 1930s, asked,

> If we have in our churches women's organizations, what have we got? Haven't we got two churches? We have one church made up of men and women, with a social program, an educational program, and a religious program. Then we have a separation of women, with identical programs except worship. We do not want to divide what is spoken of as "the church" and "the women." [17]

The problem is that Speer's reservations were a century late and came only when the women's organizations were threatening the leadership monopoly of the clergy and the ecclesiastical bureaucracy. When the leadership of women had been displacing only deacons, ruling elders, and ordinary laymen, Speer's spiritual ancestors had been recommending and encouraging women's societies as a means of ensuring the continuance of their control of the ecclesiastical power structure.

Speer went on to add: "The great danger is that the women will think that their society is the only thing they have to work over." [18] This was not a significant danger, for by the time that Speer wrote, the more progressive women had already begun making plans for "working over" the whole church. Politically, however, the Presbyterian women met their match in the 1920s and early 1930s when the Presbyterian General

16. Boyd and Brackenridge, 59.
17. Boyd and Brackenridge, 60-61.
18. Robert E. Speer, "Conference of Fifteen," 15-16; as quoted in Boyd and Brackenridge, 60-61.

Assembly incorporated the women's societies into the regular boards of the church and appointed some women, a minority, to those boards. But philosophically the women were far from beaten. The clergy, eager to gain control of such a prolific source of cash, were quite willing to put women on boards of the denomination. Thus another major step toward the complete feminization of the church was taken, again with the help of liberal clergymen.

In addition to elevating women to the governing boards of the churches, the foreign missions movement led by women created the first international ecumenical missionary agency, the World Missionary Committee of Christian Women. Like the Sunday School movement, the women's foreign missions movement abandoned the whole counsel of God and substituted a superficial creed that virtually everyone, except a Christian, could agree to. And like the Sunday School movement, the foreign missions movement fueled the ecumenism of modern times.

The Deaconess Movement

The third major device for the feminization of the church in the nineteenth century was the deaconess movement.

Like higher criticism, the deaconess movement was imported from Germany where a clergyman named Theodore Fliedner of Kaiserswerth developed the office in 1836. Fliedner toured the United States touting his innovation and inspiring William Passavant of the Evangelical Alliance of the Lutheran Church to begin the deaconess work in America. Passavant's work did not survive the Civil War, but after the War, the work began again. Methodists and Episcopalians were among the first denominations to establish deaconess orders in the U.S. Soon Lutheran and German Reformed churches had orders of deaconesses, and Congregationalists, Baptists, and Presbyterians were planning theirs. Between 1870 and the end of the century, over 140 deaconess homes were opened in the United States. There were nearly 2000 deaconesses, with the Methodist church having the majority of them, more than 1200.

This movement attracted the support of some prominent Presbyterian theologians: A. A. Hodge, Charles Augustus Briggs, Alexander T. McGill, and Benjamin Warfield. The General Assembly of 1889 appointed a committee led by Warfield to present recommendations the following year. As a result of those recommendations, the 1890 General Assembly sent the presbyteries an overture that recognized what it called the apostolic origins of the order of deaconesses and specified the election, not the ordination, of deaconesses "in a manner similar to that appointed for deacons, and set apart by prayer." The presbyteries, not being sufficiently progressive or imaginative to see the apostolic origins of this new order of Protestant nuns, defeated the overture. Not being easily dissuaded, the 1892 General Assembly sent down a similar overture, but omitted the claim to apostolic authority. The presbyteries accepted this overture. About ten years later the first Presbyterian deaconess school opened its doors in Baltimore. The Presbyterians, being the most Calvinist of the major denominations, were generally the laggards in the feminist developments of the nineteenth century. They were surpassed by the more progressive Unitarians, Methodists, Baptists, and Holiness groups.

From the election of deaconesses it was but a short but very significant step to the ordination of women as deacons. The United Presbyterian Church of North America installed women deacons in 1906; the Cumberland Presbyterian Church in 1921. In 1923, the Presbyterian Church in the United States of America jumped on the bandwagon. Now that women could be ordained, it was only a matter of time before they would be ordained elders and ministers. In 1932, the Ruling Elders Association of the PCUSA welcomed women into its ranks, despite the dissenting votes of some members.

Allies Against the Truth: Liberal Clergymen and Women

During the nineteenth century, aggressive women took advantage of the confusion among the clergy and developed their own bases of power within the churches. They created, as Robert Speer remarked, a church within a church, and frequently the women's organizations were more effective in raising money, though women ordinarily had no independent source of income, than the official organizations of the church.

This is not to say that the women accomplished all this themselves. Far from it. They were encouraged and assisted by some members of the clergy, especially the more liberal clergy, who, if they did not accept all the doctrines of the women's rights movement, needed the help of the women in raising money. Clergymen frequently preached on behalf of women's societies. As early as 1815 the Presbyterian General Assembly, which had not mentioned women in the decades since its first assembly in 1789, solicited women's aid for "indigent students in Theological Seminary," and in 1818 and 1819 the General Assembly specifically approved women's work in organizing Sunday Schools.[19]

The women responded to their clergymen friends by offering them avid support. The English writer Frances Trollope commented on the relationship between American clergymen and women in the first half of the eighteenth century:

> It is from the clergy only that the women of America receive that sort of attention which is so dearly valued by every female heart throughout the world. With the priests of America the women hold that degree of influential importance which in the countries of Europe is allowed them throughout all orders and ranks of society...and in return for this they seem to give their hearts and souls into their keeping. I never saw or read of any country where religion had so strong a hold upon the women or a slighter hold upon the men.[20]

The alliance between ambitious women and liberal clergymen is evidenced in a dozen different ways. For example, the Female Missionary Society of the Western District in Utica, New York, began employing home missionaries in 1813 and sent out the recently converted Charles Finney on a nation-wide missionary tour in 1824. Finney was ordained a Presbyterian minister in that same year, and his career links the feminization of theology and church leadership. Thomas Murphy, a Presbyterian minister, published a book on pastoral theology in 1877 in which he suggested that women join in prayer meetings, form pastors' aid associations to encourage membership and attendance, visit the aged, the sick, and the poor, and organize for benevolent work. "Women," he wrote, "have the piety, they have the feeling, they have the tact, they more generally have the time, to do such work, and hence they can do it more efficiently than men."[21]

Clergymen pandered to the ladies in the churches by asking for their help. Please notice how extensive this clergyman's list is:

19. Boyd and Brackenridge, 9.

20. As quoted in Ann Douglas, *The Feminization of American Culture* (New York: Alfred A. Knopf, 1977), 100-101.

21. Thomas Murphy, *Pastoral Theology: The Pastor in the Various Duties of His Office* (Philadelphia, 1877), 290-297; as quoted in Boyd and Brackenridge, 14.

We look to you, ladies, to raise the standard of character in our own sex; we look to you to guard and fortify those barriers, which still exist in society, against the encroachments of impudence and licentiousness. We look to you for the continuance of domestic purity, for the revival of domestic religion, for the increase of our charities and the support of what remains of religion in our private habits and publick institutions.[22]

The view that women are more suited than men for these duties in particular and for Christianity in general is a major feature of the effeminate theology of the nineteenth century. It was espoused by clergymen and women alike. Mary James, a prominent Presbyterian, believed,

> What a heritage is given us, Christ is to be King of Kings. His people (the Church) are the laborers who are to go forth to battle for him, and as two-thirds of the church are women, what a large part of the work belongs to us.... [W]oman is the lever to lift up the nations of the Earth.[23]

William Wilberforce, whose name has been invoked by some Neo-evangelicals eager to find their roots, believed that women are "the medium of our intercourse with the heavenly world, the faithful repositories of the religious principle for the benefit of the present and of the rising generation." There is, Wilberforce maintained, a "more favorable disposition to religion in the female sex."[24]

Not to be outdone in asserting the religious superiority of women, the women themselves expressed views such as these:

> By entrusting to woman a revelation of himself, God has pointed out whom he intends for his missionaries upon Earth, – the disseminators of his Spirit, the diffusers of his Word. Let men enjoy in peace and triumph the intellectual kingdom which is theirs, and which doubtless was intended for them; let us participate in its privileges without desiring to share its domination. The moral world is ours – ours by position; ours by qualification; ours by the very indication of God himself, who has

22. Quoted in Jane Rendall, *The Origins of Modern Feminism: Women in Britain, France, and the United States, 1780-1860* (New York: Schocken Books, 1984), 78.

23. Mary E. James, *Home Mission Monthly*, Volume 1, 17; as quoted in Boyd and Brackenridge, 16.

24. William Wilberforce, *A Practical View of the prevailing religious system of professed Christians in the higher and middle classes in this country, contrasted with real Christianity* (London, 1797), 435; as quoted in Rendall, 75.

deigned to put in woman's heart the only feeling...which affords the faintest representation of his most inextinguishable love to us, his erring and strayed children.[25]

Frances Willard, the president of the Women's Christian Temperance Union, expressed similar views:

> The strongest argument in favor of a woman ministry is found in woman herself, in her sympathetic and intuitional nature, in her high moral sense, in her deep and fervent religious spirit. The mother element in woman's character gives her a peculiar power in religion.... I think it is impossible, from the very nature of the case, for any man to do it as woman can.... [I]n the gifts and graces of a woman's nature there is that which so qualifies her for this work that the synod or council that forbids her entrance upon it is acting in opposition to the higher power that ordains through gifts of mind and character, and through deep spiritual aspirations, certain women to this divine work.... Now I notice in my missionary exchanges, and in late missionary literature, that the need of female evangelists for the foreign field is being recognized in conservative circles; not Quakers and Methodists, but Calvinists are saying, "The women of heathen lands must be reached by the ministry of their Christian sisters," and Dr. Thoburn, in an article written for the *Advocate*, goes so far as to say the ordinances will have to be administered by women to the inmates of the zenanas, for one generation at least.... I believe the preaching of the Gospel by women missionaries will dispel the prejudice against woman's preaching in the home church, much as the services of the medical missionaries have altered the home sentiment about lady physicians. [26]

The peculiar superiority of women for religion is summed up in this nineteenth century verse:

> A woman Satan chose at first, to bring on man the fall;
> A woman God has chose at last, for to restore us all.
> As by a woman death must come, so life must come the same,
> And they that eat the fruit she gives, may bless God's holy name. [27]

---

25. Sarah Lewis, *Woman's Mission* (London, 1839), 128-129; as quoted in Rendall, 75.
26. Frances E. Willard, *Women in the Pulpit* (Boston: D. Lathrop, 1888), 94-101; as quoted in Ruether and Keller, 208-212.
27. Joanna Southcott, as quoted in Rendall, 103

Until the nineteenth century the clear Scriptural prohibitions on women speaking in any leadership capacity in church meetings was enforced by orthodox, and even by some unorthodox, churches. After the Reformation, women first rose to prominence in the sects: the Quakers, the Moravians, the Shakers and other similar charismatic, pietistic, anabaptist, and mystical groups.

More than a millennium earlier, women had risen to positions of prominence in disorderly churches, such as that at Corinth, and in various heretical sects. Irenaeus noted that women were attracted to heretical groups in the second century, especially the Gnostics. Tertullian denounced "These heretical women – how audacious they are! They have no modesty; they are bold enough to teach, to engage in argument, to enact exorcisms, to undertake cures, and, it may be, even to baptize!"[28] Tertullian asserted that "It is not permitted for a woman to speak in the church, nor is it permitted for her to teach, nor to baptize, nor to offer [the eucharist], nor to claim for herself a share in any masculine function – not to mention any priestly office."[29] One modern woman, sympathetic to feminism, wrote:

> Among such gnostic groups as the Valentinians, women were considered equal to men; some were revered as prophets; others acted as teachers, traveling evangelists, healers, priests, perhaps even bishops.... At least three heretical circles that retained a masculine image of God [the Gnostics, like some modern sects, had a feminine or epicene god] included women who took positions of leadership – the Marcionites, the Montanists, and the Carpocratians. But from the year 200, we have no evidence for women taking prophetic, priestly, and episcopal roles among orthodox churches.[30]

Margaret Fell Fox, wife of George Fox, wrote *Women's Speaking Justified, Proved and Allowed of by the Scriptures* in 1668. The Quakers had developed the idea and practice of women's meetings, which functioned as a church within their church long before the more orthodox Protestant denominations adopted similar practices. It was no accident that several early nineteenth century feminists and abolitionists were Quaker

28. As quoted in Elaine Pagels, *The Gnostic Gospels* (New York: Random House, 1981), 71-72.

29. Pagels, 72.

30. Pagels, 72-73.

preachers: Susan B. Anthony and Lucretia Mott, to name two. Influencing the rise of women in foreign missions, the Moravians developed the idea of married couples as partners in mission, the so-called "militant marriage." And Ann Lee, the illiterate woman who claimed to be the female Messiah needed to complete the family of God, exacerbated the early feminism of the sects by founding the Shakers.

Orthodoxy on the Defensive

But in the seventeenth century the more orthodox churches still understood, believed, and obeyed the Bible. Here, for example, is what John Cotton wrote on the question of women speaking in church in 1650:

> It is apparent by the scope and context of both those Scriptures [1 Corinthians 13:34 and 1 Timothy 2:11, 12] that a woman is not permitted to speak in the Church in two cases:
>
> 1. By way of teaching, whether in expounding or applying Scripture. For this the Apostle accounteth an act of authority which is unlawful for a woman to usurp over the man, II Tim. ii, 13. And besides the woman is more subject to error than a man, ver. 14. and therefore might soon prove a seducer if she became a teacher.
>
> 2. It is not permitted to a woman to speak in the Church by way of propounding questions though under pretense of desire to learn, for her own satisfaction; but rather it is required she should ask her husband at home.
>
> For under pretense of questioning for learning ['s] sake, she might so propound her questions as to teach her teachers; or if not so, yet to open a door to some of her own weak and erroneous apprehensions, or at least soon exceed the bounds of womanly modesty.

Cotton continued to explain that the divine proscriptions of women speaking in church in no way prevent a woman from singing the *Psalms* in church or giving an account of her sins when being disciplined by the church.[31]

---

31. John Cotton, "Singing of Psalms a Gospel-Ordinance. 1650," in Edmund Clarence Stedman and Ellen Mackey Hutchinson, eds., *A Library of American Literature from the Earliest Settlement to the Present Time*, Vol. 1 (New York: Charles L. Webster & Company, 1888), 254-270; as quoted in Rosemary Radford Ruether and Rosemary Skinner Keller, eds., *Women and Religion in America*, Vol. 2 (San Francisco: Harper and Row, 1983), 190-192.

Soon after Cotton wrote, the first beginnings of feminization troubled the church in America. The Anne Hutchinson affair of 1637 had resulted in a loss of power by the men in the church, and a gain in power by the clergy. To quote two historians,

> Although laymen maintained their power in secular matters, by the 1650s they found themselves silenced within many churches: Ministers prevented them from asking questions after sermons and lectures, participating in disciplinary cases, or relating their own spiritual experiences before the church.... As lay ecclesiastical authority declined, fewer and fewer men joined New England churches, and by the late seventeenth century females dominated church membership rolls.[32]

Early in the nineteenth century, Albert Barnes, pastor of First Presbyterian Church in Philadelphia, was tried for heresy for his belief in unlimited atonement, and acquitted. Barnes expressed his opinion that Paul's injunction that women be silent in church was a "positive, explicit, and universal rule. There is no ambiguity in the expressions and there can be no difference of opinion in regard to their meaning."[33] In 1872 a writer in *The Presbyterian* remarked, "Our *Confession of Faith* and *Form of Government* say nothing on the subject [of women speaking in church meetings] simply because it never entered the head of any man in the Westminster Assembly that such a thing would ever be attempted in our denomination."[34] In the South Robert L. Dabney thundered that public preaching by women was "a frontal attack on God's truth and divine kingdom and should be vigorously opposed with all the force that the church could muster."[35] In 1891 Dabney condemned the

32. Martha Tomhave Blauvelt and Rosemary Skinner Keller, "Women and Revivalism: The Puritan and Wesleyan Traditions," in Ruether and Keller, eds., 317.

33. Albert Barnes, *Notes Explanatory and Practical on the Epistles of Paul to the Corinthians* (London, 1837), 189; as quoted in Boyd and Brackenridge, 91. Barnes is typical of the double-mindedness on the role of women in the church of some Presbyterian clergymen in the nineteenth century. While advocating the silence of women, Barnes also advocated the appointment, if not the ordination, of women as deaconesses: "It is clear from the New Testament that there was an order of women in the church known as deaconesses. Their existence is expressly affirmed in early ecclesiastical history. The *Apostolical Constitution* book III says, 'Ordain a deaconess who is faithful and holy for the ministries toward the women' " (as quoted in Ruether and Keller, 281).

34. H. J. V., *The Presbyterian*, March 2, 1872, 2; as quoted in Boyd and Brackenridge, 91-92.

35. Robert Louis Dabney, "The Public Preaching of Women," *The Southern Presbyterian Review*, October 1879, 689-713.

women's movement as "part and parcel of French Jacobinism, that travesty of true republicanism, which caused the reign of terror in France, and which disorganizes every society which it invades."[36]

In 1882 Cyrus Cort had written that even though we might not understand "the grounds or the propriety of his [Paul's] emphatic prohibition of women praying or speaking in Christian assemblies, certain it is that such is his teaching...in the most explicit and didactic terms."[37]

Confusion and Compromise

But the views of some nineteenth-century Presbyterian clergymen were ambiguous and wavering, and they grew still more shaky as the century wore on. As early as 1827 Charles Finney's support of women praying in public caused a controversy in the Presbyterian Church, but the controversy was not resolved. Those ministers opposed to Finney could not muster the votes needed to condemn Finney's encouragement of women praying. (This, of course, is not surprising, given the manner in which Finney was supported by ambitious women and ordained by the clergy.)

In 1832 the Presbyterian General Assembly, by a vote of 126 to 122, circulated a letter to the churches that expressed the Assembly's views on women praying in public. It contained a pregnant exception to the Scriptural rule of silence: Women were allowed to speak, teach, pray, and do all the things prohibited to them in meetings at which men were present, if there were no men present. The letter said, "Meetings of pious women by themselves, for conversation and prayer, whenever they can conveniently be held, we entirely approve.... [But] to teach and exhort, or to lead in prayer, in public and promiscuous assemblies, is clearly forbidden to women in the Holy Oracles."[38] This exception, approved by the highest governing body of the Presbyterian Church, and similar statements made by other churches at the time, allowed women to establish their own missionary, educational, and diaconal societies within the church and to dominate both the Sunday School movement

36. Robert Louis Dabney, "Let Women Keep Silence in the Church," *The Christian Observer*, October 7, 1891, 1; as quoted in Boyd and Brackenridge, 208.

37. Cyrus Cort, "Women Preaching Viewed in the Light of God's Word and Church History," *Reformed Quarterly Review*, 29 (January 1882), 129; as quoted in Ruether and Keller, 200.

38. Boyd and Brackenridge, 94.

in the early part of the century and the foreign missions movement later in the century. Women, the early religious feminists argued, were permitted to teach other women, and children as well. They were prohibited only from teaching adult men. Two-thirds of the church thus became students of aggressive women leaders. It was only a matter of time before the remaining third, adult men, would also become disciples of women.

Another embarrassment arose. The women's meetings were frequently attended, not by a layman, but by the pastor. If women could speak and teach and pray in the presence of the pastor, then why not other, and presumably lesser, men? Were ministers already so effeminate that they did not count as men when attending women's meetings? Feminist leaven was hard at work in the nineteenth-century churches.

As is frequently the case, it was the younger clergymen who sought to overturn the mandate of Scripture on the matter. Writing in *The Presbyterian* in 1872, an anonymous author reported that "Our younger Presbyterian ministers advocate, with all their might, females praying in mixed assemblies, and do not hesitate to declare, publicly and loudly, that there is not a word within the lids of the Bible against it. They seem to think that there can be no revivals of religion without it. They are not satisfied with female prayer-meetings." [39]

In 1874, by a vote of 211 to 84, the Presbyterian General Assembly passed another resolution on the subject of women speaking in public. This resolution expressed skepticism on the whole issue: "The Assembly expresses no opinion as to the scriptural view of women's right to speak or pray in the social prayer-meetings, but commits the whole subject to the discretion of the pastors and elders of the churches." [40] What had been so clear only 40 years earlier was now lost in a cloud of feminist fog. A generation of new clergymen had come of age.

Some of these Presbyterian clergymen were more vociferous than others in attacking Scripture. Israel See, the minister at the Wickliffe Presbyterian Church in Newark, New Jersey, invited two women attending the national convention of the Women's Christian Temperance Union to speak at his church in 1876. During his subsequent trial for this

39. "Encouragement to Christian Women," *The Presbyterian*, March 2, 1872, 1; as quoted in Boyd and Brackenridge, 98.
40. Boyd and Brackenridge, 100.

violation of divine law, See interpreted the commands of Paul in ways to which we became accustomed in the twentieth century. First, See argued, Paul's commands to the Corinthians did not necessarily apply to Newarkians. Second, Paul was silencing babbling or gossiping women, not educated, intelligent, up-to-date, modern, nineteenth-century women. Third, Joel's prophecy, "Your sons and your daughters shall prophesy," means that women are commanded to preach. This twisting of Scripture was beyond the endurance of the reporter for *The New York Times* covering See's trial. He challenged See to interpret another passage: "Your young men shall see visions and your old men shall dream dreams" by ordering the young men of his congregation to see visions and by providing comfortable pews and headrests for the old men.[41] In the late nineteenth century the laws of logic were more familiar to newspaper reporters than to many clergymen. If there is no such disparity now, it is not because clergymen have improved their command of logic.

Mr. See, however, made one valid argument, and it was the argument that was the undoing of the more conservative clergy. He argued that since women were already permitted to speak at small, social religious gatherings, they could not be prevented from speaking at larger meetings, simply because the Bible makes no distinction between large and small meetings. By this argument, See laid bare the falsity of the premise of the more conservative, but not quite Biblical, clergy.

One of the more conservative clergymen published an essay in the *Presbyterian Review* in April 1889 titled "Woman's Position and Work in the Church." Samuel Niccolls is an example of the confusion of the clergy about the whole issue, for while condemning women teachers and preachers, he advocates women deacons:

> There is not a solitary hint [in the New Testament] of a woman being placed in the position of an apostle, evangelist, pastor, elder, or ruler. There is indeed, good reason to believe that she ministered in the diaconate, and in this sense she occupied an official position on the staff of the church.... [But] the arguments used in its favor [that is, in favor of ordaining women to the full work of the Gospel ministry]...are antiscriptural. They are at best of that negative character which teaches, by artful exegesis, that the Scriptures did not mean what they say, and what the whole Church for eighteen centuries believed that they teach.

41. Boyd and Brackenridge, 103.

They [the arguments favoring women teachers] are contradicted by the testimony of history and experience. Exceptional cases of women possessing special gifts for public life, or who have been called to a providential mission, do not justify the repeal of laws which are established on general principles. Deborah's career would not warrant the establishment of military schools for the training of women for the profession of arms....

The argument for woman's preaching, based upon her superior qualifications, if admitted, proves too much. It shows that men are usurpers in the pulpit, ought never to have been there, and ought to leave it as soon as a sufficient number of women can be trained to occupy it....

[T]he great proportion of women who have already assumed the office of public teaching in the pulpit have departed from the rule of sound doctrine in their teachings.... [But] we do not see any scriptural reason why woman should not be placed in the diaconate, and thus have official position on the staff of the Church. Thousands of noble women – as missionaries, Bible-readers, and visitors – are virtually exercising that office without the title. Let no man forbid them.[42]

In the same year, 1889, George P. Hays, moderator of the General Assembly of 1884, former president of Washington and Jefferson College, and distinguished Presbyterian pastor and theologian, wrote a book titled *May Women Speak?* In the book he asserted that there were no restrictions on the role of women in the church. His booklet was published under the auspices of the WCTU and received wide distribution among church women.[43]

The President of the Women's Christian Temperance Union, Frances Willard, had published *Women in the Pulpit* a year earlier. She had been asked to write an article on women and preaching by the male editors of *The Homiletic Monthly*, but the article grew into a book in which Mrs. Willard wrote:

It is estimated that there are in the United States five hundred women who have already [1888] entered the pulpit as evangelists, and at least a score (exclusive of the 350 Quaker preachers) who are pastors, of whom several have been regularly ordained. The denominations that have or-

42. Samuel J. Niccolls, "Woman's Position and Work in the Church," *Presbyterian Review* 10 (April 1889), 267-279; as quoted in Ruether and Keller, 234-238.

43. Ruether and Keller, 108. The WCTU, of course, was an alliance of clergy and women against men's vices.

dained women are the Methodist, Baptist, Free Baptist, Congregational, Universalist, and Unitarian.[44]

Benjamin Warfield

By the time Benjamin Warfield published his article "Paul on Women Speaking in Church," in *The Presbyterian* in 1919, the damage had already been done. Warfield's position was that held by the church for almost nineteen centuries, but it had been undermined by the feminization of theology. In fact, Warfield himself had obscured the truth by publicly endorsing the deaconess movement thirty years earlier. But in 1919 his views were quite clear and thoroughly orthodox:

> The intermediate verses [in *1 Corinthians* 14] only make it plain that precisely what the apostle is doing is forbidding women to speak at all in the church. His injunction of silence he pushes so far that he forbids them even to ask questions; and adds with special reference to that, but through that to the general matter, the crisp declaration that "it is indecent" – for that is the meaning of the word – "for a woman to speak in church."
>
> It would be impossible for the apostle to speak more directly or more emphatically than he has done here. He requires women to be silent at church-meetings. For that is what "in the churches" means; there were no church buildings then. And he has not left us in doubt as to the nature of these church-meetings. He had just described them in verses 26*ff*. They were of the general character of our prayer meetings. Note the words, "let him be silent in the church," in verse 30, and compare them with "let them be silent in the churches," in verse 34. The prohibition of women speaking covers thus all public church-meetings – it is the publicity, not the formality of it, which is the point. And he tells us repeatedly that this is the universal law of the church. He does more than that. He tells us that it is the commandment of the Lord, and emphasizes the word "Lord" (verse 37).
>
> The passage in *1 Timothy* 2:11*ff*. is just as strong....
>
> In the face of these two absolutely plain and emphatic passages, what is said in *1 Corinthians* 11:5 cannot be appealed to in mitigation or modification....
>
> What then must be noted, in conclusion, is: (1) That the prohibition of speaking in the church to women is precise, absolute, and all-inclu-

44. Frances E. Willard, *Women in the Pulpit* (Boston: D. Lathrop, 1888), 94-101; as quoted in Ruether and Keller, 208.

sive. They are to keep silent in the churches – and that means in all the public meetings for worship; they are not even to ask questions....

As clear and as orthodox as Warfield's statement was – and one hears nothing like it from any seminary today – it was too little too late. What was needed by 1919 was a complete reconstruction of philosophy and theology on a Biblical foundation, for theology, not just church leadership, had been feminized.

The Feminization of Theology

At the beginning of the nineteenth century, despite growing apostasy, Calvinism was still the dominant theology of America. Its zenith had occurred fifty years earlier when Jonathan Edwards had preached and published in New England, but Christians at the beginning of the century still subscribed to a rather thorough summary of Christian theology. By the end of the nineteenth century all that had changed. The simplification of doctrine achieved by the Sunday School movement, the perversion of Christianity and the emotional peddling of quasi-Christian ideas by the revivalists, the onslaught of Darwinism, and the philosophical and theological attack on reason had transformed American religion. Calvinism had been displaced by an anti-intellectual movement, and a superficial, sentimental creed had become the new American religion. The senior Henry James, himself a fugitive from Calvinism, observed in mid-century that "religion in the old virile sense has disappeared, and been replaced by a feeble Unitarian sentimentality."[45] In the late nineteenth century Charles Spurgeon complained, "There has got abroad a notion, somehow, that if you become a Christian you must sink your manliness and turn milksop."

What makes Christianity virile is its emphasis on the intellect, on logic, and on systematic thinking. Almost alone among the religions of the world, Christianity is the religion of the mind, not of the feelings, the imagination, or the will. Pagan religions emphasize those things, but in Christianity, revelation is verbal, propositional, and consists of the communication of information to be understood and believed. The believer is justified and sanctified through knowledge. There are literally hundreds of verses in the Bible that emphasize knowledge, truth, mind, and understanding, including the first and greatest command-

45. Quoted in F. W. Dupee, *Henry James: His Life and Writings* (New York, 1956). 11.

ment: "You shall love the Lord your God with all your heart, with all your soul, with all your mind, and with all your strength."

Peter tells us that God's "divine power has given to us all things that pertain to life and godliness through the knowledge of him who called us...." John says that "we know that the Son of God has come and has given us an understanding, that we may know him who is true; and we are in him who is true, in his Son Jesus Christ. This is the true God and eternal life." Paul commands us, "Brethren, do not be children in understanding; however, in malice be babes, but in understanding be mature." Christ prayed, "Sanctify them by your truth. Your Word is truth." David wrote the longest *Psalm* extolling God's propositional revelation to man:

> Your Word is a lamp to my feet and a light to my path.... I have more understanding than all my teachers, for your testimonies are my meditation. I understand more than the ancients, because I keep your precepts.... The entrance of your words gives light; it gives understanding to the simple.... The entirety of your Word is truth.

Moses refers to God as the God of truth. The entire book of *Proverbs*, especially the first nine chapters, praises knowledge, understanding, and wisdom, and commands all, especially the young, to get knowledge:

> To know wisdom and instruction, to perceive the words of understanding, to receive the instruction of wisdom, justice, judgment, and equity; to give prudence to the simple, to the young man knowledge and discretion – A wise man will hear and increase learning, and a man of understanding will attain wise counsel.... The fear of the Lord is the beginning of knowledge, but fools despise wisdom and instruction.

Finally, the *Westminster Confession of Faith*, which is the best summary yet written of what the Bible teaches, declares that God "is truth itself," and grounds the authority of the Bible on its truth.

It is this emphasis on knowledge, logic, truth, and understanding that makes Christianity a masculine religion. Perhaps it is because God is masculine that Christianity emphasizes knowledge and understanding. The absence of a feminine deity characterizes Christianity and two of its major heresies, Judaism and Islam. This is in stark contrast to the pagan religions of Greece, Rome, Egypt, Babylonia, Africa, India, Europe, and North America. Pagan religions, religions not based upon any part of the Bible, all have feminine deities. Pagan religions emphasize will, feelings, desires, and emotions. Christianity has no female deities, nor does it emphasize either the emotions or the will.

Early American Christianity

Because the first Americans were Calvinists, that is, Biblical Christians, American theology was a masculine religion. The historian Moses Coit Tyler wrote of Calvinist New England:

> In its inception New England was not an agricultural community, nor a manufacturing community, nor a trading community: It was a thinking community; an arena and mart for ideas; its characteristic organ being not the hand, nor the heart, nor the pocket, but the brain.... Probably no other community of pioneers ever so honored study.... Theirs was a social structure with its cornerstone resting on a book....[46]

The feminization of theology in the nineteenth-century was fundamentally an attack on Christian intellectualism and a defense of the role of feelings in religion. In 1726 Cotton Mather had written his *Directions for a Candidate of the Ministry* in which he argued that learning of a general kind was the second most important qualification for a minister, after piety. He recommended that a well-trained minister should know Latin, Greek, Hebrew, Rhetoric, Logic, Natural Philosophy, Mathematics, Astronomy, and Divinity.

The Erring Nineteenth Century

But the nineteenth-century ladies thought otherwise. Catherine Beecher, daughter of Lyman Beecher and sister of Henry Ward Beecher and Harriet Beecher Stowe, believed that women ought to control education, and women are inevitably opposed to Calvinist "theological theories...as seemingly opposing the moral sense and common sense of mankind."[47] Ann Douglas, a modern feminist who has astutely analyzed the alliance between the liberal clergy and middle-class women in nineteenth-century America, pointed out that Catherine's brother, Henry Ward Beecher, "like all his siblings, made his dead mother the rationale and center for a feminized theology.... [He] told his hearers

46. Moses Coit Tyler, *A History of American Literature, 1607-1765* (Ithca, 1949), 85-86; as quoted in Richard Hofstadter, *Anti-Intellectualism in American Life* (New York, 1962), 59.

47. Catherine E. Beecher, *Common Sense Applied to Religion*, xii and *Letters on the Difficulties of Religion* (Hartford, 1857); as quoted in Douglas, 104.

that a mother's love is 'a revelation of the love of God.'"[48] In 1853 Bela Bates Edwards of Andover Seminary remarked that people considered "an intellectual clergyman...deficient in piety and an eminently pious ministry...deficient in intellect."[49]

This anti-intellectualism was characteristic not only of the liberals, but of the conservatives as well. Many professing Christians today regard the various religious awakenings and revivals in American history as recoveries of true religion. But a more accurate assessment is found in a biography of Mary Baker Eddy:

> The important thing about the revivalist movement sweeping the rural United States was that it shifted the ground from hardheaded logic to undisciplined emotion, from doctrine to piety, from an educated ministry to lay preachers and itinerant evangelists who felt themselves moved by "the Sperrit" but who might be all but illiterate. There was a general feeling that in getting away from the intellectual foundations of the past the revivalists were getting back to the conditions of primitive Christianity and recapturing a religious enthusiasm....[50]

The liberal, effeminate theologians, heretical as they were, were not original thinkers. They took their ideas from the secular philosophers that preceded and surrounded them. Before piety could be opposed to knowledge and intellect, it had to be separated from them. This separation was achieved by the secular philosophers, some of whom were romantics, others materialists, and still others positivists.

The Philosophical Background

August Comte, who developed what he called New Christianity, made a sharp distinction between the theological mode of thought, which is to be rejected, and religious feeling, without which society cannot be unified. One finds the same separation between theology and feeling in Ludwig Feuerbach, one of the most raucous materialists of the early nineteenth century. John Tyndall, a British physicist and natural philosopher, and probably the most lucid proponent of materialism in nineteenth century England, explicitly declared – and one can find a similar declaration in many other materialists, including the enormously popular

48. Douglas, 110.
49. Douglas, 144.
50. Robert Peel, *Mary Baker Eddy, The Years of Discovery, 1821-1875* (New York, 1972), 48.

American novelist Ayn Rand – that "the facts of religious feeling are to me as certain as the facts of physics." Religion, according to Tyndall, is "a force, mischievous if permitted to intrude on the region of knowledge...but being capable of being guided to noble issues in the region of *emotion*, which is its proper and elevated sphere."[51]

Thomas Henry Huxley, certainly no Christian, attacked theological dogma because he wished to enable man to start "cherishing the noblest and most human of man's emotions, by worship...at the Altar of the Unknown."[52]

At the beginning of the twentieth century the American psychologist William James maintained that

> When we survey the whole field of religion, we find a great variety in the thoughts that have prevailed there; but the feelings on the one hand and the conduct on the other are almost always the same, for Stoic, Christian, and Buddhist saints are practically indistinguishable in their lives. The theories which Religion generates, being thus variable, are secondary; and if you wish to grasp her essence, you must look to the feelings and the conduct as being the more constant elements.[53]

The reader has noticed, of course, that James refers to "Religion" with a feminine adjective. He continues the passage using feminine pronouns and adjectives. William James was the son of Henry James, Sr., a dropout from Princeton Seminary. The father and son illustrate the feminization of theology in the nineteenth century.

But to return to the beginning of our story: At the end of the eighteenth century and the beginning of the nineteenth, the philosophical and theological foundations for the feminization of theology were laid by two German philosophers and a German theologian, Immanuel Kant, Friedrich Jacobi, and Friedrich Schleiermacher. Kant argued that God is not an object of knowledge; according to Kant, we can know only the objects of sensation as formed by the categories of the mind. We can never know anything as it is in itself; and we can certainly never

---

51. John Tyndall, *Addresses Delivered Before the British Association in Belfast* (New York, 1875), 63-64; as quoted in Maurice Mandelbaum, *History, Man, and Reason* (Baltimore, 1971), 29.

52. Mandelbaum, 30.

53. William James, *The Varieties of Religious Experience*, in *Theology in America*, Sydney Ahlstrom, editor (Indianapolis, 1967), 518.

know God, for he is not an object of sensation. In Kant the disjunction between theory and practice became a chasm. The existence of God cannot be proved, but we ought to act *as if* God existed. His existence has practical value, but no constitutive importance. The immortality of the soul cannot be proved, but we ought to act *as if* we were immortal. Rather than morality being based on theology, as it is in Christianity, Kant insisted that theology is based on morality. Moral practice comes first, and theology tags along, never quite reaching the level of knowledge.[54]

After Kant, the intellect belonged to science, not religion. No longer were science and religion talking about the same universe. After Kant, if one wished to know, he must turn to science. Christianity could not furnish knowledge of God, for God was unknowable. The role Kant left to religion was that of a prop for ethics. The religious man became the ethical man, not the knowledgeable man. Those who say that Christianity is not a creed or a doctrine, but a way of life, though they are almost certainly ignorant of the fact and probably proud of their ignorance, are disciples of the false Immanuel – Kant, not Christ.

But Kant, while digging the canyon between knowledge and religion, including Christianity, did not finish the job. Freidrich Jacobi, who described himself as a pagan in his head but a Christian in his heart, developed the head/heart separation so common in modern religion, and taught that God was apprehended through feeling. Friedrich Schleiermacher was a faithful disciple of both Kant and Jacobi in one very significant sense: He too denied that religion was a matter of knowledge. Unlike Kant, however, and like Jacobi, he based religion entirely upon feeling, the feeling of absolute dependence.

Schleiermacher emerged from German romanticism in 1799 to publish his famous *On Religion: Speeches to Its Cultured Despisers*. In speaking to the "cultured despisers" of religion, Schleiermacher said: "Religion is for you at one time a way of thinking, a faith, a peculiar way of contemplating the world, and of combining what meets us in the world: at another it is a way of acting, a peculiar desire and love, a special kind of conduct and character."[55] By this statement, Schleiermacher was rejecting both the orthodox conception of Christianity as a system of truths

54. See Gordon H. Clark, *Thales to Dewey: A History of Philosophy*.
55. Friedrich Schleiermacher, *On Religion: Speeches to Its Cultured Despisers* (New York, 1958), 27.

and the Kantian conception of religion as an aid to morality. Schleier-macher denied that religion was either thinking or acting; it was feel-ing. "Feelings are exclusively the elements of religion, and none are excluded.... Ideas and principles are all foreign to religion.... If ideas and principles are to be anything, they must belong to knowledge, which is a different department of life from religion."[56]

If religion consists in feeling, then Schleiermacher was quite correct when he instructed his readers to contemplate their own navels: "But I must direct you to your own selves. You must apprehend a living move-ment. You must know how to listen to yourselves before your own consciousness.... Thus, as a feeling person, you can become an object to yourself and you can contemplate your own feeling."[57] Both sentimen-tality and subjectivism spring from Schleiermacher. They are the twin heresies of modern religion masquerading as Christianity. They per-vade Protestant and Roman Catholic, conservative and liberal, liturgi-cal and charismatic churches.

Schleiermacher believed that "To seek and to find this infinite and eternal factor in all that lives and moves, in all growth and change, in all action and passion, and to have and to know life itself only in immediate feeling – that is religion."[58] If religion is feeling, it follows that "Chris-tian doctrines are accounts of the Christian religious affections set forth in speech."[59] Doctrines, which Schleiermacher called symbols, may vary from religion to religion, and even from person to person. "Thousands might be moved religiously in the same way, and yet each, led, not so much by disposition, as by external circumstances, might designate his feelings by different symbols."[60] To those who are preoccupied with doctrines, the people Schleiermacher scornfully calls "systematizers," Schleiermacher wrote: "Nothing is of less importance to religion, for it knows nothing of deducing and connecting."[61]

Schleiermacher did not believe that religion could be charged with any wrong. What could be accused of wrong-doing was not religion, but the dogma that corrupted it.

56. Schleiermacher, 46
57. Schleiermacher, 41, 46.
58. Schleiermacher, 40.
59. C. W. Christian, *Schleiermacher* (Waco, 1979), 89.
60. Christian, 52-53.
61. Christian, 53.

Blame those who corrupt religion, who flood it with an army of for-
mulas and definitions, and seek to cast it into the fetters of a so-called
system. What is it in religion about which men have quarreled and made
parties and kindled wars? About definitions, the practical sometimes,
the theoretical always, both of which belong elsewhere.... But religion
does not, even once, desire to bring those who believe and feel to one
belief and one feeling.... [E]ach seer is a new priest, a new mediator, a
new organ.... [62]

Those who say that creeds and confessions divide and destroy the
unity of the church are, unwittingly, disciples of Schleiermacher. Ignorant men, who call themselves "practical" and are proud of their practical wisdom and common sense, are always the unwitting slaves of
some defunct theologian or philosopher.

In *On Religion* Schleiermacher wrote, "I ask, therefore, that you turn
from everything usually reckoned religion, and fix your regard on the
inward emotions and dispositions...."[63]

Significantly, Schleiermacher pointed out that these feelings, this piety, religion itself, dwells peculiarly in women: "The feeling may dwell
in many sound and strong, as for example in almost all women, without
ever having been specially a matter of contemplation."[64]

What follows from all of this, and what Schleiermacher was eager to
point out, is that if religion is different from its expressions, then those
expressions can be changed and religion still maintained. The peculiar
doctrinal expressions of the religious feelings, the expressions that we
call Christian theology, are not part of the essence of Christianity, and
the doctrines can therefore be changed whenever necessary or desirable. Doctrines are a matter of the head, but religion is a matter of the
heart. With Schleiermacher, the antithesis between the head and the
heart, which pervades virtually all theology today, conservative as well
as liberal, became the fundamental basis for religion. Schleiermacher
understood the revolutionary nature of the changes he was proposing,
for he referred to himself as the "midwife of a new Christianity."[65] Comte,
as you recall, had made the same claim, but he said it in French, not
German.

62. Christian, 55.
63. Christian, 18.
64. Christian, 47.
65. Christian, 12.

The influence of Schleiermacher and romanticism spread quickly throughout Europe and the United States. In mid-century Charles Finney, the heretical Presbyterian revivalist, attacked the seminaries because they attempted to "give young men intellectual strength, to the almost entire neglect of cultivating their moral feelings.... [The student's] intellect improves, and his heart lies waste."[66]

The Head and the Heart

In May 1850 Edwards A. Park, a professor at Andover Theological Seminary in Massachusetts, gave a speech to the Congregational ministers of Massachusetts assembled in Boston. Titled "The Theology of the Intellect and That of the Feelings," Park's speech suggested that there were two sorts of theology, and two sorts of truth. Park began his speech by illustrating his point: A father tells the literal truth about astronomy to his children, but they "learned nothing from him but falsehood."[67] "But," he said, "I have also heard of a mother who, with a woman's tact, so exhibited the general features of astronomical science that although her statements were technically erroneous," her children still learned more truth than those of the father who spoke the literal truth. "The theology of the heart," Park wrote, "...need not always accommodate itself to scientific changes, but may often use its old statements, even if, when literally understood, they be incorrect...."[68]

Charles Hodge of Princeton Seminary answered Park in a series of three articles in which he maintained that there was only one Christian theology, not two, and Park's construction, which Hodge maintained was similar to Schleiermacher's, undermined the infallibility and authority of Scripture.[69] While Hodge attacked the faculty psychology presupposed by Park's theory of two theologies that might contradict each other, he did not exegete the teachings of the Bible on the nature of man. The antithesis between the head and the heart, on which both Schleiermacher and Park relied so heavily, is not derived from the Bible.

---

66. Charles Finney, *Lectures on Revivals of Religion*, 435-436; as quoted in Hofstadter, 94.

67. Edwards A. Park, "The Theology of the Intellect and That of the Feelings," *Bibliotheca Sacra*, 1850, 45-46.

68. Park, 39.

69. Charles Hodge, "The Theology of the Intellect and That of the Feelings," *Essays and Reviews* (New York), 539-633.

Unfortunately, some of the most conservative Christian theologians have spoken carelessly, as though the heart, by which they seem to mean the emotions, were more important than the head. This error was reinforced by the romantic movement, which believed that life is deeper than logic, and by the materialists, who taught that religious emotions are facts, but religious doctrines are fairy tales. Today the antithesis between the head and the heart, and the obvious superiority of the heart, is accepted in all churches.

But the Bible makes no such disjunction: "For as a man thinks in his heart, so is he." "Why do you think evil in your hearts?" "Every intent of the thoughts of his heart was only evil continually." "He was grieved in his heart." "The imagination of man's heart is evil from his youth." "When he sees you he will be glad in his heart." There are more than 750 occurrences of the word *heart* in the Old Testament alone. Many of those verses would be utter nonsense if the word were translated "emotion."

It is obvious to anyone who cares to study the Scriptures rather than secular psychology that a person's heart thinks, wills, remembers, imagines, plans, and suffers emotions. The *heart* is simply the Scriptural name for the unitary self, the person, the inward man, who does all these things. And it is thinking that makes all these things possible. As a man thinks in his heart, so is he.

The un-Biblical antithesis between the heart and the head shaped popular religion in the nineteenth century and still shapes it today. The masculine component, the head, was subordinated to the feminine component, the heart. Revivalism was based upon this subordination, for a premise of revivalism is that it is not enough to believe with one's head, one must also trust with one's heart. When this writer was a teenager, the minister of the church he attended was fond of saying that some people would miss Heaven by twelve inches, the distance between the head and the heart, for they believed with their heads, but not with their hearts. Sometimes this is stated in a slightly different form: In order to be saved, one must trust a person, not believe a creed.

The Biblical contrast is not between the head and the heart, but between the heart and the lips, between what one thinks or believes, and what one professes. *Isaiah* 29:13 says, "These people draw near to me with their mouths and honor me with their lips, but have removed their hearts far from me."

Within the church and society at large, the disjunction between the head and the heart was applied to men and women: Men were cold, rational, logical, intellectual; women were warm, loving, emotional, trusting, feeling, affectionate, and compassionate. This natural superiority of women made them the natural repositories of virtue and religion.

Modern Gnosticism

In good heterodox fashion, some religionists in the nineteenth century were quite willing to carry this false disjunction and misunderstanding of Christianity right into their doctrine of God itself. A. B. Simpson (1843-1919), the founder of the first Bible Institute in North America in 1883, the Missionary Training College for Home and Foreign Missions, and co-founder of the Christian and Missionary Alliance Church, wrote an article called "Our Mother God." In the article Simpson declared:

> The heart of Christ is not only the heart of a man but has in it also the tenderness and gentleness of a woman. Jesus was not a man in the rigid sense of manhood as distinct from womanhood, but, as the Son of Man, the complete Head of Humanity, He combined in Himself the nature both of man and woman.... [I]n the Old Testament we find God revealing Himself under the sweet figure of motherhood....and this aspect of His blessed character finds its perfect manifestation in the Holy Ghost, our Mother God.[70]

Mary Baker Eddy, the founder of Christian Science, held similar views, and Christian Scientists today pray to "Our Father-Mother God." Eddy wrote, "We have not as much authority, in Divine Science, for considering God masculine, as we have for considering him feminine, for Love imparts the highest idea of Deity."[71] Another female-founded cult, the Shakers, "believe[d] in One God – not three male beings in one, but Father and Mother."[72]

A century earlier a Scotch Presbyterian named James Fordyce had published his *Sermons to Young Women* in which he opined that "the

70. A. B. Simpson, "Our Mother God," in *When the Comforter Came;* as quoted in Janette Hassey, *No Time for Silence* (Grand Rapids, 1986), 16.

71. Reuther and Keller, 65.

72. Anna White and Leila Taylor, *Shakerism: Its Meaning and Message* (Columbus, 1904), 255-258; as quoted in Reuther and Keller, 64.

spirit of devotion depends on sentiment, rather than ratiocination; on the feelings of gratitude and wonder, joy and sorrow, triumph and contribution, hope and fear, rather than on theological disquisition however profound...." Woman, he felt, had been placed by providence "in circumstances peculiarly advantageous for the exercises of devotion...."[73] The famous Dr. Benjamin Rush, signer of the *Declaration of Independence*, declared that "the female breast is the natural soil of Christianity."[74]

This view, so alien to the Bible, implied that a religion so natural to women was somehow unnatural to men. Just as the emotions were not fallen, as was the intellect, so women's hearts were the "natural soil" of Christian faith. This denial of the doctrine of total depravity encouraged women to be aggressive in religious exercises and activities, and demanded that men relegate religion to their mothers, wives, sisters, and daughters.

Some Ramifications

But the natures of God and man were not the only doctrines affected by the feminization of theology. Once begun, the process of feminization occurred rapidly in many different doctrines: The revivalism of the nineteenth century, particularly the work of Charles Finney, transformed theology from Calvinism into Arminianism, from the sovereignty of God to the free will of man. A God who sovereignly plans and omnipotently acts is just too masculine too endure. A God who pleads and pines is much more palatable to the modern mind.

The death of Christ, in the hands of a man like Horace Bushnell, became a way for God to affect the feelings of men, rather than to satisfy the justice of an angry God. God was a God of love, not truth, justice, or holiness. His primary characteristic became mercy, not sovereignty or justice. He had no wrath to be assuaged. The doctrine of the Atonement was transformed – from propitiation to moral influence.

Under the process of feminization, the importance of doctrine gave way to the centrality of experience. This can be observed in the American hymns written during the nineteenth century, as well as in the the-

73. Blauvelt, in Reuther and Keller, 13.
74. Blauvelt, in Reuther and Keller, 3.

ology. Unlike the eighteenth century hymns of Isaac Watts, the nineteenth century hymns of Fanny Crosby, Frances Havergal, Philip Bliss, and others, including an increasing number of women, emphasized the feelings and emotions of the singer rather than the majesty of God. The Unitarians were particularly prolific, publishing 15 separate hymnbooks between 1830 and 1865. Austin Phelps of Andover Seminary, the seminary at which Edwards Park taught, co-authored with Park and Daniel Furber the most important book on hymnology in America during the nineteenth century. Carrying out Park's theory of two theologies, those of the intellect and of the feelings, Phelps explained that hymns express the "heart of the church." They are to act as a kind of "tonic to the worshipper." What ought to be avoided in hymns, according to Phelps, was "an excess of the analytic element."[75] Unpleasant subjects such as death, punishment, and Hell, ought to be minimized.[76]

The feminization of theology in the nineteenth century substituted a new messiah for the historical Christ. Since religion consists in feelings, not knowledge, the historical Jesus disappeared together with the Jesus in Heaven, interceding for his people; and the Jesus in one's heart became the new Saviour. The written word was eclipsed by the alleged promptings of the Holy Spirit, and the twentieth-century charismatic movement is simply a logical development of the theology of feeling, whether it be found in Schleiermacher, Finney, or Parks.

Religious and philosophical ideas – Arminianism, revivalism, modernism, Kantianism – all incorporating a virulent anti-intellectualism, worked together to shape the Church Effeminate of the nineteenth and twentieth centuries. By the mid-nineteenth century the two largest churches in the United States were the Roman Church-State and the Methodist. The Calvinists had been defeated. The old virile religion whose passing Henry James lamented declined even further in the decadent twentieth century. The professed descendants of Hodge and Warfield sound more and more like the modernists of the late nineteenth century. Nevertheless, we may be confident that the teaching of God's truth will have the precise effect that he intends, whether it be

75. Austin Phelps, Edwards A. Park, and Daniel L. Furber, *Hymns and Choirs* (Andover, 1860), 52, 80-81, 79, 123; as quoted in Douglas, 219.

76. Sandra Sizer, in her *Gospel Hymns and Social Religion* (Philadelphia) quantified the tendency of nineteenth-century hymnody toward subjectivism by analyzing themes expressed in hymns. Her findings confirm these conclusions.

destruction or edification. When God wills, the apostasy of the present age will be judged and his truth once again understood and believed. Then the Church Effeminate will disappear, and the Church will be the Church Triumphant.

15

On the Councils and the Church[1]

Martin Luther

JUST AS THEY [Roman Catholic apologists] scream about the fathers and the councils, without knowing what fathers and councils are, only to drown out our voices with mere letters, so they also scream about the church. But as for saying what, who, and where the church is, they do not render either the church or God even the service of asking the question or thinking about it. They like very much to be regarded as the church, as pope, cardinals, bishops, and yet to be allowed, under this glorious name, to be nothing but pupils of the devil, desiring nothing more than to practice sheer knavery and villainy.

Well then, setting aside various writings and analyses of the word "church," we shall this time confine ourselves simply to the *Children's Creed*, which says, "I believe in one holy Christian church, the communion of saints." Here the creed clearly indicates what the church is, namely, a communion of saints, that is, a crowd [*Hauffe*] or assembly of people who are Christians and holy, which is called a Christian holy assembly, or church. Yet this word "church" [*Kirche*] is not German and does not convey the sense or meaning that should be taken from this article.

In *Acts* 19[:39] the town clerk uses the word *ecclesia* for the congregation or the people who had gathered at the market place, saying, "It shall be settled in the regular assembly." Further, "When he said this, he dismissed the assembly" [verse 41]. In these and other passages the *ecclesia* or church is nothing but an assembly of people, though they probably were heathens and not Christians. It is the same term used by town councilmen for their assembly which they summon to the city hall. Now there are many peoples in the world; the Christians, however, are

1. *Martin Luther's Basic Theological Writings,* Timothy F. Lull, editor (Minneapolis, 1989), 540.

a people with a special call and are therefore called not just *ecclesia*, "church," or "people," but *sancta catholica Christiana*, that is, "a Christian holy people" who believe in Christ. That is why they are called a Christian people and have the Holy Spirit, who sanctifies them daily, not only through the forgiveness of sin acquired for them by Christ (as the Antinomians foolishly believe), but also through the abolition, the purging, and the mortification of sins, on the basis of which they are called a holy people. Thus the "holy Christian church" is synonymous with a Christian and holy people or, as one is also wont to express it, with "holy Christendom," or "whole Christendom." The Old Testament uses the term "God's people."

If the words, "I believe that there is a holy Christian people," had been used in the *Children's Creed*, all the misery connected with this meaningless and obscure word ("church") might easily have been avoided. For the words "Christian holy people" would have brought with them, clearly and powerfully, the proper understanding and judgment of what is, and what is not, the church. Whoever would have heard the words "Christian holy people" could have promptly concluded that the pope is no people, much less a holy Christian people. So too the bishops, priests, and monks are not holy, Christian people, for they do not believe in Christ, nor do they lead a holy life, but are rather the wicked and shameful people of the devil. He who does not truly believe in Christ is not Christian or a Christian. He who does not have the Holy Spirit against sin is not holy. Consequently, they cannot be "a Christian holy people," that is, *sancta et catholica ecclesia*.

But since we use this meaningless word "church" in the *Children's Creed*, the common man thinks of the stone house called a church, as painted by the artists; or, at best, they paint the apostles, disciples, and the mother of God, as on Pentecost, with the Holy Spirit hovering over them. This is still bearable; but they are the holy Christian people of a specific time, in this case, the beginning. *Ecclesia* however, should mean the holy Christian people, not only of the days of the apostles, who are long since dead, but to the end of the world, so that there is always a holy Christian people on Earth, in whom Christ lives, works, and rules, *per redemptionem*, "through grace and the remission of sin," and the Holy Spirit, *per vivificationem et sanctificationem*, "through daily purging of sin and renewal of life," so that we do not remain in sin but are enabled and obliged to lead a new life, abounding in all kinds of good works, as the Ten Commandments or the two tables of Moses' law command, and not in old, evil works. That is Paul's teaching. But the pope, with his followers, has applied both the name and the image of the church to himself and to his vile, accursed mob, under the meaningless word *ecclesia*, "church," etc.

Nevertheless, they give themselves the right name when they call themselves *ecclesia* (that is, if we interpret this term to agree with their way of life), either *Romana* or *sancta*, but do not add (as, indeed, they cannot) *catholica*. For *ecclesia* means "a people"; that they are, just as the Turks too, are *ecclesia*, "a people." *Ecclesia Romana* means "a Roman people"; that they are too, and indeed much more Roman than the heathen of ancient times were. *Ecclesia Romana sancta* means "a holy Roman people"; that they are too, for they have invented a holiness far greater than the holiness of Christians, or than the holy Christian people possess. Their holiness is a Roman holiness, *Romanae ecclesiae*, a holiness "of the Roman people," and they are now even called *sanctissimi*, *sacrosancti*, "the most holy," as Virgil speaks of a "holy thirst for gold,"[2] and Plautus of "the most holy one of all"[3] for they cannot stand Christian holiness. Therefore they are not entitled to the name "Christian church" or "Christian people," if for no other reason than that "Christian church" is a name and "Christian holiness" an entity common to all churches and all Christians in the world; therefore it is called "catholic." But they have little, if any, regard for this common name and holiness; instead, they invented a special, higher, different, better holiness than that of others. This is to be known as *sanctitas Romana et ecclesiae Romanae sanctitas*, that is, "Roman holiness and the holiness of the Roman people."

For Christian holiness, or the holiness common to Christendom, is found where the Holy Spirit gives people faith in Christ and thus sanctifies them, *Acts* 15[:9], that is, he renews heart, soul, body, work, and conduct, inscribing the commandments of God not on tables of stone, but in hearts of flesh, 2 *Corinthians* 3[:3]. Or, if I may speak plainly, he imparts true knowledge of God, according to the first table, so that those whom he enlightens with true faith can resist all heresies, over-

---

2. *Sacra fames, sacra hostia*. Virgil (70-19 B.C.), a Roman poet, in *Aeneid*, III, 57. See H. Rushton Fairclough (trans.), *Virgil: Eclogues, Georgics, Aeneid I-III* (*The Loeb Classical Library* [2nd ed., rev.; Cambridge: Harvard University Press, 1956]), 352. Luther, quoting from memory, leaves out the term "gold" (*auri*).

3. *Omnium sacerrumus*. Plautus (d. 184 B.C.), another Roman poet, in *Mostellaria*, IV, 2, 67. Henry T. Riley (trans.), *The Comedies of Plautus* (2 vols, London, 1884), II, 500.

come all false ideas and errors, and thus remain pure in faith in opposition to the devil. He also bestows strength, and comforts timid, despondent, weak consciences against the accusation and turmoil of sin, so that the souls do not succumb or despair, and also do not become terrified of torment, pain, death, and the wrath and judgment of God, but rather, comforted and strengthened in hope, they cheerfully, boldly, and joyfully overcome the devil. He also imparts true fear and love of God, so that we do not despise God and become irritated and angry with his wondrous judgments, but love, praise, thank, and honor him for all that occurs, good or evil. That is called new holy life in the soul, in accordance with the first table of Moses. It is also called *tres virtutes theologicas*, "the three principal virtues of Christians," namely, faith, hope, and love; and the Holy Spirit, who imparts, does, and effects this (gained for us by Christ) is therefore called "sanctifier" or life-giver." For the old Adam is dead and cannot do it, and in addition has to learn from the law that he is unable to do it and that he is dead; he would not know this of himself.

In accordance with the second table, he also sanctifies the Christians in the body and induces them willingly to obey parents and rulers, to conduct themselves peacefully and humbly, to be not wrathful, vindictive, or malicious, but patient, friendly, obliging, brotherly, and loving, not unchaste, not adulterous or lewd, but chaste and pure with wife, child, and servants, or without wife and child. And on and on: They do not steal, are not usurious, avaricious, do not defraud, etc., but work honorably, support themselves honestly, lend willingly, and give and help wherever they can. Thus they do not lie, deceive, and backbite, but are kind, truthful, faithful, and trustworthy, and do whatever else the commandments of God prescribe. That is the work of the Holy Spirit, who sanctifies and also awakens the body to such a new life until it is perfected in the life beyond. That is what is called "Christian holiness." And there must always be such people on Earth, even though it may be but two or three, or only children. Unfortunately, only a few of them are old folks. And those who are not, should not count themselves as Christians; nor should they be comforted with much babbling about the forgiveness of sins and the grace of Christ, as though they were Christians – like the Antinomians do.

For they, having rejected and being unable to understand the Ten Commandments, preach much about the grace of Christ, yet they strengthen and comfort only those who remain in their sins, telling them not to fear and be terrified by sins, since they are all removed by Christ. They see and yet they let the people go on in their public sins, without any renewal or reformation of their lives. Thus it becomes quite evident that they truly fail to understand the faith and Christ, and thereby abrogate both when they preach about it. How can he speak lightly about the works of the Holy Spirit in the first table – about comfort, grace, forgiveness of sins – who does not heed or practice the works of the Holy Spirit in the second table, which he can understand and experience, while he has never attempted or experienced those of the first table? Therefore it is certain that they neither have nor understand Christ or the Holy Spirit, and their talk is nothing but froth on the tongue, and they are as already said, true Nestoriuses and Eutycheses, who confess or teach Christ in the premise, in the substance, and yet deny him in the conclusion or *idiomata*; that is, they teach Christ and yet destroy him through their teaching.

All this then has been said about Christian holiness, which the pope does not want. He has to have one that is much holier, namely, that found in the prescription of chasubles, tonsures, cowls, garb, food, festivals, days, monkery, nunning, masses, saint-worship, and countless other items of an external, bodily, transitory nature. Whether one lives under it without faith, fear of God, hope, love, and whatever the Holy Spirit, according to the first table, effects, or in misbelief, uncertainty of heart, doubts, contempt of God, impatience with God, and false trust in works (that is, idolatry), not in the grace of Christ and his merit, but in the atonement by works, even selling the surplus ones to others and taking in exchange all the goods and wealth of the world as well earned – all that is of no consequence because a man may be holier than Christian holiness itself.

Thus, in the second table it matters not that they teach disobedience toward parents and rulers, that they even murder, make war, set people against each other, envy, hate, avenge, are unchaste, lie, steal, are usurious, defraud, and indulge in every villainy to the utmost. Just throw a surplice over your head and you are holy in accordance with the Roman church's holiness, and you can indeed be saved without the Christian holiness. But we will pay no attention to these filthy people, for any effort expended on them will be futile. "God's wrath has come upon them at last," as Paul says [1 Thessalonians 2:16]. Instead, we shall discuss the church among ourselves.

Well then, the *Children's Creed* teaches us (as was said) that a Christian holy people is to be and to remain on Earth until the end of the world. This is an article of faith that cannot be terminated until that which it believes comes, as Christ promises, "I am with you always, to the close of the age" [*Matthew* 28:20]. But how will or how can a poor confused person tell where such Christian holy people are to be found in this world? Indeed, they are supposed to be in this life and on Earth, for they of course believe that a heavenly nature and an eternal life are to come, but as yet they do not possess them. Therefore, they must still be in this life and remain in this life and in this world until the end of the world. For they profess, "I believe in another life"; thereby they confess that they have not yet arrived in the other life, but believe in it, hope for it, and love it as their true fatherland and life, while they must yet remain and tarry here in exile – as we sing in the hymn about the Holy Spirit, "As homeward we journey from this exile. Lord, have mercy." We shall now speak of this.

First, the holy Christian people are recognized by their possession of the holy Word of God. To be sure, not all have it in equal measure, as Paul says [*1 Corinthians* 3:12-14]. Some possess the Word in its complete purity, others do not. Those who have the pure Word are called those who "build on the foundation with gold, silver, and precious stones"; those who do not have it in its purity are the ones who "build on the foundation with wood, hay, and straw," and yet will be saved through fire. More than enough was said about this above. This is the principal item, and the holiest of holy possessions [*Heiligthum*], by reason of which the Christian people are called holy; for God's Word is holy and sanctifies everything it touches; it is indeed the very holiness of God, Romans 1[:16], "It is the power of God for salvation to every one who has faith," and *1 Timothy* 4 [:5], "Everything is consecrated by the Word of God and prayer." For the Holy Spirit himself administers it and anoints or sanctifies the Christian church with it rather than with the pope's chrism, with which he anoints or consecrates fingers, garb, cloaks, chalices, and stones. These objects will never teach one to love God, to believe, to praise, to be pious. They may adorn the bag of maggots [*Madensack*], but afterward they fall apart and decay with the chrism and whatever holiness it contains, and with the bag of maggots itself.

Yet this holy possession is the true holy possession, the true ointment that anoints unto life eternal, even though you cannot have a papal crown or a bishop's hat, but must die bare and naked, just like children (in fact, all of us), who are baptized naked and without any adornment. But we are speaking of the external word, preached orally by men like you and me, for this is what Christ left behind as an external sign, by which his church, or his Christian people in the world, should be recognized. We also speak of this external word as it is sincerely believed and openly professed before the world, as Christ says, "Every one who acknowledges me before men, I also will acknowledge before my Father and his angels" [*Matthew* 10:32]. There are many who know it in their hearts, but will not profess it openly. Many possess it, but do not believe in it or act by it, for the number of those who believe in and act by it is small – as the parable of the seed in *Matthew* 13[:4-8] says that three sections of the field receive and contain the seed, but only the fourth section, the fine and good soil, bears fruit with patience.

Now, wherever you hear or see this Word preached, believed, professed, and lived, do not doubt that the true *ecclesia sancta catholica*, "a Christian holy people" must be there, even though their number is very small. For God's Word "shall not return empty," *Isaiah* 55[:11], but must have at least a fourth or a fraction of the field. And even if there were no other sign than this alone, it would still suffice to prove that a Christian, holy people must exist there, for God's Word cannot be without God's people, and conversely, God's people cannot be without God's Word. Otherwise, who would preach or hear it preached, if there were no people of God? And what could or would God's people believe, if there were no Word of God?

This is the thing that performs all miracles, effects, sustains, carries out, and does everything, exorcises all devils, like pilgrimage-devils, indulgence-devils, bull-devils, brotherhood-devils, saint-devils, mass-devils, purgatory-devils, monastery-devils, priest-devils, mob-devils, insurrection-devils, heresy-devils, all pope-devils, also Antinomian-devils, but not without raving and rampaging, as is seen in the poor men mentioned in *Mark* 1[:23-26] and 9[:17-29]. No, he must depart with raving and rampaging as is evidenced by Emser,[4] Eck,[5] Snot-nose,[6]

---

4. Jerome Emser (1478-1527), a humanist who became an adviser to Duke George of Saxony, Catholic ruler of Saxony and an enemy of Luther. See Luther's polemic tract *To the Leipzig Goat* (1521). PE 3, 275-286.

5. John Eck (1486-1543), known for his debate with Luther at Leipzig in 1518.

6. *Rotzleffel*, a German term for "impudent young rascal" and Luther's name for John Cochlaeus (1479-1552), a Catholic theologian who was a fanatic opponent of the

Schmid,[7] Wetzel,[8] Bumpkin, Boor, Churl, Brute, Sow, Ass, and the rout of his screamers and scribes. They all are the devil's mouths and members, through whom he raves and rampages. But it does them no good. He must take his leave; he is unable to endure the power of the Word. They themselves confess that it is God's Word and Holy Scripture, claiming, however, that one fares better with the fathers and the councils. Let them go their way. It is enough for us to know how this chief holy possession purges, sustains, nourishes, strengthens, and protects the church, as St. Augustine also says, "The church is begotten, cared for, nourished, and strengthened by the Word of God." But those who persecute and condemn it identify themselves by their own fruits.

Reformation and the author of *Memoirs on the Actions and Writings of Martin Luther* (1549), a polemic biography of Luther.

7. John Faber (1478-1541), the son of a smith (*faber* in Latin) and bishop in Vienna. He had been writing polemic tracts against Luther since 1521.

8. Used as a name for dogs and as a pun on George Wetzel (1501-1573), who was originally a follower of Luther, but since 1533 had been an opponent of the Reformation and a protege of Duke George of Saxony.

16

The Relation of Church and State

Charles Hodge[1]

T HIS IS AN exceedingly complicated and difficult subject. There are three aspects under which it may be viewed.

I. The actual relation which at different times and in different countries has subsisted between the two institutions.

II. The theory devised to justify or determine the limits of such existing relation.

III. The normal relation, such as should exist according to the revealed will of God, and the nature of the state and of the church.

Constantine

Before the conversion of Constantine, the church was of course so far independent of the state that she determined her own faith, regulated her worship, chose her officers, and exercised her discipline without any interference of the civil authorities. Her members were regarded as citizens of the state, whose religious opinions and practices were, except in times of persecution, regarded as matters of indifference. It is probable that much the same liberty was accorded to the early Christians as was granted by the Romans to the Jews, who were not only allowed, in ordinary cases, to conduct their synagogue services as they pleased, but to decide matters of dispute among themselves, according to their own laws. It is also stated that churches were allowed to hold real estate before the profession of Christianity by the Emperor.

1. Charles Hodge was perhaps the most influential American Presbyterian theologian of the nineteenth century, an instructor at Princeton Seminary for decades, and the author of many books, including his three volume *Systematic Theology*. This essay originally appeared in the *Princeton Review* in 1863. It has been reprinted in *The Reformation of the Church*, edited by Iain H. Murray, and published by The Banner of Truth Trust, Edinburgh, 1957.

When Constantine declared himself a Christian, he expressed the relation which was henceforth to subsist between church and state, by saying to certain bishops, "God has made you the bishops of the internal affairs of the church, and me the bishop of its external affairs." This saying has ever since been, throughout a large portion of Christendom, the standing formula for expressing the relation of the civil magistrate to the kingdom of Christ.

According to this statement, it belongs to the church, through her own organs, to choose her officers, to regulate all matters relating to doctrine, to administer the Word and sacraments, to order public worship, and to exercise discipline. And to the state it belongs to provide for the support of the clergy, to determine the sources and amount of their incomes, to fix the limits of parishes and dioceses, to provide places of public worship, to call together the clergy, to preside in their meetings, to give the force of laws to their decisions, and to see that external obedience at least was rendered to the decrees and acts of discipline.

And this, in general terms, was the actual relation between the two institutions under the Roman emperors and in many of the states which rose after the dissolution of the Roman Empire. But it is easy to see that the distinction between the internal affairs which belonged to the bishops, and the external which belonged to the civil ruler, is too indefinite to keep two mighty bodies from coming into collision. If the magistrate provided the support of the bishops and sustained them in their places of influence, he felt entitled to have a voice in saying who should receive his funds and use that influence. If he was to enforce the decisions of councils as to matters of faith and discipline, he must have some agency in determining what those decisions should be. If he was to banish from his kingdom those whom the clergy excluded from the church, he must judge whether such exclusion was in itself just. And on the other hand, if the church was recognized as a divine institution, with divinely constituted government and powers, she would constantly struggle to preserve her prerogatives from the encroachments of the state and to draw to herself all the power requisite to enforce her decisions in the sphere of the state into which she was adopted, which she of right possessed in her own sphere as a spiritual, and, in one sense voluntary, society.

Simple and plausible, therefore, as the relation between the church and state, as determined by Constantine, may at first sight appear, the whole history of the church shows that it cannot be maintained. Either the church will encroach on the peculiar province of the state, or the state upon that of the church. It would require an outline of ecclesiastical history, from Constantine to the present day, to exhibit the conflicts and vacillations of these two principles. The struggle, though protracted and varied in its prospects, was decided in favour of the church, which under the papacy gained a complete ascendancy over the state.[2]

The Middle Ages

The papal world constituted one body, of which the pope, as Vicar of Christ, was the head. This spiritual body claimed a divine right to make its own laws, appoint its own officers, and have its own tribunals, to which alone its officers were amenable, and before whom all persons in the state, from the highest to the lowest, could be cited to appear. All ecclesiastical persons were thus withdrawn from the jurisdiction of the state; while all civil persons were subject to the jurisdiction of the church. The church being the infallible judge of all questions relating to faith and practice, and it being the obvious duty of all men to receive the decisions and obey the injunctions of an infallible authority, the state was bound to receive all those decisions and enforce all those commands. The civil magistrate had no judgment or discretion in the case: He was but the secular arm of the church, with whose judgments, no matter how injurious he might regard them to his own prerogative or to the interests of his people, he had no right to interfere. The church, however, claimed the right to interfere in all the decisions of the civil power; because she only could judge whether those decisions were or were not inimical to the true faith, or consistent with the rule of duty. Hence arose what is called the indirect power of the church in the temporal affairs of the state. Even without going to the extreme of claiming for the pope, by divine right, a direct sovereignty over the Christian world, moderate Romanists of the Italian school claimed for the pope this indirect power in the civil affairs of kingdoms; that is, power of deciding whether any law or measure was or was not hurtful to the church, and either to sanction or to annul it. And in case any sovereign should persist in a course pronounced by an infallible authority hurtful to the church, the obligation of obedience on the part of his subjects was declared to be at an end, and the sovereign deposed.

2. In the East, it was the state that prevailed over the church. – *Editor.*

In most cases, the actual relation between the church and state is determined historically, *i.e.*, by the course of events, and then a theory invented to explain and justify it; but in the case of the papacy, it is probable the theory preceded and produced the actual relation. On the assumption of the external unity of the whole church under a visible head and of the infallibility of that visible body when speaking through its appropriate organ, the relation of the church to the state – which Gregory strove to realize, and which did for ages subsist – is the normal relation; and it is therefore, at the present day, the very theory which is held by the great body of Romanists.

In practice, however, it was found intolerable; and therefore, especially in France, and later in Austria, the kings have resisted this domination and asserted that as the state no less than the church is of divine origin, the former has the right to judge whether the acts and decisions of the church are consistent with the rights and interests of the state. The kings of France, therefore, claimed indirect power in the affairs of the church; and exercised the right of giving a *placet*, as it was called, to acts of the church; that is, they required that such acts should be submitted to them and receive their sanction before taking effect in their dominions.

As the Reformation involved the rejection of the doctrine of the visible unity of the church under one infallible head, it of necessity introduced a change in the relation between the state and the church. This relation, however, was very different in different countries, and that difference was evidently not the result of any preconceived theory, but of the course of events. It was, therefore, one thing in England, another in Scotland, and another in Germany.

The Church of England

With regard to England, it may be said, in general terms, that the Reformation was effected by the civil power. The authority by which all changes were decreed, was that of the king and Parliament. The church passively submitted, subscribing articles presented for acceptance, and adopting forms of worship and general regulations prescribed for her use. This fact is so inconsistent with the high-church theory that every effort is made by advocates of that theory to evade its force and to show that the change was the work of the church itself. It is admitted, however, by Episcopal writers themselves that in the time of Henry and

Edward, the great majority both of the clergy and the people, *i.e.* the church, was opposed to the Reformation.

Henry rejected the authority of the pope, though he adhered to the doctrines of Romanism. He declared himself by Act of Parliament the head of the church and required all the bishops to give up their sees, suspending them from office, and then made each take out a commission from the crown in which it was declared that all ecclesiastical power flowed from the sovereign, and that the bishops acted in his name and by virtue of power derived from him.

The six Articles were framed by his authority, in opposition to Cranmer and the real Reformers, and enacted by Parliament and made obligatory under severe penalties upon all the clergy. These Articles affirm all the distinguishing doctrines of Romanism. The clearest proof that they rested on the authority of the king is, that as soon as he died they were discarded, and a doctrinal formulary of an opposite character adopted.

Under Edward VI, the actual practice was for the crown to appoint a certain number of the clergy to prepare the requisite formularies or measures; and then these, if approved by the king, were published in his name and enforced by Parliament. The convocation and the clergy then gave their assent. It was thus the *Prayer Book* was prepared and introduced. Thus, too, the *Articles of Religion* were, under Edward, the act of the civil power alone. They were drawn up under Cranmer's direction with the assistance of other divines, but they were not the work of the Convocation, as their preamble would seem to imply; nor were they set forth by any authority but that of the Crown. Under Elizabeth they were revised by the Convocation.

The actual relation of the church to the state in England is sufficiently indicated by these facts. The king was declared to be the supreme head of the church, *i.e.*, the source of authority in its government, and the supreme judge of all persons and causes ecclesiastical, of whatever kind. The clergy were brought with great difficulty to make this acknowledgment, and therefore it cannot be said to be the spontaneous act of the church. It was rather a usurpation. It is said that the acknowledgment was made with the saving clause, *quantum per Christi legem licet*, with regard to which there is a dispute whether it was in the first acknowledgment. The preponderance of evidence, so far as we know, is against it; and certain it is, it is not now in the oath. And it can make little difference, because the very end of the oath was to declare that Christ did allow the king the power which he claimed and exercised.

The king then, as head of the church, changed the form of worship, introduced new articles of faith, suspended and appointed bishops, visited all parts of the church to reform abuses, issued edicts regulating matters of discipline, granted commissions to the bishops to act in his name, and by Act of Parliament declared that all jurisdiction – spiritual and temporal – emanates from him, and that all proceedings in the episcopal courts should be in his name.

These principles have ever been acted on in the Church of England, though with less flagrancy of course in the settled state of the church than at the Reformation. All the proceedings, however, of Elizabeth; all the acts of James I against the Puritans; of Charles I in Scotland, in the introduction of episcopacy into that country; of Charles II at his restoration; and even of William III at the Revolution, when the non-juring bishops were excluded, were founded on the assumption of the absolute power of the state over the church. And everything still rests on that foundation. The king still appoints all the bishops and has the legal right to suspend them; all the binding authority of the *Articles* and *Prayer Book* rests on Acts of Parliament. No man can be refused admission to the church, no matter what his opinions or character, against the will of the state; and no man can be excommunicated but by civil process; and the ultimate decision, even in the trial of a bishop for heresy, is rendered by the King in Council.

Different theories have been devised to justify this entire subordination of the church to the state. The early Reformers (Cranmer especially) were thoroughly Erastian and held that the king was entrusted with the whole care of his subjects, as well concerning the administration of the Word, as in things civil and political; and as he had under him civil officers to act in his name, so he had church officers, the one class being assigned, appointed, and selected by the authority of the king as much as the other. Cranmer did not even hold to the necessity of any ordination by church officers, considering the king's commission all-sufficient. This whole theory rests on an exorbitant notion of the regal power.

A second theory supposes that there is no difference between a Christian state and a church. A church is a people professing Christianity, and they may adopt what form of government they please. This supposes not only that the details of church government are not prescribed in Scripture, but that there is no government in the hands of church officers at all ordained by Christ; but in whatever way the will of the sovereign power, *i.e.* of the people, is expressed and exercised, is, as to its form, legitimate; and hence the best and most healthful form of church government is that which most fully identifies the church with the state. This is the doctrine of Dr. Arnold. Though this theory, if sound, might justify the existing state of things in England, it cannot justify the Reformation; for that was not carried on by the people, *i.e.* the church in its state capacity, but by civil authority despite both the clergy and the people.

High churchmen take different grounds. Some admit the irregularity in the mode of proceeding under Henry and Elizabeth, but justify it on the ground of necessity, or of extraordinary emergency, calling for the exercise of extraordinary powers. Others, as Mr. Palmer, deny that the church is responsible for those acts, or that she is to be judged by the preamble of Acts of Parliament, or by the claims or acts of the crown, but exclusively by her own declarations and acts. And he endeavors to show that all the leading facts of the Reformation were determined by the church. To do this, however, he is obliged to maintain that what the king did on the advice of a few divines was done by the church, which is as unreasonable as to refer the sanitary or legal regulations of a kingdom to the authority of the physicians or lawyers who may be consulted in drawing them up.

Mr. Palmer falls back on the theory suggested by Constantine, which assigns the internal government of the church to bishops, and the external to the king. He accordingly denies that the king can, either by himself or by officers deriving their authority from him, pronounce definitions of faith, administer the Word or sacraments, or absolve or excommunicate. He may, however, convene synods and preside in them; sanction their decisions, and give them the force of laws; he may refuse to sanction them, if contrary to the doctrines of the Catholic church, or injurious to the state; he may receive appeals from church courts; preserve subordination and unity in the church; prevent, by civil pains and penalties, all secession from her communion; and found and endow new bishoprics.

This doctrine rests on the assumption,

1. That it is the design of the state, and the duty of its officers, to promote and sustain religion by civil pains and penalties;

2. That the church is a divine institution, with a prescribed faith and discipline; and

3. That the marks of the true church are so plain that no honest man can mistake them.

The only point in which this system differs from the papal doctrine on this subject is that it allows the civil magistrate discretion whether he will enforce the decisions of the church or not. This difference arises from the fact that Tractarians do not pretend that provincial synods are infallible, and with such only has the king anything to do; whereas Romanists maintain that the pope, speaking *ex cathedra*, is infallible. There is room, therefore, for discretion in reference to the decisions of the former, but none in reference to those of the latter.

Mr. Palmer, however, is far from maintaining that the actual state of things corresponds with his theory, and most Tractarians are loud in their complaints of the bondage under which the church in England is now groaning.

Lutherans

In Germany the course of the Reformation was very different from what it was in England, and consequently the relation between the church and state received a different form. The movement took its rise, and was guided in all its progress, in the former country by Luther and his associates, and was sanctioned cordially by the people. He did not wait to be called up by the Elector to denounce the errors of popery, or to reform its abuses. He did both, and the people joined him. They besought the civil authorities to sanction these changes and to protect and aid them in carrying them out. And the Electors slowly and cautiously granted their sanction. The Reformation here, therefore, did not proceed from the state, but really and truly from the church, *i.e.* the clergy and people, and the state sanctioned and joined it. Had the bishops generally cooperated in the work, it is probable, from the frequent declarations of Luther and Melanchthon, they would in Germany, as in Sweden, have been allowed – not as a matter of right, but of expediency – to retain the executive power in their hands. But as they had not only greatly neglected all discipline in the church, and finally sided with Rome, the Reformers called on the Electors to appoint consistories, to be composed, as they expressed it, "of honest and learned men," to supply the deficiency. These bodies were at first designed simply to administer discipline. They were to be church courts, for the trial and punishment of spiritual offences. As, however, the bishops withdrew, the powers of the consistories were enlarged, and they became on the one hand the organ of the church. As the members of these consistories are appointed by the state, and as they are the organs of administering both the internal and external affairs of the state, the prince is, in Lutheran countries, the real possessor of church power, *i.e.* it is regarded as inhering in him. The whole administration of its affairs is in his hands, and whatever changes are introduced are made by his authority. Accordingly, the union of the Lutheran and Reformed churches and the introduction of a new liturgy was the act of the late king of Prussia. At first it was only advisory on his part, but he subsequently began to coerce compliance with his will. This extreme exercise of authority, however, met with great opposition, and was, by a large part of the church, considered as transcending the legitimate power of the state. The present king disclaims such power, and says he wishes to know the mind of the church, and stands ready to carry out her wishes if consistent with his conscience.

The actual power of the state in Lutheran countries was the result of the Reformation and not of a theory of what ought to be the relation of the church and state. Different theories have been suggested, in order to give form and intelligibility to this relation. The most common is that the prince is there, and, by the will of the church heir to the power of the bishops. His power is therefore called an episcopate. This theory includes the following points.

1. Civil and ecclesiastical government are distinct.

2. The object of church government is mainly the preservation of the truth.

3. Church power belongs by the ordinance of God to the church itself and to the prince as the highest member of the church, and, since the religious peace, by the legal devolution on him of the power of the bishops.

4. This authority is, however, only external, a *potestas externa*, in the exercise of which he is bound to act according to the judgment of the clergy, and the people have the right to assent or dissent. This is the doctrine of the three orders, as it is called; that is, that church power belongs to the church as composed of prince, clergy, and people.

5. Hence the prince possesses civil and ecclesiastical power in different ways and on different subjects. This is considered the orthodox,

established doctrine of the Lutheran Church on the relation of the church and state. It is the doctrine of all the older, eminent theologians of that church. The other theories are the Territorial, *i.e.* Erastian; the collegiate (voluntary union); and the Hegelian – that the state is God's kingdom; the church but a form of the state. The prince is the point of unity, having the full power of both. He appoints (not merely confirms) bishops, prescribes liturgies, and gives the contents as well as the binding form to all church decisions.

The Reformed Church

According to the Reformed Church of Geneva, Germany, France, Holland, and Scotland, the relation of state and church is taught in the following propositions as given and sustained by Turretin, Lec. 28, Ques. 34.

1. Various rights belong to the Christian magistrate in reference to the church.

This authority is confined within certain limits, and is essentially different from that of pastors. These limits are thus determined:

(a) The magistrate cannot introduce new articles of faith, or new rites or modes of worship.

(b) He cannot administer the Word and sacraments.

(c) He does not possess the power of the keys.

(d) He cannot prescribe to pastors the form of preaching or administration of sacraments.

(e) He cannot decide on ecclesiastical affairs, or on controversies of faith, without consulting the pastors.

On the other hand:

(a) He ought to establish the true religion, and when established, faithfully uphold it, and if corrupted, restore and reform it.

(b) He should, to the utmost, protect the church by restraining heretics and disturbers of its peace by propagating and defending the true religion and hindering the confession of false religions.

(c) Provide proper ministers, and sustain them in the administration of the Word and sacraments, according to the Word of God, and found schools as well for the church as the state.

(d) See that ministers do their duty faithfully according to the canons of the church and the laws of the land.

(e) Cause that confessions of faith and ecclesiastical constitutions, agreeable to the Scriptures, be sanctioned, and when sanctioned adhered to.

(f) To call ordinary and extraordinary synods, to moderate in them, and to sanction their decisions with his authority.

The question, "whether the state can rightfully force its subject to profess the faith," is answered in the negative. The question – "whether heretics should be capitally punished," – is answered in the affirmative, provided their heresy is gross and dangerous to the church and state, and provided they are contumacious and malignant in the defence and propagation of it.

The *Westminster Confession*, as adopted by the Church of Scotland, taught the same general doctrine. The 23rd chapter of that *Confession* contains the following clause:

> The civil magistrate may not assume to himself the administration of the Word and sacraments, or the power of the keys of the kingdom of Heaven, yet he hath the authority, and it is his duty, to take order that unity and peace be preserved in the church, that the faith of God be kept pure and entire, that all blasphemies and heresies be suppressed, all corruptions and abuses in worship and discipline be prevented or reformed, and all the ordinances of God duly settled, administered, and observed; for the better effecting whereof he hath power to call synods, to be present at them, and to provide that whatsoever is transacted in them be according to the mind of God.

When this *Confession* was adopted by our church in 1729, this clause was excepted, or adopted only in a qualified manner; and when our present constitution was adopted in 1789, it and the corresponding passages in the *Larger Catechism* were omitted. It has, however, always been part of the *Confession* of the Church of Scotland (and was, it is believed, retained in the *Cambridge* and *Saybrooke Platforms* as adopted in New England).

In words, this clause seems to cover all the ground taken by Mr. Palmer. History shows, however, that the church in Scotland has ever been, in a great measure, independent of the state, and for generations in conflict with it. The practical interpretation, therefore, of the doctrine here taught, has been to deny to the civil magistrate any real control in ecclesiastical affairs.

The late Dr. Cunningham, in one of his tracts, occasioned by the recent controversies, thus expounds the doctrine of this passage.

1. He says, by the civil magistrate is to be understood the supreme civil power; and that the *Confession* merely teaches what the civil ruler will find to be his duty when he comes to the study of the Word of God.

2. That the rule of all his judgments is the Word of God.

3. That the *Confession* denies to the civil magistrate all right to the ministration of the Word and sacraments, or to the power of the keys, that is, to the management of the ordinary affairs of the church of Christ; and states, that as it is the duty of every private person to judge for himself whether the doctrines, discipline, and decisions of a church are according to the Word of God, and if so, then to receive, obey, and promote them; so also it is the duty of the civil magistrate, in his sphere, and in the exercise of his legitimate authority and influence, to do the same.

In that branch of the Reformed church which was transported to this country by the Puritans and established in New England, this same doctrine as to the duty of the magistrate and relation to the church and state was taught, though under a somewhat modified form. The New England theory was more of a theocracy. All civil power was confined to the members of the church, no person being either eligible to office, or entitled to the right of suffrage, who was not in full communion of some church. The laws of the church became thus the laws of the land, and the two institutions were in a measure merged together. The duty of the magistrate to make and enforce laws for the support of religion, for the suppression of heresy and punishment of heretics, was clearly taught. John Cotton even wrote a book to prove that persecution was a Christian duty.

The theory on which this doctrine of the Reformed church is founded, is,

1. That the state is a divine institution, designed for promoting the general welfare of society, and as religion is necessary to that welfare, religion falls legitimately within the sphere of the state.

2. That the magistrate, as representing the state, is, by divine appointment, the guardian of the law, to take vengeance on those who transgress, and for the praise of those who obey; and as the law consists of two tables, one relating to our duties to God, and the other to our duties to men, the magistrate is, *ex officio*, the guardian of both tables and bound to punish the infractions of the one as well as of the other.

3. That the Word of God determines the limits of the magistrate's office in reference to both classes of his duties; and as, under the Old Testament, there was a form of religion with its rites and officers prescribed which the magistrate could not change, so there is under the New. But under the Old, we find with this church government the kings were required to do, and in fact did do, much for the support and reformation of religion and the punishment of idolaters; so they are now bound to act on the same principles, making the pious kings of the Old Testament their model.

The American Church

The doctrine current among us on this subject is of very recent origin. It was unknown to the ancients before the advent. In no country was religion disconnected with the state. It was unknown to the Jews. The early Christians were not in circumstances to determine the duty of Christian magistrates to the Christian church. Since the time of Constantine, in no part of Christendom and by no denomination has the ground been assumed, until a recent period, that the state and church should be separate and independent bodies. Yet to this doctrine the public mind in this country has already been brought, and to the same conclusion the convictions of God's people in all parts of the world seem rapidly tending. On what grounds, then, does this novel, yet sound, doctrine rest? This question can only be answered in a very general and superficial manner on the present occasion.

1. In the first place it assumes that the state, the family, and the church are all divine institutions, having the same general end in view, but designed to accomplish that end by different means. That as we cannot infer from the fact that the family and the state are both designed to promote the welfare of men, that the magistrate has the right to interfere in the domestic economy of the family; so neither can we infer from the church and state having the same general end, that the one can rightfully interfere with the affairs of the other. If there were no other institution than the family, we might infer that all the means now used by the church and state, for the good of men, might properly be used by the family; and if there were no church, as a separate institution of God, then we might infer that the family and the state were designed to accomplish all that could be effected. But as God has instituted the family for domestic training and government; the state, that we may lead quiet

and peaceable lives; and the church for the promotion and extension of true religion, the three are to be kept distinctive within their respective spheres.

2. That the relative duties of these several institutions cannot be learned by reasoning *a priori* from their design, but must be determined from the Word of God. And when reasoning from the Word of God, we are not authorized to argue from the Old Testament economy because that was avowedly temporary and has been abolished, but must derive our conclusions from the New Testament. We find it there taught:

(a) That Christ did institute a church separate from the state, giving it separate laws and officers.

(b) That he laid down the qualifications of those officers and enjoined on the church, not on the state, to judge of their possession by candidates.

(c) That he prescribed the terms of admission to and the grounds of exclusion from the church, and left with the church its officers to administer these rules.

These acts are utterly inconsistent with Erastianism and with the relation established in England between the church and state.

3. That the New Testament, when speaking of the immediate design of the state and the official duties of the magistrate, never intimates that he has those functions which the common doctrine of the Lutheran and Reformed church assign him. This silence, together with the fact that those functions are assigned to the church and church officers, is proof that it is not the will of God that they should be assumed by the state.

4. That the only means which the state can employ to accomplish many of the objects said to belong to it, *viz.* pains and penalties, are inconsistent with the example and commands of Christ; with the rights of private Christians, guaranteed in the Word of God (*i.e.*, to serve God according to the dictates of his conscience); are ineffectual to the true end of religion, which is voluntary obedience to the truth; and productive of incalculable evil. The New Testament, therefore, does not teach that the magistrate is entitled to take care that true religion is established and maintained; that right men are appointed to church offices; that those officers do their duty, that proper persons be admitted, and improper persons be rejected from the church; or that heretics be punished. And on the other hand, by enjoining all these duties upon the

church, as an institution distinct from the state, it teaches positively that they do not belong to the magistrate, but to the church. If to this it be added that experience teaches that the magistrate is the most unfit person to discharge these duties; that his attempting it has always been injurious to religion and inimical to the rights of conscience, we have reason to rejoice in the recently discovered truth that the church is independent of the state, and that the state best promotes her interests by letting her alone.

PART 4

AUTOCRATS IN THE CHURCH

"You know that the rulers of the Gentiles lord it over them,
and those who are great exercise dominion over them.
Yet it shall not be so among you;
but whoever desires to become great among you,
let him be your servant,
and whoever desires to be first among you,
let him be your slave,
just as the Son of Man did not come to be served,
but to serve,
and to give his life a ransom for many."
Matthew 20:25-28

17

The Roman Church-State[1]

John Calvin

How MUCH the ministry of the Word and sacraments should weigh with us, and how far reverence for it should extend, so as to be a perpetual badge for distinguishing the church, has been explained; for we have shown, first, that wherever it exists entire and unimpaired, no errors of conduct, no defects should prevent us from giving the name of church;[2] and, secondly, that trivial errors in this ministry ought not to make us regard it as illegitimate. Moreover, we have shown that the errors to which such pardon is due, are those by which the fundamental doctrine of religion is not injured, and by which those articles of religion, in which all believers should agree, are not suppressed, while, in regard to the sacraments, the defects are such as neither destroy nor impair the legitimate institution of their Author. But as soon as falsehood has forced its way into the citadel of religion, as soon as the sum of necessary doctrine is inverted, and the use of the sacraments is destroyed, the death of the church undoubtedly ensues, just as the life of man is destroyed when his throat is pierced, or his vitals mortally wounded. This is clearly evinced by the words of Paul when he says that the church is "built upon the foundation of the apostles and prophets, Jesus Christ himself being the chief cornerstone" (*Ephesians* 2:20). If the church is founded on the doctrine of the apostles and prophets, by which believers are enjoined to place their salvation in Christ alone, then if

---

1. John Calvin, *Institutes of the Christian Religion*, Henry Beveridge, translator. Eerdmans, 1970, II, 304-314.

2. French, "Secondement, qu'encore il y ait quelques petites fautes, ou en la doctrine ou aux sacremens qu'icelui no laisse point d'avoir sa vigeur." – Secondly, that though there may be some little faults either in doctrine or in the sacraments, the church ceases not to be in vigor.

that doctrine is destroyed, how can the church continue to stand? The church must necessarily fall whenever that sum of religion, which alone can sustain it, has given way. Again, if the true church is "the pillar and ground of the truth" (1 Timothy 3:15), it is certain that there is no church where lying and falsehood have usurped the ascendancy.

Since this is the state of matters under the papacy, we can understand how much of the church there survives.[3] There, instead of the ministry of the Word, prevails a perverted government, compounded of lies, a government which partly extinguishes, partly suppresses, the pure light. In place of the Lord's Supper, the foulest sacrilege has entered, the worship of God is deformed by a varied mass of intolerable superstitions; doctrine (without which Christianity exists not) is wholly buried and exploded, the public assemblies are schools of idolatry and impiety. Wherefore, in declining fatal participation in such wickedness, we run no risk of being disseered from the church of Christ. The communion of the church was not instituted to be a chain to bind us in idolatry, impiety, ignorance of God, and other kinds of evil, but rather to retain us in the fear of God and obedience of the truth. They, indeed, vaunt loudly of their church,[4] as if there was not another in the world; and then, as if the matter were ended, they make out that all are schismatics who withdraw from obedience to that church which they thus depict, that all are heretics who presume to whisper against its doctrine (see section 5). But by what arguments do they prove their possession of the true church? They appeal to ancient records which formerly existed in Italy, France, and Spain, pretending to derive their origin from those holy men who, by sound doctrine, founded and raised up churches, confirmed the doctrine, and reared the edifice of the church with their blood; they pretend that the church thus consecrated by spiritual gifts and the blood of martyrs was preserved from destruction by a perpetual succession of bishops. They dwell on the importance which Irenaeus, Tertullian, Origen, Augustine, and others attached to this succession (see section 3). How frivolous and plainly ludicrous these allegations are, I will enable any, who will for a little consider the matter with me, to understand without any difficulty. I would also exhort our opponents to give their serious attention, if I had any hope of being able to benefit

3. See chapter 1, section 10; chapter 2, section 10; chapter 8, section 12.
4. French, "Je sais bien que les flatteurs du Pape magnifient grandement leur Eglise."
– I know that the flatterers of the Pope greatly extol their Church.

them by instruction; but since they have laid aside all regard to truth, and make it their only aim to prosecute their own ends in whatever way they can, I will only make a few observations by which good men and lovers of truth may disentangle themselves from their quibbles. First, I ask them why they do not quote Africa, and Egypt, and all Asia, just because in all those regions there was a cessation of that sacred succession, by the aid of which they vaunt of having continued churches. They therefore fall back on the assertion, that they have the true church, because ever since it began to exist it was never destitute of bishops, because they succeeded each other in an unbroken series. But what if I bring Greece before them? Therefore, I again ask them, why they say that the church perished among the Greeks among whom there never was any interruption in the succession of bishops – a succession, in their opinion, the only guardian and preserver of the church? They make the Greeks schismatics. Why? Because, by revolting from the apostolic See, they lost their privilege. What? Do not those who revolt from Christ much more deserve to lose it? It follows, therefore, that the pretence of succession is vain, if posterity do not retain the truth of Christ, which was handed down to them by their fathers, safe and uncorrupted, and continue in it.

In the present day, therefore, the pretence of the Romanists is just the same as that which appears to have been formerly used by the Jews, when the Prophets of the Lord charged them with blindness, impiety, and idolatry. For as the Jews proudly vaunted of their temple, ceremonies, and priesthood, by which with strong reason, as they supposed they measured the church, so instead of the church, we are presented by the Romanists with certain external masks, which often are far from being connected with the church, and without which the church can perfectly exist. Wherefore, we need no other argument to refute them than that which Jeremiah opposed the foolish confidence of the Jews – namely, "Trust ye not in lying words, saying, The temple of the Lord, the temple of the Lord, the temple of the Lord are these" (*Jeremiah* 7:4). The Lord recognizes nothing as his own, save when his Word is heard and religiously observed. Thus, though the glory of God sat in the sanctuary between the cherubim (*Ezekiel* 10:4), and he had promised that he would there have his stated abode, still when the priests corrupted his worship by depraved superstitions, he transferred it elsewhere, and left the place without any sanctity. If that temple which seemed consecrated for the perpetual habitation of God could be abandoned by God and become profane, the Romanists have no ground to pretend that God is so bound to persons or places, and fixed to external observances, that he must remain with those who have only the name and semblance of a church. This is the question which Paul discusses in the *Epistle to the Romans*, from the ninth to the twelfth chapter. Weak consciences were greatly disturbed, when those who seemed to be the people of God not only rejected, but even persecuted the doctrine of the Gospel. Therefore, after expounding doctrine, he removes this difficulty, denying that those Jews, the enemies of the truth, were the church, though they wanted nothing which might otherwise have been desired to the external form of the church. The ground of his denial is that they did not embrace Christ. In the *Epistle to the Galatians,* when comparing Ishmael with Isaac, he says still more expressly that many hold a place in the church to whom the inheritance does not belong, because they were not the offspring of a free parent. From this he proceeds to draw a contrast between two Jerusalems, because, as the law was given on Mount Sinai, but the Gospel proceeded from Jerusalem, so many who were born and brought up in servitude confidently boast that they are the sons of and of the church; nay, where they are themselves degenerate, proudly despise the genuine sons of God. Let us also, in like manner, when we hear that it was once declared from Heaven, "Cast out the bondmaid and her son," trust to this inviolable decree, and boldly despise their unmeaning boasts. For if they plume themselves on external profession, Ishmael also was circumcised: If they found on antiquity, he was the firstborn: And yet we see that he was rejected. If the reason is asked, Paul assigns it (*Romans* 9:6) that those only are accounted sons who are born of the pure and legitimate seed of doctrine. On this ground God declares that he was not astricted to impious priests, though he had made a covenant with their father Levi, to be their angel, or interpreter (*Malachi* 2:4); nay, he retorts the false boasts by which they were wont to rise against the Prophets – namely, that the dignity of the priesthood was to be held in singular estimation. This he himself willingly admits: And he disputes with them, on the ground that he is ready to fulfil the covenant, while they, by not fulfilling it on their part, deserve to be rejected. Here, then, is the value of succession when not conjoined with imitation and corresponding conduct: Posterity, as soon as they are convicted of having revolted from their origin, are deprived of all honor;

unless, indeed, we are prepared to say, that because Caiaphas succeeded many pious priests (nay, the series from Aaron to him was continuous) that accursed assembly deserved the name of church. Even in earthly governments, no one would bear to see the tyranny of Caligula, Nero, Heliogabalus, and the like, described as the true condition of a republic, because they succeeded such men as Brutus, Scipio, and Camillus.[5] That in the government of the church especially, nothing is more absurd than to disregard doctrine, and place succession in persons. Nor, indeed, was anything further from the intention of the holy teachers, whom they falsely obtrude upon us, than to maintain distinctly that churches exist, as by hereditary right, whenever and wherever bishops have been uniformly succeeded by bishops. But while it was without controversy that no change had been made in doctrine from the beginning down to their day, they assumed it to be a sufficient refutation of all their errors, that they were opposed to the doctrine maintained constantly, and with unanimous consent, even by the apostles themselves. They have, therefore, no longer any grounds for proceeding to make a gloss of the name of the church, which we regard with due reverence; but when we come to definition, not only (to use the common expression) does the water adhere to them, but they stick in their own mire, because they substitute a vile prostitute for the sacred spouse of Christ. That the substitution may not deceive us, let us, among other admonitions, attend to the following from Augustine. Speaking of the church, he says, "She herself is sometimes obscured, and, as it were, beclouded by a multitude of scandals; sometimes, in a time of tranquillity, she appears quiet and free; sometimes she is covered and tossed by the billows of tribulation and trial" – (Augustine ad Vincent, Epistle 48). As instances, he mentions that the strongest pillars of the church often bravely endured exile for the faith, or lay hid throughout the world.

In this way the Romanists assail us in the present day, and terrify the unskillful with the name of church, while they are the deadly adversar-

5. French, "Or tant s'en faut que cela ait lieu, que mesmes aux gouvernemens terrestres il ne seroit point supportable. Comme il n'y a nul propos de dire que la tyrannie de Caligula, Neron, Heliogabale, et leures semblables soit le vrai etat de la cité de Rome, pourcequ'ils ont succedé aux bons governeurs qui etoient establis par la peuple." – No, so far is this from being the case, that even in earthly governments it would not be supportable. As there is no ground for saying that the tyranny of Caligula, Nero, and Heliogabalus, and the like, is the true state of the city of Rome, because they succeeded the good governors who were established by the people.

ies of Christ. Therefore, although they exhibit a temple, a priesthood, and other similar masks, the empty glare by which they dazzle the eyes of the simple should not move us in the least to admit that there is a church where the Word of God appears not. The Lord furnished us with an unfailing test when he said, "Every one that is of the truth hears my voice" (John 18:37). Again, "I am the good shepherd, and know my sheep, and am known of mine." "My sheep hear my voice, and I know them, and they follow me." A little before he had said, when the shepherd "puts forth his own sheep, he goes before them, and the sheep follow him; for they know his voice. And a stranger will they not follow, but will flee from him: for they know not the voice of strangers" (John 10:14, 4, 5). Why then do we, of our own accord, form so infatuated an estimate of the church, since Christ has designated it by a sign in which is nothing in the least degree equivocal, a sign which is everywhere seen, the existence of which infallibly proves the existence of the church while its absence proves the absence of everything that properly bears the name of church? Paul declares that the church is not founded either upon the judgments of men or the priesthood, but upon the doctrine of the apostles and the prophets (Ephesians 2:20). Nay, Jerusalem is to be distinguished from Babylon, the church of Christ from a conspiracy of Satan, by the discriminating test which our Saviour has applied to them, "He that is of God, hears God's words: You therefore hear them not, because you are not of God" (John 8:47). In short, since the church is the kingdom of Christ, and he reigns only by his Word, can there be any doubt as to the falsehood of those statements by which the kingdom of Christ is represented without his scepter, in other words, without his sacred Word?

As to their charge of heresy and schism, because we preach a different doctrine, and submit not to their laws, and meet apart from them for prayer, baptism, the administration of the Supper, and other sacred rites, it is indeed a very serious accusation, but one which needs not a long and labored defense. The name of heretics and schismatics is applied to those who, by dissenting from the church, destroy its communion. This communion is held together by two chains – viz., consent in sound doctrine and brotherly charity. Hence the distinction which Augustine makes between heretics and schismatics is, that the former corrupt the purity of the faith by false dogmas, whereas the latter sometimes, even while holding the same faith, break the bond of union (Augustine, Lib.

Quaest. in Evang. Matth.). But the thing to be observed is that this union of charity so depends on unity of faith, as to have in it its beginning, its end, in fine, its only rule. Let us therefore remember, that whenever ecclesiastical unity is commended to us, the thing required is that while our minds consent in Christ, our wills also be united together by mutual goodwill in Christ. Accordingly Paul, when he exhorts us to it, takes for his fundamental principle that there is "one God, one faith, one baptism" (*Ephesians* 4:5). Nay, when he tells us to be "of one accord, of one mind," he immediately adds, "Let this mind be in you which was also in Christ Jesus" (*Philippians* 2:2, 5); intimating, that where the Word of the Lord is not, it is not a union of believers, but a faction of the ungodly.

Cyprian also, following Paul, derives the fountain of ecclesiastical concord from one bishopric of Christ, and afterwards adds, "There is one church, which by increase from fecundity is more widely extended to a multitude, just as there are many rays of the Sun, but one light, and many branches of a tree, but one trunk upheld by the tenacious root. When may streams flow from one fountain, though there seems wide-spreading numerosity from the overflowing copiousness of the supply, yet unity remains in the origin. Pluck a ray from the body of the Sun, and the unity sustains no division. Break a branch from a tree, and the branch will not germinate. Cut off a stream from a fountain, that which is thus cut off dries up. So the church, pervaded by the light of the Lord, extends over the whole globe, and yet the light which is everywhere diffused is one" (Cyprian, *De Simplicit. Praelat.*). Words could not more elegantly express the inseparable connection which all the members of Christ have with each other. We see how he constantly calls us back to the head. Accordingly, he declares that when heresies and schisms arise, it is because men return not to the origin of the truth, because they seek not the head, because they keep not the doctrine of the heavenly Master. Let them go now and clamor against us as heretics for having withdrawn from their church, since the only cause of our estrangement is that they cannot tolerate a pure profession of the truth. I say nothing of their having expelled us by anathemas and curses. The fact is more than sufficient to excuse us, unless they would also make schismatics of the apostles, with whom we have a common cause. Christ, I say, forewarned his apostles, "They shall put you out of the synagogues" (*John* 16:2). The synagogues of which he speaks were then held to be lawful churches. Seeing then it is certain that we were cast out, and we are prepared to show that this was done for the name of Christ, the cause should first be ascertained before any decision is given either for or against us. This, however, if they choose, I am willing to leave them; to me it is enough that we behoved to withdraw from them in order to draw near to Christ.

The place which we ought to assign to all the churches on which the tyranny of the Romish idol has seized will better appear if we compare them with the ancient Israelitish church, as delineated by the prophets. So long as the Jews and Israelites persisted in the laws of the covenant, a true church existed among them; in other words, they by the kindness of God obtained the benefits of a church. True doctrine was contained in the law, and the ministry of it was committed to the prophets and priests. They were initiated in religion by the sign of circumcision, and by the other sacraments trained and confirmed in the faith. There can be no doubt that the titles with which the Lord honored his church were applicable to their society. After they forsook the law of the Lord, and degenerated into idolatry and superstition, they partly lost the privilege. For who can presume to deny the title of the church to those with whom the Lord deposited the preaching of his Word and the observance of his mysteries? On the other hand, who may presume to give the name of church, without reservation, to that assembly by which the Word of God is openly and with impunity trampled under foot – where his ministry, its chief support, and the very soul of the church, is destroyed?

What then? (someone will say); was there not a particle of the church left to the Jews from the date of their revolt to idolatry? The answer is easy. First I say that in the defection itself there were several gradations; for we cannot hold that the lapses by which both Judah and Israel turned aside from the pure worship of God were the same. Jeroboam, when he fabricated the calves against the express prohibition of God, and dedicated an unlawful place for worship, corrupted religion entirely. The Jews became degenerate in manners and superstitious opinions before they made any improper change in the external form of religion. For although they had adopted many perverse ceremonies under Rehoboam, yet, as the doctrine of the law and the priesthood, and the rites which God had instituted, continued at Jerusalem, the pious still had the church in a tolerable state. In regard to the Israelites, matters which, up to the time of Ahab, had certainly not been reformed, then became worse. Those who succeeded him, until the overthrow of the kingdom, were partly like him, and partly (when they wished to be somewhat better) followed the example of Jeroboam, while all, without exception, were wicked and idolatrous. In Judea different changes now and then took place, some kings corrupting the worship of God by false and superstitious inventions, and others attempting to reform it, until, at length, the priests themselves polluted the temple of God by profane and abominable rites.

Now then let the papists, in order to extenuate their vices as much as possible, deny, if they can, that the state of religion is as much vitiated and corrupted with them as it was in the kingdom of Israel under Jeroboam. They have a grosser idolatry, and in doctrine are not one whit more pure; rather, perhaps, they are even still more impure. God, nay, even those possessed of a moderate degree of judgment, will bear me witness, and the thing itself is too manifest to require me to enlarge upon it. When they would force us to the communion of their church, they make two demands upon us – first, that we join in their prayers, their sacrifices, and all their ceremonies; and, secondly, that whatever honor, power, and jurisdiction, Christ has given to his church, the same we must attribute to theirs. In regard to the first, I admit that all the prophets who were at Jerusalem, when matters there were very corrupt, neither sacrificed apart nor held separate meetings for prayer. For they had the command of God, which enjoined them to meet in the temple of Solomon, and they knew that the Levitical priests, whom the Lord had appointed over sacred matters, and who were not yet discarded, how unworthy soever they might be of that honor, were still entitled to hold it[6] (*Exodus* 29:9). But the principal point in the whole question is that they were not compelled to any superstitious worship, nay, they undertook nothing but what had been instituted by God. But in these men, I mean the papists, where is the resemblance?

Scarcely can we hold any meeting with them without polluting ourselves with open idolatry. Their principal bond of communion is undoubtedly in the Mass, which we abominate as the greatest sacrilege.

---

6. French, "Ils savoient que les pretres Levitiques, combien qu'ils fussent indignes d'un tel office, neantmoins pourcequ'ils avoient eté ordonnez de Dieu, et n'etoient point encore deposés, devoient etre recognus pour ministres legitimes, ayant le degré de pretrise." – They knew that the Levitical priests, although they were unworthy of such an office, nevertheless, because they had been ordained of God, and were not yet deposed, were to be recognized as lawful ministers, having the rank of priesthood.

Whether this is justly or rashly done will be elsewhere seen (see chapter 18; see also Book II, chapter 15, section 6). It is now sufficient to show that our case is different from that of the prophets, who, when they were present at the sacred rites of the ungodly, were not obliged to witness or use any ceremonies but those which were instituted by God. But if we would have an example in all respects similar, let us take one from the kingdom of Israel. Under the ordinance of Jeroboam, circumcision remained, sacrifices were offered, the law was deemed holy, and the God whom they had received from their fathers was worshiped; but in consequence of invented and forbidden modes of worship, everything which was done there God disapproved and condemned. Show me one prophet or pious man who once worshiped or offered sacrifice in Bethel. They knew that they could not do it without defiling themselves with some kind of sacrilege. We hold, therefore, that the communion of the church ought not to be carried so far by the godly as to lay them under a necessity of following it when it has degenerated to profane and polluted rites.

With regard to the second point, our objections are still stronger. For when the church is considered in that particular point of view as the church, whose judgment we are bound to revere, whose authority acknowledge, whose admonitions obey, whose censures dread, whose communion religiously cultivate in every respect, we cannot concede that they have a church, without obliging ourselves to subjection and obedience. Still we are willing to concede what the prophets conceded to the Jews and Israelites of their day, when with them matters were in a similar, or even in a better condition. For we see how they uniformly exclaim against their meetings as profane conventicles, to which it is not more lawful for them to assent than to abjure God (*Isaiah* 1:14). And certainly if those were churches, it follows, that Elijah, Micaiah, and others in Israel, Isaiah, Jeremiah, Hosea, and those of like character in Judah, whom the prophets, priests, and people of their day, hated and execrated more than the uncircumcised, were aliens from the church of God. If those were churches, then the church was no longer the pillar of the truth, but the stay of falsehood, not the tabernacle of the living God, but a receptacle of idols. They were, therefore, under the necessity of refusing consent to their meetings, since consent was nothing else than impious conspiracy against God. For this same reason, should any one acknowledge those meetings of the present day, which are contaminated by idolatry, superstition, and impious doctrine, as churches, full communion with which a Christian must maintain so far as to agree with them even in doctrine, he will greatly err. For if they are churches, the power of the keys belongs to them, whereas the keys are inseparably connected with the Word which they have put to flight. Again, if they are churches, they can claim the promise of Christ, "Whatsoever you bind," etc.; whereas, on the contrary, they discard from their communion all who sincerely profess themselves the servants of Christ. Therefore, either the promise of Christ is vain, or in this respect, at least, they are not churches. In fine, instead of the ministry of the Word, they have schools of impiety, and sinks of all kinds of error. Therefore, in this point of view, they either are not churches, or no badge will remain by which the lawful meetings of the faithful can be distinguished from the meetings of Turks.

Still, as in ancient times, there remained among the Jews certain special privileges of a church, so in the present day we deny not to the papists those vestiges of a church which the Lord has allowed to remain among them amid the dissipation. When the Lord had once made his covenant with the Jews, it was preserved not so much by them as by its own strength, supported by which it withstood their impiety. Such, then, is the certainty and constancy of the divine goodness, that the covenant of the Lord continued there and his faith could not be obliterated by their perfidy; nor could circumcision be so profaned by their impure hands as not still to be a true sign and sacrament of his covenant. Hence the children who were born to them the Lord called his own (*Ezekiel* 16:20), though, unless by special blessing, they in no respect belonged to him. So having deposited his covenant in Gaul, Italy, Germany, Spain, and England, when these countries were oppressed by the tyranny of Antichrist, he, in order that his covenant might remain inviolable, first preserved baptism there as an evidence of the covenant; – baptism, which, consecrated by his lips, retains its power in spite of human depravity; secondly, he provided by his providence that there should be other remains also to prevent the church from utterly perishing. But as in pulling down buildings the foundations and ruins are often permitted to remain, so he did not suffer Antichrist either to subvert his church from its foundation, or to level it with the ground (though, to punish the ingratitude of men who had despised his Word, he allowed a fearful shaking and dismembering to take place), but was pleased that amid the devastation the edifice should remain, though half in ruins.

Therefore, while we are unwilling simply to concede the name of church to the papists, we do not deny that there are churches among them. The question we raise only relates to the true and legitimate constitution of the church, implying communion in sacred rites, which are the signs of profession, and especially in doctrine.[7] Daniel and Paul foretold that Antichrist would sit in the temple of God (*Daniel* 9:27; *2 Thessalonians* 2:4); we regard the Roman Pontiff as the leader and standard-bearer of that wicked and abominable kingdom.[8] By placing his seat in the temple of God, it is intimated that his kingdom would not be such as to destroy the name either of Christ or of his church. Hence, then, it is obvious that we do not at all deny that churches remain under his tyranny; churches, however, which by sacrilegious impiety he has profaned, by cruel domination has oppressed, by evil and deadly doctrines like poisoned potions has corrupted and almost slain; churches where Christ lies half buried, the Gospel is suppressed, piety is put to flight, and the worship of God almost abolished; where, in short, all things are in such disorder as to present the appearance of Babylon rather than the holy city of God. In one word, I call them churches, inasmuch as the Lord there wondrously preserves some remains of his people, though miserably torn and scattered, and inasmuch as some symbols of the church still remain – symbols especially whose efficacy neither the craft of the devil nor human depravity can destroy. But as, on the other hand, those marks to which we ought especially to have respect in this discussion are effaced, I say that the whole body, as well as every single assembly, want the form of a legitimate church.

7. French, "Mais nous contendons seulement du vrai etat de l'Eglise, qui emporte communion, tant en doctrine, qu'en tout que appartient à la profession de notre Chretienté;" – But we contend only for the true state of the church, implying communion, as well as everything which pertains to the profession of our Christianity.

8. The French adds, "Pour le moins en l'Eglise Occidentale;" – At least in the Western church.

18

The Grand Inquisitor[1]

Fyodor Dostoyevsky

MY STORY is laid in Spain, in Seville, in the most terrible time of the Inquisition, when fires were lighted every day to the glory of God, and in the splendid act of faith the wicked heretics were burnt. Oh, of course, this was not the coming in which He will appear according to His promise at the end of time in all His heavenly glory, and which will be sudden 'as lightning flashing from east to west.' No, He visited His children only for a moment, and there where the flames were crackling round the heretics. In His infinite mercy He came among men in that human shape in which He walked among men for three years fifteen centuries ago. He came down to the 'hot pavement' of the southern town in which on the day before almost a hundred heretics had, 'for the greater glory of God'[2] been burned by the cardinal, the Grand Inquisitor, in a magnificent 'act of faith.' They had been burned in the presence of the king, the court, the knights, the cardinals, the most charming ladies of the court, and the whole population of Seville.

"He came softly, unobserved, and yet, strange to say, everyone recognized Him.... This might be one of the best passages in the poem. I mean, why they recognized Him.... The people are irresistibly drawn to

---

1. *The Brothers Karamazov* has been acclaimed as Dostoyevsky's best novel, and certainly "The Grand Inquisitor" is his most perceptive piece of theology. He grasps the enormity of the perversion of Christianity espoused by large, professedly Christian churches, and he condenses that perversion to these ideas: miracle, mystery, and authority, the three temptations of Christ in the wilderness. Christ rejected those temptations, but those who claim to be his representatives on Earth have not: "We have corrected Thy work and have founded it upon miracle, mystery, and authority. And men rejoiced that they were again led like sheep." The speaker is Ivan Karamazov. – *Editor.*

2. This, of course, is the slogan of the Jesuits: *ad majoram gloriam Dei.* – *Editor.*

Him; they surround Him; they flock about Him; follow Him. He moves silently in their midst with a gentle smile of infinite compassion. The sun of love burns in His heart; light and power shine from His eyes; and their radiance, shed on the people, stirs their hearts with responsive love. He holds out His hands to them, blesses them, and a healing virtue comes from contact with Him, even with His garments. An old man in the crowd, blind from childhood, cries out: 'O Lord, heal me and I shall see Thee!' And, as it were, scales fall from his eyes and the blind man sees Him. The crowd weeps and kisses the earth under His feet. Children throw flowers before Him, sing, and cry Hosanna. 'It is He! It is He!' all repeat. 'It must be He; it can be no one but Him!' He stops at the steps of the Seville cathedral at the moment when the weeping mourners are bringing in a little open white coffin. In it lies a child of seven, the only daughter of a prominent citizen. The dead child lies hidden in flowers. 'He will raise your child,' the crowd shouts to the weeping mother. The priest, coming to meet the coffin, looks perplexed, and frowns, but the mother of the dead child throws herself at His feet with a wail. 'If it is Thou, raise my child!' she cries, holding out her hands to Him. The procession halts, the coffin is laid on the steps at His feet. He looks with compassion, and His lips once more softly pronounce 'Maiden, arise!' And the maiden arises. The little girl sits up in the coffin and looks around smiling, with wide-open wondering eyes, holding a bunch of white roses they had put in her hand.

"There are cries, sobs, confusion among the people, and at that moment the cardinal himself, the Grand Inquisitor, passes by the cathedral. He is an old man, almost ninety, tall and erect, with a withered face and sunken eyes, in which there is still a gleam of light. He is not dressed in his brilliant cardinal's robes, as he was the day before, when he was burning the enemies of the Roman Church – at this moment he is wearing his coarse, old, monk's cassock. At a distance behind him come his gloomy assistants and slaves and the 'holy guard.' He stops at the right of the crowd and watches it from a distance. He sees everything; he sees them set the coffin down at His feet, sees the child rise up. His face darkens. He knits his thick gray brows and his eyes gleam with a sinister fire. He holds out his finger and bids his guards arrest Him. And such is his power, so completely are the people cowed into submission and trembling obedience to him, that the crowd immediately makes way for the guards. And in the midst of deathlike silence the guards lay hands on Him and lead Him away. The crowd instantly bows down to the earth, like one man, before the old Inquisitor. He blesses the people in silence and passes on.

"The guards lead their Prisoner to the close, gloomy vaulted prison in the ancient palace of the Holy Inquisition and lock Him in it. The day passes and is followed by the dark burning 'breathless' night of Seville. The air is 'fragrant with laurel and lemon.' In the pitch darkness the iron door of the prison is suddenly opened and the Grand Inquisitor himself comes in with a light in his hand. He is alone. The door is closed at once behind him. He stands in silence and for a minute or two gazes into His face. At last he goes up slowly, sets the light on the table and speaks.

" 'Is it Thou? Thou?' But receiving no answer, he adds at once, 'Don't answer, be silent. What canst Thou say, indeed? I know too well what Thou wouldst say. And Thou hast no right to add anything to what Thou hadst said of old. Why, then, art Thou come to hinder us? For Thou hast come to hinder us, and Thou knowest that. But dost Thou know what will be tomorrow? I know not who Thou art and care not to know whether it is Thou or only a semblance of Him. But tomorrow I shall condemn Thee and burn Thee at the stake as the worst of heretics. And the very people who have today kissed Thy feet, tomorrow at the faintest sigh from me will rush to heap up the embers of Thy fire. Knowest Thou that? Yes, maybe Thou knowest it,' he added with thoughtful penetration, never for a moment taking his eyes off the Prisoner."

"I don't quite understand, Ivan. What does it mean?" Alyosha, who had been listening in silence, asked with a smile. "Is it simply a fantasy, or a mistake on the part of the old man – some impossible mistaken identity?"

"Take it as the last," said Ivan, laughing, "if you are so corrupted by modern realism that you can't stand fantasy. If you like it to be a case of mistaken identity, let it be so. It is true," he went on, laughing, "the old man was ninety, and he might well have been crazy over his set idea. He might have been struck by the appearance of the Prisoner. It might in fact, be simply his ravings, the delusion of an old man of ninety, overexcited by the 'act of faith' of a hundred heretics the day before. But does it matter to us after all whether it was a mistake of identity or a wild fantasy? All that matters is that the old man should speak out, should speak openly of what he has thought in silence for ninety years."

"And the Prisoner too is silent? Does He look at him and not say a word?"

"That's inevitable," Ivan laughed again. "The old man has told Him He hasn't the right to add anything to what He has said of old. One may say it is the most fundamental feature of Roman Catholicism, in my opinion at least. 'All has been given by Thee to the Pope,' they say. 'And all, therefore, is still in the Pope's hands, and there is no need for Thee to come now at all. Thou must not meddle for the time, at least.' That's how they speak and write too – the Jesuits, at any rate. I have read it myself in the works of their theologians.

"'Hast Thou the right to reveal to us one of the mysteries of that world from which Thou hast come,' my old man asks Him, and answers the question for Him. 'No. Thou hast not; that Thou mayest not add to what has been said of old, and mayest not take from men the freedom which Thou didst exalt when Thou was on Earth. Whatsoever Thou revealest anew will encroach on men's freedom of faith; for it will be manifest as a miracle, and the freedom of their faith was dearer to Thee than anything else in those days fifteen hundred years ago. Didst Thou not often say then: "I will make you free"? But now Thou has seen these "free men," the old man adds suddenly, with a pensive smile. 'Yes, we've paid dearly for it,' he goes on, looking sternly at Him, 'but at last we have completed that work in Thy name. For fifteen centuries we have been wrestling with Thy freedom, but now it is ended and over for good. Dost Thou not believe that it's over for good? Thou lookest meekly at me and deignest not even to be angry with me. But let me tell Thee that now, today, people are more persuaded than ever that they have perfect freedom, yet they have brought their freedom to us and laid it humbly at our feet. But that has been our doing. Was this what Thou didst? Was this Thy freedom?'"

"I don't understand," Alyosha broke in again. "Is he ironical, is he joking?"

"No. Not at all! He claims it is a merit for himself and his Church that at last they have vanquished freedom and have done so to make men happy. 'For now' (he is speaking of the Inquisition, of course) 'for the first time it has become possible to think of the happiness of men. Man was created a rebel; and how can rebels be happy? Thou wast warned,' he says to Him. 'Thou hast had no lack of warnings, but Thou didst not listen to those warnings. Thou didst reject the only way by which men might be made happy. But, fortunately, departing Thou didst hand on the work to us. Thou hast promised, Thou hast established by Thy Word, Thou hast given to us the right to bind and to unbind, and now, of course, Thou canst not think of taking it away. Why, then, hast Thou come to hinder us?' "

"And what's the meaning of 'no lack of warnings'?" asked Alyosha.

"Why, that's the chief part of what the old man must say."

" 'The wise and dread spirit, the spirit of self-destruction and non-existence,' the old man goes on, 'the great spirit talked with Thee in the wilderness, and we are told in the books that he "tempted" Thee. Is that so? And could anything truer be said than what he revealed to Thee in three questions which Thou didst reject, and which in the books is called "the temptation"? And yet if there has ever been on Earth a real miracle, it took place on that day, on the day of the three temptations. The statement of those three questions was itself the miracle.... Imagine simply for the sake of argument that those three questions of the dread spirit had perished utterly from the books, and that we had to restore them and to invent them anew. To do so we had gathered together all the wise men of the Earth – rulers, chief priests, learned men, philosophers, poets – and had set them to the task of inventing three questions, such as would not only fit the occasion but express in three words, three human phrases, the whole future history of the world and of humanity. Dost Thou believe that all the wisdom of the Earth united could have invented anything in depth and force equal to the three questions which were actually put to Thee then by the wise and mighty spirit in the wilderness? From those questions alone, from the miracle of their statement, we can see that we have here to do not with the fleeting human intelligence, but with the absolute and eternal. For in those three questions the whole subsequent history of mankind is, as it were, brought together into one whole, and foretold. In them are united all the unsolved historical contradictions of human nature. At the time it could not be so clear, since the future was unknown. But now that fifteen hundred years have passed, we see that everything in those three questions was so justly divined and foretold, and has been so truly ful-filled, that nothing can be added to them or taken from them.

" 'Judge Thyself who was right – Thou or he who questioned Thee then? Remember the first question. Its meaning was this: "Thou wouldst go into the world, and art going with empty hands, with some promise of freedom which men in their simplicity and their natural unruliness cannot even understand, which they fear and dread – for nothing has ever been more insupportable for a man and a human society than freedom. But seest Thou these stones in this parched and barren wilderness? Turn them into bread, and mankind will run after Thee like a flock of sheep, grateful and obedient, though forever trembling, lest Thou withdraw Thy hand and deny them Thy bread." But Thou wouldst not deprive man of freedom and didst reject the offer, thinking, what is that freedom worth, if obedience is bought with bread? Thou didst reply that man lives not by bread alone. But dost Thou know that for the sake of that earthly bread the spirit of the Earth will rise up against Thee and will strive with Thee and overcome Thee? And all will follow him, crying: "Who can compare with this beast? He has given us fire from Heaven!" Dost Thou know that the ages will pass, and humanity will proclaim by the lips of their sages that there is no crime, and therefore no sin; there is only hunger? "Feed men, and then ask of them virtue!" that's what they'll write on the banner, which they will raise against Thee, and with which they will destroy Thy temple. Where Thy temple stood will rise a new building; the terrible tower of Babel will be built again. And though, like the one of old, it will not be finished, yet Thou mightest have prevented that new tower and have cut short the sufferings of men for a thousand years; for they will come back to us after a thousand years of agony with their tower. They will seek us again, hidden underground in the catacombs, for we shall be again persecuted and tortured. They will find us and cry to us: "Feed us, for those who have promised us fire from Heaven haven't given it!" And then we shall finish building their tower, for he finishes the building who feeds them. And we alone shall feed them in Thy name, declaring falsely that it is in Thy name. Oh, never, never can they feed themselves without us! No science will give them bread so long as they remain free. In the end they will lay their freedom at our feet, and to say to us: "Make us your slaves, but feed us." They will understand at last, that freedom and bread enough for all are inconceivable together. Never, never will they be able to have both together! They will be convinced, too, that they can never be free, for they are weak, vicious, worthless and rebellious.

" 'Thou didst promise them the bread of Heaven, but, I repeat again, can it compare with earthly bread in the eyes of the weak, ever sinful

314

and ignoble race of man? And if for the sake of the bread of Heaven thousands and tens of thousands shall follow Thee, what is to become of the millions and tens of thousands of millions of creatures who will not have the strength to forgo the earthly bread for the sake of the heavenly? Or dost Thou care only for the tens of thousands of the great and strong, while the millions, numerous as the sands of the sea, who are weak but love Thee, must exist only for the sake of the great and strong? No, we care for the weak, too. They are sinful and rebellious, but in the end they too will become obedient. They will marvel at us and look on us as gods, because we are ready to endure the freedom which they have found so dreadful and to rule over them – so awful it will seem to them to be free. But we shall tell them that we are Thy servants and rule them in Thy name. We shall deceive them again, for we will not let Thee come to us again. That deception will be our suffering, for we shall be forced to lie.

" 'This is the significance of the first question in the wilderness, and this is what Thou hast rejected for the sake of that freedom which Thou has exalted above everything. Yet in this question lies hidden the great secret of this world. Choosing "bread," Thou wouldst have satisfied the universal and everlasting craving of humanity – to find someone to worship. So long as man remains free he strives for nothing so incessantly and so painfully as to find someone to worship. But man seeks to worship what is established beyond dispute, so that all men would agree at once to worship it. For these pitiful creatures are concerned not only to find what one or the other can worship, but also to find something that all would believe in and worship; what is essential is that all may be together in it. This craving for community of worship is the chief misery of every man individually and of all humanity from the beginning of time. For the sake of common worship they've slain each other with the sword. They have set up gods and challenged one another: "Put away your gods and come and worship ours, or we will kill you and your gods!" And so it will be to the end of the world, even when gods disappear from the Earth; they will fall down before idols just the same. Thou didst know, Thou couldst not but have known, this fundamental secret of human nature. But Thou didst reject the one infallible banner which was offered Thee to make all men bow down to Thee alone – the banner of earthly bread. And Thou hast rejected it for the sake of freedom and the bread of Heaven.

" 'Behold what Thou didst further. And again in the name of free-dom! I tell Thee that man is tormented by no greater fear than to find someone quickly to whom he can hand over that gift of freedom with which he is born. But only one who can appease his conscience can take over his freedom. In bread there was offered Thee an invincible banner; give bread, and man will worship Thee, for nothing is more certain than bread. But if someone else gains possession of his conscience – oh! then he will cast away Thy bread and follow after him who has ensnared his conscience. In that Thou wast right. For the secret of man's being is not only to live but also to have something to live for. Without a stable conception of the object of life, man would not consent to go on living, and would rather destroy himself than remain on Earth, though he had bread in abundance. That is true. But what happened? Instead of taking men's freedom from them, Thou didst make it greater than ever! Didst Thou forget that man prefers peace, and even death, to freedom of choice in the knowledge of good and evil? Nothing is more seductive for man than his freedom of conscience, but nothing is a greater cause of suffering. And behold, instead of giving a firm foundation for setting the conscience of man at rest forever, Thou didst choose all that is ex-ceptional, vague, and puzzling. Thou didst choose what was utterly beyond the strength of men, acting as though Thou didst not love them at all – Thou who didst come to give Thy life for them! Instead of taking possession of men's freedom, Thou didst increase it, and burdened the spiritual kingdom of mankind with its sufferings forever. Thou didst desire man's free love, that he should follow Thee freely, enticed and taken captive by Thee. In place of the rigid ancient law, man must hereafter with free heart decide for himself what is good and what is evil, having only Thy image before him as a guide. But didst Thou not know he would at last reject even Thy image and Thy truth, if he is weighed down with the fearful burden of free choice? They will cry aloud at last that the truth is not in Thee, for they could not have been left in greater confusion and suffering than Thou has caused, laying upon them so many cares and unanswerable problems.

" 'So that, in truth, Thou didst Thyself lay the foundation for the destruction of Thy kingdom, and no one is more to blame for it. Yet what was offered Thee?

" 'There are three powers, three powers alone, able to conquer and to hold captive forever the conscience of these impotent rebels for their happiness – those forces are miracle, mystery and authority. Thou hast rejected all three and hast set the example for doing so. When the wise and dread spirit set Thee on the pinnacle of the temple and said to Thee, "If Thou wouldst know whether Thou art the Son of God, then cast Thyself down, for it is written: The angels shall hold him up lest he fall and bruise himself, and Thou shalt know then whether Thou art the Son of God and shalt prove then how great is Thy faith in Thy Father." But Thou didst refuse and wouldst not cast Thyself down. Oh! of course, Thou didst proudly and well like God. But the weak, unruly race of men, are they gods? Oh Thou didst know then that in taking one step, in making one movement to cast Thyself down, Thou wouldst be tempting God and have lost all Thy faith in Him, and wouldst have been dashed to pieces against that Earth which Thou didst come to save. And the wise spirit that tempted Thee would have rejoiced. But I ask again, are there many like Thee? And couldst Thou believe for one moment that men, too, could face such a temptation? Is the nature of men such, that they can reject miracles and at the great moments of their life, the moments of their deepest, most agonizing spiritual difficulties, cling only to the free verdict of the heart? Oh, Thou didst know that Thy deed would be recorded in books, would be handed down to remote times and the utmost ends of the Earth, and Thou didst hope that man, following Thee, would cling to God and not ask for a miracle. But Thou didst not know that when man rejects miracles he rejects God too; for man seeks not so much God as the miraculous. And as man cannot bear to be without the miraculous, he will create new miracles of his own for himself, and will worship deeds of sorcery and witchcraft though he might be a hundred times over a rebel, heretic and infidel. Thou didst not come down from the cross when they shouted to Thee, mocking and reviling Thee: "Come down from the cross and we will believe that Thou art He." Thou didst not come down, for again Thou wouldst not enslave man by a miracle, and didst crave faith given freely, not based on miracles.

" 'Thou didst crave for free love and not the base raptures of the slave before the might that has overawed him forever. But Thou didst think too highly of men therein, for they are slaves, of course, though rebellious by nature. Look round and judge, fifteen centuries have passed, look upon them. Whom hast Thou raised up to Thyself? I swear, man is weaker and baser by nature than Thou hast believed him! Can he, can he do what Thou didst? By showing him so much respect, Thou didst, as it were, cease to feel for him, for Thou didst ask far too much from him – Thou who has loved him more than Thyself! Respecting him less, Thou wouldst have asked less of him. That would have been more like love, for his burden would have been lighter. He is weak and vile. He is weak and vile though he is everywhere now rebelling against our power, and proud of rebellion! It is the pride of a child and a schoolboy. They are little children rioting and barring out the teacher at school. But their childish delight will end; it will cost them dearly. They will cast down temples and drench the earth with blood. But they will see at last the foolish children, that, though they are rebels, they are impotent rebels, unable to keep their own rebellion. Bathed in their foolish tears they will recognize at last that He who created them rebels must have meant to mock at them. They will say this in despair, and their utterance will be a blasphemy which will make them more unhappy still, for man's nature cannot bear blasphemy, and in the end always avenges it on itself. And so unrest, confusion and unhappiness – that is the present lot of man after Thou didst bear so much for his freedom!

" 'Thy great prophet tells in vision and in image, that he saw all those who took part in the first resurrection and that there were of each tribe twelve thousand. But if there were so many of them – they must have been not men but gods. They had borne Thy cross, they had endured scores of years in the barren, hungry wilderness, living upon locusts and roots – and Thou mayest indeed point with pride at those children of freedom, of free love, of free and splendid sacrifice for Thy name. But remember that they were only some thousands; and what of the rest? And how are the other weak ones to blame, because they could not endure what the strong have endured? How is the weak soul to blame that it is unable to receive such terrible gifts? Canst Thou have simply come to the elect and for the elect? If so, it is mystery and we cannot understand it. And if it is a mystery, we too have a right to preach a mystery, and to teach men that it's not the free judgment of their hearts, not love that matters, but a mystery which they must follow blindly, even against their conscience. So we have done. We have corrected Thy work and have founded it upon *miracle, mystery* and *authority*. And men rejoiced that they were again led like sheep, and that the terrible gift that had brought them such suffering, was, at last lifted from their hearts. Were we right teaching them this? Speak! Did we not

love mankind, so meekly acknowledging their feebleness, lovingly light-
ening their burden, and permitting their weak nature even sin with our
sanction? Why hast Thou come now to hinder us? And why dost thou
look silently and searchingly at me with Thy mild eyes? Be angry. I
don't want Thy love, for I love Thee not. And what use is it for me to
hide anything from Thee? Don't I know to Whom I am speaking? All
that I can say is known to Thee already. And is it for me to conceal from
Thee our mystery? Perhaps it is Thy will to hear it from my lips. Listen,
then. We are not working with Thee, but with *him* – that is our mystery.
It's long – eight centuries – since we have been on his side and not on
Thine.

"'Just eight centuries ago, we took from him, the wise and mighty
spirit in the wilderness, what Thou didst react with scorn, that last gift
he offered Thee, showing Thee all the kingdoms of the Earth. We took
from him Rome and the sword of Caesar, and proclaimed ourselves
sole rulers of the Earth, though we have not yet been able to complete
our work. But whose fault is that? Oh, the work is only beginning, but
it has begun. It has long to await completion and the Earth has yet
much to suffer, but we shall triumph and shall be Caesars, and then we
shall plan the universal happiness of man. But Thou mightest have taken
even then the sword of Caesar. Why didst Thou reject that last gift?
Thou wouldst have accomplished all that man seeks on Earth – that is,
someone to worship, someone to keep his conscience, and some means
of uniting all in one unanimous and harmonious ant heap, because the
craving for universal unity is the third and last anguish of men. Mankind as a whole has always striven to organize a universal state. There
have been many great nations with great histories, but the more highly
they were developed the more unhappy they were, for they felt more
acutely than other people the craving for worldwide union. The great
conquerors, Timours and Genghis Khans, whirled like hurricanes over
the face of the Earth striving to subdue its people, and they too were
but the unconscious expression of the same craving for universal unity.
Hadst Thou taken the world and Caesar's purple, Thou wouldst have
founded the universal state and have given universal peace. For who
can rule men if not he who holds their conscience and their bread in his
hands?

"'We have taken the sword of Caesar, and in taking it, of course,
have rejected Thee and followed him. Oh, ages are yet to come of the

confusion of free thought, of their science and cannibalism. For having begun to build their tower of Babel without us, they will end, of course, with cannibalism. But then the beast will crawl to us and lick our feet and spatter them with tears of blood. And we shall sit upon the beast and raise the cup, and on it will be written: "Mystery." But then, and only then, the reign of peace and happiness will come for men. Thou art proud of Thine elect, but Thou hast only the elect, while we give rest to all. And besides, how many of those elect, those mighty ones who could become elect, have grown weary waiting for Thee, and have transferred and will transfer the powers of their spirit and the warmth of their heart to the other camp, and end by raising their free banner against Thee? Thou didst Thyself lift up that banner. But with us all will be happy and will no more rebel nor destroy one another as under Thy freedom. Oh, we shall persuade them that they will only become free when they renounce their freedom to us and submit to us. And shall we be right or shall we be lying? They will be convinced that we are right, for they will remember the horrors of slavery and confusion to which Thy freedom brought them. Freedom, free thought and science, will lead them into such straits and will bring them face to face with such marvels and insoluble mysteries, that some of them, the fierce and rebellious, will destroy themselves. Others, rebellious but weak, will destroy one another. The rest, weak and unhappy, will crawl fawning to our feet and whine to us: "Yes, you were right, you alone possess His mystery, and we come back to you. Save us from ourselves!"

" 'Receiving bread from us, they will see clearly that we take the bread made by their hands from them, to give it to them, without any miracle. They will see that we do not change the stones to bread, but in truth they will be more thankful for taking it from our hands than for the bread itself! For they will remember only too well that in old days, without our help, even the bread they made turned to stones in their hands, while since they have come back to us, the very stones have turned to bread in their hands. Too, too well they know the value of complete submission! And until men know that, they will be unhappy. Who is most to blame for their not knowing it? Speak! Who scattered the flock and sent it astray on unknown paths?

" 'But the flock will come together again and will submit once more, and then it will be once and for all. Then we shall give them the quiet humble happiness of weak creatures such as they are by nature. Oh, we shall persuade them at last not to be proud, for Thou didst lift them up and thereby taught them to be proud. We shall show them that they are weak, that they are only pitiful children, but that childlike happiness is the sweetest of all. They will become timid and will look to us and will huddle close to us in fear, as chicks to the hen. They will marvel at us and will be awestricken before us, and will be proud at our being so powerful and clever, that we have been able to subdue such a turbulent flock of thousands of millions. They will tremble impotently before our wrath, their minds will grow fearful, they will be quick to shed tears like women and children, but they will be just as ready at a sign from us to pass to laughter and rejoicing, to happy mirth and childish song. Yes, we shall set them to work, but in their leisure hours we shall make their life like a child's game, with children's songs and innocent dance. Oh, we shall allow them even sin; they are weak and helpless, and they will love us like children because we allow them to sin. We shall tell them that every sin will be atoned, if it is done with our permission. We shall tell them that we allow them to sin because we love them, and the punishment for these sins we take upon ourselves. And we shall take it upon ourselves, and they will adore us as their Saviour because we have taken on their sins before God. And they will have no secrets from us. We shall allow or forbid them to live with their wives and mistresses, to have or not to have children – according to whether they have been obedient or disobedient – and they will submit to us gladly and cheerfully. The most painful secrets of the conscience, all, all they will bring to us, and we shall have an answer for all. And they will be glad to believe our answer, for it will save them from the great fear and terrible agony they endure at present in making a free decision for themselves. And all will be happy, all the millions of creatures except the hundred thousand who rule over them. For only we, we who guard the mystery, shall be unhappy. There will be thousands of millions of happy ones and a hundred thousand sufferers who have taken upon themselves the curse of the knowledge of good and evil. Peacefully, they will die, peacefully in Thy name, and beyond the grave they will find nothing but death. But we shall keep the secret, and for their happiness we shall allure them with the reward of Heaven and eternity. Though if there were anything in the other world, it certainly would not be for such as they.

" 'It is prophesied that Thou wilt come again in victory, thou wilt come with Thy chosen, the proud and strong. But we will say that they have only saved themselves, but we have saved all. We are told that the harlot that sits upon the beast, and holds in her hands the *mystery*, shall be put to shame, that the weak will rise up again, and will rend her royal purple and will strip naked her loathsome body. But then I will stand up and point out to Thee the thousand millions of happy creatures who have known no sin. And we who have taken their sins upon us for their happiness will stand up before Thee and say: "Judge us if thou canst and darest." Know that I fear Thee not. Know that I too have been in the wilderness, I too have lived on roots and locusts, I too prized the freedom with which Thou hast blessed men, and I too was striving to stand among Thy elect, along the strong and powerful, thirsting "to make up the number." But I awakened and would not serve madness. I turned back and joined the ranks of those *who have corrected thy work*. I left the proud and went back to the humble, for the happiness of the humble.

" 'What I say to Thee will come to pass, and our dominion will be built up. I repeat, tomorrow Thou shalt see that obedient flock who at a sign from me will hasten to heap up the hot cinders about the pile on which I shall burn Thee for coming to hinder us. For if anyone has ever deserved our fires it is Thou. Tomorrow I shall burn Thee.... I have spoken.' "

Ivan stopped. He had been carried away as he talked and spoke with excitement. Now he suddenly smiled.

Alyosha had listened in silence. Toward the end he was greatly moved and seemed several times on the point of interrupting, but he restrained himself. Now his words came with a rush.

"But...that's absurd!" he cried. "Your poem is in praise of Jesus, not in blame of Him – as you meant it to be. And who will believe you about freedom? Is that the way to understand it? That's not the idea of it in the Orthodox Church... That's Rome and not even the whole of Rome, it's false – those are the worst Catholics, the Inquisitors, and Jesuits!... And there could not be such a fantastic creature as your Inquisitor. What are these sins of mankind that they take upon themselves? Who are these keepers of the mystery who have taken some curse upon themselves for the happiness of mankind? When have they been seen? We know the Jesuits. They are spoken ill of, but surely they are not what you describe? They are not that at all, not at all....they are simply the Romish army for the earthly sovereignty of the world in the future, with the pontiff of Rome for Emperor.... That's their ideal, but there's no sort of mystery about it.... It's simple lust for power, for filthy earthly gain, for domination – something like a universal serfdom with them as masters – that's all they stand for. They don't even believe in God perhaps. Your suffering Grand Inquisitor is a mere fantasy."

"Wait, wait," laughed Ivan. "How upset you are! A fantasy you say, let it be so! Of course it's a fantasy. But let me say: Do you really think that the Roman Catholic movement of the last centuries is actually nothing but the lust for power, for filthy earthly gain? Is that Father Paissy's teaching"

"No, no, on the contrary, Father Paissy did once say something rather the same as you.... But of course it's not the same, not at all the same," Alyosha quickly corrected himself.

"A precious admission, in spite of your 'not at all the same.' I ask you why your Jesuits and Inquisitors have united simply for vile material gain? Why can there not be among them one martyr oppressed by great sorrow and loving humanity? You see, only suppose that there was one such man among all those who desire nothing but filthy material gain – if there's only one like my old Inquisitor, who had himself eaten roots in the desert and made frenzied efforts to subdue his flesh to make himself free and perfect. But yet all his life he loved humanity, and suddenly his eyes were opened, and he saw that it is no great moral blessedness to attain perfection and freedom, if at the same time one gains the conviction that millions of God's creatures have been created as a mockery, that they will never be capable of using their freedom, that these poor rebels can never turn into giants to complete the tower, that it was not for such geese that the great idealist dreamt his dream of harmony. Seeing all that he turned back and joined – the clever people. Surely that could have happened?"

"Joined what clever people?" cried Alyosha, completely carried away. "They have no such great cleverness and no mysteries and secrets.... Perhaps nothing but atheism, that's all their secret. Your Inquisitor does not believe in God, that's his secret!"

"What if he doesn't believe in God! At last you have guessed it. It's perfectly true that that's the whole secret. But isn't that suffering, at least for a man like that, who has wasted his whole life in the desert and yet could not shake off his incurable love of humanity? In his old age he reached the clear conviction that nothing but the advice of the great dread spirit could build up a tolerable sort of life for the feeble, unruly 'incomplete, empirical creatures created in jest.' And so, convinced of this, he sees that he must follow the counsel of the wise spirit, the dread spirit of death and destruction, and accept lying and deception, and lead men consciously to death and destruction. He sees that he must deceive them all the way so that they may not notice where they are being led, that the poor blind creatures may at least on the way think themselves happy. And note, the deception is in the name of Him in whose ideal the old man had so fervently believed all his life. Is not that tragic? And if only one such stood at the head of the whole army 'filled with the lust for power only for the sake of filthy gain' – would not one such be enough to make a tragedy? More than that, one such standing at the head is enough to create the actual leading idea of the Roman Church with all its armies and Jesuits, its highest idea. I tell you frankly that I firmly believe that there has always been such a man among those who stood at the head of the movement. Who knows, there may have been some such even among the Roman popes. Who knows, perhaps the spirit of that accursed old man who loves mankind so obstinately in his own way, is to be found even now in a whole multitude of such old men, existing not by chance but by agreement. Perhaps these old men formed a secret league long, long ago for the guarding of the mystery, to guard it from the weak and the unhappy, so as to make them happy. No doubt it is so and so it must be indeed. I believe that even among the Masons there's something of the same mystery and that that's why the Catholics detest the Masons. They feel that the Masons are breaking up the unity of the idea, while it is so essential that there should be one flock and one shepherd.... But from the way I defend my idea you might think that I am angry at your criticism. Enough of it."

"Maybe you are a Mason yourself!" said Alyosha suddenly. "You don't believe in God," he added, speaking this time very sorrowfully. He felt that his brother was looking at him ironically. "How does your poem end?" he asked, suddenly looking down. "Or was that the end?"

"I meant to end it like this. When the Inquisitor stopped speaking he waited some time for his Prisoner to answer him. His silence weighed down upon him. He saw that the Prisoner had listened carefully all the time, looking gently in his face. But evidently He did not want to reply. The old man longed for Him to say something, however bitter and terrible. But He suddenly approached the old man in silence and softly kissed him on the forehead. That was his answer. The old man shuddered. His lips moved. He went to the door, opened it and said to Him: 'Go, and come no more.... Come not at all, never, never!' And he let Him out into the dark alleys of the town. The Prisoner went away."

"And the old man?"

"This kiss glows in his heart, but the old man holds to his idea."

19

Episcopacy

Jeremiah Burroughs[1]

Editor's Note:

E PISCOPAL CHURCH government has always been opposed by Christians, and the Reformation encouraged that opposition in the sixteenth century. William Tyndale denied the legitimacy of episcopal church government in his *Practice of Prelates* in 1530. When, in the seventeenth century, opposition to bishops increased, writers who criticized episcopacy were punished by the autocrats in the church. Alexander Leighton, for example, was whipped, branded in the face, had his ears cut off, his nose slit, and imprisoned for publishing his *Sion's Plea against the Prelacy* in 1628. Charles I's attempt to impose bishops on Presbyterian Scotland brought about his and their downfall in England. To raise money for his army he was forced to summon Parliament in 1640, after a hiatus of ten years, and opposition to king and bishop burst forth. When the Long Parliament met in November 1640, petitions for church reform poured in, especially directed against episcopacy. The "Root and Branch" petition from London, which bore 15,000 signatures, stated that:

> Whereas the government of Archbishops and Lord Bishops, etc., hath proved very prejudicial and dangerous both to the church and Commonwealth...we therefore most humbly pray and beseech this honorable Assembly, the premises considered, that the said government, with all its dependencies, roots and branches, may be abolished...and the government according to God's Word may be rightly placed among us.

1. Burroughs is the author to whom this criticism of the *Petition for the Prelates* is attributed. This excerpt is taken from *The Reformation of the Church*, edited by Iain H. Murray and published by The Banner of Truth Trust, 1965. The Editor's note relies on and is adapted from *The Reformation of the Church*.

To counter this document, which was the basis of a Root and Branch Bill introduced into the House of Commons in May 1641, the advocates of episcopacy drew up the *Petition for the Prelates*, pleading for the maintenance of the established government of the Church of England.

The Long Parliament viewed the reformation of episcopacy as a necessity, but there was no unanimity over the extent to which reform should be carried. Some regarded the removal of all political power from the bishops as sufficient (a step which was accomplished in 1642 when episcopal seats in the House of Lords were abolished). Others desired the reduction of diocesan episcopacy to a more primitive form in which a bishop would be only a "first among equals" in a local presbytery. The prevalent Puritan view, however, regarded as unscriptural the claim that a bishop was anything more than a preaching elder in a local congregation: The Scriptures teach that these two names – *bishop* and *elder* – belong to one office and that there is no other permanent order of teachers besides presbyters. This conviction triumphed in 1643 when Parliament abolished episcopacy and joined with Scotland in drawing up the famous *Solemn League and Covenant*, in which the two nations pledged to extirpate church government by archbishops and bishops and to seek "the reformation of religion in the kingdoms of England and Ireland, in doctrine, worship, discipline, and government, according to the Word of God and the example of the best Reformed Churches."

Political reform of the church, however, did not last even 20 years. After 1660 the monarchy and bishops were restored. The increasingly latitudinarian attitude toward Scripture that developed in the latter part of the seventeenth century led to the view that Scripture does not determine the question of the form of church government and therefore the preservation of episcopacy may be argued from considerations which lie outside the scope of Scripture. The whole controversy ended largely until the Tractarian Movement of the 1830s revived it. According to the Tractarian position, there can be no true church without diocesan bishops in lineal succession from the apostles. Such a belief rests on an essentially Roman Catholic definition of the church; so it is not surprising to find that those who hold it today regard episcopacy as necessary not only for the Church of England but for all churches as a prerequisite for the reunion of Christendom. Because those who defend this view do not accept Scripture as the sole means of knowing God's will for the church, they find no inconsistency in asserting that episcopacy is to be revered because of its "Divine origin," even though the episcopal system is not appointed in the Word of God. This modern view is similar to the defense of episcopacy by opponents of the Puritans. The twentieth century has witnessed a widespread abandonment of any attempt to reject episcopacy on scriptural grounds – largely because apostasy in the churches has made them indifferent to Biblical authority. Some churches have turned to episcopacy – Charismatic, Reconstructionist, and even some Reformed churches.

Burroughs' examination of the *Petition for the Prelates* begins with a note to the reader, followed by the text of the *Petition*, followed by Burroughs' own criticism of the *Petition*.

Episcopacy:
The *Petition for the Prelates* Examined

To the reader:

It will seem nothing strange, that amidst so many petitions against prelacy, from all the parts of the Kingdom, someone should set forth, and appear for it; if we consider how many papists and popishly affected have for many years found peace and ease under the shadow thereof; how many members of the prelatical hierarchy do feel their foundations shaken, and their hopes blasted; how many worldly men do fear the yoke of Christ, and shun to be brought under the obedience of the Gospel; and how many there be that are mistaken with the concept of the external pomp and glory of the church, of the governing of the church by the rules of human policy, and of the dangers which may ensue upon alterations. We know that even Ba'al had the men of the city who pleaded for him: that cursed Jericho found favor with Hiel the Bethelite, that many cried out, Great is Diana; and that the ruin of Babylon, although a matter of Hallelujah to the godly, who find in her the blood of prophets, and of saints, is bewailed and lamented by the merchants of the Earth, and such as have lived deliciously with her. The prelacy was of late grown to such greatness in this kingdom that it were a wonder, if it should not find some to uphold it; and yet to such insolence, that it were a wonder, if at this opportunity, it should not fall. We do for our parts find ourselves bound, both to warn, and call upon all men to be wise, and to observe the wonderful work of God, lest haply they be found fighting against God; and also to remove stumbling blocks out of the way, that the weak be not hindered or discouraged in praying and petitioning for Reformation, which is all that is aimed at, in these following pages.

The Petition for the Prelates

That whereas there has of late a petition subscribed by many (who pretend to be inhabitants of this city) been delivered, received, and read in this honorable House, against the ancient, present, and by law established government of the church, and that not so much for the reformation of bishops, as for the utter subversion and extirpation of episcopacy itself. We whose names are underwritten to show there be many, and those of the better sort of the inhabitants of this city, otherwise and better minded, do humbly represent unto this honorable House these following considerations:

1. That episcopacy is as ancient as Christianity itself in this Kingdom.

2. That bishops were the chief instruments in the reformation of the church against popery, and afterwards the most eminent martyrs for the Protestant religion, and since, the best and able champions for the defense of it.

3. That since the Reformation, the times have been very peaceable, happy, and glorious, notwithstanding episcopal government of the church, and therefore that this government can be no cause of our unhappiness.

4. We conceive that not only many learned, but diverse other godly persons, would be much scandalized and troubled in conscience if the government of episcopacy, conceived by them to be an apostolical institution, were altered, and since there is so much care taken, that no man should be offended in the least ceremony, we hope there will be some, that such men's consciences may not be pressed upon, in a matter of an higher nature and consequence, especially considering that this government by episcopacy is not only lawful and convenient for edification, but likewise suitable and agreeable to the civil policy and government of this state.

5. That this government is lawful, it appears by the immediate, universal and constant practice of all the Christian world grounded upon Scripture, from the apostles' time to this last age; for above 1,500 years together. It being utterly incredible, if not impossible, that the whole

church for so long a time, should not discover by God's Word this government to be unlawful, if it had been so: To which may be added, that the most learned Protestants, even in those very churches which now are not governed by bishops, do not only hold the government by episcopacy to be lawful, but wish that they themselves might enjoy it.

Again, that the government by episcopacy is not only lawful, but convenient for edification, or as much, or more conducive to piety and devotion than any other, it appears because no modest man denies that the primitive times were most famous for piety, constancy, and perseverance in the faith, notwithstanding more frequent and more cruel persecutions, than ever have been since, and yet it is confessed, that the church in those times was governed by bishops.

Lastly: That the government of the church by episcopacy is most suitable to the frame and form of the civil government here in this Kingdom, it appears by the happy and flourishing union of them both, for so long a time together, whereas no man can give us an assurance how any church government besides this (whereof we have had so long experience) will suit and agree with the civil policy of this state: And we conceive it may be of dangerous consequence for men of settled fortunes to hazard their estates, by making so great an alteration, and venturing upon a new form of government, whereof neither we, nor our ancestors have had any trial, or experience; especially considering that those, who would have episcopacy to be abolished, have not yet agreed, nor (as we are verily persuaded) ever will or can agree upon any other common form of government to succeed in the room of it, as appears by the many different and contrary drafts, and platforms they have made and published, according to the several humors and sects of those that made them, whereas, seeing every great alteration in a church or state must needs be dangerous, it is just and reasonable that whosoever would introduce a new form instead of an old one, should be obliged to demonstrate and make it evidently appear aforehand: that the government he would introduce is proportionably so much better, than that he would abolish, as may recompense the loss we may sustain, and may be worthy of the hazard we in must run, in abolishing the one, and in introducing and settling of the other. But this we are confident can never be done, in regard of this particular.

And therefore our humble and earnest request to the honorable

House is, that as well in this consideration, as all the other aforesaid, we may still enjoy that government, which most probably holds its institution from the apostles and most certainly its plantation with our Christian faith itself in this Kingdom, where it has ever since flourished and continued for many ages without interruption or alteration, whereby it plainly appears, that as it is the most excellent government in itself: so it is the most suitable, most agreeable, and every way most proportionable to the civil constitutions and temper of this state: and therefore we pray and hope will always be continued, and preserved in it and by it, notwithstanding the abuses and corruptions which in so long tract of time through the errors or negligence of men have crept into it, which abuses and corruptions being all of them (what and how many soever they may be) but merely accidental to episcopacy. We conceive and hope, there may be a Reformation of the one, without destruction of the other, which is the humble Suit of, etc.

The Petition for the Prelates Briefly Examined

[Petition for the Prelates:] We whose names are underwritten, to show there be many and those of the better sort of the inhabitants of this city, otherwise and better minded, do humbly represent unto this honorable House, these considerations.

[Response:] How much better these petitioners are than the former [the signers of the "Root and Branch" petition], let not their own judgments, but their work determine. We will not examine their minds, what they think, but their considerations, what they publish, Which are:

1. *That episcopacy is as ancient as Christianity itself in this Kingdom.*

This is a consideration to gain time by; how far about must we go to search all antiquity, before the strength of this consideration can come to an issue. The most speedy and best way of determining is to go to that which is most ancient, the certain infallible rule.

History tells us that Christianity came into England by Simon Zelotes, and Joseph of Arimathaea,[2] who lived in the times of penning that Scripture which must be the rule of our church government; put us not off, therefore, with the rust of your antiquity, but give us the gold of divine truth.

2. This was a generally accepted belief of the period. There is no historical evidence for the tradition, although Christianity may have been introduced into England as early as the apostolic age.

If wheresoever mention is made of bishops in the history of antiquity, you bring it to prove the lawfulness of your bishops in controversy, you abuse the reader; for we say that bishops indeed are ancient, but such bishops as the Scriptures speak of, namely, presbyters in several congregations. St. Patrick in his time had founded in Ireland three hundred and sixty-five churches, and ordained so many bishops. Eusebius tells us of one Soticus, bishop of the Village of Comanbind; Theodoret of Mares, bishop of a small town called Solicha; Jerome of Asclepias, bishop of a small town in Africa. What antiquity relates concerning the government of churches within themselves, and how smaller churches in villages came to be under the power of pastors of greater churches in cities, is very observable. Thus we find it written. The policy of the churches was like that of members in one body, where all suffer together, and are helpful each to other: Hence we have so many epistles to churches and teachers written to others, which came neither from subjection or authority, but from love and desire of edifying; but because the light of the Gospel, set up in the same one city, by little and little did enlighten the lesser towns adjacent, therefore those churches did acknowledge and reverence that city, from whence the light of the Gospel sprung to them, as their mother; and did consult with the officers thereof in controversies and things pertaining to the church; and if any thing were not well done, they did admonish and freely rebuke one another, and friendly subject each to other. Those that excelled in gifts lorded it not over others, but ministered unto them; but those churches where the apostles and other eminent men taught, were of great esteem and honored accordingly. But this custom afterwards grew to a law, as appears by the Nicene Council, where some churches, with their bishops, are made subject by law, and compelled to obey some other one church and her bishop. And in this age, namely, the second century, the story saith, it cannot be showed by the testimony of any approved author, that of so many churches as were planted by the apostles, any one did arrogate superiority over others, by divine or apostolical authority, neither did other churches acknowledge, or honor any one of them as superior, whose bishop should have power to appoint ceremonies or make decrees, to which all should be bound.

The constitution of diocesan bishops in England was first in imitation of the heathens, who had their Archflamins and Flamins, instead whereof that the Christians might gain them to their religion, the seat of the Archflamins of London, York, and Chester were changed into the sees of three Archbishops, and of the Flamins into the sees of Bishops; and one Devotus, Bishop of Winchester, had all the possessions of the pagan Flamins, even twelve miles compass round about the city conferred upon him and his clergy, in which were contained thirty-two villages.

The Christian world knew no diocese made up of many parishes till the year 267, as Polydore Vergil testifies; therefore, diocesan bishops cannot be so ancient as Christianity in England. Suppose bishops were so ancient, as you pretend, yet they may be Antichristian, because the Scripture tells us that Antichrist began to work in the apostles' time.

2. *That bishops were the chief instruments in the reformation of the church against popery.*

That some good men should not see the evil of episcopacy in the darkness of popery, it is no marvel.

If their places were therefore good, because the men were instruments of reformation, then now their places are naught, because they are inlets and instruments of so much corrupting innovation.

Most of the bishops then were the chief hinderers of the reformation, witness Martin Bucer in a speech of his to King Edward: Your Majesty (saith he) does see, that this restoring again the kingdom of Christ, which we require, yea, which the salvation of us all requires, may in no wise be expected to come of the bishops, seeing there be so few among them which do understand the power and proper offices of this kingdom, and very many of them by all means (which possibly they can and dare) either oppose themselves against it, or defer and hinder it.

Had not King Edward, though young, set his heart for reformation more than the best of the bishops, it had never proceeded so far as it did. When Cranmer and Ridley pressed him to permit his sister the Lady Mary to have Mass in her house, the King having heard what they could say, replied out of the Scriptures so fully, that they were enforced to give place to his replication, and grant the same to be true. Then they after long debating with his Majesty in this manner, labored politically in another sort, and alleged what dangers the denying thereof might bring to his Grace, what breach of amity on the Emperor's part, what troubles, what unkindnesses, and what occasions sundry ways it would enforce, unto whom the King answered, willing them to content themselves, for he would, he said, spend his life, and all he had, rather than to agree and grant to that he knew to be against the truth. The which when the bishops heard, notwithstanding they urged him still to grant, and would by no means have his nay. Then the good King seeing their importunate suit, in the end his tender heart bursting out into bitter weeping and sobbing, he desired them to be content; whereat the bishops wept as fast as he and acknowledged the good King had more divinity in his little finger, than they had in all their bodies.

3. *Bishops were most eminent martyrs.*

Of many bishops there were some few martyrs, but what bishops were they? Latimer, upon the coming forth of the six *Articles* in King Henry VIII's time, did freely and of his own accord, resign his bishopric, and when he put off his rochet, suddenly he skipped for joy, feeling his shoulders so light, being discharged (as he said) of so heavy a burden, and gloried in the title of a *Quondam*. Hooper was another and he made supplication to the King, desiring his Highness either to discharge him of the bishopric, or else to dispense with him of such ceremonial orders as were required of him. Also concerning ceremonies, he saith thus: Behold how fearful a thing it is, though the intent be never so good, even to adorn and beautify the institutions, decrees, and ordinances of God, with any device of man, without the appointment of God in his Word; yea, it is no less abominable in the sight of God, than if a man should accuse him of ignorance and foolishness. Speaking of the Supper of the Lord, he saith, The outward preparation the more simple it is, the better it is, and the nearer the institution of Christ and his apostles. If you have bread, wine, a table, and a fair tablecloth, be not solicitous and careful for the rest, seeing they are things brought in, not by Christ, but by popes. He also speaks expressly against kneeling at the Lord's Supper, the surplice, with all the monuments, tokens, and leavings of papistry, and that excommunication should not be done by the bishop alone, but by the bishop and all the parish.

Ridley also, when they put on his episcopal robes for his degradation, he vehemently inveighed against that apparel, calling it foolish and abominable, yea too fond for a vice in a play.

Bishop Ferrar was another martyr, and he was so strongly set against their superstitious ceremonies that they made an article against him for refusing to wear a square cap.

What bishops have you more that were martyrs, except Cranmer?

And you see what manner of men these were, and by that little taste of their non-conformity, you may judge they would have been as forward to the work of reformation as any other, had they lived in these times.

If some bishops, being martyrs, argues the goodness of their place, then other bishops, being persecutors of the martyrs, as Bonner and Gardiner, argues the evil of their places.

If you account so highly of the testimony of martyrs, hear what that famous martyr the Lord Cobham in Henry V's time says, that the pope is the great head of Antichrist, the priests and prelates and monks the body, and friars the tail.

4. And since were the best champions for the defense of it.

The most famous champions we have had in England for the truth have been such as have either been fully against bishops, or that have held presbyters and bishops to be all one.

Doctor Barnes was condemned for saying thus, I will never believe, nor can ever believe, that one may by the law of God be Bishop of two or three cities, yea of a whole country, for that is contrary to the doctrine of Paul, who writing unto Titus, commands that he should ordain a Bishop in every town.

Master Tyndale in his book of *The Obedience of a Christian Man*, page 114, says, As thou canst heal no disease, except thou begin at the root, so canst thou preach against no mischief, except thou begin at the Bishops.[3] Moreover, in his defense of the English translation, he saith: These overseers, which now we call Bishops, after the Greek word, were always abiding in one place, to govern the congregation there.

Doctor Reynolds, as great a champion for the truth as any of the Prelates, in his letter to Sir Francis Knollys, requiring his resolution, whether the authority Bishops have amongst us be God's own ordinance, answers negatively, and proves at large by writers old and new, that the now Archbishop Doctor Bancroft was in an error for preaching otherwise.

Doctor Fulke against the Rhemists upon *Titus* 1:5 affirms that, albeit for order and seemly government, there was always one principal, to whom by long use of the church the name Bishop was applied, yet in the Scripture a bishop and an elder is of one order and authority.

3. Tyndale, *Doctrinal Treatises* (Parker Society, 1848), 186.

Doctor Whitaker, in his *Answer* to Campion's ten reasons, says, that *jure divino*, a presbyter and bishop are both one, and if Arius were an heretic for saying so, Jerome certainly was akin to the same heretic.

We might produce many others, as Doctor Humphry Holland, Deacon, Bale, Fox, Bradford, and others, which of necessity we forbear, to prevent tediousness. Only one who himself was a Bishop, and one of the chief champions against Papists, yet acknowledged Episcopacy not to be by divine right; for citing a place out of Austin, affirming that the office of a Bishop is above the office of a Priest, after the names of honor which the custom of the church hath now attained, he adds himself, but not by authority of the Scripture; where also he consents to that of Jerome, Let Bishops understand that they are above Priests, rather of custom, than of any truth or right of Christ's Institution; and this he does in opposition to Harding, pleading superiority of Bishops.[4]

5. *Since the Reformation the times have been very peaceable, happy, and glorious, notwithstanding episcopal government.*

To whom have the times been so? Indeed Bishops and their creatures have lived in pomp, but how many hundreds of faithful laborious ministers have been cast out from all their means of livelihood, themselves and their families put to lamentable extremities? How many have been imprisoned and brought to untimely ends there? How many have been driven out of their dear country? What reproaches and contempt hath been cast upon those that remain? No reformed church in all the world can show such lamentable miseries, that their ministers and people have been put unto for their consciences, and that in things of as low a nature, as in England can be showed.

For that prosperity we have had, no thanks to Bishops; for the lower Bishops were, as in Queen Elizabeth's time, the greater was our prosperity: But since the Bishops grew to that height (they were lately in) our prosperity hath been as much lessened, witness the lamentable complaints and outcries of the whole Kingdom against the miseries caused by them. If the lower they were, the more prosperous we were, then if they were not at all, we may very well expect more prosperity than ever.

This [episcopal] argument of prosperity is the same that heathens brought against Christians. One Symmachus against whom Prudentius wrote in an *Epistle to Theodosius the Emperor* used this argument

---

4. The author referred to is John Jewel, Bishop of Salisbury.

to persuade continuance in the old religion of the Romans, because their Commonwealth had been most fully flourishing all the time they worshiped Jupiter, Apollo, and their other gods. So likewise the heathen persecutors of Christians used to say, when any evil befell them: Now are we not so fortunate as we were wont to be, because we suffer the Christians, and because we worship not our gods with that zeal as formerly.

6. *We conceive that many learned and godly persons would be much scandalized and troubled in conscience if the government by episcopacy were altered.*

We confess, in things indifferent, that governors in commanding and all men in practicing ought to be very careful in giving offence; the Scripture lays down rules for ordering us in things indifferent, which bind governors as well as others. The apostles had as much authority in the church as ever any since, and yet they durst not enjoin a thing indifferent, which was offensive, but counted it necessary to abstain from that which was offensive, though in its own nature indifferent as in the matter of eating blood, *Acts* 15. But in such things wherein we are not at all left to our liberty, the rules of offence take no place; if any will be offended for doing our duty, we must not therefore forbear.

The keeping in of Bishops in these times wherein God so clearly opposes them will be the greatest offence that ever was given to the people of England and other reformed churches, and a special hardening of our adversaries, even the papists themselves, who do extremely contend for episcopacy to be *jure divino*, witness that book of Franciscus à Sancta Clara, called *Apologia pro Episcopis*; and that Canon of the Council of Trent: If any man shall say, that Bishops are not above Presbyters, let him be Anathema. And that you may see what a dangerous offence it is, consider what mischievous inferences they make from thence; as that the ministers of all reformed churches (where episcopacy is not) are no true ministers, and their ministry to be altogether invalid, and their churches to be no true churches; witness that of Jansenius, cited by Voetius: The Bishop only may call and ordain Elders, and whosoever in case of necessity be ordained by the church and Presbyters, he is no presbyter, and his whole ministry is invalid. Also that of the papists, cited by Gerardus, saith thus: The papist laying this foundation, that Bishops are above Presbyters *jure divino*, do infer, that Luther had no power of ordaining ministers, because he was no Bishop, but only a

Presbyter, and by consequence, that there are no true ministers in our churches. And no marvel, if papists say so abroad, when our late Archprelate in open court at home called Reverend Master Calvin rascal, and said of those Protestant churches, that they were no churches, because they had no Bishops; now what a scandal this is, let the world judge.

7. *That episcopacy is not only lawful, but convenient for edification.*

What edification have we by Bishops, unless edification of altars, images, and popery? But for edification of souls by the Word, who are greater enemies thereunto than Bishops? Preaching twice a day is sufficient to put a conformable minister into their black book, yea, to suspend him from his ministry. In catechizing they forbid any further exposition than the giving the bare grammatical sense of their form. And for prayer, wherein the apostle makes it a chief work of the ministers of the Gospel, to give themselves to prayer as well as the ministry of the Word, they will suffer no other than reading in a book and saying over the fifty-fifth Canon.

In other reformed churches, where are no Bishops, in every congregation there is a preaching minister, but for England, where is now a settled maintenance for the ministry, and as many able men as in any other place; yet there are divers thousands of congregations without a preaching ministry, and for one sermon they preach themselves, they hinder many hundreds. It is little good that prelates do in this kind. More of God and his Kingdom hath appeared in some one congregation, where a minister hath been whom they have silenced or deprived, than in all the Bishops' families in England; could any godly minister endure such a parish as Lambeth is, if he had such power to reform as the Archprelate had?

When the Parliament hath examined what men the prelates have put into places, it will appear what edification people have had by their means; what places have been more miserably provided for in all the Kingdom, than those that prelates and cathedrals have had the disposing of? Neither hath this been through some particular personal corruptions, but the whole Kingdom can witness how generally this hath been ever since the Reformation; and if this be your edification, we beseech the Lord in mercy to deliver us from it.

8. *Episcopacy is suitable and agreeable to the civil policy and government of this State.*

What is by divine institution is agreeable to all States, and what is against it cannot be agreeable to any Christian government.

We see by our neighbors how agreeable it hath been to civil government; hath it not endangered to bring all things into confusion amongst them?

We ourselves have had full experience how the prelates and that faction have stopped the course of Law, and lifted up themselves above it. Priests in parishes above the magistrates there, and Bishops above the nobles. The government of our Kingdom is by Parliamentary and common law, but they seek to rule against either, as appears by their Commission, which they have got for the High Commission. In the copy whereof these are their words: That you our said Commissioners, and every of you, shall diligently and faithfully execute this our Commission, and every part and branch thereof in manner and form aforesaid, and according to the true meaning thereof, notwithstanding any appellation, provocation, privilege or exemption in that behalf to be had, made, pretended or alleged by any person or persons, resident or dwelling in any place or places, exempt or not exempt within these our Realms of England, and Ireland, and the Dominion of Wales, any our laws, statutes, proclamations, or other grants, privilege, or ordinances which be or may seem contrary to the premises notwithstanding.

King Philip the husband of Queen Mary thought it so inconsistent with civil government by the nobility, that upon his death-bed, calling his son unto him, he gave him this counsel: If you intend to rule by your nobles, keep your Bishops low, and if you would rule by your Bishops, keep your nobles low. What disturbance in civil states this power of prelates with kings hath made, our English records do sufficiently testify, which no true English spirit can read or relate without a saddened spirit. Matthew Paris in his *History* tells us of the great power that Peter, Bishop of Winchester, and Peter Rivall, the Bishop's cousin, with other adherents, had with King Henry III. Great complaints were made, that by their counsel the King's heart was turned from the love of his subjects, and the hearts of them from him, and discord was sown amongst them; and that by the said counsel of the foresaid Bishop and his fellows, King John, the King's father, lost first the hearts of his barons, after that lost Normandy, and after that other lands also, and in the end wasted all his treasure, and the Kingdom for a long time after had no quiet. By the said counsel also, England that was the prince of provinces, became a tributary. Moreover, through their wicked counsel, saith the story, at this present, great perturbation seemed to hang over the realm; for if it had not been for their counsel, and if that true justice and judgment might have been administered unto the King's subjects, these tumults had never been stirred, and the King might have had his land unwasted, and his treasure unconsumed. The said Bishop impiously tells the nobles, that the King right well might call unto him what foreigners and strangers he listed by whom he might be able to bridle his proud and rebellious subjects, and so to keep them in awe and good order: Whereupon the nobles in great perturbation departed, promising amongst themselves in this case (which touched the state of the whole realm) they would constantly join together, even unto death.

The great divisions in the Commonwealth presently after Constantine's times were made by the Bishops; which the historians of those times do plentifully testify.

This is not our judgment alone; hear what Master Tyndale saith in his book of Christian obedience: Woe unto the realms where Bishops are of the King's Counsel: as profitable are they verily unto the realms with their counsels, as wolves unto the sheep, or the foxes unto the geese.

In France the Reformed churches not under Bishops are as good and faithful subjects unto their Prince, and so acknowledged by himself, though of another religion, as any he hath. Hence it appears, that that government which is not prelatical may stand with the peace and civil order of a State as well as it.

9. *That this government is lawful, appears by the immediate and constant practice of all the Christian world, grounded upon Scripture from the apostles' time to this last age, for above fifteen hundred years together.*

To that which they say, it is grounded upon Scripture, we shall speak afterwards, but to say that this was the practice of all the Christian world for fifteen hundred years is a bold assertion. We find in history that the Church of Scotland was not governed by Bishops till between four or five hundred years after Christ, although it had flourished in the Christian religion two or three hundred years before.

We answer as before, it is true indeed, that in all times for fifteen hundred years there were bishops, but in this time of the apostles and presently after, bishops were much different from that they are now, as

1. Then they were parochial, not diocesan.

2. Even in those times when episcopacy began to grow to some height, yet the election of bishops was by the whole church, but it is not so now.

3. There was not that superiority of them over other ministers as there is now.

4. They challenged not the power of ordination and church censures to themselves, as now they do.

These four we undertake now to show you briefly, because ere long you shall have them discussed more largely upon another occasion.

For the first – Bishops were parochial, not diocesan; for these were bishops of villages and small towns, as Sozomen in his seventh book testifies; and according to Eusebius, churches wherein were bishops, were parishes.

Ignatius saith, Every church should have her communion table, and every church her bishop.

And Cyprian saith, The bounds of a church were not greater than a bishop might call together the whole multitude about the affairs of it.

For the second – These bishops were chosen by the whole church. Ambrose saith, That is truly and certainly a divine election of a bishop is made by the whole church.

Platina tells us, that Ludovicus the Second commanded by his letters that the Romans should choose their own bishop, not looking for strangers to meddle in it, for it belonged to the citizens.

Ambrose complains to Nepotianus of the great disorder in the clergy, that they run to Bishops Suffragans, certain times of the year, and bringing some sum of money, they are ordained being chosen of none; and the Bishop without any lawful election is chosen in private of the Canons or Prebendaries only, without the knowledge of the people.

For the third – They had not superiority over other ministers, as they have now.

The *Helvetian Confession*, 5. 12, hath these words, Equal power is given to all ministers of the church: from the beginning no one preferred himself before another, saving only for order, someone did call them together, propounded the matters that were to be consulted of, and gathered the voices.

The honor of a bishop being taken from the rest of the ministers, and given to one, was the first step to papacy.

Power of ordination belonged likewise to presbyters, for besides the evidence of Scripture, the third Canon of the Council of Carthage says: The Bishop giving the blessing, let all the elders there present lay on their hands.

That they had not the power of church censures to themselves Cyprian saith, that the presbyters and other church officers have as well power to absolve, as the Bishop. And in another place, For as much as absolution belongs unto all, I alone dare not do it.

And Augustine, It helps much to make the party more ashamed, that he be excommunicated by the whole church.

Jerome, The elders have interest in other censures of the church, and the church itself in excommunication.

Now if there be such difference between our Bishops and the former, why do you again bring their antiquity? Your repetition leads us in our answer to come again to the same thing; may not all see how egregiously you seek to deceive the reader with great words, in pretending that diocesan Bishops were of so long standing, because bishops were. We see by this deceit how dangerous it is to take words that are common to many things, and appropriate them to a particular; if it once gain the appropriation of a name or title, it will soon challenge the thing itself, and the keeping up the name after it hath been afore no marvel though men contend so much for keeping the name of Bishops. We find in the notes of the Rhemists upon that place, 1 Timothy 6. v. 20, that they contend much for the keeping their old terms. Let us keep our forefathers' words (say they) and we shall easily keep our old faith; let them say amendment, let us say penance, let them say the Lord's Supper, let us say the Mass, let them say the communion table, let us say the altar, let them say elders, ministers, let us say priest, let them say superintendent, let us say Bishop, etc. They and we all have experience what power words and names have; the spirit of these Rhemists hath been lately in many of our men, they began to alter the former language, but told you at first they meant no hurt by the words and names they put upon things, and now in this controversy about episcopacy, their chief prevailing argument is the very word *bishop*, which we acknowledge to be a Scripture word, but applied so as they do, to a certain kind of superior officer in the ministry of their own devising, when God gives it to all ministers of the Gospel; this we say hath much evil in it, and the retaining of it, in this sense, is very dangerous.

10. *The most learned Protestants in those churches which now are not gov-*

erned by Bishops do not only hold the government to be lawful, but wish that they themselves may enjoy it.

This is boldly said, but we know quite the contrary to be true, both by their writings and by those that have lived amongst them. Gerard, in whom we may see the mind of the reformed churches as much as in any, saith: We do not acknowledge any inequality of jurisdiction that bishops have over presbyters *jure divino*, seeing the contrary may be gathered out of Scripture, as from *Acts* 20.17-18, and divers other places by him cited. He also brings the testimony of Jerome, Ambrose, Austin, Sedulius, Primasius, Chrysostom, Theodoret, Oecumenius, and Theophylact, and answers the contrary arguments of Bellarmine. Chamierus also, who fully knew the mind of the reformed churches, saith thus: That in the first beginning of the churches, there were no such Bishops as were afterwards instituted, to wit, such as *suo jure* were over the clergy, such saith he, were not instituted by Christ and his apostles, and because that is best which is first, it were better for the churches, if they were all esteemed to be of equal right and degree; and when that distinct order of the bishops from the presbyters was first brought in, the bishops were not the monarchs of the church, nor had power over the clergy, but only some of the chief were chosen to go before others in deliberation and composing of matters. And lest you should think the judgment of the divines of the Reformed churches to be altered, take what Voetius, Professor of Utrecht, hath formerly written, and of late said. What he hath written, you may read in his learned tractate *De desperata causa Papatus*; where amongst much against episcopacy, he hath these passages: We have more than abundantly proved, that pretended episcopacy is not *jure divino*. Again, either we are not heretics in this point, or the fathers and doctors are heretics with us. And that you might flatter yourselves in conceiting that the reformed churches wish for your government, he saith, We who have not that order of Bishops, stand not in need of them from the English. And for his speech, when Bishop Hall's book in defense of episcopacy came forth, he said, What will this poor fellow do? He hath of late read many lectures against the superiority and jurisdiction of the Bishops.

11. *Again, the government of episcopacy, etc.*

Here you repeat the argument of antiquity again, and cry up your great Diana, but concerning the episcopacy of the primitive times, we have said enough before. The bringing this over again, with so fair a gloss, is but to deceive the world.

12. *That the government of the church by episcopacy is most suitable to the frame of the civil government in this Kingdom, appears by the happy and flourishing union of them both for so long a time together.*

Considering what persecutions and distractions there have been in both Kingdoms, by means of them, neither we nor the other Kingdom have cause to boast much of flourishing happiness.

What good hath been by the union of the Kingdoms, cannot be attributed to the prelates; but what evil hath come by the disunion, hath been apparently by them.

13. *No man can give us assurance how any church government besides this will suit well the civil policy of this State.*

Whatsoever we desire in this kind is no other than according to the Word, and we and you may assure ourselves, that so long as we walk according to that rule, peace shall be upon us, and upon the Israel of God.

This is an argument pagans have used against the Christians: We have worshiped our gods all this while, and if we bring in any new way of worship, we know not what the issue will be.

We are already sure that episcopal government hath been a woeful trouble and disturbance to ours and other States, as hath been showed before.

14. *We conceive it may be of dangerous consequence for men of settled fortunes to hazard their estates, etc.*

This seems to be a threatening clause, as if some mischievous thing were intended by the episcopal party, suitable to the expression of one who laboring to promote the petition, urged it with this argument, that there would be no living for men in England, unless they would subscribe to it.

15. *Those who would have episcopacy abolished, have not yet agreed, nor as we are persuaded ever can or will agree upon any other common form of government.*

If episcopacy were gone, the agreement would be easy, as we see in Scotland; while episcopacy was amongst them, there was no small disagreement, but since the removal thereof, they are of one heart and mind.

There is no government in any Reformed church from which there are so many rents, under which there are so many divisions, as the government of episcopacy which we have in England.

Many men are afraid to discover themselves freely, for fear if episcopacy hold, it will be hereafter revenged upon them, having had so much experience of the cruelty of men in that place, whereas if it were down, they would be more free to show their opinions, and to close with their brethren in the truth.

Reformed churches in all places do agree, and why should not we think there would be agreement amongst us, if episcopacy were removed?

They who seem most to differ, yet they differ not one from another so much, as they all differ from episcopacy. They profess one to another, that they can walk as brethren together in enjoying communion one with another in peace and love.

You seem to rejoice in the supposal of dissentions between others, thinking thereby to gain time, but that you may see there is not so vast a difference amongst us as you think, in these things we are all agreed.

Church discipline is to be learned from the plain and perfect Word of God, and in such particulars as are common to the church with other societies, is to be directed by the light of nature, the church observing always the general rules of the Word.

A particular church consists of such as in the use of the ordinances of Christ do join together in one body and society, to walk in all the ways of Christ. Neither are there any other members of a particular church, but such as in profession are believers and saints.

The church may have no office nor office-bearers, but such as are by divine appointment, which are elders or deacons, or more particularly, pastors, teachers, elders, and deacons, by which Christ hath provided for all the necessities of the church.

Although the civil and ecclesiastical government be different kinds of governments, yet it is a principal part of the civil magistrate, who is keeper of both Tables, to have a care of the church, and to exercise his authority for the preserving of religion, and for the peace and safety of the church, and where the magistrate does his duty, it is a special blessing of God, and he is to be obeyed in all things lawful.[5]

Each particular church hath her own power and authority, and the

5. Burroughs not only seems to favor a four office view of the church, but an active role for civil government in church affairs as well.

use and benefit of all the ordinances of Christ. Neither is there anything to be done without the express or tacit consent of the congregation, in matters which are proper and peculiar to a particular church, whether in election or ordination of ministers, or in admitting or excommunicating of members.

It is in many respects expedient both for the members of each church, whether ministers or people, and for the right governing and well-being of the particular churches in a nation professing the Christian religion, that besides their particular assemblies and elderships, they convene by their commissioners, ministers, and elders in greater assemblies, that matters that concern all the churches within their bounds respective may, with common advice and consent, be agreed upon for their good and edification.

16. *It is just and reasonable, that whosoever would introduce a new form, should be obliged to demonstrate aforehand, that the government he would introduce be better than the other, and able to recompense the loss thereof.*

There can be no loss of an evil, and therefore you need not call for a recompense either before or after, seeing prelacy is an evil, as we have proved and shall prove, it is neither to be recompensed, nor moderated, nor reserved, but presently and wholly to be taken away, whatever the consequence may be. The presence of an error hinders men from seeing the truth; if the government be for the present hurtful, and the exercise mischievous to others, we need not, we ought not to spare it till we know what shall come in the room.

And further we all see a platform before us amongst our brethren in the reformed churches, which we conceive would give satisfaction in the main, being according to the former six Propositions, and what alteration is to be made in such things wherein one reformed church differs from another, the same may be effected with more peace than the episcopacy can be continued.

17. *We may still enjoy that government which most probably holds its institution from the apostles.*

We are glad you suspect your cause so far, having no other than a sandy foundation of probability; what an evil is it that so many thousands have suffered such sore things, in souls and bodies, in estates, liberties, and names, for mere probabilities! We bless God we have more to say for our cause against episcopacy than probables, and our reasons from Scripture are these.

The whole charge of all the affairs of the Church of Ephesus was left to the elders, *Acts* 20, where Saint Paul tells them, that the Holy Ghost had made them overseers over that flock which they were *poimainein*, and the word signifies in the judgment of all, both to feed and to rule.

Whatsoever you make to belong to episcopacy, as episcopacy, is either matter of jurisdiction, or ordination. Jurisdiction does not belong to the Bishop; for our Saviour Christ saith, Go tell the church, which to interpret of one man, is against that place, because he saith, Whatsoever ye bind, against the course of Scripture, because one man is never called a church, and against common sense, because the word *church*, there signifies an assembly. And for ordination, the apostle saith unto Timothy, The gift that is in thee, which was given thee by prophecy, with the laying on of the hands of the presbytery, 1 *Timothy* 4:14, therefore ordination also belongs unto the elders.

We find no rules nor instructions in Scripture for the ordering of Bishops, as distinguished from elders, pastors, and teachers, and therefore we cannot believe that there is any such distinct office. *Judicent nobis loca*, as Voetius speaks, let them show us those places of Scripture, where is that peculiar ministry, and where are those special instructions which belong to the Bishops alone, and not unto other pastors?

We find in the judgment of the Holy Ghost, that a bishop and an elder are all one, as appears in *Acts* 20, by comparing the seventeenth verse with the twenty-eighth; those that are called elders in the seventeenth are called bishops in the twenty-eighth; which the English translates "overseers" and only here. So *Titus* 1:5 compared with verse 7 where those who are said to be elders in the fifth verse, are each of them called a bishop in the seventh; otherwise there should be no force in the particle, "for." This is the arguing of the apostle, ordain elders, verse 5, if any be blameless, verse 6, for a bishop must be blameless, verse 7.

One Bishop now has jurisdiction over diverse counties and hundreds of churches, but in the apostle's times, there were diverse bishops in every city, *Titus* 1: 5: Elders in every city; who (as we have proved before) are the same with bishops, *Philippians* 1:1, bishops and deacons at Philippi; it is certain in these places they [the citizens] were not all Christians, it is most likely, very few of them, and yet those few had divers bishops set over them; other kind of Bishops than these the Scripture knows not. Yet in these times the elders had extraordinary gifts, as appears *James* 5, where the apostle sets down a rule for all churches in those times, that when any was sick, the elders should anoint him with oil, and so he should recover; if the elders had then miraculous gifts, and yet there were divers appointed for every city, then it cannot be conceived, that now when elders have no such extraordinary gifts, yet that one should be set over many counties, it may be thousands of congregations.

The Scripture acknowledges no superiority or inferiority between officers of the same kind. One apostle was not over another, nor one evangelist over another, nor one prophet over another (indeed the Scripture saith, the spirits of the prophets are subject to the prophets, but the subjection was mutual, one not having more power over another, than that other had over him), neither is one deacon over another; and what color of reason can be given, that one pastor or teacher should have power over another.

There is no mention in Scripture of any under an apostle or evangelist that did perform any work of office in any place but in his own particular church; the apostles and evangelists which are made distinct officers in the 4th of *Ephesians*, had their commission general for all places without any limitation; but in this latitude of the commission, they have no successors. There was no place where apostles or evangelists came, but they had the same power, which we suppose none of our Bishops dare arrogate to themselves. If therefore they succeed not apostles and evangelists in the largeness of their commission, then their succession must be of those pastors and teachers, whom we find the Holy Ghost hath set over particular congregations.

If church officers be not limited to several congregations, then there is no limitation by any divine institution, and if so, then a pastor may have many, yea, all churches in the world under him, and so the popedom must be granted at most inconvenient, and not against any divine institution. If it should be said, that though one can oversee divers, yet it follows not that he can oversee all, we answer, that no man can oversee divers, but by substitutes, and by substitutes he may oversee all, and so the difference will be only in the inconvenience, and not in the unlawfulness, which is in the nature of the thing. You have here our arguments, and if they be weighed without prejudice, surely you yourselves will judge them to be more than probabilities. We have not answered to every passage of this *Petition*, for we find many tautologies. Only one passage there is more, which we cannot pass by, to which we answer briefly, and then we have done.

18. *You say that this government by Bishops hath continued many ages without any alteration.*

If an alteration be made unto the better, what cause hath any to complain, *nullus pudor est ad melior a transire*, Ambrose, *Epist.* 31 ad Valent. It is no shame to change for the better.

If this government hath been without any alteration, then it is the same every way it was before the Reformation, and if so, then it is the very same Antichrist had retained many hundreds of years. Now we will leave it to the consideration of any indifferent man whether he can think in his conscience that it is any way probable, that Antichrist should retain the government of Christ so long in the simplicity and purity of it. Is it not the great design of Antichrist to lift up himself above Christ and his people? And by what means could he more readily effect this, than by corrupting the government? Had he not power to do it, seeing for many years he did what he listed in the church? All doctrines that stood in his way, he hath corrupted, and can it be thought, that he should leave government entire, according to institution, which was most opposite to his design? Pride and arrogancy cause men above all things to seek to bring government under their own wills; and whoever since the beginning of the world swelled with more pride and arrogancy than Antichrist hath done? which appears by his interdicting of kingdoms, and bringing princes under his feet. But now we hope God will stir up the spirits of the princes of the Earth to cast off with indignation that base bondage and Babylonish tyranny they have so long been under; for which, both we and all the churches of God, both do, and shall cry to Heaven to hasten.

20

Secrets of Church Polity[1]

John Witherspoon

Editor's Introduction

O NE OF THE most notable of early American Presbyterians was John Witherspoon, sixth president of the College of New Jersey at Princeton (Jonathan Edwards had been the third president of this institution that later was known as Princeton University); the only clergyman and educator to sign the *Declaration of Independence*; principal author of the form of church government for the Presbyterian Church in the U.S.A. adopted in 1788; member of the New Jersey provincial Congress and the Continental Congress; educator of presidents, vice presidents, justices of the United States Supreme Court, state and federal legislators, and dozens of Presbyterian ministers; and author of many essays and sermons, among which is *Ecclesiastical Characteristics: or, the Arcana of Church Policy*, from which these excerpts are taken.

In 1766, when Witherspoon was invited by the board of trustees at the College of New Jersey to become Princeton's sixth president, he was the leader of the popular or orthodox faction in the Church of Scotland. Thirteen years before, at the age of 30, he had anonymously published *Ecclesiastical Characteristics* in order to ridicule the clergymen of the moderate party. In 1754 – while on a fundraising trip to Scotland with Gilbert Tennent – the Reverend Samuel Davies, president of the College, read Witherspoon's satire on the Scots clergy and remarked that its humor was "not inferior to that of Dean Swift."

Enormously popular with the laity, *Ecclesiastical Characteristics* ran into seven editions and was the first of Witherspoon's works to be pub-

1. This essay is reprinted from *The Trinity Review.*

lished in America. According to Witherspoon, the *Ecclesiastical Charac-teristics* "make a complete system for the education and accomplish-ment of a moderate clergyman, for his guidance in public judgment, and his direction as to private practice." The book was the focus of rage and resentment among the powerful moderate clergymen of Scotland, and Witherspoon was forced to defend the satire before the Synod of Glasgow. He did so brilliantly, and we have included here part of that defense.

Our reasons for reprinting part of Witherspoon's work are several: First, not many Americans know anything about Witherspoon, even though he was certainly one of the most influential Christians of his generation. Second, those who have heard his name do not seem to be aware that he wrote brilliant satire. Third, many of those who profess to be Christians seem to think that satire is somehow un-Christian, yet it is, perhaps, the only form of humor found in Scripture. Certainly Elijah mocked the priests of Ba'al, Paul mocked the Judaizers, and Jesus mocked the Pharisees. Satire, sarcasm, and ridicule, used in defense of the truth, are legitimate weapons; for falsehood is, among other things, ludicrous. Finally, there are just as many clergymen in 1987 as there were in 1753 who deserve to be ridiculed. Some of Witherspoon's Max-ims are as appropriate today as they were two centuries ago. Here are Witherspoon's own words from *Serious Apology for the Ecclesiastical Char-acteristics:*

> The *Ecclesiastical Characteristics* is evidently a satire upon clergymen of a certain character. It is a satire too, which everybody must see was intended to carry in it no small measure of keenness and severity. This was to be expected from the nature and design of the performance. A satire that does not bite is good for nothing. Hence it necessarily follows that it is essential to this manner of writing to provoke and give of-fence.... The rage and fury of many ministers in Scotland, when this pamphlet was first published, is known almost to all its readers. The most opprobrious names were bestowed upon the concealed author, and the most dreadful threatenings uttered, in case they should be so fortunate as to discover and convict him.
>
> ...[W]hat first induced me to write was a deep concern for the declin-ing interest of religion in the Church of Scotland, mixed with some indignation at what appeared to me a strange abuse of church-author-ity.... I am altogether at a loss to know what is the argument in reason, or the precept in Scripture, which makes it criminal to censure ministers

when they deserve it.... I hold it as a first principle that as it is in them doubly criminal and doubly pernicious, so it ought to be exposed with double severity.... [I]f, in any case, erroneous doctrine, or degeneracy of life, is plain and visible, to render them completely odious, must certainly be a duty. When it is not done, it provokes men to conclude that the clergy [are] all combined together, like "Demetrius and the craftsmen," and more concerned for their own power and credit, than for the interest and benefit of those committed to their charge....

There have been, within these few years, writings published in Scotland directly leveled against religion itself, taking away the very foundation of morality, treating our Redeemer's name with contempt and derision, and bringing in doubt the very being of God. Writings of this kind have been publicly avowed, and the names of the authors prefixed. Now, where has been the zeal of the enemies of the *Characteristics* against such writings? Have they moved for the exercise of discipline against the writers? ...Does this not tempt men to say, as was said an age ago by Molière in France, or by some there, on occasion of a play of his called *Tartuffe*, That a man may write what he pleases against God Almighty in perfect security; but if he write against the characters of the clergy in power, he is ruined forever...?

[I]t seems very reasonable to believe, that as human beings are never at a stand, a church and a nation, in a quiet and peaceable state, is always growing insensibly worse, till it be either so corrupt as to deserve and procure exterminating judgments, or in the infinite mercy of God, by some great shock or revolution, is brought back to simplicity and purity, and reduced, as it were, to its first principles.... [I]t is every man's duty to do all in his power to retard the progress of corruption, by strictness and tenderness in his own personal walk, fidelity and vigilance in the duties of a public station, and a bold and open testimony against every thing contrary to the interest of true and undefiled religion.

In his *Speech in the Synod of Glasgow,* Witherspoon pulled no punches with his critics:

[M]ust the least attempt to show that there are corruptions among the clergy be an unpardonable crime? I have seen it insisted on in print, that as soon as the liberty of the press is taken away, there is an end of every shadow of liberty. And as of late years it hath been very frequent to borrow from what is customary in the civil government, and apply it to the church, I shall beg leave to borrow this maxim, and to affirm, that so soon as it is not permitted in general to lash the characters of churchmen, there is established a sacerdotal tyranny, which always was, and always will be, of the most cruel, relentless, and illegal kind....

To conclude, Sir, though I will never approve of, or give my consent for establishing a practice which I think unjust and tyrannical; yet as to my own case, I will even submit to be interrogated by this very party upon this just, this self-evidently just, condition, that the ministers of that Presbytery do submit themselves to be interrogated by me in turn, on their doctrine....

Let us now turn to *Ecclesiastical Characteristics*.

Maxim I

All ecclesiastical persons, of whatever rank, whether principals of colleges, professors of divinity, ministers, or even probationers, that are suspected of heresy, are to be esteemed men of great genius, vast learning, and uncommon wont and are, by all means, to be supported and protected.

All moderate men have a kind of fellow-feeling with heresy, and as soon as they hear of any one suspected, or in danger of being prosecuted for it, zealously and unanimously rise up in his defense. This fact is unquestionable. I never knew a moderate man in my life that did not love and honor a heretic, or that had not an implacable hatred at the persons and characters of heresy-hunters; a name with which we have thought proper to stigmatize these sons of Belial, who begin and carry on prosecutions against men for heresy in church-courts.

It is related of the apostle John, and an ugly story it is, that upon going into a public bath, and observing the heretic Cerethinus there before him, he retired with the utmost precipitation, lest the edifice should fall, and crush him, when in company with such an enemy of the truth. If the story be true, the apostle's conduct was ridiculous and wild... ; however, whether it be true or not, the conduct of all moderate men is directly opposite. As to the justice of this maxim, many solid reasons may be given for it. Compassion itself, which is one of the finest and most benevolent feelings of the human heart, moves them to the relief of their distressed brother. Another very plain reason may be given for it: Moderate men are, by their very name and constitution, the reverse, in all respects, of bigoted zealots. Now, it is well known, that many of this last sort, both clergy and common people, when they hear of a man suspected of heresy, conceive an aversion at him, even before they know anything of the case; nor after he is acquitted (as they are all of them commonly in our church-courts) can they ever come to entertain a favorable opinion of him. The reverse of this is to be as early and vigorous in his defense, as they are in his prosecution, and as implicit in our belief of his orthodoxy, as they are in their belief of his error....

This brings to mind another reason for the maxim, *viz*. That heretics, being so nearly related to the moderate men, have a right to claim their protection out of friendship and personal regard....

Maxim II

When any man is charged with loose practices, or tendencies to immorality, he is to be screened and protected as much as possible; especially if the faults laid to his charge be, as they are incomparably well termed in a sermon, preached by a hopeful youth that made some noise lately, "good humored vices."

The reason upon which this maxim is founded, may be taken from the reasons for the former, "mutatis mutandis"; there being scarcely any of them that does not hold equally in both cases. A libertine is a kind of practical heretic; and is to be treated as such....

I must not, however, omit taking notice, to prevent mistakes, of one exception that must be made from this maxim; that is, that when the person to whose charge any faults are laid, is reputed orthodox in his principles, in the common acceptation of that word,... in that case they are all to be taken for granted as true, and the evil of them set forth in the liveliest colors. In consequence of this, he is to be prosecuted and torn to pieces on account of these crimes. But if it so happen, that he cannot be convicted upon a trial, then it is best to make use of things as they really are; that is, to express suspicions, to give ingenious and dubious hints, and if possible, ruin him without any trial at all....

Maxim III

It is a necessary part of the character of a moderate man, never to speak of the Confession of Faith but with a sneer; to give sly hints, that he does not thoroughly believe it; and to make the word orthodoxy a term of contempt and reproach.

The *Confession of Faith*, which we are now all laid under a disagreeable necessity to subscribe, was framed in times of hot religious zeal; and therefore it can hardly be supposed to contain anything agreeable to our sentiments in these cool and refreshing days of moderation. So true is this, that I do not remember to have heard any moderate man speak well of it, or recommend it, in a sermon, or private discourse, in my time. And, indeed, nothing can be more ridiculous, than to make a fixed standard for opinions, which change just as the fashions of clothes and dress. No complete system can be settled for all ages, except the maxims I am now compiling and illustrating, and their great perfection lies in their being ambulatory, so that they may be applied differently, with the change of times.

Upon his head some may be ready to object: That if the *Confession of Faith* be built upon the sacred Scriptures, then, change what will, it cannot, as the foundation upon which it rests, remains always firm and the same. In answer to this, I beg leave to make a very new, and therefore striking comparison: When a lady looks in a mirror, she sees herself in a certain attitude and dress, but in her native beauty and color; should her eye, on a sudden, be tinctured with the jaundice, she sees herself all yellow and spotted; yet the mirror remains the same faithful mirror still, and the alteration arises not from it, but from the object that looks at it. I beg leave to make another comparison: When an old philosopher looked at the evening-star, he beheld nothing but a little twinkling orb, round and regular like the rest; but when a modern views it with a telescope, he talks of phases, and horns, and mountains, and what not; now this arises not from any alteration in the star, but from his superior assistance in looking at it. The application of both these similitudes I leave to the reader.

But besides these general reasons, there is one very strong particular reason why moderate men cannot love the *Confession of Faith*; moderation evidently implies a large share of charity, and consequently a good and favorable opinion of those that differ from our church; but a rigid adherence to the *Confession of Faith*, and high esteem of it, nearly borders upon, or gives great suspicion of harsh opinions of those that differ from us: and does not experience rise up and ratify this observation? Who are the narrow-minded, bigoted, uncharitable persons among us? Who are the severe censurers of those that differ in judgment? Who are the damners of the adorable Heathens, Socrates, Plato, Marcus Antonius, &c.? In fine, who are the persecutors of the inimitable heretics among ourselves? Who but the admirers of this antiquated composition, who pin their faith to other men's sleeves, and will not endure one jot less or different belief from what their fathers had before them! It is therefore plain, that the moderate man, who desires to inclose all intelligent beings in one benevolent embrace, must have an utter abhorrence at that vile hedge of distinction, the *Confession of Faith*.

I shall briefly mention a trifling objection to this part of our character. – That by our subscription we sacrifice sincerity, the queen of virtues, to private gain and advantage. To which I answer, in the first place, That the objection proves too much, and therefore must be false, and can prove nothing: for allowing the justice of the objection, it would follow, that a vast number, perhaps a majority, of the clergy of the Church of England are villains; their printed sermons being, many of them, diametrically opposite to the articles which they subscribe. Now, as this supposition can never be admitted by a charitable man, the objection from whence it flows, as a necessary consequence, must fall to the ground.

But further, what is there more insincere in our subscriptions, than in those expressions of compliment and civility, which all acknowledge lawful, although they rarely express the meaning of the heart! The design is sufficiently understood in both cases; and our subscriptions have this advantage above forms of compliment, in point of honesty, that we are at a great deal of pains usually to persuade the world that we do not believe what we sign; whereas the complaisant gentleman is very seldom at any pains about the matter.

What is said might suffice in so clear a case; but I am here able to give a proof of the improvement of the age, by communication to the reader a new way of subscribing the *Confession of Faith*, in a perfect consistency with sincerity, if that be thought of any consequence: It is taken from the method of attesting some of our gentlemen elders to the general assembly. Many insist that they ought to be attested, and do attest them, as qualified in all respects, if the attestors are wholly ignorant about the matter; because, in that case, there is not evidence to the contrary, and the presumption ought to lie on the favorable side. Now, as every new discovery should be applied to all the purposes for which it may be useful, let this method be adopted by the intrants into the ministry, and applied to their subscription of the *Confession to Faith*. Nothing is more easy than for them to keep themselves wholly ignorant of what it contains; and then they may, with a good conscience, subscribe it as true, because it ought to be so.

Maxim IV

A good preacher must not only have all the above and subsequent principles of moderation in him, as the source of everything that is good; but must, over and over, have the following special marks and signs of a talent for preaching:

1. *His subjects must be confined to social duties.*

2. *He must recommend them only from rational considerations, viz. the beauty and comely proportions of virtue, and its advantages in the present life, without any regard to a future state of more extended self-interest.*

3. *His authorities must be drawn from heathen writers, none, or as few as possible, from Scripture.*

4. *He must be very unacceptable to the common people.*

Maxim V

A minister must endeavor to acquire as great a degree of politeness, in his carriage and behavior, and to catch as much of the air and manner of a fine gentleman, as possibly he can.

This maxim is necessary, because without it the former could not be attained to. Much study is a great enemy to politeness in men, just as a great care of household affairs spoils the free careless air of a fine lady, and whether politeness is to be sacrificed to learning, let the impartial world judge. Besides, the scheme which I have permitted the moderate man to study does actually supercede the use of all other learning, because it contains a knowledge of the whole, and the good of the whole; more than which, I hope, will be allowed to be not only needless, but impossible.

This scheme excels in brevity; for it may be understood in a very short time, which, I suppose, prompted a certain clergyman to say, that any student might get as much divinity as he would ever have occasion for in six weeks.... Agreeably to all this have we not seen in fact, many students of divinity brought up in hot-beds, who have become speakers in general assemblies, and strenuous supporters of a falling church, before their beards were grown, to the perfect astonishment of an observing world?... Then there will be no need at all for the critical study of the Scriptures, for reading large bodies of divinity, for an acquaintance with church history, or the writings of those poor creatures the Christian fathers....

We find that moderate men have mostly, by constitution, too much spirit to submit to the drudgery of the kinds of learning above-mentioned, and despise all those who do so. There is no controversy now about Arian, Arminian, Pelagian, or Socinian tenets.... This shows, by the by, the injustice and malignity of those poor beings the Seceders, who cry out of erroneous doctrines in the church, and assert that Arminianism is publicly taught by many. It is known that they mean the moderate men, when they speak so; and yet I will venture to affirm, that there are not a few young men of that character, who, if they were asked, could not tell what the five Arminian articles are, so little do they regard Arminianism.... It will perhaps be objected against this maxim, That the moderate party commonly set up on a pretence of being more learned than their adversaries; and are, in fact, thought to be very learned in their sermons by the vulgar, who, for that reason hate them. Now, as to their pretending to be more learned than their adversaries, it is most just; for they have, as has been shown, got hold of the sum-total of learning, although they did not calculate it themselves. And as to their being thought learned in their sermons by the vulgar, it is sufficient for that purpose that they be unintelligible. Scattering a few phrases in their sermons...will easily persuade the people that they are learned: and this persuasion is, to all intents and purposes, the same thing as if it were true.

Maxim XI

The character which moderate men give their adversaries of the orthodox party must always be that of "knaves" or "fools"; and, as occasion serves, the same person (if it will pass) may be represented as a "knave" at one time, and as a "fool" at another.

Maxim XII

As to the world in general, a moderate man is to have great charity for Atheists and Deists in principle, and for persons that are loose and vicious in their practice; but none at all for those that have a high profession of religion, and a great pretence to strictness in their walk and conversation.

...[T]he very meaning of charity is to believe without evidence; it is not charity at all to believe good of a man when we see it, but when we do not see it. It is with charity in sentiment, as with charity in supplying the wants of the necessitous; we do not give alms to the rich but to the

poor. In like manner, when there are all outward appearances of goodness, it requires no charity to believe well of the persons: but when
there are none at all, or perhaps very many to the contrary, then I will
maintain it is charity, and charity in its perfection, to believe well of
them. Some object to this, Well, since it is your will, have charity for
them; but have charity also for such as are apparently good. Oh! the
stupid world! and slow of heart to conceive! Is it not evident to a demonstration, that if the appearance of wickedness be the foundation of
charity, the appearance of goodness, which is its opposite, must be the
foundation of a quite contrary judgment, viz. suspecting, or rather believing ill of them? If any still insist, That if not charity, yet justice
should incline us to believe well of them? as I have seemingly confessed;
I answer, That we have no occasion for justice, if we have charity; for
charity is more than justice, even as the whole is more than a part: But
though I have supposed... that justice requires this, yet it is not my sentiment; for the persons meant being usually great enemies to us, are
thereby cut off from any claim in justice to our good opinion, and being
also, as have been proved, improper objects of charity, it remains that
we should hate them with perfect hatred, as in fact we do.

Maxim XIII

*All moderate men are joined together in the strictest bond of union and do
never fail to support and defend one another to the utmost, be the cause they are
engaged in what it will.*

Time would fail me, if I should go through all the excellencies of this
crowning maxim; and therefore I shall only further observe, that it excels all the known principles of action for clearness and perspicuity. In
order to determine which side to choose in a disputed question, it requires no long discussions of reason, no critical inquiry into the truth of
controverted facts, but only some knowledge of the characters of men;
a study much more agreeable, as well as more common, than that of
books. To speak more properly, it requires no study at all of any kind;
for, as to the gross, or general tendency of a character, common fame
communicates the impression, and seldom or never deceives us.

Calvinism and the Church[1]

N. S. McFetridge

WHAT THEN, do we mean by Calvinism? I will let one answer who has gained the right to answer, and than whom no one is better qualified to answer – the Rev. Dr. Archibald Alexander Hodge.

He says:

"Calvinism" is a term used to designate, not the opinions of an individual, but a mode of religious thought or a system of religious doctrines of which the person whose name it bears was an eminent expounder. There have been from the beginning only three generically distinct systems of doctrine, or modes of conceiving and adjusting the facts and principles understood to be revealed in the Scriptures: the Pelagian, which denies the guilt, corruption and moral impotence of man, and makes him independent of the supernatural assistance of God. At the opposite pole is the Calvinistic, which emphasizes the guilt and moral impotence of man, exalts the justice and sovereignty of God, and refers salvation absolutely to the undeserved favor and new creative energy of God. Between these comes the manifold and elastic system of compromises once known as Semi-Pelagianism, and in modern times as Arminianism, which admits man's original corruption, but denies his guilt; regards redemption as a compensation for innate, and consequently irresponsible, disabilities; and refers the moral restoration of the individual to the co-operation of the human with the divine energy, the determining factor being human will.[2]

We have here, in succinct form, an accurate definition of the two systems of theology which are in active operation today, and which, Dr.

1. This is an excerpt from chapter one of McFetridge's *Calvinism in History*. It is reprinted from *The Trinity Review.*
2. *Johnson's Cyclopedia*, article "Calvinism."

Pusey says, "are now, and probably for the last time, in conflict"[3]– Calvinism and Arminianism, the former taking its name from John Calvin, a Frenchman, born in 1509, and the latter taking its name from James Herman or (in Latin dress) Arminius, a Dutchman, born in 1560. These men did not originate the systems of doctrine which bear their names, but only expounded them more fully and developed them into a more perfect form. The same views were maintained at least as early as the fourth century when Augustine and Pelagius stood in much the same attitude to each other as Calvin and Arminius in the sixteenth century. Hence Calvinism is frequently and correctly called Augustinianism; and Arminianism, Semi-Pelagianism. These are the two systems which are now most extensively held, and with the one or the other of them all other Christian theological systems have organic sympathies.

Out of Arianism grew Socinianism, and out of that modern Unitarianism, which makes Christ neither a man nor God, but a created being somewhere above angels and between humanity and Deity.[4] And while Arminianism is neither Arian nor Socinian nor Unitarian, these all are Arminian. As the writer of the article "Arminianism" in the *American Cyclopedia* says, "Every new phase of Arianism, to this day, is infallibly Arminian, though the organic connection of the two is not so manifest from the distinctively Arminian side, at least in modern times."

Their organic connection might be easily traced, and their natural affinity easily shown, did it come within our present purpose. But there are other connections and affinities of these doctrines which demand our present consideration. Each of these two systems, Calvinism and Arminianism, has an organic connection and a natural affinity with a distinct form of church government – the Calvinistic with the presbyterial and independent form, and the Arminian with the prelatical or episcopal form. As a matter of fact, this has always been so. The *Roman* Episcopal Church has always been, as a Church, Arminian in doctrine, although her *Thirty-nine Articles of Faith* are Calvinistic. I once asked a learned Episcopal rector how it came that while his *Confession of Faith* is Calvinistic his Church is Arminian. Smiling, he replied, "The Calvinism in the *Articles* is so weak that you could drive a horse and cart through it at some points!"

3. His *Letter to the Archbishop of Canterbury*.
4. See Channing's *Works*, and Joseph Cook's exposition of them in *The Independent*, March 1880.

That, I presume, accounts for it. It is not strong enough to hold the Church up to it or to resist the powerful tendency of episcopacy to Arminian doctrines. The Methodist Episcopal Church also is, as a Church, Arminian. The fact, then, is that Arminianism and episcopacy do naturally sympathize and affiliate. There is that in the Arminian doctrines of emotions and works which leads directly to the external forms and ceremonies of prelacy or episcopacy.

On the other hand, the Reformed churches which took the Presbyterian form of government have always been Calvinistic. As the Rev. Albert Barnes says, "There are no permanent Arminian, Pelagian, or Socinian presbyteries, synods, general assemblies on Earth. There are no permanent instances where these forms of belief or unbelief take on the presbyterian forms of ecclesiastical administration where they would be long retained."[5]

This connection between the *doctrine* and the *form of worship* is not superficial or accidental, but inherent. A system of doctrine, as Pelagianism, which teaches salvation by our own good works or, as Arminianism, which teaches salvation partly by works and partly by grace, of necessity sympathizes and affiliates with rites and ceremonies, and lays, in the very spirit of it, the foundation for a ritualistic service. Romanism, which is rigid Arminianism, and Presbyterianism, which is strict Calvinism, are the very antipodes of each other, and have always been in the most uncompromising hostility. Hence the historical fact that the higher the "Churchman" the more intensely Arminian he is. "It is a conspicuous fact of English history," says Dr. Hodge, "that high views as to the prerogatives of the ministry have always antagonized Calvinistic doctrines."[6] Hence also the simple republican form of worship in the Calvinistic churches.

Buckle, who, himself a fatalist, cannot be charged with partiality toward any church, says:

> It is an interesting fact that the doctrines which in England are called Calvinistic have always been connected with a democratic spirit, while those of Arminianism have found most favor among the aristocratic, or protective, party. In the republics of Switzerland, of North America and of Holland, Calvinism was always the popular creed. On the other hand,

---

5. As quoted by Breed, *Presbyterianism Three Hundred Years Ago*, 11.
6. *Johnson's Cyclopedia*, article "Calvinism."

in those evil days immediately after the death of Elizabeth, when our liberties were in imminent peril, when the Church of England, aided by the Crown, attempted to subjugate the consciences of men, and when the monstrous claim of the divine right of episcopacy was first put forward – then it was that Arminianism became the cherished doctrine of the ablest and most ambitious of the ecclesiastical party. And in that sharp retribution which followed, the Puritans and Independents, by whom the punishment was inflicted, were, with scarcely an exception, Calvinists; nor should we forget that the first open movement against Charles proceeded from Scotland, where the principles of Calvin had long been in the ascendant.[7]

Thus we see how Arminianism, taking to an aristocratic form of church government, tends toward a monarchy in civil affairs, while Calvinism, taking to a republican form of church government, tends toward a democracy in civil affairs.

Allow me to quote again from this eminent English author. He says,

[T]he first circumstance by which we must be struck is, that Calvinism is a doctrine for the poor and Arminianism for the rich. A creed which insists upon the necessity of faith must be less costly than one which insists upon the necessity of works. In the former case the sinner seeks salvation by the strength of his belief; in the latter one he seeks it by the fullness of his contributions.... This is the first great practical divergence of the two creeds.... It is also observable that the Church of Rome, whose worship is addressed mainly to the senses, and which delights in splendid cathedrals and pompous ceremonies, has always displayed against the Calvinists an animosity far greater than she has done against any other Protestant sect.

Continuing in this strain, he observes what he calls "the aristocratic tendency of Arminianism and the democratic tendency of Calvinism" and says: "The more any society tends to equality, the more likely it is that its theological opinions will be Calvinistic; while the more a society tends toward inequality, the greater the probability of those opinions being Arminian."[8]

These views of this writer are abundantly confirmed by the history bearing upon the subject. The historical fact is that Arminianism tends

---

7. *History of English Civilization*, I, 611.
8. *History of English Civilization*, I, 612-613.

to beget and to foster classes and castes in society, and to build up a gorgeous ritual wherever it gains a foothold. And so it comes to be true, on the other hand, what the historian Bancroft observes, that "a richly-endowed Church always leads to Arminianism and justification by works."[9]

Now let us glance at the explanation of this historical fact.

The prelatical or episcopal form of church government, which has always been connected with Arminian doctrines, asserts that all church power is vested in the clergy; while the republican form, which has always accompanied Calvinistic doctrines, asserts that all church power is vested in the church; that is, in the people. This is a radical difference, and "touches the very essence of things." If all the power be in the clergy, then the people are practically bound to passive obedience in all matters of faith and practice. Thus the one system subjects the people to the autocratic orders of a superior, the center principle of monarchy and despotism; while the other system elevates the people to an equality in authority, the center principle of democracy.

On this point I will quote a few sentences from the late Dr. Charles Hodge. "The theory," he observes,

> that all church power vests in a divinely constituted hierarchy begets the theory that all civil power vests, of divine right, in kings and nobles. And the theory that church power vests in the church itself, and all church officers are servants of the church, of necessity begets the theory that civil power vests in the people, and that civil magistrates are servants of the people. These theories God has joined together, and no man can put them asunder. It was therefore by an infallible instinct that the unfortunate Charles of England said, "No Bishop, no King;" by which he meant that if there is no despotic power in the church, there can be no despotic power in the state, or if there be liberty in the church, there will be liberty in the state.[10]

We find, then, these three propositions proved by historical fact and logical sequence: First, Arminianism associates itself with an episcopal form of church government, and Calvinism with a republican form of church government; second, episcopacy fosters ideas of inequality in society and of monarchy and one-man power in civil affairs; and, third,

9. *History of the United States*, IX, 503.
10. *What Is Presbyterianism?* 11. Charles I may have repeated this statement, but James I seems to have said it earlier. – *Editor.*

Arminianism is unfavorable to civil liberty, and Calvinism is unfavorable to despotism. The despotic rulers of former days were not slow to observe the correctness of these propositions, and, claiming the divine right of kings, feared Calvinism as republicanism itself.

Now, consider, for a moment, some of the reasons which lie in the system of Calvinism for its strong hostility to all despotism and its powerful influence in favor of civil liberty.

One reason for this may be found in the boundary line which it draws between church and state. It gives to each its distinct sphere, and demands that the one shall not assume the prerogatives of the other. In this it differs from Lutheranism, "which soon settled down at peace with princes, while Calvinism was ever advancing and ever contending with rulers of the world;"[11] and from the Anglican system, which began with Henry VIII as its head in place of the pope. This distinction between church and state is, as the eminent Yale professor, Dr. Fisher, remarks, "the first step, the necessary condition, in the development of religious liberty, without which civil liberty is an impossibility."[12]

Another reason is found in the republican character of its polity. Its clergy are on a perfect equality. No one of them stands higher in authority than another. They are all alike bishops. Its laymen share equally with its clergymen in all official acts – in the discussion and decision of all matters of doctrine and practice. They have a most important part given them in the right of choosing and calling their own pastor. By being thus rulers in the church they are taught to claim and exercise the same liberty in the state. It is this feature of the Calvinistic system which has, from the first, exalted the layman. It constitutes, not the clergy, but the Christian people, the interpreter of the divine will. To it the voice of the majority is the voice of God, and the issue, therefore, is, as Bancroft observes, "popular sovereignty."[13]

Another reason why Calvinism is favorable to liberty lies in its theology. "The sense of the exaltation of the Almighty Ruler," says Dr. Fisher,

> and of his intimate connection with the minutest incidents and obligations of human life, which is fostered by this theology, dwarfs all earthly

11. Dr. Henry B. Smith, *Faith and Philosophy.*
12. *History of the Reformation.*
13. *History of the United States,* I, 44, 461. Of course, this is caricature; Calvinists do not believe that the voice of the people is the voice of God; Rousseauists do. Calvinists believe that the voice of Scripture is the voice of God. – *Editor.*

potentates. An intense spirituality, a consciousness that this life is but an infinitesimal fraction of human existence, dissipates the feeling of personal homage for men, however high their station, and dulls the luster of all earthly grandeur.... The Calvinist, unlike the Romanist, dispenses with a human priesthood, which has not only often proved a powerful direct auxiliary to temporal rulers, but has *educated the sentiments to a habit of subjection,* which renders submission to such rulers more facile and less easy to shake off.[14]

Its doctrine of predestination also is calculated to have a tremendous influence on the political character of its adherents. This has not escaped the notice of historians. Bancroft, who, while adopting another religious creed, has awarded to Calvinism the palm for its influence in favor of religious and civil liberty, remarks that

the political character of Calvinism, which, with one consent and with instinctive judgment, the monarchs of that day feared as republicanism, is expressed in a single word – *predestination.* Did a proud aristocracy trace its lineage through generations of a highborn ancestry, the republican Reformers, with a loftier pride, invaded the invisible world, and from the book of life brought down the record of the noblest enfranchisement, decreed from eternity by the King of kings.... They went forth in confidence... and, standing surely amidst the crumbling fabric of centuries of superstition, they had faith in one another; and the martyrdoms of Cambray, the fires of Smithfield, the surrender of benefices by two thousand nonconforming Presbyterians, attests their perseverance.[15]

This doctrine of predestination inspires a resolute, almost defiant, freedom in those who deem themselves the subjects of God's electing grace; in all things they are more than conquerors through the confidence that nothing shall be able to separate them from the love of God. No doctrine of the dignity of human nature, of the rights of man, of national liberty, of social equality, can create such a resolve for the freedom of the soul as this personal conviction of God's favoring and protecting sovereignty. He who has this faith feels that he is compassed about with everlasting love, guided with everlasting strength; his will is the tempered steel that no fire can melt, no force can break. Such faith is free-

14. See Fisher's *History of the Reformation.*
15. *History of the United States,* II, 461.

dom and this spiritual freedom is the source and strength of all other freedom.[16]

And here let it be remarked that events follow principles; that mind rules the world; that thought is more powerful than cannon; that "all history is in its inmost nature religious";[17] and that, as John von Muller says, "Christ is the key to the history of the world...." In the formation of the modern nations religion performed a principal part. The great movements out of which the present [1882] civilized nations sprung were religious through and through....

So, then, enemies themselves being witness, Paul had laid down the grand truth which Luther found in his study of the Augustinian theology and of the Bible. The Arminianism of the Church of Rome had so perverted that truth, and so wrapped it over with its "works of righteousness," as to make it practically unknown. It was not until Luther had grasped it clearly and firmly in his intellect and heart that it became again a living thing and a mighty force. Henceforth the secret power and stirring watchword of the Reformation was justification by faith alone. It was this cleanly-cut and strong theology which began the Reformation, and which carried it on through fire and flood, through all opposition and terror and persecution and misery, to its glorious consummation. When in the great toil and roar of the conflict the fiery nature of Luther began to chill, and he began to temporize with civil rulers, it was this same uncompromising theology of the Genevan school which heroically and triumphantly waged the conflict to the end. I but repeat the testimony of history, friendly and unfriendly to Calvinism, when I say that had it not been for the strong, unflinching, systematic spirit and character of the theology of Calvin, the Reformation would have been lost to the world....

This was the Calvinism which flashed forth in the great reforming days – the spirit which, when Romanists and despots claimed the right to burn all who differed from them, inspired men and women and youth to go forth, Bible and sword in hand, to the greatest daring, appealing for the justice of their cause and the victory of their arms to the Lord of Hosts. This was the spirit which acted in those men "who attracted to

---

16. *The United States as a Nation*, 30, by Joseph Thompson, D.D., LL.D.
17. H. B. Smith, *Faith and Philosophy*.

their ranks almost every man in Western Europe who hated a lie";…who, though they did not utterly destroy Romanism, "drew its fangs, and forced it to abandon that detestable principle that it was entitled to murder those who dissented from it." This was the spirit out of which came, and by which was nourished, the religious and civil liberties of Christendom; of which Bancroft says, "More truly benevolent to the human race than Solon, more self-denying than Lycurgus, the genius of Calvin infused enduring elements into the institutions of Geneva, and made it for the modern world the impregnable fortress of popular liberty, the fertile seed-plot of democracy." [18]

In 1815 John Adams wrote these significant words:

> The apprehensions of episcopacy contributed, fifty years ago, as much as any other cause to arouse the attention, not only of the inquiring mind, but of the common people, and urge them to close thinking on the constitutional power of Parliament over the colonies…. In Virginia the Church of England was established by law in exclusion, and without toleration, of any other denomination. In New York it displayed its essential character of intolerance. Large grants of land were made to it, while other denominations could obtain none….

In the same letter he adduces facts to prove what he terms "the bigotry, intrigue, intolerance and persecution" of the Establishment, and to confirm his statement that the threat of episcopacy was one of the chief causes of the revolt of the colonies against Great Britain. It might be difficult to separate monarchy and episcopacy in the minds of the dissenting colonists, for they regarded them as twins; but to one who is acquainted with the struggle of the seventeenth and eighteenth centuries, it will be evident enough that the dissenters feared episcopacy quite as much as they feared monarchy, and that this fear was among the first and mightiest influences which led to the war against King George….

The two great springs by which men are moved are sentiment and idea, feeling and conviction; as these control, so the moral character will be shaped. The man of sentiment, of feeling, is the man of instability….

Now, the appeal of Arminianism is chiefly to the sentiments. Regarding man as having the absolutely free moral control of himself, and as

18. *Essays.*

able at any moment to determine his own eternal state, it naturally applies itself to the arousing of his emotions. Whatever can lawfully awaken the feelings it considers expedient. Accordingly, the senses, above all things, must be addressed and affected. Hence, the Arminian is, religiously, a man of feeling, of sentiment, and consequently disposed to all those things which interest the eye and please the ear. His morality, therefore, as depending chiefly upon the emotions, is, in the nature of the case, liable to frequent fluctuation, rising or falling with the wave of sensation upon which it rides. Calvinism, on the other hand, is a system which appeals to idea rather than sentiment, to conscience rather than to emotion. In its view all things are under a great and perfect system of divine laws, which operate in defiance of feeling, and which must be obeyed at the peril of his soul. Regarding the sinner as unable of himself even to exercise faith unto salvation, it throws him not upon his feelings, but upon his convictions, and turns him away from man and all human efforts to the God who made him....

Another prominent characteristic of Calvinistic morality is its courageousness. This follows from the former. Conscience and courage go together. Conscience makes "cowards" or heroes "of us all." To change the conscience you must first change the idea. But this is not easily done. Sentiment, or feeling, may pass through a thousand changes in a moment, and carry its possessor in so many directions; but conviction holds steadfastly on in the same unvarying way until by some brighter light it discovers its error and turns aside. Hence the men of conscience are, other things being equal, the brave men, the bold men, the courageous men. Calvinism, by appealing to conscience and emphasizing duty, begets a moral heroism which has been the theme of song and praise for three centuries....

If we now turn to the fruits of Calvinism in the form of devoted Christians and in the number of churches established, we shall see that it has been the most powerful evangelistic system of religious belief in the world. Consider with what amazing rapidity it spread over Europe, converting thousands upon thousands to a living Christianity. In about twenty-five years from the time when Calvin began his work, there were two thousand places of Calvinistic worship, and almost half a million worshippers, in France alone. When Ambrose Willie, a man who had studied theology at the feet of Calvin in Geneva, preached at Emonville Bridge, near Tournay, in 1556, twenty thousand people assembled to hear him. Peter Gabriel had also for an audience in the same year, near Haarlem, "tens of thousands...."

These are but two of the many examples of the intense awakening produced by the earnest preaching of the Calvinistic doctrines. So great were the effects that in three years after this time a General Synod was held in Paris, at which a *Confession of Faith* was adopted. Two years after the meeting of the Synod – that is in 1561 – the Calvinists numbered one-fourth of the entire French population. And in less than half a century this so-called harsh system of belief had penetrated every part of the land, and had gained to its standards almost one-half of the population and almost every great mind in the nation....

Many are accustomed to think that revivals belong particularly to the Methodist Church, whereas, in fact, that Church has never yet inaugurated a great national or far-spreading revival. Her revivals are marked with localism; they are connected with particular churches, and do not make a deep, abiding and general impression on society. The first great Christian revival occurred under the preaching of Peter in Jerusalem, who employed such language in his discourse or discourses as this: "Him, being delivered by the determinate counsel and foreknowledge of God, you have taken, and by wicked hands have crucified and slain." That is Calvinism rigid enough.

22

The New Babylonian Captivity of the Church

Godwell A. Chan[1]

THOUGH THE Romans conquered the Greeks militarily, the Greeks conquered the Romans intellectually. The Romans' ideology and philosophy could not escape the dominance of Greek thought. Whose was the real victory? Like the Romans, the heirs of the Reformation at the end of the twentieth century proved unable to escape the theology of Roman Catholicism. The Reformation had broken the chains that had captured the consciences of men, but her children are now busily welding them back on. Just as the Jewish nation was carried away from their Temple into captivity to Babylon, so Christians are being carried away from Scripture into captivity by man-made rules. After five hundred years, the church has come full circle. The mortal wound is healing.

Three Walls

In his essay *To the Christian Nobility of the German Nation,* Luther attacked three tyrannical abuses of authority by the Roman ecclesiastics. Luther called the three abuses "three walls" that the Roman Church had built to protect itself from all criticism. The first wall is the distinction between the clergy and the laity. The second wall is the sole authority of the Roman Church to interpret Scripture. The third wall that Roman Catholicism set up to protect itself is that only the pope can call a council – that the Roman Church is not answerable to any council that it itself has not called. Or, to put these three walls another way, laymen

---

1. G. A. Chan is a free-lance writer living in New York. This essay is reprinted from *The Trinity Review.*

can't say clergymen are wrong; if laymen use Scripture, their interpretations are faulty since they do not have any seminary training; and, even if their interpretation and application could be correct, the clergymen still are not answerable to the laymen. The observant reader will immediately perceive that Protestantism has not escaped these central ideas of Roman ecclesiology.

> The Romanists have very cleverly built three walls around themselves. Hitherto they have protected themselves by their walls in such a way that no one has been able to reform them....
>
> In the first place, when pressed by the temporal power they have made decrees and declared that the temporal power had no jurisdiction over them, but that, on the contrary, the spiritual power is above the temporal. In the second place, when the attempt is made to reprove them with Scriptures, they raised the objection that only the pope may interpret Scripture. In the third place, if threatened with a council, their story is that no one may summon a council but the pope.
>
> In this way they have cunningly stolen our three rods from us, that they may go unpunished. They have ensconced themselves within the safe stronghold of these three walls so that they can practice all the knavery and wickedness which we see today....
>
> May God help us, and give us just one of those trumpets with which the walls of Jericho were overthrown to blast down these walls of straw and paper in the same way and set free the Christian rod for the punishment of sin, [and] bring to light the craft and deceit of the devil, to the end that through punishment we may reform ourselves and once more attain God's favor [10-12].

The first wall, the class distinction between "full-time" Christian workers (*i.e.*, pastors, missionaries, seminarians) and ordinary Christians, is apparent today. Clergymen are sought out to pray for the sick, or to lay their hands on them, as if the clergy have a direct toll-free line to God, and as if the prayers of fellow Christians are of lower value. The views of pastors are usually accepted at face value without a comparison with the Scriptures. Even with those in part-time ministries, or unofficial positions, there seems to be an ecclesiastical caste system. The choirs' alleged function, for example, is to "offer a sacrifice of songs to God on behalf of the congregation," as if the robed choir members were mediators between God and ordinary men. Women seek spiritual help from the wives of pastors, regardless of whether they have any spiritual gifts or not, as if one can marry into the spiritual aristocracy. In fact, in Chinese churches, wives of pastors actually are called by the title "Mrs. Pastor." Children born to pastors have an automatic status above ordinary children. And if they choose to enter the ministry, they can be hired without strict consideration of whether they have the necessary spiritual gifts, just like the Roman Church used to assign pastoral positions to relatives and illegitimate children regardless of their qualifications. And if you think that Protestantism has rid itself of Roman vestments, look at the choir and priestly robes and listen to the rationale for having them.

Luther blasted down this first wall with 1 *Peter* 2:9, that all Christians are priests before God, and therefore need no mediator other than Christ; and *Revelation* 5:9-10, that all Christians are kings also by the blood of Christ, and therefore can have no class distinction. Christ does not have two bodies, Luther said; one spiritual and one temporal, but Christ is one head over one body. That some are preachers is so because of their calling by the election of fellow Christians to fulfill certain functions, not status. They are "nothing else but an office holder" (14). If they should abuse that trust or calling, they may be deposed (as we will see in Luther's third treatise). For example, if one is called to fulfill the office of preaching, and in time it is obvious that he has not the gift of preaching, he may be deposed, or as Jay Adams says, given "an honorable discharge." Luther wrote:

> To put it still more clearly: Suppose a group of earnest Christian laymen were taken prisoners and set down in a desert without an episcopally ordained priest among them. And suppose they were to come to a common mind there and then in the desert and elect one of the number...to baptize, say mass, pronounce absolution, preach the Gospel. Such a man would be as truly a priest as though he had been ordained by all the bishops and popes in the world. That is why in cases of necessity anyone can baptize and give absolution. This would be impossible if we were not all priests.... Augustine, Ambrose, and Cyprian each became a bishop in this way [13].

Many denominations are unwilling to ordain to the ministry anyone who has not a seminary degree, even though he has the spiritual gift and qualifications. Many churches are unwilling to depose anyone for lack of spiritual gifts as long as he has a seminary degree.

This wall of class distinction was set up by the Roman Church, and re-established by the modern Protestants, in order to make the clergy immune to any criticism from the laity. The laity ought to respect the clergy by not disagreeing with them. "Touch not the Lord's anointed," the clergymen intone, as if all Christians were not the Lord's anointed.

Now, should the laity appeal to the Scripture for the authority to criticize errors, the Roman Church and modern Protestantism retreat behind the second wall of immunity: The interpretation of Scripture can properly be done only by the clergy class. Though the Protestant churches have no popes, nor a doctrine of ecclesiastical infallibility, the idea is nevertheless prominent. Take, for example, the common practice of "stacking up rabbis." "Pastor so-and-so says this," or, "Dr. so-and-so says that," as if their interpretations are, if not infallible, at least better than the laity's. I often remind my Sunday School class not to say, "the Sunday School teacher says this or that." If they are convinced that what was taught was Biblical, they should say, "The Bible says this." "It is written" should settle all debates. It is true that I, too, often quote from others, like Luther and Calvin, but I do this as an *ad hominem* method. Because my audience could not escape the idea that somehow the clergy is above the laity, I often quote respected theologians to them. Because my opponents claim to be evangelicals, I quote the Reformers against them. By their own hands I cover their own mouths. In the same way Calvin and Luther quoted Augustine and the church fathers against their opponents. Jesus also quoted their own words to the Pharisees in *ad hominem* fashion. Luther wrote,

> If it were to happen that the pope and his cohorts were wicked and not true Christians, were not taught by God and were without understanding, and at the same time some obscure person had a right understanding, why should the people not follow the obscure man? ...
>
> Besides, if we are all priests, as was said above, and all have one faith, one Gospel, one [baptism], why should we not also have the powers to test and judge what is right or wrong in matters of faith?
>
> If God spoke then through an ass against a prophet [*Numbers* 2:21-25], why should he not be able even now to speak through a righteous man against the pope? Similarly, St. Paul rebukes St. Peter as a man in error in *Galatians* 2. Therefore, it is the duty of every Christian to espouse the cause of the faith, to understand and defend it, and to denounce every error [20-22].

Luther was that "obscure person." When he nailed the ninety-five theses on the doors of Castle Church, all he wanted was an open dialogue with the Roman Church. He had no plans to start any sort of revolution. The antagonistic reaction of the Roman Church took him by surprise, and her persecution propelled him to "stardom," to the limelight, so to speak, and made him the father of the Reformation. So it was with Calvin, whose only wish in life was to be an obscure scholar writing down his studies. But the insatiable hatred of Satan simply would not leave them alone. In his madness he sought to destroy every one of God's people, and, unknowingly and against his will, he instigated the very occasions which thrust the defenders of the faith onto the world's stage and broadcast throughout the world the very message he sought to suppress. Had Satan left them alone in obscurity, perhaps the world might still be lying in ignorance of justification by faith alone, the bondage of the will, predestination, limited atonement, etc.

The third wall of immunity with which Romanism protects itself is the pope's sole authority to call a council. If the laity are to accuse the clergy, Luther said, they "must naturally call the church together." But if the right to "take the case to the people," so to speak, is taken away, then the clergy are immune to all criticism. Luther noted that the council at Jerusalem (*Acts* 15) was called together by Christians, and "even the Council of Nicæa, the most famous of all councils," was not called nor confirmed by the clergy of Rome. Luther wrote:

> The third wall falls of itself when the first two are down. When the pope acts contrary to the Scripture, it is our duty to stand by the Scriptures, to reprove him and to constrain him, according to the Word of Christ, *Matthew* 18:15-17, "if your brother sins against you, go tell it to him...." But if I am to accuse him before the church, I must naturally call the church together [22].

Obviously, Luther considered erroneous teachings "sins," liable to confrontation according to the rules of church discipline laid out in *Matthew* 18 and *Luke* 17. (The first two steps of church discipline, that of one-to-one or two-to-one, do not apply in this case, since public teaching or preaching already involves more than two or three people. Confrontations of erroneous teaching must be public for the sake of those who had been taught the wrong doctrines.) When a friend of mine wrote letters to several members of his church to correct some teachings of the pastor, the wife of the assistant pastor censured him because she said he should have gotten the pastor's approval first before sending out the letters. This is obviously designed to shield the ecclesiastical class from criticism. Should the pastor have edited the letter first? Luther wrote,

> Would it not be unnatural if a fire broke out in a city and everybody were to stand by and let it burn on and on and consume everything that could be burnt because nobody had the authority of the mayor, or because, perhaps, the fire broke out in the mayor's house? In such a situation is it not the duty of every citizen to arouse and summon the rest? How much more should this be done in the spiritual city of Christ if a fire of offense breaks out, whether in the papal government, or anywhere else! The same argument holds if an enemy were to attack a city. The man who first roused the others deserves honor and gratitude. Why, then, should he not deserve honor who makes known the presence of the enemy from Hell and rouses Christian people and calls them together [23-24]?

After Luther explained these three walls which Romanism had erected to protect itself, he went on to list many specific ways in which the Roman Church takes captive the consciences of men. The Babylonian captivity of the church begins when the Word of God is ignored and, in its place, a ton of commandments after the traditions of men is installed. Luther derides these man-made laws with great sarcastic humor. Here are some samples:

> And when a lackey comes along from Rome he should be given a strict order to keep out, to jump into the Rhine or the nearest river, and give the Romish ban with all its seals and letters a nice, cool dip [46].
> It is actually a greater sin to silence or suppress the Word and worship of God than if one had strangled twenty popes at one time ... [71].
> One of the reasons this [man-made] law is called "spiritual" is that it comes from the spirit: not from the Holy Spirit but from the evil spirit [72].

No wonder many clergymen and seminaries want to keep their congregations and students in ignorance of Luther and the Reformation!

The Babylonian Captivity

In *The Babylonian Captivity of the Church,* Luther continued his attack on the captivity of men's consciences to man-made rules. He attacked sacramentalism, clericalism, and monasticism. Fundamentally, however, Luther was really criticizing Rome's haphazard and whimsical way of interpreting the Scripture every which way it pleased and then holding men's consciences captive under such interpretations. Luther was attacking false opinions which were "generally held" and "firmly believed" (152). He wrote, "I am attacking a different matter, an abuse perhaps impossible to uproot, since through the century-long custom and the common consent of men it has become so firmly entrenched that it would be necessary to abolish most of the books now in vogue..." (152).

This statement can easily be applied to the doctrines currently in vogue in so-called Protestant churches, such as: the free will of man, the universal love of God, the universal atonement of Christ, etc. These falsehoods are so entrenched in modern minds that they more than qualify to be called the modern Babylonian captivity of the church. Men's consciences are so enslaved that they are reluctant to leave churches that teach these heresies. Their reluctance may be due to one of the following reasons:

1. They are ignorant. No one has shown them the truth from the Bible.

2. They are arrogant. Though shown the truth from the Bible, they refuse to admit that they are wrong.

3. They are stupid. Though shown the truth, they do not understand it; and/or, they do not understand the difference between the truth and their errors. (Those who advocate contradiction seem to be of this class.)

4. They are apathetic. Truth is not important to them.

None of these possibilities reflects well on them. Ignorance, arrogance, stupidity, indifference – these are the inevitable results of the Babylonian captivity of the church. Or, 5. They do, in fact, understand and believe the truth, but they have not yet left that church in order actively to teach the truth and actively to combat errors. Such people ought to be commended for their continuous efforts.

Other than this one, there aren't any good reasons for staying in a church that propagates a false gospel. Some may object that since there are no perfect churches on Earth, one might as well stay where he is. But though there are no perfect churches on Earth, this does not imply that there are no churches that preach the Gospel. Luther tried to reform the church from within, but he was kicked out. Though against the tide, though feeling like a drop in the ocean, Luther contended:

> But my Christ lives, and we must be careful to give more heed to the Word of God than to all the thoughts of men and of angels. I will perform the duties of my office and bring to light the facts in the case. As I have received the truth freely [*Matthew* 10:8], I will impart it without malice.... I do my part faithfully so that no one may be able to cast on me the blame for his lack of faith and his ignorance of the truth when we appear before the judgment seat of Christ [153].

One example Luther cited of Rome's whimsical interpretations is that she denies the cup to the laity in the Lord's Supper on the basis that in *John* 6:51, Jesus said, "I am the living bread," and not, "I am the living cup" (127). She conveniently forgets the next few verses: "Unless you eat My flesh and drink My blood.... For My flesh is food indeed, and My blood is drink indeed" (53, 55). Luther replies, first, that the interpretation is out of context. And secondly, the text is misapplied to the Lord's Supper, for the passage in *John* 6 is referring to spiritual food and drink, as Jesus says, "My words are spirit and life" (63). The sacramentalism of denying the cup to the laity, but giving both bread and cup to the clergy, accentuates Romanism's separation of two classes of people in the church. And when anyone in the laity confronts such errors, even on the basis of Scripture, the ecclesiastical aristocracy claims the sole authority to interpret Scripture.

This kind of out-of-context interpretation and haphazard application of the Scripture is rampant in Protestant churches today. And when Luther used the correct passage which applies to the Lord's Supper, 1 *Corinthians* 11, the Roman Church rebutted that this passage applied only to the Corinthian church, and not to all churches. Today, the prohibition of women preaching is also brushed aside on the pretext that it only applies to the first-century Corinthians. Of this whimsical method of hermeneutics, Luther wrote, "[I]f we permit one institution of Christ to be changed, we make all of his laws invalid, and any man may make bold to say that he is not bound by any other law or institution of Christ.

For a single exception, especially in the Scriptures, invalidates the whole" (135).

Romanism is both anti-Scriptural and, like many of their Protestant theological brothers who revel in contradictions, anti-logical: "[W]hen the Scripture is on our side and against them, they will not allow themselves to be bound by any force of logic" (134).

When silenced by Luther's arguments, the Roman Church resorted to smearing Luther. Luther rejoiced in this. He wrote,

> [I]t is a pleasure to be blamed and accused by heretics and perverse sophists, since to please them would be the height of impiety. Besides, the only way in which they can prove their opinions and disprove contrary ones is by saying, "That is Wycliffite, Hussite, heretical!" They carry this feeble argument always on the tip of their tongues, and they have nothing else [146].

In other words, when shown from the Scripture itself that Romanism is wrong, Rome spat the label "heretic" in the face of Luther, with no Scriptural foundation whatsoever. To shield themselves from criticism, the modern Romanists in Protestant clothing also have a few favorite pithy platitudes to spit out: "love," "unity," and especially "judge not." Meanwhile, they criticize their critics with such labels as "heresy hunters," "schismatics," "Lone Rangers," etc. These abusive labels are nothing but convenient methods of diversion from the discussion at hand. Why debate the issue when one can resort to character assassination?

The call to "judge not" the clergy for the sake of "love and unity" is a good example of the Babylonian captivity of the church. First, it exemplifies the class distinction. The ecclesiastical elite may criticize anyone they please, especially those who disagree with them, but no one is allowed to criticize the clergy without drawing down their heavy curses. "Judge not us, but let us judge you!" In direct contradiction to this man-made rule, the Bible expressly commands that all teachings should be judged: "Let the prophets speak, but let the people judge" (1 Corinthians 14:29; see also 1 Thessalonians 5:21, 1 John 4:1). Second, it demonstrates the pick-and-choose method of hermeneutics. The Bible clearly states that both love and unity must be in the context of the truth (1 Corinthians 13:6; Ephesians 4:13; Philippians 3:15-16). Yet, the modern Romanists in Protestant clothing insist on a love and unity devoid of truth, in fact, against the truth. And it is highly ironical, indeed hypocritical, that those who advocate "judge not" and "love and unity," should at the same time judge those who judge them, and advocate hatred toward and separation from those who criticize them. Now, which is better: to avoid people whose speaking truth causes divisions, or people whose heresies bring unity?

In attacking sacramentalism, Luther did not merely argue against transubstantiationism, or the denial of the cup to the laity. He attacked Romanism's doctrine of *opus operatum* – that the sacrament is effective without regard to any faith or lack of faith on the part of the person for whom it is performed. From pages 152 to 165, Luther carefully expounded the utmost importance of faith. Faith is to believe in the promises of God from the Word of God. Faith gives rise to hope and love. And without faith, hope, and love, there can be no service to God. In the sacraments, it is the explanation of the promises of God, followed by faith on the part of the person receiving the sacraments, which makes the sacraments effective. The ceremonies are signs to remind of the promises of God. Without faith, ceremonies are not good works. Luther wrote,

> For anyone can easily see that these two, promises and faith, must necessarily go together. For without the promise there is nothing to be believed: while without faith the promise is useless, since it is established and fulfilled through faith. [Luther is saying that faith is intellectual assent to the propositional promises of God.] [160].
>
> It is already easy to see what is the inevitable result of this extinguishing of the faith, namely, the most godless superstition of works. For where faith dies and the word of faith is silenced, these works and the prescribing of works immediately crowd into their place. By them [works] we have been carried away out of our own land, as into a Babylonian captivity, and despoiled of all our precious possessions [166].

The practice of deliverance is one example of godless superstition in the modern church. That modern evangelicalism is buzzing with works like Sardis is the direct effect of its loss of Biblical faith. Men's consciences are held in captivity to the fear of facing Judgment Day without works rather than a fear of being without Christ. "Must I go empty-handed?" goes the hymn, as if the works of our hands could contribute anything at the Judgment Day. Today, even faith is measured in terms of works: the more money one gives, the more his *faith*; the more committees one is on, the more his *faith*; the more the involvement, activities, services, fasts, short-term missionary trips, etc., etc. Luther accused them: "Blind and godless Pharisees, who measure righteousness and holiness by the greatness, number, or other quality of the works! But God measures them by faith alone, and with him there is no difference among works, except insofar as there is a difference in faith" (199).

Faith comes from the Word of God. In attacking monasticism, Luther attacked the fundamental evil that supports monasticism, the evil of man-made rules over Scriptures, and the tendency to spiritual snobbery on the basis of works:

> But whatever is without the warrant of Scripture is most hazardous and should by no means be urged upon any one, much less established as a common and public mode of life ... [201].

> For in the religious order, there is scarcely one in many thousands who is not more concerned about his works than about faith, and on the basis of this madness, they claim superiority over each other, as being "stricter" or "laxer," as they call it [202].

On this subject, Calvin wrote: "For there are always superstitious little fellows who dream up something new to win admiration for themselves." And: "[Some] will try to win praise for humility through ensnaring themselves in many observances, from which God has with good reason willed us to be free and exempt" (*Institutes of the Christian Religion*, IV, XII, 27, and XIII, 3). Fasting is one such example. And to those who contemplate entering "full time" or short-term ministry, Luther wrote:

> Therefore I advise no one to enter any religious order or the priesthood...unless he is forearmed with this knowledge and understands that the works of monks and priests, however holy and arduous they may be, do not differ one whit in the sight of God from the works of the rustic laborer in the field or the woman going about her household tasks, but that all works are measured before God by faith alone... [202-203].

Next, Luther attacked the sacramentalism of marriage. The Roman Church asserts that marriage is a sacrament on the basis of *Ephesians* 5:31-32, where the Latin *Vulgate* has "the two shall become one. This is a great sacrament." Luther replied:

> This argument, like the others, betrays great shallowness and a careless and thoughtless reading of Scripture. Nowhere in all of the Holy

Scripture is the word *sacramentum* employed in the sense in which we use the term... [221].

... Plainly, it was their ignorance of both words and things that betrayed them. They clung to the mere sound of the words, indeed, to their own fancies. For, having once arbitrarily taken the word *sacramentum* to mean a sign, they immediately, without thought or scruples, made a "sign" of it every time they came upon it in the Holy Scriptures. Such new meanings of words, human customs, and other things have they dragged into the Holy Scriptures. They have transformed the Scriptures according to their own dreams, making anything out of any passage whatsoever.... For they employ them all after their own arbitrary judgment, learned from the writings of men, to the detriment of both the truth of God and of our salvation [222].

Once again it is plain that Luther was not attacking merely sacramentalism, nor marriage, but the method of twisting Scriptures, and then holding men's consciences captive to such interpretations. The Greek in *Ephesians* 5:31-32 should be properly translated "mystery," not "sacrament."

One good example of such "shallowness and thoughtless reading of Scriptures," of "ignorance of words," of taking certain words "arbitrarily every time they came upon the word" – one good example is the arbitrary interpretation of the word "world" in *John* 3:16 to mean "every single person." In fact, the Chinese Bible does not have "world," but "people of the world," implying universalism. Another example is *1 Timothy* 3:11, where some English Bible translations have "deaconess." The Chinese Bible also has "deaconess," though in the margin it notes that the word does not appear in the original Greek. Notwithstanding, pastors tenaciously "cling to the mere sound of the words," insisting on their own arbitrary interpretations, thereby showing their ignorance, and their tyranny over men, "learned from the writings of men, to the detriment of both the truth of God and our salvation."

Luther stated the crux of the matter in these words:

But most of all we should guard against impairing the authority of the Holy Scriptures. For those things which have been delivered to us by God in the sacred Scriptures must be sharply distinguished from those that have been invented by men in the church, no matter how eminent they may be for saintliness and scholarship [224].

It is a shameful and wicked slavery for a Christian man, who is free, to be subject to any but heavenly and divine ordinances [243].

Though Luther attacked all seven of Rome's sacraments, ordination will be the last one considered in this brief article. Even though Protestants no longer consider ordination as a sacrament, they nevertheless prove unable to extricate themselves from some ideas inherent in Romanism. Rome asserts that ordination is indelible – *character indelibilis* – the idea that "once a priest, always a priest." The Council of Trent (1563) condemned anyone who argues that priests can once again become laymen, even if they do not exercise the ministry of the Word of God. This is, once again, the first wall which Luther complained about. To the contrary, Luther maintained that whoever does not preach the Word, the Gospel, ought to be deposed.

...[W]hoever does not preach the Word, though he was called by the church to do this very thing, is no priest at all, and that the sacrament of ordination can be nothing else than a certain rite by which the church chooses its preachers. For this is the way a priest is defined in *Mal.* 2[:7]: "The lips of a priest should guard knowledge, and men should seek instruction from his mouth, for he is the messenger of the Lord of hosts...." They are also called pastors because they are to pasture, that is, to teach [245].

O the disgrace that these monstrous priests bring upon the church of God! Where are there any bishops or priests who even know the Gospel, not to speak of preaching it? Why then do they boast of being priests?... The duty of a priest is to preach, and if he does not preach he is as much a priest as a picture of a man is a man.... It is the ministry of the Word [not merely the ordination] that makes the priest and the bishop.

Therefore my advice is: Begone, all of you that would live in safety; flee, young men, and do not enter upon this holy estate, unless you are determined to preach the Gospel, and can believe you are made not one whit better than the laity through this "sacrament" of ordination [247-8].

Whoever, therefore, does not know or preach the Gospel is not only no priest or bishop, but he is a kind of pest to the church... [249].

The "Protestant" churches are plagued with such pests.

The reader is reminded of what Luther said about the Gospel in *The Bondage of the Will*. It is *not* "God loves everyone," nor "Christ died for everyone," nor "Man has the free will to believe," nor "God sincerely desires the salvation of all men." Such are false gospels. And anyone preaching these doctrines ought to get the Gehenna away from the pulpit!

Granted, ordained pastors are sometimes deposed due to public scandals. But there seems to be a popular opinion that it is not a scandal when men without the requisite spiritual gifts are ordained to the ministry. The congregation of one pastor (a friend of mine) complained that he preached nothing, multiplying words without point or lesson. I sympathize with the congregation for having to endure terrible sermons week after week, full of nothing but pithy platitudes. I also sympathize with my friend. So, I sent him books on sermon improvements; but it seems that he simply does not have the requisite spiritual gift. After years of status quo, some in the congregation finally left the church because the senior pastor simply will not fire my friend. This is un-Biblical. This is a remnant of Romanism, a spiritual tyranny enslaving the sheep to spiritual starvation. (The modern Protestant equivalent to Rome's *character indelibilis* seems to be the seminary degree.)

The early church may have been corrupted much the same way Protestant churches are being corrupted today. First, there may have been the appointment to leadership of those without the requisite spiritual gifts. Many churches, for example, appoint novices, recent converts, and seminary graduates who have not been tested first. Some churches even appoint unbelievers to various services (*e.g.*, choir). The rationale behind it is that the novice, or the unbeliever, will learn as he goes, or will acquire the zeal for God as he serves in the church. This is contrary to the Bible directives (1 *Timothy* 3:6; 3:10; *Titus* 1:9). Second, these leaders in turn appoint others to the leadership who are just as ignorant of the Bible as they. Since they are ignorant of the Bible they adopt worldly solutions to the problems they face. One example I could give is a meeting I was in some years ago, where pastors and leaders were deciding salary policy. Almost an hour of worldly solutions (*e.g.*, kinds of degrees, number of years of experience, *etc.*) later, I asked, "What does the Bible say?" They were stunned and silenced as if with a totally unheard-of idea. They had never even thought of consulting the Bible. After a moment or two of this stunned silence, they all went back to discussing worldly solutions, as if my question never existed, somehow sucked into the Twilight Zone. After one or two generations of this kind of leadership, the church will be completely dominated by unbelieving professors. The Babylonian captivity will then be complete.

The Freedom of the Christian

Believe it or not, this third treatise begins with an open letter, almost conciliatory in tone, to Pope Leo X. Luther assured the pope that he was not attacking him personally, being, he said, "conscious of the beam in my own eye." But toward false doctrines, Luther gave not the least compromise.

> I have, to be sure, sharply attacked ungodly doctrines in general, and I have snapped at my opponents, not because of their bad morals, but because of their ungodliness [in doctrines]. Rather than repent this in the least, I have determined to persist in that fervent zeal and to despise the judgment of men, following the example of Christ who in his zeal called his opponents "a brood of vipers," "blind fools," "hypocrites," "children of the devil" [*Matthew* 23:13, 17, 33; *John* 8:44]. Paul branded Magus [Elymas the magician] as the "son of the devil...full of all deceit and villainy" [*Acts* 13:10], and he calls others "dogs," "deceivers," and "adulterers" [*Philippians* 3:2; 2 *Corinthians* 11:13; 2:17]. If you will allow people with sensitive feelings to judge, they would consider no person more stinging and unrestrained in his denunciations than Paul. Who is more stinging than the prophets? Nowadays, it is true, we are made so sensitive by the raving crowd of flatterers that we cry out that we are stung as soon as we meet with disapproval. When we cannot ward off the truth with any other pretext, we flee from it by ascribing it to a fierce temper, impatience, and immodesty. What is the good of salt if it does not bite? Of what use is the edge of a sword if it does not cut? "Cursed is he who does the work of the Lord deceitfully" [*Jeremiah* 48:10].
>
> I have no quarrel with any man concerning his morals but only concerning the Word of truth. In all other matters I will yield to any man whatsoever; but I have neither the power nor the will to deny the Word of God [267-268].

As mentioned above, instead of facing the issue at hand, the modern counterparts often flee behind slogans of "unity," "love," "judge not." These platitudes conveniently change the subject of doctrinal discussions, and immediately throw subtle insinuations (of temper, impatience, immodesty) at the one trying to bring forth the truth. The same with Luther. Though Luther attacked not the immoral character of the popes, but only their doctrines (in obedience to 1 *Corinthians* 14:29), his own character was often assassinated. The true descendants of the Reformation can expect nothing less.

After this somewhat conciliatory dedication, Luther began his discussion of the freedom of a Christian. Christian freedom begins and continues with the doctrine of justification by faith alone. Once a Christian understands that righteousness comes by faith and faith alone, without any works, all man-made rules and traditions in the world cannot bind his conscience. Luther said, "there is no more terrible disaster with which the wrath of God can afflict men than a famine of the hearing of his Word" (*Amos* 8:11). He was referring to preaching Christ and the doctrine of justification by faith alone, for the ignorance of any aspect of this doctrine of grace will lead to spiritual captivity. If you sit in a church year in and year out and have never come to a right understanding of this doctrine, you can be sure that it is no different from sitting in a Roman Catholic Church all those years.

Faith alone, on the other hand, does not make the Christian lawless. Though he may disregard man-made rules, he is not free from the Word of God. He may not give up his Christian liberty for the sake of those who stubbornly put a premium on the rules of man; in fact, he must be an offense to them. But to the brother weak in faith, he must take care not to be a stumbling block for the sake of love. "A Christian is a perfectly free lord of all, subject to none," said Luther. Yet, too, "a Christian is a perfectly dutiful servant of all, subject to all." Luther explained:

> Our faith in Christ does not free us from works but from false opinion concerning works.... Hence the Christian must take a middle course and face those two classes of men. He will meet first the unyielding, stubborn ceremonialists.... There he must resist, do the very opposite, and offend them boldly lest by their impious views they drag many with them into error. In the presence of such men it is good to eat meat, break the fasts, and for the sake of the liberty of faith do other things which they regard as the greatest of sins. Of them we must say, "Let them alone; they are blind guides." According to this principle Paul would not circumcise Titus when the Jews insisted that he should [*Galatians* 2:3], and Christ excused the apostles when they plucked ears of grain on the Sabbath [*Matthew* 12:1-8].... The other class of men whom a Christian will meet is simple-minded, ignorant men, weak in the faith.... Since they do and think as they do, not because they are stubbornly wicked, but only because their faith is weak, the fasts and things which they consider necessary must be observed to avoid giving them offense. This is the command of love which would harm no one but would serve all men. It is not by their fault that they are weak, but by that of their

pastors who have taken them captive with the snares of their traditions and have wickedly used these traditions as rods with which to beat them. They should have been delivered from these pastors by the teachings of faith and freedom.... [311-312].

... Therefore fight strenuously against the wolves, but for the sheep and not also against the sheep.... Use your freedom constantly and consistently in the sight of and despite the tyrants and the stubborn so that they also may learn that they are impious, that their laws are of no avail for righteousness, and that they had no right to set them up [313].

Over time, traditions of men, even traditional interpretations of certain verses, have a way of creeping up from behind and gradually becoming the laws of God. The Christian, freed by Christ through faith in the Gospel, must ever be on guard against losing his freedom. He must ever watch and pray against the Babylonian captivity of the church. And, as Luther opposed the Roman Church, we must clearly and boldly oppose the Babylonian captivity of the so-called Protestant churches.

23

The Reconstructionist Road to Rome[1]

John W. Robbins

THIS BOOK [*The Sociology of the Church: Essays in Reconstruction,* by James B. Jordan] is a collection of fourteen essays:

1. Reconstructing the Church: A Conservative Ecumenical Agenda
2. The Sociology of the Church: A Systematic Approach
3. The Sociology of the Church: A Biblico-Historical Approach
4. The Three Faces of Protestantism
5. Conversion
6. The Effective Church Splitter's Guide
7. Propositions on Pentecostalism
8. Christian Zionism and Messianic Judaism
9. Should Churches Incorporate?
10. How Biblical Is Protestant Worship?
11. God's Hospitality and Holistic Evangelism
12. Triumphalistic Investiture
13. A Liturgy of Malediction
14. A Liturgy of Healing,

some of which were previously published.

Influences on Jordan's Thought

Jordan includes an eight-page Preface that furnishes us with some insight into the influences on his thought. His family was variously Methodist, Lutheran, Baptist, and Moravian; he attended a Roman Catholic elementary school and his young mind was shaped by the Sisters of the Sacred Heart; he was confirmed in a Lutheran church; later he was influenced by Campus Crusade, the Navigators, Francis Schaeffer,

---

1. This essay is reprinted from *The Trinity Review.*

C. S. Lewis, Billy Graham, Cornelius Van Til, and Reformed and Westminster Theological Seminaries. Jordan holds two degrees from Westminster Seminary, the M.A.R. and the Th.M., where he studied under another Master of Theology, John M. Frame. Frame has described him as "one of the most interesting and able students I ever taught at Westminster Theological Seminary.... Jim is one of these 'Theonomists' or 'Christian Reconstructionists' who believes that these mysterious biblical laws are still binding, even upon New Testament believers." Jordan has been a prolific writer for the Reconstructionist movement, producing several books, scores of essays, and functioning as a pastor of the Reconstructionist church in Tyler, Texas. He was editor of *Christianity and Civilization*, and his essays are published by Gary North's Institute for Christian Economics.

Jordan discloses that "My intellectual formation as a presuppositionalist has been due to the writings of Cornelius Van Til and Rousas John Rushdoony, and also to various classes I was privileged to take under Greg Bahnsen at Reformed Theological Seminary and John M. Frame at Westminster Theological Seminary.... Norman Shepherd of Westminster Seminary tremendously reoriented my thinking about the covenant and the sacraments" (xi). (Norman Shepherd was removed from the Seminary's faculty for his views regarding justification by works.)

Jordan also thanks Vern Poythress (Van Tilian and member of the Westminster Seminary faculty), Ray Sutton (Van Tilian Reconstructionist and former president of the Philadelphia Seminary of the Reformed Episcopal Church), Lewis Bulkeley (then an elder of the Reconstructionist church in Tyler, Texas), Geddes MacGregor (neo-orthodox), Louis Bouyer (Roman Catholic charismatic), Alexander Schmemann (Russian Orthodox), Gary North (Van Tilian Reconstructionist), Michael Gilstrap (Van Tilian Reconstructionist), Craig Bulkeley, the late Robert Dwelle, and the late David Chilton (all Van Tilian Reconstructionists). Jordan says that he is relying on "two schools of thought": "Vantilian presuppositionalism and Christian Reconstructionism" (1).

Fallacious Arguments

Jordan wastes no time launching an attack on Christianity. Apparently because he could quote no greater, he quotes himself saying, " 'to discuss religion only in terms of ideas or doctrine is to reduce religion to an ideology.' A true presuppositionalist will not fall into the trap of the 'primacy of the intellect and doctrine...' "(x). Notice the words "only," "primacy," "reduce," and "ideology."

The word "primacy" implies that there is something secondary; the word "only" implies that there is nothing else. By sliding from one idea to the other, Jordan hopes to get those who agree with his first sentence to swallow his second as well, with no argument presented. He is trying to smuggle in his anti-intellectual, anti-doctrinal view of Christianity, right at the start of the book. As his book later shows, he seems obsessed with destroying the notion of the primacy of the intellect.

To clarify the argument, no Christian discusses Christianity "only in terms of ideas or doctrine," but Christianity definitely teaches the primacy of doctrine: "He who keeps my doctrine will not see death ever" (*John* 8:51); "he who believes in me has everlasting life" (*John* 6:47); "If you instruct the brethren in these things, you will be a good minister of Jesus Christ, nourished in the words of faith and of the good doctrine which you have carefully followed" (*1 Timothy* 4:6); "Whoever transgresses and does not abide in the doctrine of Christ does not have God. He who abides in the doctrine of Christ has both the Father and the Son" (*2 John* 9). What makes Christianity different from other philosophies and theologies, different from Buddhism, Eastern Orthodoxy, Neo-orthodoxy, Roman Catholicism, and existentialism, is its doctrine. Any other differences, such as the behavior of Christians, are effects of that doctrine.

We Must Listen to Rome

Jordan continues to prepare us for what is to come later in his book: "*[W]e must be open to the values in other Christian traditions* – even Roman Catholic and Eastern Orthodox traditions" (11, Jordan's emphasis).

It may come as a surprise to some readers, but several members of the Reconstructionist church in Tyler, Texas, the church with which Gary North, Ray Sutton, James Jordan, David Chilton, and other Reconstructionist writers have long been associated, left that church and joined the Roman Catholic Church. Other Reconstructionists across the country have also joined the Roman Church. One reason for such defections is that their theology – their doctrine – especially the doctrine of the church, represented by this book, is quasi-Romanist.

Excommunication

One of the measures of Jordan's fascination with Rome is the importance that he places on excommunication. Thus he argues that Christ could associate with sinful people ("publicans, harlots, and sinners") because they were not excommunicated; "How could Jesus, the spotless Son of God, associate with such evil people? Simple: They were (a) members of the visible church.... They were (b) not excommunicate from that visible church. They were (c) willing to listen to what he had to say.... Notice that Jesus *ate and drank* with them. It requires a clever bit of nominalism to miss the sacramental implications of this" (15, Jordan's emphasis).

This is a ludicrous statement. Jesus did not fraternize with publicans, harlots, and sinners because they were church members, and ostracize non-church members. He ate and drank with them because they were sinners. They were not church members in good standing, as Jordan alleges. Neither was the woman at the well, who not only drank with him but also gave him water to drink. (Think of the sacramental implications of that!) It was precisely *because* these people were outcasts and sinners, not church members, that the Pharisees were so indignant when Jesus ate and drank with them. They were outcasts, dregs of society, not upstanding church members like the Pharisees. Jesus explains this to the Pharisees when he commands them: "Go and learn what this means: 'I desire mercy and not sacrifice.' For I did not come to call the righteous, but sinners, to repentance" (*Matthew* 9:13). Furthermore, in *John* 9, Jesus seeks out a man – itself a rare thing for Jesus to do – who has been excommunicated from the visible church by the Antichristian religious leaders of the visible church. To that excommunicated man Jesus reveals his identity. In his eagerness to inflate the importance and power of the visible church, Jordan has twisted the meaning of Christ's fellowship with sinners. Jesus' followers, at least those who were "church members," were routinely thrown out of the synagogue. It was a matter of policy for the religious leaders to excommunicate Christians. Jesus himself was murdered by church members in good standing – the religious leaders.

Imagining a sacramental or ritual meaning in Jesus' ordinary eating and drinking is another example of Jordan's overheated and ludicrous imagination. He apparently wants to turn every meal (and, one supposes, every shower) into a sacrament. Indeed, much of what he writes in this book is based on his imagination and is unsupported speculation. He apparently wants to revive not only the Roman Church-State, but also the speculative theology of the Dark Ages, which he calls the "Christian centuries."

Of course, Jordan tries to frighten critics by using an argument from intimidation: "It requires a clever bit of nominalism to miss the sacramental implications of this." Well, if this be nominalism, let us make the most of it. Christ's eating and drinking with sinners was no more a sacrament than his eating and drinking with Joseph and Mary and his brothers. Like Rome, Jordan wants to multiply sacraments. He writes: "The sacramental system in the Roman Catholic Church is hardly perfect, but the way Protestants have come to handle the crises and 'conversions' of life has not proven adequate either. It should be on our agenda to give serious consideration to reforming our teaching and practice in this area" (161). Jordan does not even entertain the possibility that Scripture alone should determine the number of sacraments. Later on he repudiates the regulative principle of worship.[2]

Episcopalians, Elites, and Dominion

Jordan has a fondness for the Episcopalian Church as well. The Reconstructionist church in Tyler is now [1992] affiliated with the Reformed Episcopal Church, after earlier affiliations with Presbyterian and other Episcopal organizations.

Jordan believes that the Episcopalians have exercised more "social dominion" than the Baptists or Presbyterians. The Episcopal Church teaches, says Jordan, "the primacy of the institutional church" (16). "The Episcopalians identify, promote, protect, and prosper their best men. They provide large salaries, good homes, secure retirements. For their scholar Bishops, they provide domestic servants and secretaries..." (16). Presbyterians and Baptists don't do this, and that is why Cornelius Van Til's writings are not in "polished English style," even though he was the "most brilliant" of the "best thinkers" (17).

---

2. Other factions in the Reconstructionist movement have also repudiated the regulative principle – Steven Schlissel, the *Chalcedon Report,* and Douglas Wilson, to name three.

Jordan is an elitist:

> We can contrast this [the Baptist and Presbyterian practice of starving scholars] with the armies of scholars maintained by Rome, and the small cadre maintained in Episcopalian circles. The difference is marked, and points to the fundamental difference between these two groups. The catholic party (Roman and Anglican) is frankly elitist. It strives to convert and control the elite in society, and it arms its best men for that task, giving them time for reflection and writing. The evangelical party (Presbyterian and Baptist, especially the latter) is infected largely with the heresy of democracy, and believes (wrongly) that the conversion of society comes with the conversion of the masses [17; see page 19 for more about the heresy of democracy].

Democracy is a heresy, says Jordan, which has "infected" (it seems to be a disease as well) Presbyterians and Baptists. He scorns misguided evangelicals, who, unlike the enlightened Romanists, believe that the conversion of society means the conversion of the masses. Doesn't Jordan realize that the proposition is tautological? Just who is society, unless it is the "masses"? Apparently Jordan has another notion of "society" in mind. He also seems to want to restrict the meaning of the word "church" to the elite as well. Despite his seminary training, he does not know the meaning of *ekklesia*.

Christ thought that the conversion of society meant the conversion of the masses: "The fields are white for harvest." That is why he spent so much time with the common people, rather than with the church leaders. Christ was loved by the people, hated by the elite, and commanded that his Gospel be preached to every creature, not just to the elite. Jordan, unlike Christ, exercises a preferential option for the elite.

In recent years Reconstructionists have spent much time and energy denying that they are elitists who wish to impose their views from the top down. But Jordan disagrees: "Americans (evangelicals) like to believe the myth that society is transformed from the 'bottom up' and not from the 'top down' "(17). Jordan appeals directly to the power of kings: "Good kings produced a good nation; bad kings a bad nation. The order is always seen from the top down..." (17).

Church Organization

Lest anyone think that his elitist view of society has nothing to do with the church, Jordan continues: "There are rulers and governors –

a hierarchy – in the church" (18). There are rulers and governors, of course, in the Roman Church-State, but not in the Christian churches. There is no hierarchy in the Christian church. There are elected officers, called elders and deacons. The church on Earth is a republic, not a monarchy or an aristocracy. Christ and the apostles explicitly condemned the exercise of dominion in church and state. That is something the Gentiles – the unbelievers – do. Christians do not act that way.

Jordan denounces the "modern Presbyterians" who reject the "Episcopalian notion of the Bishop as a separate office" (19). Apparently Jordan does not realize that rejection of hierarchy is not a modern innovation at all; it is in fact, the meaning of Presbyterianism. It is not the "modern Presbyterians" who are infected with the heresy of democracy, but James Jordan who is infected with the heresy of dominion, commonly called episcopacy, popery, or prelacy. Hear his most awful accusation: "they ["modern Presbyterians"] really *do not want dominion*" (19). Since Christ commanded us not to have dominion over men, Jordan's condemnation is praise. Attempting to curse, he praises us.

After berating Presbyterians for a while, Jordan belittles the "masses": "The production of literature aimed at the masses has its place, of course; but it does not affect the transformation of society. It is a legitimate ministry, but it will not change the world" (20). One wonders if this applies to printing Bibles.

The spread of Christianity in the first three centuries after Christ changed the world. That transformation – that turning the world upside down, as Luke reports – was accomplished largely by ordinary men and women: those whom Jordan contemptuously calls the masses. It was not done by kings. Kings did their best to stop it. A thousand years later the Reformers once again turned the world upside down – despite the best efforts of kings, popes, and other wicked spirits in high places – by publishing, writing, and preaching in the vernacular, the language of the common people. Had Luther's *Theses* never been translated from the Latin, had they remained in the language of the elite, there would have been no Reformation, and Luther would have been snuffed out like so many other Christian victims of the Roman Church-State.

The problem, Jordan tells us, is that the masses are too stupid: "It has never been possible to reduce hard, intellectual, elitist theology to the level of the common man" (20). It is more likely that the people, at least the elect, are too smart to swallow the paradoxical, anti-intellectual, elitist theology of Jordan and his ilk.

Tradition

Another strength of Episcopalianism, says Jordan, is tradition:

[T]he English church never *reacted* against the Medieval tradition, and sought to conserve the best that was there. All the Reformers were experts in the early church, and also in the Medieval theologians. After a century, however, the other Reformed groups had begun to ignore the Fathers and the Medievals. [This would be about the time of the Westminster Assembly.] The myth arose that the Medieval church was wholly evil from A.D. 606 on. *The great advances of the Christian centuries were overlooked. The real accomplishments of the Papal See were rejected"* [20-21, emphasis mine].

Jordan does not condescend to tell us common folk what these "great advances" and "real accomplishments" were. Perhaps the suppression of the Bible? Perhaps the Inquisition? Notice that Jordan calls the Dark Ages "the Christian centuries." He, like so many other elitists, longs for the medieval glory of chivalry, serfdom, and superstition. Those were the days when the visible church had dominion.

The Primacy of the Visible Church

Another strength or Episcopalianism is that

the Episcopalian churches have put the visible church in the first place, before theology and before personalities.... [T]hey permit various theologies to exist under the common umbrella of the institutional church.... The Episcopal churches bind their people to the church and to the traditions by the careful and plenary use of profound symbol and beautiful ritual [21].

Jordan espouses the ideology of the ecumenical movement, putting the organization, the organized church, first, and theology second. This clearly indicates the preference Reconstructionists have for power (dominion) over truth. This agenda – one church, many theologies – is Antichristian. God prefers theological truth to organization and ritual:

Hear the Word of the Lord, you rulers of Sodom [Israel]; give ear to the law of our God, you people of Gomorrah [Israel]: "To what purpose is the multitude of your sacrifices to me?" says the Lord. "I have had enough of burnt offerings of rams and the fat of fed cattle. I do not delight in the blood of bulls, or of lambs or goats. When you come to appear before me, who has required this from your hand, to trample my courts? Bring no more futile sacrifices; incense is an abomination to me. The new moons, the sabbaths, and the calling of assemblies – I cannot endure iniquity and the sacred meeting. Your new moons and your appointed feasts my soul hates; they are a trouble to me, I am weary of bearing them. When you spread out your hands, I will hide my eyes from you; even though you make many prayers, I will not hear. Your hands are full of blood."

God grants primacy, not to the visible church, but to his doctrine. His idea of unity is unity of mind, of doctrine, of theology, not unity of organization: "Now I plead with you, brethren, by the name of our Lord Jesus Christ, that you all speak the same thing, and that there be no division among you, but that you be perfectly joined together in the same mind and in the same judgment" (*1 Corinthians* 1:10; see also *1 Corinthians* 13:11; *Philippians* 1:27; *1 Peter* 3:8, etc.). God wants one theology in many churches; Jordan wants many theologies within one organization. Jordan, a Van Tilian, does not get the relationship between the one and the many straight.

But the Episcopal Church is not perfect, Jordan reveals. Its weakness is that "it does not excommunicate anyone," Jordan says. The Roman Church-State, however, has solved that problem: "the answer to this problem is seen *only* in the Roman Catholic church.... [T]here is no reticence about disciplining apostates" (22, my emphasis). The Roman Church-State has always been eager to silence its opposition. They were the original dominion theologians. And it is *only* the Roman Church-State that has solved the problem of disobedient members, Jordan says.

A little later in the book (page 71), Jordan muses about whether a liberal Episcopal Church is a true church:

> They still have officers. The sacraments are still rightly administered (far more so than in Reformed churches, since *Christ is made visible weekly* [emphasis added]). The Word is still sung in the liturgy and in the *psalms*, and read in appointed readings, even if the sermons are heretical. On the basis of what we have seen, such a church should be counted and treated as part of the church of Jesus Christ.

The same goes for the Roman Church-State: "We should be quite clear on this. Regardless of what they might sometimes have said, the Reformers continued to recognize that the Roman Catholic Church was in some sense part of the true church" (74). This was their view, he says, "regardless of what they might sometimes have said:" (Later in the book Jordan writes: "the Roman Church is still pervaded by superstition and heresy.... Roman Catholicism today presents its people with a choice between bleeding statues and revolutionary Marxism.... Yes, the Roman Church has a powerful witness, but it is a witness that is 10% gospel and 90% error" [133-134]).

Church Intimidation

Moreover, Jordan thunders, an individual cannot simply leave a church: "If an individual leaves a local church, without transferring, then he has apostatized from the church. He is no longer part of the church of Christ" (74). Jordan stops short of saying the former church member is going to Hell, but he wants the reader to draw that conclusion. He clearly means: Outside the (visible) church there is no salvation. But with most churches today, there is no salvation *inside* the visible church. A high churchman like Jordan, lusting for dominion over men, cannot permit the masses, the common people, simply to leave a church. They must be scared into staying, even if the church is a liberal Episcopal or the Roman Church-State itself. "Intimidation," Jordan believes, "is a good thing. People should be intimidated by the church [that is, the clergy]" (276).

Jordan tells us that laymen, common men, cannot challenge church leaders:

> It is not the place of non-officers to provoke such confrontations [about heresy and false doctrine]. The layman (or, general officer) should approach a special officer [of the church] whom he trusts, and ask him to provoke the confrontation. If there are no special officers who care enough to fight for orthodoxy, then the general officer should quietly and peaceably transfer to another church. God never blesses insurrection, even if the cause is just [72n.].

Worship

On page 26, under the subhead "Worship," Jordan returns to his attack on truth: After asserting that truth is "more than a mere intellectual ideology" (notice the pejorative use of "mere" and "ideology" again), Jordan informs us that truth is a "dialogue" between man and God. Moreover, because it is "more" than intellectual, truth takes many forms: "The Word is read to us, taught to us, preached to us, made visible to us in the Supper, sprinkled upon us in baptism, embodied to us in the lifestyle of Godly men and women."

This may be acceptable poetry, since there seem to be no standards for poetry these days, but it is not Christian theology. Truth is not a dialogue; it is a divine monologue. Truth is always and only intellectual, always and only propositional. Jordan has embraced the superstitious notions of the Gentiles, along with their views of the church.

In worship, according to Jordan, we engage in "the triple act of sacrifice." Please notice the word "sacrifice." The first act is confession – why this is a sacrifice Jordan does not say. Why worship consists of sacrifices, he does not say. He is enthralled by the rites and rituals – the sacrifices – of the Old Testament.

This fixation on the sacrificial system of the Old Testament is the result of the Reconstructionists' belief in the "abiding validity of the law in exhaustive detail." If the details of the law are still valid, then it is immaterial what *Hebrews* or *Romans* or *Galatians* says on the matter. The Reconstructionists' peculiar view of the law logically compels them to regard the Old Testament as if Christ had never come and the New Testament had never been written. It will not be too long (if it has not happened already) before the Reconstructionists realize that during the Dark Ages (what Jordan calls the "Christian centuries") attempts were made to reinstitute Old Testament laws in detail. When that happens, their followers will be regaled with books about how wonderful the Dark Ages were.

The second act of sacrifice, Jordan says, is the Offertory (this is the only act that Jordan capitalizes, perhaps indicating its importance to him). The reading of Scripture and the sermon "is all designed to lead us to the second act of sacrifice: the Offertory.... Thus the offering plates are brought down front to the minister, who holds them up before God ('heave offering') and gives them to Him" (27). In this second act of sacrifice, notice that the offering plates are elevated, and the Scripture and sermon are only preliminaries to the offering. At least Jordan is consistent with the rest of his theology when he puts money before truth. Jordan defends not only the elevation of the collection plates, but of the bread and wine as well: "[C]learly there is nothing wrong, then, with lifting up the collection plates, and the bread and wine... toward Heaven during the offertory prayer.... Lifting up the offering and the elements is thoroughly evangelical, Biblical, and Reformed" (269). He says that he does not lift them to be worshiped, but to offer them to God.

The third act of sacrifice is the "Eucharist." At the end of the service, the people are "ordered" (Jordan's word) to leave. The mention of the Eucharist gets Jordan's mind on eating: "Worship is a dance.... The Greek notions of the primacy of internal feeling, or the primacy of the intellect, have nothing to do with Scripture. In fact, if anything, the Scriptures give us the *primacy of eating*" (31). He quotes Alexander Schmemann quoting the German materialist Ludwig Feuerbach: "He [man] is indeed 'that which he eats...' " (31). One can think only of Paul's condemnation of those "whose god is their belly." Jordan writes, "By eat, we mean *eat*: a good chewable hunk of bread and a good-sized glass of real shalom-inducing wine" (230).

"At the climax of worship," Jordan pontificates, "is the Lord's Supper. Jesus did not say, 'Understand this in memory of Me.' What He actually said was '*Do* this *as a memorial* of Me.' The doing takes precedence over any theory of what is being done.... [I]n terms of the sacrament, doing is more important [than knowing]" (31-32).

This, of course, is Antichristian nonsense. If we truly had no theory, if eating bread and drinking wine were more important than knowing theology, the Supper, and the church, would be pointless. It was the Church at Corinth, one supposes, that came closest to practicing Jordan's primacy of eating and doing. That is why Paul read them the riot act. He told them to eat at home and to stop getting drunk. He also explained the meaning of the Supper to them – again.

"Doing" is so important to Jordan that he calls for worship to be characterized by "singing, falling down, kneeling, dancing, clapping, processions, and so forth. The recovery of all these things for worship...must be our eventual goal" (32).

Jordan continues to misrepresent the Lord's Supper: "As we noted above, the inauguration of the Lord's Supper preceded its interpretation. Jesus did not at that point give an explanation of it. He just said to do it" (33). Jesus' explanation may be found in *Matthew* 26:26-29; *Mark* 14:22-25; and *Luke* 22:14-22.

Jordan is driven to this bizarre position because he wishes to deny the primacy of the intellect. Perhaps a few words from Peter will suffice as an answer: "His divine power has given to us all things that pertain to life and godliness through the knowledge of him who called us...." Peter says all things we need come through knowledge. One factor that distinguishes Christianity from religions is its emphasis on understanding, on knowledge, and on doctrine. False religions appeal to the feelings, to the will, to the emotions, to sinful desires, to aesthetics. Christianity appeals to the mind. And it is that appeal that Jordan wants to deny. He seeks an "emotionally satisfying worship service" (229).

Jordan attacks Protestantism: "[W]hen the church falls into teaching without doing, as in Protestantism," it falls into perverted practices: "extreme negative sabbatarianism," "the altar call ritual," "Pentecostalism," and "extreme negative views of worship that reject all kinds of worship actions commanded in the Bible (such as kneeling, dancing, processions, etc.)" (34).

Jordan's Fascination with the Miraculous

Pentecostalism appears, he says, because "the weekly *miracle of Christ's special presence* is not maintained" (emphasis added, 34). He obviously regards the Lord's Supper not just as a memorial but as both a miracle and a sacrifice, a miracle and sacrifice that are performed weekly by the priest: "The sacrament, as a memorial, is also a continuing miracle. The fascination with the miraculous that has crippled the American churches since the days of the Great Awakening can only be overcome when the Lord's Supper is once again part of the center of our worship.... As a miraculous memorial, the sacrament has a real influence. It is never neutral.... The sacrament works positively in response to faith, but it also works negatively in response to faithlessness. In this sense, we must say that the sacrament does indeed work *ex opere operato*" (40).

How presenting a weekly miracle will end the fascination with the miraculous, Jordan does not explain. It certainly has not ended it in the Roman Church-State, which has been in the miracle-mongering business for centuries. No Pentecostal or charismatic church or cult has ever promoted "miracles" as assiduously as the mother of all cults, the Roman Church-State. Oral Roberts, Pat Robertson, Robert Tilton, and the whole Pentecostal and charismatic movements are tyros and novices compared to Rome. It would seem that a weekly miracle only panders to and encourages interest in the miraculous. Moreover, why does Jordan object to interest in the miraculous if he wants miracles to be performed weekly? Finally, Jordan has taken another step away from the Reformation and back to the Dark Ages by saying that the sacraments work magically, *ex opere operato.*

Speculative Theology

Jordan resumes his attack on the intellect and truth: "Because the pluriform revelation in Word and Sacrament is a reflex of the triunity of God, it will always ultimately evade our attempts to explain it rationally" (40). It is a standard ploy of theologians who do not know what they are talking about to use big words and say that doctrine X cannot be explained rationally. That is designed to relieve them of responsibility for talking nonsense. It also allows them to impugn the intelligence of the masses who do not understand their sesquipedalian nonsense.

Much of Jordan's book is pious speculation unsullied by vulgar and common truth. After all, if one has given up on logic and rationality, all that is left is speculation. For example, under the heading, "Church Rulers," Jordan writes: "That [Divine] council is seen initially in *Genesis* 1:26, and had then only three members. Had Adam persevered, he and Eve would have been the next two" (42). Or take this example of his speculative theology: "For their own good, Adam and Eve were cast out of the Garden. Just as the Lord's Supper causes the faithless to become sick and die, so the Tree of Life would have caused Adam to die had he eaten of it. Thus, for his own good Adam was prevented from eating the sacrament" (106).

God contradicts Jordan: Adam would not have died, he would have lived forever: "Then the Lord God said, 'Behold, the man has become like one of us, to know good and evil. And now, lest he put out his hand and take also of the tree of life, and eat, and live forever' – therefore the Lord God sent him out of the garden of Eden...'" (*Genesis* 3:22-23). Jordan is determined to have his own theology, no matter what the Bible says.

"The Woman Question"

Discussing the role of women in the church, Jordan gives a convoluted explanation of 1 *Corinthians* 14 in which only men may speak at certain church meetings, and women may speak at others. A few pages later, he returns to "The Woman Question" and tells us that a woman may prophesy, speak for her husband, be a judge, make judgments in the church, instruct men, be a priestess, be a teacher, be a magistrate, and be a deacon (44-49).

A Liturgy of Hate

For special occasions, Jordan recommends cursing as part of the worship service. "It is the church," he bellows, "that binds and looses on Earth" (280). "She is only to bind on Earth what she knows has been bound in Heaven," and that is easily discerned. Here are some excerpts from the liturgy Jordan's Reconstructionist church has used:

> *Presiding Elder.* "Tonight we bring before you the names of _____, who have attacked the church of Jesus Christ. We ask you to join with us in praying that God will pour out His wrath upon them, and upon all in alliance with them in this sinful act....
>
> (Praying) "Almighty and Most terrible God, Judge of all men living and dead, we bring before You _____ (here name the persons being cursed), who have brought an attack upon the integrity of Your holy government on the Earth. We as Your anointed office-bearers now ask that You place Your especial curse upon these people, and upon all in alliance with them. We ask You to pour out the fire of Your wrath upon them, and destroy them, that Your church may be left in peace..." [281-282].

What heinous persecution provoked this vitriol? It seems that a former teacher at the church's school had filed for unemployment benefits (280-281). Well, add another chapter to Foxe's *Martyrs*. One wonders what Jordan would recommend were the church actually to be persecuted. In any event, one need only contrast his suggested liturgy with the instructions Peter gives us about rulers in *1 Peter* 2:13-23.

A Liturgy of Healing

Jordan includes an essay by this title in the book. The gist of it is this: "God generally wants His people able, strong, and healthy. He has instituted the rite of unction..." (290). Jordan also believes in haunted houses (252). Presumably he would favor the rite of exorcism as well.

Clothing and Clerical Costumes

In an essay titled "Triumphalistic Investiture," Jordan longs for the days when clothing marked one's station in life:

> [T]he industrial revolution, coupled with democratic notions of society, have [sic] completely separated us from all human traditions in this area. Nowadays, men dress in "business suits" regardless of their profession; earlier, this was not so. In traditional societies, clothing gave a visible indication of the status of a person.... Democracy has impoverished us to the extent that this is no longer so [264].

Jordan is very concerned with status. Speaking of the distinctive clothing of the priests in the Old Testament, he tells us that "there is no reason to presume any change in principle here" (264). He argues at length for the reintroduction of clerical costumes, "since Rome is no longer a problem" (275). "Practically speaking," he writes, "we should be careful not to introduce too much, but bring the people along. In the area of vestments, a simple white alb or surplice (the white robe of the Bible) and a colored stole (the strip of cloth that represents the 'easy yoke' of Christ's service, the colors variable with the liturgical season) should be sufficient. But we should not be afraid to think about more glorious apparel at some later time" (277).

Justification Not by Faith Alone

Jordan apparently believes in salvation by works. He writes: "Paul goes on to speak [in *Romans* 2] of Gentiles who did not have the law, but who did the things contained in the law. The plain implication here is that such Gentiles were saved (by their *faithful* obedience)" (107).

The Four Spiritual Laws

In his essay on conversion, Jordan defends the "Four Spiritual Laws." He defends telling everyone that God has a wonderful plan for his life. He also defends telling all men that God loves them and Christ died for them. "God does offer salvation to all men, covenantally speaking" (158). This is the Arminian preaching that Herman Hoeksema perceptively predicted (in *The Clark-Van Til Controversy*) would result from the paradoxical theology of Van Til.

Glossolalia (A Gift), Irrationalism (Another Gift), the Regulative Principle (Bad), and the Real Presence (Good)

Jordan writes:

> Glossolalia, modern tongues-speaking, is not a foreign language, but
> a natural reflex or capacity of the human body, like weeping, laughter,
> or hysteria.... [G]lossolalia is a God-given gift to man, which can be used
> for good, but which also can be abused. Like any other human action,
> the practice of glossolalia should be directed as a thank offering to God.
> The use of glossolalia in prayer is no more problematic in principle than
> the use of laughter or weeping in prayer.... The modern Pentecostal
> movement is an irrationalistic reaction against an overly rationalistic
> culture and church. The Reformation produced an overly rationalistic
> church.... The failure to maintain the Real Presence in the sacraments,
> and to keep the Eucharist at the center of weekly worship, also served to
> de-mystify and overly intellectualize Christian experience.... The cat-
> echisms produced in Reformed churches to train youth concern the
> definitions of doctrinal terms, and bear no resemblance to the whole-
> life orientation of that Biblical catechism, the book of Proverbs.... Irratio-
> nalism can also be used for good or for ill.... We need to repudiate the
> historic Protestant stoic and intellectualistic interpretations of worship
> (the regulative principle), and reintroduce cultivated musical and artis-
> tic beauty in worship.... We need to reintroduce the mystery of the
> Eucharist as Christ's Real Presence in our midst, as the center of special
> worship, weekly, with our children not excluded... [171-174].

Church and State

Jordan asserts a medieval view of the church's prerogatives: "Once
upon a time [Jordan should begin all his essays with this phrase], it was
understood that the sacramental body of the church was the primary
form of 'incorporation' on the Earth, and that all other corporations
were secondary in comparison to the church" [189-190].

The church, according to Jordan, is even prior to the family: "The
church performed marriages, maintained marriage certificates and birth
records, granted divorces, etc., thus showing that the corporation of
the family is an extension of the life of Christ and the Blessed Trinity in
the world" (190). The church is prior to the state as well: "The church
ordained kings, showing that the corporation of the state is an exten-

sion of the work of Christ in the world.... Let the state come to the church and request incorporation!" (190).

After espousing the papist view of the church, he continues:

> No church should heed a summons to appear before the court of the state. Church officers may and should appear as a courtesy, by "special appearance," but not as if the church herself is on trial.... The church, her laws, her ordinances, her decrees, her property, etc., are simply not under the inspection of the state.... To be sure, when they have a gun to your head, you give them your wallet. If the state refuses to honor the principle of jurisdiction and threatens to close down a given local church, she may choose to pay a bribe to state officials.... This has been the tactic of the Roman Catholic Church for centuries. She maintains lawyers and gives outward compliance to all laws, pretending deceptively to be under the rule of the state.... We as Protestants (Reformed Catholics) may well take our cue from this [192].

Man

Jordan's worldview includes a non-Christian view of man:

> [T]he Bible teaches neither a bipartite nor a tripartite view of man.... Man is a spirit in bodily form, not a spirit housed in a body. It is Greek philosophy that teaches that man is a soul or spirit housed in a body.... [P]agan man assumes that there is some immortal soul living inside his body, which soul or spirit is his true self, and this soul will go on living in some other place after the physical body dies... [222-223].

Does this last sentence sound familiar? It should. What Jordan calls "Greek philosophy" and "pagan" is the teaching of Scripture. Paul, for example, refers to our bodies as tents and houses (2 *Corinthians* 5:1, 4). Christ tells us not to be afraid of him who can destroy the body but not the soul. Peter repeatedly refers to his body as a tent (2 *Peter* 1:14). Paul says to be absent from the body is to be present with the Lord (2 *Corinthians* 5:6, 8).

Jordan uses his peculiar view of man to launch another attack on the intellect and on preaching: "Under the influence of Greek thought, Christianity began to hold that man is divided into various parts or faculties, and that the most important of these parts is the intellect. This notion is called the doctrine of the primacy of the intellect." From this statement and Jordan's repeated denunciation of the primacy of the intellect, one can only conclude that Jordan does not think that the most important part of man is his intellect. One wonders what it is.

He continues: "Because the brain was regarded as the most important part of man, the most important work of the church was to communicate intellectual information to that brain." Here Jordan lapses into behaviorism, confusing the intellect, the mind, with the brain. One should expect this of a person who thinks that "man is a spirit in bodily form." To such a person, it would seem plausible that the brain is the bodily form of the mind, and Jordan's mistake is easily understandable. Jordan betrays his preference for the physical on page 237, where, speaking of the Lord's Supper, he writes, "The invitation is to a real meal, one at which Christ is present as Host. Real food, physical food, is to be eaten" (237). Notice that *real* means *physical*.

Preaching

According to Jordan, the pernicious result of the primacy of the intellect for the church has been the "primacy of preaching" rather than "the primacy of the Word." The primacy of preaching leads to the primacy of the preacher. Jordan wants the Word "experienced," "made visible," "sung," "prayed," "obeyed and implemented" (224). Once again Jordan plays the trick of sliding from "primacy" to "only." This writer knows of no church that preaches but refuses to sing, or pray, or celebrate the Lord's Supper. That does not stop Jordan, however. He launches into an extended attack on the primacy of the preacher. His entire diatribe may be answered by referring to Jesus' command to teach and make disciples of every creature, and Paul's rhetorical question, How will they hear without a preacher? The problem with contemporary churches is not the primacy of the preacher, but the fact that there is only one preacher per church. Such was not the case in the apostolic churches.

I shall conclude simply by saying that Christian Reconstructionist James Jordan has written a book telling us that Protestantism is bad and Romanism is good. Many Reconstructionists have acted on that information and joined the Roman Church-State. Reconstructionism, as exemplified in this book, has a heretical view of the church.

24

The Abolition of Vestments

John à Lasco[1]

IT IS MY BELIEF that among all things in the church of Christ, some
ought to be preserved perpetually, some are indifferent, but others
are not on any account to be tolerated. Those that ought to be permanent in the church are the pure teaching of the prophets and apostles,
which ought to be set forth diligently through God's ministers to the
flock of Christ, as the food of the soul. Additional to this are the sacraments of Baptism and the Lord's Supper administered according to the
apostolic rite described in three apostolic *Gospels;* to these ecclesiastical
discipline is most fittingly joined. But whatever things are done for the

---

1. Born into the Polish nobility, Lasco studied in Italy, Paris, and Basle before returning to Poland where positions of honor in the Roman Church-State had been assigned
to him since childhood: "I was once a Pharisee of repute, adorned with many roles and
dignities, splendidly endowed with many and rich benefices from the days of my boy-
hood." In 1538, however, when Lasco was Archdeacon of Warsaw, he declined the
King's offer of the bishopric of Cujavia and instead relinquished all his titles and went
into exile. Thereafter he served in poor and persecuted churches in the Rhineland and
Belgium before crossing to England at the invitation of Cranmer in 1548.

In his letter of invitation Archbishop Cranmer had written, "We are desirous of
setting forth in our churches the true doctrine of God, and have no wish to adapt it to
all tastes, or to deal in ambiguities." The Polish reformer returned to his work in East
Friesland in 1549, but again traveled to England in 1550 in the face of increasing persecution. Thus Lasco was back in London in the critical year of the Vestment Controversy, and he was the most theologically able of those Reformers, who, like Hooper,
were concerned for a more decided policy of reform based on a recognition of the
regulative principle of Scripture.

Besides his intellectual powers and charm of character, Lasco was a forceful leader,
and King Edward gave him permission to organize the 5,000 member "Strangers'
Church," composed of refugees, according to principles which had not been put into
practice in the English Church. In a statement à Lasco made after the death of Edward, he declared that the young king was a knowing supporter of the plan that the
refugees "should have churches of their own in which they should freely regulate all

useful and convenient administration of the Word and sacraments are indifferent; so long as they have their source in the Scriptures let there be no prohibition, let their usefulness to the church be clear, and let there be no tyranny which strangles men's consciences. Of this kind are questions of gathering at this or that hour of day in church, using this or that sort of speech in administration of the sacraments, and celebrating the Lord's Supper once or more often in the year.

The things which ought definitely to be kept out of the church are twofold: Certain things are so obviously impious that they can never deceive even those who are but little instructed in the Word of God, such as the worship of images, adoration of the bread and wine, profanation of the Lord's Supper by the mass, invocation of the sacraments, prayer for the dead, and innumerable similar monstrosities which Antichrist has brought into Christ's church. There are other things, intro-

---

things according to primitive methods, without any regard to existing rites: so that the English churches might be incited to embrace apostolic purity." Nicholas Ridley recognized the implications of having such a large congregation that claimed freedom from the jurisdiction and ecclesiastical acts of the English Church in the heart of London, and he contested the right of the refugees to worship in ways other than those laid down in English law.

This document was first printed by the English Puritans in 1566 in a collection of tracts titled *The Fortress of the Fathers*. The following is a fresh English translation by David Clines of Lasco's original Latin manuscript. The manuscript is dated September 20, in the fifth year of Edward's reign. It thus belongs to the period of the Vestment Controversy in which Lasco, in contrast to the mediating roles adopted by Martin Bucer and Peter Martyr, gave forthright support to the position taken by Hooper.

Other documents of Lasco's throwing light on the Edwardian period of the English Reformation have still to be printed in English, particularly Letter 29 in Abraham Kuyper's Latin edition of Lasco's works, in which the Reformer gives his reasons to Cranmer for those differences in practice in the "Stranger's Church" to which Ridley objected, and states what he believed to be the scriptural case to establish that: "Nothing ought to be added to public worship concerning which God has given no command."

After the death of Edward, Lasco, returning to the Continent with members of his congregation, was shipwrecked on the Danish coast, and only after many hardships reached Friesland and later Frankfurt. In 1556 he returned to Poland, but the early promise of a great Reformation in that country was terminated by the Reformer's death on January 8, 1560. One of his last letters was to the new Queen Elizabeth, urging her to follow the religious policy of her late brother. Testimonies to the worth of this forgotten Reformer can be found in the words of many of his contemporaries, including Cranmer, Latimer, Hooper, and Calvin. This document is reprinted with permission from *The Reformation of the Church*, Iain Murray, editor, published by The Banner of Truth Trust, 1965.

duced by the same Antichrist, which contend strongly with Christian liberty, obscure Christ, increase hypocrisy, and bring pride into the church. At the same time, however, they bear upon them the appearance of utility and splendor. Of this sort are appointed fast days, limitation of foods, much singing which is not understood in the church, the playing of organs, and the use of vestments in the administration of the sacraments. There is not now the space to record how much harm has crept into the church from these individual things, and how much more could creep in if they are not abolished; I can here only treat of the use of vestments, because they must by no means be tolerated any longer in the reformed church of Christ by a pious teacher. Although much can be thought out in its defense by ingenious men, we regard not the reasonings of man's intellect but rely upon the command of the divine will.

First, by means of the argument by which Christ and the prophets together with the apostles expel from the church human dogmas and inventions as a plague (*Matthew* 12, *Isaiah* 29, *Colossians* 2), I too am convinced that vestments are a human invention which ought to be removed from the church. A witness of this is Polydore Vergil, Book 6, *De Inventoribus Rerum,* chapter 12. The practice has been borrowed from the Hebrews that priestly vestments should be consecrated along with the altar covers and other things necessary for temple use, and that the vestments themselves should be assigned to priests and other initiates, so that they might put them on when they were about to perform their sacred duties. Pope Stephen I was the first among us to lay down that this should be done. For in the beginnings of the new religion, the priests used not to put on anything extra when they were going to carry out divine service, since they were anxious rather to clothe themselves inwardly with spiritual virtues and put off the vices of the flesh than to put on new apparel.[2] Now I conclude that if they did not change their clothes before performing sacred duties, then they used none for them that were admitted into the ministry of the Gospel. Laying on of hands with fasting and prayer was sufficient for Paul and Barnabas. Paul, when he carefully laid down all the duties of a bishop for Timothy and Titus, made no mention of special vestments and other ceremonies. It is clear

2. These comments apply to any special apparel, whether one calls them vestments, robes, or gowns. To be inconspicuous, elders ought to dress in ordinary clothing. – *Editor.*

enough from the decree of Celestinus, the first bishop of Rome, that the use of vestments did not pervade all the churches at once; these are his words against special vestments of this kind for bishops:

> We ought to be distinguished, he says, from the common people or from others by our teaching, not our dress; our behavior, not our appearance; and our purity of mind, not our clothing, for if we begin to be anxious for novelty, we shall trample under foot the order handed down to us by our fathers, and make a place for empty superstitions. Therefore we ought not to lead the simple minds of the faithful to such things, but should teach them rather than deceive them. Nor is an imposition to be made on their eyes, but rather precepts should be poured upon their minds.

Thus far Celestinus.

However we cannot deny, since our people are prone to superstition, that before his time the use of certain kinds of vestments, though quite simple, had crept into many churches. Certainly Sylvester gave the opportunity, but Charlemagne finished the matter, as the histories witness. Thus it is clear that the use of special vestments in the church for ecclesiastical personages is a human invention, and is for this cause to be done away with if there were no more.

Those who wish to retain the use of vestments in the church as a divine institution refer to the priesthood of Aaron. But let them take a little care of what they are saying, for according to the Scriptures Christ is a priest according to the order not of Aaron but of Melchizedek, and the priesthood of Aaron has in Christ been abolished, together with all its parts, among which we number vestments. And thus Christ, the very wisdom of the Father, did not use in divine service any new or special kind of vestments or prescribe their use, for the foreshadowing priesthood was done away with by the true priest Christ. All those therefore who bring back Aaronic vestments into the church defile the priesthood of Christ, as if there should be need of shadows when there is the light itself. Nor will there be room for your defense that you are not recalling the whole Aaronic priesthood, but only a part thereof, and he who receives part does not receive the whole; but it is undoubted that the whole foreshadowing priesthood of Aaron is to be rejected, because it is abrogated. And all those who restore again those things which have been destroyed and by the authority of the divine Word are without doubt transgressors of the divine law (*Galatians* 2). Furthermore, Paul rightly teaches (*Galatians* 4), "The handmaid is to be cast out, along with her son" – signifying that all bondage of the law after the rising of the Gospel's light is to be cast out; and it means that we should on no account allow ourselves to be moved from our liberty in Christ.

Now it is clear that teaching and commandment of a special kind of vestments in God's ministry is a transgression of the divine law because Aaronic priesthood is thus recalled.

If anyone is induced by the foregoing argument to deny that vestments are part of the Aaronic priesthood, and says that by a certain expression of liberty they were introduced by the Roman bishops to adorn the order of the priesthood, even so he has not produced sufficient reason why they should be retained. We know that the Roman pope is the very Antichrist; wherefore his priesthood also is Antichristian, by which the whole priesthood of Christ is utterly trampled upon. But forasmuch as the principal part of the papistical priesthood consists in ceremonies, anointing, shaving of hair, mitres, and vestments (for without these things they do not regard anyone as a bishop, and by the quality of these ornaments they judge them of the bishop) it follows that if we condemn the pope's priesthood because it is of Antichrist, we ought also to avoid all its parts and manifestations. For the more the pious and Christian heart loves the sacrilegious marks of the papistical priesthood, the more the Christian priesthood is defiled. Wherefore he who hates the priesthood of Antichrist ought also to hate its individual manifestations. Again, he who loves the part cannot hate the whole.

Moreover, if it is agreed that the pope's priesthood with all its marks is the priesthood of Antichrist (and every work of Antichrist is a work of Satan), we ought not to promote it but destroy it, if indeed we wish to be co-workers with Christ, who came to destroy the works of the devil, as the Scriptures testify.

Nor let us imagine that anyone may, of his own authority, institute, abolish, or keep, the use of these vestments; for all power is given for edification (as Paul says) and not for destruction. And in the same place he says, "We can do nothing against the truth, but for the truth." And edification is to build the faithful upon Christ, in faith, hope, and love, and in innocence of life, by always stretching out towards what is more perfect; but vestments promote none of these things; nay rather they obscure the face of Christ, they induce a certain connection with the profane priesthood of Antichrist, or a falling back to the shadows of Aaron from the body of Christ. It is the truth for which apostolic men and Christian magistrates ought to labor. It is certain that Christ is content with that order which he himself left, and that the shadows should no more be sought. Wherefore they will labor for the truth, not against it, by recalling those things which Christ destroyed and abolished.

In this regard Paul simply admitted nothing into the church unless it edified, that is, increased godliness. Special vestments in the ministry do not edify but destroy; they are therefore not to be tolerated. Nor do those things edify which provide an imaginary occasion for piety, but they must provide Christians with a compelling opportunity for piety. But vestments, on the contrary, sometimes increase pride in those who use them, sometimes hypocrisy, sometimes both. It is very easy for them to provide an opportunity for hypocrisy, indeed it is unavoidable; if there is really in oneself that virtue which you imagine to be signified by vestments, why do you receive a reward from men by declaring it? But there is not, and the hypocrite in you is shown up, who is a different man from what you appear to be. Nor will you escape if you say that no inner virtue is signified by these private garments, but that of the office is indicated. What then was it that indicated the office of the apostles? Was it vestments or the Spirit of the Lord and love of the church and of Christ? His disciples do not forget their office when they take off these vestments. Why do they not rather meditate upon the Word of the Lord day and night and by it correct their ways, for it penetrates to the inmost recesses of the heart, while vestments can move only the outward man. What did Christ demand of Peter the third time that his office should be indicated in feeding the sheep? Indeed, nothing but love.

Moreover, there is a danger that a reputation of merit or some such foolish thing should be occasioned by the idea that the dignity of the ministers or the sacraments or the preaching of the Word is violated unless it is supplied with this useless and pernicious clothing.

This fear alone of human merit should move us to exclude from the temple vestments, together with the other ceremonies introduced by human invention.

It is an impious thing to furnish an occasion of stumbling in this way to the weak for whom Christ died. Experience has taught how easy it is to put one's trust in these things, so much so that he who does not consider or care for these things does not seem to be able to escape the imputation of impiety. Nor is it possible that they should excuse themselves by claiming that in vestments there resides nothing either of good or bad. For in order for us to grant this, you would have to argue that this was realized by those emperors when first vestments were introduced by the bishops. We are not born for ourselves alone, but that we should serve the church and also posterity; it cannot but be that to leave to them the religion of Christ in as pure a form as possible is a thing most pleasing to God. No dying man willingly leaves to his sons a will unless it is provided with all that is necessary to remove all cause of contention. Why do we not show the same diligence and faithfulness in reference to the testament of God?

I know that it is objected by some that sacred services are adorned by vestments. Nay, they are much obscured. For vestments assail the eyes of men and remove their minds from the contemplation of the sacred things which are taking place in the sacraments and lead them to the pleasures of the senses. Holy simplicity commends the institutions of God. Through them are given to us the example of Christ and the apostles and the early church, which it is safer and more holy and more useful to imitate than to pervert and to condemn Christ by acting otherwise. Here I add what Paul remarked concerning the doctrines of men which "have an appearance of wisdom and humility of mind and afflicting of the body, not through any honor to the satisfying of the flesh" (*Colossians* 2).

Tyranny finally is brought in and vestments are imposed whether they are wanted or not. And this tyranny brings it about that if something is of itself free and indifferent, it ceases to be indifferent. Paul instructs Christians in plain words not to put themselves under tyranny or superstitions. Thus, "If you are dead to the elements of this world," etc. And again, "Do not become servants of men." And indeed it is a most hard slavery to be compelled to a certain kind of vestment in the church, which savors of paganism or the Aaronic priesthood or the heresy of Antichrist, and which is in so many ways pernicious, and useful in no way at all.

But why does it please us so much to strain ourselves with popish filth? Why do we not give the same honor to the priesthood of Jesus Christ as the popish priests give to the priesthood of Antichrist? There is not the slightest thing prescribed by him (no matter how far he differs from Christ) which they do not most religiously observe; why do we for our part not obey Christ in everything, content with his simple truth?

Finally, since Paul commands us to beware of every kind of evil, and we have shown that to prescribe vestments in the administration of holy things is truly an evil, who will not judge that they should be avoided, for they are indeed a human invention, parts of the Aaronic or papistical priesthood, edifying nothing, but begetting pride, hypocrisy, and the reputation of merit.

Certain objections are made by the advocates of these vestments to which it will be sufficient to subjoin brief answers, for they will hardly refute our previous arguments.

Objection. In indifferent matters the weakness of our brethren is to be considered, according to the example of the apostles.

Answer. You would surely deny that those things are indifferent which obscure the priesthood of Christ, and produce from themselves nothing except hypocrisy, sects, and pride in the church, have no source in the Scriptures, and are commanded with tyranny unworthy of Christians. The apostles are never said to have done such things; let us not falsely pervert the pious concern of the apostles for the founding of the church of Christ. Again, since our opponents claim that the understanding of the weak is to be taken account of, why do they not allow a free use to the strong? And when will the weak better learn that these things are stupid, foolish, and pernicious, than when they see them abrogated? How can the simple and ignorant think otherwise than that some godliness consists in those things that yet remain, when they see so many other things which were used in times past done away? Thus infirmity is not helped, but rather harmed, if vestments or similar ceremonies are retained. For they are retained for the sake of the reputation of merit, and we measure the dignity of the sacraments by external things.

Further, they bring forward the decree of the magistrate concerning the retention of vestments. Indeed the piety, prudence, and goodwill of our magistrate is well-known to me, so that when he perceives carefully the danger of these ceremonies, he would rejoice that there are some who wish to run in the law of the Lord, and make the path plain for others, so that he might restore everything to the integrity of the apostolic order. They know that to them is given power in the church for edification, not for destruction, that they should stand for the truth, not against the truth. And since the ready piety of our magistrate is well known, I doubt that blame can be withheld if anyone under his patronage wishes to defend tyrannically human traditions, or to force them upon others against their will, contrary to the commandment of God. But those things which we have ourselves chosen are apt to please us more than those which God's laws prescribe. Nor need there be any fear of uproar if human dogmas and those superstitions by which we provoke the anger of God are removed from the church; nay rather we ought to hope for greater peace and tranquillity in the kingdom the nearer we come to the institutions of Christ and the further we retreat from Antichrist. The prudence of human reason is deceptive, which seeks for itself and promises to itself peace by illegitimate means. Saul, by seeking the favor of God with the forbidden sacrifices of the Amalekites, foolishly destroyed himself. There is one way of safety if we altogether turn to repentance: Believe the Gospel of Christ, walk in innocence of life, and retain nothing in the church which does not either have the express Word of God, or else take its infallible origin from that source. Then let true pastors, zealous for teaching, be set over the churches, and let dumb and wicked pastors be shut out; thus king will flourish with people, according to the promises of God often repeated by His prophets.

PART 5

The Growth of the Church

"All authority has been given to me in Heaven and on Earth.
Go therefore and make disciples of all the nations,
baptizing them in the name of the Father
and of the Son
and of the Holy Spirit,
teaching them to observe all things that I have commanded you;
and lo, I am with you always, even to the end of the age."
Matthew 28:18-20

Then those who gladly received his Word were baptized;
and that day about three thousand souls were added.
And they continued steadfastly in the apostles' doctrine
and fellowship, in the breaking of bread, and in prayers.
Acts 2:41-42

25

Ought the Church to Pray for Revival?[1]

Herman Hanko

IF ONE WERE TO ask the question, "Ought the church to pray for revival?" the answer almost surely would be a resounding "Yes." Anyone who has a love in his heart for the church and who is concerned about the cause of Zion is aware of the fact that the church is by no means in a healthy condition. It is simply a fact that, from a doctrinal point of view, today's church has, at best, become doctrinally indifferent and, at worst, allowed all kinds of heresies to creep into her confession. From a doctrinal point of view, the church is not strong.

The same is true if one measures the strength of the church from the viewpoint of her spiritual walk. The church is spiritually very weak. It is characterized by worldliness and carnality. The commandments of the Lord are openly broken by its members. The Lord's Day is desecrated. The name of God is taken in vain. Fornication, adultery, and immorality flourish in the church as if they were plants in a heavily fertilized soil.

It is no different if we consider the church from the viewpoint of her zeal. Anyone who is at all concerned about the church cannot help but see that the church has lost her zeal for Christ and for the cause of the truth; lost her spiritual energies; and become spiritually lethargic, spiritually cold, and sunken in formalism so that the vibrancy that ought to characterize her seems to be gone. And the church has, without any doubt whatsoever, come under the condemnation of the Lord in His letter to the Church of Ephesus, "You have lost your first love."

From all of these points of view it would seem immediately evident to anyone who concerns himself with the welfare of the church that

---

1. This essay is reprinted from *The Trinity Review*.

the church is in need of revival. And so it has happened, too, that the cry for revival has become increasingly loud, widespread, and urgent.

Let me give you just a few instances of this.

Ian Paisley, who is perhaps the best known and most powerful man in Northern Ireland, has publicly gone on record as stating that he is "convinced that before he dies the Lord will send revival to the church." And the Lord has told him, so he claims, that he will be an instrument in such revival. A great deal of the work which he carries on is geared to bringing about revival in the church of his land and in the church throughout the world.

Martyn Lloyd-Jones, whose influence has been so great and who has cast his long shadow not only over the British Isles where he labored all his life, but also over America, has said publicly, and has written in his books that "the last hope of the church in our day is revival" (*The Welsh Revival of 1904*, Introduction).

The Banner of Truth, which has been instrumental in the excellent work of re-publishing innumerable Puritan classics and which sponsors the Banner of Truth Conferences, plays a large role, if not a crucial role, in the growing clamor for revival and in the growing interest in revival which characterizes the church of our day. At their conferences they speak of the need for revival, they lecture concerning revival, and they pray for revival.

David Bellington has said: "Revivalism is a strand within the evangelical tradition." The same thing is true in the Reformed churches. The following prayer appeared this past year in a magazine of a Reformed church: "Lord, for our souls, families, churches, missions, schools, and nations we desperately need revival. The times are dark. Thy judgments are imminent" (*The Banner*, January 1990, 7). And so revival has become an important and an urgent cry that arises from a church concerned about the spiritual welfare of God's heritage.

The question that faces us is this: "Is it proper, is it Biblical, is it Reformed to pray for and seek revival in the church?" To that question the Reformed faith must give a resounding "No!" Revival is wrong. Revival is contrary to the Scriptures. Revival is at odds with the Reformed faith. To pray for revival is to go against the will of God and is to grieve the Holy Spirit.

What Is Revival?

Before we enter into any kind of an analysis of revivals we must be careful that we understand what we mean by this term. Many have used the term "revival" in a very broad sense. They have used "revival," for example, to describe those incidents in the history of the nation of Judah when, under the leadership of a good king (such as Asa or Jehoshaphat or Hezekiah or Josiah), the nation of Judah returned to the true worship of Jehovah after a period of idolatry and grievous sin. Although Scripture uses the word "revival" in the Old Testament, this term must be understood in the context of Israel's theocracy and before the time of the outpouring of the Spirit on Pentecost. It had therefore an entirely different connotation.

This broad meaning of revival has also sometimes been applied to various reformations in the church, such as the great Protestant Reformation of the 16th century, the rise of Puritanism in the British Isles, and the separation in the Netherlands from the State Church under the leadership of Brummelkamp, Van Raalte, Scholte, and others. But none of these events, either in the Old or New Testament, is rightly called a revival. They were church reformations, but to confuse church reformation with revival is a serious historical and theological mistake.

There are others who speak of revival, especially in evangelical and fundamentalistic circles, as referring to that kind of preaching which goes sometimes under the name of "revivalistic" preaching – preaching after the order of Dwight L. Moody, the Sankeys, and, in our own time, such men as Billy Graham. It is common for churches who have become spiritually lethargic to call in a revival preacher who attempts to instill new life into a congregation, gain new converts to Christ, and solicit from members of the church new commitments to the Lord Jesus. On a much broader scale, efforts are made by such powerful revival preachers as Billy Graham to bring revival to whole cities or countries. The Reformed faith has a quarrel with that type of preaching, particularly with its decisionism, its whole approach to the preaching of the Gospel, and its idea of the church. But we are not particularly interested in this either, although some of the things which are characteristic of revivals in the narrower sense of the word are characteristic also of revival preaching.

When I speak of "revival" I am using the word in a much more limited sense than that, but in the sense in which it is used time and time again in church circles today. Perhaps it is best for us to take our definition of "revival" from one who himself is an ardent proponent of revival (or was until the Lord took him from this life), Martyn Lloyd-Jones. In his book, *Revival: An Historical and Theological Survey*, he defines "revival" in these terms: "Revival is an experience in the life of the church when the Holy Spirit does an unusual work." The key word in that definition is the word "unusual." At unexpected times and in unexpected ways, the Holy Spirit enters the church to bring about unusual events in the lives of men which bring about drastic change in the lives of men and churches.

There have been many such revivals since the time of the Protestant Reformation. Some of the more important ones were the Welsh Revivals of 1859 and 1904; the Irish Revival of 1859; the revivals of 18th century England, under the leadership of John Wesley and his brother Charles, the great hymn-writer, as well as George Whitefield, who also came to America to promote revivals. In America, perhaps the best-known revival is the Great Awakening in New England in the time of Jonathan Edwards in 1734-1735 and again in 1740. And Jonathan Edwards, himself a minister at that time in the church of Northampton, Massachusetts, was a leading figure in the revival movement. George Whitefield came from England to join Edwards in this work. There were other such revivals in the eastern part of America, as in the early 1800s under the preaching of Charles Finney.

When Martyn Lloyd-Jones defines revivals in the terms that he uses in his book, these are the revivals to which he specifically refers and these are the revivals which he says are the last hope of the church in our day. If the Lord is not pleased to send revivals, the end has come for the church.

So the question is: What characterizes all these revivals? What do they have in common? What are the unusual aspects of the work which the Holy Spirit performs which makes these revivals different from the Spirit's ordinary and common work?

The distinctive features of such revivals are, first of all, that they come especially at a time when a church is characterized by the two great evils of worldly-mindedness and dead formalism in her life, confession, and worship. The church has been conformed to the world and, as a result, has died spiritually. It is at such a time, if revival is to come, that it comes as an unusual working of the Spirit.

Such revival is always characterized by and has its beginning in a work of the Spirit which brings about, in the people upon whom the Spirit falls, a deep and profound, an extraordinarily disturbing consciousness of sin. It is an effusion of the Spirit, an outpouring of the Spirit in unusual measure, an outpouring of the Spirit in great abundance, so to speak, which brings about and manifests itself in a profound and even unnerving and frighteningly disturbing conviction of sin.

But this conviction of sin takes on the outward form of very strange and very peculiar happenings. If you read the literature on revival, the books on the Welsh revival or the Great Awakening which describe the New England revivals, they are all filled with the dominant theme that the conviction of sin brought about by the Holy Spirit manifests itself in extraordinary and unusual forms. It comes about in such a way that those who are brought under the conviction of sin are so completely under the control of forces beyond their power that they cry out and groan and shout. They fall down in fits of despair. They are, in their awful agonies of soul, seized by fierce tremors of the body, shaking of the limbs, strange contortions, so that they roll about on the floor, sometimes in agony. They fall into what amounts almost to a catatonic state in which they are immobile and rigid, and during which time they see visions of the flames of Hell and of demons which come seeking their souls – all of which are intended to portray to them in graphic and unusual ways the horror of sins and the fury of God against the formalism and worldliness which characterized their life. All revivals, without exception, were accompanied by phenomena of this sort. Sometimes within a congregation, as the minister was preaching, the disturbances, the groanings, the shouting, the pleading, the crying became so loud and so boisterous that it became impossible for the minister to go on. He had to quit his preaching and dismiss the services.

In the second place, that kind of an unusual and extraordinary working of the Spirit bringing about conviction of sin was soon followed in many people, if not most, by experiences of total rapturous joy. When the conviction of sin was removed and the Spirit worked in the hearts of those under the conviction of sin, the rapture of their salvation was indefinable and indescribable. They were cast into ecstasies of joy and were carried on the wings of rapture into the very presence of God

himself where they were given the privilege of seeing visions and receiving revelations which they could scarcely describe. They experienced a closeness and fellowship with God which tore at the heart. I
have, for example, a description of one such ecstatic experience which,
as a matter of fact, characterized the leader of the Welsh revival in 1904.

> One Friday night last spring, when praying by my bedside before retir-
> ing, I was taken up to a great expanse without time and space. It was
> communion with God. Before this I had a far off God. I was frightened
> that night but never since. So great was my shivering that I rocked the
> bed. And my brother, being awakened, took hold of me thinking I was
> ill. After that experience, I was awakened every night a little after one
> o'clock. This was most strange for, through the years, I slept like a rock
> and no disturbance in my room would awaken me. From that hour, I
> was taken up into the divine fellowship for about four hours. What it
> was, I cannot tell you except that it was divine. About five o'clock I was
> again allowed to sleep on till about nine. At this time I was again taken
> up into the same experience in the early hours of the morning, until
> about twelve or one o'clock. This went on for about three months (*The
> Welsh Revival of 1904*, Efion Evans, Evangelical Press of Wales, 1969).

This is by no means the most unusual of experiences, literally hundreds and hundreds of which are reported in the literature on revival.
And this was, indeed, the state to which revivals were intended to lead
one. The prayers that ascend today from the hearts and minds of so
many have this as the goal: that an experience such as this would become the experience of every believer.

One leader of the Welsh revival received a vision of "unprecedented
excitement" which is described as follows: "His spiritual perception had
been considerably developed and he could not fail to draw inspiration
and motivation from those supernatural, extrabiblical [notice the ter-
minology, HH] revelations. There was no question in my mind as to
their authenticity or authority" (Evans, 191). The result of that kind of
an experience is one in which one withdraws, as it were, into direct
union and fellowship with God and which gives to one a rapturous joy
and an other-worldly peace and tranquility of heart.

This experience brings one into such close union with God and experience of fellowship with him that it defies human description. It is a
wholly emotional and completely ethereal absorption into mystical
union with God himself, and it has resulted in a kind of revival in the

church, which manifested itself in a new zeal for the cause of God and a new zeal for missions and for the conversion of souls, and has brought the church to a state of spiritual strength such as she had not known in all of her existence.

This is what is meant by revival. When you hear prayers for revival, when you hear people speak of the need of revival, this is what is meant. This is the *unusual* work of the Holy Spirit which characterizes revivals.

This is what revivalism is all about. I know that there have been those who have warned of the excesses of revivalism. Jonathan Edwards himself wrote a book in which he specifically condemned the excesses that were present in the New England revivals. And Samuel Miller, the old Presbyterian Calvinist, himself an ardent defender of revival, delivered an extraordinarily lengthy speech warning against its dangers. Nevertheless, this is what characterizes revivals. These are the unusual outpourings of the Spirit. Those who engage in such things have made a return to Roman Catholic mysticism.

That kind of revival is what men seek for today as the cure for the church's ills. That kind of revival is inimical to the Reformed faith and must be condemned by every believer who loves the truth of the Scriptures.

The Mysticism of Revivals

What are the Scriptural and confessional objections to revival? The answer to that question is, in the first place, that revival is characterized by mysticism.

Mysticism has an interesting history in the church of the Lord Jesus Christ. It first made an appearance very early in the history of the church, as early as the third century; and the great church father, Tertullian, made the mistake at the end of his life of joining a mystical movement called Montanism. But mysticism did not really come into its own until the Middle Ages, during the period when the Roman Catholic Church was ruling supreme in Europe. That is striking because the mysticism of the Middle Ages was also a reaction to worldliness and carnality in the church and to the dead, cold formalism of Roman Catholicism. The mysticism that developed in the Middle Ages, however, had a highly developed theology. I cannot go into many of the details, but it is very interesting that mysticism had as its goal what is called "union with God," a phrase which sounds not only perfectly innocuous, but also like something eminently desirable in the life of the child of God. What could be better than union with God? Mysticism spoke of this, however, in such a way that union with God was attained through a series of steps which one had to go through in order to reach that high goal. Now, without going into any kind of detail concerning these steps, the last step that was to be taken before union with God could be achieved was called by the medieval mystics "the dark night of the soul." It was as if the steps to union with God led first of all downward to the dark night of the soul, only then to spring out of the dark night into that rapturous, joyful, other-worldly union with God.

It is very striking that the Roman Catholic idea of mysticism found a certain analogy in the thinking of the Puritans. Now, I know when I say anything bad about the Puritans it is almost as if I am beating a sacred cow. And I do not want to leave the impression that the Puritans are of no value. The works which they produced, especially the early Puritans, can be read even today by any child of God with a great deal of pleasure and spiritual benefit, so much so that I would urge you to read Puritan literature. And, in fact, I can think of little devotional literature that is better to read than Puritan literature. That does not alter the fact, however, that they were wrong, desperately wrong, in their conception of Christian experience. What the medieval mystics called the "dark night of the soul" became, in Puritan thinking, "the conviction of sin" or "being under the conviction of sin."

But the mysticism of Roman Catholicism was carried directly into Protestant thinking through the revivals of John Wesley in the 18th century. It may surprise you to know that prior to his Aldersgate experience, at which time John Wesley considered himself to have been converted, he steeped himself deeply in the writings of Roman Catholic medieval mystics, read them avidly, devoured them, as he says, and was even instrumental in publishing a great number of these Roman Catholic works. That mysticism stayed with him all his life. Robert G. Tuttle, in a book titled *Mysticism in the Wesleyan Tradition,* points this out very clearly. Tuttle, by the way, is himself a Methodist, an admirer of John Wesley, and is pleased and thankful for the fact that Roman Catholic mysticism became a part of Protestant thinking through the work of John Wesley.

John Wesley and the Puritans are the fathers of revivalism. In fact, so much is that so that an acknowledged authority on revivalism goes so far as to say: "The Puritans gave to the English-speaking world what may be called the classical school of Protestant belief in revival" *(The Puritan Hope,* Iain Murray, The Banner of Truth, 1971, 4).

All the trappings of mysticism are present in revivalism. The idea of "the dark night of the soul" has become known as "being under the conviction of sin"; the experiences according to which one defines genuine conversion are the experiences of the mystics; the rapturous joys that grip one and that carry one to realms unknown and into union with God are the rapturous joys of the mystics of the Middle Ages. The emphasis on visions and dreams, special, extra-Biblical revelations, the guidance of the Spirit through these revelations – all these things belong to the tradition of mysticism.

It is interesting that a crucial and integral part of mysticism was also the performing of miracles – exorcism and miracles of healing. I say this because that immediately ought to bring to our minds the obvious relationship revivalism and the charismatic movement. These two have much in common – so much in common, in fact, that those who promote revivals even go so far as to say that before a revival can come it is necessary that the church have a second outpouring of the Spirit. This is charismatic language indeed! In fact, those who promote revivals have, in many instances, been, if not supporters, then encouragers of the charismatic movement, and unwilling to condemn it. Are you aware of the fact, for example, that Dr. Martyn Lloyd-Jones was himself a strong supporter of the charismatic movement? You can find that in several of his books. You can understand some of what he says, for example, in his sermons on *Ephesians,* especially *Ephesians* 4 and 5, if you are aware of his leanings toward the charismatics. There has always been the closest relationship between revivalism and the charismatic movement because both are characterized by mysticism.

One can perhaps understand the need people feel for revival. In these times of spiritual darkness and lethargy, when our own spiritual life is so cold, there is something about revivalism that brings with it a promise that is eminently attractive. By a cultivation of the inner life, by a special effusion of the Spirit, by an outpouring from above in which the Spirit enters the heart in unusual and powerful ways, one is transported into the very presence of God Himself, there to be united with God in this totally other worldly, rapturous, emotional joy which transcends anything that can be found in this world. There is a siren song in that.

There is a particularly sensuous appeal of Satan in that sort of thing. And the colder one's spiritual life becomes, the more that sort of a thing seems to be desirable.

Nevertheless, mysticism is contrary to the Scriptures and the Reformed faith. It is contrary to the Reformed faith because mysticism, in all its forms, places all the emphasis on the human emotions. It is a theology of emotions, a theology of feeling. Perhaps that is exactly its great appeal in our day. We live in an age in which feeling is everything. Feeling is the end-all and be-all of life. And when this siren song of rapturous, emotional joy of union with God comes dinning in our ears at times when our lives seem barren and cold, it seems as if the emotional high of mysticism is eminently desirable. But it is a siren song that leads to destruction.

Mysticism has little regard for doctrine. With its emphasis on feelings and emotions, it makes light of the knowledge of the truth. In this respect it also stands at odds with the Reformed faith. The Reformed faith has always emphasized the importance of knowledge as an essential part of faith. It takes seriously the warning in Hosea – "My people perish for lack of *knowledge.*" The Reformed faith believes in the importance of doctrinal soundness, of confession of faith in harmony with the Scriptures. Revivalism shows little interest in doctrine; it is much more concerned about emotions.

This manifests itself in two ways. It manifests itself first of all in a carelessness or indifference toward doctrine, even to the point where it considers doctrine a detriment to true spiritual life. Consider, for example, this quote which is taken from the book of Ian R. K. Paisley. He writes about someone involved in a revival who was asked concerning whether or not he was a Calvinist. This is his answer: "I would not wish to be more or less a Calvinist than our Lord and his apostles. But I do not care to talk on mere points of doctrine. I would rather speak of the experience of salvation in the soul" (*The '59 Revival,* Valiant Press, London).

Secondly, this influence of mysticism on revivalism often results in crass and false doctrine. This can be illustrated from *The Memoirs of Charles G. Finney* (Zondervan Publishing, 1989). Charles Finney was a revivalist of the 19th century who worked in the Northeastern part of the United States. In these *Memoirs* he tells us of how he repudiated all the fundamental doctrines of Calvinism, including the vicarious nature of the atonement of Jesus Christ, in the interests of preaching revival. He writes:

> But my studies, so far as he was concerned as my teacher, were little else than controversy. He held to the Presbyterian doctrine of original sin, or that the human *constitution* was morally depraved. He held also, that men were utterly unable to comply with the terms of the Gospel, to repent, to believe, or to do anything that God required them to do. That while they were free to all evil, in the sense of being able to commit any amount of sin, yet they were not free in regard to all that was good. That God had condemned men for their sinful *nature,* and for this, as well as for their transgressions, they deserved eternal death, and were under condemnation. He held also that the influences of the Spirit of God on the minds of men were *physical* acting directly upon the substance of the soul. That men were passive in regeneration; and in short he held all those doctrines that logically flow from the fact of a nature *sinful in itself.* These doctrines I could not receive. I could not receive his views on the subject of atonement, regeneration, faith, repentance, the slavery of the will, or any of their kindred doctrines (48).

Throughout the book Finney consistently repudiates and even mocks Calvinism and all it stands for. He speaks openly of free will and of universal atonement, and even embraces the Arminian doctrine of perfectionism – that the converted man can free himself from all known sins. Interestingly enough, he even explains that he adopted what is today known as "the altar call" (which he called "summoning sinners to the anxious seat") because he believed that this method would be a solution to the constant backsliding of those who earlier had claimed to be converted. Revivalism substitutes emotions for sound doctrine. Although this cannot be said of all revivalists, notably of such men as Jonathan Edwards and George Whitefield, nevertheless for the most part revivalism at best is disinterested in and careless of doctrine; at worst, it is an enemy of the truth.

Faith, as our *Heidelberg Catechism* says, is, though also confidence in Christ, a certain knowledge whereby I hold for true all that God has revealed in His Word. That is the amazing wonder of the Scriptures. When I appropriate the Scriptures and lay hold on their truth and receive as true all that they teach, I lay hold on Christ. Not by some emotional high, not by reducing religion to some kind of a spiritual shot of adrenaline, but by laying hold on the truth of the Scriptures.

And in that way I lay hold on Christ and on God and live in fellowship with him. Faith, the faith that brings assurance, true assurance, an assurance not built on the shifting sands of emotional experiences which are here today and gone tomorrow, but a faith which is solid as a rock, a faith which withstands the onslaughts of Satan, a faith which says with Job, "I know that my Redeemer lives," a faith which is the calm, quiet confidence of victory over all our enemies, over the devil and his hosts and even our own flesh, the faith which is the victory that overcomes the world – *that* faith is knowledge.

A Wrong View of Conversion

All of that brings us to another objection which a Reformed man brings against revivals: the theory of conversion which is inherent in revivalism and which is specifically taught by those who still promote revivals today.

Once again I have to go back to the Puritans, specifically the later Puritans, the Puritans at the time of the Marrow controversy in the early part of the 18th century, including the so-called Marrow men: Thomas Boston, the Erskine brothers, and others. They emphasized that when the law was preached in the church then the Holy Spirit could make the law and the preaching of the law instrumental in bringing people under the conviction of sin. Read, for example, the diary of Robert M'Cheyne, an old Puritan divine of this school, and you will find a diary that is filled with this sort of thing. Under the preaching of the law, men came under the conviction of sin. That conviction of sin manifested itself in all of these strange phenomena which we described. Sometimes this happened to a greater degree than others, but all agree that law-preaching manifested itself especially in such terrible fears of Hell and of damnation which so gripped the soul of a man that he was overcome by them. He saw that his condition was hopeless, he understood that the only way of escape was by a power greater than himself. This was how the Spirit worked, first of all, through the preaching of the law.

The wrong of this was that this conviction of sin was apart from the work of regeneration. It was what the Puritans called "preparatory grace." It was what sometimes was called the "work of the Spirit in His prompting," a phrase that carried with it the idea that the sinner was prompted to seek Christ. Or, it created a man who was sometimes called "a seeker" – not regenerated, not converted, not saved, not a child of God, but one who possessed that work of the Holy Spirit which, as a preparatory grace, enabled him to "seek" for salvation. To that man had to be directed the preaching of the Gospel which brought the urgency of taking Christ, taking hold of Christ, or, as the Puritans were wont to express it, "closing with Christ." But whether one under the conviction of sin would actually "close with Christ" was not certain. He could feel deep sorrow for sin. He could experience the torments of a guilty conscience. He could long for deliverance and salvation. But the outcome remained uncertain and the possibility existed that he could still go to Hell.

It was in this context that the Puritans developed their ideas concerning the free offer of the Gospel. One must preach the Gospel and preach Christ's love for all, urging men to "close with Christ." This could only be done on the basis of the fact that in some sense Christ, as Thomas Boston put it, was dead for all. Boston did not want to say that Christ died for all. He insisted only that Christ was dead for all. But in this way Christ's death could serve as a "warrant" to all who heard the Gospel to close with Christ. None could say: I will not close with Christ because he did not die for me. Salvation was offered freely.

The preaching of the Gospel, therefore, which urged one to take Christ into his life, was preaching that made salvation dependent upon the individual, who was put in this state of preparatory grace, whether or not at that crucial point in his life he would indeed take Christ into his heart. What he did would result in his salvation or in his damnation. Such a one, in other words, who had these promptings of the Spirit, who was prepared – the Puritans, as you know, developed a theory of "preparationism" – by the Spirit, and put in a spiritual frame of mind either to accept Christ or reject Him, is now left with a decision resting in his hands.

That is their view of conversion. But that view is fundamentally Arminian. It places the salvation of the sinner in the hands of the sinner himself. It places the salvation of the sinner in the choice or the free will of man, although it is a will prepared by the Spirit. It makes salvation less than sovereign and is, therefore, opposed to the Reformed faith.

This error, which arose 150 years after Dordt, is already condemned in the *Canons of Dordt*: "We condemn the errors of those who teach that the unregenerate man is not really nor utterly dead in sin, nor destitute of all powers unto spiritual good, but that he can yet hunger and thirst after righteousness and life, and offer the sacrifice of a contrite and broken spirit, which is pleasing to God" (*Canons* III, IV, B, Article 3). That, says our *Canons*, is the error of Arminianism which puts salvation in the hands of man.

Revivalism adopts this same view of conversion and thus holds to the false doctrine that salvation rests in man's hands. I know that the Puritans would dispute this because they want to appear as proponents of sovereign grace. Nevertheless, they teach that there is a common grace worked by the Spirit in the hearts of all, which grace puts all in a spiritual position to accept or reject Christ. Christ is presented through preaching as eminently desirable, as the one who can deliver sinners. And sinners, on their part, though thirsting for deliverance, though seeing the riches of Christ, though understanding that in Him alone is escape from sin, though even praying to be regenerated, may nevertheless still be lost.

This brings us to the theory of conversion promoted by revivalism in a more specific way. Conversion is, in revivalism, something that is accompanied by some kind of unusual and extraordinary experience. This element has always characterized mysticism, either in medieval Roman Catholic thought, in John Wesley's work, in Puritan theology, or in revivalistic thinking today. It so happened, when revivals took place, that those who supposedly came to this pinnacle of rapturous joy when the soul was united to God had to undergo a very rigorous examination on the part of the ministers and the elders of the church to determine whether such a conversion was indeed genuine. And the criterion which was used to determine the genuineness of such a conversion was the genuineness of the experience through which one passed. All of this presupposed not only that a man could give a rational and intelligible account of his conversion, but also that it was within the power of the minister and the elders of the church to evaluate that conversion, to pass judgment upon it, and to determine whether or not it was indeed genuine. They believed that the devil was lurking about, especially at times of revival, attempting to imitate the work of the Holy Spirit and giving people wrong experiences, experiences that arose out of delusion. The devil would bring people to a false and carnal security in which they had no faith in Christ at all, but an imitation, a counterfeit faith that would only lead them more rapidly to Hell. The ministers and elders, especially in the Great Awakening during the time of Jonathan Edwards, would, surprisingly enough, claim to be able to tell with almost one hundred percent accuracy, whether the conversion of a particular individual was indeed genuine or whether it was devil-inspired. So many were the conversions and so busy were the ministers and elders that sometimes these examinations went on, during periods of revival, day and night. There was no time for preaching. There was no time for pastoral work. There was no time for sermon preparation, because of the vast amounts of time which were consumed examining the character of conversions.

Further, such conversions, sudden and profound, not only became the test of whether one was a genuine Christian, but also served as the ground of personal assurance of salvation. Indeed, without such extraordinary experiences, assurance was impossible.

All of this is inimical to the Reformed faith. No man who is genuinely Reformed can teach that kind of doctrine of conversion. The Reformed doctrine of conversion is something quite different.

Conversion in Reformed thought, and this is explicitly stated in our *Heidelberg Catechism* in Lord's Day 33, is not an unusual, once-for-all, extraordinary, inexplicable experience through which one passes from the "dark night of the soul" to rapturous union with God. But conversion is a daily characteristic of a believing, regenerated child of God. Conversion ought to take place and does take place every day of his life. As long as the believing child of God lives here in this world, he is a believer who does battle with sin, not only in the world about him, but in his own flesh. He is not yet perfect. He is not yet brought into the everlasting joy that shall be the inheritance of the people of God in glory. Here he is in the church militant. Here he must do battle. Here he carries with him the body of his death.

Conversion is, as Lord's Day 33 expresses it, "a daily killing of the old man." That is, conversion is a deep, daily sorrow for sin. Yet it is also a quickening of the new man. It is a daily joy that one finds at the foot of the cross when one brings the burden of his sins to Calvary. A daily conversion, a daily battle, a daily fleeing from sin, a daily hastening to the cross with an increasingly urgent longing to leave this life (which is nothing but a continual death) in order to be at last in the everlasting perfection of Heaven – that is conversion.

Revivalism scorns this. It mocks the humble sinner, the humble child of God who fights daily against the sins of his flesh. It has no time or patience for the daily battle which the believer fights. It looks for the spectacular. Like Elijah of old it has never learned that God is not in the earthquake, in the fire, or in the strong wind; but only in the still, small voice. Revivalism has not learned what Zechariah had to learn: "Not by might, not by power, but by My Spirit, saith Jehovah of Hosts. Who hath despised the day of little things?" Looking for the spectacular, for the exciting, for the unusual, looking for that which can serve as some kind of ground for assurance, they find nothing but sinking sand, shaky ground on which to build one's faith and hope and joy. Nevertheless, conversion is in the daily, bitter, and fierce battle against sin; it is carried on in the hearts and lives of the elect children of the covenant; it is characteristic of the faithful child of God all his life long. This is the work of conversion and this is the true work of the Spirit.

We must not mock this. We must not turn away from this as if it is a kind of carnal security, a self-deception, an easy religion. It is not. It is the hard way. It is the way of daily struggle. It is the way of groanings and tears. It is the way of fleeing to the cross. It is the way of casting one's self down in shame at the foot of Calvary. But it is the way of the joy of salvation in the blood of Christ. And that Christ is the Christ that is appropriated by faith....

Conclusion

Do we pray for revival? No. May we pray for revival? No. Does this mean that we are not troubled about the condition of the church? We ought to be and we are. And this precisely means that the Reformed church is and always ought to be a reforming church.

But we must not confuse church reformation with revivalism. The two are completely different. Church reformation is the calling of all the people of God always. But church reformation begins with the child of God on his knees confessing his sins. There is not anything more important in church reformation than this. If it does not start with the Christian daily confessing his sins, there will not be church reformation.

In confessing his sin and hastening to the cross one has the beginnings of true church reformation. On our knees we seek the welfare of Zion. On our knees we seek the peace of Jerusalem. We do not pray for revival, unusual outpourings of the Spirit, but we pray for the courage and the grace of the Holy Spirit to be steadfast in the battle; not to waver, not to compromise, not to be overcome with fear, but to stand fast in the cause of the truth.

And if it comes to that, as it has in the church of Christ many times, one must reform the church by leaving a church that will have nothing any longer of the truth of the Gospel. That is reformation. That is what we seek. That is our calling. May God grant that to us, may God grant that mighty work of the Spirit which brings the sinner to his knees but which makes him strong and courageous in the assurance of the cross in the battle in the church here below.

26

The Great Revival of Religion, 1740-1745[1]

Charles Hodge

THE GREAT REVIVAL, which about a hundred years ago visited so extensively the American churches, is so much implicated with the ecclesiastical history of our own denomination, that the latter cannot be understood without some knowledge of the former. The controversies connected with the revival are identical with the disputes which resulted in the schism which divided the Presbyterian Church in 1741. Before entering, therefore, upon the history of that event, it will be necessary to present the reader with a general survey of that great religious excitement, which arrayed in conflicting parties the friends of religion in every part of the country. This division of sentiment could hardly have occurred, had the revival been one of unmingled purity. Such a revival, however, the church has never seen. Every luminous body is sure to cause shadows in every direction and of every form. Where the Son of Man sows wheat, the evil one is sure to sow tares. It must be so. For it needs be that offences come, though woe to those by whom they come.

The men who, either from their character or circumstances, are led to take the most prominent part, during such seasons of excitement, are themselves often carried into extremes, or are so connected with the extravagant, that they are sometimes the last to perceive and the slowest to oppose the evils which so frequently mar the work of God, and burn over the fields which he had just watered with his grace. Opposition to these evils commonly comes from a different quarter; from wise and good men who have been kept out of the focus of the

1. This is an excerpt from Charles Hodge's *Constitutional History of the Presbyterian Church in the United States*. This essay is reprinted from *The Trinity Review*.

excitement. And it is well that there are such opposers, else the church would soon be over-run with fanaticism.

The term "revival" is commonly used in a very comprehensive sense. It includes all the phenomena attending a general religious excitement; as well those which spring from God, as those which owe their origin to the infirmities of men. Hence those who favor the work, for what there is divine in it, are often injuriously regarded as the patrons of its concomitant irregularities, and those who oppose what is unreasonable about it, are as improperly denounced as the enemies of religion. It is, therefore, only one expression of that fanaticism which haunts the spirit of revivals, to make such a work a touchstone of character; to regard all as good who favor it, and all as bad who oppose it. That this should be done during the continuance of the excitement, is an evil to be expected and pardoned; but to commit the same error in the historical review of such a period, would admit of no excuse....

That the state of religion did rapidly decline after the revival, we have abundant and melancholy evidence. Even as early as [March] 1744, President [Jonathan] Edwards says, "the present state of things in New England is, on many accounts, very melancholy. There is a vast alteration within two years." God, he adds, was provoked at the spiritual pride and self-confidence of the people, and withdrew from them, and "the enemy has come in like a flood in various respects, until the deluge has overwhelmed the whole land. There had been from the beginning a great mixture, especially in some places, of false experiences and false religion with true; but from this time the mixture became much greater, and many were led away into sad delusions."

In another letter, dated May 23, 1749, he says, "as to the state of religion in these parts of the world, it is, in general, very dark and melancholy." In the preceding October, when writing to Mr. Erskine of Edinburgh, he communicates to him an extract from a letter to himself from Governor Belcher of New Jersey, who says, "The accounts which I receive from time to time, give me too much reason to fear that Arminianism, Arianism, and even Socinianism, in destruction to the doctrines of grace, are daily propagated in the New England colleges."

In 1750, he writes to Mr. McCulloch in the following melancholy strain:

> It is indeed now a sorrowful time on this side of the ocean. Iniquity abounds, and the love of many waxes cold. Multitudes of fair and high professors, in one place or another, have sadly backslidden, sinners are

desperately hardened; experimental religion is more than ever out of credit with far the greater part; and the doctrines of grace and those principles in religion which do chiefly concern the power of godliness, are far more than ever, discarded. Arminianism and Pelagianism have made a strange progress within a few years. The Church of England in New England, is, I suppose, treble what it was seven years ago. Many professors are gone off to great lengths in enthusiasm and extravagance in their notions and practices. Great contentions, separations, and confusions in our religious state prevail in many parts of the land.

In 1752, in a letter to Mr. Gillespie, relating to his difficulties with his congregation, he says, "It is to be considered that these things have happened when God is greatly withdrawn, and religion was very low, not only in Northampton, but all over New England." The church in Stonington, Connecticut, was torn to pieces by fanaticism, and a separate congregation erected. The excellent pastor of that place, the Rev. Mr. Fish, a warm friend of the revival, exerted himself in vain to stem the torrent; "and other ministers," he says,

> that came to our help carried on the same design of correcting the false notions which new converts had embraced about religion; particularly the late judicious and excellent Mr. David Brainerd, who, in this desk, exposed and remonstrated against the same errors, and told me that such false religion as prevailed among my people, had spread almost all the land over.

That false doctrines increasingly prevailed after the revival is strongly asserted in the letter of Edwards already quoted. Other proofs of the fact might easily be adduced. The Rev. John Graham, in a sermon preached in 1745, complains that many had gone forth who preached not the Gospel of our Lord Jesus Christ, who denied the doctrines of personal election, of original sin, of justification by the perfect righteousness of Christ, imputed by an act of sovereign grace; instantaneous regeneration by the divine energy of special irresistible grace; and of the final perseverance of the saints. "The Pelagian and Arminian errors," he adds,

> cannot but be exceedingly pleasing to the devil; and such as preach them most successfully, are the greatest instruments of supporting his kingdom in the world, and his dominion in the hearts of men. What necessity is then laid upon ministers of the Gospel, who see what danger

precious souls are in by the spread and prevalence of such pernicious errors, which are like a fog or smoke, sent from the bottomless pit on purpose to prevent the shining of the Gospel sun into the hearts of men, to be very close and strict in searching into the principles of such as are candidates for the sacred ministry.

Somewhat later, President Clap found it necessary, on account of the increasing prevalence of error, to write a formal defense of the doctrines of the New England churches. The leading features of the new divinity, of which he complained, were,

1. That the happiness of the creature is the great end of creation.

2. That self-love is the ultimate foundation of all moral obligation.

3. That God cannot control the acts of free agents.

4. That he cannot certainly foreknow, much less decree such acts.

5. That all sin consists in the voluntary transgression of known law; that Adam was not created in a state of holiness, but only had a power to act virtuously; and every man is now born into the world in as perfect a state of rectitude as that in which Adam was created.

6. The actions of moral agents are not free, and consequently have no moral character, unless such agents have plenary ability and full power to the contrary. Hence it is absurd to suppose that God should implant grace or holiness in any man, or keep him from sin.

7. Christ did not die to make satisfaction for sin, and hence there is no need to suppose him to be essentially God, but only a perfect and glorious creature. No great weight ought to be laid upon men's believing Christ's divinity, or any of those speculative points which have been generally received as the peculiar and fundamental doctrines of the Gospel; but we ought to have charity for all men, let their speculative principles be what they may, provided they lead moral lives.

These doctrines were a great advance of the Arminian or even Pelagian errors over which President Edwards lamented, and show what might indeed be expected, that the churches had gone from bad to worse.

This is certainly a gloomy picture of the state of religion so soon after a revival, regarded as the most extensive the country had ever known. It is drawn not by the enemies, but in a great measure by the best and wisest friends of religion....

This low state of religion, and extensive departure from the truth, in that part of the country where the revival had been most extensive, is certainly *prima facie* proof that there must have been something very wrong in the revival itself. It may, however, be said, that the decay of religion through the land generally, is perfectly consistent with the purity of the revival and the flourishing state of those particular churches which had experienced its influence. The facts of the case, unfortunately, do not allow us the benefit of this assumption. It is no doubt true, that in some congregations...religion was in a very desirable state, in the midst of the general decline; but it is no less certain, that in many instances, in the very places where the revival was the most remarkable, the declension was the most serious. Northampton itself may be taken as an illustration.

> That church was pre-eminently a city set upon a hill. Mr. [Solomon] Stoddard, during a remarkably successful ministry, had drawn the attention of American Christians for fifty-seven years. He had also been advantageously known in the mother country. Mr. Edwards had been their minister for twenty-three years. In the respect paid to him as a profound theological writer, he had no competitor from the first establishment of the colonies, and even then, could scarcely find one in England or Scotland. He had also as high a reputation for elevated and fervent piety as for superiority of talents. During the preceding eighty years, that church had been favored with more numerous and powerful revivals than any church in Christendom.

This account, though given in the characteristically large style of Edwards' biographer, is no doubt in the main correct. Here then, if anywhere, we might look for the most favorable results of the revival. During the religious excitement in the years 1734 and 1735, within six months, more than three hundred persons, whom Edwards regarded as true converts, were received into the church. In 1736, the whole number of communicants was six hundred and twenty, including almost the whole adult population of the town. The revival of 1740-1742, was considered still more pure and wonderful. What was the state of religion in this highly favored place, soon after all these revivals? In the judgment of Edwards himself it was deplorably low, both as to Christian temper and adherence to sound doctrine. In 1744, when an attempt was made to administer discipline somewhat injudiciously, it is true, as to the manner of doing it, it was strenuously resisted. The whole town was thrown into a blaze. Some of the accused "refused to appear; others, who did appear, behaved with a great degree of insolence, and contempt for the authority of the church and little or nothing could be done further in the affair." From 1744 to 1748, not a single application was made for admission to the church. In 1749, when it became known that Edwards had adopted the opinion that none ought to be admitted to the Lord's Supper but such as gave satisfactory evidence of conversion, "the town was put into a great ferment; and before he was heard in his own defense, or it was known by many what his principles were, the general cry was to have him dismissed." That diversity of opinion between a pastor and his people on such a practical point, should lead to a desire for a separation, might not be very discreditable to either party. But when it is known that on this occasion the church treated such a man as Edwards, who not only was an object of veneration to the Christian public, but who behaved in the most Christian manner through the whole controversy, with the greatest injustice and malignity, it must be regarded as proof positive of the low state of religion among them. They refused to allow him to preach on the subject in dispute; they pertinaciously resisted the calling of a fair council to decide the matter; they insisted on his dismission without making any provision for his expensive family; and when his dismission had taken place, they shut their pulpit against him even when they had no one else to occupy it. On the unfounded suspicion that he intended to form a new church in the town, they presented a remonstrance containing direct, grievous, and criminal charges against him, which were really gross slanders. This was not the offence of a few individuals. Almost the whole church took part against Edwards. Such treatment of such a man certainly proves a lamentable state of religion, as far as Christian temper is concerned. With regard to orthodoxy the case was not much better. Edwards in a letter to Erskine, in 1750, says, there seemed to be the utmost danger that the younger generation in Northampton would be carried away with Arminianism as with a flood; that it was not likely that the church would choose a Calvinist as his successor, and that the older people were never so indifferent to things of this nature.

The explanation which has been proposed of these extraordinary facts is altogether unsatisfactory. It is said that the custom which had long prevailed in Northampton, of admitting those to the Lord's Supper who gave no sufficient evidence of conversion, sufficiently accounts for all this ill conduct on the part of the church. But where were the three hundred members whom Edwards regarded as "savingly brought home to Christ," within six months, during the revival of 1734-5? Where were all the fruits of the still more powerful revival of 1740-42? The vast majority of the members of the church had been brought in by Edwards himself and of their conversion he considered himself as having sufficient evidence. The habit of free admission to the Lord's table, therefore, by no means accounts for the painful facts above referred to. After all that had been published to the world of the power of religion in Northampton, the Christian public were entitled to expect to see the people established in the truth, and an example in holiness to other churches. Instead of this, we find them resisting the administration of discipline in less than eighteen months after the revival; alienated from their pastor; indifferent to the truth, and soon driving from among them the first minister of his age, with every aggravating circumstance of ingratitude and injustice. It is all in vain to talk of the religion of such a people. This fact demonstrates that there must have been something wrong in these revivals, even under the eye and guidance of Edwards, from the beginning. There must have been many spurious conversions, and much false religion which at the time were regarded as genuine. This assumption is nothing more than the facts demand, nor more than Edwards himself frequently acknowledged.

There is the most marked difference between those of his writings which were published during the revival, and those which appeared after the excitement had subsided. In the account which he wrote in 1736, of the revival of the two preceding years, there is scarcely an intimation of any dissatisfaction with its character. Yet, in 1743, he speaks of it as having been very far from pure; and in 1751 he lamented his not having had boldness to testify against some glaring false appearances, and counterfeits of religion, which became a dreadful source of spiritual pride, and of other things exceedingly contrary to true Christianity. In like manner, in the contemporaneous account of the revival of 1740-42 he complains of nothing but of some disorders introduced toward the close of the year 1742, from other congregations; whereas, in his letters written a few years later, he acknowledges that many things were wrong from the first. This is, indeed, very natural. While in the midst of the excitement, seeing and feeling much that he could not but regard as the result of divine influence, he was led to encourage many things which soon brought forth the bitter fruits of disorder and corruption. His correspondence affords abundant evidence how fully sensible he became of the extent to which this revival was corrupted with false religion. When his Scottish friends had informed him of the religious excitement then prevailing in some parts of Holland, he wrote to Mr. Erskine, June 28, 1751, expressing his anxiety that the people might be led to "distinguish between true and false religion; between those experiences which are from the saving influence of the Spirit of God, and those which are from Satan transformed into an angel of light." He wished that they had the experience of the church of God in America, on this subject, as they would need all the warning that could be given them. "The temptation," he adds, "to religious people in such a state to countenance the glaring, shining counterfeits of religion, without distinguishing them from the reality," is so strong that they can hardly be restrained from committing the mistake. In reference to the wish of the Dutch ministers to have attestations of the permanently good effects of the revivals in Scotland and America, he says,

> I think it fit they should know the very truth in the case, and that things should be represented neither better nor worse than they are. If they should be represented worse, it would give encouragement to unreasonable opposers; if better it might prevent a most necessary caution among the true friends of the awakening. There are, undoubtedly, very many instances in New England, in the whole, of the perseverance of such as were thought to have received the saving benefit of the late revivals of religion, and of their continuing to walk in newness of life as becomes saints; instances which are incontestable. But I believe the proportion here is not so great as in Scotland. I cannot say that the greater portion of the supposed converts give reason to suppose, by their conversation, that they are true converts. The proportion may, perhaps, be more truly represented by the proportion of the blossoms on a tree which abide and come to mature fruit, to the whole number of blossoms in the spring....

These passages give a melancholy account of the results of the great religious excitement now under consideration. In the preceding estimate, Edwards does not speak of those who were merely awakened, or who were for a time the subjects of serious impressions, but of those who were regarded as converts. It is of these, he says, that only a small portion proved to be genuine. If this be so, it certainly proves that apart from the errors and disorders universally reprobated by the judicious friends of the revival, there were serious mistakes committed by those friends themselves. If it was difficult then, it must be much more so now, to detect the causes of the spurious excitement which then so extensively prevailed. Two of these causes, however, are so obvious that they can hardly fail to attract attention. These were laying too much stress on feelings excited through the imagination, and allowing, and indeed encouraging the free and loud manifestation of feeling during public or social worship.

It is one office of the imagination to recall and reconstruct conceptions of any object which affects the senses. It is by this faculty that we form mental images, or lively conceptions of the objects of sense. It is to this power that graphic descriptions of absent or imaginary scenes are addressed; and it is by the agency of this faculty that oratory, for the most part, exerts its power over the feelings. That a very large portion of the emotions so strongly felt, and so openly expressed during this revival, arose not from spiritual apprehensions of divine truth, but from mere imaginations or mental images, is evident from two sources; first, from the descriptions given of the exercises themselves; and, secondly, from the avowal of the propriety of this method of exciting feeling in connection with religious subjects. Had we no definite information as to this point, the general account of the effects of the preaching of [George] Whitefield and others would satisfy us that, to a very great extent, the results were to be attributed to no supernatural influence, but to the natural powers of oratory. There is no subject so universally interesting as religion, and therefore there is none which can be made the cause of such general and powerful excitement; yet it cannot be doubted that had Whitefield selected any worthy object of benevolence or patriotism, he would have produced a great commotion in the public mind. When therefore he came to address men on a subject of infinite importance, of the deepest personal concern, we need not be surprised at the effects which he produced. The man who could thaw the icy propriety of [Viscount] Bolingbroke; who could extort gold from [Benjamin] Franklin, though armed with a determination to give only copper; or set Hopkinson, for the time being, beside himself; might be expected to control at will the passions of the young, the ignorant, and the excitable. It was far from being denied or questioned that his preaching was, to an extraordinary degree, attended by a divine influence. That influence is needed to account for the repentance, faith, and holiness, which were in a multitude of cases the result of his ministrations.

It is not needed, however, to account for the loud outcries, faintings, and bodily agitations which attended his course. These are sufficiently explained by his vivid descriptions of Hell, of Heaven, of Christ, and a future Judgment, addressed to congregated thousands of excited and sympathizing hearers, accompanied by the most stirring appeals to the passions, and all delivered with consummate skill of voice and manner. It was under such preaching, the people, as he tells us, soon began to melt, to weep, to cry out, and to faint. That a large part of these results was to be attributed to natural causes, can hardly be doubted; yet who could discriminate between what was the work of the orator, and what was the work of the Spirit of God? Who could tell whether the sorrow, the joy, and the love expressed and felt, were the result of lively imaginations, or of spiritual apprehensions of the truth? The two classes of exercises were confounded; both passed for genuine, until bitter experience disclosed the mistake. It is evident that Whitefield had no opportunity of making any such discrimination; and that for the time at least, he regarded all meltings, all sorrowing, and all joy following his fervid preaching, as evidence of the divine presence. It is not, however, these general accounts so much as the more particular detail of the exercises of the subjects of this revival, which shows how much of the feeling then prevalent was due to the imagination. Thus Edwards speaks of those who had a lively picture in their minds of Hell as a dreadful furnace, of Christ as one of glorious majesty, and of a sweet and gracious aspect, or as of one hanging on the cross, and blood running from his wounds. Great stress was often laid upon these views of "an outward Christ," and upon the feeling resulting from such conceptions. Though Edwards was from the beginning fully aware that there was no true religion in such exercises; and though in his work on the *Affections,* written in 1746, he enters largely on the danger of delusion from this source, it is very evident that at this period he was not properly impressed with a sense of guarding against this evil. Just after stating how commonly such mental pictures were cherished by the people, he adds, "surely such things will not be wondered at by those who have observed how any strong affections about temporal matters will excite lively ideas and pictures of different things in the mind." In his sermon on the distinguishing marks of a work of the Spirit of God, he goes much further. He there says, "Such is our nature, that we cannot think of things invisible without some degree of imagination. I dare appeal to any man of the greatest powers of mind, whether he is able to fix his thoughts on God, or Christ, or the things of another world without imaginary ideas attending his meditation." By imaginary ideas, he means mental images, or pictures.[2] In the same connection, he adds, "the more engaged the mind is, and the more intense the contemplation and affection, still the more lively and strong will the imaginary idea ordinarily be." Hence, he insists, "that it is no argument that a work is not a work of the Spirit of God, that some who are the subjects of it, have been in a kind of ecstasy, wherein they have been carried beyond themselves, and have had their minds transported in a train of strong and pleasing imaginations, and of visions, as though they were rapt up even to Heaven, and there saw glorious sights."

It is not to be denied that there is a legitimate use of the imagination in religion. The Bible often addresses itself to this faculty. The descriptions which it gives of the future glory of the church, and of Heaven itself are little else than a series of images; not that we should conceive of the millennium as of a time when the lion and lamb shall feed together, or of Heaven as a golden city, but that we may have a more lively impression of the absence of all destructive passions, when Christ shall reign on Earth, and that we may learn to think of Heaven as a state of surpassing glory. In all such cases, it is the thought which the figure is meant to convey, and not the figure itself, that the mind rests upon in all truly religious exercises. When, on the other hand, the mind fixes on the image, and not upon the thought, and inflames itself with these imaginations, the result is mere curious excitement. So far then as the imagination is used to render the thoughts which the understanding forms of spiritual things distinct and vivid, so far may it minister to our religious improvement. But when it is made a mere chamber of imagery, in which the soul alarms or delights itself with specters, it becomes the source of all manner of delusions.

It may still further be admitted, that images borrowed from sensible objects often mix with and disturb the truly spiritual contemplations of the Christian, but this is very different from teaching that we cannot think of God, or Christ, or spiritual subjects, without some pictorial representations of them. If such is the constitution of our nature that

2. The connection between empiricism and idolatry can be clearly seen in this paragraph. – *Editor.*

we must have such imaginary ideas of God himself then we ought to have and to cherish them. But by the definition, these ideas are nothing but the reproduction and varied combinations of past impressions on the senses. To say, therefore, that we must have such ideas of God, is to say that we must conceive of him and worship him under some corporeal form, which is nothing but refined idolatry, and is as much forbidden as the worship of stocks or stones. It certainly needs no argument to show that we cannot form any pictorial representation of a spirit, and least of all, of God; or that such representations of Christ or Heaven cannot be the source of any truly religious affections. What have such mental images to do with the apprehension of the evil of sin, of the beauty of holiness, of the mercy of God, or the merits of Christ, or with any of those truths on which the mind acts when under the influence of the Spirit of God?

From the accounts of this revival already quoted, from the detail given of the experience of many of its subjects, and especially from the arguments and apologies just referred to, it is evident that one great source of the false religion, which it is admitted, then prevailed, was the countenance given to these impressions on the imagination and to the feelings thus excited. It was in vain to tell the people they must distinguish between what was imaginary and what was spiritual; that there was no religion in these lively mental images, when they were at the same time told that it was necessary they should have them, and that the more intense the religious affection, the more vivid would these pictures be. Under such instruction they would strive to form such imaginations; they would dote on them, inflame themselves with them, and consider the vividness of the image, and the violence of the consequent emotion, as the measure of their religious attainment. How deeply sensible Edwards became of the evil which actually arose from this source may be learned from his work on the *Affections*. When an "affection arises from the imagination, and is built upon it, as its foundation instead of a spiritual illumination or discovery, then is the affection, however elevated, worthless and vain." And in another place he says,

> When the Spirit of God is poured out, to begin a glorious work, then the old Serpent, as fast as possible, and by all means, introduces this bastard religion, and mingles it with the true; which has from time to time, brought all things into confusion. The pernicious consequence of it is not easily imagined or conceived of until we see and are amazed

with the awful effects of it, and the dismal desolation it has made. If the revival of true religion be very great in its beginning, yet if this bastard comes in, there is danger of its doing as Gideon's bastard, Abimelech, did, who never left until he had slain all his threescore and ten true-born sons, excepting one, that was forced to flee. The imagination or phantasy seems to be that wherein are formed all those delusions of Satan, which those are carried away with, who are under the influence of false religion, and counterfeit graces and affections. Here is the devil's grand lurking-place, the very nest of foul and delusive spirits.

If Edwards, who was *facile princeps* among the friends of this revival, could, during its early stages, fall into the error of countenancing the delusions which he afterwards so severely condemned, what could be expected of Whitefield and others, who at this time, (dates must not be neglected, a few years made a great difference both in persons and things) passed rapidly from place to place, neither making nor being able to make, the least distinction between the effects of an excited imagination, and the exercises of genuine religion? That they would test the experience of their converts by its fruits, is not denied; but that they considered all the commotions which attended their ministrations as proofs of the Spirit's presence is evident from their indiscriminate rejoicing over all such manifestations of feeling. These violent agitations produced through the medium of the imagination, though sufficiently prevalent, during the revival in this country, were perhaps still more frequent in England, under the ministrations of Wesley, and, combined with certain peculiarities of his system, have given to the religion of the Methodists its peculiar, and, so far it is peculiar, its undesirable characteristic.

Another serious evil was the encouragement given to loud outcries, faintings, and bodily agitations during the time of public worship. It is remarkable that these effects of the excitement prevailed generally, not only in this country, but also in Scotland and England. The fanatical portion of the friends of the revival not only encouraged these exhibitions, but also regarded them as proofs of the presence and power of the Spirit of God. The more judicious never went to this extreme, though most of them regarded them with favor. This was the case with Whitefield, Edwards, and Blair.

The manner in which Whitefield describes the scenes at Nottingham and Fagg's Manor, and others of a similar character, shows that he did not disapprove of these agitations. He says he never saw a more glorious sight, than when the people were fainting all round him, and crying out in such a manner as to drown his own voice. Edwards took them decidedly under his protection. He not only mentions, without the slightest indication of disapprobation, that his church was often filled with outcries, faintings, and convulsions, but takes great pains to vindicate the revival from all objection on that account. Though such effects were not, in his view, any decisive evidence of the kind of influence by which they were produced, he contended that it was easy to account for their being produced by a "right influence and a proper sense of things." He says, ministers are not to be blamed for speaking of these things

> as probable tokens of God's presence, and arguments of the success of preaching, because I think they are so indeed. I confess that when I see a great outcry in a congregation, I rejoice in it much more than merely in an appearance of solemn attention, and a show of affection by weeping. To rejoice that the work of God is carried on calmly and without much ado, is in effect to rejoice that it is carried on with less power, or that there is not so much of the influence of God's Spirit.

In the same connection he says that when these outcries, faintings, and other bodily effects attended the preaching of the truth, he did not "scruple to speak of them, to rejoice in them, and bless God for them," as probable tokens of his presence.

The Boston ministers, on the other hand, appear to have disapproved of these things entirely, as they mention their satisfaction that there had been little or nothing of such "blemishes of the work" among their churches. The same view was taken of them by President Dickinson, William Tennent of Freehold, and many others.

That the fanatics, who regarded these bodily agitations and outcries as evidences of conversion, committed a great and dangerous mistake, need not be argued; and that Edwards and others, who rejoiced over and encouraged them, as probable tokens of the favor of God, fell into an error scarcely less injurious to religion, will, at the present day, hardly be questioned. That such effects frequently attend religious excitements is no proof that they proceed from a good source. They may owe their origin to the corrupt, or at least merely natural feelings, which always mingle, to a greater or less degree, with strong religious exercises. It is a matter of great practical importance to learn what is the true cause of these effects; to ascertain whether they proceed from those feelings which

449

are produced by the Spirit of God, or from those which arise from other sources. If the former, we ought to rejoice over them; if the latter, they ought to be repressed and discountenanced.

That such bodily agitations owe their origin not to any divine influence, but to natural causes, may be inferred from the fact that these latter are adequate to their production. They are not confined to those persons whose subsequent conduct proves them to be the subjects of the grace of God; but, to say the least, are quite as frequently experienced by those who know nothing of true religion. Instead, therefore, of being referred to those feelings which are peculiar to the people of God, they may safely be referred to those which are common to them and to unrenewed men. Besides, such effects are not peculiar to what we call revivals of religion; they have prevailed, in seasons of general excitement, in all ages and in all parts of the world, among pagans, papists, and every sect of fanatics which has ever disgraced the Christian church. We are, therefore, not called upon to regard such things with much favor, or to look upon them as probable tokens of the presence of God. That the bodily agitations attendant on revivals of religion are of the same nature, and attributable to the same cause, as the convulsions of enthusiasts, is in the highest degree probable, because they arise under the same circumstances, are propagated by the same means, and cured by the same treatment. They arise in seasons of great, and especially of general excitement; they, in a great majority of cases, affect ignorant rather than the enlightened, those in whom the imagination predominates over the reason, and especially those who are of a nervous temperament, rather than those of an opposite character. These affections all propagate themselves by a kind of infection. This circumstance is characteristic of this whole class of nervous diseases. Physicians enumerate among the causes of epilepsy "seeing a person in convulsions." This fact was so well known, that the Romans made a law, that if any one should be seized with epilepsy during the meeting of the *comitia*, the assembly should be immediately dissolved. This disease occurred so frequently in those exciting meetings, and was propagated so rapidly, that it was called the *morbus comitialis*. Among the enthusiasts who frequented the tomb of the Abbé Paris, in the early part of the last century, convulsions were of frequent occurrence, and never failed to prove infectious. During a religious celebration in the church of Saint Roch, at Paris, a young lady was seized with convulsions, and within half an hour between fifty and sixty were similarly affected. A multitude of facts of the same kind might be adduced. Sometimes such affections become epidemic, spreading over whole provinces. In the fifteenth century, a violent nervous disease, attended with convulsions, and other analogous symptoms, extended over a great part of Germany, especially affecting the inmates of the convents. In the next century something of the same kind prevailed extensively in the south of France. These affections were then regarded as the result of demoniacal possessions, and in some instances, multitudes of poor creatures were put to death as demoniacs.

The bodily agitations attending the revival, were in like manner propagated by infection. On their first appearance in Northampton, a few persons were seized at an evening meeting, and while others looked on they soon became similarly affected; even those who appear to have come merely out of curiosity did not escape. The same thing was observable at Nottingham, Fagg's Manor, and other places, under the preaching of Whitefield. It was no less obvious in Scotland. It was exceedingly rare for any one to be thus affected in private; but in the public meetings, when one person was seized, others soon caught the infection. In England, where these affections were regarded at least at first, by Wesley, as coming from God, and proofs of his favor, they were very violent, and spread with great rapidity, seizing, at times, upon opposers as well as friends. Thus on one occasion, it is stated, that a Quaker who was present at one meeting, and inveighed against what he called the dissimulation of these creatures, caught the contagious emotion himself and even while he was biting his lips and knitting his brows, dropt down as if he had been struck by lightning. "The agony he was in," says Wesley, "was even terrible to behold; we besought God not to lay folly to his charge, and he soon lifted up his head and cried aloud, 'Now I know thou art a prophet of the Lord.' " On another occasion, under the preaching of the Rev. Mr. Berridge, a man who had been mocking and mimicking others in their convulsions, was himself seized. "He was," says the narrator,

> the most horrible human figure I ever saw. His large wig and hair were coal-black, his face distorted beyond all description. He roared incessantly, throwing and clapping his hands together with his whole force. Some of his brother scoffers were calling for horsewhips, till they saw him extended on his back at full length; they then said he was dead; and

indeed the only sign of life was the working of his breast, and the distortions of his face, while the veins of his neck were swelled as if ready to burst. His agonies lasted some hours; then his body and soul were eased.

"At another meeting," he says,

a stranger who stood facing me, fell backward to the wall, then forward on his knees, wringing his hands and roaring like a bull. His face at first turned quite red, then almost black. He rose and ran against the wall, till Mr. Keeling and another held him. He screamed out, "Oh! what shall I do! Oh, for one drop of the blood of Christ!" As he spoke, God set his soul at liberty; he knew his sins were blotted out; and the rapture he was in seemed too great for human nature to bear.

One woman tore up the ground with her hands, filling them with dust and with the hard trodden grass, on which I saw her lie as one dead. Some continued long as if they were dead, but with a calm sweetness in their looks. I saw one who lay two or three hours in the open air, and being then carried into the house, continued insensible another hour, as if actually dead. The first sign of life she showed, was a rapture of praise intermixed with a small joyous laughter.

These accounts, however, must be read in detail, in order to have any adequate conception of the nature and extent of these dreadful nervous affections. Wesley at one time regarded them as direct intimations of the approbation of God. Preaching at Newgate, he says, he was led insensibly, and without any previous design, to declare strongly and explicitly, that God willed all men to be saved, and to pray that, if this was not the truth of God, he would not suffer the blind to go out of the way; but if it was, he would bear witness to his word.

Immediately one and another sunk to the earth; they dropt on every side as thunderstruck. In the evening I was again pressed in spirit to declare that Christ gave himself a ransom for all. And almost before we called upon him to set to his seal, he answered. One was so wounded by the sword of the Spirit, that you would have imagined she could not live a moment. But immediately his abundant kindness was shown, and she loudly sang of his righteousness.

The various bodily exercises which attended the Western revivals in our own country, in the early part of the present century, were of the same nature, and obeyed precisely the same laws. They began with what was called the falling exercise; that is, the person affected would fall on the ground helpless as an infant. This was soon succeeded, in many places, by a species of convulsions called the jerks. Sometimes it would affect the whole body, jerking it violently from place to place, regardless of all obstacles; at others, a single limb would be thus agitated. When the neck was attacked, the head would be thrown backwards and forwards with the most fearful rapidity. There were various other forms in which this disease manifested itself, such as whirling, rolling, running, and jumping. These exercises were evidently involuntary. They were highly infectious, and spread rapidly from place to place; often seizing on mere spectators, and even upon those who abhorred and dreaded them.

Another characteristic of these affections, whether occurring among pagans, papists, or Protestants, and which goes to prove their identity, is, that they all yield to the same treatment. As they arise from impressions on the nervous system through the imagination, the remedy is addressed to the imagination. It consists in removing the exciting causes, that is, withdrawing the patient from the scenes and contemplations which produced the disease; or in making a strong counter-impression, either through fear, shame, or sense of duty. The possessions, as they were called, in the south of France, were put a stop to by the wisdom and firmness of certain bishops, who insisted on the separation and seclusion of all the affected. On another occasion, a strange nervous agitation, which had for some time, to the great scandal of religion, seized periodically on all the members of a convent, was arrested by the magistrates bringing up a company of soldiers, and threatening with severe punishment the first who should manifest the least symptom of the affection. The same method has often been successfully resorted to. In like manner the convulsions attending revivals have been prevented or arrested by producing the conviction that they were wrong or disgraceful. They hardly ever appeared, or at least continued, where they were not approved and encouraged. In Northampton, where Edwards rejoiced over them, they were abundant; in Boston, where they were regarded as "blemishes," they had nothing of them. In Sutton, Massachusetts, they were "cautiously guarded against," and consequently never appeared, except among strangers from other congregations. Only two or three cases occurred in Elizabethtown, under President Dickinson, who considered them as "irregular heats," and those few were speedily regulated. There was nothing of the kind at Freehold, where William Tennent set his face against all such manifestations of enthusiasm. On the other hand, they followed Davenport and other fanatical preachers, almost wherever they went. In Scotland, they were less encouraged than they were here, and consequently prevailed less. In England, where Wesley regarded them as certainly from God, they were fearful both as to frequency and violence. The same thing was observed with regard to the agitations attending the Western revivals. The physician already quoted says: "Restraint often prevents a paroxysm. For example, persons always attacked by this affection in churches where it is encouraged, will be perfectly calm in churches where it is discouraged, however affecting may be the service, and however great the mental excitement." It is also worthy of consideration that these bodily affections are of frequent occurrence at the present day, among those who continue to desire and encourage them.

It appears, then, that these nervous agitations are of frequent occurrence in all times of strong excitement. It matters little whether the excitement arise from superstition, fanaticism, or from the preaching of the truth. If the imagination be strongly affected, the nervous system is very apt to be deranged, and outcries, faintings, convulsions, and other hysterical symptoms, are the consequence. That these effects are of the same nature whatever may be the remote cause, is plain, because the phenomena are the same; the apparent circumstances of their origin the same; they all have the same infectious nature, and are all cured by the same means. They are, therefore, but different forms of the same disease; and, whether they occur in a convent or a camp meeting, they are no more a token of the divine favor than hysteria or epilepsy.

It may still be said, that, although they do sometimes arise from other causes, they may be produced by genuine religious feeling. This, however, never can be proved. The fact that undoubted Christians experience these effects, is no proof that they flow from a good source; because there is always a corrupt mixture in the exercises of the most spiritual men. These affections *may*, therefore, flow from the concomitants of genuine religious feelings, and not from those feelings themselves. And that they do in fact flow from that source, may be assumed, because in other cases they certainly have that origin; and because all the known effects of true religious feelings are of a different character. Those apprehensions of truth which arise from divine illumination do not affect the imagination, but the moral emotions, which are very different in their nature and effects from the feelings produced by a heated fancy. This view of the subject is greatly confirmed by the consideration that there is nothing in the Bible to lead us to regard these bodily affections as the legitimate effects of religious feeling. No such results followed the preaching of Christ, or his apostles. We hear of no general outcries, faintings, convulsions, or ravings in the assemblies which they addressed. The scriptural examples cited by the apologists of these exhibitions are so entirely inapplicable as to be of themselves sufficient to show how little countenance is to be derived from the Bible for such irregularities. Reference is made, for example, to the case of the jailer at Philippi who fell down at the apostles' feet; to *Acts* ii. 37 ("Now when they heard this, they were pricked in their heart, and said, Men and brethren, what shall we do?") and to the conversion of Paul. It is, however, too obvious to need remark, that in no one of these cases was either the effect produced, or the circumstances attending its production, analogous to the hysterical convulsions and outcries now under consideration.

The testimony of the Scriptures is not merely negative on this subject. Their authority is directly opposed to all such disorders. They direct that all things should be done decently and in order. They teach us that God is not the God of confusion, but of peace, in all the churches of the saints. These passages have particular reference to the manner of conducting public worship. They forbid every thing which is inconsistent with order, solemnity, and devout attention. It is evident that loud outcries and convulsions are inconsistent with these things, and therefore ought to be discouraged. They cannot come from God, for he is not the author of confusion. The apology made in Corinth for the disorders which Paul condemned was precisely the same as that urged in defense of these bodily agitations. We ought not to resist the Spirit of God, said the Corinthians; and so said all those who encouraged these convulsions. Paul's answer was that no influence which comes from God destroys our self-control. "The spirits of the prophets are subject to the prophets." Even in the case of direct inspiration and revelation, the mode of communication was in harmony with our rational nature, and left our powers under the control of reason and the will. The man, therefore, who felt the divine afflatus had no right to give way to it, under circumstances which would produce noise and confusion. The prophets of God were not like the Pythoness of the heathen temples;

nor are the saints of God converted into whirling dervishes by any influence of which he is the author. There can be little doubt that Paul would have severely reprobated such scenes as frequently occurred during the revival of which we are speaking. He would have said to the people substantially what he said to the Corinthians. If any unbeliever or ignorant man come to your assemblies, and hear one shouting in ecstasy, another howling in anguish; if he see some falling, some jumping, some lying in convulsions, others in trances, will he not say, You are mad? But if your exercises are free from confusion, and your discourses addressed to the reason, so as to convince and reprove, he will confess that God is among you of a truth.

Experience, no less than Scripture, has set the seal of reprobation upon these bodily agitations. If they are of the nature of an infectious nervous disease, it is as much an act of infatuation to encourage them, as to endeavor to spread epilepsy over the land. It is easy to excite such things, but when excited, it is very difficult to suppress them, or to arrest their progress; and they have never prevailed without the most serious mischief. They bring discredit upon religion, they give great advantage to infidels and gainsayers, and they facilitate the progress of fanaticism. When sanctioned, the people delight in them, as they do in all strong excitement. The multitude of spurious conversions, the prevalence of false religion, the rapid progress of fanaticism, and the consequent permanent declension of religion immediately after the great revival, are probably to be attributed to the favor shown to these bodily agitations, as much as to any one cause.

Besides the errors above specified, which were sanctioned by many of the best friends of the revival, there were others which, though reprobated by the more judicious, became, through the patronage of the more ardent, prolific sources of evil. There was from the first a strong leaven of enthusiasm, manifesting itself in the regard paid to impulses, inspirations, visions, and the pretended power of discerning spirits. This was decidedly opposed by Edwards, by the Boston clergy, by Tennent, and many others. Whitefield, on the contrary, was, especially in the early part of his career, deeply infected with this leaven. When he visited Northampton, in 1740, Edwards endeavored to convince him of the dangerous tendency of this enthusiastic spirit, but without much success. He had such an idea of what the Scriptures mean by the guidance of the Spirit, as to suppose that by suggestions, impressions, or sudden

recollection of texts of the Bible, the Christian's duty was divinely revealed, even as to the minutest circumstance, and that at times even
future events were thus made known. On the strength of such an impression he did not hesitate publicly to declare that his unborn child
would prove to be a son. "An unaccountable but very strong impression," that he should preach the Gospel, was regarded as a revelation of
the purpose of God respecting him. The question whether he should
return to England was settled to his satisfaction by the occurrence to his
mind of the passage. When Jesus was returned, the people gladly received him. These few examples are enough to illustrate the point in
hand.

In Whitefield there was much to counteract the operation of this
spirit, which in others produced its legitimate effects. When Davenport
was asked by the Boston ministers the reason of any of his acts, his
common reply was, God commanded me. When asked whether he was
inspired, he answered, they might call it inspiration, or what they pleased.
The man who attended him he called his armor-bearer, because he was
led to take him as a follower, by opening on the story of Jonathan and
his armor-bearer. He considered it also as revealed that he should convert as many persons at a certain place as Jonathan and his armor-bearer
slew of the Philistines.

This was the only one of the forms in which this spirit manifested
itself. Those under its influence pretended to a power of discerning
spirits, of deciding at once who was and who was not converted; they
professed a perfect assurance of the favor of God founded not upon
scriptural evidence, but inward suggestion. It is plain that when men
thus give themselves up to the guidance of secret impressions, and attribute divine authority to suggestions, impulses, and casual occurrences,
there is no extreme of error or folly to which they may not be led. They
are beyond the control of reason or the Word of God. They have a
more direct and authoritative communication of the divine will than
can be made by any external and general revelation. They of course act
as if inspired and infallible. They are commonly filled with spiritual
pride, and with a bitter denunciatory spirit. All these results were soon
manifested to a lamentable extent during this revival. If an honest man
doubted his conversion, he was declared unconverted. If any one was
filled with great joy, he was pronounced a child of God. These enthusiasts paid great regard to visions and trances, and would pretend in

them to have seen Heaven or Hell, and particular persons in the one or the other. They paid more attention to inward impressions than to the Word of God. They laid great stress on views of an outward Christ, as on a throne, or upon the cross. If they did not feel a minister's preaching, they maintained he was unconverted, or legal. They made light of all meetings in which there was no external commotion. They had a remarkable haughtiness and self-sufficiency, and a fierce and bitter spirit of zeal and censoriousness.

The origin and progress of this fanatical spirit is one of the most instructive portions of the history of this period. In 1726, a religious excitement commenced in New Milford, Connecticut, which was at first of a promising character, but was soon perverted. Its subjects opened a communication with the enthusiasts of Rhode Island, and began to speak slightly of the Bible, especially of the *Psalms* of David, and to condemn the ministers of the Gospel and civil magistrates. They organized themselves into a separate society, and appointed officers not only to conduct their meetings, but also to regulate their dress. They made assurance essential to faith; they undervalued human learning and despised the ordinances of baptism and the Lord's supper. They laid claim to sinless perfection, and claimed that the standing ministers were unfit to preach, and that the people ought to leave them. One of the leaders of this company was a man named Ferris, who entered Yale College in 1729. A contemporary writer says of this gentleman, He told me he was certain not one in ten of the communicants in the church in New Haven could be saved; that he should have a higher seat in Heaven than Moses; that he knew the will of God in all things, and had not committed any sin for six years. He had a proud and haughty spirit, and appeared greatly desirous of applause. He obtained a great ascendancy over certain of the students, especially Davenport, Wheelock and Pomeroy, who lived with him most familiarly. He remained in college until 1732, and then returned to New Milford. He ultimately became a Quaker preacher.

Such was the origin of that enthusiastical and fanatical spirit, which swept over the New England churches. Messrs. Wheelock and Pomeroy seem soon to have escaped from its influence; but Davenport remained long under its power, and was the cause of incalculable mischief. He was settled as pastor of the church in Southhold, Long Island. In March 1740, he became satisfied that God had revealed to him that his kingdom was coming with great power, and that he had an extraordinary call to labor for its advancement. He assembled his people on one occasion, and addressed them, continuously, for nearly twenty-four hours; until he became quite wild. After continuing for some time his exciting labors in his own neighborhood, he passed over into Connecticut. The best and most favorable account of his erratic course is given by the Rev. Mr. Fish, who knew him intimately. The substance of this account, given nearly in the language of its author, is as follows.

The good things about him, says this writer, were, that he was a fast friend of the doctrines of grace; fully declaring the total depravity, the deplorable wretchedness and danger, and utter inability of men by the fall. He preached with great earnestness the doctrines of man's dependence on the sovereign mercy of God; of regeneration; of justification by faith, &c. The things that were evidently and dreadfully wrong about him were, that he not only gave full liberty to noise and outcries, but also promoted them with all his power. When these things prevailed among the people, accompanied with bodily agitations, the good man pronounced them tokens of the presence of God. Those who passed immediately from great distress to great joy, he declared, after asking them a few questions, to be converts; though numbers of such converts, in a short time, returned to their old way of living, and were as carnal, wicked, and void of experience, as ever they were. He was a great favorer of visions, trances, imaginations, and powerful impressions in others, and made such inward feelings the rule of his own conduct in many respects.

This is a formidable array of evils. Yet as the friends of the revival testify to their existence, no conscientious historian dare either conceal or extenuate them. There was too little discrimination between true and false religious feeling. There was too much encouragement given to outcries, faintings, and bodily agitations, as probable evidence of the presence and power of God. There was, in many, too much reliance on impulses, visions, and the pretended power of discerning spirits. There was a great deal of censoriousness, and of a sinful disregard of ecclesiastical order. The disastrous effects of these evils, the rapid spread of false religion, the dishonor and decline of true piety, the prevalence of erroneous doctrines, the division of congregations, the alienation of Christians, and the long period of subsequent deadness in the church, stand up as a solemn warning to Christians, and especially to Christian ministers in all times to come. It was thus, in the strong language of Edwards, the devil prevailed against the revival. "It is by this means that the daughter of Zion in this land, now lies in such piteous circumstances, with her garments rent, her face disfigured, her nakedness exposed, her limbs broken, and weltering in the blood of her own wounds, and in nowise able to rise, and this so soon after her late great joys and hopes."

27

The Power of the Word[1]

Martin Luther

D EAR FRIENDS, you heard yesterday the chief characteristics of a Christian man, that his whole life and being is faith and love. Faith is directed toward God, love toward man and one's neighbor, and consists in such love and service for him as we have received from God without our work and merit. Thus, there are two things: the one, which is the most needful, and which must be done in one way and no other; the other, which is a matter of choice and not of necessity, which may be kept or not, without endangering faith or incurring Hell. In both, love must deal with our neighbor in the same manner as God has dealt with us; it must walk the straight road, straying neither to the left nor to the right. In the things which are "musts" and are matters of necessity, such as believing in Christ, love nevertheless never uses force or undue constraint. Thus the mass is an evil thing, and God is displeased with it, because it is performed as if it were a sacrifice and work of merit. Therefore it must be abolished. Here there can be no question or doubt, any more than you should ask whether you should worship God. Here we are entirely agreed: The private masses must be abolished. As I have said in my writings,[2] I wish they would be abolished everywhere and only the ordinary evangelical mass be retained. Yet Christian love should not employ harshness here nor force the matter. However, it should be preached and taught with tongue and pen that to hold mass in such a manner is sinful, and yet no one should be dragged away from it by the hair; for it should be left to God, and his Word should be allowed to work alone, without our work or interference. Why? Because it is not in

1. The second sermon, March 10, 1522.
2. In the *Open Letter to the Christian Nobility* (1520), PE 2, 61-164, and *The Babylonian Captivity of the Church* (1520), PE 2, 170-293.

my power or hand to fashion the hearts of men as the potter molds the clay and fashion them at my pleasure [*Ecclus.* 33:13]. I can get no farther than their ears; their hearts I cannot reach. And since I cannot pour faith into their hearts, I cannot, nor should I, force any one to have faith. That is God's work alone, who causes faith to live in the heart. Therefore we should give free course to the Word and not add our works to it. We have the *jus verbi* [right to speak] but not the *executio* [power to accomplish]. We should preach the Word, but the results must be left solely to God's good pleasure.

Now if I should rush in and abolish it by force, there are many who would be compelled to consent to it and yet not know where they stand, whether it is right or wrong, and they would say: I do not know if it is right or wrong; I do not know where I stand; I was compelled by force to submit to the majority. And this forcing and commanding results in a mere mockery, an external show, a fool's play, man-made ordinances, sham-saints, and hypocrites. For where the heart is not good, I care nothing at all for the work. We must first win the hearts of the people. But that is done when I teach only the Word of God, preach the Gospel, and say: Dear lords or pastors, abandon the mass, it is not right, you are sinning when you do it; I cannot refrain from telling you this. But I would not make it an ordinance for them, nor urge a general law. He who would follow me could do so, and he who refused would remain outside. In the latter case the Word would sink into the heart and do its work. Thus he would become convinced and acknowledge his error, and fall away from the mass; tomorrow another would do the same, and thus God would accomplish more with his Word than if you and I were to merge all our power into one heap. So when you have won the heart, you have won the man – and thus the thing must finally fall of its own weight and come to an end. And if the hearts and minds of all are agreed and united, abolish it. But if all are not heart and soul for its abolishment – leave it in God's hands, I beseech you, otherwise the result will not be good. Not that I would again set up the mass; I let it lie in God's name. Faith must not be chained and imprisoned, nor bound by an ordinance to any work. This is the principle by which you must be governed. For I am sure you will not be able to carry out your plans. And if you should carry them out with such general laws, then I will recant everything that I have written and preached and I will not support you. This I am telling you now. What harm can it do you? You still have your faith in God, pure and strong so that this thing cannot hurt you.

Love, therefore, demands that you have compassion on the weak, as all the apostles had. Once, when Paul came to Athens (*Acts* 17 [:16-32]), a mighty city, he found in the temple many ancient altars, and he went from one to the other and looked at them all, but he did not kick down a single one of them with his foot. Rather he stood up in the middle of the market place and said they were nothing but idolatrous things and begged the people to forsake them; yet he did not destroy one of them by force. When the Word took hold of their hearts, they forsook them of their own accord, and in consequence the thing fell of itself. Likewise, if I had seen them holding mass, I would have preached to them and admonished them. Had they heeded my admonition, I would have won them; if not, I would nevertheless not have torn them from it by the hair or employed any force, but simply allowed the Word to act and prayed for them. For the Word created Heaven and Earth and all things [*Psalm* 33:6]; the Word must do this thing, and not we poor sinners.

In short, I will preach it, teach it, write it, but I will constrain no man by force, for faith must come freely without compulsion. Take myself as an example. I opposed indulgences and all the papists, but never with force. I simply taught, preached, and wrote God's Word; otherwise I did nothing. And while I slept [compare *Mark* 4:26-29], or drank Wittenberg beer with my friends Philip [Melanchthon] and [Nicholas von] Amsdorf, the Word so greatly weakened the papacy that no prince or emperor ever inflicted such losses upon it. I did nothing; the Word did everything. Had I desired to foment trouble, I could have brought great bloodshed upon Germany; indeed, I could have started such a game that even the emperor would not have been safe. But what would it have been? Mere fool's play. I did nothing; I let the Word do its work. What do you suppose is Satan's thought when one tries to do the thing by kicking up a row? He sits back in Hell and thinks: Oh, what a fine game the poor fools are up to now! But when we spread the Word alone and let it alone do the work, that distresses him. For it is almighty and takes captive the hearts, and when the hearts are captured the work will fall of itself. Let me cite a simple instance. In former times there were sects, too, Jewish and Gentile Christians, differing on the law of Moses with respect to circumcision. The former wanted to keep it, the latter not. Then came Paul and preached that it might be kept or not, for it was of no consequence, and also that they should not make a "must" of it, but leave it to the choice of the individual; to keep it or not was immaterial [1 Corinthians 7:18-24; Galatians 5:1]. So it was up to the time of Jerome, who came and wanted to make a "must" out of it, desiring to make it an ordinance and a law that it be prohibited. Then came Augustine and he was of the same opinion as Paul: it might be kept or not, as one wished. Jerome was a hundred miles away from Paul's opinion. The two doctors bumped heads rather hard, but when Augustine died, Jerome was successful in having it prohibited. After that came the popes, who also wanted to add something and they, too, made laws. Thus out of the making of one law grew a thousand laws, until they have completely buried us under laws. And this is what will happen here, too; one law will soon make two, two will increase to three, and so forth.

Let this be enough at this time concerning the things that are necessary, and let us beware lest we lead astray those of weak conscience [1 Corinthians 8:12].

28

What Is Evangelism?[1]

Gordon H. Clark

WHEN A congregation and its pastor decide to pay special attention to evangelism, they may invite a recommended speaker, set aside two weeks for meetings, and scatter advertisements around the neighborhood. But there is a great deal more to evangelism than this. One must ask, What kind of man is the recommended evangelist? What kind of music will be introduced? What kind of sermon does he preach? What will be the tone of the meetings? There are also other questions. What preparations should the church make before the evangelist comes? What sort of follow-up should be scheduled for the week after the evangelist leaves? And this last question points out the fact that evangelism is not limited to special meetings with special speakers. If a pastor and congregation wish to pay attention to evangelism, they may conclude that evangelism is a year-round affair, and possibly they may finally decide that an outside speaker is not so important after all. The pastor himself may be more important. And the ordinary members of the congregation may be the most important of all. These are points that the following pages will consider.

Evangelism is an indispensable part of *a* church's program because evangelism is an indispensable part of *the* church's program. If the church does not continually win people to Christ, the church will die. And it looks as if the church were dying. Many denominations are not keeping up with the growth of the population in the West. The growth of the population in the East gives a still more pessimistic picture. In the times of the apostles, the Lord added to the church daily those who were being saved. This occurred daily. How many local congregations can

1. This essay is taken from *Today's Evangelism: Counterfeit or Genuine?* The Trinity Foundation, 1990, 1-3, 33-62.

say that they add new members daily? There may be some, but I do not happen to know where they are. Most churches do not have large increases. And in many cases, increases do not mean that people are coming to accept Christ. They may merely mean that many people are moving to the suburbs, so that the suburban churches grow, while the downtown churches die. It may also mean that the particular congregation is an efficient country club, or political action group, having nothing to do with apostolic Christianity. Growth is not necessarily the result of evangelism.

What is the cause of the present evil days? Is it personal sin on the part of church members that hinders growth? Maybe it is. Is it the pressure of secular society in the post-Christian age that blocks out the message from the people's minds? Maybe it is. Is it because the message is not preached? Well, that is often the case, too. Or again, is it because God had planned a great apostasy at the end of the age, and now that that time has arrived, God is blinding the minds of the people so that hearing they do no hear? This could be so, too.

Nevertheless, God's command still rests on us to preach the Gospel to every creature. The church always has been and always will be a minority group in this world; its numbers may be decreasing at the present time; but the church must not die. It will not die. The present members will all die in a few years, if the Lord does not soon return, and new members must be sought. They will be sought. They will all be found. God will not permit his church to be extinguished. Now, our question is, How may we preserve the church? God will preserve the church, but only through the efforts of his servants. It is we who must do the work. Evangelism is indispensable. Somehow the church must gather in new people.

Somehow, but how? There are many methods in actual use. Surely some are better than others. Since the problem is serious and important, careful thought should be given to how evangelization should be conducted. Some methods may be good in one situation and bad in another. Some may do more harm than good. Bingo is one of these. No, if a church wants to pay attention to evangelism, it should not thoughtlessly plunge ahead. It must face the questions that different methods pose, carefully consider the probable effects, and then choose deliberately what the situation requires. Too often inertia produces an automatic acceptance of customary procedures. Evangelistic services have become stereotyped. They all follow the same form. Happy singing, impassioned address, altar call with pleading, shaking hands, signing cards, love offering, and good-bye till the next campaign. Well, once in a while the form should be scrutinized. If it is a good method, it will survive scrutiny. If it has weak spots, it can be improved. And if it is unbiblical, it should be scrapped. Since these are dark days for the church, it is all the more important to examine the whole procedure now. It is all the more reprehensible to react automatically and go through some familiar motions. Evangelism requires very serious consideration....

If the heedless evangelist gives no thought to the place or desirability of emotion and experience in his services, if now it is clear that he should, then all the more should he stop a moment to ask what evangelism is. At first he might simply snort at such a question. Doesn't he know good and well what evangelism is? Isn't he a professional evangelist? Evangelism is what he does, and his doing it makes it evangelism.

If, on the other hand, the activity is to be Christian and not mere entertainment, one might acknowledge that Christ and the apostles had some idea of evangelism. And just perhaps our practices should be judged by theirs. Even the usage of the word in the New Testament should be informative.

To *evangelize* is to preach the Gospel. The Gospel is the *evangel*. In Greek the word is *evangelion*. The verb too, translated *preach* or *proclaim*, has the same root. It is *evangelidzomai*. The noun occurs about 75 times in the New Testament: four times in *Matthew*, and five times in *Mark*. The opening words of the second *Gospel* are, "The beginning of the Gospel..." and the account, the Gospel itself, follows. The Gospel is what Mark wrote down, or at least what Mark wrote down is the beginning of the Gospel.

Mark 1:15 commands us to "believe in the Gospel."[2] Some people make a distinction between *believing* a written account and *believing in* a person. This verse undermines such a distinction. Really, when one *believes in* a person, he believes the words the person speaks – he believes his promises and his asserted ability to perform. This is what saying that we trust a person means.

2. In Greek the object of the verb *believe* can be a simple noun in the dative case, or a noun preceded by the prepositions *en*, *eis*, or *epi*, and sometimes *peri*. There seems to be no obvious distinction in meaning among these forms. In Hebrew also two prepositions are possible.

The other references in *Mark* (8:35, 10:29, 13:10, 14:9, and 16:15) all indicate that the Gospel is a *message* that must be published, proclaimed, or preached. That the Gospel is a message is emphasized in *Acts* 15:7: "Peter rose up" in the Jerusalem Council, "and said…God chose among us that the Gentiles by my mouth should hear the word of the Gospel and believe." The words came from Peter's mouth, and these words are what these Gentiles believed.

In addition to *Romans* 1:9 and 10:16, chapter 2:16 says, "God shall judge… according to my Gospel." Paul had been preaching certain standards of justice; he had been condemning sin; he was in the process of exposing the wickedness of the Jews. In this verse he says that God's judgment will be based on the principles of justice that he has been expounding. To be sure, chapter 2 does not expound the entire Gospel; but the Gospel contains these principles by which God judges. If we today are to preach the Gospel, rather than some other message, the ideas of this chapter, *Romans* 2, must be included. Some recent books on evangelism say they should not.

It would be tedious to quote all 75 verses that use the word *Gospel*, but *1 Corinthians* 15:1 contains a part of the message not mentioned in *Romans* 2. In brief it says, "The Gospel which I preached unto you [explains]…how that Christ died for our sins…and that he rose again the third day…." This is the Gospel "by which also you are saved." The Gospel therefore is a message, not an emotion. And as a message it is received by the intellect, not the emotions. In *Philippians* 1:27 Paul tells us to let our conversation or conduct accord with the Gospel, which we can do by being of one mind, striving together for the faith of the Gospel. Note that Paul tells us to be of one mind. He does not tell us to be of one emotion. Now, since as *Colossians* 1:5 says, the Gospel is the Word of Truth, its reception has to be an intellectual act. Truth cannot be received by the emotions. A message is something intelligible. It is something to be understood. If the facts of Christ's death and resurrection were not to be understood, then music and painting could replace preaching and words; for the arts can stimulate emotion, but they cannot convey the Gospel.[3] See also *Colossians* 1:23.

The verb *evangelize* occurs over 50 times in the New Testament. It is most often translated *preach*. There is no point in multiplying quota-

3. See the next chapter, "Art and the Gospel."

tions. The Gospel is clearly a message to be proclaimed, understood, and in order for a person to be saved, believed. John Brown of Edinburgh in *An Exposition of the Epistle of Paul to the Galatians,* chapter 3, verse 23, said, "But before faith came.... Some interpreters understand by 'faith' Jesus Christ, whom they represent as the object of faith.... In a strict propriety of language it is not Jesus Christ personally considered, but the truth about Jesus Christ, which is the object of faith..." (170).

The point is particularly appropriate for the present days of apostasy. The liberals use the name *Jesus Christ,* and some other historic terms, as symbols to evoke pious emotions. The phrases often sound good. But after a little study we discover that their Jesus was not born of a virgin, never raised Lazarus from the dead, and never himself came out of the tomb. Their Jesus is an empty name without intellectual content, a mere emotional idol. Real Christians believe the truth about Jesus: that he actually was virgin-born, that he actually said, "The Son of Man came...to give his life a ransom for many," and that this is precisely what he did on the cross. It is the intellectual content, the message, that counts.

There is more to be said about the Gospel message. In particular an explanation is needed of the way an evangelist's evaluation of emotion causes him to alter the message, either by the inclusion of certain topics or by the exclusion of others. However, before showing how an evangelist selects his message, the aim of the evangelist should be considered.

The unthinking evangelist has a ready-made answer with respect to his aim. Obviously his aim is to win souls. Why does this need thought? Is it not obvious? No, it is not quite obvious. In fact, this simple, unthinking answer is too simple and too unthinking. If this is the limit of the evangelist's aim, his conduct of an evangelistic campaign will more likely be somewhat unscriptural.

That there can be no misunderstanding, let it be made quite clear that this answer is not exactly wrong. Of course the preaching of the Gospel aims at the salvation of souls. It was said at the outset that the church must gather in those that are being saved, unless it is to die in this generation. And the zeal of some thoughtless evangelists is highly commendable in itself, even if it is not according to knowledge. It would be most gratifying if all who had knowledge had the same degree of zeal as some of our enthusiastic brethren. Nevertheless the answer is too simple.

It is too simple because it is too short, too ambiguous, and too easily misunderstood. Yet, if properly defined, it is entirely scriptural. Jude in verse 23 says, "Others [you are to] save, snatching them out of the fire." *James* 5:20 says, "he that converts a sinner...shall save a soul from death." *1 Timothy* 4:16 reads, "Take heed, for in doing this you shall save both yourself and them that hear you." In *1 Corinthians* 9:22 the apostle claims that "I am made all things to all men that I might save some." Compare *Romans* 11:14. Peter in *Acts* 2:40 tells his audience, "Save yourselves."

But is it true that a man can save himself? Did Paul save anybody? Can one man convert another? What about grace? Is not salvation of the Lord? James, who in the verse quoted says that one man should convert another, also says, "There is one lawgiver who is able to save and destroy." And he also says, "The engrafted Word...is able to save your souls." The angel told Joseph to call his name Jesus, "for he shall save his people from their sins." And the children of Israel, in times of repentance, called on the Lord to save them. Then of course there is that very familiar verse, "By grace are you saved, through faith, and that not of yourselves, it is the gift of God."

In salvation, or more particularly, in regeneration, in the production of faith, how much is to be attributed to the sinner? How much is to be attributed to God? There are not many, I suppose there are not any, American fundamentalist evangelists who accept the views of Pelagius. This monk of the fifth century took the idea of saving yourself very seriously. Each man really saved himself. The messenger could repeat to him the commandments of God, and God had been gracious in giving the law, but all else was to be accomplished by the person himself. He was able to keep God's commandments; sin had no great hold on him; and by becoming law abiding, he would save himself. But I have never heard any evangelists talk like this. There are, however, some people I would not call evangelists who talk very much like this. These are the liberals who want us to get "involved" in all sorts of street demonstrations, who want us to engineer boycotts of firms that manufacture munitions for our nation, who want us to disrupt orderly procedures of democratic government, and thus we shall save ourselves – from what and to what I cannot tell.

Nearly all the popular evangelists split up the credit a bit more equitably. Some credit goes to the evangelist, some to the person converted, and of course a fair percentage to God. The evangelist preaches the message, and as James said, the word preached saves the man. (Is this just what James said?) Then, of course, God and only God can regenerate. But God regenerates only those who by their own will have manufactured their faith in Jesus Christ. Faith is not a gift; it is something we ourselves do. And until we do it, God will not help.

Then there are other preachers; they are not what anybody would call popular evangelists; and these men say something immensely different. To be sure, they grant that the evangelist does something. The aim of evangelism, that is, the aim of preaching the Gospel, is to present to the sinner the message to be believed. Faith comes by hearing, and hearing by the Word of God. The Christian witness certainly has a part in the process of salvation. But it is not the decisive part. The sinner has a part, too. He must listen to the message. We can say more. He must understand the message. If a missionary went to the Chinese or the Zambians and preached in English, they could not understand him, and they would not believe the Gospel because they would not have heard the message. Understanding is essential, but it is not decisive, for many people hear the message and understand it very well, but they do not believe it. For example, Saul as a young man heard the message. He understood it better than most of the Christians did. It was because he understood it so well that he became a persecutor. Jesus is God; he said to himself: This is blasphemy; these people must be exterminated. So he harried them, beat them, and imprisoned them. He understood the Gospel, but he did not believe it. Note also that when he believed, it was the same Gospel he had earlier heard. Later on, when he had retired to Arabia for meditation and for revelation, he learned more. God told him additional truths. These he learned directly from God, for he did not confer with those who were apostles before him. He conferred with God. But at the moment of conversion, he understood no more than he had already heard.

This brings the discussion to the matter of faith or belief. Now, who does this? To whom is the credit due? Not the evangelist, of course, unless you wish to credit him with extreme powers of persuasion. It is to the credit either of the sinner or of God. One thing is clear. It is the sinner who believes. God is not the believer. It is we who must have faith. If God can be said to have faith in any sense, it is entirely irrelevant to the problem of evangelism. The sinner has the faith. No one else.

But is the credit his? The familiar verse quoted before is "For by grace are you saved through faith; and that not of yourselves: It is the gift of God."[4] Here the apostle tells us by revelation that faith is the gift of God. The credit then belongs to God. A man in the exercise of his natural powers given him by creation may understand the Gospel; but no sinner by the exercise of his natural powers believes that Jesus is Lord. This belief is the gift of God. Of course, it is the sinner who believes; no one else can believe for him, not even God. Believing is a mental act, and it is individual and personal. But it is God and God alone who causes a man to believe. The man simply does the act because God made him do it. It is to God's credit – or in more Scriptural language, it is to the praise of the glory of his grace, and of his mere good pleasure.

There is more to it than this. God has a method by which he causes a sinner to believe. Saul was a sinner, unregenerate, dead in trespasses and sins. So at one time were the Ephesians. So were we. But God, who is rich in mercy, even when we were dead in sins, has raised us from the dead with Christ, for by grace are you saved, not of works, lest any man should boast. Evangelist John calls this action of God regeneration. He says that those who believe have been born, not of the will of the flesh, but they have been born of God. The other three evangelists usually refer to this as God's giving us life. Now, faith is the exercise of the powers of spiritual life. A dead man cannot exercise the functions of life. A spiritually dead man cannot believe. As Jesus said to the Pharisees, "How can you believe?" The dead cannot believe. Therefore God must give the dead sinner life, and the first function of that new life is to believe the Gospel. The glory therefore is God's.

This is why there is a third aim for the evangelist. And this third aim is the most important and most profound. The ultimate aim is not to convert sinners. Nor is it to preach the Gospel. It is to glorify God. After speaking about the unsearchable riches of Christ, Paul says that God created the universe in order that his manifold wisdom should be revealed (by means of the church, which is built up by evangelism) to the principalities and powers in the heavenly realm. The glory then belongs

---

4. Those who say that the word *faith* in Greek is feminine, and the word *that* is neuter, and that therefore the demonstrative pronoun cannot refer to faith, know very little Greek. Many evangelists know very little Greek. They should learn that feminine abstract nouns frequently take neuter pronouns, and that even feminine concrete nouns sometimes take neuter pronouns.

to God, in or by means of the church and Jesus Christ, to all generations of the age of ages. Amen.

To glorify God it is necessary to preach the Gospel. If the aim were to save souls, maybe some persuasive *hocus pocus* could produce results as spectacular as those seen in mammoth meetings. But it is God with whom we have to do, God, before whose eyes all things are open and manifest. *Hocus pocus* may impress men, but it cannot fool God. To glorify God, his message must be preached. Alterations, dilutions, additions, falsifications are prohibited. Now, just what this message is, what parts of it should be preached, what parts should not be preached, and whether musical saws and klaxon horns should be used – all these things are decided upon by the evangelist largely on the ground of his notion of the role of emotion in evangelism. How this is so can be seen by a study of a small booklet titled *Fundamentalism and Evangelism* by John R. W. Stott. I wish to show how he distorts the Biblical Gospel because of his views on the aim of evangelism and his evaluation of emotion and intellect.

In chapter 1 Mr. Stott makes some admirable statements about the Bible. He notes that if Christ were sinless, he must have told the truth. He was inerrant (page 17). Although he seems to avoid the words *inerrant* and *infallible* with respect to the apostles, Mr. Stott remarks on their claim to divine authority. "They teach with dogmatic emphasis." And "Paul boldly links together God's teaching and his own apostolic charge." In addition, there are several other excellent statements on the nature of Scripture. All this should be taken as Mr. Stott's acceptance of the doctrine of verbal and plenary inspiration and his adherence to the complete truth, the inerrancy and infallibility of Scripture in its entirety.

Unfortunately, in the United States at least, some so-called Evangelicals are claiming to accept the "authority" of Scripture, even while asserting that it contains errors. I know one queer duck who says he believes in infallibility but not in inerrancy. Or is it the other way around? Liberals are often dishonest. Since by and large they commit perjury when they take their ordination vows – accepting the *Westminster Confession* in the vow, but not believing many of the doctrines it enumerates – it is not wise to trust their use of words. The best words I know for the present situation are: *verbal plenary inspiration*, and *inerrant* and *infallible*.

Now, I am far from accusing Mr. Stott of dishonesty. Fifty years ago his words would have been taken as synonymous with or equivalent to the Reformation doctrine of verbal and plenary inspiration. The trouble is that liberal laxness with language, and the deliberate attempt to confuse people in order to gain political power in the churches, makes it difficult to know what an honest man wants to say.

If Mr. Stott did not accept the Bible as the inerrant Word of God, I would not take the trouble, in a book on evangelism, to object to his view of the emotions and the content of the Gospel. These are matters that can be discussed only on the basis of Scripture. If one of us believes the Bible and the other does not, no progress could be made in discussion. One might show that the Bible teaches this or that, while the other could reply, Of course it does, but I do not accept it. The latter person uses an external criterion to judge which parts of the Bible are true and which parts are false. His external criterion is probably some form of empirical philosophy. But the Bible-believer cannot base his arguments on such a platform, but on revelation only. Assuming now that Mr. Stott does in fact believe the Bible, one can profitably discuss with him whether the Scripture teaches such and such, and whether one of us is introducing something foreign and secular into our view of the Scriptural message. This is the nature of my criticism. I wish to show that his view of emotion, of mind, of the Biblical word *heart* is not Scriptural, and that because of mistaken views on these terms, he alters the contents of the Gospel.

Chapter 2 of his booklet (it has only two chapters for a total of 41 pages) is headed "Evangelism," and it begins with an account of the mind or understanding. After a very few admissions that man is not like a mule that has no understanding and that we should love the Lord with all our mind, Mr. Stott puts some pages of emphasis on the fact that the mind of man is sinful. One of his conclusions is that "we will need to be cautious in relying too greatly on the mind when making an evangelistic appeal."

He immediately makes some concessions. The evangelist will seek to give a reasoned and reasonable exposition of God's plan of salvation. We must remember that "the New Testament represents conversion in terms of our response not to a Person but to the truth." He also notes that the apostles "reason and argue" with their hearers. These concessions are admirable. But why should not these Scriptural themes have received the emphasis; why should not the concession have been simply to be a little cautious?

In these days particularly, so it seems to me, a strong emphasis on the intellect is necessary. The temper of the times is nihilistic. The authors are irrationalistic. Nothing is true. One must act on hunches. One must decide blindly. Logic is deceptive. Argument is decadent. Thus we have dialectical theologians, existentialists, hippies, and violent street demonstrations. In view of all this, it is good to repeat what the Scripture says. It says a great deal. One could go through 1 John, the Proverbs, passages in 1 Corinthians, and many individual verses, but here for an example two chapters of Ephesians will be used.

In Ephesians 1:8 Paul tells us that God has abounded to us in all wisdom and prudence. He does not mean that God acted wisely and prudently. He means that God makes us act wisely and prudently. He does this by making known to us the secret of his will. In verse 13 we hear the Word of Truth. In the seventeenth verse Paul prays that God grant us a spirit of wisdom in knowing him, which comes about by the eyes of our heart being enlightened. In a moment or two it will be shown that heart is a Scriptural expression for mind. It does not mean emotions. Here the heart is enlightened so that knowledge results. And Paul continues to pray that we should know a great deal (verse 18).

The second chapter of Ephesians does not use the word knowledge, but it is full of knowledge that we should learn. Then in chapter 3 the emphasis on knowledge resumes. God made known something to Paul, and as we read him we can understand his understanding about the secret that God has now more fully revealed. In verse 8 Paul brings to light, that is, makes known, the administration of God's plan – God who created the world so that principalities and powers should know the wisdom of God. In 3:18 Paul prays that we may grasp or understand the breadth and length of God's love; and then he makes a very paradoxical statement: This love exceeds knowledge, but we are to have knowledge of this love that exceeds knowledge. He almost says we should know the unknowable. What is more, we are to know what exceeds knowledge in order to be filled to all the fullness of God. The whole is an amazing paragraph. Its emphasis on knowledge is most important today.

Contrasted with this passage of Scripture, Mr. Stott's denigration of the mind is all the more distressing, for when he comes to speak of emotion, he does not say that the emotions are sinful. Everything he says in subsection (ii) is in commendation of the emotions.

This perverse evaluation is certainly not Scriptural. Mr. Stott tries to make it seem so by saying, "Jesus told us to love the Lord our God with all our *heart* as well as with all our mind." But Mr. Stott seems to have little idea of what the term *heart* means in Scripture. His context shows that he thinks the Bible is talking about the emotions when it uses the word *heart*. But if anyone would take a few moments and look up every instance of the word in the Old Testament, he would find that about 75 percent of the time it means the mind. The remaining one-fourth of the instances is divided between the will and the emotions. Strictly the word *heart*, it seems to me, means "the whole personality." And the proportion shows that the mind is the most important factor in the whole personality. At any rate, the word *heart* is not the equivalent of emotion.

Now, before going on and showing how this unscriptural view causes Mr. Stott to alter the contents of the Gospel, I think it essential to stress the fact that man is sinful. And if man is sinful, so is his mind. So are his emotions.

The Scripture pictures an unregenerate farmer doing his spring plowing, and it says that even the plowing of the wicked is sin. No matter what an unregenerate man does, it is a sin. This Biblical theme is well summarized by the *Westminster Confession* in chapter 16, paragraph 7: "Works done by unregenerate men, although, for the matter of them, they may be things which God commands…yet, because they proceed not from a heart purified by faith…they are therefore sinful…. And yet their neglect of them is more sinful and displeasing to God."

Let strong emphasis therefore be placed on the sinfulness of man. Man is dead in sins and is totally unable to do any spiritual good. For this reason an evangelist may well be cautious in relying too greatly on the mind. He should be cautious in relying too greatly on the man. The evangelist should rely wholly on the Holy Ghost to regenerate his auditors.

But though we should not rely "too greatly" on the mind for something it cannot do, still the mind, sinful though it is, can exercise its natural functions. Mr. Stott says, "the human mind is both finite and fallen, and will neither understand nor believe without the gracious work of the Holy Spirit" (23). Most emphatically, the unregenerate man cannot believe or have faith without the irresistible work of the Holy Spirit. But he can understand the Gospel with the mind as it is. If he could not understand the message, why preach it? Why in particular should a missionary spend years in hard labor learning a foreign language, if his hearers cannot understand the message? Why should he not preach to them in English? In the providence of God, faith, though it is the gift of God, is given through hearing. And it is not through hearing an unknown tongue, but through understanding an intelligible message.

With this distortion of the Scriptural position, it is not surprising that Mr. Stott fails to insist on the preaching of the Gospel as the Gospel is found in the Bible. There are probably other factors besides his view of the emotions that contribute to this result. He seems to be influenced by some phases of the current dialectical theology. Yet this influence is not very far removed from the matter of the emotions, for the dialectical theologians do not hold the intellect in esteem, as did the Reformed. Some of them explicitly repudiate logic and intelligibility. If they do not explicitly arouse the emotions, they may nonetheless be thought of as mystics.

In contradiction to the Bible and to Paul's example, Mr. Stott says that "Our objective is not to unfold to him [the unsaved person] 'the whole counsel of God' but to proclaim the essential core of the Christian gospel." In this connection, note very carefully that Paul claimed that he was innocent of the blood of all men because he had declared all the counsel of God. There is no hint that an evangelist should be silent and omit certain sections of God's revelation. Admittedly a preacher must begin at the point where his hearers find themselves. When Paul preached to the Jews, he did not have to repeat all the Old Testament. Much of it he could take for granted. But when Paul preached on Mars Hill, he could not assume that the Athenians had a knowledge of the Old Testament, or even of its basic theism. So that was where he began. But there is no hint that that is where he wanted to end. His hearers walked out on him; but had they stayed, he would have continued.

Mr. Stott says, "It is commonly accepted today that within the New Testament itself a distinction is made between the *kerugma* (the proclamation of the gospel) and the *didaché* (the instruction of converts)." True, this idea is commonly accepted today. It is one of the most important parts of the anti-Scriptural theories of the dialectical theologians. And it should be resisted by those who believe the Bible.

For one thing, the idea of finding a kernel, or a few important themes, and discarding the rest as unessential, raises the question as to how one should distinguish what is important from what is unimportant. In the history of modernism, from Friedrich Schleiermacher to contemporary times, this kernel has contracted to zero. Modern modernism no longer has even God. God is dead. The kernel is an existential experience or a march on a picket line or the disrupting of democratic procedures in favor of mob violence.

No doubt Mr. Stott would object most strongly to such irresponsible actions; but when a person begins to pare off parts of the Gospel as unessential, there is no stopping point.

That the paring off and omissions have no stopping point can be seen by reflecting on another of Mr. Stott's statements. He says, "The evangelist cannot be expected to usurp the task of the pastor or the teacher. Nor can he, especially in an interdenominational mission, trespass into disputed and controversial fields."

These two sentences are full of misunderstanding and confusion. Note than the word *usurp* is a loaded word. Its use is to picture the evangelist as doing something that it is not his business to do. But if the evangelist's duty is to preach the Gospel, he must preach what the pastor preaches, and he does so without usurpation. An itinerant evangelist should be looked upon as a person who in some way can make a more forceful appeal than the pastor. The pastor is without honor in his own pulpit. The stranger is a bit exceptional. He attracts a little extra attention. But the message must be the same, the same Biblical message, without turning aside to the right or the left, without addition or subtraction.

In the next place, Mr. Stott's second sentence is impossible of attainment. I have never known an evangelist to avoid all controversial topics. Dr. Billy Graham, when in Indianapolis, spent ten minutes attacking Presbyterian doctrine. He told his audience that it was useless to pray for the people who had come forward in response to his invitation. Not even God could help them. They could rely only on their own will. He also said many other controversial things. So too did this evangelist whose preaching I described on the first page of *Biblical Predestination*, from whose use of words I chose the title of that work. In fact, I must say that

I strongly detest the hypocrisy of evangelists who object to others preaching on controversial themes and themselves do the same. Does it not occur to them that if our preaching is controversial because it conflicts with theirs, theirs is just as controversial because it conflicts with ours? They make such an accusation against us so as to deflect attention from their own methods. Now, I do not condemn controversy. The whole of the Bible is controversial. What I detest is hypocrisy.

Now, for all of Mr. Stott's complaint against controversial topics, he himself is engaging in controversy by recommending his type of evangelism. It is controversial to pare off parts of the Gospel. Any paring is controversial. Even after he has pared, controversy remains. It is clear that Mr. Stott stops paring before the Atonement is discarded. But the Atonement is a very controversial doctrine. And I wish to controvert what Mr. Stott says about the Atonement.

The Bible teaches that Christ's death was a propitiatory sacrifice. The modernist *Revised Standard Version* mistranslates the Greek text in an effort to omit propitiation. Now, Mr. Stott says, "We emphatically do not believe that he did this to placate and buy off the anger of God." On the contrary, we emphatically do believe it. Only it is not the same "we." Mr. Stott is engaging in interdenominational controversy. Some groups do not believe that Christ gave his life as a ransom, a payment to the Father, to buy off sinners from the Father's wrath. Some do so believe. So do the Scriptures. *Romans* 1:18 is a verse that speaks of God's wrath and anger. Christ's denunciations of the Pharisees stress the wrath of God. Hell is the punishment inflicted on the unsaved, and is referred to as the wrath to come. Christ interposed himself as a propitiatory sacrifice to save his own from this wrath. He is called the Lamb of God, and the whole Mosaic sacrificial system anticipates this final sacrifice. Even the covenant with Noah, which the Dispensationalists try to reduce to politics, and in which they see no reference to the Atonement, speaks of placating an angry God. This idea is obscured in the *King James Version* and the *American Version* as well. These translations say that God smelled a sweet odor. But the *Koehler-Baumgartner Lexicon* (the latest lexicon at this writing) gives just one meaning to the Hebrew word transliterated *niychoach*: appeasement (*Beschwichtigung*). The "smell of appeasement" then means the placating odor. See also the verbal usage in *Ezekiel* 5:13, "I will appease my anger." Hence the correct translation of *Genesis* 8:20-21 is, "And Noah built an altar unto the Lord...and offered burnt offer-

ings on the altar. And the Lord smelled the placating odor." This anticipation of Christ's sacrifice in the Old Testament and explanations of his
sacrifice in the New agree that he was the propitiation for our sins. He
turned aside God's wrath and anger, which we deserved.

To deny this, as Mr. Stott does, is at the very least to initiate a controversy at the very center of the Gospel. In my opinion, it is something
much worse: It is a rejection of the Gospel. Do away with Christ's propitiation and his satisfaction of the Father's justice, and you do away
with Christianity. I pray that Mr. Stott does not mean what his words say.

But his words are clear, and they must be rejected if one is to be true
to the Bible. Speaking of the "fact" of the cross, Mr. Stott says, "Our
desire is that men should believe that fact, not accept our explanations.
'Christ died for our sins' is enough without any further elucidation.
Moreover, our appeal is never that men should accept a theory about
the Cross but that they should receive a Person who died for them" (35).

These statements are one hundred percent wrong. They should be
denied with all vehemence. They are completely anti-Scriptural and
totally destructive of Biblical Christianity.

In the first place, Mr. Stott's antithesis here between receiving a Person and believing a theory is inconsistent with the Scripture references
he himself previously quoted to the effect that the New Testament represents conversion in terms of our response not to a person but to the
truth. In addition, John Brown of Edinburgh was quoted on this point
just a page or two ago. For further emphasis note also this passage from
Klaas Runia, in his *Reformation Today*: "One of the most popular slogans
in contemporary theology is that truth in the New Testament does not
mean doctrinal truth about Christ but a personal knowledge of Christ.
We believe that such a contrast between propositional conceptual truth
(truth about) and personal truth (knowledge 'of') is utterly foreign to
the New Testament" (56).

In the second place, Mr. Stott's antithesis between a fact and a theory
contradicts the whole New Testament. The "fact" of the Cross is that
the Romans executed a man by nailing him to a post. It is also a "fact"
that there were two other men crucified that day. From the standpoint
of "fact" all three fit the description. But if there is any difference between the significance of Christ's death and the death of the thieves, it
is a matter of "explanation" and not of "fact." Death may be "fact"; but
propitiation is an explanation or theory. And it is the theory that counts.

In the third place, when Mr. Stott says, " 'Christ died for our sins' is enough without any further elucidation," he contradicts his previous words and contradicts Scripture as well. He contradicts his previous words because the phrase "for our sins" itself goes beyond "fact" and is a theory. He contradicts Scripture because 1 *Corinthians* says, "Christ died for our sins *according to the Scriptures*." The Scriptures give a great deal of further elucidation. The theory that "Christ died for our sins...without...further elucidation" is a poor theory and an anti-Scriptural one.

Some people think that Christ died for our sins as an example to us of courage or martyrdom. His death exerts a moral influence on us. In this sense Christ died for our sins. But preaching the death of Christ in this sense never saved anyone. Those who study the history of theology know that there was a patristic theory explaining that Christ paid his ransom to the devil. Hugo Grotius expounded a governmental theory. The evangelist does not preach the Gospel unless he expounds the Scriptural theory.

No evangelist can preach the Atonement without relying on a theory. The word *Atonement* itself is the name of and the result of a theory. The word *Satisfaction*, used earlier, and unfortunately replaced by the word *Atonement*, is also the name of and the result of a theory. It is the name of the Scriptural theory. And unless this theory is preached, the Atonement, the Satisfaction, the Gospel is not preached. Therefore, we may say that Mr. Stott espouses a theory, that his theory is not Scriptural, and that it is controversial. May few evangelists follow his advice.

More recently Mr. Stott has published a much less offensive book, *Our Guilty Silence* (Eerdmans, 1967). In the interval it seems that the author has read and profited by the publications of Dr. J. I. Packer (pages 90, 102). Since this more recent book aims mainly at encouraging evangelistic effort, large sections are beyond reproach. Evangelism needs to be encouraged. Even doctrinally it contains several excellent statements. For example, "we are not to preach a vague Christ, but a precise and particular Christ, namely the Christ of the New Testament" (31); and "If we now ask what Christ did to secure salvation for sinners, the chief answer is: He died" (33); and "He gave himself as a ransom once" (34). Mr. Stott even refers to the sentiment "Impart a minimum of truth...without doctrinal formulation" – a sentiment he seems to have shared in his earlier book – but adds here "With this viewpoint the apostles would certainly have disagreed." On the next page he reinforces this excellent remark with the assertion, "To preach the gospel means preaching Christian dogma" (50-51).

One must unfortunately note, however, that the chief point about Christ's ministry, namely his death, is not an adequate account of the Gospel; nor even the better reference to his death as a ransom is sufficiently precise and particular. Neither the phrase "preaching Christian dogma" nor the most commendable observation that the apostles did not approve of a mere minimum of truth without doctrinal formulation defines the extent of the message to be preached.

In spite of these improvements this more recent book repeats rather than retracts some of the most objectionable features of the earlier one. Perhaps the approach of Holman Hunt's *The Light of the World*, where Christ is portrayed as unable to enter the heart of man, may be passed off as the artistic taste and theological ignorance of an old pensioner (82). But one cannot so shrug off Mr. Stott's plain statement that "the order of events to which the apostles commonly bear witness is that faith is antecedent to life. It is by believing that we live" (104). That this assertion does not mean merely that the daily life I now live in the flesh, I live by the faith of the Son of God, is very clear from the context. The question was, "Does regeneration precede conversion?" Calvinists argue that since man is dead in sin, he cannot repent and believe until he is born from above. This is what Mr. Stott quotes and denies. He conditions regeneration on a faith somehow produced before the sinner is raised from the dead.

To support his contention he says, "It is dangerous to argue from analogy and say 'dead men cannot....' " Mr. Stott ignores the fact that it was not the Calvinists who originated this analogy. The analogy is Scriptural. But if anyone wants plain univocal speech, let him remember the words, "The carnal mind is enmity against God." This is not an analogy.

In addition to belittling Scriptural analogy, Mr. Stott's quotation refers to *John* 3:15-16, 5:25, and 20:31. The first two verses hardly support the Arminian view. Nor does the last. *John* 20:31 reads, "But these are written that you might believe that Jesus is the Christ, the Son of God, and that believing you might have life through his name." If the last clause means that believing produces regeneration, then the first clause would have to mean that John's authorship produces faith. Both clauses are purpose clauses; they would have to be explained similarly. The verse can easily be translated, "These things are written...that believers may have life." The participial substantive points out the group of people who live. There is no way an Arminian can show by this verse that faith causes regeneration or that regeneration and faith are not simultaneous. The difficulty arises only because regeneration, like birth, is momentary, but faith continues throughout life.

The verse on which Mr. Stott puts most emphasis is *John* 5:25; at least he quotes it and not the other: "The dead will hear the voice of the Son of God, and those that hear will live" (104). On the basis of these words the author asserts that faith antecedes regeneration and that it is dangerous to trust the Scriptural analogy between death and sin. A reply to this argument is very easy to make. In my little book, *Biblical Predestination,*[5] I have quoted nearly 500 verses that form a background into which Mr. Stott's interpretation will not fit. *Romans* 3:11-12, 18 say, "There is none that seeks after God.... There is none that does good.... There is no fear of God before their eyes." Now faith is a seeking after God, at least it is something good, and it involves a pious fear of God. It must therefore follow regeneration, for Paul denies that these things are true of the unregenerate. These are only three of the 500 verses. One other is particularly appropriate because it occurs in the immediate context, in fact it is the preceding verse, *John* 5:24, which says, "The one who hears my words...has passed from death to life." Hearing in the present tense is the evidence that the one who was dead became alive in the perfect tense and so remains alive forever.

This quotation is not a mere analogy, even a Scriptural analogy, but a literal statement that life precedes hearing. An analogy might be Lazarus who heard Christ say, "Lazarus, come forth!" Lazarus had to have been resurrected a moment before he heard – unless one were to say his soul in Paradise heard and came back. One sure thing – his decayed corpse did not hear. Or, if one wish an example of similar linguistic usage in a modern setting, one may suppose that a physician, speaking of babies, says, Those that breathe will live. Does this mean that breath produces life, that breath antecedes life, or simply that the baby to continue living must breathe?

It is instructive to note also the dilemma in which Mr. Stott gets tangled by his attempt to recognize the work of the Holy Spirit while maintain-

5. Now called simply *Predestination*. – *Editor*.

ing his Arminian interpretations. On pages 108-109 he writes, " 'No one can come to me unless the Father draw him.' We need to hear much more in the Church on this 'no one can,' this natural inability of men to believe in Christ…. [To which I say, Amen.] Jesus also said, 'You are not willing to come….' The human mind finds it impossible neatly to resolve the tension between this 'cannot' and this 'will not.' " My comment is that Mr. Stott's inability to resolve this tension does not prove that some other mind cannot. Those who accept the clear Calvinistic senses of the Scriptural texts find that the tension is imaginary.

In contrast with Mr. Stott's non-evangelical views, I would like to commend to all readers the excellent statement of the Gospel made by J. I. Packer on pages 57-73 of his *Evangelism and the Sovereignty of God*. The title of the subsection is "What Is the Evangelistic Message?" Mr. Packer is very clear that it is not "Christ died for our sins…without …further elucidation." This is why he takes thirteen pages to summarize it. He apologizes for shortening it, as unfortunately it must be in a small book. The summary is divided into four parts. The first part is the thesis that the evangelistic message is a message about God. "It tells us who he is, what his character is, what his standards are, and what he requires of us, his creatures." Even in this opening sentence, we breathe a fresh, new atmosphere, full of sound theology, with the hope of reasonable elucidation. His second point is that the Gospel is a message about sin. After three pages on sin, Mr. Packer adds three subheads under sin: "(i) Conviction of sin is essentially an awareness of a wrong relationship with God…. (ii) Conviction of sin always involves conviction of sins…. (iii) Conviction of sin always includes conviction of sinfulness…." His third point is "The Gospel is a message about Christ," under which he has two subpoints: "(i) We must not present the person of Christ apart from his saving work…. (ii) We must not present the saving work of Christ apart from his person…." Finally, the fourth point is, "The Gospel is a summons to faith and repentance." Here is a man who obviously knows a great deal about the Gospel. He wants the message proclaimed. He has the right ideas about evangelism, and it would do every Christian good to read his book.

There are nonetheless certain points on which I believe Mr. Packer to be woefully wrong. He is not wrong about the Gospel, but I believe he is wrong in evaluating the people who hear the Gospel and perhaps accept it, or seem to accept it. In defending the sovereignty of God, he appeals to Christian or apparently Christian experience and says that all Christians believe in prayer, and that a person who prays acknowledges God's sovereignty. He also says, "You have never for one moment supposed that the decisive contribution to your salvation was yours and not God's." He also says, "You pray for the conversion of others."

Now, it is clear that any Christian who prays for the conversion of others and who never for a moment thinks that his action was decisive admits, at least tacitly, the sovereignty of God. But there are so many in professedly Christian evangelistic services who do no such things. In Indianapolis, as I said a moment ago, I heard Billy Graham tell his audience not to pray for the conversion of those who had come forward, because not even God himself could help them. The decisive thing was their own choice. Mr. Packer knows the message, but I fear he does not realize the extent of the opposition.[6]

There is another point at which I would like to suggest a correction of what Mr. Packer says. It seems to me that he goes astray because he imports into the religious argument an analogy from science, an analogy that science does not itself justify. Mr. Packer distinguishes between a paradox, which can be solved and explained by a little ingenuity, and an antinomy, which he says is insoluble. His scientific example is the two theories of light, the wave theory and the corpuscular theory, both of which scientists use, but which are mutually incompatible. Then Mr. Packer says that there are antinomies in the Bible. The antinomy between divine sovereignty and human responsibility is one such.

It seems to me that a misunderstanding of science at this point led the author into a misunderstanding of the Bible. If the Bible contradicts itself, as clearly as the wave theory contradicts the corpuscular theory, we will be forced to abandon the Bible. No one in his right mind can believe contradictions. In fact, if the antinomy is as he says it is, God himself is faced with an insoluble puzzle. And if something is insoluble for God, then God cannot be trusted. Packer tells us that God has given us this antinomy, and if he has given it to us, is that not enough? Cannot we trust God? The answer is that we cannot trust contradictions and insoluble antinomies, no matter who gives them to us. If someone told me to believe that the number two was both even and odd, I would

6. This is a most perceptive comment, and it explains Packer's later involvement in the ecumenical movement called Evangelicals and Catholics Together, as well as his lifelong affiliation with the apostate Anglican Church. – *Editor*

conclude that this someone was not God. God, anyone I could think of as God, does not talk nonsense, and insoluble antinomies are nonsense. They are just as much nonsense as it would be to say that the path of a point equidistant from a given point has three right angles along it.

But if we see what modern science can do with its two theories of light, and if we pay just a little attention to sovereignty and responsibility, these unfortunate consequences never arise. The laws of science should not be considered as intended descriptions of natural motions. They should be considered as directions for operating in a physics laboratory. They are methods for producing desired results. This, in brief, is the theory of operationalism, which I have defended in *The Philosophy of Science and Belief in God*. It is always possible to use either of two mutually exclusive methods for producing the same desired result. To cure milk fever in cows, one may use the antiseptic Lugol, or one may use compressed air. Both work satisfactorily. Hence, in manipulating light, a physicist may use either theory, or if for a particular purpose the two are not equally satisfactory, for Lugol cannot do everything compressed air can do and vice versa, the physicist can use one for one purpose and the other for another.

As for sovereignty and responsibility, it is relatively easy to see that they are not antinomies. Sovereignty and free will would be an antinomy and contradiction; for sovereignty means that God controls all things, including our wills, and free will means that God does not control our wills. This is a clear contradiction. Only an insane person could believe both of these. But responsibility does not mean free will. Responsibility means that God can demand from us a response. God can hold us to account. Far from conflicting with sovereignty, this is an exercise of sovereignty. If there were no sovereignty, if there were no superior to hold us accountable, there would be no responsibility. For further elucidation, see my small book on *Biblical Predestination*.

Another but smaller booklet than J. I. Packer's *Evangelism and the Sovereignty of God* is Iain Murray's *The Invitation System*, published by The Banner of Truth Trust. Evangelism would flourish today if a thousand American ministers would read these two small books. Mr. Murray stresses preaching the Gospel. His opening words are, "An invariable characteristic of true preaching has been the assurance that the proclamation of the Gospel is the divinely ordained means for the conviction and conversion of sinners."

The booklet, however, deals chiefly with the deplorable practices in evangelistic services, which practices hinder the progress of or obscure the clarity of the Gospel. The particular practice singled out for examination is that of inviting members of the audience to come forward at the end of the sermon. Connected with this coming forward are an after-meeting, signing cards, and perhaps visiting the people in their homes after the campaign.

The method seems to have been invented by Charles Finney in the middle of the nineteenth century. Mr. Murray notes that it was unknown in Britain until recently. Now, anything Finney did or said is suspect, or worse. He was a disaster. Years and decades after his evangelistic campaigns he was still preventing men from believing the Gospel. Still, one cannot argue that because Finney stood on a platform, no evangelist should stand on a platform. Possibly even inviting the audience to walk down to the front could be a good thing.

It could of course be bad. It could be bad in itself – unlike standing on a platform; or it could be bad merely in some accidental aspects that happen to be widely used at present. Mr. Murray picks out several such. For example, the evangelist often leaves it unclear why a person should come forward. I have heard evangelists give such wide invitations that virtually the whole audience could come forward. Those who wished to accept Christ, those who wanted a new experience, those who had doubts and perplexities, those who wanted the evangelist to pray for them – all come to the front! Then the next day's newspaper could give the number that responded.

Even if the invitation is more restricted, there are difficulties. Remarks Mr. Murray, "Is the walk forward an outward declaration of an inner saving decision already made by the hearer in his seat, just as an 'act of witness'? Why then are they told to 'come forward and receive Christ'?" The author describes in some detail the confusion observed in evangelistic services between receiving Christ and a public profession of having received him. There is Scriptural warrant for the latter; but none for receiving Christ by coming forward. Coming forward ought not to be explained as coming to receive Christ. To do so is like interpreting John 8:38 to mean that "continuing in the Word" is the method by which one becomes a Christian, instead of the act of one who is already a Christian. Similarly John 15:8 does not say that fruit-bearing is the process by which we become Christians. Coming forward in a service therefore may be a public profession of having become a Christian, but it cannot be understood as coming to Christ.

In a following section Mr. Murray examines certain psychological arguments. Evangelists use them to defend their methods. Non-Christians use them to reduce evangelism to the naturalistic power of mass appeal. He quotes Billy Graham's calling the attention of the audience to the hundreds coming forward, and claiming that "tens of thousands will have come to know Christ" in this manner.

The theology that underlies this use of an invitation is given by Harold J. Ockenga. He says, "Some Reformed theologians teach that regeneration by the Holy Spirit precedes conversion. The evangelical position is that regeneration is conditioned upon repentance, confession, and faith." This is remarkable ignorance on Ockenga's part. It is not true that "some" Reformed theologians teach that regeneration precedes conversion. *All* Reformed theologians do. Second, Ockenga tries to exclude these Reformed theologians from the evangelical fold. He contrasts the Reformation theology with the "evangelical view." According to Ockenga, therefore, none of the Puritans was evangelical. To support his bad theology Ockenga relies on his ignorance of Greek grammar in his exegesis of *Ephesians* 2:8. He wants faith to be the result of human ability, an ability found in every man before regeneration; he does not want faith to be a gift from God.

When such unscriptural ideas are held, it is no wonder that the invitation to come forward is either confused or completely bad.

It does seem to me, however, that Mr. Murray has restricted his attention to one aspect or one form of "coming forward." His warnings against adulterating the Gospel with bad Greek and worse theology are well taken. Nevertheless, good theology and great clarity can make use of inviting people to come forward. The present writer insists that evangelism is preaching the Gospel; that a few sermons are inadequate; that as much elucidation as possible must be given. If this be so, then an evangelist, after having explained how Christ satisfied the justice of his Father because of man's disobedience to and depravity before God, and after having declared the Resurrection and its implications, can very well invite those who are interested to come forward and enter counseling sessions for the purpose of a clearer and a more extensive understanding. This is much more necessary now than it was in Britain before the time of Finney.

In those days many people heard the Gospel weekly. Some were catechized in their homes. Very few in Britain were as ignorant as today's American populace. If the people of that happy age needed instruction, the need is tenfold greater now. Why cannot the method of coming forward be used to set up classes for Bible study? Cards could be signed: They could be signed as class cards in college, for admission to classes projected ahead of time and ready to receive the people. Thus when properly used the method of coming forward is just as good as the method of standing on a platform while preaching. The essential thing is the message preached.

The same principle applies to hillbilly singing. If it detracts from the message, it is bad. If it were used with a moderately well educated audience, with people who have some taste in music, it would so detract, by repelling them. On the other hand, I cannot agree with a friend of mine who says that good Reformed theology requires that only Bach should be used. Oh dear, no Mozart and not even Handel's *Messiah*? Personally I prefer good music, just as I prefer good grammar; but the Scripture does not specify what style of music must be used. As the *Westminster Confession* says, "There are circumstances concerning the worship of God and government of the church, common to human actions and societies, which are to be ordered by the light of nature and Christian prudence."

In conclusion, the Gospel is a message, a message that Mr. Packer and Mr. Murray understand very well and that some others do not. Evangelism is a matter of proclaiming that message. If the message is not proclaimed all the hillbilly music in Kentucky and Tennessee will not make the service evangelistic. If the message is proclaimed, the accidents can be as they may; the effort is *ipso facto* evangelism.

29

Art and the Gospel[1]

Gordon H. Clark

IN THE United States, both within and without the churches, Christianity has many enemies. There are the scientific and not-so-scientific atheists who have tremendous influence in public education. There are the murderous abortionists, and criminals of all types. But none of these is the subject of this article. Within the churches, Neo-orthodoxy, more Neo than orthodox, reduces the Bible to the level of *Aesop's Fables*. Also within the churches is another group, some of whom have been influenced by Herman Dooyeweerd and H. R. Rookmacher, some whose background is too diverse to trace, who wish to substitute art for the Gospel. Perhaps they are not technically existentialists, but they dislike intellect and truth just as much. The exact views of these people vary considerably. Some see further into the implications than others. Since this diversity makes it awkward to speak of the group as a whole, the present article will select one particular member. The selection is defensible because the gentleman, Leland Ryken, has edited and written a preface for an anthology entitled *The Christian Imagination* (Baker Book House, 1981). Consider now this quotation from the Preface:

> The imagination is what enables us to produce and enjoy the arts.... The imagination is one way we know the truth. For truth, including religious truth, is not solely the province of the reason or intellect. For example, one can experience the truth about God and salvation while listening to Handel's *Messiah*. But how? Not primarily through reason, but through the senses (hearing), emotions, and the combination of mind, senses, and emotions that I call the imagination.

1. Reprinted from *The Trinity Review*.

A pastor friend of mine...first knew that Jesus rose from the grave...not during the sermon, but with the sound of the trumpets that concluded the service [one Easter morning].... Not surely with the intellect, but with the senses.... Truth, I repeat, does not come to us solely through the reason and intellect.

Consider the way truth comes to us in the Bible. If you asked an adult Sunday School class what topics are covered in the Old Testament *Psalms*, the list would look something like this: God, providence, guilt.... Such a list leans decidedly toward the abstract.... But consider an equally valid list of topics...dogs, honey, grass, thunder.... It touches our emotions far more vividly than the first list does. In the Bible truth does not address only the rational intellect.... Handel's *Messiah* is as important to us as a Christmas sermon.

Because the ideas expressed in these paragraphs attract the adherence of many who profess Christianity, they should be scrutinized with care. One good thing can be said: The author tries to define his term *imagination*: It is what enables us to enjoy the arts. Later he more explicitly defines it as the combination of mind, senses, and emotions. That no major philosopher had ever used the term in that sense is irrelevant, for every author has the right to define his terms as he pleases. He must, however, adhere to his own definition, and the definition must be suitable to the development of the subject. Yet, though the stated definition includes mind, the general tenor of the passage is inimical to mind. Furthermore, if imagination is the complex of all these factors, including the mind, what can the author mean by saying that the imagination is one way to know the truth. What other way could there be? The definition as given includes one's entire consciousness. It fails to distinguish imagination from any other conscious action. Without using one's mind, senses, or emotions, what truths could possibly be learned, and what would the learning process be? The definition is so all-inclusive that it is utterly useless in distinguishing between any two methods of learning. Because of this vacuity, because the author obviously wants to find at least two ways to truth – one without the intellect – and because of the next-to-last sentence in the quotation, it seems that the author wishes to learn some things through the emotions alone.

One must ask whether or not even the enjoyment of the arts depends more on the mind than on the emotions. Critics of painting examine the brushwork; they evaluate the relation between light and dark areas (*e.g.* Rembrandt's drawing of the beggar, his daughter, her baby son, and the householder); and they analyze the composition. Composition requires careful thought on the part of both artist and critic. Such analyses are intellectual, not emotional; and I can hardly imagine that Rembrandt's drawing arouses much emotion in anyone. If the biographer of Leonardo da Vinci had his facts right, it would seem that this prince of painters was completely non-emotional; or if not completely, his emotion was one of continuing anger. Then too, Milton Nahm's book on *The Aesthetic Response* sharply distinguishes it from emotion.

However, aesthetics is neither the main difficulty with the quoted passage nor of much importance to Christianity. A more, a much more serious difficulty is the author's view of truth. Maybe he has no view of truth, at least no clear view; but he certainly seems to be talking about two kinds of truth. He says, "Religious truth is not solely the province of reason." Presumably the truths of physics and zoology are truths of reason. Even this is doubtful, for he says that truth – presumably all truth, and therefore religious truths as well, but also the laws of physics – is not solely intellectual. I doubt that many physicists would agree, and it would be interesting to see how Ryken would answer their disclaimer. Our trouble here is to discover what he means by *truth*. Statements, propositions, predicates attached to subjects are true (or false). But how could a nocturne or one of Rodin's sculptures be true? The sculpture might resemble its model, and the proposition "The sculpture resembles its model" would be a truth; but how could a bronze or marble statute be a truth? Only propositions can be true. If I merely pronounce a word – *cat, college, collage* – it is neither true nor false: It does not say anything. But if I say "The cat is black" or "The collage is abominable," I speak the truth (or falsehood as the case may be). But *cat*, all by itself and without previous context, is neither true nor false. Note that the *Psalms*, which the author tries to use as a support, do not simply say *dogs, honey, grass*, and *thunder*: They say that the grass withers, the honey is sweet, and so on, all of which are propositions. And if the words *grass* and *thunder* touch one's emotions "far more vividly" than the words *God* and *guilt*, there is something radically wrong with that person's emotions. Better to have no emotions at all. Emotions are hard to control; they are not only distressing to the one who has them, they are also disconcerting to his friends.

If the author's peculiar aesthetics is relatively unimportant, and if his undefined view of truth is a more serious flaw, the implications of such a defective view of truth are disastrous for the preaching of the Gospel.

It is undoubtedly true that "one can experience the truth about God and salvation while listening to Handel's *Messiah*." The reason is that *The Messiah* gives the words of Scripture. Of course, one can have the experience of boredom, or a bright idea on investment policy, or a decision as to which restaurant one will take his girlfriend afterward while listening to *The Messiah*. But if one has thoughts of God and salvation while and because of the oratorio, they come by reason of the Scriptural words. The music adds little or nothing. In fact, the reason why many people do not have thoughts about God while listening, is that the music distracts them.

The use of the word *while* is a propaganda device: Literally the sentence is true, but the writer means something else. Fortunately, after inducing a favorable response on the part of the reader by the word *while*, he actually says what he means, twice. First, a pastor first believed Jesus rose from the dead, not during a sermon which told him so, but with (of course *with* is ambiguous too) the sound of the concluding fanfare. At any rate, the pastor did not believe in the resurrection with his mind or intellect: He sensed it. One might grant that he sensed the noise of the trumpets; but how can anyone today sense Christ's resurrection? This is utter nonsense, and the final line of the quotation shows how anti-Christian the whole viewpoint is.

He says, "Handel's *Messiah* is as important to us as a Christmas sermon." Naturally, if the Christmas sermon in a liberal church centers on Santa Claus, and not on the incarnation of the Second Person of the Trinity, Handel's music might be as important, the equal importance being about zero. But of course the writer means that the music is as important as the words. If this were so, there would be no necessity to preach the Gospel and ask people to believe the good news.

But art is no substitute for Gospel information. In Clowes Hall at Butler University in Indianapolis there hangs a gigantic tapestry which depicts the miraculous draft of fishes. It is supposed to be a great work of art. Now, on one occasion, I accompanied a group of Japanese professors through the place, and one of them asked me, "What is the story?" No amount of art appreciation could give him the information the Bible gives. That Christ was God and that he worked miracles during his incarnation is understood only through the intellectual understanding of words. Nor would a blast of trumpets help.

If the writer's views were true, the work of missionaries would be enormously easier. They would not have to learn a difficult language. They could just put on a recording of Handel and conversions would follow. Why didn't Paul think of that? Don't preach the Gospel, don't give information, just play some music! Poor Paul; he said, Faith comes by hearing the Word of God. No tapestry, no sculpture, no fanfare. But it is Paul who defines what Christianity is. Anything else is something else.

PART 6

THE PURITY AND PEACE
OF THE CHURCH

And this I pray, that your love may abound still more and more
in knowledge and all discernment,
that you may approve the things that are excellent,
that you may be sincere and without offense
till the day of Christ,
being filled with the fruits of righteousness
which are by Jesus Christ,
to the glory and praise of God.
Philippians 1:9-11

30

The Necessity of Reforming the Church[1]

John Calvin

FIRST, THEN, the question is not, whether the church labors under diseases both numerous and grievous (this is admitted even by all moderate judges), but whether the diseases are of a kind the cure of which admits not of longer delay, and as to which, therefore, it is neither useful nor becoming to await the result of slow remedies. We are accused of rash and impious innovation, for having ventured to propose any change at all on the former state of the church. What! Even if it has not been done either without cause or imperfectly? I hear there are persons who, even in this case, do not hesitate to condemn us; their opinion being that we were indeed right in desiring amendment, but not right in attempting it. From such persons, all I would ask at present is, that they will for a little [while] suspend their judgment until I shall have shown from fact that we have not been prematurely hasty – have not attempted anything rashly, anything alien from our duty – have, in fine, done nothing until compelled by the highest necessity. To enable me to prove this, it is necessary to attend to the matters in dispute.

We maintain, then, that at the commencement – when God raised up Luther and others, who held forth a torch to light us into the way of salvation, and who, by their ministry, founded and reared our churches – those heads of doctrine in which the truth of our religion, those in which the pure and legitimate worship of God, and those in which the salvation of men are comprehended, were in a great measure obsolete. We maintain that the use of the sacraments was in many ways vitiated

---

1. Calvin published this tract in 1543 and addressed it to Charles V, Roman Catholic Emperor of the Holy Roman Empire, and to the Diet of Spires. This excerpt is from the edition published in 1995 by Protestant Heritage Press, P.O. Box 180922, Dallas, Texas 75218.

and polluted. And we maintain that the government of the church was converted into a species of foul and insufferable tyranny. But, perhaps these averments have not force enough to move certain individuals until they are better explained. This, therefore, I will do, not as the subject demands, but as far as my ability will permit. Here, however, I have no intention to review and discuss all our controversies; that would require a long discourse, and this is not the place for it. I wish only to show how just and necessary the causes were which forced us to the changes for which we are blamed. To accomplish this, I must take up together the three following points.

First, I must briefly enumerate the evils which compelled us to seek for remedies.

Secondly, I must show that the particular remedies which our reformers employed were apt and salutary.

Thirdly, I must make it plain that we were not at liberty any longer to delay putting forth our hand, inasmuch as the matter demanded instant amendment.

The Evils Which Compelled Us to Seek Remedies

The first point, as I merely advert to it for the purpose of clearing my way to the other two, I will endeavor to dispose of in a few words; but in wiping off the heavy charge of sacrilegious audacity and sedition, founded on the allegation that we have improperly, and with intemperate haste, usurped an office which did not belong to us, I will dwell at greater length.

If it be inquired, then, by what things chiefly the Christian religion has a standing existence amongst us, and maintains its truth, it will be found that the following two not only occupy the principal place, but comprehend under them all the other parts, and consequently the whole substance of Christianity: that is, a knowledge, *first,* of the mode in which God is duly worshiped; and, *secondly,* of the source from which salvation is to be obtained. When these are kept out of view, though we may glory in the name of Christians, our profession is empty and vain. After these come the sacraments and the government of the church, which, as they were instituted for the preservation of these branches of doctrine, ought not to be employed for any other purpose; and, indeed, the only means of ascertaining whether they are administered purely and in due form, or otherwise, is to bring them to this test. If any one is desirous of a clearer and more familiar illustration, I would say, that rule in the church, the pastoral office, and all other matters of order, resemble the body, whereas the doctrine which regulates the due worship of God, and points out the ground on which the consciences of men must rest their hope of salvation, is the soul which animates the body, renders it lively and active, and, in short, makes it not to be a dead and useless carcass.

As to what I have yet said, there is no controversy among the pious, or among men of right and sane mind.

Let us now see what is meant by the due worship of God. Its chief foundation is to acknowledge him to be, as he is, the only source of all virtue, justice, holiness, wisdom, truth, power, goodness, mercy, life, and salvation; in accordance with this, to ascribe and render to him the glory of all that is good, to seek all things in him alone, and in every want have recourse to him alone. Hence arises prayer, hence praise and thanksgiving – these being attestations to the glory which we attribute to him. This is that genuine sanctification of his name which he requires of us above all things. To this is united adoration, by which we manifest for him the reverence due to his greatness and excellency; and to this ceremonies are subservient, as helps or instruments, in order that, in the performance of divine worship, the body may be exercised at the same time with the soul. Next after these comes self-abasement, when, renouncing the world and the flesh, we are transformed in the renewing of our mind and living no longer to ourselves, submit to be ruled and actuated by him. By this self-abasement we are trained to obedience and devotedness to his will, so that his fear reigns in our hearts, and regulates all the actions of our lives.

That in these things consists the true and sincere worship which alone God approves, and in which alone he delights, is both taught by the Holy Spirit throughout the Scriptures, and is also, antecedent to discussion, the obvious dictate of piety. Nor from the beginning was there any other method of worshiping God, the only difference being, that this spiritual truth, which with us is naked and simple, was under the former dispensation wrapped up in figures. And this is the meaning of our Saviour's words, "The hour is coming, and now is, when the true worshipers shall worship the Father in Spirit and in truth" (John 4:23). For by these words he meant not to declare that God was not worshiped by the fathers in this spiritual manner, but only to point out a distinction in the external form: That is, that while they had the Spirit shadowed forth by many figures, we have him in simplicity. But it has always been an acknowledged point, that God, who is a spirit, must be worshiped in Spirit and in truth.

Moreover, the rule which distinguishes between pure and vitiated worship is of universal application, in order that we may not adopt any device which seems fit to ourselves, but look to the injunctions of him who alone is entitled to prescribe. Therefore, if we would have him to approve our worship, this rule, which he everywhere enforces with the utmost strictness, must be carefully observed. For there is a twofold reason why the Lord, in condemning and prohibiting all fictitious worship, requires us to give obedience only to his own voice. First, it tends greatly to establish his authority that we do not follow our own pleasure, but depend entirely on his sovereignty; and, secondly, such is our folly, that when we are left at liberty, all we are able to do is to go astray. And then when once we have turned aside from the right path, there is no end to our wanderings, until we get buried under a multitude of superstitions. Justly, therefore, does the Lord, in order to assert his full right of dominion, strictly enjoin what he wishes us to do, and at once reject all human devices which are at variance with his command. Justly, too, does he, in express terms, define our limits, that we may not, by fabricating perverse modes of worship, provoke his anger against us.

I know how difficult it is to persuade the world that God disapproves of all modes of worship not expressly sanctioned by his Word. The opposite persuasion which cleaves to them, being seated, as it were, in their very bones and marrow, is, that whatever they do has in itself a sufficient sanction, provided it exhibits some kind of zeal for the honor of God. But since God not only regards as fruitless, but also plainly abominates, whatever we undertake from zeal to his worship, if at variance with his command, what do we gain by a contrary course? The words of God are clear and distinct, "Obedience is better than sacrifice." "In vain do they worship me, teaching for doctrines the commandments of men," (1 Samuel 15:22; Matthew 15:9). Every addition to his Word, especially in this matter, is a lie. Mere "will worship" (ἐθελοθρησκεία) is vanity. This is the decision, and when once the judge has decided, it is no longer time to debate.

Will your imperial majesty now be pleased to recognize, and will you, most illustrious princes, lend me your attention, while I show how utterly at variance with this view are all the observances, in which, throughout the Christian world in the present day, divine worship is made to consist? In word, indeed, they concede to God the glory of all that is good; but, in reality, they rob him of the half, or more than the half, by partitioning his perfections among the saints. Let our adversaries use what evasions they may, and defame us for exaggerating what they pretend to be trivial errors, I will simply state the fact as every man perceives it. Divine offices are distributed among the saints as if they had been appointed colleagues to the supreme God, and, in a multitude of instances, they are made to do his work, while he is kept out of view. The thing I complain of is just what everybody confesses by a vulgar proverb. For what is meant by saying, "the Lord cannot be known for apostles," unless it be that, by the height to which apostles are raised, the dignity of Christ is sunk, or at least obscured? The consequence of this perversity is that mankind, forsaking the fountain of living waters, have learned, as Jeremiah tells us, to hew them out "cisterns, broken cisterns, that can hold no water" (*Jeremiah* 2:13). For where is it that they seek for salvation and every other good? Is it in God alone? The whole tenor of their lives openly proclaims the contrary. They say, indeed, that they seek salvation and every other good in him; but it is mere pretence, seeing they seek them elsewhere.

Of this fact, we have clear proof in the corruptions by which prayer was first vitiated, and afterwards in a great measure perverted and extinguished. We have observed that prayer affords a test whether or not suppliants render due glory to God. In like manner, will it enable us to discover whether, after robbing him of his glory, they transfer it to the creatures. In genuine prayer, something more is required than mere entreaty. The suppliant must feel assured that God is the only being to whom he ought to flee, both because he only can succor him in necessity; and also, because he has engaged to do it. But no man can have this conviction unless he pays regard both to the command by which God calls us to himself, and to the promise of listening to our prayers which is annexed to the command. The command was not thus regarded when the generality of mankind invoked angels and dead men promiscuously with God, and the wiser part, if they did not invoke them instead of God, at least regarded them as mediators, at whose intercession God granted their requests.

Where, then, was the promise which is founded entirely on the intercession of Christ? Passing by Christ, the only Mediator, each betook himself to the patron who had struck his fancy, or if at any time a place was given to Christ, it was one in which he remained unnoticed, like some ordinary individual in a crowd. Then, although nothing is more repugnant to the nature of genuine prayer than doubt and distrust, so much did these prevail, that they were almost regarded as necessary, in order to pray aright. And why was this? Just because the world understood not the force of the expressions in which God invites us to pray to him, engages to do whatsoever we ask in reliance on his command and promise, and sets forth Christ as the Advocate in whose name our prayers are heard. Besides, let the public prayers which are in common use in churches be examined. It will be found that they are stained with numberless impurities. From them, therefore, we have it in our power to judge how much this part of divine worship was vitiated. Nor was there less corruption in the expressions of thanksgiving. To this fact, testimony is borne by the public hymns, in which the saints are lauded for every blessing, just as if they were the colleagues of God.

Then what shall I say of adoration? Do not men pay to images and statues the very same reverence which they pay to God? It is an error to suppose that there is any difference between this madness and that of the heathen. For God forbids us not only to worship images, but also to regard them as the residence of his divinity, and worship it as residing in them. The very same pretexts which the patrons of this abomination employ in the present day were formerly employed by the heathen to cloak their impiety. Besides, it is undeniable that saints – nay, their very bones, garments, shoes, and images – are adored even in the place of God.

But some subtle disputant will object that there are diverse species of adoration: that the honor of *dulia* [*veneration*], as they term it, is given to saints, their images, and their bones; and that *latria* [*worship*] is reserved for God as due to him only, unless we are to except *hyperdulia* [*high veneration*], a species which, as the infatuation increased, was invented to set the blessed virgin above the rest. As if these subtle distinctions were either known or present to the minds of those who prostrate themselves before images. Meanwhile, the world is full of idolatry not less gross, and if I may so speak, not less capable of being felt, than was the ancient idolatry of the Egyptians, which all the prophets everywhere so strongly reprobate. I am merely glancing at each of these corruptions, because I will afterwards more clearly expose their demerits.

I come now to ceremonies, which, while they ought to be grave attestations of divine worship, are rather a mere mockery of God. A new Judaism, as a substitute for that which God had distinctly abrogated, has again been reared up by means of numerous puerile extravagancies, collected from different quarters; and with these have been mixed up certain impious rites, partly borrowed from the heathen, and more adapted to some theatrical show than to the dignity of our religion. The first evil here is that an immense number of ceremonies, which God had by his authority abrogated once for all, have been again revived. The next evil is that while ceremonies ought to be living exercises of piety, men are vainly occupied with numbers of them that are both frivolous and useless. But by far the most deadly evil of all is that after men have thus mocked God with ceremonies of one kind or other, they think they have fulfilled their duty as admirably as if these ceremonies included in them the whole essence of piety and divine worship.

With regard to self-abasement, on which depends regeneration to newness of life, the whole doctrine was entirely obliterated from the minds of men, or, at least, half buried, so that it was known to few, and to them but slenderly. But the spiritual sacrifice which the Lord in an especial manner recommends is to mortify the old and be transformed into a new man. It may be, perhaps, that preachers stammer out something about these words, but that they have no idea of the things meant by them is apparent even from this – that they strenuously oppose us in our attempt to restore this branch of divine worship. If at any time they discourse on repentance, they only glance, as if in contempt, at the points of principal moment, and dwell entirely on certain external exercises of the body, which, as Paul assures us, are not of the highest utility (*Colossians* 2:23; *1 Timothy* 4:8). What makes this perverseness the more intolerable is that the generality, under a pernicious error, pursue the shadow for the substance, and, overlooking true repentance, devote their whole attention to abstinences, vigils, and other things, which Paul terms "beggarly elements" of the world.

Having observed that the Word of God is the test which discriminates between his true worship and that which is false and vitiated, we thence readily infer that the whole form of divine worship in general use in the present day is nothing but mere corruption. For men pay no regard to what God has commanded, or to what he approves, in order that they may serve him in a becoming manner, but assume to themselves a license of devising modes of worship, and afterwards obtruding them upon him as a substitute for obedience. If in what I say I seem to exaggerate, let an examination be made of all the acts by which the generality suppose that they worship God. I dare scarcely except a tenth part as not the random offspring of their own brain. What more would we? God rejects, condemns, abominates all fictitious worship, and employs his Word as a bridle to keep us in unqualified obedience. When shaking off this yoke, we wander after our own fictions, and offer to him a worship, the work of human rashness, how much soever it may delight ourselves, in his sight it is vain trifling, nay, vileness and pollution. The advocates of human traditions paint them in fair and gaudy colors; and Paul certainly admits that they carry with them a show of wisdom; but as God values obedience more than all sacrifices, it ought to be sufficient for the rejection of any mode of worship, that it is not sanctioned by the command of God.

We come now to what we have set down as the second principal branch of Christian doctrine: that is, knowledge of the source from which salvation is to be obtained. Now, the knowledge of our salvation presents three different stages. First, we must begin with a sense of individual wretchedness, filling us with despondency as if we were spiritually dead. This effect is produced when the original and hereditary depravity of our nature is set before us as the source of all evil – a depravity which begets in us distrust, rebellion against God, pride, avarice, lust, and all kinds of evil concupiscence; and making us averse to all rectitude and justice, [it] holds us captive under the yoke of sin; and when, moreover, each individual, on the disclosure of his own sins, feeling confounded at his turpitude, is forced to be dissatisfied with himself, and to account himself and all that he has of his own as less than nothing; then, on the other hand, conscience (being cited to the bar of God) becomes sensible of the curse under which it lies, and, as if it had received a warning of eternal death, learns to tremble at the divine anger. This, I say, is the first stage in the way to salvation, when the sinner, overwhelmed and prostrated, despairs of all carnal aid, yet does not harden himself against the justice of God, or become stupidly callous, but, trembling and anxious, groans in agony, and sighs for relief.

From this he should rise to the second stage. This he does when, animated by the knowledge of Christ, he again begins to breathe. For to one humbled in the manner in which we have described, no other course remains but to turn to Christ, that through his interposition he may be delivered from misery. But the only man who thus seeks salvation in Christ is the man who is aware of the extent of his power: that is, acknowledges him as the only priest who reconciles us to the Father, and his death as the only sacrifice by which sin is expiated, the divine justice satisfied, and a true and perfect righteousness acquired; who, in fine, does not divide the work between himself and Christ, but acknowledges it to be by mere gratuitous favor that he is justified in the sight of God. From this stage also he must rise to the third, when instructed in the grace of Christ, and in the fruits of his death and resurrection, he rests in him with firm and solid confidence, feeling assured that Christ is so completely his own, that he possesses in him righteousness and life.

Now, see how sadly this doctrine has been perverted. On the subject of original sin, perplexing questions have been raised by the Schoolmen, who have done what they could to explain away this fatal disease; for in their discussions they reduce it to little more than excess of bodily appetite and lust. Of that blindness and vanity of intellect whence unbelief and superstition proceed, of inward depravity of soul, of pride, ambition, stubbornness, and other secret sources of evil, they say not a word. And sermons are not a whit more sound. Then, as to the doctrine of free will, as preached before Luther and other reformers appeared, what effect could it have but to fill men with an overweening opinion of their own virtue, swelling them out with vanity, and leaving no room for the grace and assistance of the Holy Spirit?

But why dwell on this? There is no point which is more keenly contested, none in which our adversaries are more inveterate in their opposition, than that of justification: namely, as to whether we obtain it by faith or by works. On no account will they allow us to give Christ the honor of being called our righteousness, unless their works come in at the same time for a share of the merit. The dispute is not, whether good works ought to be performed by the pious, and whether they are accepted by God and rewarded by him; but whether, by their own worth, they reconcile us to God; whether we acquire eternal life as their price; whether they are compensations which are made to the justice of God, so as to take away guilt; and whether they are to be confided in as a ground of salvation.

We condemn the error which enjoins men to have more respect to their own works than to Christ, as a means of rendering God propitious, of meriting his favor, and obtaining the inheritance of eternal life: in short, as a means of becoming righteous in his sight. First, they plume themselves on the merit of works, as if they laid God under obligations to them. Pride such as this, what is it but a fatal intoxication of soul? For instead of Christ, they adore themselves, and dream of possessing life while they are immersed in the profound abyss of death. It may be said that I am exaggerating on this head, but no man can deny the trite doctrine of the schools and churches to be, that it is by works we must merit the favor of God, and by works acquire eternal life; that any hope of salvation unpropped by good works is rash and presumptuous; that we are reconciled to God by the satisfaction of good works, and not by a gratuitous remission of sins; that good works are meritorious of eternal salvation, not because they are freely imputed for righteousness through the merits of Christ, but in terms of law; and that men, as often as they lose the grace of God, are reconciled to him, not by a free pardon, but by what they term works of satisfaction – these works being supplemented by the merits of Christ and martyrs, provided only the sinner deserves to be so assisted. It is certain that before Luther became known to the world, all men were fascinated by these impious dogmas; and even in the present day, there is no part of our doctrine which our opponents impugn with greater earnestness and obstinacy.

Lastly, there was another most pestilential error, which not only occupied the minds of men, but was regarded as one of the principal articles of faith, of which it was impious to doubt: that is, that believers ought to be perpetually in suspense and uncertainty as to their interest in the divine favor. By this suggestion of the devil, the power of faith was completely extinguished, the benefits of Christ's purchase destroyed, and the salvation of men overthrown. For, as Paul declares, that faith only is Christian faith which inspires our hearts with confidence, and emboldens us to appear in the presence of God (*Romans* 5:2). On no other view could his doctrine in another passage be maintained: that is, that "we have received the Spirit of adoption, whereby we cry, Abba, Father" (*Romans* 8:15).

But what is the effect of that hesitancy which our enemies require in their disciples, save to annihilate all confidence in the promises of God? Paul argues that "If they which are of the law be heirs, faith is made void, and the promise made of none effect" (*Romans* 4:14). Why so? Just because the law keeps a man in doubt, and does not permit him to entertain a sure and firm confidence. But they, on the other hand, dream of a faith, which, excluding and repelling man from that confidence which Paul requires, throws him back upon conjecture, to be tossed like a reed shaken by the wind. And it is not surprising that after they had once founded their hope of salvation on the merit of works, they plunged into all this absurdity. It could not but happen, that from such a precipice they should have such a fall. For what can man find in his works but materials for doubt, and, finally, for despair? We thus see how error led to error.

Here, mighty emperor, and most illustrious princes, it will be necessary to recall to your remembrance what I formerly observed: that is, that the safety of the church depends as much on this doctrine as human life does on the soul. If the purity of this doctrine is in any degree impaired, the church has received a deadly wound; and, therefore, when I shall have shown that it was for the greater part extinguished, it will be the same as if I had shown that the church had been brought to the very brink of destruction. As yet, I have only alluded to this in passing, but by-and-by I will unfold it more clearly.

I come now to those things which I have likened to the body: that is, government and the dispensation of the sacraments, of which, when the doctrine is subverted, the power and utility are gone, although the external form should be faultless. What, then, if there was no soundness in them externally or internally? And it is not difficult to demonstrate that this was the fact.

First, in regard to the sacraments, ceremonies devised by men were placed in the same rank with the mysteries instituted by Christ. For seven sacraments were received without any distinction, though Christ appointed two only, the others resting merely on human authority. Yet to these the grace of God was held to be annexed, just as much as if Christ had been present in them. Moreover, the two which Christ instituted were fearfully corrupted. Baptism was so disguised by superfluous additions, that scarcely a vestige of pure and genuine baptism could be traced; while the holy Supper was not only corrupted by extraneous observances, but its very form was altogether changed.

What Christ commanded to be done, and in what order, is perfectly clear. But in contempt of his command, a theatrical exhibition was got

507

up, and substituted for the Supper. For what resemblance is there between the mass and the true supper of our Lord? While the command of Christ enjoins believers to communicate with each other in the sacred symbols of his body and blood, the thing seen at mass ought more properly to be termed excommunion. For the priest separates himself from the rest of the assembly, and devours apart that which ought to have been brought forward into the midst and distributed. Then, as if he were some successor of Aaron, he pretends that he offers a sacrifice to expiate the sins of the people.

But where does Christ once mention sacrifice? He bids us take, eat, and drink. Who authorizes men to convert *taking* into *offering?* And what is the effect of the change but to make the perpetual and inviolable edict of Christ yield to their devices?

This is, indeed, a grievous evil. But still worse is the superstition which applies this work to the living and the dead, as a procuring cause of grace. In this way the efficacy of Christ's death has been transferred to a vain theatrical show, and the dignity of an eternal priesthood wrested from him to be bestowed upon men.

If, at any time, the people are called to communion, they are admitted only to half a share. Why should this be? Christ holds forth the cup to all, and bids all drink of it. In opposition to this, men interdict the assembly of the faithful from touching the cup. Thus the signs, which by the authority of Christ were connected by an indissoluble tie, are separated by human caprice. Besides, the consecration, both of baptism and of the mass, differs in no respect whatever from magical incantations. For by breathings and whisperings, and unintelligible sounds, they think they work mysteries. As if it had been the wish of Christ, that in the performance of religious rites his Word should be mumbled over, and not rather pronounced in a clear voice. There is no obscurity in the words by which the Gospel expresses the power, nature, and use of baptism. Then, in the Supper, Christ does not mutter over the bread, but addresses the apostles in distinct terms, when he announces the promise and subjoins the command, "This do in remembrance of me." Instead of this public commemoration, they whisper out secret exorcisms, fitter (as I have observed), for magical arts than sacraments.

The first thing we complain of here is, that the people are entertained with showy ceremonies, while not a word is said of their significance and truth. For there is no use in the sacraments unless the thing which the sign visibly represents is explained in accordance with the Word of God. Therefore, when the people are presented with nothing but empty figures, with which to feed the eye, while they hear no doctrine which might direct them to the proper end, they look no further than the external act. Hence that most pestilential superstition, under which, as if the sacraments alone were sufficient for salvation, without feeling any solicitude about faith or repentance, or even Christ himself, they fasten upon the sign instead of the thing signified by it. And, indeed, not only among the rude vulgar, but in the schools also, the impious dogma everywhere obtained, that the sacraments were effectual by themselves, if not obstructed in their operation by mortal sin; as if the sacraments had been given for any other end or use than to lead us by the hand to Christ.

Then, in addition to this, after consecrating the bread by a perverse incantation, rather than a pious rite, they keep it in a little box, and occasionally carry it about in solemn state, that it may be adored and prayed to instead of Christ. Accordingly, when any danger presses, they flee to that bread as their only protection, use it as a charm against all accidents, and, in asking pardon of God, employ it as the best expiation; as if Christ, when he gave us his body in the sacrament, had meant that it should be prostituted to all sorts of absurdity. For what is the amount of the promise? Simply this – that as often as we received the sacrament, we should be partakers of his body and blood. "Take," says he, "eat and drink; this is my body, this is my blood. This do in remembrance of me." Do we not see that the promise is on either side enclosed by limits within which we must confine ourselves if we would secure what it offers? Those, therefore, are deceived who imagine that, apart from the legitimate use of the sacrament, they have anything but common and unconsecrated bread.

Then, again, there is a profanation common to all these religious rites: That is, that they are made the subjects of a disgraceful traffic, as if they had been instituted for no other purpose than to be subservient to gain. Nor is this traffic conducted secretly or bashfully; it is plied openly, as at the public mart. It is known in each particular district how much a mass sells for. Other rites, too, have their fixed prices. In short, anyone who considers must see that churches are just ordinary shops, and that there is no kind of sacred rite which is not there exposed for sale.

Were I to go over the faults of ecclesiastical government in detail, I should never have done. I will, therefore, only point to some of the grosser sort, which cannot be disguised.

And, first, the pastoral office itself, as instituted by Christ, has long been in desuetude. His object in appointing bishops and pastors, or whatever the name be by which they are called, certainly was, as Paul declares, that they might edify the church with sound doctrine. According to this view, no man is a true pastor of the church who does not perform the office of teaching. But, in the present day, almost all those who have the name of pastors have left that work to others. Scarcely one in a hundred of the Bishops will be found who ever mounts the pulpit in order to teach. And no wonder; for bishoprics have degenerated into secular principalities. Pastors of inferior rank, again, either think that they fulfill their office by frivolous performances altogether alien from the command of Christ, or, after the example of the Bishops, throw even this part of the duty on the shoulders of others. Hence the letting of sacerdotal offices is not less common than the letting of farms. What would we more? The spiritual government which Christ recommended has totally disappeared, and a new and mongrel species of government has been introduced, which, under whatever name it may pass current, has no more resemblance to the former than the world has to the kingdom of Christ.

If it be objected that the fault of those who neglect their duty ought not to be imputed to the order, I answer, first, that the evil is of such general prevalence, that it may be regarded as the common rule; and, secondly, that, were we to assume that all the Bishops, and all the presbyters under them, reside each in his particular station, and do what in the present day is regarded as professional duty, they would never fulfill the true institution of Christ. They would sing or mutter in the church, exhibit themselves in theatrical vestments, and go through numerous ceremonies, but they would seldom, if ever, teach. According to the precept of Christ, however, no man can claim for himself the office of bishop or pastor who does not feed his flock with the Word of the Lord.

Then while those who preside in the church ought to excel others, and shine by the example of a holier life, how well do those who hold the office in the present day correspond in this respect to their vocation! At a time when the corruption of the world is at its height, there is no order more addicted to all kinds of wickedness. I wish that by their innocence they would refute what I say. How gladly would I at once retract. But their turpitude stands exposed to the eyes of all – exposed their insatiable avarice and rapacity – exposed their intolerable pride and cruelty. The noise of indecent revelry and dancing, the rage of gaming, and entertainments, abounding in all kinds of intemperance, are in their houses only ordinary occurrences, while they glory in their luxurious delicacies, as if they were distinguished virtues.

To pass over other things in silence, what impurity in that celibacy which of itself they regard as a title to esteem! I feel ashamed to unveil enormities which I had much rather suppress, if they could be corrected by silence. Nor will I divulge what is done in secret. The pollutions which openly appear are more than sufficient. How many priests, pray, are free from whoredom? Nay, how many of their houses are infamous for daily acts of lewdness? How many honorable families do they defile by their vagabond lusts? For my part, I have no pleasure in exposing their vices, and it is no part of my design; but it is of importance to observe what a wide difference there is between the conduct of the priesthood of the present day, and that which true ministers of Christ and his church are bound to pursue.

Not the least important branch of ecclesiastical government is the due and regular election and ordination of those who are to rule. The Word of God furnishes a standard by which all such appointments ought to be tested, and there exist many decrees of ancient councils which carefully and wisely provide for every thing which relates to the proper method of election. Let our adversaries then produce even a solitary instance of canonical election, and I will yield them the victory. We know the kind of examination which the Holy Spirit, by the mouth of Paul (epistles of *Timothy* and *Titus*), requires a pastor to undergo, and that which the ancient laws of the fathers enjoin. At the present day, in appointing Bishops, is anything of the kind perceived? Nay, how few of those who are raised to the office are endowed even slenderly with those qualities without which they cannot be fit ministers of the church? We see the order which the apostles observed in ordaining ministers, that which the primitive church afterwards followed, and, finally, that which the ancient canons require to be observed. Were I to complain that at present this order is spurned and rejected, would not the complaint be just? What, then, should I say that everything honorable is trampled upon, and promotion obtained by the most disgraceful and flagitious proceedings? The fact is of universal notoriety. For ecclesiastical honors are either purchased for a set price, or seized by the hand of violence, or secured by nefarious actions, or acquired by sordid sycophancy. Occasionally even, they are the hire paid for panderism and similar services. In short, more shameless proceedings are exhibited here than ever occur in the acquisition of secular possessions.

And would that those who preside in the church, when they corrupt its government, only sinned for themselves, or at least injured others by nothing but by their bad example! But the most crying evil of all is, that they exercise a most cruel tyranny, and that a tyranny over souls. Nay, what is the vaunted power of the church in the present day, but a lawless, licentious, unrestricted domination over souls, subjecting them to the most miserable bondage?

Christ gave to the apostles an authority similar to that which God had conferred on the prophets, an authority exactly defined: that is, to act as his ambassadors to men. Now, the invariable law is that he who is entrusted with an embassy must faithfully and religiously conform to his instructions. This is stated in express terms in the apostolical commission, "Go and teach all nations whatsoever things I have delivered unto you." Likewise "preach" (not anything you please), but the "Gospel" [*Matthew* 28:19-20]. If it is asked what the authority is with which their successors were invested, we have the definition of Peter which enjoins all who speak in the church to speak "the oracles" of God [*1 Peter* 4:11].

Now, however, those who would be thought the rulers of the church arrogate to themselves a license to speak whatsoever they please, and to insist that as soon as they have spoken they shall be implicitly obeyed. It will be averred that this is a calumny, and that the only right which they assume is that of sanctioning by their authority what the Holy Spirit has revealed. They will, accordingly, maintain that they do not subject the consciences of believers to their own devices or caprice, but only to the oracles of the Spirit, which, being revealed to them, they confirm and promulgate to others.

Forsooth an ingenious pretext! No man doubts that in whatever the Holy Spirit delivers by their hands they are to be unhesitatingly obeyed. But when they add that they cannot deliver anything but the genuine oracles of the Holy Spirit, because they are under his guidance, and that all their decisions cannot but be true, because they sit in chairs of verity, is not this just to measure their power by their caprice? For if all their decrees, without exception, are to be received as oracles, there is no limit to their power. What tyrant ever so monstrously abused the patience of his subjects as to insist that everything he proclaimed should be received as a message from Heaven! Tyrants, no doubt, will have their edicts obeyed, be the edicts what they may. But these men demand much more. We must believe that the Holy Spirit speaks when they obtrude upon us what they have dreamed.

We see, accordingly, how hard and iniquitous the bondage is in which, when armed with this power, they have enthralled the souls of the faithful. Laws have been piled above laws, to be so many snares to the conscience. For they have not confined these laws to matters of external order, but applied them to the interior and spiritual government of the soul. And no end was made until they amounted to that immense multitude, which now looks not unlike a labyrinth. Indeed, some of them seem framed for the very purpose of troubling and torturing consciences, while the observance of them is enforced with not less strictness than if they contained the whole substance of piety. Nay, though in regard to the violation of the commands of God, either no question is asked, or slight penances are inflicted, anything done contrary to the decrees of men requires the highest expiation. While the church is oppressed by this tyrannical yoke, anyone who dares to say a word against it is instantly condemned as a heretic. In short, to give vent to our grief is a capital offense. And in order to ensure the possession of this insufferable domination, they, by sanguinary edicts, prevent the people from reading and understanding the Scriptures, and fulminate against those who stir any question as to their power. This excessive rigor increases from day to day, so that now on the subject of religion it is scarcely permitted to make any inquiry at all.

At the time when divine truth lay buried under this vast and dense cloud of darkness; when religion was sullied by so many impious superstitions; when by horrid blasphemies the worship of God was corrupted, and his glory laid prostrate; when by a multitude of perverse opinions, the benefit of redemption was frustrated, and men, intoxicated with a fatal confidence in works, sought salvation anywhere rather than in Christ; when the administration of the sacraments was partly maimed and torn asunder, partly adulterated by the admixture of numerous fictions, and partly profaned by traffickings for gain; when the government of the church had degenerated into mere confusion and devastation; when those who sat in the seat of pastors first did most vital injury to the church by the dissoluteness of their lives, and, secondly, exercised a cruel and most noxious tyranny over souls, by every kind of error, leading men like sheep to the slaughter; then Luther arose, and after him others, who with united counsels sought out means and methods by which religion might be purged from all these defilements, the doctrine of godliness restored to its integrity, and the church raised out of its calamitous into somewhat of a tolerable condition. The same course we are still pursuing in the present day....

To return to the division which we formerly adopted. All our controversies concerning doctrine relate either to the legitimate worship of God, or to the ground of salvation. As to the former, unquestionably we do exhort men to worship God neither in a frigid nor a careless manner; and while we point out the mode, we neither lose sight of the end, nor omit anything which bears upon the point. We proclaim the glory of God in terms far loftier than it was wont to be proclaimed before, and we earnestly labor to make the perfections in which his glory shines better and better known. His benefits toward ourselves we extol as eloquently as we can, while we call upon others to reverence his majesty, render due homage to his greatness, feel due gratitude for his mercies, and unite in showing forth his praise. In this way there is infused into their hearts that solid confidence which afterwards gives birth to prayer; and in this way, too, each one is trained to genuine self-denial, so that his will being brought into obedience to God, he bids farewell to his own desires. In short, as God requires us to worship him in a spiritual manner, so we most zealously urge men to all the spiritual sacrifices which he recommends.

Even our enemies cannot deny our assiduity in exhorting men to expect the good which they desire from none but God, to confide in his power, rest in his goodness, depend on his truth, and turn to him with the whole heart; to recline upon him with full hope, and recur to him in necessity: that is, at every moment to ascribe to him every good thing which we enjoy, and show we do so by open expressions of praise. And that none may be deterred by difficulty of access, we proclaim that a complete fountain of blessings is opened up to us in Christ, and that out of it we may draw for every need. Our writings are witnesses, and our sermons witnesses, how frequent and sedulous we are in recommending true repentance, urging men to renounce their own reason and carnal desires, and themselves entirely, that they may be brought into obedience to God alone, and live no longer to themselves, but to him. Nor, at the same time, do we overlook external duties and works of charity, which follow on such renovation. This I say, is the sure and unerring form of worship, which we know that he approves, because it is the form which his word prescribes, and these the only sacrifices of the Christian church which have his sanction.

Since, therefore, in our [Reformed] churches, only God is adored in pious form without superstition; since his goodness, wisdom, power, truth, and other perfections, are there preached more fully than anywhere else; since he is invoked with true faith in the name of Christ, his mercies celebrated both with heart and tongue, and men constantly urged to a simple and sincere obedience; since, in fine, nothing is heard but what tends to promote the sanctification of his name, what cause have those who call themselves Christians to be so inveterate against us? First, loving darkness rather than light, they cannot tolerate the sharpness with which we, as in duty bound, rebuke the gross idolatry which is everywhere beheld in the world. When God is worshiped in images, when fictitious worship is instituted in his name, when supplication is made to the images of saints, and divine honors paid to dead men's bones; against these, and similar abominations, we protest, describing them in their true colors. For this cause, those who hate our doctrine inveigh against us, and represent us as heretics who have dared to abolish the worship of God, as of old approved by the church. Concerning this name of *church*, which they are ever and anon holding up before them as a kind of shield, we will shortly speak. Meanwhile, how perverse, when these flagitious corruptions are manifest, not only to defend them, but cloak their deformity, by impudently pretending that they belong to the genuine worship of God!

Both parties confess that in the sight of God idolatry is an execrable crime. But when we attack the worship of images, our adversaries immediately take the opposite side, and lend their support to the crime which they had verbally concurred with us in condemning. Nay, what is more ridiculous, after agreeing with us as to the term in Greek, it is no sooner turned into Latin than their opposition begins. For they strenuously defend the worship of images, though they condemn idolatry – ingenious men denying that the honor which they pay to images is worship; as if, in comparing it with ancient idolatry, it were possible to see any difference. Idolaters pretended that they worshiped the celestial gods, though under corporeal figures which represented them. What else do our adversaries pretend? But does God accept of such excuses? Did the prophets cease to rebuke the madness of the Egyptians, when, out of the secret mysteries of their theology, they drew subtle distinctions under which to screen themselves? What, too, do we suppose the brazen serpent, whom the Jews worshiped, to have been, but something which they honored as a representation of God? "The Gentiles," says Ambrose (in *Psalm* 118), "worship wood, because they think it an image of God, whereas the invisible image of God is not in that which is seen, but specially in that which is not seen." And what is it that is done in the present day? Do they not prostrate themselves before images, as if God were present in them? Did they not suppose the power and grace of God attached to pictures and statues, would they flee to them when they are desirous to pray?

I have not yet adverted to the grosser superstitions, though these cannot be confined to the ignorant, since they are approved by public consent. They adorn their idols now with flowers and chaplets, now with robes, vests, zones, purses, and frivolities of every kind. They light tapers and burn incense before them, and carry them on their shoulders in solemn state. When they pray to the image of Christopher or Barbara, they mutter over the Lord's Prayer and the angel's salutation. The fairer or dingier the images are, the greater is their excellence supposed to be. To this is added a new recommendation from fabulous miracles. Some they pretend to have spoken, others to have extinguished a fire in the church by trampling on it, others to have removed of their own accord to a new abode, others to have dropped from Heaven. While the whole world teems with these and similar delusions (and the fact is perfectly notorious), we, who have brought back the worship of the one God to the rule of his word – we, who are blameless in this matter, and have purged our churches, not only of idolatry but of superstition also – are accused of violating the worship of God, because we have discarded the worship of images: that is, as we call it, *idolatry,* but as our adversaries will have it, *idolodulia.*

But, besides the clear testimonies which are everywhere met with in Scripture, we are also supported by the authority of the ancient church. All the writers of a purer age describe the abuse of images among the Gentiles as not differing from what is seen in the world in the present day; and their observations on the subject are not less applicable to the present age than to the persons whom they then censured.

As to the charge which they bring against us for discarding images, as well as the bones and relics of saints, it is easily answered. For none of these things ought to be valued at more than the brazen serpent, and the reasons for removing them were not less valid than those of Hezekiah for breaking it. It is certain that the *idolmania,* with which the minds of men are now fascinated, cannot be cured otherwise than by removing bodily the source of the infatuation. And we have too much experience of the absolute truth of St. Augustine's sentiment (*Ep.* 49): "No man prays or worships looking on an image without being impressed with the idea that it is listening to him." And, likewise (in *Psalm* 115:4): "Images, from having a mouth, eyes, ears, and feet, are more effectual to mislead an unhappy soul than to correct it, because they neither speak, nor see, nor hear, nor walk." Also, "The effect in a manner extorted by the external shape is, that the soul living in a body, thinks a body which it sees so very like its own must have similar powers of perception."

As to the matter of relics, it is almost incredible how impudently the world has been cheated. I can mention three relics of our Saviour's circumcision; likewise fourteen nails which are exhibited for the three by which he was fixed to the cross; three robes for that seamless one on which the soldiers cast lots; two inscriptions that were placed over the cross; three spears by which our Saviour's side was pierced, and about five sets of linen clothes which wrapped his body in the tomb. Besides, they show all the articles used at the institution of the Lord's Supper, and an infinite number of similar impositions. There is no saint of any celebrity of whom two or three bodies are not in existence. I can name the place where a piece of pumice stone was long held in high veneration as the skull of Peter. Decency will not permit me to mention fouler exhibitions. Undeservedly, therefore, are we blamed for having studied to purify the church of God from such pollutions.

In regard to the worship of God, our adversaries next accuse us, because, omitting empty and childish observances tending only to hypocrisy, we worship God more simply. That we have in no respect detracted from the spiritual worship of God is attested by fact. Nay, when it had in a great measure gone into desuetude, we have reinstated it in its former rights. Let us now see whether the offence taken at us is just. In regard to doctrine, I maintain that we make common cause with the prophets.

For, next to idolatry, there is nothing for which they rebuke the people more sharply than for falsely imagining that the worship of God consisted in external show. For what is the sum of their declarations? That God dwells not, and sets no value on ceremonies considered only in themselves; that he looks to the faith and truth of the heart; and that the only end for which he commanded, and for which he approves them, is that they may be pure exercises of faith, and prayer, and praise. The writings of all the prophets are full of attestations to this effect. Nor, as I have observed, was there anything for which they labored more.

Now, it cannot, without effrontery, be denied that when our reformers appeared, the world was more than ever smitten with this blindness. It was therefore absolutely necessary to urge men with these prophetical rebukes, and draw them off, as by force, from that infatuation, that they might no longer imagine that God was satisfied with naked ceremonies, as children are with shows. There was a like necessity for urging the doctrine of the spiritual worship of God – a doctrine which had almost vanished from the minds of men. That both of these things have been faithfully performed by us in times past, and still are, both our writings and our sermons clearly prove.

In inveighing against ceremonies themselves, and also in abrogating a great part of them, we confess that there is some difference between us and the prophets. They inveighed against their countrymen for confining the worship of God to external ceremonies, but still ceremonies which God himself had instituted; we complain that the same honor is paid to frivolities of man's devising. They, while condemning superstition, left untouched a multitude of ceremonies which God had enjoined, and which were useful and appropriate to an age of tutelage; our business has been to correct numerous rites which had either crept in through oversight, or been turned to abuse – and which, moreover, by no means accorded with the time. For, if we would not throw everything into confusion, we must never lose sight of the distinction between the old and the new dispensations, and of the fact that ceremonies, the observance of which was useful under the law, are now not only superfluous, but vicious and absurd.

When Christ was absent and not yet manifested, ceremonies, by shadowing him forth, cherished the hope of his advent in the breasts of believers; but now that his glory is present and conspicuous, they only obscure it. And we see what God himself has done. For those ceremonies which he had commanded for a time he has now abrogated forever. Paul explains the reason: first, that since the body has been manifested in Christ, the types have, of course, been withdrawn; and, secondly, that God is now pleased to instruct his church after a different manner (*Galatians* 4:5; *Colossians* 2:4, 14, 17). Since, then, God has freed his church from the bondage which he had imposed upon it, can anything, I ask, be more perverse than for men to introduce a new bondage in place of the old? Since God has prescribed a certain economy, how presumptuous to set up one which is contrary to it, and openly repudiated by him.

But the worst of all is that though God has so often and so strictly interdicted all modes of worship prescribed by man, the only worship paid to him consisted of human inventions. What ground, then, have our enemies to vociferate that in this matter we have given religion to the winds? First, we have not laid even a finger on anything which Christ does not discountenance as of no value, when he declares that it is vain to worship God with human traditions. The thing might, perhaps, have been more tolerable if the only effect had been that men lost their pains by an unavailing worship; but, since as I have observed, God in many passages forbids any new worship unsanctioned by his word; since he declares that he is grievously offended with the presumption which invents such worship, and threatens it with severe punishment; it is clear that the reformation which we have introduced was demanded by a strong necessity.

I am not unaware how difficult it is to persuade the world that God rejects and even abominates everything relating to his worship that is devised by human reason. The delusion on this head is owing to several causes: "Every one thinks highly of his own," as the old proverb expresses it. Hence the offspring of our own brain delights us, and besides, as Paul admits, this fictitious worship often presents some show of wisdom [*Colossians* 2:23]. Then, as it has for the most part an external splendor which pleases the eye, it is more agreeable to our carnal nature, than that which alone God requires and approves, but which is less ostentatious. But there is nothing which so blinds the understandings of men, and misleads them in their judgments in this matter, as hypocrisy. For while it is incumbent on true worshipers to give the heart and mind, men are always desirous to invent a mode of serving God of a totally different description, their object being to perform to him certain bodily observances, and keep the mind to themselves. Moreover, they imagine that when they obtrude upon him external pomp, they have, by this artifice, evaded the necessity of giving themselves. And this is the reason why they submit to innumerable observances which miserably fatigue them without measure and without end, and why they choose to wander in a perpetual labyrinth, rather than worship God simply in spirit and in truth....

Reformation Required Without Delay

But how deservedly soever we complain that the doctrine of truth was corrupted, and the whole body of Christianity sullied by numerous blemishes, still our censurers deny that this was cause sufficient for so disturbing the church, and, in a manner, convulsing the whole world.

We, indeed, are not so stupid as not to perceive how desirable it is to avoid public tumults, nor so savage as not to be touched, and even to shudder in our inmost soul, on beholding the troubled condition in which the church now is. But with what fairness is the blame of existing commotions imputed to us, when they have not been, in the least degree, excited by us? Nay, with what face is the crime of disturbing the church laid to our charge by the very persons who obviously are the authors of all these disturbances? This is just the case of the wolves complaining of the lambs.

When Luther at first appeared, he merely touched, with a gentle hand, a few abuses of the grossest description, now grown intolerable. And he did it with a modesty which intimated that he had more desire to see them corrected, than determination to correct them himself. The opposite party forthwith sounded to arms; and when the contention was more and more inflamed, our enemies deemed it the best and shortest method to suppress the truth by cruelty and violence. Accordingly, when our people challenged them to friendly discussion, and desired to settle disputes by calm arguments, they were cruelly persecuted with sanguinary edicts, until matters have been brought to the present miserable pass.

Nor is this calumny against us without precedent. With the very same charge which we are now forced to hear, wicked Ahab once upbraided Elijah: that is, that he was the disturber of Israel. But the holy prophet by his reply acquitted us. "I," says he, "have not troubled Israel, but you and your father's house, in that you have forsaken the commandments of the Lord, and you have followed Baalim" (1 Kings 18:17-

18). It is unfair, therefore, to load us with odium, on account of the fierce contest concerning religion which this day rages in Christendom, unless, indeed, it be thought proper first to condemn Elijah, with whom we have a common defense. His sole excuse is that he had fought only to vindicate the glory and restore the pure worship of God, and he retorts the charge of exciting contention and disturbances upon those who stirred up tumults as a means of resisting the truth.

And what is it that we have done hitherto, and what do we even now, but strive that the one God may be worshiped amongst us, and that his simple truth may reign in the church? If our adversaries deny this, let them, at least, convict us of impious doctrine before they charge it upon us, as a fault, that we dissent from others. For what were we to do? The only terms on which we could purchase peace were to betray the truth of God by silence. Though, indeed, it would not have been enough to be silent, unless we had also, by tacit consent, approved of impious doctrine, of open blasphemies against God, and the most degrading superstitions. What else, then, at the very least, could we do, than testify with a clear voice that we had no fellowship with impiety? We have, therefore, simply studied to do what was our duty. That matters have blazed forth into hostile strife is an evil, the blame of which must rest with those who chose to confound Heaven and Earth, rather than give a place to pious and sound doctrine – their object being, by whatever means, to keep possession of the tyranny which they had usurped.

It ought to be sufficient, and more than sufficient, for our defense, that the sacred truth of God, in asserting which we sustain so many contests, is on our side, whereas our adversaries, in contending with us, war not so much against us as God himself. Then it is not of our own accord that we engage in this fervor of contention. It is their intemperance which has dragged us into it against our expectation. Let the result, then, have been what it may, there is no reason why we should be loaded with hatred. For as it is not ours to govern events, neither is it ours to prevent them. But there is an ancient practice which the wicked have resorted to in all ages: that is, to take occasion from the preaching of the Gospel to excite tumult, and then to defame the Gospel as the cause of dissension – dissension which, even in the absence of opportunity, they wickedly and eagerly court. And, as in the primitive church, the prophecy behooved to be fulfilled, that Christ should be to his own countrymen a stone of stumbling and rock of offense, so it is not surprising if the same thing holds true in our time also. It may well indeed be thought strange for the builders to reject the stone which ought to occupy the principal place in the foundation, but as this happened at the beginning, in the case of Christ, let it not surprise us that it is also a common event in the present day.

Here I entreat your imperial majesty, and you, most illustrious princes, that as oft as this unhappy rending of the church, and the other countless evils which have sprung from dissension, either occur to your own thoughts, or are suggested by others, you would, at the same time, call to mind, that Christ has been set up as a sign to be spoken against, and that his Gospel, wherever it is preached, instantly inflames the rage and resistance of the wicked. Then, from conflict a shock must necessarily ensue. Hence the uniform fate of the Gospel, from its first commencement, has been, and always will be, even unto the end, to be preached in the world amid great contention. But it is the part of the prudent to consider from what source the evil springs. Whoever does this will readily free us from all blame. It certainly behooved us to bear testimony to the truth, as we have done. Woe to the world if it chooses to challenge Christ to combat, rather than embrace the peace which he offers! The man who will not bear to be corrected will undoubtedly be crushed by him....

But someone will ask, how are the appropriated revenues [from priests and monks] administered? Certainly not in a manner altogether free from blame, but still in a manner far better and holier than by our enemies. Out of them, at all events, true ministers are supported, who feed their flocks with the doctrine of salvation, whereas, formerly, churches left utterly destitute of pastors were burdened with the payment of them. Wherever schools or hospitals for the poor existed they remain; in some instances their revenues have been increased; in none have they been diminished. In many places, also, in lieu of monasteries, hospitals have been established where there were none before; in others new schools have been erected, in which not only have regular salaries been given to the masters, but youths also are trained, in the hope of being afterwards of service to the church.

In fine, churches derive many advantages in common from these revenues, with which, before, only monks and priests were gorged. Nor is it a small portion which is devoted to extraordinary expenses, though these are well entitled to be taken into account. It is certain that much more is consumed when matters are in disorder, than would be if proper arrangements were made among the churches. But nothing could be more unjust than to deny to our princes and magistrates the right of making expenditure of this kind, not for their private benefit, but to meet the public necessities of the church. Besides, our adversaries forget to deduct their spoliations and unjust exactions, by which communities were pillaged for sacrifices, of which they are now relieved. But there is one reason which renders all this discussion, in a great measure, superfluous. More than three years ago, our princes declared their readiness to make restitution, provided the same course were enforced against those who detain a much larger amount for a less honorable cause, and who are guilty of much greater corruption in the administration of it. Our princes, therefore, stand bound to your imperial majesty by their promise. The document also is before the world; so that this should not be any hindrance to uniformity of doctrine.

The last and principal charge which they bring against us is, that we have made a schism in the church. And here they boldly maintain against us, that in no case is it lawful to break the unity of the church. How far they do us injustice, the books of our authors bear witness. Now, however, let them take this brief reply – that we neither dissent from the church, nor are aliens from her communion. But, as by this specious name of church, they are wont to cast dust in the eyes even of persons otherwise pious and right-hearted, I beseech your imperial majesty, and you, most illustrious princes, *first,* to divest yourselves of all prejudice, that you may give an impartial ear to our defense; *secondly,* not to be instantly terrified on hearing the name of church, but to remember that the prophets and apostles had, with the pretended church of their days, a contest similar to that which you see us have in the present day with the Roman pontiff and his whole train. When they, by the command of God, inveighed freely against idolatry, superstition, and the profanation of the temple, and its sacred rites; against the carelessness and lethargy of priests; and against the general avarice, cruelty, and licentiousness; they were constantly met with the objection which our opponents have ever in their mouths – that by dissenting from the common opinion, they violated the unity of the church. The ordinary government of the church was then vested in the priests. They had not presumptuously arrogated it to themselves, but God had conferred it upon them by his law. It would occupy too much time to point out all the instances. Let us, therefore, be contented with a single instance, in the case of Jeremiah.

He had to do with the whole college of priests, and the arms with which they attacked him were these, "Come, and let us devise devices against Jeremiah; for the law shall not perish from the priest, nor counsel from the wise, nor the word from the prophet" (*Jeremiah* 18:18) They had among them a high priest, to reject whose judgment was a capital crime, and they had the whole order to which God himself had committed the government of the Jewish church concurring with them. If the unity of the church is violated by him, who, instructed solely by divine truth, opposes himself to ordinary authority, the prophet must be a schismatic; because, not at all deterred by such menaces from warring with the impiety of the priests, he steadily persevered.

That the eternal truth of God, preached by the prophets and apostles, is on our side, we are prepared to show, and it is indeed easy for any man to perceive. But all that is done is to assail us with this battering-ram, "Nothing can excuse withdrawal from the church." We deny out and out that we do so. With what, then, do they urge us? With nothing more than this, that to them belongs the ordinary government of the church. But how much better right had the enemies of Jeremiah to use this argument? To them, at all events, there still remained a legal priesthood, instituted by God; so that their vocation was unquestionable. Those who, in the present day, have the name of prelates, cannot prove their vocation by any laws, human or divine. Be it, however, that in this respect both are on a footing, still, unless they previously convict the holy prophet of schism, they will prove nothing against us by that specious title of church.

I have thus mentioned one prophet as an example. But all the others declare that they had the same battle to fight – wicked priests endeavoring to overwhelm them by a perversion of this term *church*. And how did the apostles act? Was it not necessary for them, in professing themselves the servants of Christ, to declare war upon the synagogue? And yet the office and dignity of the priesthood were not then lost. But it will be said that, though the prophets and apostles dissented from wicked priests in doctrine, they still cultivated communion with them in sacrifices and prayers. I admit they did, provided they were not forced into idolatry. But which of the prophets do we read of as having ever sacrificed in Bethel? Which of the faithful, do we suppose, communicated in impure sacrifices, when the temple was polluted by Antiochus, and profane rites were introduced into it?

On the whole, we conclude that the servants of God never felt themselves obstructed by this empty title of church when it was put forward to support the reign of impiety. It is not enough, therefore, simply to throw out the name of *church,* but judgment must be used to ascertain which is the true church, and what is the nature of its unity. And the thing necessary to be attended to, first of all, is, to beware of separating the church from Christ its Head. When I say Christ, I include the doctrine of his Gospel, which he sealed with his blood. Our adversaries, therefore, if they would persuade us that they are the true church, must, first of all, show that the true doctrine of God is among them; and this is the meaning of what we often repeat, that is, that the uniform characteristics of a well-ordered church are the preaching of sound doctrine, and the pure administration of the sacraments. For, since Paul declares (*Ephesians* 2:20) that the church is "built upon the foundation of the apostles and prophets," it necessarily follows that any church not resting on this foundation must immediately fall. I come now to our opponents.

They, no doubt, boast in lofty terms that Christ is on their side. As soon as they exhibit him in their word we will believe it, but not sooner. They, in the same way, insist on the term *church.* But where, we ask, is that doctrine which Paul declares to be the only foundation of the church? Doubtless your imperial majesty now sees that there is a vast difference between assailing us with the reality and assailing us only with the name of "church." We are as ready to confess as they are that those who abandon the church, the common mother of the faithful, the "pillar and ground of the truth," revolt from Christ also; but we mean a church which, from incorruptible seed, begets children for immortality, and, when begotten, nourishes them with spiritual food (that seed and food being the Word of God), and which, by its ministry, preserves entire the truth which God deposited in its bosom. This mark is in no degree doubtful, in no degree fallacious, and it is the mark which God himself impressed upon his church, that she might be discerned thereby. Do we seem unjust in demanding to see this mark? Wherever it exists not, no face of a church is seen. If the name, merely, is put forward, we have only to quote the well known passage of Jeremiah, "Trust you not in lying words, saying, The temple of the Lord, The temple of the Lord,

The temple of the Lord, are these" (*Jeremiah* 7:4). "Is this house, which is called by my name, become a den of robbers in your eyes?" (*Jeremiah* 7:11).

In like manner, the unity of the church, such as Paul describes it, we protest we hold sacred, and we denounce anathema against all who in any way violate it. The principle from which Paul derives unity is that there is "one Lord, one faith, one baptism, one God and Father of all," who hath called us into one hope (*Ephesians* 4:4-5). Therefore, we are one body and one spirit, as is here enjoined, if we adhere to God only, for example, be bound to each other by the tie of faith. We ought, moreover, to remember what is said in another passage, "that faith comes by the Word of God" [*Romans* 10:17]. Let it, therefore, be a fixed point, that a holy unity exists amongst us, when, consenting in pure doctrine, we are united in Christ alone. And, indeed, if concurrence in any kind of doctrine were sufficient, in what possible way could the church of God be distinguished from the impious factions of the wicked? Wherefore, the apostle shortly after adds, that the ministry was instituted "for the edifying of the body of Christ, till we all come in the unity of the faith, and of the knowledge of the Son of God: That we be no more children tossed to and fro, and carried about with every wind of doctrine, but speaking the truth in love, may grow up into him in all things, which is the Head, even Christ" (*Ephesians* 4:12-15). Could he more plainly comprise the whole unity of the church in a holy agreement in true doctrine, than when he calls us back to Christ and to faith, which is included in the knowledge of him, and to obedience to the truth? Nor is any lengthened demonstration of this needed by those who believe the church to be that sheepfold of which Christ alone is the shepherd, and where his voice only is heard, and distinguished from the voice of strangers. And this is confirmed by Paul, when he prays for the Romans, "The God of patience and consolation grant you to be like-minded one toward another, according to Christ Jesus; that ye may with one mind and one mouth glorify God, even the Father of our Lord Jesus Christ" (*Romans* 15:5-6).

Let our opponents, then, in the first instance, draw near to Christ, and then let them convict us of schism, in daring to dissent from them in doctrine. But, since I have made it plain that Christ is banished from their society, and the doctrine of his Gospel exterminated, their charge against us simply amounts to this, that we adhere to Christ in preference to them. For what man, pray, will believe that those who refuse to be led away from Christ and his truth, in order to deliver themselves into the power of men, are thereby schismatics, and deserters from the communion of the church? I certainly admit that respect is to be shown to priests, and that there is great danger in despising ordinary authority. If, then, they were to say, that we are not at our own hand to resist ordinary authority, we should have no difficulty in subscribing to the sentiment. For we are not so rude, as not to see what confusion must arise when the authority of rulers is not respected. Let pastors, then, have their due honor – an honor, however, not derogatory in any degree to the supreme authority of Christ, to whom it behooves them and every man to be subject. For God declares, by Malachi, that the government of the Israelitish church was committed to the priests, under the condition that they should faithfully fulfill the covenant made with them, that is, that their "lips should keep knowledge," and expound the law to the people (*Malachi* 2:7). When the priests altogether failed in this condition, he declares, that, by their perfidy, the covenant was abrogated and made null. Pastors are mistaken if they imagine that they are invested with the government of the church on any other terms than that of being ministers and witnesses of the truth of God. As long, therefore, as, in opposition to the law and to the nature of their office, they eagerly wage war with the truth of God, let them not arrogate to themselves a power which God never bestowed, either formerly on priests, or now on bishops, on any other terms than those which have been mentioned.

But, because they hold that the communion of the church is confined to a kind of regimen which they have struck out for themselves, they think it sufficient to decide the victory in their favor, when they point to our alienation from the Romish See. But to this vaunted primacy of the Romish See it is not difficult to reply. It is a subject, however, on which I will not here enter, both because it would occupy too much time, and because it has been amply discussed by our writers. I will only beg your imperial majesty, and most illustrious princes, to listen to Cyprian, when he points out a better method of ascertaining the true communion of the church, than that of referring it, as our opponents do, to the Roman pontiff alone. For, after placing the only source of ecclesiastical concord in the episcopal authority of Christ, which episcopal authority he affirms that each bishop, to the extent to which it has been communicated, holds entire, he thus proceeds:

There is one church, which, by the increase of its fruitfulness, spreads into a multitude, just as there are many rays of the Sun, but only one light, many branches in a tree, but one trunk, upheld by its tenacious root; and when many streams flow from one fountain, though, from the copiousness of the supply, there seems a division into parts, still, in regard to the origin, unity is preserved. Separate a ray from the body of the Sun, the unity of the light is not divided. Break a branch from a tree; that which is broken cannot germinate. Cut off a stream from the fountain, and it dries up. So, also, the church of God, irradiated with light, sends its beams over the whole world. Still it is one light which is everywhere diffused. The unity of the body is not violated (Cyprian, *De Unitat. Ecclesi.*).

Heresies and schisms, therefore, arise when a return is not made to the origin of truth, when neither the Head is regarded, nor the doctrine of the heavenly Master preserved. Let them then show us a hierarchy in which the bishops are distinguished, but not for refusing to be subject to Christ, in which they depend upon him as the only Head, and act solely with reference to him, in which they cultivate brotherly fellowship with each other, bound together by no other tie than his truth; then, indeed, I will confess that there is no anathema too strong for those who do not regard them with reverence, and yield them the fullest obedience. But is there anything like this in that false mask of hierarchy on which they plume themselves? The Roman pontiff alone as Christ's vicar is in the ascendant, and domineers without law and without measure, after the manner of a tyrant, nay, with more abandoned effrontery than any tyrant. The rest of the body is framed more according to his standard than that of Christ. The light of which Cyprian speaks is extinguished, the copious fountain cut off; in short, the only thing exhibited is the tallness of the tree, but a tree dissevered from its root.

I am aware that our adversaries have good reason for laboring so strenuously to maintain the primacy of the Romish See. They feel that on it both themselves and their all depend. But your part, most invincible emperor, and most illustrious princes, is to be on your guard in order that they may not with vain glosses deceive you, as they are wont to deceive the unwary. And, first, this vaunted supremacy, even themselves are forced to confess, was established by no divine authority, but by the mere will of man. At least, when we give proof of this fact, though they do not expressly assent, they seem as if ashamed to maintain the opposite. There was a time, indeed, when they audaciously perverted certain passages of Scripture to confirm this palpable falsehood; but as soon as we came to close quarters, it was found easy to pluck out of their hands the bits of lath, to which, when at a distance, they had given the appearance of swords. Abandoned, accordingly, by the Word of God, they flee for aid to antiquity. But here, also, without much ado, we dislodge them. For both the writings of holy fathers, the acts of councils, and all history, make it plain that this height of power, which the Roman pontiff has now possessed for about four hundred years, was attained gradually, or rather was either craftily crept into, or violently seized. But let us forgive them this, and let them take for granted that primacy was divinely bestowed on the Romish See, and has been sanctioned by the uniform consent of the ancient church; still there is room for this primacy only on the supposition that Rome has both a true church and a true bishop. For the honor of the seat cannot remain after the seat itself has ceased to exist. I ask, then, in what respect the Roman pontiff performs the duty of a bishop, so as to oblige us to recognize him as a bishop? There is a celebrated saying of Augustine, "Bishopric is the name of an office, and not a mere title of honor." And ancient synods define the duties of a bishop to consist in feeding the people by preaching the Word, in administering the sacraments, in curbing clergy and people by holy discipline, and, in order not to be distracted from these duties, in withdrawing from all the ordinary cares of the present life. In all these duties, presbyters ought to be the bishop's coadjutors. Which of them do the pope and his cardinals pretend to perform? Let them say, then, on what ground they claim to be regarded as legitimate pastors, while they do not, with their little finger, in appearance even, touch any part of the duty.

But let us grant all these things – that is, that he is a bishop who entirely neglects every part of his duty, and that [in] a church which is destitute, as well of the ministry of the Word as of the pure administration of the sacraments – still, what answer is made when we add not only that these are wanting, but that everything which exists is directly the reverse? For several centuries that See has been possessed by impious superstitions, open idolatry, [and] perverse doctrines, while those great truths, in which the Christian religion chiefly consists, have been suppressed. By the prostitution of the sacraments to filthy lucre, and other abominations, Christ has been held up to such extreme derision, that he has in a manner been crucified afresh. Can she be the mother of all churches, who not only does not retain, I do not say the face, but even a single lineament, of the true church, and has snapped asunder all those bonds of holy communion by which believers should be linked together?

The Roman pontiff is now opposing himself to the reviving doctrines of the Gospel, just as if his head were at stake. Does he not, by this very fact, demonstrate that there will be no safety for his See unless he can put to flight the kingdom of Christ? Your imperial majesty is aware how wide a field of discussion here opens upon me. But to conclude this point in a few words: I deny that See to be apostolical, wherein nought is seen but a shocking apostasy; I deny him to be the vicar of Christ, who, in furiously persecuting the Gospel, demonstrates by his conduct that he is Antichrist; I deny him to be the successor of Peter, who is doing his utmost to demolish every edifice that Peter built; and I deny him to be the head of the church, who by his tyranny lacerates and dismembers the church, after dissevering her from Christ, her true and only Head. Let these denials be answered by those who are so bent on chaining the hierarchy of the church to the Romish See, that they hesitate not to subordinate the sure and tried doctrines of the Gospel to the authority of the pope. Yea, I say, let them answer; only do you, most invincible emperor, and most illustrious princes, consider whether, in so calling upon them, the thing I ask is just or unjust.

From what has been said, it will doubtless be easy for you to perceive how little attention is due to the calumny of our adversaries, when they accuse us of impious presumption, and as it were inexpiable audacity, in having attempted to purify the church from corruption, both in doctrine and ceremonies, without waiting for the beck of the Roman pontiff. They say we have done what private individuals have no right to do. But, in regard to ameliorating the condition of the church, what was to be hoped from him to whom we were required to give place? Any man who considers how Luther and the other reformers acted at the outset, and how they afterwards proceeded, will deem it unnecessary to call upon us for any defense. When matters were still entire, Luther himself humbly besought the pontiff that he would be pleased to cure the very grievous disorders of the church. Did his supplication succeed? The evils having still increased, the necessity of the case, even had Luther been silent, should have been stimulus enough to urge the pope to delay no longer. The whole Christian world plainly demanded this of him, and he had in his hands the means of satisfying the pious wishes of all. Did he do so? He now talks of impediments. But if the fact be traced to its source, it will be found that he has all along been, both to himself and to others, the only impediment.

But why insist on these lighter arguments? Is it not in itself alone an argument of sufficient clearness and sufficient weight, that, from the commencement up to the present time, he gives us no hope of transacting with him until we again bury Christ, and return to every impiety which formerly existed, that he may establish them on a firmer basis than before? This, unquestionably, is the reason why still, in the present day, our opponents so strenuously maintain that we had no right to intermeddle with the revival of the church – not that the thing was not necessary (this it was too desperate effrontery to deny), but because they are desirous that as well the safety as the ruin of the church should be suspended on the mere beck and pleasure of the Roman pontiff.

Let us now attend to the only remedy left us by those who think it impiety to move a finger, how great soever the evils by which the church is oppressed. They put us off to a universal council. What? If the major part, from obstinacy, rush upon their own destruction, must we therefore perish along with them, when we have the means of consulting for our own safety? But they tell us it is unlawful to violate the unity of the church, and that unity is violated if any party decide an article of faith by themselves, without calling in the others. Then they enlarge on the inconveniences to which such a course might lead – that nothing could be expected but fearful devastation and chaotic confusion, were each people and nation to adopt for itself its peculiar form of faith. Things like these might be said justly, and even appositely to the occasion, if any one member of the church, in contempt of unity, should of its own accord separate itself from the others. But that is not the point now in dispute.

I wish, indeed, it were possible for all the monarchs and states of the Christian world to unite in a holy league, and resolve on a simultaneous amendment of the present evils. But since we see that some are averse to amelioration, and that others, involved in war or occupied with other cares, cannot give their attention to the subject, how long, pray, must we, in waiting for others, defer consulting for ourselves? And more freely to explain the source of all our evils, we see that the Roman pontiff, if he can prevent it, will never permit all churches to unite, I do not say in due consultation, but in assembling any council at all. He will, indeed, as often as he is asked, give promises in abundance, provided he sees all the ways shut up, and all modes of access interrupted, while he has in his hand obstructions which he can every now and then throw in, so as never to want pretexts for tergiversation. With a few exceptions, he has all the cardinals, Bishops, and abbots, consenting with him in this matter, since their only thought is how to retain possession of their usurped tyranny. As to the welfare or destruction of the church, it gives them not the least concern....

Such indications, however, ought not only to move us by their actual aspect; they ought also to remind us of coming vengeance. Divine worship being vitiated by so many false opinions, and perverted by so many impious and foul superstitions, the sacred majesty of God is insulted with atrocious contumely, his holy name profaned, his glory only not trampled under foot. Nay, while the whole Christian world is openly polluted with idolatry, men adore, instead of him, their own fictions. A thousand superstitions reign – superstitions which are just so many open insults to him. The power of Christ is almost obliterated from the minds of men, the hope of salvation is transferred from him to empty, frivolous, and nugatory ceremonies, while there is a pollution of the sacraments not less to be execrated. Baptism is deformed by numerous additions, the holy Supper is prostituted to all kinds of ignominy, religion throughout has degenerated into an entirely different form.

If we are negligent in remedying these evils, God assuredly will not forget himself. How could he who declares that he will not allow his honor to be in any way impaired, fail to interpose when it is cast down and destroyed? How could he who threatens with destruction all the nations among whom prophecy shall have failed, permit our open and contumacious contempt of the prophecies to go unpunished? How could he who punished a slight stain on his Supper so severely in the Corinthians, spare us in presuming to pollute it with so many unutterable blasphemies? How could he who, by the mouths of all his prophets, testifies and proclaims that he is armed with vengeance against idolatry, leave untouched in us so many monstrous idolatries? Assuredly he does not so leave them, for we see how, sword in hand, he urges and pursues us. The Turkish war now occupies the minds of all, and fills them with alarm. It well may. Consultations are held to prepare the means of resistance. This, too, is prudently and necessarily done. All exclaim that there is need of no ordinary dispatch. I admit that there cannot be too much dispatch, provided, in the meantime, the consultation which ought to be first, the consultation how to restore the church to its proper state, is neither neglected nor retarded. Already delays more than enough have been interposed. The fuel of the Turkish war is within, shut up in our bowels, and must first be removed, if we would successfully drive back the war itself.

In [the] future, therefore, as often as you shall hear the croaking note – "The business of reforming the church must be delayed for the present; there will be time enough to accomplish it after other matters are transacted" – remember, most invincible emperor, and most illustrious princes, that the matter on which you are to deliberate is, whether you are to leave to your posterity some empire or none. Yet, why do I speak of posterity? Even now, while your own eyes behold, it is half bent, and totters to its final ruin. In regard to ourselves, whatever be the event, we will always be supported, in the sight of God, by the consciousness that we have desired both to promote his glory and do good to his church; that we have labored faithfully for that end; that, in short, we have done what we could. Our conscience tells us that in all our wishes, and all our endeavors, we have had no other aim. And we have essayed, by clear proof, to testify the fact. And, certainly, while we feel assured that we both care for and do the work of the Lord, we are also confident that he will by no means be wanting either to himself or to it.

But be the issue what it may, we will never repent of having begun, and of having proceeded thus far. The Holy Spirit is a faithful and unerring witness to our doctrine. We know, I say, that it is the eternal truth of God that we preach. We are, indeed, desirous, as we ought to be, that our ministry may prove salutary to the world; but to give it this effect belongs to God, not to us. If, to punish, partly the ingratitude, and partly the stubbornness of those to whom we desire to do good, success must prove desperate, and all things go to worse, I will say what it befits a Christian man to say, and what all who are true to this holy profession will subscribe: We will die, but in death even be conquerors, not only because through it we shall have a sure passage to a better life, but because we know that our blood will be as seed to propagate the divine truth which men now despise.

31

Idolatry [1]

J. C. Ryle

Flee from idolatry (1 Corinthians 10:14).

THE TEXT which heads this page may seem at first sight to be hardly needed in England. In an age of education and intelligence like this, we might almost fancy it is waste of time to tell an Englishman to "flee from idolatry."

I am bold to say that this is a great mistake. I believe that we have come to a time when the subject of idolatry demands a thorough and searching investigation. I believe that idolatry is near us, and about us, and in the midst of us, to a very fearful extent. The second commandment, in one word, is in peril. "The plague is begun."

Without further preface, I propose in this paper to consider the four following points:

I. *The definition of idolatry.* What is it?

II. *The cause of idolatry.* Whence comes it?

III. *The form idolatry assumes in the visible church of Christ.* Where is it?

IV. *The ultimate abolition of idolatry.* What will end it?

I feel that the subject is encompassed with many difficulties. Our lot is cast in an age when truth is constantly in danger of being sacrificed to toleration, charity, and peace, falsely so called. Nevertheless, I cannot forget, as a clergyman, that the Church of England is a church which has "given no uncertain sound" on the subject of idolatry; and, unless I am greatly mistaken, truth about idolatry is, in the highest sense, truth for the times.

---

1. Reprinted from J. C. Ryle, *Warnings to the Churches.* The Banner of Truth Trust, 1967.

I. Let me, then, first of all supply *a definition of idolatry*. Let me show *what it is*.

It is of the utmost importance that we should understand this. Unless I make this clear, I can do nothing with the subject. Vagueness and indistinctness prevail upon this point, as upon almost every other in religion. The Christian who would not be continually running aground in his spiritual voyage must have his channel well buoyed, and his mind well stored with clear definitions.

I say then, that *"idolatry is a worship in which the honor due to God in Trinity, and to him only, is given to some of his creatures, or to some invention of his creatures."* It may vary exceedingly. It may assume exceedingly different forms, according to the ignorance or the knowledge – the civilization or the barbarism, of those who offer it. It may be grossly absurd and ludicrous, or it may closely border on truth, and admit of being most speciously defended. But whether in the adoration of the idol of Juggernaut, or in the adoration of the host in St. Peter's at Rome, the principle of idolatry is in reality the same. In either case the honor due to God is turned aside from him, and bestowed on that which is not God. And whenever this is done, whether in heathen temples or in professedly Christian churches, there is an act of *idolatry*.

It is not necessary for a man formally to deny God and Christ in order to be an idolater. Far from it. Professed reverence for the God of the Bible and actual idolatry are perfectly compatible. They have often gone side by side, and they still do so. The children of Israel never thought of renouncing God when they persuaded Aaron to make the golden calf. "These be thy gods," they said ("thy *Elohim*"), "which brought thee up out of the land of Egypt." And the feast in honor of the calf was kept as "a feast unto the Lord" (Jehovah) (*Exodus* 32:4, 5). Jeroboam, again, never pretended to ask the ten tribes to cast off their allegiance to the God of David and Solomon. When he set up the calves of gold in Dan and Bethel, he only said, "It is too much for you to go up to Jerusalem: Behold thy gods, O Israel ("thy *Elohim*"), which brought thee up out of the land of Egypt" (1 *Kings* 12:28). In both instances, we should observe, the idol was not set up as a rival to God, but under the pretence of being a help – a steppingstone to his service. But, in both instances, a great sin was committed. The honor due to God was given to a visible representation of him. The majesty of Jehovah was offended. The second commandment was broken. There was, in the eyes of God, a flagrant act of *idolatry*.

Let us mark this well. It is high time to dismiss from our minds those loose ideas about idolatry, which are common in this day. We must not think, as many do, that there are only two sorts of idolatry – the spiritual idolatry of the man who loves his wife, or child, or money more than God; and the open, gross idolatry of the man who bows down to an image of wood, or metal, or stone, because he knows no better. We may rest assured that idolatry is a sin which occupies a far wider field than this. It is not merely a thing in Hindustan, that we may hear of and pity at missionary meetings; nor yet is it a thing confined to our own hearts, that we may confess before the mercy-seat upon our knees. It is a pestilence that walks in the church of Christ to a much greater extent than many suppose. It is an evil that, like the man of sin, "sits in the very temple of God" (2 *Thessalonians* 2:4). It is a sin that we all need to watch and pray against continually. It creeps into our religious worship insensibly, and is upon us before we are aware. Those are tremendous words which Isaiah spoke to the formal Jew – not to the worshiper of Ba'al, remember, but to the man who actually came to the temple (*Isaiah* 66:3): "He that kills an ox is as if he slew a man; he that sacrifices a lamb, as if he cut off a dog's neck; he that offers an oblation, as if he offered swine's blood; he that burns incense, as if he blessed an idol."

This is that sin which God has especially denounced in his Word. One commandment out of ten is devoted to the prohibition of it. Not one of all the ten contains such a solemn declaration of God's character, and of his judgments against the disobedient: "I the Lord thy God am a jealous God, visiting the iniquity of the fathers upon the children unto the third and fourth generation of them that hate me" (*Exodus* 20:5). Not one, perhaps, of all the ten is so emphatically repeated and amplified, and especially in the fourth chapter of the book of *Deuteronomy*.

This is the sin, of all others, to which the Jews seem to have been most inclined before the destruction of Solomon's temple. What is the history of Israel under their judges and kings but a melancholy record of repeated falling away into idolatry? Again and again we read of "high places" and false gods. Again and again we read of captivities and chastisements on account of idolatry. Again and again we read of a return to the old sin. It seems as if the love of idols among the Jews was naturally bone of their bone and flesh of their flesh. The besetting sin of the Old Testament church, in one word, was idolatry. In the face of the most elaborate ceremonial ordinances that God ever gave to his people, Israel was incessantly turning aside after idols, and worshiping the work of men's hands.

This is the sin, of all others, which has brought down the heaviest judgments on the visible church. It brought on Israel the armies of Egypt, Assyria, and Babylon. It scattered the ten tribes, burned up Jerusalem, and carried Judah and Benjamin into captivity. It brought on the Eastern churches, in later days, the overwhelming flood of the Saracenic invasion, and turned many a spiritual garden into a wilderness. The desolation which reigns where Cyprian and Augustine once preached, the living death in which the churches of Asia Minor and Syria are buried, are all attributable to this sin. All testify to the same great truth which the Lord proclaims in *Isaiah*: "My glory will I not give to another" (*Isaiah* 42:8).

Let us gather up these things in our minds, and ponder them well. Idolatry is a subject which, in every church of Christ that would keep herself pure, should be thoroughly examined, understood, and known. It is not for nothing that St. Paul lays down the stern command, "Flee from idolatry."

II. Let me show, in the second place, *the cause to which idolatry may be traced. Whence comes it?*

To the man who takes an extravagant and exalted view of human intellect and reason, idolatry may seem absurd. He fancies it too irrational for any but weak minds to be endangered by it.

To a mere superficial thinker about Christianity, the peril of idolatry may seem very small. Whatever commandments are broken, such a man will tell us, professing Christians are not very likely to transgress the second.

Now, both these persons betray a woeful ignorance of human nature. They do not see that there are secret roots of idolatry within us all. The prevalence of idolatry in all ages among the heathen must necessarily puzzle the one – the warnings of Protestant ministers against idolatry in the church must necessarily appear uncalled for to the other. Both are alike blind to its cause.

The cause of all idolatry is the natural corruption of man's heart. That great family disease, with which all the children of Adam are infected from their birth, shows itself in this, as it does in a thousand other ways. Out of the same fountain from which "proceed evil thoughts, adulteries, fornications, murders, thefts, covetousness, wickedness, deceit," and the like (*Mark* 7:21, 22) – out of that same fountain arise false views of God, and false views of the worship due to him; and, therefore, when the Apostle Paul tells the Galatians (*Galatians* 5:20) what are the "works of the flesh," he places prominently among them "idolatry."

A religion of some kind man will have. God has not left himself without a witness in us all, fallen as we are. Like old inscriptions hidden under mounds of rubbish – like the almost-obliterated underwriting of Palimpsest manuscripts,[2] – even so there is a dim *something* engraven at the bottom of man's heart, however faint and half-erased – a *something* which makes him feel he must have a religion and a worship of some kind. The proof of this is to be found in the history of voyages and travels in every part of the globe. The exceptions to the rule are so few, if indeed there are any, that they only confirm its truth. Man's worship in some dark corner of the Earth may rise no higher than a vague fear of an evil spirit, and a desire to propitiate him; but a worship of some kind man will have.

But then comes in the effect of the fall. Ignorance of God, carnal and low conceptions of his nature and attributes, earthly and sensual notions of the service which is acceptable to him, all characterize the religion of the natural man. There is a craving in his mind after something he can see, and feel, and touch in his Divinity. He would fain bring his god down to his own crawling level. He would make his religion a thing of sense and sight. He has no idea of the religion of heart, and faith, and spirit. In short, just as he is willing to live on God's Earth, but, until renewed by grace, a fallen and degraded life, so he has no objection to worship after a fashion, but, until renewed by the Holy Ghost, it is always with a fallen worship. In one word, idolatry is a natural product of man's heart. It is a weed, which like the earth uncultivated, the heart is always ready to bring forth.

And now does it surprise us, when we read of the constantly recurring idolatries of the Old Testament church – of Peor, and Ba'al, and

2. "Palimpsest" is the name given to ancient parchment manuscripts which have been twice written over, that is, the work of a comparatively modern writer has been written over or across the work of an older writer. Before the invention of cheap paper, the practice of so writing over an old manuscript was not uncommon. The object of the practice, of course, was to save expense. The misfortune was that the second writing was often far less valuable than the first.

Moloch, and Chemosh, and Ashtaroth – of high places and hill altars, and groves and images – and this in the full light of the Mosaic ceremonial? Let us cease to be surprised. It can be accounted for. There is a cause.

Does it surprise us when we read in history how idolatry crept in by degrees into the church of Christ – how little by little it thrust out Gospel truth, until, in Canterbury, men offered more at the shrine of Thomas à Becket, than they did at that of the Virgin Mary, and more at that of the Virgin Mary, than at that of Christ? Let us cease to be surprised. It is all intelligible. There is a cause.

Does it surprise us when we hear of men going over from Protestant churches to the Church of Rome, in the present day? Do we think it unaccountable, and feel as if we ourselves could never forsake a pure form of worship for one like that of the pope? Let us cease to be surprised. There is a solution for the problem. There is a cause.

That cause is nothing else but the corruption of man's heart. There is a natural proneness and tendency in us all to give God a sensual, carnal worship, and not that which is commanded in his Word. We are ever ready, by reason of our sloth and unbelief, to devise visible helps and stepping-stones in our approaches to him, and ultimately to give these inventions of our own the honor due to him. In fact, idolatry is all natural, downhill, easy, like the broad way. Spiritual worship is all of grace, all up-hill, and all against the grain. Any worship whatsoever is more pleasing to the natural heart than worshiping God in the way which our Lord Christ describes, "in spirit and in truth" (John 4:23).

I, for one, am not surprised at the quantity of idolatry existing, both in the world and in the visible church. I believe it perfectly possible that we may yet live to see far more of it than some have ever dreamed of. It would never surprise me if some mighty personal Antichrist were to arise before the end – mighty in intellect, mighty in talents for government, aye, and mighty, perhaps, in miraculous gifts too. It would never surprise me to see such an one as him setting up himself in opposition to Christ, and forming an infidel conspiracy and combination against the Gospel. I believe that many would rejoice to do him honor, who now glory in saying, "We will not have this Christ to reign over us." I believe that many would make a god of him, and reverence him as an incarnation of truth, and concentrate their idea of hero-worship on his person. I advance it as a *possibility*, and no more. But of this at least I am certain – that no man is less safe from danger of idolatry than the man who now sneers at every form of religion; and that from infidelity to credulity, from atheism to the grossest idolatry, there is but a single step. Let us not think, at all events, that idolatry is an old-fashioned sin, into which we are never likely to fall. "Let him that thinks he stands, take heed lest he fall." We shall do well to look into our own hearts: The seeds of idolatry are all there. We should remember the words of St. Paul: "Flee from idolatry."

III. Let me show, in the third place, *the forms which idolatry has assumed, and does assume in the visible church. Where is it?*

I believe there never was a more baseless fabric than the theory which obtains favor with many – that the promises of perpetuity and preservation from apostasy belong to the visible church of Christ. It is a theory supported neither by Scripture nor by facts. The church against which "the gates of Hell shall never prevail," is not the visible church, but the whole body of the elect, the company of true believers out of every nation and people. The greater part of the visible church has frequently maintained gross heresies. The particular branches of it are never secure against deadly error, both of faith and practice. A departure from the faith – a falling away – a leaving of first love in any branch of the visible church, need never surprise a careful reader of the New Testament.

That idolatry would arise, seems to have been the expectation of the apostles, even before the canon of the New Testament was closed. It is remarkable to observe how Paul dwells on this subject in his *Epistle to the Corinthians*. If any Corinthian called a brother was an idolater, with such an one the members of the church "were not to eat" (*1 Corinthians* 5:11). "Neither be ye idolaters, as were some of our fathers" (*1 Corinthians* 10:7). He says again, in the text which heads this paper, "My dearly beloved, flee from idolatry" (*1 Corinthians* 10:14). When he writes to the Colossians, he warns them against "worshiping of angels" (*Colossians* 2:18). And John closes his first *Epistle* with the solemn injunction, "Little children, keep yourselves from idols" (*1 John* 5:21). It is impossible not to feel that all these passages imply an expectation that idolatry would arise, and that soon, among professing Christians.

The famous prophecy in the fourth chapter of the first *Epistle to Timothy* contains a passage which is even more directly to the point: "The Spirit speaks expressly, that in the latter times some shall depart from the faith, giving heed to seducing spirits, and doctrines of devils" (*1*

Timothy 4:1). I will not detain my readers with any lengthy discussion of that remarkable expression, "doctrines of devils." It may be sufficient to say that our excellent translators of the Bible are considered for once to have missed the full meaning of the apostle in their rendering of the word translated as "devils" in our version, and that the true meaning of the expression is, "doctrines about departed spirits." And in this view, which, I may as well say, is maintained by all those who have the best right to be heard on such a question, the passage becomes a direct prediction of the rise of that most specious form of idolatry, the *worship of dead saints.* (See Mode's *Works.*)

The last passage I will call attention to is the conclusion of the ninth chapter of *Revelation.* We there read, at the twentieth verse: "The rest of the men which were not killed by these plagues, yet repented not of the works of their hands, that they should not worship devils" (this is the same word, we should observe, as that in the *Epistle to Timothy,* just quoted), "and idols of gold, and silver, and brass, and stone, and wood: which neither can see, nor hear, nor walk." Now, I am not going to offer any comment on the chapter in which this verse occurs. I know well there is a difference of opinion as to the true interpretation of the plagues predicted in it. I only venture to assert, that it is the highest probability these plagues are to fall upon the visible church of Christ; and the highest improbability that John was here prophesying about the heathen, who never heard the Gospel. And this once conceded, the fact that idolatry is *a predicted sin of the visible church* does seem most conclusively and forever established.

And now, if we turn from the Bible to facts, what do we see? I reply unhesitatingly, that there is unmistakable proof that Scripture warnings and predictions were not spoken without cause, and that idolatry has actually arisen in the visible church of Christ, and does still exist.

The rise and progress of the evil in former days, we shall find well summed up in the *Homily* of the Church of England, on "Peril of Idolatry." To that *Homily* I beg to refer all churchmen, reminding them once for all, that in the judgment of the *Thirty-nine Articles,* the *Book of Homilies* "contains a godly and wholesome doctrine, and necessary for these times." There we read, how, even in the *fourth century,* Jerome complains, "that the errors of images have come in, and passed to the Christians from the Gentiles;" and Eusebius says, "We do see that images of Peter and Paul, and of our Saviour himself be made, and tables be painted, which I think to have been derived and kept indifferently by an heathenish custom." There we may read, how "Pontius Paulinus, Bishop of Nola, in the *fifth century,* caused the walls of the temples to be painted with stories taken out of the Old Testament; that the people beholding and considering these pictures might the better abstain from too much surfeiting and riot. But from learning by painted stories, it came by little and little to idolatry." There we may read how Gregory I, Bishop of Rome, in the beginning of the *seventh century,* did allow the free having of images in churches. There we may read how Irene, mother of Constantine VI, in the *eighth century,* assembled a Council at Nicæa, and procured a decree that images should be put up in all the churches of Greece, and that honor and worship should be given to the said images. And there we may read the conclusion with which the *Homily* winds up its historical summary, "that laity and clergy, learned and unlearned, all ages, sorts, and degrees of men, women and children of whole Christendom, have been at once drowned in abominable idolatry, of all other vices most detested by God, and most damnable to man, and that by the space of 800 years and more."

This is a mournful account, but it is only too true. There can be little doubt the evil began even before the time just mentioned by the *Homily* writers. No man, I think, need wonder at the rise of idolatry in the primitive church who considers calmly the excessive reverence which it paid, from the very first, to the visible parts of religion. I believe that no impartial man can read the language used by nearly all the fathers about the church, the bishops, the ministry, baptism, the Lord's Supper, the martyrs, the dead saints generally – no man can read it without being struck with the wide difference between their language and the language of Scripture on such subjects. You seem at once to be in a new atmosphere. You feel that you are no longer treading on holy ground. You find that things which in the Bible are evidently of second-rate importance, are here made of first-rate importance. You find the things of sense and sight exalted to a position in which Paul, and Peter, and James, and John, speaking by the Holy Ghost, never for a moment placed them. It is not merely the weakness of uninspired writings that you have to complain of; it is something worse; it is a new system. And what is the explanation of all this? It is, in one word, that you have got into a region where the malaria of idolatry has begun to arise. You perceive the first workings of the mystery of iniquity. You detect the buds of that huge system of idolatry which, as the *Homily* describes, was afterwards formally acknowledged, and ultimately blossomed so luxuriantly in every part of Christendom.

But let us now turn from the past to the present. Let us examine the question which most concerns ourselves. Let us consider in what form idolatry presents itself to us as a sin of the visible church of Christ in our own time.

I find no difficulty in answering this question. I feel no hesitation in affirming that idolatry never yet assumed a more glaring form than it does *in the Church of Rome at this present day.*

And here I come to a subject on which it is hard to speak, because of the times we live in. But the whole truth ought to be spoken by ministers of Christ, without respect of times and prejudices. And I should not lie down in peace, after writing on idolatry, if I did not declare my solemn conviction that idolatry is one of the crying sins of which the Church of Rome is guilty. I say this in all sadness. I say it, acknowledging fully that we have our faults in the Protestant church; and practically, perhaps, in some quarters, not a little idolatry. But from formal, recognized, systematic idolatry, I believe we are almost entirely free. While, as for the Church of Rome, if there is not in her worship an enormous quantity of systematic, organized idolatry, I frankly confess I do not know what idolatry is.

(*a*) To my mind, it is idolatry to have images and pictures of saints in churches, and to give them a reverence for which there is no warrant or precedent in Scripture. And if this be so, I say there is *idolatry in the Church of Rome.*

(*b*) To my mind, it is idolatry to invoke the Virgin Mary and the saints in glory, and to address them in language never addressed in Scripture except to the Holy Trinity. And if this be so, I say there is *idolatry in the Church of Rome.*

(*c*) To my mind, it is idolatry to bow down to mere material things, and attribute to them a power and sanctity far exceeding that attached to the ark or altar of the Old Testament dispensation; and a power and sanctity, too, for which there is not a tittle of foundation in the Word of God. And if this be so, with the holy coat of Treves, and the wonderfully-multiplied wood of the true cross, and a thousand other so-called relics in my mind's eye, I say there is *idolatry in the Church of Rome.*

(*d*) To my mind, it is idolatry to worship that which man's hands have made – to call it God, and adore it when lifted up before our eyes. And if this be so, with the notorious doctrine of transubstantiation, and the elevation of the host in my recollection, I say there is *idolatry in the Church of Rome.*

(e) To my mind, it is idolatry to make ordained men mediators between ourselves and God, robbing, as it were, our Lord Christ of his office, and giving them an honor which even apostles and angels in Scripture flatly repudiate. And if this be so, with the honor paid to popes and priests before my eyes, I say there is *idolatry in the Church of Rome.*

I know well that language like this jars the minds of many. Men love to shut their eyes against evils which it is disagreeable to allow. They will not see things which involve unpleasant consequences. That the Church of Rome is an *erring* Church, they will acknowledge. That she is *idolatrous,* they will deny.

They tell us that the reverence which the Romish Church gives to saints and images does not amount to idolatry. They inform us that there are distinctions between the worship of "latria" and "dulia," between a mediation of redemption, and a mediation of intercession, which clear her of the charge. My answer is that the Bible knows nothing of such distinctions; and that, in the actual practice of the great bulk of Roman Catholics, they have no existence at all.[3]

They tell us that it is a mistake to suppose that Roman Catholics really worship the images and pictures before which they perform acts of adoration; that they only use them as helps to devotion, and in reality look far beyond them. My answer is that many a heathen could say just as much for his idolatry – that it is notorious, in former days, they did say so – and that in Hindustan many idol-worshipers do say so at the present day. But the apology does not avail. The terms of the second commandment are too stringent. It prohibits *bowing down,* as well as worshiping. And the very anxiety which the Church of Rome has often displayed to exclude that second commandment from her catechisms is of itself a great fact which speaks volumes to a candid observer.

They tell us that we have no evidence for the assertions we make on this subject; that we found our charges on the abuses which prevail

3. "Latria" and "dulia" are two Greek words, both meaning "worship" or "service," but the former being a stronger word than the latter. The Roman Catholic admits that the worship of "latria" may not be given to saints, but maintains that "dulia" may be given. [Such a distinction is not supported by Scriptural usage. – *Editor.*]

among the ignorant members of the Romish communion; and that it is absurd to say that a church containing so many wise and learned men is guilty of idolatry. My answer is that the devotional books in common use among Roman Catholics supply us with unmistakable evidence. Let any one examine that notorious book, *The Garden of the Soul,* if he doubts my assertion, and read the language there addressed to the Virgin Mary. Let him remember that this language is addressed to a woman, who, though highly favored, and the mother of our Lord, was yet one of our fellow-sinners – to a woman who actually confesses her need of a Saviour for herself. She says, "My spirit hath rejoiced in God my Saviour" (*Luke* 1:47). Let him examine this language in the light of the New Testament, and then let him tell us fairly, whether the charge of idolatry is not fully made out. But I answer, beside this, that we want no better evidence than that which is supplied in the city of Rome itself. What do men and women do under the light of the pope's own countenance? What is the religion that prevails around St. Peter's and under the walls of the Vatican? What is Romanism at Rome, unfettered, unshackled, and free to develop itself in full perfection? Let a man honestly answer these questions, and I ask no more. Let him read such a book as Seymour's *Pilgrimage to Rome,* or Alford's *Letters,* and ask any visitor to Rome if the picture is too highly colored. Let him do this, I say, and I believe he cannot avoid the conclusion that Romanism in perfection is a gigantic system of church-worship, sacrament-worship, Mary-worship, saint-worship, image-worship, relic-worship, and priest-worship – that it is, in one word, a *huge organized idolatry.*

I know how painful these things sound to many ears. To me it is no pleasure to dwell on the shortcomings of any who profess and call themselves Christians. I can say truly that I have said what I have said with pain and sorrow.

I draw a wide distinction between the accredited dogmas of the Church of Rome and the private opinions of many of her members. I believe and hope that many a Roman Catholic is in heart inconsistent with his profession, and is better than the Church to which he belongs. I cannot forget the Jansenists, and Quesnel, and Martin Boos. I believe that many a poor Italian at this day is worshiping with an idolatrous worship, simply because he knows no better. He has no Bible to instruct him. He has no faithful minister to teach him. He has the fear of the priest before his eyes, if he dares to think for himself. He has no money to enable him to get away from the bondage he lives under, even if he feels a desire. I remember all this; and I say that the Italian eminently deserves our sympathy and compassion. But all this must not prevent my saying that the Church of Rome is an *idolatrous Church*.

I should not be faithful if I said less. The church of which I am a minister has spoken out most strongly on the subject. The *Homily* on "Peril of Idolatry," and the solemn protest following the Rubrics, at the end of our *Prayer Book* Communion Service, which denounces the adoration of the sacramental bread and wine as "idolatry to be abhorred of all faithful Christians," are plain evidence that I have said no more than the mind of my own church. And in a day like this – when some are disposed to secede to the Church of Rome, and many are shutting their eyes to her real character, and wanting us to be reunited to her – in a day like this, my own conscience would rebuke me if I did not warn men plainly that the Church of Rome is an idolatrous church, and that if they will join her they are *"joining themselves to idols."*

But I may not dwell longer on this part of my subject. The main point I wish to impress on men's minds is this – that idolatry has decidedly manifested itself in the visible church of Christ, and nowhere so decidedly as in the Church of Rome.

IV. And now let me show, in the last place, the *ultimate abolition of all idolatry. What will end it?*

I consider that man's soul must be in an unhealthy state who does not long for the time when idolatry shall be no more. That heart can hardly be right with God which can think of the millions who are sunk in heathenism, or honor the false prophet Mahomet, or daily offer up prayers to the Virgin Mary, and not cry, "O my God, what shall be the end of these things? How long, O Lord, how long?"

Here, as in other subjects, the sure word of prophecy comes in to our aid. The end of all idolatry shall one day come. Its doom is fixed. Its overthrow is certain. Whether in heathen temples, or in so-called Christian churches, idolatry shall be destroyed at the second coming of our Lord Jesus Christ.

Then shall be fulfilled the prophecy of Isaiah, "The idols he shall utterly abolish." (*Isaiah* 2:18). Then shall be fulfilled the words of Micah (5:13): "Their graven images also will I cut off, and their standing images out of the midst of thee, and thou shalt no more worship the work of thine hands." Then shall be fulfilled the prophecy of Zephaniah (2:11):

"The Lord will be terrible unto them: for he will famish all the gods of the Earth; and men shall worship him, every one from his place, even all the isles of the heathen." Then shall be fulfilled the prophecy of Zechariah (13:2): "It shall come to pass at that day, saith the Lord of hosts, that I will cut off the names of the idols out of the land, and they shall no more be remembered." In a word, the 97th *Psalm* shall then receive its full accomplishment: "The Lord reigns: Let the Earth rejoice; let the multitude of isles be glad thereof. Clouds and darkness are round about him: righteousness and judgment are the habitation of his throne. A fire goes before him, and burns up his enemies round about. His lightnings enlightened the world: The Earth saw, and trembled. The hills melted like wax at the presence of the Lord, at the presence of the Lord of the whole Earth. The heavens declare his righteousness, and all the people see his glory. Confounded be all they that serve graven images, that boast themselves of idols: Worship him, all ye gods."

The second coming of our Lord Jesus Christ is that blessed hope which should ever comfort the children of God under the present dispensation. It is the pole-star by which we must journey. It is the one point on which all our expectations should be concentrated. "Yet a little while, and he that shall come will come, and will not tarry" (*Hebrews* 10:37). Our David shall no longer dwell in Adullam, followed by a despised few, and rejected by the many. He shall take to himself his great power, and reign, and cause every knee to bow before him.

Till then our redemption is not perfectly enjoyed; as, Paul tells the Ephesians, "We are sealed unto the day of redemption" (*Ephesians* 4:30). Till then our salvation is not completed; as Peter says, "We are kept by the power of God through faith unto salvation ready to be revealed in the last time" (*1 Peter* 1:5). Till then our knowledge is still defective; as Paul tells the Corinthians: "Now we see through a glass darkly; but then face to face: now I know in part; then shall I know even also as I am known" (*1 Corinthians* 13:12). In short, our best things are yet to come.

But in the day of our Lord's return every desire shall receive its full accomplishment. We shall no more be pressed down and worn out with the sense of constant failure, feebleness, and disappointment. In his presence we shall find there is a *fulness* of joy, if nowhere else; and when we awake up after his likeness we shall be *satisfied*, if we never were before (*Psalm* 16:11; 17:15.)

There are many abominations now in the visible church, over which we can only sigh and cry, like the faithful in Ezekiel's day (*Ezekiel* 9:4). We cannot remove them. The wheat and the tares will grow together until the harvest. But a day comes when the Lord Jesus shall once more purify his temple, and cast forth everything that defiles. He shall do that work of which the doing of Hezekiah and Josiah were a faint type long ago. He shall cast forth the images, and purge out idolatry in every shape.

Who is there now that longs for the conversion of the heathen world? You will not see it in its fulness until the Lord's appearing. Then, and not till then, will that often-misapplied text be fulfilled: "A man shall cast his idols of silver, and his idols of gold, which they made each one for himself to worship, to the moles and to the bats" (*Isaiah* 2:20).

Who is there now that longs for the redemption of Israel? You will never see it in its perfection till the Redeemer comes to Zion. Idolatry in the professing church of Christ has been one of the mightiest stumblingblocks in the Jews' way. When it begins to fall, the veil over the heart of Israel shall begin to be taken away (*Psalm* 102:16).

Who is there now that longs for the fall of Antichrist, and the purification of the Church of Rome? I believe that will never be until the winding up of this dispensation. That vast system of idolatry may be consumed and *wasted* by the Spirit of the Lord's mouth, but it shall never be *destroyed* excepting by the brightness of his coming (2 *Thessalonians* 2:8).

Who is there now that longs for a perfect church – a church in which there shall not be the slightest taint of idolatry? You must wait for the Lord's return. Then, and not til then, shall we see a perfect church, a church having neither spot nor wrinkle, nor any such thing (*Ephesians* 5:27), a church of which all the members shall be regenerate, and every one a child of God.

If these things be so, men need not wonder that we urge on them the study of prophecy, and that we charge them above all to grasp firmly the glorious doctrine of Christ's second appearing and kingdom. This is the "light shining in a dark place" to which we shall do well to take heed. Let others indulge their fancy, if they will, with the vision of an imaginary "church of the future." Let the children of this world dream of some "coming man" who is to understand everything, and set everything right. They are only sowing to themselves bitter disappointment. They will awake to find their visions baseless and empty as a dream. It is to such as these that the prophet's words may be well applied: "Behold, all ye that kindle a fire, that compass yourselves about with sparks: Walk in the light of your fire, and in the sparks that ye have kindled. This shall ye have of mine hand; ye shall lie down in sorrow" (*Isaiah* 50:11).

But let your eyes look right onward to the day of Christ's second advent. That is the only day when every abuse shall be rectified, and every corruption and source of sorrow completely purged away. Waiting for that day, let us each work on and serve our generation; not idle, as if nothing could be done to check evil, but not disheartened because we see not yet all things put under our Lord. After all, the night is far spent, and the day is at hand. Let us wait, I say, on the Lord.

If these things be so, men need not wonder that we warn them to beware of all leanings toward the Church of Rome. Surely, when the mind of God about idolatry is so plainly revealed to us in his Word, it seems the height of infatuation in anyone to join a church so steeped in idolatries as the Church of Rome. To enter into communion with her, when God is saying, "Come out of her, that ye be not partakers of her sins, and receive not of her plagues" (*Revelation* 18:4) – to seek her when the Lord is warning us to leave her – to become her subjects when the Lord's voice is crying, "Escape for thy life, flee from the wrath to come"; all this is mental blindness indeed, a blindness like that of him, who, though forewarned, embarks in a sinking ship, a blindness which would be almost incredible, if our own eyes did not see examples of it continually.

We must all be on our guard. We must take nothing for granted. We must not hastily suppose that we are too wise to be ensnared, and say, like Hazael, "Is thy servant a dog, that he should do this thing?" Those who preach must cry aloud and spare not, and allow no false tenderness to make them hold their peace about the heresies of the day. Those who hear must have their loins girt about with truth, and their minds stored with clear prophetical views of the end to which all idol-worshippers must come. Let us all try to realize that the latter ends of the world are upon us, and that the abolition of all idolatry is hastening on. Is this a time for a man to draw nearer to Rome? Is it not rather a time to draw further back and stand clear, lest we be involved in her downfall? Is this a time to extenuate and palliate Rome's manifold corruptions, and refuse to see the reality of her sins? Surely we ought rather to be doubly jealous of everything of a Romish tendency in religion, doubly careful that we do not connive at any treason against our Lord Christ, and doubly ready to protest against unscriptural worship of every description. Once more, then, I say, let us remember that the destruction of all idolatry is certain, and remembering that, *beware of the Church of Rome.*

The subject I now touch upon is of deep and pressing importance, and demands the serious attention of all Protestant churchmen. It is vain to deny that a large party of English clergy and laity in the present day are moving Heaven and Earth to reunite the Church of England with the idolatrous Church of Rome. The publication of that monstrous book, Dr. Pusey's *Eirenicon*, and the formation of a "Society for Promoting the Union of Christendom," are plain evidence of what I mean. He that runs may read.

The existence of such a movement as this will not surprise any one who has carefully watched the history of the Church of England during the last forty years. The tendency of Tractarianism and Ritualism has been steadily toward Rome. Hundreds of men and women have fairly and honestly left our ranks, and become downright papists. But many hundreds more have stayed behind, and are yet nominal churchmen within our pale. The pompous semi-Romish ceremonial which has been introduced into many churches has prepared men's minds for changes. An extravagantly theatrical and idolatrous mode of celebrating the Lord's Supper has paved the way for transubstantiation. A regular process of *unprotestantizing* has been long and successfully at work. The poor old Church of England stands on an inclined plane. Her very existence, as a Protestant church, is in peril.

I hold, for one, that this Romish movement ought to be steadily and firmly resisted. Notwithstanding the rank, the learning, and the devotedness of some of its advocates, I regard it as a most mischievous, soul-ruining and unscriptural movement. To say that re-union with Rome would be an insult to our martyred Reformers, is a very light thing; it is far more than this: It would be a sin and an offence against God! Rather than be re-united with the idolatrous Church of Rome, I would willingly see my own beloved church perish and go to pieces. Rather than become popish once more, she had better die!

Unity in the abstract is no doubt an excellent thing, but unity without truth is useless. Peace and uniformity are beautiful and valuable, but peace without the Gospel – peace based on a common Episcopacy, and not on a common faith – is a worthless peace, not deserving of the name. When Rome has repealed the decrees of Trent, and her additions to the Creed, when Rome has recanted her false and unscriptural doctrines, when Rome has formally renounced image-worship, Mary-worship, and transubstantiation, then, and not till then, it will be time to talk of re-union with her. Till then there is a gulf between us which cannot be honestly bridged. Till then I call on all churchmen to resist to the death this idea of reunion with Rome. Till then let our watchwords be "No peace with Rome! No communion with idolaters!" Well says the admirable Bishop Jewel, in his *Apology*, "We do not decline concord and peace with men; but we will not continue in a state of war with God that we might have peace with men! If the pope does indeed desire we should be reconciled to him, he ought first to reconcile himself to God." This witness is true! Well would it be for the Church of England, if all her Bishops had been like Jewel!

I write these things with sorrow. But the circumstances of the times make it absolutely necessary to speak out. To whatever quarter of the horizon I turn, I see grave reason for alarm. For the true church of Christ I have no fears at all. But for the Established Church of England, and for all the Protestant churches of Great Britain, I have very grave fears indeed. The tide of events seems running strongly against Protestantism and in favor of Rome. It looks as if God had a controversy with us, as a nation, and was about to punish us for our sins.

I am no prophet. I know not where we are drifting. But at the rate we are going, I think it quite within the verge of possibility that in a few years the Church of England may be reunited to the Church of Rome. The Crown of England may be once more on the head of a papist. Protestantism may be formally repudiated. A Romish Archbishop may once more preside at Lambeth Palace. Mass may be once more said at Westminster Abbey and St. Paul's. And one result will be that all Bible-reading Christians must either leave the Church of England, or else sanction idol-worship and become idolaters! God grant we may never come to this state of things! But at the rate we are going, it seems to me quite possible.

And now it only remains for me to conclude what I have been saying, by mentioning some safeguards for the souls of all who read this paper. We live in a time when the Church of Rome is walking amongst us with renewed strength and loudly boasting that she will soon win back the ground that she has lost. False doctrines of every kind are continually set before us in the most subtle and specious forms. It cannot be thought unseasonable if I offer some practical safeguards against idolatry. What it is, whence it comes, where it is, what will end it – all this we have seen. Let me point out how we may be safe from it, and I will say no more.

(1) Let us arm ourselves, then, for one thing, with a *thorough knowledge of the Word of God*. Let us read our Bibles more diligently than ever, and become familiar with every part of them. Let the Word dwell in us richly. Let us beware of anything which would make us give less time, and less heart, to the perusal of its sacred pages. The Bible is the sword of the Spirit – let it never be laid aside. The Bible is the true lantern for a dark and cloudy time – let us beware of traveling without its light. I strongly suspect – if we did but know the secret history of the numerous secessions from our church to that of Rome, which we deplore – I strongly suspect that in almost every case one of the most important steps in the downward road would be found to have been a neglected Bible – more attention to forms, sacraments, daily services, primitive Christianity, and so forth, and diminished attention to the written Word of God. The Bible is the King's highway. If we once leave that for any by-path, however beautiful, and old, and frequented it may seem, we must never be surprised if we end with worshiping images and relics, and going regularly to a confessional.

(2) Let us arm ourselves, in the second place, with a *godly jealousy about the least portion of the Gospel*. Let's beware of sanctioning the slightest attempt to keep back any jot or tittle of it, or to throw any part of it into the shade by exalting subordinate matters in religion. When Peter withdrew himself from eating with the Gentiles, it seemed but a little thing; yet Paul tells the Galatians, "I withstood him to the face, because he was to be blamed" (*Galatians* 2:11). Let us count nothing little that concerns our souls. Let us be very particular whom we hear, where we go, and what we do, in all the matters of our own particular worship, and let us care nothing for the imputation of squeamishness and excessive scrupulosity. We live in days when great principles are involved in little acts, and things in religion, which fifty years ago were utterly indifferent, are now by circumstances rendered indifferent no longer. Let us beware of tampering with anything of a Romanizing tendency. It is foolishness to play with fire. I believe that many of our perverts and seceders began with thinking there could be no mighty harm in attaching a *little* more importance to certain outward things than they once

did. But once launched on the downward course, they went on from one thing to another. They provoked God, and he left them to themselves! They were given over to strong delusion, and allowed to believe a lie (2 *Thessalonians* 2:11). They tempted the devil, and he came to them! They started with trifles, as many foolishly call them. They have ended with downright idolatry.

(3) Let us arm ourselves, last of all, with *clear, sound views of our Lord Jesus Christ,* and of the salvation that is in him. He is the "image of the invisible God," the express "image of his person," and the true preservative against all idolatry, when truly known. Let us build ourselves deep down on the strong foundation of his finished work upon the cross. Let us settle it firmly in our minds that Christ Jesus has done everything needful in order to present us without spot before the throne of God, and that simple, childlike faith on our part is the only thing required to give us an entire interest in the work of Christ. Let us not doubt that having this faith, we are completely justified in the sight of God – will never be more justified if we live to the age of Methuselah and do the works of the Apostle Paul – and *can* add nothing to that complete justification by any acts, deeds, words, performances, fastings, prayers, almsdeeds, attendance on ordinances, or anything else of our own.

Above all let us keep up continual communion with the person of the Lord Jesus! Let us abide in him daily, feed on him daily, look to him daily, lean on him daily, live upon him daily, draw from his fulness daily. Let us realize this, and the idea of other mediators, other comforters, other intercessors, will seem utterly absurd. "What need is there?" we shall reply: "I have Christ, and in him I have all. What have I to do with idols? I have Jesus in my heart, Jesus in the Bible, and Jesus in Heaven, and I want nothing more!"

Once let the Lord Christ have his rightful place in our hearts, and all other things in our religion will soon fall into their right places – church, ministers, sacraments, ordinances, all will go down, and take the second place.

Except Christ sits as Priest and King upon the throne of our hearts, that little kingdom within will be in perpetual confusion. But only let him be "all in all" there, and all will be well. Before him every idol, every Dagon shall fall down. Christ rightly known, Christ truly believed, and Christ heartily loved, is the true preservative against ritualism, Romanism, and every form of idolatry.

Note

I ask every reader of this paper to read, mark, learn, and inwardly digest the language of the following declaration. It is the declaration which, under the "Act of Settlement" and by the law of England, every Sovereign of this country, at his or her coronation, must "make, subscribe, and audibly repeat." It is the declaration, be it remembered, which was made, subscribed and repeated by Her Gracious Majesty, Queen Victoria.

"I, Victoria, do solemnly and sincerely, in the presence of God, profess, testify, and declare that I do believe that in the Sacrament of the Lord's Supper there is not any transubstantiation of the elements of bread and wine into the body and blood of Christ, at or after the consecration thereof, by any person whatsoever; and that the invocation or adoration of the Virgin Mary or any other Saint, and the sacrifice of the mass, as they are now used in the Church of Rome, are superstitious and *idolatrous*. And I do solemnly, in the presence of God, profess, testify, and declare, that I do make this declaration, and every part thereof, in the plain and ordinary sense of the words read unto me, as they are commonly understood by English Protestants, without any evasion, equivocation or mental reservation, and without any dispensation already granted me for this purpose by the pope or any other authority or person whatsoever, or without any hope of any such dispensation from any person or authority whatsoever, or without thinking that I am or can be acquitted before God or man, or absolved of this declaration or any part thereof, although the pope, or any person or persons or power whatsoever, shall dispense with or annul the same, or declare that it was null and void from the beginning."

May the day never come when British Sovereigns shall cease to make the above declaration!

32

Pharisees and Sadducees[1]

J. C. Ryle

Then Jesus said unto them, "Take heed and beware of the leaven of the Pharisees and of the Sadducees" (Matthew 16:6).

EVERY WORD spoken by the Lord Jesus is full of deep instruction for Christians. It is the voice of the Chief Shepherd. It is the Great Head of the church speaking to all its members – the King of kings speaking to his subjects – the Master of the house speaking to his servants – the Captain of our salvation speaking to his soldiers. Above all, it is the voice of him who said, "I have not spoken of myself: The Father which sent me, he gave me a commandment what I should say and what I should speak" (*John* 12:49). The heart of every believer in the Lord Jesus ought to burn within him when he hears his Master's words: He ought to say, "This is the voice of my beloved" (*Canticles* 2:8).

And every kind of word spoken by the Lord Jesus is of the greatest value. Precious as gold are all his words of doctrine and precept; precious are all his parables and prophecies; precious are all his words of comfort and of consolation; precious, not least, are all his words of caution and of warning. We are not merely to hear him when he says, "Come unto me, all ye that labor, and are heavy laden"; we are to hear him also when he says, "Take heed and beware."

I am going to direct attention to one of the most solemn and emphatic warnings which the Lord Jesus ever delivered: "Take heed and beware of the leaven of the Pharisees and of the Sadducees." Upon this text I wish to erect a beacon for all who desire to be saved, and to preserve some souls, if possible, from making shipwreck. The times call

1. Reprinted from J. C. Ryle, *Warnings to the Churches*. The Banner of Truth Trust, 1967.

loudly for such beacons: The spiritual shipwrecks of the last twenty-five years have been deplorably numerous. The watchmen of the church ought to speak out plainly now, or forever hold their peace.

I. First of all, I ask my readers to observe *who they were to whom the warning of the text was addressed.*

Our Lord Jesus Christ was not speaking to men who were worldly, ungodly, and unsanctified, but to his own disciples, companions, and friends. He addressed men who, with the exception of the apostate Judas Iscariot, were right-hearted in the sight of God. He spoke to the twelve apostles, the first founders of the church of Christ, and the first ministers of the Word of salvation. And yet even to them he addressed the solemn caution of our text: "Take heed and beware."

There is something very remarkable in this fact. We might have thought that these apostles needed little warning of this kind. Had they not given up all for Christ's sake? They had. Had they not endured hardship for Christ's sake? They had. Had they not believed Jesus, followed Jesus, loved Jesus, when almost all the world was unbelieving? All these things are true; and yet to them the caution was addressed: "Take heed and beware." We might have imagined that at any rate the disciples had but little to fear from the "leaven of the Pharisees and of the Sadducees." They were poor and unlearned men, most of them fishermen or publicans; they had no leanings in favor of the Pharisees and the Sadducees; they were more likely to be prejudiced against them than to feel any drawing toward them. All this is perfectly true; yet even to them there comes the solemn warning: "Take heed and beware."

There is useful counsel here for all who profess to love the Lord Jesus Christ in sincerity. It tells us loudly that the most eminent servants of Christ are not beyond the need of warnings, and ought to be always on their guard. It shows us plainly that the holiest of believers ought to walk humbly with his God, and to watch and pray, lest he fall into temptation, and be overtaken in a fault. None is so holy, but that he may fall – not finally, not hopelessly, but to his own discomfort, to the scandal of the church, and to the triumph of the world: None is so strong but that he may for a time be overcome. Chosen as believers are by God the Father, justified as they are by the blood and righteousness of Jesus Christ, sanctified as they are by the Holy Ghost – believers are still only men: They are yet in the body, and yet in the world. They are ever near temptation: They are ever liable to err, both in doctrine and in practice.

Their hearts, though renewed, are very feeble; their understanding, though enlightened, is still very dim. They ought to live like those who dwell in an enemy's land, and every day to put on the armor of God. The devil is very busy: He never slumbers or sleeps. Let us remember the failings of Noah, and Abraham, and Lot, and Moses, and David, and Peter; and remembering them, be humble, and take heed lest we fall.

I may be allowed to say that none need warnings so much as the ministers of Christ's Gospel. Our office and our ordination are no security against errors and mistakes. It is, alas, too true, that the greatest heresies have crept into the church of Christ by means of ordained men. Neither Episcopal ordination, nor Presbyterian ordination, nor any other ordination confers any immunity from error and false doctrine. Our very familiarity with the Gospel often begets in us a hardened state of mind. We are apt to read the Scriptures, and preach the Word, and conduct public worship, and carry on the service of God, in a dry, hard, formal, callous spirit. Our very familiarity with sacred things, except we watch our hearts, is likely to lead us astray. "Nowhere," says an old writer, "is a man's soul in more danger than in a priest's office." The history of the church of Christ contains many melancholy proofs that the most distinguished ministers may for a time fall away. Who has not heard of Archbishop Cranmer recanting and going back from those opinions he had defended so stoutly, though, by God's mercy, raised again to witness a glorious confession at last? Who has not heard of Bishop Jewel signing documents that he most thoroughly disapproved, and of which signature he afterwards bitterly repented? Who does not know that many others might be named, who at one time or another, have been overtaken by faults, have fallen into errors, and been led astray? And who does not know the mournful fact that many of them never came back to the truth, but died in hardness of heart, and held their errors to the last?

These things ought to make us humble and cautious. They tell us to distrust our own hearts and to pray to be kept from falling. In these days, when we are specially called upon to cleave firmly to the doctrines of the Protestant Reformation, let us take heed that our zeal for Protestantism does not puff us up, and make us proud. Let us never say in our self-conceit, "I shall never fall into Popery or Neologianism: Those views will never suit me." Let us remember that many have begun well and run well for a season, and yet afterwards turned aside out of the right way. Let us take heed that we are spiritual men as well as Protestants, and real friends of Christ as well as enemies of Antichrist. Let us pray that we may be kept from error, and never forget that the twelve apostles themselves were the men to whom the Great Head of the church addressed these words: "Take heed and beware."

II. I propose, in the second place, to explain *what were those dangers against which our Lord warned the apostles.* "Take heed," he says, "and beware of the leaven of the Pharisees and of the Sadducees."

The danger against which he warns them is false doctrine. He says nothing about the sword of persecution, or the open breach of the Ten Commandments, or the love of money, or the love of pleasure. All these things no doubt were perils and snares to which the souls of the apostles were exposed; but against these things our Lord raises no warning voice here. His warning is confined to one single point: "The leaven of the Pharisees and of the Sadducees." We are not left to conjecture what our Lord meant by that word "leaven." The Holy Ghost, a few verses after the very text on which I am now dwelling, tells us plainly that by leaven was meant the "doctrine" of the Pharisees and of the Sadducees. Let us try to understand what we mean when we speak of the "doctrine of the Pharisees and of the Sadducees."

(a) The doctrine of the Pharisees may be summed up in three words – they were formalists, tradition-worshipers, self-righteous. They attached such weight to the traditions of men that they practically regarded them of more importance than the inspired writings of the Old Testament. They valued themselves upon excessive strictness in their attention to all the ceremonial requirements of the Mosaic law. They thought much of being descended from Abraham, and said in their hearts, "We have Abraham for our father." They fancied because they had Abraham for their father that they were not in peril of Hell like other men, and that their descent from him was a kind of title to Heaven. They attached great value to washings and ceremonial purifyings of the body, and believed that the very touching of the dead body of a fly or gnat would defile them. They made a great ado about the outward parts of religion, and such things as could be seen of men. They made broad their phylacteries, and enlarged the fringes of their garments. They prided themselves on paying great honor to dead saints, and garnishing the sepulchres of the righteous. They were very zealous to make proselytes. They thought much of having power, rank, and preeminence, and of being called by men, "Rabbi, Rabbi." These things, and many such-like things, the Pharisees did. Every well-informed Christian can find these things in the *Gospels of Matthew* and *Mark*. (See *Matthew* 15 and 23; *Mark* 7.)

All this time, be it remembered, they did not formally deny any part of the Old Testament Scripture. But they brought in, over and above it, so much of human invention, that they virtually put Scripture aside, and buried it under their own traditions. This is the sort of religion, of which our Lord says to the apostles, "Take heed and beware."

(b) The doctrine of the Sadducees, on the other hand, may be summed up in three words – free-thinking, skepticism, and rationalism. Their creed was one far less popular than that of the Pharisees, and, therefore, we find them less often mentioned in the New Testament Scriptures. So far as we can judge from the New Testament, they appear to have held the doctrine of degrees of inspiration; at all events they attached exceeding value to the Pentateuch above the other parts of the Old Testament, if indeed they did not altogether ignore the latter. They believed that there was no resurrection, no angel, and no spirit, and tried to laugh men out of their belief in these things, by supposing hard cases, and bringing forward difficult questions. We have an instance of their mode of argument in the case which they propounded to our Lord of the woman who had had seven husbands, when they asked, "In the resurrection, whose wife shall she be of the seven?" And in this way they probably hoped, by rendering religion absurd, and its chief doctrines ridiculous, to make men altogether give up the faith they had received from the Scriptures.

All this time, be it remembered, we may not say that the Sadducees were downright infidels: This they were not. We may not say they denied revelation altogether: This they did not do. They observed the law of Moses. Many of them were found among the priests in the times described in the *Acts of the Apostles*. Caiaphas who condemned our Lord was a Sadducee. But the practical effect of their teaching was to shake men's faith in any revelation, and to throw a cloud of doubt over men's minds, which was only one degree better than infidelity. And of all such kind of doctrine – free thinking, skepticism, rationalism – our Lord says, "Take heed and beware."

Now the question arises, Why did our Lord Jesus Christ deliver this warning? He knew, no doubt, that within forty years the schools of the

Pharisees and the Sadducees would be completely overthrown. He that knew all things from the beginning, knew perfectly well that in forty years Jerusalem, with its magnificent temple, would be destroyed, and the Jews scattered over the face of the Earth. Why then do we find him giving this warning about "the leaven of the Pharisees and of the Sadducees"?

I believe that our Lord delivered this solemn warning for the perpetual benefit of that church which he came on Earth to found. He spoke with a prophetic knowledge. He knew well the diseases to which human nature is always liable. He foresaw that the two great plagues of his church upon Earth would always be the doctrine of the Pharisees and the doctrine of the Sadducees. He knew that these would be the upper and nether millstones, between which his truth would be perpetually crushed and bruised until he came the second time. He knew that there always would be Pharisees in spirit, and Sadducees in spirit, among professing Christians. He knew that their succession would never fail, and their generation never become extinct – and that though the names of Pharisees and Sadducees were no more, yet their principles would always exist. He knew that during the time that the church existed, until his return, there would always be some that would add to the Word, and some that would subtract from it – some that would stifle it, by adding to it other things, and some that would bleed it to death, by subtracting from its principal truths. And this is the reason why we find him delivering this solemn warning: "Take heed and beware of the leaven of the Pharisees and of the Sadducees."

And now comes the question, Had not our Lord Jesus Christ good reason to give this warning? I appeal to all who know anything of church history, Was there not indeed a cause? I appeal to all who remember what took place soon after the apostles were dead. Do we not read that in the primitive church of Christ, there rose up two distinct parties; one ever inclined to err, like the Arians, in holding less than the truth – the other ever inclined to err, like the relic worshipers and saint worshipers, in holding more than the truth as it is in Jesus? Do we not see the same thing coming out in after times, in the form of Romanism on the one side and Socinianism on the other? Do we not read in the history of our own Church of two great parties, the Non-jurors on the one side, and the Latitudinarians on the other? These are ancient things. In a short paper like this it is impossible for me to enter more fully into them.

They are things well known to all who are familiar with records of past days. There always have been these two great parties – the party representing the principles of the Pharisee, and the party representing the principles of the Sadducee. And therefore our Lord had good cause to say of these two great principles, "Take heed and beware."

But I desire to bring the subject even nearer at the present moment. I ask my readers to consider whether warnings like this are not especially needed in our *own* times. We have, undoubtedly, much to be thankful for in England. We have made great advances in arts and sciences in the last three centuries, and have much of the form and show of morality and religion. But I ask anybody who can see beyond his own door, or his own fireside, whether we do not live in the midst of dangers from false doctrine?

We have amongst us, on the one side, a school of men who, wittingly or unwittingly, are paving the way into the Church of Rome – a school that professes to draw its principles from primitive tradition, the writings of the fathers, and the voice of the church – a school that talks and writes so much about the church, the ministry, and the sacraments, that it makes them like Aaron's rod, swallow up everything else in Christianity – a school that attaches vast importance to the outward form and ceremonial of religion – to gestures, postures, bowings, crosses, piscinas, sedilia, credence-tables, rood screens, albs, tunicles, copes, chasubles, altar cloths, incense, images, banners, processions, floral decorations, and many other like things, about which not a word is to be found in the Holy Scriptures as having any place in Christian worship. I refer, of course, to the school of churchmen called Ritualists. When we examine the proceedings of that school, there can be but one conclusion concerning them. I believe whatever be the meaning and intention of its teachers, however devoted, zealous, and self-denying, many of them are, that upon them has fallen the mantle of the Pharisees.

We have, on the other hand, a school of men who, wittingly or unwittingly, appear to pave the way to Socinianism – a school which holds strange views about the plenary inspiration of Holy Scripture – stranger views about the doctrine of sacrifice, and the Atonement of our Lord and Saviour Jesus Christ – strange views about the eternity of punishment, and God's love to man – a school strong in negatives, but very weak in positives – skilful in raising doubts, but impotent in laying them – clever in unsettling and unscrewing men's faith, but powerless to offer any firm rest for the sole of our foot. And, whether the leaders of this school mean it or not, I believe that on them has fallen the mantle of the Sadducees.

These things sound harsh. It saves a vast deal of trouble to shut our eyes, and say, "I see no danger," and because it is not seen, therefore not to believe it. It is easy to stop our ears and say, "I hear nothing," and because we hear nothing, therefore to feel no alarm. But we know well who they are that rejoice over the state of things we have to deplore in some quarters of our own Church [of England]. We know what the Roman Catholic thinks; we know what the Socinian thinks. The Roman Catholic rejoices over the rise of the Tractarian party: The Socinian rejoices over the rise of men who teach such views as those set forth in modern days about the atonement and inspiration. They would not rejoice as they do if they did not see their work being done, and their cause being helped forward. The danger, I believe, is far greater than we are apt to suppose. The books that are read in many quarters are most mischievous, and the tone of thought on religious subjects, among many classes, and especially among the higher ranks, is deeply unsatisfactory. The plague is abroad. If we love life, we ought to search our own hearts, and try our own faith, and make sure that we stand on the right foundation. Above all, we ought to take heed that we ourselves do not imbibe the poison of false doctrine, and go back from our first love.

I feel deeply the painfulness of speaking out on these subjects. I know well that plain speaking about false doctrine is very unpopular, and that the speaker must be content to find himself thought very uncharitable, very troublesome, and very narrow-minded. Thousands of people can never distinguish differences in religion. To the bulk of men a clergyman is a clergyman, and a sermon is a sermon, and as to any difference between one minister and another, or one doctrine and another, they are utterly unable to understand it. I cannot expect such people to approve of any warning against false doctrine. I must make up my mind to meet with their disapprobation, and must bear it as I best can.

But I will ask any honest-minded, unprejudiced Bible reader to turn to the New Testament and see what he will find there. He will find many plain warnings against false doctrine: "Beware of false prophets" – "Beware lest any man spoil you through philosophy and vain deceit" – "Be not carried about with divers and strange doctrines" – "Believe not every spirit, but try the spirits whether they be of God" (*Matthew*

7:15; *Colossians* 2:8; *Hebrews* 13:9; *1 John* 4:1). He will find a large part of several inspired epistles taken up with elaborate explanations of true doctrine and warnings against false teaching. I ask whether it is possible for a minister who takes the Bible for his rule of faith to avoid giving warnings against doctrinal error?

Finally, I ask any one to mark what is going on in England at this very day. I ask whether it is not true that hundreds have left the Established Church and joined the Church of Rome within the last thirty years? I ask whether it is not true that hundreds remain within our pale, who in heart are little better than Romanists, and who ought, if they were consistent, to walk in the steps of [John Henry] Newman and [Henry] Manning, and go to their own place? I ask again whether it is not true that scores of young men, both at Oxford and Cambridge, are spoiled and ruined by the withering influence of skepticism, and have lost all positive principles in religion? Sneers at religious newspapers, loud declarations of dislike to "parties," high-sounding, vague phrases about "deep thinking, broad views, new light, free handling of Scripture, and the effete weakness of certain schools of theology," make up the whole Christianity of many of the rising generation. And yet, in the face of these notorious facts, men cry out, "Hold your peace about false doctrine. Let false doctrine alone!" I cannot hold my peace. Faith in the Word of God, love to the souls of men, the vows I took when I was ordained, alike constrain me to bear witness against the errors of the day. And I believe that the saying of our Lord is eminently a truth for the times: "Beware of the leaven of the Pharisees and of the Sadducees."

III. The third thing to which I wish to call attention is *the peculiar name by which our Lord Jesus Christ speaks of the doctrines of the Pharisees and of the Sadducees.*

The words which our Lord used were always the wisest and the best that could be used. He might have said, "Take heed and beware of the doctrine, or of the teaching, or of the opinions of the Pharisees and of the Sadducees." But he does not say so: He uses a word of a peculiar nature: He says, "Take heed and beware of the *leaven* of the Pharisees and of the Sadducees."

Now we all know what is the true meaning of the word "leaven." It is what we commonly call yeast – the yeast which is added to the lump of dough in making a loaf of bread. This yeast, or leaven, bears but a small proportion to the lump into which it is thrown; just so, our Lord would have us know, the first beginning of false doctrine is but small compared to the body of Christianity. It works quietly and noiselessly; just so, our Lord would have us know, false doctrine works secretly in the heart in which it is once planted. It insensibly changes the character of the whole mass with which it is mingled; just so, our Lord would have us know, the doctrines of the Pharisees and Sadducees turn everything upside down, when once admitted into a church or into a man's heart. Let us mark these points: They throw light on many things that we see in the present day. It is of vast importance to receive the lessons of wisdom that this word "leaven" contains in itself.

False doctrine does not meet men face to face, and proclaim that it is false. It does not blow a trumpet before it, and endeavor openly to turn us away from the truth as it is in Jesus. It does not come before men in broad day, and summon them to surrender. It approaches us secretly, quietly, insidiously, plausibly, and in such a way as to disarm man's suspicion, and throw him off his guard. It is the wolf in sheep's clothing, and Satan in the garb of an angel of light, who have always proved the most dangerous foes of the church of Christ.

I believe the most powerful champion of the Pharisees is not the man who bids you openly and honestly come out and join the Church of Rome: It is the man who says that he agrees on all points with you in *doctrine*. He would not take anything away from those evangelical views that you hold; he would not have you make any change at all; all he asks you to do is to *add* a little more to your belief, in order to make your Christianity perfect. "Believe me," he says, "we do not want you to give up anything. We only want you to hold a few more clear views about the church and the sacraments. We want you to add to your present opinions a little more about the office of the ministry, and a little more about episcopal authority, and a little more about the *Prayer Book,* and a little more about the necessity of order and of discipline. We only want you to add *a little more* of these things to your system of religion, and you will be quite right." But when men speak to you in this way, then is the time to remember what our Lord said, and to "take heed and beware." This is the leaven of the Pharisees, against which we are to stand upon our guard.

Why do I say this? I say it because there is no security against the doctrine of the Pharisees, unless we resist its principles in their beginnings. Beginning with a "little more about the church," you may one day place the church in the room of Christ. Beginning with a "little more about the ministry," you may one day regard the minister as "the mediator between God and man." Beginning with a "little more about the sacraments," you may one day altogether give up the doctrine of justification by faith without the deeds of the law. Beginning with a "little more reverence for the *Prayer Book*," you may one day place it above the holy Word of God himself. Beginning with a "little more honor to Bishops," you may at last refuse salvation to every one who does not belong to an Episcopal Church. I only tell an old story: I only mark out roads that have been trodden by hundreds of members of the Church of England in the last few years. They began by carping at the Reformers, and have ended by swallowing the decrees of the Council of Trent. They began by crying up Laud and the Non-jurors, and have ended by going far beyond them, and formally joining the Church of Rome. I believe that when we hear men asking us to "add a little more" to our good old plain Evangelical views, we should stand upon our guard. We should remember our Lord's caution: "Of the leaven of the Pharisees take heed and beware."

I consider the most dangerous champion of the Sadducee school is not the man who tells you openly that he wants you to lay aside any part of the truth, and to become a freethinker and a sceptic. It is the man who begins with quietly insinuating doubts as to the position that we ought to take up about religion – doubts whether we ought to be so positive in saying "this is truth, and that falsehood," – doubts whether we ought to think men wrong who differ from us on religious opinions, since they *may* after all be as much right as we are. It is the man who tells us we ought not to condemn anybody's views, lest we err on the side of want of charity. It is the man who always begins talking in a vague way about God being a God of love, and hints that we ought to believe perhaps that all men, whatever doctrine they profess, will be saved. It is the man who is ever reminding us that we ought to take care how we think lightly of men of powerful minds, and great intellects *(though they are Deists and skeptics)*, who do not think as we do, and that, after all, "great minds are all more or less, taught of God!" It is the man who is ever harping on the difficulties of inspiration, and raising questions whether all men may not be found saved in the end, and whether all may not be right in the sight of God. It is the man who crowns this kind of talk by a few calm sneers against what he is pleased to call "old-fashioned views," and "narrow-minded theology," and "bigotry," and the "want of liberality and charity," in the present day. But when men begin to speak to us in this kind of way, then is the time to stand upon our guard. Then is the time to remember the words of our Lord Jesus Christ, and "to take heed and beware of leaven."

Once more, why do I say this? I say it because there is no security against Sadduceeism, any more than against Phariseeism, unless we resist its principles in the bud. Beginning with a little vague talk about "charity," you may end in the doctrine of universal salvation, fill Heaven with a mixed multitude of wicked as well as good, and deny the existence of Hell. Beginning with a few high-sounding phrases about intellect and the inner light in man, you may end with denying the work of the Holy Ghost, and maintaining that Homer and Shakespeare were as truly inspired as Paul, and thus practically casting aside the Bible. Beginning with some dreamy, misty idea about "all religions containing more or less truth," you may end with utterly denying the necessity of missions, and maintaining that the best plan is to leave everybody alone. Beginning with dislike to "Evangelical religion," as old-fashioned, narrow, and exclusive, you may end by rejecting every leading doctrine of Christianity – the atonement, the need of grace, and the divinity of Christ. Again I repeat that I only tell an old story: I only give a sketch of a path which scores have trodden in the last few years. They were once satisfied with such divinity as that of Newton, Scott, Cecil, and Romaine; they are now fancying they have found a more excellent way in the principles which have been propounded by theologians of the Broad school! I believe there is no safety for a man's soul unless he remembers the lesson involved in those solemn words, "Beware of the leaven of the Sadducees."

Let us beware of the *insidiousness* of false doctrine. Like the fruit of which Eve and Adam ate, it looks at first sight pleasant and good, and a thing to be desired. Poison is not written upon it, and so people are not afraid. Like counterfeit coin, it is not stamped "bad": It passes current from the very likeness it bears to the truth.

Let us beware of the *very small beginnings* of false doctrine. Every heresy began at one time with some little departure from the truth. There is only a little seed of error needed to create a great tree. It is the little stones that make up the mighty building. It was the little timbers that made the great ark that carried Noah and his family over a deluged world. It is the little leaven that leavens the whole lump. It is the little flaw in one link of the chain cable that wrecks the gallant ship, and drowns the crew. It is the omission or addition of one little item in the doctor's prescription that spoils the whole medicine, and turns it into poison. We do not tolerate quietly a little dishonesty, or a little cheating, or a little lying: Just so, let us never allow a little false doctrine to ruin us, by thinking it is but a "little one," and can do no harm. The Galatians seemed to be doing nothing very dangerous when they "observed days and months, and times and years;" yet Paul says, "I am afraid for you" (*Galatians* 4:10, 11).

Finally, let us beware of supposing that *we at any rate are not in danger.* "Our views are sound: Our feet stand firm: Others may fall away, but we are safe!" Hundreds have thought the same, and have come to a bad end. In their self-confidence they tampered with little temptations and little forms of false doctrine; in their self-conceit they went near the brink of danger; and now they seem lost forever. They appear given over to a strong delusion, so as to believe a lie. Some of them have exchanged the *Prayer Book* for the *Breviary,* and are praying to the Virgin Mary, and bowing down to images. Others of them are casting overboard one doctrine after another, and bid fair to strip themselves of every sort of religion but a few scraps of Deism. Very striking is the vision in *Pilgrim's Progress*, which describes the hill Error as "very steep on the farthest side;" and "when Christian and Hopeful looked down they saw at the bottom several men dashed all to pieces by a fall they had from the top." Never, never let us forget the caution to beware of "leaven;" and if we think we stand, let us "take heed lest we fall."

33

The Good Fight of Faith[1]

J. Gresham Machen

And the peace of God, which passes all understanding, shall keep your hearts and minds through Christ Jesus (Philippians 4:7).

Fight the good fight of faith (1 Timothy 6:12).

THE APOSTLE Paul was a great fighter. His fighting was partly against external enemies – against hardships of all kinds. Five times he was scourged by the Jews, three times by the Romans; he suffered shipwreck four times; and was in perils of waters, in perils of robbers, in perils by his own countrymen, in perils by the heathen, in perils in the city, in perils in the wilderness, in perils in the sea, in perils among false brethren. And finally he came to the logical end of such a life, by the headsman's axe. It was hardly a peaceful life, but was rather a life of wild adventure. Lindbergh, I suppose, got a thrill when he hopped off to Paris, and people are in search of thrills today; but if you wanted a really unbroken succession of thrills, I think you could hardly do better than try knocking around the Roman Empire of the first century with the Apostle Paul, engaged in the unpopular business of turning the world upside down.

But these physical hardships were not the chief battle in which Paul was engaged. Far more trying was the battle that he fought against the enemies in his own camp. Everywhere his rear was threatened by an all-engulfing paganism or by a perverted Judaism that had missed the real purpose of the Old Testament law. Read the *Epistles* with care, and you

---

1. This is the last sermon preached by Professor Machen at Princeton Theological Seminary.

see Paul always in conflict. At one time he fights paganism in life, the notion that all kinds of conduct are lawful to the Christian man, a philosophy that makes Christian liberty a mere aid to pagan license. At another time he fights paganism in thought, the sublimation of the Christian doctrine of the resurrection of the body into the pagan doctrine of the immortality of the soul.

At still another time, he fights the effort of human pride to substitute man's merit as the means of salvation for Divine grace; he fights the subtle propaganda of the Judaizers with its appeal to the Word of God. Everywhere we see the great apostle in conflict for the preservation of the church. It is as though a mighty flood were seeking to engulf the church's life; dam the break at one point in the levee, and another break appears somewhere else. Everywhere paganism was seeping through; not for one moment did Paul have peace; always he was called upon to fight.

Fortunately, he was a true fighter; and by God's grace he not only fought, but he won. At first sight indeed he might have seemed to have lost. The lofty doctrine of Divine grace, the center and core of the Gospel that Paul preached, did not always dominate the mind and heart of the subsequent church. The Christianity of the Apostolic Fathers, of the Apologists, of Irenaeus is very different from the Christianity of Paul. The church meant to be faithful to the apostle; but the pure doctrine of the Cross runs counter to the natural man, and not always, even in the church, was it fully understood. Read the *Epistle to the Romans* first, and then read Irenaeus, and you are conscious of a mighty decline. No longer does the Gospel stand out sharp and clear; there is a large admixture of human error; and it might seem as though Christian freedom, after all, were to be entangled in the meshes of a new law.

The human instruments which God uses in great triumphs of faith are no pacifists, but great fighters like Paul himself. Little affinity for the great apostle has the whole tribe of considerers of consequences, the whole tribe of the compromisers ancient and modern. The real companions of Paul are the great heroes of the faith. But who are those heroes? Are they not true fighters, one and all? Tertullian fought a mighty battle against Marcion; Athanasius fought against the Arians; Augustine fought against Pelagius; and as for Luther, he fought a brave battle against kings and princes and popes for the liberty of the people of God. Luther was a great fighter; and we love him for it. So was Calvin; so were John

Knox and all the rest. It is impossible to be a true soldier of Jesus Christ and not fight.

God grant that you – students in this seminary – may be fighters, too! Probably you have your battles even now; you have to contend against sins gross or sins refined; you have to contend against the sin of slothfulness and inertia; you have, many of you, I know very well, a mighty battle on your hands against doubt and despair. Do not think it strange if you fall thus into diverse temptations. The Christian life is a warfare after all. John Bunyan rightly set it forth under the allegory of a Holy War; and when he set it forth, in his greater book, under the figure of a pilgrimage, the pilgrimage too, was full of battles.

There are indeed, places of refreshment on the Christian way; the House Beautiful was provided by the King at the top of the Hill Difficulty, for the entertainment of pilgrims, and from the Delectable Mountains could sometimes be discerned the shining towers of the City of God. But just after the descent from the House Beautiful, there was the battle with Apollyon and the Valley of Humiliation, and later came the Valley of the Shadow of Death. Yes, the Christian faces a mighty conflict in this world. Pray God that in that conflict you may be true men; good soldiers of Jesus Christ, not willing to compromise with your great enemy, not easily cast down, and seeking ever the renewing of your strength in the Word and ordinances and prayer!

If you decide to stand for Christ, you will not have an easy life in the ministry. Of course, you may try to evade the conflict. All men will speak well of you if, after preaching no matter how unpopular a Gospel on Sunday, you will only vote against that Gospel in the councils of the church the next day; you will graciously be permitted to believe in supernatural Christianity all you please if you will only act as though you did not believe in it, if you will only make common cause with its opponents. Such is the program that will win the favor of the church. A man may believe what he pleases, provided he does not believe anything strongly enough to risk his life on it and fight for it. "Tolerance" is the great word. Men even ask for tolerance when they look to God in prayer. But how can any Christian possibly pray such a prayer as that? What a terrible prayer it is, how full of disloyalty to the Lord Jesus Christ!

There is a sense, of course, in which tolerance is a virtue. If by it you mean tolerance on the part of the state, the forbearance of majorities toward minorities, the resolute rejection of any measures of physical compulsion in propagating either what is true or what is false, then of course, the Christian ought to favor tolerance with all his might and main, and ought to lament the widespread growth of intolerance in America today. Or if you mean by tolerance forbearance toward personal attacks upon yourself, or courtesy and patience and fairness in dealing with all errors of whatever kind, then again tolerance is a virtue. But to pray for tolerance apart from such qualifications, in particular to pray for tolerance without careful definition of that of which you are to be tolerant, is just to pray for the breakdown of the Christian religion; for the Christian religion is intolerant to the core.

There lies the whole offense of the Cross – and also the whole power of it. Always the Gospel would have been received with favor by the world *if* it had been presented merely as one way of salvation; the offense came because it was presented as the only way, and because it made relentless war upon all other ways. God save us, then, from this "tolerance" of which we hear so much. God deliver us from the sin of making common cause with those who deny or ignore the blessed Gospel of Jesus Christ! God save us from the deadly guilt of consenting to the presence as our representatives in the church of those who lead Christ's little ones astray; God make us, whatever else we are, just faithful messengers, who present, without fear or favor, not our word, but the Word of God.

But if you are such messengers, you will have the opposition, not only of the world, but increasingly, I fear, of the Church. I cannot tell you that your sacrifice will be light. No doubt it would be noble to care nothing whatever about the judgment of our follow men. But to such nobility I confess that I for my part have not quite attained, and I cannot expect you to have attained to it. I confess that academic preferments, easy access to great libraries, the society of cultured people, and in general the thousand advantages that come from being regarded as respectable people in a respectable world – I confess that these things seem to me to be in themselves good and desirable things. Yet the servant of Jesus Christ, to an increasing extent, is being obliged to give them up. Certainly, in making that sacrifice we do not complain; for we have something with which all that we have lost is not worthy to be compared. Still, it can hardly be said that any unworthy motives of self-interest can lead us to adopt a course which brings us nothing but reproach.

Where, then, shall we find a sufficient motive for such a course as that; where shall we find courage to stand against the whole current of the age, where shall we find courage for this fight of faith? I do not think that we shall obtain courage by any mere lust of conflict. In some battles that means may perhaps suffice. Soldiers in bayonet practice were sometimes, and for all I know still are, taught to give a shout when they thrust their bayonets at imaginary enemies; I heard them doing it even long after the armistice in France. That serves, I suppose, to overcome the natural inhibition of civilized man against sticking a knife into human bodies. It is thought to develop the proper spirit of conflict. Perhaps it may be necessary in some kinds of war. But it will hardly serve in this Christian conflict. In this conflict I do not think we can be good fighters simply by being resolved to fight. For this battle is a battle of love; and nothing ruins a man's service in it so much as a spirit of hate.

No, if we want to learn the secret of this warfare, we shall have to look deeper; and we can hardly do better than turn again to that great fighter, the Apostle Paul. What was the secret of his power in the mighty conflict; how did he learn to fight?

The answer is paradoxical; but it is very simple. Paul was a great fighter because he was at peace. He who said, "Fight the good fight of faith," spoke also of "the peace of God which passes all understanding"; and in that peace the sinews of his war were found. He fought against the enemies that were without because he was at peace within; there was an inner sanctuary in his life that no enemy could disturb. There, my friends, is the great central truth. You cannot fight successfully with beasts, as Paul did at Ephesus; you cannot fight successfully against evil men, or against the devil and his spiritual powers of wickedness in high places, unless when you fight against those enemies there is One with Whom you are at peace.

But if you are at peace with that One, then you can care little what men may do. You can say with the apostles, "We must obey God rather than men"; you can say with Luther, "Here I stand, I cannot do otherwise, God help me. Amen"; you can say with Elisha, "They that be with us are more than they that be with them"; you can say with Paul, "it is God that justifies, who is he that condemns?" Without that peace of God in your hearts, you will strike little terror into the enemies of the Gospel of Christ. You may amass mighty resources for the conflict; you may be great masters of ecclesiastical strategy; you may be very clever, and very zealous too; but I fear that it will be of little avail. There may be a tremendous din; but when the din is over, the Lord's enemies will be in possession of the field. No, there is no other way to be a really good fighter. You cannot fight God's battle against God's enemies unless you are at peace with him.

But how shall you be at peace with him? Many ways have been tried. How pathetic is the age-long effort of sinful man to become right with God; sacrifice, lacerations, almsgiving, morality, penance, confession! But alas, it is all of no avail. Still there is that same awful gulf. It may be temporarily concealed; spiritual exercises may conceal it for a time; penance or the confession of sin unto men may give a temporary and apparent relief. But the real trouble remains; the burden is still on the back; Mount Sinai is still ready to shoot forth flames; the soul is still not at peace with God. How then shall peace be obtained?

My friends, it cannot be attained by anything in us. Oh, that that truth could be written in the hearts of every one of you! Oh, that it could be written in letters of flame for all the world to read! Peace with God cannot be attained by any act or any mere experience of man; it cannot be attained by good works, neither can it be attained by confession of sin, neither can it be attained by any psychological results of an act of faith. We can never be at peace with God unless God first be at peace with us. But how can God be at peace with us? Can he be at peace with us by ignoring the guilt of sin? by descending from his throne? by throwing the universe into chaos? by making wrong to be the same as right? by making a dead letter of his holy law, "The soul that sins, it shall die"? by treating his eternal laws as though they were the changeable laws of man?

Oh, what an abyss were the universe if that were done, what a mad anarchy, what a wild demon-riot! Where could there be peace if God were thus at war with himself; where could there be a foundation if God's laws were not sure? Oh, no, my friends, peace cannot be attained for man by the great modern method of dragging God down to man's level; peace cannot be attained by denying that right is right and wrong is wrong; peace can nowhere be attained if the awful justice of God stand not forever sure.

How then can we sinners stand before that Throne? How can there be peace for us in the presence of the justice of God? How can he be just and yet justify the ungodly? There is one answer to these questions. It is not our answer. Our wisdom could never have discovered it.

It is God's Answer. It is found in the story of the cross. We deserved eternal death because of sin; the eternal Son of God, because he loved us, and because He was sent by the Father who loved us too, died in our stead, for our sins, upon the cross. That message is despised today; upon it the visible church as well as the world pours out the vials of its scorn, or else does it even less honor by paying it lip-service and then passing it by. Men dismiss it as a "theory of the atonement," and fall back upon the customary commonplaces about a principle of self-sacrifice, or the culmination of a universal law, or a revelation of the love of God, or the hallowing of suffering, or the similarity between Christ's death and the death of soldiers who perished in the great war.

In the presence of such blindness, our words often seem vain. We may tell men something of what we think about the cross of Christ, but it is harder to tell them what we feel. We pour forth our tears of gratitude and love; we open to the multitude the depths of our souls; we celebrate a mystery so tender, so holy, that we might think it would soften even a heart of stone. But all to no purpose. The cross remains foolishness to the world, men turn coldly away, and our preaching seems but vain. And then comes the wonder of wonders! The hour comes for some poor soul, even through the simplest and poorest preaching; the message is honored, not the messenger; there comes a flash of light into the soul, and all is as clear as day. "He loved me and gave himself for me," says the sinner at last, as he contemplates the Saviour upon the cross. The burden of sin falls from the back, and a soul enters into the peace of God.

Have you yourselves that peace, my friends? If you have, you will not be deceived by the propaganda of any disloyal church. If you have the peace of God in your hearts, you will never shrink from controversy; you will never be afraid to contend earnestly for the Faith. Talk of peace in the present deadly peril of the church, and you show, unless you be strangely ignorant of the conditions that exist, that you have little inkling of the true peace of God. Those who have been at the foot of the cross will not be afraid to go forth under the banner of the cross to a holy war of love.

Where are you going to stand in the great battle which now rages in the church? Are you going to curry favor with the world by standing aloof; are you going to be "conservative liberals" or "liberal conservatives" or "Christians who do not believe in controversy," or anything else so self-contradictory and absurd? Are you going to be Christians, but not Christians overmuch? Are you going to stand coldly aloof when God's people fight against ecclesiastical tyranny at home and abroad? Are you going to excuse yourselves by pointing out personal defects in those who contend for the Faith today? Are you going to be disloyal to Christ in external testimony until you can make all well within your own soul? Be assured, you will never accomplish your purpose if you adopt such a program as that. Witness bravely to the Truth that you already understand, and more will be given to you; but make common cause with those who deny or ignore the Gospel of Christ, and the enemy will forever run riot in your life.

There are many hopes that I cherish for you men, with whom I am united by such ties of affection. I hope that you may be gifted preachers; I hope that you may have happy lives; I hope that you may have adequate support for yourselves and for your families; I hope that you may have good churches. But I hope something for you far more than all that. I hope above all that, wherever you are and however your preaching may be received, you may be true witnesses for the Lord Jesus Christ; I hope that there may never be any doubt where you stand, but that always you may stand squarely for Jesus Christ, as he is offered to us, not in the experiences of men, but in the blessed written Word of God.

Many have been swept from their moorings by the current of the age; a church grown worldly often tyrannizes over those who look for guidance to God's Word alone. But this is not the first discouraging time in the history of the church; other times were just as dark, and yet always God has watched over his people, and the darkest hour has sometimes preceded the dawn. So even now God has not left himself without a witness. In many lands there are those who have faced the great issue of the day and have decided it aright, who have preserved true independence of mind in the presence of the world; in many lands there are groups of Christian people who in the face of ecclesiastical tyranny have not been afraid to stand for Jesus Christ. God grant that you may give comfort to them as you go forth from this seminary; God grant that you may rejoice their hearts by giving them your hand and your voice. To do so you will need courage. Far easier is it to curry favor with the world by abusing those whom the world abuses, by speaking against controversy, by taking a balcony view of the struggle in which God's servants are engaged.

But God save you from such a neutrality as that! It has a certain worldly appearance of urbanity and charity. But how cruel it is to burdened souls; how heartless it is to those little ones who are looking to the church for some clear message from God! God save you from being so heartless and so unloving and so cold! God grant, instead, that in all humility but also in all boldness, in reliance upon God, you may fight the good fight of faith. Peace is indeed yours, the peace of God which passes all understanding. But that peace is given you, not that you may be onlookers or neutrals in love's battle, but that you may be good soldiers of Jesus Christ.

34

Apostolic Fears[1]

J. C. Ryle

I fear, lest by any means, as the serpent beguiled Eve by his subtlety, so your minds should be corrupted from the simplicity that is in Christ. (2 Corinthians 11:3).

THE TEXT which heads this page contains one part of the experience of a very famous Christian. No servant of Christ perhaps has left such a mark for good on the world as the Apostle Paul. When he was born the whole Roman Empire, excepting one little corner, was sunk in the darkest heathenism; when he died the mighty fabric of heathenism was shaken to its very center, and ready to fall. And none of the agents whom God used to produce this marvelous change did more than Saul of Tarsus, after his conversion. Yet even in the midst of his successes and usefulness we find him crying out, "I fear."

There is a melancholy ring about these words which demands our attention. They show a man of many cares and anxieties. He who supposes that St. Paul lived a life of ease, because he was a chosen apostle, wrought miracles, founded churches, and wrote inspired epistles, has yet much to learn. Nothing can be more unlike the truth! The eleventh chapter of the *Second Epistle to the Corinthians* tells a very different tale. It is a chapter which deserves attentive study. Partly from the opposition of the heathen philosophers and priests, whose craft was in danger – partly from the bitter enmity of his own unbelieving countrymen – partly from false or weak brethren – partly from his own thorn in the flesh – the great Apostle of the Gentiles was like his Master, "a man of sorrows and acquainted with grief" (*Isaiah* 53:3).

1. Reprinted from J. C. Ryle, *Warnings to the Churches*. The Banner of Truth Trust [1967] 1992, 122-141.

But of all the burdens which Paul had to carry, none seems to have weighed him down so much as that to which he refers, when he writes to the Corinthians – "the care of all the churches" (2 *Corinthians* 11:28). The scanty knowledge of many primitive Christians – their weak faith, their shallow experience, their dim hope, their low standard of holiness – all these things made them peculiarly liable to be led astray by false teachers, and to depart from the faith. Like little children, hardly able to walk, they required to be treated with immense patience. Like exotics in a hothouse, they had to be watched with incessant care. Can we doubt that they kept their apostolic founder in a state of constant tender anxiety? Can we wonder that he says to the Colossians, "What great conflict I have for you"? – and to the Galatians, "I marvel that ye are so soon removed from him who called you into the grace of Christ unto another gospel." – "O foolish Galatians, who has bewitched you?" (*Colossians* 2:1; *Galatians* 1:6; 3:1). No attentive reader can study the *Epistles* without seeing this subject repeatedly cropping up. And the text I have placed at the head of this paper is a sample of what I mean: "I fear, lest by any means, as the serpent beguiled Eve by his subtlety, so your minds should be corrupted from the simplicity that is in Christ." That text contains three important lessons, which I wish to press on the attention of all my readers. I believe in my conscience they are lessons for the times.

I. First, the text shows us a spiritual *disease to which we are all liable, and which we ought to fear.* That disease is corruption of our minds: "I fear lest your minds be corrupted."

II. Secondly, the text shows us an *example which we ought to remember, as a beacon:* "The serpent beguiled Eve by *his subtlety.*"

III. Thirdly, the text shows us *a point about which we ought specially to be on our guard.* That point is corruption "from the simplicity that is in Christ."

The text is a deep mine, and is not without difficulty. But let us go down into it boldly, and we shall find it contains much precious metal.

I. First, then, there is *a spiritual disease, which we ought to fear:* "corruption of mind."

I take "corruption of mind" to mean injury of our minds by the reception of false and un-Scriptural doctrines in religion. And I believe the sense of the apostle to be, "I fear lest your minds should imbibe erroneous and unsound views of Christianity. I fear lest you should take up, as truths, principles which are not the truth. I fear lest you should depart from the faith once delivered to the saints, and embrace views which are practically destructive of the Gospel of Christ."

The fear expressed by the apostle is painfully instructive, and at first sight may create surprise. Who would have thought that under the very eyes of Christ's own chosen disciples – while the blood of Calvary was hardly yet dry, while the age of miracles had not yet passed away – who would have thought that in a day like this there was any danger of Christians departing from the faith? Yet nothing is more certain than that "the mystery of iniquity" began already to work before the apostles were dead (2 Thessalonians 2:7). "Even now," says John, "there are many antichrists" (1 John 2:18). And no fact in church history is more clearly proved than this – that false doctrine has never ceased to be the plague of Christendom for the last eighteen centuries. Looking forward with the eye of a prophet, Paul might well say *"I fear:"* – "I fear not merely the corruption of your morals, but of your minds."

The plain truth is that *false doctrine* has been the chosen engine which Satan has employed in every age to stop the progress of the Gospel of Christ. Finding himself unable to prevent the Fountain of Life being opened, he has labored incessantly to poison the streams which flow from it. If he could not destroy it, he has too often neutralized its usefulness by addition, subtraction, or substitution. In a word he has "corrupted men's minds."

(a) False doctrine soon overspread the primitive church after the death of the apostles, whatever some may please to say of primitive purity. Partly by strange teaching about the Trinity and the person of Christ, partly by an absurd multiplication of new-fangled ceremonies, partly by the introduction of monasticism and a man-made asceticism, the light of the church was soon dimmed and its usefulness destroyed. Even in Augustine's time, as the preface to the English *Prayer Book* tells us, "Ceremonies were grown to such a number that the estate of Christian people was in worse case concerning this matter than were the Jews." Here was the corruption of men's minds.

(b) False doctrine in the Middle Ages so completely overspread the church that the truth as it is in Jesus was well nigh buried or drowned. During the last three centuries before the Reformation, it is probable that very few Christians in Europe could have answered the question, "What must I do to be saved?" Popes and cardinals, abbots and priors,

archbishops and Bishops, priests and deacons, monks and nuns were, with a few rare exceptions, steeped in ignorance and superstition. They were sunk into a deep sleep, from which they were only partially roused by the earthquake of the Reformation. Here, again, was the "corruption of men's minds."

(c) False doctrine since the days of the Reformation has continually been rising up again, and marring the work which the Reformers began. Neologianism in some districts of Europe, Socinianism in others, formalism and indifferentism in others, have withered blossoms which once promised to bear good fruit, and made Protestantism a mere barren form. Here, again, has been the "corruption of the mind."

(d) False doctrine, even in our own day and under our own eyes, is eating out the heart of the Church of England and periling her existence. One school of churchmen does not hesitate to avow its dislike to the principles of the Reformation, and compasses sea and land to Romanize the Establishment. Another school, with equal boldness, speaks lightly of inspiration, sneers at the very idea of a supernatural religion, and tries hard to cast overboard miracles as so much lumber. Another school proclaims liberty to every shade and form of religious opinion, and tells us that all teachers are equally deserving our confidence, however heterogeneous and contradictory their opinions, if they are only clever, earnest, and sincere. To each and all the same remark applies. They illustrate the "corruption of men's minds."

In the face of such facts as these, we may well lay to heart the words of the apostle in the text which heads the paper. Like him we have abundant cause to feel afraid. Never, I think, was there such need for English Christians to stand on their guard. Never was there such need for faithful ministers to cry aloud and spare not. "If the trumpet give an uncertain sound, who shall prepare himself for the battle?" (1 Corinthians 14:8).

I charge every loyal member of the Church of England to open his eyes to the peril in which his own Church stands, and to beware lest it takes damage through apathy and a morbid love of peace. Controversy is an odious thing; but there are days when it is a positive duty. Peace is an excellent thing; but, like gold, it may be bought too dear. Unity is a mighty blessing; but it is worthless if it is purchased at the cost of truth. Once more I say, Open your eyes and be on your guard.

The nation that rests satisfied with its commercial prosperity, and neglects its national defenses, because they are troublesome or expensive, is likely to become a prey to the first Alaric, or Attila, or Tamerlane, or Napoleon who chooses to attack it. The church which is "rich, and increased with goods," may think it has "need of nothing," because of its antiquity, orders, and endowments. It may cry *"Peace, peace,"* and flatter itself it shall see no evil. But if it is not careful about the maintenance of sound doctrine among its ministers and members, it must never be surprised if its candlestick is taken away.

I deprecate, from the bottom of my heart, despondency or cowardice at this crisis. All I say is, let us exercise a godly fear. I do not see the slightest necessity for forsaking the old ship, and giving it up for lost. Bad as things look inside our ark, they are not a whit better outside. But I do protest against that careless spirit of slumber which seems to seal the eyes of many churchmen, and to blind them to the enormous peril in which we are placed by the rise and progress of false doctrine in these days. I protest against the common notion so often proclaimed by men in high places, that *unity* is of more importance than sound doctrine, and *peace* more valuable than truth. And I call on every reader who really loves the Church of England to recognize the dangers of the times, and to do his duty, manfully and energetically, in resisting them by united action and by prayer. It was not for nothing that our Lord said, "He that has no sword, let him sell his garment and buy one" (*Luke* 22:36). Let us not forget Paul's words, "Watch: Stand fast in the faith. Quit you like men: Be strong" (*1 Corinthians* 16:13). Our noble Reformers bought the truth at the price of their own blood, and handed it down to us. Let us take heed that we do not basely sell it for a mess of pottage, under the specious names of unity and peace.

II. Secondly, the text shows us an *example we shall do well to remember, as a beacon:* "The serpent beguiled Eve by his subtlety."

I need hardly remind my readers that Paul in this place refers to the story of the fall in the third chapter of *Genesis*, as a simple historical fact. He does not afford the least countenance to the modern notion that the book of *Genesis* is nothing more than a pleasing collection of myths and fables. He does not hint that there is no such being as the devil, and that there was not any literal eating of the forbidden fruit, and that it was not really in this way that sin entered into the world. On the contrary, he narrates the story of the third of *Genesis* as a veracious history of a thing that really took place.

You should remember, moreover, that this reference does not stand

alone. It is a noteworthy fact that several of the most remarkable histories and miracles of the Pentateuch are expressly mentioned in the New
Testament, and always as historical facts. Cain and Abel, Noah's ark, the
destruction of Sodom, Esau's selling his birthright, the destruction of
the first-born in Egypt, the passage of the Red Sea, the brazen serpent,
the manna, the water flowing from the rock, Balaam's ass speaking – all
these things are named by the writers of the New Testament, and named
as matters of fact and not as fables. Let that never be forgotten. Those
who are fond of pouring contempt on Old Testament miracles, and
making light of the authority of the Pentateuch, would do well to consider whether they know better than our Lord Jesus Christ and the
apostles. To my mind, to talk of *Genesis* as a collection of myths and
fables, in the face of such a text of Scripture as we have before us in this
paper, sounds alike unreasonable and profane. Was Paul mistaken or
not when he narrated the story of the temptation and the fall? If he was,
he was a weak-minded credulous person, and may have been mistaken
on fifty other subjects. At this rate there is an end of all his authority as
a writer! From such a monstrous conclusion we may well turn away
with scorn. But it is well to remember that much infidelity begins with
irreverent contempt of the Old Testament.

The point, after all, which the apostle would have us mark in the
history of Eve's fall, is the "subtlety" with which the Devil led her into
sin. He did not tell her flatly that he wished to deceive her and do her
harm. On the contrary, he told her that the thing forbidden was a thing
that was "good for food, and pleasant to the eyes, and to be desired to
make one wise" (*Genesis* 3:6). He did not scruple to assert that she might
eat the forbidden fruit and yet "not die." He blinded her eyes to the
sinfulness and danger of transgression. He persuaded her to believe
that to depart from God's plain command was for her benefit and not
for her ruin. In short, "he beguiled her by his subtlety."

Now this "subtlety," Paul tells us, is precisely what we have to fear in
false doctrine. We are not to expect it to approach our minds in the
garment of error, but in the form of truth. Bad coin would never obtain
currency if it had not some likeness to good. The wolf would seldom get
into the fold if he did not enter it in sheep's clothing. Popery and infidelity
would do little harm if they went about the world under their true names.
Satan is far too wise a general to manage a campaign in such a fashion as
this. He employs fine words and high-sounding phrases, such as "catho-

licity, apostolicity, unity, church order, sound church views, free thought, broad sense, kindly judgment, liberal interpretation of Scripture," and the like, and thus effects a lodgment in unwary minds. And this is precisely the "subtlety" which Paul refers to in the text. We need not doubt that he had read his Master's solemn words in the Sermon on the Mount: "Beware of false prophets, which come to you in sheep's clothing but inwardly they are ravening wolves" (*Matthew* 7:15).

I ask your special attention to this point. Such is the simplicity and innocence of many churchmen in this day, that they actually expect false doctrine to look false, and will not understand that the very essence of its mischievousness, as a rule, is its resemblance to God's truth. A young churchman, for instance, brought up from his cradle to hear nothing but Evangelical teaching, is suddenly invited some day to hear a sermon preached by some eminent teacher of semi-Romish or semi-sceptical opinions. He goes into the church, expecting in his simplicity to hear nothing but *heresy* from the beginning to the end. To his amazement he hears a clever, eloquent sermon, containing a vast amount of truth, and only a few homeopathic drops of error. Too often a violent reaction takes place in his simple, innocent, unsuspicious mind. He begins to think his former teachers were illiberal, narrow, and uncharitable, and his confidence in them is shaken, perhaps forever. Too often, alas! it ends with his entire perversion, and at last he is enrolled in the ranks of the Ritualists or the Broad Churchmen! And what is the history of the whole case? Why a foolish forgetfulness of the lesson Paul puts forward in this text. "As the serpent beguiled Eve by his subtlety," so Satan beguiles unwary souls in the nineteenth century by approaching them under the garb of truth.

I beseech every reader of this paper to remember this part of my subject, and to stand upon his guard. What is more common than to hear it said of some false teacher in this day – "He is so good, so devoted, so kind, so zealous, so laborious, so humble, so self-denying, so charitable, so earnest, so fervent, so clever, so evidently sincere, there can be no danger and no harm in hearing him. Besides he preaches so much real Gospel: No one can preach a better sermon than he does sometimes! I never can and never will believe he is unsound." Who does not hear continually such talk as this? What discerning eye can fail to see that many churchmen expect unsound teachers to be open vendors of poison, and cannot realize that they often appear as "angels of

light," and are far too wise to be always saying all they think, and showing their whole hand and mind. But so it is. Never was it so needful to
remember the words, "The serpent beguiled Eve by his subtlety."

I leave this part of my subject with the sorrowful remark that we
have fallen upon times when *suspicion* on the subject of sound doctrine
is not only a duty but also a virtue. It is not the avowed Pharisee and
Sadducee that we have to fear, but the *leaven* of the Pharisees and
Sadducees. It is the "show of wisdom" with which Ritualism is invested
that makes it so dangerous to many minds (*Colossians* 2:23). It seems so
good, and fair, and zealous, and holy, and reverential, and devout, and
kind, that it carries away many well-meaning people like a flood. He
that would be safe must cultivate the spirit of a sentinel at a critical post.
He must not mind being laughed at and ridiculed, as one who "has a
keen nose for heresy." In days like these he must not be ashamed to
suspect danger. And if any one scoffs at him for so doing, he may well be
content to reply, "The serpent beguiled Eve by his subtlety."

III. The third and last lesson of the text remains yet to be considered.
It shows us *a point about which we ought to be especially on our guard.* That
point is called "The simplicity that is in Christ."

Now the expression before us is somewhat remarkable, and stands
alone in the New Testament. One thing at any rate is abundantly clear:
The word *simplicity* means that which is single and unmixed, in contra-
distinction to that which is mixed and double. Following out that idea,
some have held that the expression means "singleness of affection towards Christ" – we are to fear lest we should divide our affections between Christ and any other. This is no doubt very good theology; but I
question whether it is the true sense of the text. I prefer the opinion
that the expression means the simple, unmixed, unadulterated, unal-
tered doctrine of Christ – the simple "truth as it is in Jesus," on all points
– without addition, subtraction, or substitution. Departure from the
simple genuine prescription of the Gospel, either by leaving out any
part or adding any part, was the thing Paul would have the Corinthians
specially dread. The expression is full of meaning, and seems specially
written for our learning in these last days. We are to be ever jealously on
our guard, lest we depart from and corrupt the *simple* Gospel which
Christ once delivered to the saints.

The expression before us is exceedingly instructive. The principle it
contains is of unspeakable importance. If we love our souls and would

keep them in a healthy state, we must endeavor to adhere closely to the *simple doctrine of Christ,* in every jot, tittle, and particular. Once add to it or take away anything from it, and you risk spoiling the Divine medicine, and may even turn it into poison. Let your ruling principle be – "No other doctrine but that of Christ; nothing less, and nothing more!" Lay firm hold on that principle, and never let it go. Write it on the table of your heart, and never forget it.

(1) Let us settle it, for example, firmly in our minds, that there is *no way of peace* but the simple way marked out by Christ. True rest of conscience and inward peace of soul will never come from anything but direct faith in Christ himself and his finished work. Peace by auricular confession, or bodily asceticism, or incessant attendance at church services, or frequent reception of the Lord's Supper, is a delusion and a snare. It is only by coming straight to Jesus himself, laboring and heavy laden, and by believing, trusting communion with him, that souls find rest. In this matter let us stand fast in "the simplicity that is in Christ."

(2) Let us settle it next in our minds that there is *no other priest* who can be in any way a mediator between yourself and God but Jesus Christ. He himself has said, and his Word shall not pass away, "No man comes unto the Father but by me" (*John* 14:6). No sinful child of Adam, whatever be his orders, and however high his ecclesiastical title, can ever occupy Christ's place, or do what Christ alone is appointed to do. The priesthood is Christ's peculiar office, and it is one which he has never deputed to another. In this matter also let us stand fast in "the simplicity that is in Christ."

(3) Let us settle it next in our minds that there is *no sacrifice for sin* except the one sacrifice of Christ upon the cross. Listen not for a moment to those who tell you that there is any sacrifice in the Lord's Supper, any repetition of Christ's offering on the cross, or any oblation of his body and blood, under the form of consecrated bread and wine. The one sacrifice for sins which Christ offered was a perfect and complete sacrifice, and it is nothing short of blasphemy to attempt to repeat it. "By one offering he has perfected forever them that are sanctified" (*Hebrews* 10:14). In this matter also let us stand fast in the "simplicity that is in Christ."

(4) Let us settle it next in our minds that there is *no other rule of faith,* and judge of controversies, but that simple one to which Christ always referred – the written Word of God. Let no man disturb our souls by

such vague expressions as "the voice of the church, primitive antiquity, the judgment of the early fathers," and the like tall talk. Let our only standard of truth be the Bible, God's Word written. "What saith the Scripture?" "What is written?" "How do you read?" "To the law and the testimony!" "Search the Scriptures." (*Romans* 4:3; *Luke* 10:26; *Isaiah* 8:20; *John* 5:39). In this matter also let us stand fast in the "simplicity that is in Christ."

(*5*) Let us settle it next in our minds that there are *no other means of grace* in the church which have any binding authority, except those well known and simple ones which Christ and the apostles have sanctioned. Let us regard with a jealous suspicion all ceremonies and forms of man's invention, when they are invested with such exaggerated importance as to thrust into the background God's own appointments. It is the invariable tendency of man's inventions to supersede God's ordinances. Let us beware of making the Word of God of none effect by human devices. In this matter also let us stand fast in the "simplicity that is in Christ."

(*6*) Let us settle it next in our minds that *no teaching about the sacraments* is sound which gives them a power of which Christ says nothing. Let us beware of admitting that either baptism or the Lord's Supper can confer grace *"ex opere operato"* – that is, by their mere outward administration, independently of the state of heart of those who receive them. Let us remember that the only proof that baptized people and communicants have grace is the exhibition of grace in their lives. The fruits of the Spirit are the only evidences that we are born of the Spirit and one with Christ, and not the mere reception of the sacraments. In this matter also let us stand fast in the "simplicity that is in Christ."

(*7*) Let us settle it next in our minds that *no teaching about the Holy Ghost* is safe which cannot be reconciled with the simple teaching of Christ. They are not to be heard who assert that the Holy Ghost actually dwells in all baptized people, without exception, by virtue of their baptism, and that this grace within such people only needs to be "stirred up." The simple teaching of our Lord is that he dwells only in those who are his believing disciples, and that the world neither knows, nor sees, nor can receive the Holy Spirit (*John* 14:17). His indwelling is the special privilege of Christ's people, and where he is he will be seen. On this point also let us stand fast in the "simplicity that is in Christ."

(*8*) Finally let us settle it in our minds that no teaching can be thoroughly sound in which truth is not set forth in *the proportion of Christ and the apostles.* Let us beware of any teaching in which the main thing is an incessant exaltation of the church, the ministry, or the sacraments, while such grand verities as repentance, faith, conversion, holiness, are comparatively left in a subordinate and inferior place. Place such teaching side by side with the teaching of the *Gospels*, *Acts*, and *Epistles*. Count up texts. Make a calculation. Mark how little *comparatively* is said in the New Testament about baptism, the Lord's Supper, the church, and the ministry; and then judge for yourself what is the proportion of truth. In this matter also, I say once more, let us stand fast in the "simplicity that is in Christ."

The simple doctrine and rule of Christ, then – nothing added, nothing taken away, nothing substituted – this is the mark at which we ought to aim. This is the point from which departure ought to be dreaded. Can we improve on his teaching? Are we wiser than he? Can we suppose that he left anything of real vital importance unwritten, or liable to the vague reports of human traditions? Shall we take on ourselves to say that we can mend or change for the better any ordinance of his appointment? Can we doubt that in matters about which he is silent we have need to act very cautiously, very gently, very moderately, and must beware of pressing them on those who do not see with our eyes? Above all, must we not beware of asserting anything to be needful to salvation of which Christ has said nothing at all? I see only one answer to such questions as these. We must beware of anything which has even the appearance of departure from the "simplicity that is in Christ."

The plain truth is that we cannot sufficiently exalt the Lord Jesus Christ as the great Head of the church, and Lord of all ordinances, no less than as the Saviour of sinners. I take it we all fail here. We do not realize how high and great and glorious a King the Son of God is, and what undivided loyalty we owe to One who has not deputed any of his offices, or given his glory to another. The solemn words which John Owen addressed to the House of Commons, in a sermon on the "Greatness of Christ," deserve to be remembered. I fear the House of Commons hears few such sermons in the present day.

> Christ is the *way:* Men without him are Cains, wanderers, vagabonds. His is the *truth:* Men without him are liars, like the Devil of old. He is the *life:* Men without him are dead in trespasses and sins. He is the *light:* Men without him are in darkness, and go they know not whither. He is the

vine: Men that are not in him are withered branches prepared for the fire. He is the *rock:* Men not built on him are carried away with a flood. He is the *Alpha and Omega,* the first and the last, the author and the ender, the founder and finisher of our salvation. He that hath not him hath neither beginning of good nor shall have end of misery. Oh, blessed Jesus, how much better were it not to be than to be without Thee! Never to be born than not to die in Thee! A thousand Hells come short of this, eternally to want Jesus Christ.

This witness is true. If we can say *Amen* to the spirit of this passage it will be well with our souls.

And now let me conclude this paper by offering a few parting words of counsel to anyone into whose hands it may fall. I offer them not as one who has any authority but one who is affectionately desirous to do good to his brethren. I offer them especially to all who are members of the Church of England, though I believe they will be found useful by all English Christians. And I offer them as counsels which I find helpful to my own soul, and as such I venture to think they will be helpful to others.

(1) In the first place, if we would be kept from falling away into false doctrine, *let us arm our minds with a thorough knowledge of God's Word.* Let us read our Bibles from beginning to end with daily diligence, and constant prayer for the teaching of the Holy Spirit, and so strive to become thoroughly familiar with their contents. Ignorance of the Bible is the root of all error, and a superficial acquaintance with it accounts for many of the sad perversions and defections of the present day. In a hurrying age of railways and telegraphs, I am firmly persuaded that many Christians do not give time enough to private reading of the Scriptures. I doubt seriously whether English people did not know their Bibles better two hundred years ago than they do now. The consequence is that they are "tossed to and fro, and carried about with every wind of doctrine," and fall an easy prey to the first clever teacher of error who tries to influence their minds. I entreat my readers to remember this counsel, and take heed to their ways. It is as true now as ever, that the good *textuary* is the only good theologian, and that a familiarity with great leading texts, is, as our Lord proved in the temptation, one of the best safeguards against error. Arm yourself then with the sword of the Spirit, and let your hand become used to it. I am well aware that there is no royal road to Bible-knowledge. Without diligence and pains no

one ever becomes "mighty in the Scriptures." "Justification," said Charles Simeon, with his characteristic quaintness, "is by faith, but knowledge of the Bible comes by works."[2] But of one thing I am certain: There is no labor which will be so richly repaid as laborious regular daily study of God's Word.

(2) In the second place, if we could keep a straight path, as churchmen, in this evil day, *let us be thoroughly acquainted with the Thirty-nine Articles of the Church of England.* Those *Articles*, I am bold to say, are the authorized *Confession* of the Church of England, and the true test by which the teaching of every clergyman ought to be tried. The "teaching of the *Prayer Book*" is a common phrase in many mouths, and the *Prayer Book* is often held up as a better standard of churchmanship than the *Articles.* But I venture to assert that the *Articles*, and not the *Prayer Book,* are the church's standard of church doctrine. Let no one suppose that I think lightly of the *Prayer Book* because I say this. In loyal love to the liturgy, and deep admiration of its contents, I give place to no man. Taken for all in all, it is an incomparable book of devotion for the use of a Christian congregation. But the church's *Prayer Book* was never meant to be the church's fixed standard of Bible doctrine, in the same way that the *Articles* are. This was not meant to be its office: This was not the purpose for which it was compiled. It is a manual of devotion; it is not a confession of faith. Let us value it highly; but let us not exalt it to the place which the *Articles* alone can fill, and which common sense, statute law, and the express opinion of eminent divines agree in assigning to them.

I entreat every reader of this paper to search the *Articles*, and to keep up familiar acquaintance with them by reading them carefully at least once a year. Settle it in your mind that no man has a right to call himself a sound churchman who preaches, teaches, or maintains anything contrary to the church's confession of faith. I believe the *Articles* in this day are unduly neglected. I think it would be well if in all middle-class schools connected with the Church of England, they formed a part of the regular system of religious instruction. Like the famous *Westminster Confession* in Scotland, they would be found a mighty barrier against the tendency to return to Rome.

2. Too-clever-by-half theologians frequently mislead their readers. Knowledge of the Bible is a *gift,* coming directly and immediately from God: "Flesh and blood has not revealed this to you, but my Father who is in Heaven."

(3) The third and last counsel which I venture to offer is this. *Let us make ourselves thoroughly acquainted with the history of the English Reformation.* My reason for offering this counsel is my firm conviction that this highly important part of English history has of late years been undeservedly neglected. Thousands of churchmen nowadays have a most inadequate notion of the amount of our debt to our martyred Reformers. They have no distinct conception of the state of darkness and superstition in which our fathers lived, and of the light and liberty which the Reformation brought in. And the consequence is that they see no great harm in the Romanizing movement of the present day and have very indistinct ideas of the real nature and work of Popery. It is high time that a better state of things should begin. Of one thing I am thoroughly convinced: A vast amount of the prevailing apathy about the Romanizing movement of the day may be traced up to gross ignorance, both of the true nature of Popery and of the Protestant Reformation.

Ignorance, after all, is one of the best friends of false doctrine. More light is one of the great wants of the day, even in the nineteenth century. Thousands are led astray by Popery or infidelity from sheer want of reading and information. Once more I repeat, If men would only study with attention the Bible, the *Articles*, and the history of the Reformation, I should have little fear of their "minds being corrupted from the simplicity that is in Christ." They might not, perhaps, be "converted" to God, but at any rate they would not be "perverted" from the church.

35

The Separateness of the Church[1]

J. Gresham Machen

You are the salt of the Earth: But if the salt have lost his savor, wherewith shall it be salted? It is thenceforth good for nothing, but to be cast out, and to be trodden underfoot of men (Matthew 5:13).

IN THESE WORDS our Lord established at the very beginning the distinctness and separateness of the church. If the sharp distinction is ever broken down between the church and the world, then the power of the church is gone. The church then becomes like salt that has lost its savor, and is fit only to be cast out and to be trodden under foot of men.

It is a great principle, and there never has been a time in all the centuries of Christian history when it has not had to be taken to heart. The really serious attack upon Christianity has not been the attack carried on by fire and sword, by the threat of bonds or death, but it has been the more subtle attack that has been masked by friendly words; it has been not the attack from without but the attack from within. The enemy has done his deadliest work when he has come with words of love and compromise and peace. And how persistent the attack has been! Never in the centuries of the church's life has it been altogether relaxed; always there has been the deadly chemical process, by which, if it had been unchecked, the precious salt would have been merged with the insipidity of the world, and would have been henceforth good for nothing but to be cast out and to be trodden under foot of men.

The process began at the very beginning, in the days when our Lord still walked the Galilean hills. There were many in those days who

---

1. A sermon preached in the Chapel of Princeton Theological Seminary on Sunday, March 8, 1925.

heard him gladly; he enjoyed at first the favor of the people. But in that favor he saw a deadly peril; he would have nothing of a half-discipleship that meant the merging of the company of his disciples with the world. How ruthlessly he checked a sentimental enthusiasm! "Let the dead bury their dead," he told the enthusiast who came eagerly to him but was not willing at once to forsake all. "One thing you lack," he said to the rich young ruler, and the young man went sorrowfully away. Truly Jesus did not make it easy to be a follower of him. "He that is not with me," he said, "is against me." "If any man come to me, and hates not his father, and mother, and wife and children..., he cannot be my disciple." How serious a thing it was in those days to stand for Christ!

And it was a serious thing not only in the sphere of conduct but also in the sphere of thought. There could be no greater mistake than to suppose that a man in those days could think as he liked and still be a follower of Jesus. On the contrary, the offence lay just as much in the sphere of doctrine as in the sphere of life. There were "hard sayings," then as now, to be accepted by the disciples of Jesus, as well as hard commands. "I am the bread which came down from Heaven," said Jesus. It was indeed a hard saying. No wonder the Jews murmured at him. "Is not this Jesus," they said, "the son of Joseph, whose father and mother we know? How is it then that he saith, I came down from Heaven?" "How can this man give us his flesh to eat?" Jesus did not make the thing easy for these murmurers. "Then Jesus said unto them, 'Verily, verily, I say unto you, Except ye eat the flesh of the Son of man, and drink his blood, ye have no life in you.' " At that many even of his disciples were offended. "This is a hard saying," they said, "who can hear it?" And so they left him. "From that time many of his disciples went back and walked no more with him." Many of them went back – but not all. "Then said Jesus unto the twelve, 'Will ye also go away?' Then Simon Peter answered him, 'Lord, to whom shall we go? Thou hast the words of eternal life.'" Thus was the precious salt preserved.

Then came the gathering clouds, and finally the cross. In the hour of his agony they all left him and fled; apparently the movement that he had initiated was hopelessly dead. But such was not the will of God. The disciples were sifted, but there was still something left. Peter was forgiven; the disciples saw the risen Lord; the salt was still preserved.

One hundred and twenty persons were gathered in Jerusalem. It was not a large company; but salt, if it truly have its savor, can permeate the whole lump. The Spirit came in accordance with our Lord's promise, and Peter preached the first sermon in the Christian church. It was hardly a concessive sermon. "Him being delivered by the determinate counsel and foreknowledge of God, you have taken, and by wicked hands have crucified and slain." How unkind Peter was! But by that merciful unkindness they were pricked in their hearts, and three thousand souls were saved.

So there stood the first Christian church in the midst of a hostile world. At first sight it might have seemed to be a mere Jewish sect; the disciples continued to attend the temple services and to lead the life of Jews. But in reality that little company was as separate as if it had been shut off by desert wastes or the wide reaches of the sea; an invisible barrier, to be crossed only by the wonder of the new birth, separated the disciples of Jesus from the surrounding world. "Of the rest," we are told, "durst no man join himself to them." "And fear came upon every soul." So it will always be. When the disciples of Jesus are really faithful to their Lord, they inspire fear; even when Christians are despised and persecuted and harried, they have sometimes made their persecutors secretly afraid. It is not so, indeed, when there is compromise in the Christian camp; it is not so when those who minister in the name of Christ have – as was said in praise some time ago in my hearing of a group of ministers in our day – it is not so when those who minister in the name of Christ "have their ears to the ground." But it will be so whenever Christians have their ears, not to the ground, but open only to the voice of God, and when they say simply, in the face of opposition or flattery, as Peter said, "We must obey God rather than men."

But after those persecutions, there came in the early church a time of peace – deadly, menacing, deceptive peace, a peace more dangerous by far than the bitterest war. Many of the sect of the Pharisees came into the church – false brethren privily brought in. These were not true Christians, because they trusted in their own works for salvation, and no man can be a Christian who does that. They were not even true adherents of the old covenant; for the old covenant, despite the Law, was a preparation for the Saviour's coming, and the Law was a schoolmaster unto Christ. Yet they were Christians in name, and they tried to dominate the councils of the church. It was a serious menace; for a moment it looked as though even Peter, true apostle though he was at heart, were being deceived. His principles were right, but by his actions his principles, at Antioch, for one fatal moment, were belied. But it was not God's will that the church should perish; and the man of the hour was there. There was one man who would not consider consequences where a great principle was at stake, who put all personal consider- ations resolutely aside and refused to become unfaithful to Christ through any fear of "splitting the church." "When I saw that they walked not uprightly," said Paul, "according to the truth of the Gospel, I said unto Peter before them all...." Thus was the precious salt preserved.

But from another side also the church was menaced by the blandish- ments of the world; it was menaced not only by a false Judaism, which really meant opposition of man's self-righteousness to the mysterious grace of God, but also by the all-embracing paganism of that day. When the Pauline churches were planted in the cities of the Graeco-Roman world, the battle was not ended but only begun. Would the little spark of new life be kept alive? Certainly it might have seemed to be unlikely in the extreme. The converts were for the most part not men of inde- pendent position, but slaves and humble tradesmen; they were bound by a thousand ties to the paganism of their day. How could they possi- bly avoid being drawn away by the current of the time? The danger certainly was great, and when Paul left an infant church like that at Thessalonica his heart was full of dread.

But God was faithful to his promise, and the first word that came from that infant church was good. The wonder had actually been ac- complished; the converts were standing firm; they were in the world but not of the world; their distinctness was kept. In the midst of pagan impurity they were living true Christian lives. But why were they living true Christian lives? That is the really important question. And the answer is plain. They were living Christian lives because they were devoted to Christian truth. "You turned to God," says Paul, "from idols to serve the living and true God; and to wait for his Son from Heaven, whom he raised from the dead, even Jesus, which delivered us from the wrath to come." That was the secret of their Christian lives: Their Chris- tian lives were founded upon Christian doctrine – upon theism ("the living and true God"), upon Christology ("his Son...whom he raised from the dead"), and upon soteriology ("which delivered us from the wrath to come"). They kept the message intact, and hence they lived the life. So it will always be. Lives apparently and superficially Christian can perhaps sometimes be lived by force of habit, without being based upon Christian truth; but that will never do when Christian living, as in pagan Thessalonica, goes against the grain. But in the case of the Thessalonian converts the message was kept intact, and with it the Christian life. Thus again was the precious salt preserved.

The same conflict is observed in more detail in the case of Corinth. What a city Corinth was, to be sure, and how unlikely a place for a Christian church! The address of Paul's first epistle is, as Bengel says, a mighty paradox. "To the church of God which is at Corinth" – that was a paradox indeed. And in the *First Epistle to the Corinthians* we have attested in all its fullness the attempt of paganism, not to combat the church by a frontal attack, but to conquer it by the far deadlier method of merging it gradually and peacefully with the life of the world. Those Corinthian Christians were connected by many ties with the pagan life of their great city. What should they do about clubs and societies; what should they do about invitations to dinners where meat that had been offered to idols was set before the guests? What should they do about marriage and the like? These were practical questions, but they involved the great principle of the distinctness and exclusiveness of the church. Certainly the danger was very great; the converts were.

But the conflict was not merely in the sphere of conduct. More fundamentally it was in the sphere of thought. Paganism in Corinth was far too astute to think that Christian life could be attacked when Christian doctrine remained. And so pagan practice was promoted by an appeal to pagans in great danger, from the human point of view, of sinking back into the corrupt life of the world theory; the enemy engaged in an attempt to sublimate or explain away the fundamental things of the Christian faith. Somewhat after the manner of the Auburn "Affirmationists" in our day, paganism in the Corinthian church sought to substitute the Greek notion of the immortality of the soul for the Christian doctrine of the resurrection. But God had his witness; the Apostle Paul was not deceived; and in a great passage – the most important words, historically, perhaps, that have ever been penned – he reviewed the sheer factual basis of the Christian faith. "How that Christ died for our sins according to the Scriptures; and that he was buried, and that he rose again the third day according to the Scriptures." There is the foundation of the Christian edifice. Paganism was gnawing away – not yet directly, but by ultimate implication – at that foundation in Corinth, as it has been doing so in one way or another ever since, and particularly in the Presbyterian Church in the United States of America just at the present time. But Paul was there, and many of the five hundred witnesses were still alive. The Gospel message was kept distinct, in the Pauline churches, from the wisdom of the world; the precious salt was still preserved.

Then, in the second century, there came another deadly conflict. It was again a conflict not with an enemy without, but with an enemy within. The Gnostics used the name of Christ; they tried to dominate the church; they appealed to the epistles of Paul. But despite their use of Christian language they were pagan through and through. Modern scholarship, on this point, has tended to confirm the judgment of the great orthodox writers of that day. Gnosticism was at bottom no mere variety of Christian belief, no mere heresy, but paganism masquerading in Christian dress. Many were deceived; the danger was very great. But it was not God's will that the church should perish. Irenaeus was there, and Tertullian with his vehement defense. The church was saved – not by those who cried "Peace, peace, when there is no peace," but by zealous contenders for the faith. Again, out of a great danger, the precious salt was preserved.

Time would fail us to speak of Athanasius and of Augustine and the rest, but they too were God's instruments in the preservation of the precious salt. Certainly the attack in those days was subtle enough almost to deceive the very elect. Grant the semi-Arians their one letter in *homoiousios,* the smallest letter of the Greek alphabet, and Christ would have been degraded to the level of a creature, mythology would have been substituted for the living God, and the victory of paganism would have been complete. From the human point of view the life of the church was hanging by a hair. But God was watching over his own; Athanasius stood against the world; and the precious salt was preserved.

Then came the Middle Ages. How long and how dark, in some respects, was the time! It is hard to realize that eleven centuries elapsed between Augustine and Luther, yet such was the case. Never in the interval, indeed, was God altogether without his witnesses; the light still shone from the sacred page; but how dim, in that atmosphere, the light seemed to be! The Gospel might have seemed to be buried forever. Yet in God's good time it came forth again with new power – the same Gospel that Augustine and Paul had proclaimed. What stronger proof could there be that that Gospel had come from God? Where in the history of religion is there any parallel for such a revival, after such an interval, and with such a purity of faithfulness to what had formerly been believed? A Gospel that survived the Middle Ages will probably, it may well be hoped, never perish from the Earth, but will be the word of life unto the end of the world.

Yet in those early years of the sixteenth century how dark was the time! When Luther made his visit to Rome, what did he find – what did he find there in the center of the Christian world? He found paganism blatant and triumphant and unashamed; he found the glories of ancient Greece come to life in the Italian Renaissance, but with those glories the self-sufficiency and the rebellion against the God and the moral degradation of the natural man. Apparently paganism had at last won its age-long battle; apparently it had made a clean sweep over the people of God; apparently the church had at last become quite indistinguishable from the world.

But in the midst of the general wreck one thing at least was preserved. Many things were lost, but one thing was still left – the medieval church had never lost the Word of God. The Bible had indeed become a book with seven seals; it had been buried under a mass of misinterpretation never equaled perhaps until the absurdities indulged in by the Modernism of the present day – a mass of misinterpretation which seemed to hide it from the eyes of men. But at last an Augustinian monk penetrated beneath the mass of error, read the Scriptures with his own eyes, and the Reformation was born. Thus again was the precious salt preserved.

Then came Calvin and the great consistent system which he founded upon the Word of God. How glorious were even the by-products of that system of revealed truth; a great stream of liberty spread from Geneva throughout Europe and to America across the sea. But if the by-products were glorious, more glorious by far was the truth itself, and the life that it caused men to live. How sweet and beautiful a thing was the life of the Protestant Christian home, where the Bible was the sole guide and stay! Have we really devised a substitute for that life in these latter days? I think not, my friends. There was liberty there, and love, and peace with God.

But the church after the Reformation was not to have any permanent rest, as indeed it is probably not to have rest at any time in this evil world. Still the conflict of the ages went on, and paganism prepared for an assault greater and more insidious perhaps than any that had gone before. At first there was a frontal attack – Voltaire and Rousseau and the Goddess Reason and the terrors of the French Revolution and all that. As will always be the case, such an attack was bound to fail. But the enemy has now changed his method, and the attack is coming, not from without, but in far more dangerous fashion, from within. During the past one hundred years the Protestant churches of the world have gradually been becoming permeated by paganism in its most insidious form.

Sometimes paganism is blatant, as, for example, in a recent sermon in the First Presbyterian Church of New York, the burden of which was, "I Believe in Man." That was the very quintessence of the pagan spirit – confidence in human resources substituted for the Christian consciousness of sin. But what was there blatant is found in subtler forms in many places throughout the church. The Bible, with a complete abandonment of all scientific historical method and of all common sense, is made to say the exact opposite of what it means; no Gnostic, no medieval monk with his fourfold sense of Scripture, ever produced more absurd Biblical interpretation than can be heard every Sunday in the pulpits of New York. Even prayer in many quarters is made a thinly disguised means of propaganda against the truth of the Gospel; men pray that there may be peace, where peace means victory for the enemies of Christ. Thus gradually the church is being permeated by the spirit of the world; it is becoming what the Auburn Affirmationists call an "inclusive" church; it is becoming salt that has lost its savor and is henceforth good for nothing but to be cast out and to be trodden under foot of men.

At such a time, what should be done by those who love Christ? I think, my friends, that they should at least face the facts; I do not believe that they should bury their heads like ostriches in the sand; I do not think that they should soothe themselves with the minutes of the General Assembly or the reports of the Boards or the imposing rows of figures which the church papers contain. Last week it was reported that the churches of America increased their membership by 690,000. Are you encouraged by these figures? I for my part am not encouraged a bit. I have indeed my own grounds for encouragement – especially those which are found in the great and precious promises of God. But these figures have no place among them. How many of these 690,000 names do you think are really written in the Lamb's Book of Life? A small proportion, I fear. Church membership today often means nothing more, as has well been said, than a vague admiration for the moral character of Jesus; churches in countless communities are little more than Rotary Clubs. One day, as I was walking through a neighboring city, I saw, not an altar with an inscription to an unknown god, but something that filled me with far more sorrow than that could have done. I saw a church with a large sign on it, which read somewhat like this: "Not a member? Come and help us make this a better community." Truly we have wandered far from the day when entrance into the church involved confession of faith in Christ as the Savior from sin.

The trust is that in these days the ecclesiastical currency has been sadly debased. Church membership, church office, the ministry, no longer mean what they ought to mean. But what shall we do? I think, my friends, that, cost what it may, we ought at least to face the facts. It will be hard; it will seem impious to timid souls; many will be hurt. But in God's name let us get rid of shams and have reality at last. Let us stop soothing ourselves with columns of statistics, and face the spiritual facts; let us recall this paper currency and get back to a standard of gold.

When we do that, and when we come to God in prayer – with the real facts spread before him, as Hezekiah spread before him the letter of the enemy – there will be some things to cheer our hearts. God has not left himself altogether without his witnesses. Humble they may often be, and despised by the wisdom of the world; but they are not perhaps altogether without the favor of God. In China, in Great Britain, and in America there have been some who have raised their voices bravely for their Savior and Lord.

True, the forces of unbelief have not yet been checked, and none can say whether our own American Presbyterian church, which we love so dearly, will be preserved. It may be that paganism will finally control and that Christian men and women may have to withdraw from a church that has lost its distinctness from the world. Once in the course of history, at the beginning of the sixteenth century, that method of withdrawal was God's method of preserving the precious salt. But it may be also that our Church in its corporate capacity, in its historic grandeur, may yet stand for Christ. God grant that it may be so! The future at any rate is in God's hand, and in some way or other – let us learn that much from history – the salt will be preserved.

What are you going to do, my brothers, in this great time of crisis? What a time it is to be sure! What a time of glorious opportunity! Will you stand with the world? Will you shrink from controversy? Will you witness for Christ only where witnessing costs nothing? Will you pass through these stirring days without coming to any real decision? Or will you learn the lesson of Christian history? Will you penetrate, by your study and your meditation, beneath the surface? Will you recognize in that which prides itself on being modern an enemy that is as old as the hills? Will you hope, and pray, not for a mere continuance of what now is, but for a rediscovery of the Gospel that can make all things new? Will you have recourse to the charter of Christian liberty in the Word of God? God grant that some of you may do that! God grant that some of you, even though you be not now decided, may come to say, as you go forth into the world: "It is hard in these days to be a Christian; the adversaries are strong; I am weak; but thy Word is true and thy Spirit will be with me; here am I, Lord, send me."

36

The Sin of Signing
Ecumenical Declarations[1]

John W. Robbins

TODAY'S EMAIL brought an invitation from the Acton Institute of Grand Rapids, Michigan, to sign the "Cornwall Declaration on Environmental Stewardship." This "Declaration" is the latest in a long series of ecumenical religious manifestoes issued in the twentieth century. It used to be that only those who considered themselves liberals issued ecumenical pronouncements, but now those who profess to be theological conservatives – such as the signers of "Evangelicals and Catholics Together" – are issuing ecumenical Declarations as well.[2] The emailman for the Acton Institute, a Roman Catholic organization[3] located in the heartland of the Christian Reformed Church and funded in large part by nominal Protestants, explained the intention behind the "Cornwall Declaration":

> Our aim is to launch a nationwide publicity campaign near Earth Day in hope of igniting a grass-roots movement for more responsible environmental stewardship than what dominates the environmentalist movement. Jewish, Catholic, and Protestant leaders will develop, as supplements to this Declaration, their own monographs on environmental

1. Reprinted from *The Trinity Review*.
2. The principals of Evangelicals and Catholics Together, Roman priest Richard John Neuhaus and Southern Baptist Charles Colson, are also signers of the "Cornwall Declaration."
3. The Acton Institute for Religion and Liberty is not only named for a Roman Catholic, but it was founded and is headed by, not a Roman Catholic layman, but a Roman priest, Robert Sirico, a member of the Paulist order; and the Institute promotes the "economic personalism" of John Paul II. Ironically, its views are opposed to the views of Lord Acton, a nineteenth-century layman who was a bold critic of the Roman Church-State and its pretensions to power and infallibility.

stewardship in which their own theological commitments will be explicit. This enables each community to stand to its own theological positions and not be implicated by cobelligerency in the theological commitments of others. After the start of the publicity campaign, we expect to produce articles in the religious press and op-ed pieces to help spread the message. Right now we are looking for endorsements of the Declaration from scholars like yourself. Below is a list of current signers of the Declaration. If after reading the Declaration you find yourself in agreement, please sign the endorsement form that follows it and send it to the Acton Institute....

Four lists of signers follow: 13 "Jewish Signers"; 21 "Roman Catholic Signers"; 48 "Protestant Signers"; and 16 "Other Signers (religious or otherwise)." [4]

What is remarkable about the "Cornwall Declaration" is not merely the appearance of such a varied assortment of religious officials, but the language used in the invitation to sign:

> This [the publication of additional monographs] enables each [religious] community to stand to its own theological positions and not be implicated by cobelligerency in the theological commitments of the others.

This statement demonstrates the concern of the authors that the signers of the "Cornwall Declaration" would be "implicated by cobelligerency" in the views of other signers. Additional publications are needed in order to attempt to avoid such implication, for each signer is indeed implicated by the "Cornwall Declaration" in the theological views of others. The only way to avoid implication would be to argue that

---

4. The complete list of signers as of February 28, 2000, includes: JEWISH SIGNERS: Rabbi Daniel Lapin, Rabbi David Novak, Dr. Malcolm J. Sherman, Rabbi Clifford E. Librach, Rabbi Dr. Kenneth Fradkin, Rabbi Samuel B. Press, Rabbi Jonathan Ginsburg, Rabbi Dennis Prager, Rabbi Jacob Neusner, Dr. Herbert I. London, Dr. Kenneth R. Weinstein, Rabbi Ron Aigen, Mr. David N. Friedman; ROMAN CATHOLIC SIGNERS: Father Richard John Neuhaus, The Rev. Paul Hartmann, Father Robert A. Sirico, Father Kevin S. Barrett, Father Frank A. Pavone, Dr. Todd Flanders, Father J. Michael Beers, Dr. Charles Baird, Dr. Alejandro A. Chafuen, Dr. Robert Royal, Dr. Margaret Maxey, Dr. Gregory Gronbacher, Dr. Eduardo J. Echeverria, Mr. Michel Therrien, Mr. Michael B. Barkey, Dr. Kevin E. Schmiesing, Dr. Russell Hittinger, Prof. Leonard P. Liggio, Rev. Dr. Alexander A. Di Lella, Mr. Samuel Casey Carter, Mr. Paul V. Harberger, PROTESTANT SIGNERS: Mr. E. Calvin Beisner, Ms. Diane Knippers, Dr. P. J. Hill, Rev. Dr. D. James Kennedy, Mr. Michael Cromartie, Mr. Doug Bandow, Mr. David Rothbard, The Rev. Dr. H. Lee Cheek, J. Render Caines, David W. Hall, Dr. Marvin Olasky, Dr. Ronald

there is no meeting of the minds at all, which would defeat the purpose of the "Declaration." The whole point of the "Declaration" is to implicate – to closely connect – Judaism, Romanism, Protestantism, and Otherism on these issues. Additional publications may discuss differences between the religious groups, but the "Cornwall Declaration" itself implicates ("closely connects") the signers and their religions. The "Declaration" declares the signers' "shared reverence for God and His creation" (a statement that seems to suggest the signers revere the creature as well as the Creator); and it describes itself as "this declaration of our common concerns, beliefs, and aspirations." The "Declaration" mentions "Our position [singular], informed by revelation and confirmed by reason and experience"; "Our common Judeo-Christian heritage"; and it makes several references to theology. The section titled "Our Beliefs" is seven paragraphs long, and it states "theological and anthropological principles" on which the signers agree. Either these statements are true, or they are disingenuously deceptive.

The signers have not signed as individuals (that would be bad enough); they have signed as members (and officials) of religious groups: Rabbis, Priests, Elders; Jews, Romanists (erroneously called Catholics), Protestants (though they seem not to be protesting Romanism any more), and Others. The "Cornwall Declaration" is a religious document signed by religious officials. By signing this "Declaration", and others like it, Christians sin in several ways:

1. They "share [are implicated] in other people's sins."

2. They disclose that making a joint political statement is more important to them than proclaiming the whole counsel of God.

Nash, Mr. Stephen Grabill, Mr. Paul Mastin, Dr. Richard Stroup, Dr. Kenneth Chilton, Dr. Thomas Sieger Derr, Prof. Alan Gomes, Dr. George Grant, Dr. Amy Sherman, Rev. Edmund Opitz, Mr. David Noebel, Dr. Paul Cleveland, Dr. Robert G. Lee, Rev. Richard Cizik, Dr. Don Racheter, Ms. Juliana Thompson, Dr. Charles W. Colson, The Very Rev. Stephen H. Bancroft, Mr. Howard A. Ball, Rev. Donald E. Wildmon, Dr. Timothy Terrell, Dr. J. Franklin Sexton, Dr. Jay Grimstead, Dr. Philip C. Bom, Dr. Mark Y. Herring, Dr. Jo Ann Kwong, Dr. Alan Snyder, Dr. Gary Quinlivan, Mr. Tom Minnery, Dr. James Dobson, The Venerable Norman Aldred, Dr. William R. Bright, Dr. Bruce L. Edwards, Dr. Stephen Cox, Dr. Jeffrey L. Myers, Mr. David Ridenour, Mr. William H. Lash, III; OTHER SIGNERS (religious or otherwise): Mr. Paul Weyrich, Dr. Daniel Klein, Dr. George P. Khushf, Dr. John Bennett, Dr. D. Eric Schansberg, Ms. Floy Lilley, Dr. Peter Huber, Mr. John McConnell, Dr. Charles W. Rovey, Mr. Paul Driessen, Mr. Jerry Bowyer, Mr. William T. Devlin, Ms. Laurie Morrow, Dr. Jane M. Orient, Dr. Henry I. Miller, Mr. Len Munsil.

3. They violate the scores of commands in Scripture to "be separate"; to avoid "unequal yokes with unbelievers"; to be "sanctified"; to be "called out"; to have nothing to do with those who profess to be Christians but are not.

4. They speak useless words.

5. They use words that cannot communicate clear meaning.

6. They teach that the Christian worldview is not unique but shares common ground with the worldviews of Romanism, Judaism, and Otherism.

Let us examine these public sins – these scandals.

Scandal Number 1:
Real Guilt by Religious Collaboration:
"Sharing in Other People's Sins"

The Bible issues a stern warning to church officers (and to all Christians by presupposition) not to share in other people's sins: "Do not lay hands on [ordain] anyone hastily, nor share in other people's sins; keep yourself pure" (1 Timothy 5:22). Sharing in others' sins is a sin of impurity that is always to be avoided. Declarations that are acceptable to and endorsed by unbelievers as well as believers are either so vague as to be virtually meaningless – the useless, idle words that Christ warned against – or so un-Christian that unbelievers can endorse them. Any religious declaration that contained the Gospel – or even clear definitions of terms such as "God" and "revelation" – could not be sincerely and intelligently signed by an unbeliever. The "Cornwall Declaration" avoids both the Gospel and clear definitions in order to persuade unbelievers to sign.

Scandal Number 2
Inversion of Christian Priorities: Political Proclamations
Are More Important than Proclaiming the Gospel

By issuing joint religious declarations on political issues with unbelievers, Christians show that they esteem making ecumenical political statements more important than proclaiming the Gospel to those unbelievers. By their action they show that the views that unite them are more important than the Gospel that divides them. Rather than speaking face-to-face to those unbelievers about the Gospel of Jesus Christ, the Christians who signed the "Cornwall Declaration" stand shoulder-to-shoulder with unbelievers to issue joint religious statements on political matters. Issuing ecumenical manifestoes is a subtle way of disobeying the Great Commission while posturing as spokesmen for Christianity.

This inversion of Christian priorities has been a persistent and prevalent error of the twentieth century, espoused first by liberals and modernists, and now by conservatives. By adopting liberal tactics, conservatives convey a liberal message, no matter what they say.

Can the reader imagine the Apostle Paul signing a joint religious declaration with Jews, Judaizers – who apparently believed the "fundamentals of the faith" (but not justification by faith alone; for teaching that error Paul damned them) – and dissident Pagans against the policies of the Roman Empire? Can the reader imagine Jesus issuing a joint religious declaration – the "Jerusalem Declaration on Imperial Stewardship" – with the Sanhedrin, condemning the oppressive policies of Caesar? If the reader can imagine that, it shows only how far the reader is from the mind of Paul and Christ, who determined not to know anything among us but Christ crucified, to speak only the words of divine wisdom, not of human foolishness, and to be friends of God, not friends of the world: "Do you not know that friendship with the world is enmity with God? Whoever therefore wants to be a friend of the world makes himself an enemy of God" (*James* 4:4). Signing ecumenical declarations for political purposes demonstrates that Christians do not know or do not accept the priorities of Jesus and Paul.

Furthermore, the "Cornwall Declaration" discloses a misunderstanding of the theological foundation of Western civilization, which emerged only from the preaching of the Gospel, not from the doctrines of other religions, and certainly not from the tyranny and foolishness of the Roman Church-State. The "Cornwall Declaration" obscures the role of the Reformation in the development of Western civilization, not only by not mentioning it, but also by using misleading language such as "The past millennium brought unprecedented improvements in human health, nutrition, and life expectancy...." It was not "the past millennium" that brought these improvements, but the past 500 years,[5] during which God has blessed the bold proclamation and belief of his Word. That Word had been suppressed for a millennium by the Roman Church-

5. The effect of the words "the past millennium" is to credit the Roman Church-State with these improvements and to obscure the role of the Reformation.

State. The "Cornwall Declaration" ignores and thus obscures the indispensable role of the Reformation in the development of Western civilization, apparently because to tell the truth might offend some prospective signers.

Scandal Number 3
Compromise with the World:
Accepting Human Foolishness as Wisdom

When God gave the Israelites the Promised Land, he forbade them to compromise with the inhabitants of Canaan. God instituted many laws to impress upon the Israelites the absolute necessity of their being separate, sanctified, and holy: They were not to intermarry, nor to adopt the customs of the Canaanite people, nor to eat their food, nor to worship their gods. They were not to wear garments of mixed fabrics nor to plant crops of mixed seed. All these laws were designed to impress upon the Israelites the absolute necessity of remaining separate, pure, unspotted, and uncompromised. The ancient Israelites did not learn the lesson, and they were destroyed; neither have many professed Christians of the twentieth century.

By entangling themselves in such declarations, Christians hope to gain something – media attention, fame, influence, respectability, the honor of the world, power – but they endanger their own souls and the souls of others. The invitation to sign the "Cornwall Declaration" reports that

> Our aim is to launch a nationwide publicity campaign...in hopes of igniting a grass-roots movement.... After the start of the publicity campaign, we expect to produce articles in the religious press and op-ed pieces to help spread the message.

Christians who have signed this ecumenical "Declaration" have made a fool's bargain. In order to gain publicity, they have compromised the Word of God. Orange juice gains nothing by being mixed with strychnine, but poison mixed with orange juice gains more victims. Christians gain nothing by issuing joint religious declarations with unbelievers, but unbelievers and unbelief gain much by the confusion such pronouncements engender in people's minds. Truth gains nothing by being mixed with falsehood, but falsehood gains much by being mixed with truth: It can deceive more people more effectively. The honest man gains nothing by collaborating with the shady character, but the shady character gains much by collaborating with the honest man: He obtains credit and an undeserved reputation for honesty. Only falsehood, unbelief, and dishonesty can gain from such collaboration – from such ecumenical declarations. That may be one reason so many unbelievers are willing to sign these declarations: They understand better than Christians do exactly who gains and who loses from such alliances. "For the sons of this world are more shrewd in their generation than the sons of light" (*Luke* 16:8).

Scandal Number 4
Fatal Locution: "Idle Words"

Christ made several statements about the importance of words. His teaching directly contradicts the common contemporary notion that words are relatively unimportant; that only actions and deeds matter. His teaching also contradicts the premise upon which ecumenical manifestoes such as the "Cornwall Declaration" rest, that unbelievers are able sincerely and intelligently to say good words. For example, Christ said:

> Brood of vipers! How can you, being evil, speak good things? For out of the abundance of the heart the mouth speaks. A good man out of the good treasure of his heart brings forth good things, and an evil man out of the evil treasure brings forth evil things. But I say to you that for every idle [useless] word men may speak, they will give account of it in the Day of Judgment. For by your words you will be justified, and by your words you will be condemned [*Matthew* 12:34-37].

The "Cornwall Declaration" assumes and teaches that those whom Christ called evil can sincerely and intelligently say good things.

Scandal Number 5
Garbling God's Word: "An Uncertain Sound"

The Apostle Paul, a model for Christians, repeatedly prayed that he would proclaim the Gospel boldly as he ought: "that I may open my mouth boldly to make known the mystery of the Gospel, for which I am an ambassador in chains; that in it I may speak boldly, as I ought to speak" [*Ephesians* 6:18-20].

Paul and other Biblical writers also emphasized the importance of clarity:

> But now, brethren, if I come to you speaking with tongues, what shall I profit you unless I speak to you either by revelation, by knowledge, by prophesying, or by teaching? Even things without life, whether flute or harp, when they make a sound, unless they make a distinction in the sounds, how will it be known what is piped or played? For if the trumpet makes an uncertain sound, who will prepare himself for battle? So likewise you, unless you utter by the tongue words easy to understand, how will it be known what is spoken? For you will be speaking into the air [1 Corinthians 14:6-9].

Paul's fear was not that words spoken by Christians might be hard to hear, but that they would be impossible to understand because they have no univocal meaning or definite significance. Paul condemned words that are not definite and clear. Even things without life must make distinctive and definite sounds; otherwise no one can understand their significance. If harps, pipes, and trumpets must speak clearly, how much more so Christians? Hearers will not understand their meaning if their words are equivocal, vague, ambiguous, and indefinite. They will understand only if their words are univocal, clear, unambiguous, and definite.

Ecumenical manifestoes such as the "Cornwall Declaration" are not clear and unambiguous; they not only omit essential ideas and include misleading ideas, but they also deliberately use words in an equivocal fashion so that persons of various religions can sign them. This equivocation is not a minor feature of the "Cornwall Declaration"; the "Declaration" depends on using important terms ambiguously and indefinitely. Take, for example, the phrase "shared reverence for God." Not only is the term "God" used equivocally so that Protestants, Romanists, Jews, and Others, each with a different definition of the term "God," may sign the "Declaration," but the impact of the document turns on these fundamental equivocations. If a reader object that the various religions' definitions of the term "God" are not different, then the reader has missed the lessons of Scripture: The Apostle Paul disposed of the natural theology of Aristotle and Thomas Aquinas (that is, the Roman Catholic conception of God): "For since, in the wisdom of God, the world through wisdom did not know God..." (1 Corinthians 1:21). Jesus himself disposed of both the Greek and the Judaic conceptions of God in these words: "All things have been delivered to me by my Father, and no one knows the Son except the Father. Nor does anyone know the

Father except the Son and he to whom the Son wills to reveal him" (*Matthew* 11:27). Furthermore, since Jews reject the Trinity, their god is obviously a different god. And who knows what definitions of the term "god" flit about the brains of those who classify themselves as "Other"?

Not to belabor the point, but what on Earth can the "Cornwall Declaration" mean by its appeal to "revelation"? Is this personal or propositional revelation? Is it the 66 books of the Bible, or the 73 books and additional scattered fragments of the Roman Church-State? Does it include infallible encyclicals, or is it merely the Old Testament? And what does that group that calls itself "Other" think the term "revelation" means? The *Koran*? The *Book of Mormon*? Martin Luther King's *Letter from a Birmingham Jail*? The "Cornwall Declaration" is a tissue of equivocations.

Scandal Number 6
Adulterating the Word of God: Syncretism

All these scandals culminate in the last and most serious scandal: syncretism.

If it is appropriate for Christians to take public positions on economic and political issues – and it is – then they are required by God to do so as Christians, not as builders of an ecumenical tower of Babel. The real and effective message delivered by ecumenical pronouncements such as the "Cornwall Declaration" – the message delivered irrespective of what the "Declaration" itself says – is that Christianity has nothing uniquely true or important to say to the world on these matters, that Christian ideas are interchangeable and fungible with the ideas of Judaism, Romanism, and Otherism. By making joint religious declarations with unbelievers, Christians implicitly deny the uniqueness of Biblical, propositional revelation; they implicitly assert, contrary to Scripture, that men's foolishness is as good as divine wisdom; they unavoidably teach that Christianity shares important ideas and principles with unbelieving systems of thought. Christians who sign such statements fail to realize that Christianity does not have a single proposition in common with systems of unbelieving thought. That is the philosophical lesson that must be drawn from the many Biblical statements and injunctions about purity, separation, sanctification, and holiness. Those terms do not apply, in some pietistic fashion, merely to one's behavior; they apply even more strictly to one's ideas and thoughts. Ideas are not neutral, nor are they common to various systems of thought. Ideas are to be "taken captive to the obedience of Christ":

> For though we walk in the flesh, we do not war according to the flesh. For the weapons of our warfare are not carnal but mighty in God for pulling down strongholds, casting down arguments and every high thing that exalts itself against the knowledge of God, bringing every thought into captivity to the obedience of Christ... [2 *Corinthians* 10:3-5].
>
> Do not be conformed to this world, but be transformed by the renewing of your mind... [*Romans* 12:2].

Some Christians obviously think they gain something by signing such ecumenical Declarations: In this case, they hope to gain publicity. But what exactly is being publicized? It is not Christianity; it is not even Christian economics. What is being publicized is a religious document that says that whether one thinks as a Jew, a Romanist, a Protestant, or an Other really does not matter: Jews, Romanists, Protestants, and Others all agree on these principles. They share common ground. These important matters are not the exclusive domain of Christ Jesus; they are Everyman's Land. Christians may have something distinctive to say on secondary matters, but on these fundamental "theological and anthropological principles," to use the language of the "Cornwall Declaration," Christianity and Judaism, Christianity and Romanism, Christianity and Otherism speak with one voice.

This is the language of unbelief.

Those Christians who have signed the "Cornwall Declaration" have obscured the clear message of the Gospel, compromised the Christian worldview, and opposed the advance of the Kingdom of God.

37

Fundamentalism and Ecumenism[1]

Thomas M'Crie

MOURNFUL AS the divisions of the church are, and anxious as all its genuine friends must be to see them cured, it is their duty to examine carefully the plans which may be proposed for attaining this desirable end. We must not do evil that good may come; and there are sacrifices too costly to be made for the procuring of peace with fellow Christians.

Is it necessary to remind you that unity and peace are not always good, not a sure and infallible mark of a true and pure church? We know that there is a church which has long boasted of her catholic unity notwithstanding all the corruptions which pollute her communion; and that within her pale the whole world called Christian once enjoyed a profound repose, and it could be said, "Behold, the people is one, and they have all one language." It was a union and peace founded in ignorance, delusion, implicit faith, and a base subjection to human authority; and supported by the arts of compulsion and terror.

But there are other methods by which Christians may be deceived, and the interests of religion deeply injured, under the pretext or with the view of uniting its friends. Among these I know none more imposing, nor from which greater danger is to be apprehended in the present time, than that which proceeds on the scheme of principles usually styled latitudinarian.

It has obtained this name because it proclaims an undue latitude in matters of religion, which persons may take to themselves or give to others. Its abettors make light of the differences which subsists among

---

1. From Thomas M'Crie, *The Unity of the Church*, Dallas, Texas: Presbyterian Heritage Publications [1821] 1989, 106-114.

religious parties, and propose to unite them on the common principles on which they are already agreed in the way of burying the rest in silence, or of stipulating mutual forbearance and charity with respect to everything about which they may differ in opinion or in practice.

Some plead for this on the ground that the several professions of religion differ very little from one another, and are all conducive to the happiness of mankind and the honor of God, who is pleased with the various diversified modes in which men profess their regard to him, provided only they are sincere in their profession – a principle of difformity which, however congenial to the system of polytheism, is utterly eversive to a religion founded on the unity of the divine nature and will, and on a revelation which teaches us what we are to believe concerning God and what duty he requires of us.

But the ground on which this plan is ordinarily made to rest is a distinction made among the articles of religion. Some of these are called essential, or fundamental, or necessary, or principal; others circumstantial or non-fundamental, or unnecessary or less important. The former, it is pleaded, are embraced by all true Christians; the latter form the subjects of difference among them, and ought not to enter in the terms of ecclesiastical fellowship.[2] On this principle some of them would conciliate and unite all the Christian denominations, not excepting papists, Arians, and Socinians; while others restrict their plan to those called evangelical, who differ mainly in their views and practice as to the worship, order, and discipline of the church.

The distinction on which this scheme rests is itself liable to objections which appear insuperable. It is not warranted by the Word of God; and the most acute of its defenders have never been able to state it in a manner that is satisfactory, or which renders it subservient to any practical use. The Scripture, indeed, speaks of certain truths which may be called the foundation, because they are first laid, and others depend on them – first principles, or elementary truths, which are to be taught before others. But their priority or posteriority in point of order, in

2. This distinction is variously expressed. Some modern writers on the subject of communion adhere to the distinction between what is essential or not essential to salvation. Others, aware of what has been urged against it, choose to substitute the word *fundamental* in the room of *essential*; and, for security's sake, they would add a few other articles to the fundamental. But what the one or the other are they do not tell.

conception of instruction, does not determine the relative importance of doctrines, or their necessity in order to salvation. Far less does it determine the propriety of their being made to enter into the religious profession of Christians and Christian churches.

There are doctrines, too, which intrinsically, and on different accounts, may be said to have a peculiar and superior degree of importance; and this, so far as known, may properly be urged as a motive for our giving the more earnest heed to them. It is not, however, their comparative importance or utility, but their truth and the authority of him who has revealed them, which is the formal and proper reason of our receiving, professing, and maintaining them. And this applies equally to all the contents of a divine revelation. The relations of truths, especially those of a supernatural kind, are manifold and incomprehensible to us; it is not our part to pronounce a judgment on them; and if we could see them as God does, in all their extent and at once, we would behold the lesser joined to the greater, the most remote connected with the primary, by necessary and indissoluble links, and all together conspiring to form one beautiful and harmonious and indivisible whole.

Whatever God has revealed we are bound to receive and hold fast; whatever he has enjoined we are bound to obey; and the liberty which we dare not arrogate to ourselves we cannot give to others. It is not, indeed, necessary that the confession or testimony of the church (meaning by this that which is explicitly made by her, as distinguished from her declared adherence to the whole Word of God) should contain all truths. But then any of them may come to be included in it, when opposed and endangered; and it is not sufficient reason for excluding any of them that they are less important than others, or that they have been doubted and denied by good and learned men. Whatever forbearance may be exercised to persons, "the Word of the Lord," in all its extent, "must have free course and be glorified." And any act of men – call it forbearance or what you will – which serves as a screen and protection to error or sin, and prevents it from being opposed and removed by any proper means, is contrary to the divine law, and consequently is destitute of all intrinsic force and validity.

There are truths also which are more immediately connected with salvation. But who will pretend to fix those propositions which are absolutely necessary to be known in order to salvation, by all persons, of all capacities, and in all situations; or say how low a God of grace and salvation may descend in dealing with particular individuals? Or, if we determine this extreme point, who would say that it ought to fix the rule of our dealing with others, or the extent of a church's profession of faith? Is nothing else to be kept in view in settling articles of faith and fellowship, but what may be necessary to the salvation of sinners? Do we not owe a paramount regard to the glory of God in the highest, to the edifying of the body of Christ, to the advancing of the general interests of religion, and to the preserving, in purity, of those external means, by which in the economy of providence and grace, the salvation of men, both initial and progressive, may be promoted to an incalculable extent from age to age?

In fine, there is reason for complaining that the criteria or marks given for determining these fundamental or necessary articles are uncertain or contradictory. Is it alleged that "they are clearly taught in Scripture"? This is true of the others also. "That they are few and simple"? This is contradicted by their own attempts to state them. "That they are such as the Scripture has declared to be necessary"? Why then have we not yet been furnished with a catalogue of them? "That they are such as embraced by all true Christians"? Have they a secret tact by which they are to discover such characters? If not, can they avoid running into a vicious circle in reasoning, by first determining who are true Christians by their embracing certain doctrines, and then determining that these doctrines are fundamental because they are embraced by persons of that description?

Many who have contributed to give currency to this scheme have been actuated, I have no doubt, by motives which are in themselves highly commendable. They wished to fix the attention of men on matters confessedly of great importance, and were anxious to put an end to the dissensions of Christian by discovering a mean point in which the views of all might harmoniously meet. But surely those who cherish a supreme regard for divine authority will be afraid of contemning or of teaching others to think lightly of anything which bears its sacred impress. They will be disposed carefully to reconsider an opinion, or an interpretation of any part of Scripture, which seems to imply in it that God has given men a power to dispense with some of his own laws. And they will be cautious of originating or countenancing plans of communion that may involve a principle of such a complexion.

These plans are more or less dangerous according to the extent to which they are carried, and the errors or abuses which may prevail among the parties which they embrace. But however limited they may be, they set an example which may be carried to any extent. So far as it is agreed and stipulated that any truth or duty shall be sacrificed or neglected, and that any error or sin shall be treated as indifferent or trivial, the essence of latitudinarianism is adopted, room is made for further advancements, and the way is prepared for ascending, through successive generations, to the very highest degree in the scale.

38

The Unity of the Church[1]

John Calvin

IN THE LAST Book, it has been shown, that by the faith of the Gospel Christ becomes ours, and we are made partakers of the salvation and eternal blessedness procured by him. But as our ignorance and sloth (I may add, the vanity of our mind) stand in need of external helps, by which faith may be begotten in us, and may increase and make progress until its consummation, God, in accommodation to our infirmity, has added such helps, and secured the effectual preaching of the Gospel, by depositing this treasure with the church. He has appointed pastors and teachers, by whose lips he might edify his people (*Ephesians* 4:11); he has invested them with authority, and in short, omitted nothing that might conduce to holy consent in the faith, and to right order. In particular, he has instituted sacraments, which we feel by experience to be most useful helps in fostering and confirming our faith. For seeing we are shut up in the prison of the body and have not yet attained to the rank of angels, God, in accommodation to our capacity, has in his admirable providence provided a method by which, though widely separated, we might still draw near to him. Wherefore, due order requires that we first treat of the church, of its government, orders, and power; next, of the sacraments; and, lastly, of civil government; at the same time guarding pious readers against the corruptions of the papacy, by which Satan has adulterated all that God had appointed for our salvation. I will begin with the church, into whose bosom God is pleased to collect his children, not only that by her aid and ministry they may be nourished so long as they are babes and children, but may also be guided by her

---

1. John Calvin, *Institutes of the Christian Religion*, Henry Beveridge, translator, Eerdmans, 1970, II, 280-292.

maternal care until they grow up to manhood, and, finally, attain to the perfection of faith. What God has thus joined, let not man put asunder (*Mark* 10:9): To those to whom he is a Father, the church must also be a mother. This was true not merely under the Law, but even now after the advent of Christ; since Paul declares that we are the children of a new, even a heavenly Jerusalem (*Galatians* 4:26).

When in the creed we profess to believe the church, reference is made not only to the visible church of which we are now treating, but also to all the elect of God, including in the number even those who have departed this life. And, accordingly, the word used is "believe," because oftentimes no difference can be observed between the children of God and the profane, between his proper flock and the untamed herd. The particle *in* is often interpolated, but without any probable ground. I confess, indeed, that it is the more usual form, and is not unsupported by antiquity, since the Nicene Creed, as quoted in *Ecclesiastical History*, adds the preposition. At the same time, we may perceive from early writers, that the expression received without controversy in ancient times was to believe "the church," and not "in the church." This is not only the expression used by Augustine, and that ancient writer, whoever he may have been, whose treatise, *De Symboli Expositione*, is extant under the name of Cyprian, but they distinctly remark that the addition of the preposition would make the expression improper, and they give good grounds for so thinking. We declare that we believe in God, both because our mind reclines upon him as true, and our confidence is fully satisfied in him. This cannot be said of the church, just as it cannot be said of the forgiveness of sins, or the resurrection of the body. Wherefore, although I am unwilling to dispute about words, yet I would rather keep to the proper form, as better fitted to express the thing that is meant, than affect terms by which the meaning is causelessly obscured. The object of the expression is to teach us, that though the devil leaves no stone unturned in order to destroy the grace of Christ, and the enemies of God rush with insane violence in the same direction, it cannot be extinguished – the blood of Christ cannot be rendered barren and prevented from producing fruit. Hence, regard must be had both to the secret election and to the internal calling of God because he alone "knows them that are his" (2 *Timothy* 2:19); and as Paul expresses it, holds them as it were enclosed under his seal, although, at the same time, they wear his insignia, and are thus distinguished from the reprobate. But as they are a small and despised number, concealed in an immense crowd, like a few grains of wheat buried among a heap of chaff, to God alone must be left the knowledge of his church, of which his secret election forms the foundation. Nor is it enough to embrace the number of the elect in thought and intention merely. By the unity of the church we must understand a unity into which we feel persuaded that we are truly ingrafted. For unless we are united with all the other members under Christ our head, no hope of the future inheritance awaits us. Hence the church is called catholic or universal (Augustine, *Ep.* 48), for two or three cannot be invented without dividing Christ; and this is impossible. All the elect of God are so joined together in Christ, that as they depend on one head, so they are as it were compacted into one body, being knit together like its different members; made truly one by living together under the same Spirit of God in one faith, hope, and charity, called not only to the same inheritance of eternal life, but to participation in one God and Christ. For although the sad devastation which everywhere meets our view may proclaim that no church remains, let us know that the death of Christ produces fruit, and that God wondrously preserves his church, while placing it as it were in concealment. Thus it was said to Elijah, "Yet I have left me seven thousand in Israel" (1 *Kings* 19:18).

Moreover, this article of the creed relates in some measure to the external church, that every one of us must maintain brotherly concord with all the children of God, give due authority to the church, and, in short, conduct ourselves as sheep of the flock. And hence the additional expression, the "communion of saints"; for this clause, though usually omitted by ancient writers, must not be overlooked, as it admirably expresses the quality of the church; just as if it had been said, that saints are united in the fellowship of Christ on this condition, that all the blessings which God bestows upon them are mutually communicated to each other. This, however, is not incompatible with a diversity of graces, for we know that the gifts of the Spirit are variously distributed; nor is it incompatible with civil order, by which each is permitted privately to possess his own means, it being necessary for the preservation of peace among men that distinct rights of property should exist among them. Still a community is asserted, such as Luke describes when he says, "The multitude of them that believed were of one heart and of one soul" (*Acts* 4:32); and Paul, when he reminds the Ephesians, "There is one body, and one Spirit, even as ye are called in one hope of your calling" (*Ephesians* 4:4). For if they are truly persuaded that God is the common Father of them all, and Christ their common head, they cannot but be united together in brotherly love, and mutually impart their blessings to each other. Then it is of the highest importance for us to know what benefit thence redounds to us. For when we believe the church, it is in order that we may be firmly persuaded that we are its members. In this way our salvation rests on a foundation so firm and sure, that though the whole fabric of the world were to give way, it could not be destroyed. First, it stands with the election of God, and cannot change or fail, any more than his eternal providence. Next, it is in a manner united with the stability of Christ, who will no more allow his faithful followers to be dissevered from him, than he would allow his own members to be torn to pieces. We may add, that so long as we continue in the bosom of the church, we are sure that the truth will remain with us. Lastly, we feel that we have an interest in such promises as these, "In Mount Zion and in Jerusalem shall be deliverance" (*Joel* 2:32; *Obadiah* 17); "God is in the midst of her; she shall not be moved" (*Psalm* 46:5). So available is communion with the church to keep us in the fellowship of God. In the very term *communion* there is great consolation; because, while we are assured that everything which God bestows on his members belongs to us, all the blessings conferred upon them confirm our hope. But in order to embrace the unity of the church in this manner, it is not necessary, as I have observed, to see it with our eyes, or feel it with our hands. Nay, rather from its being placed in faith, we are reminded that our thoughts are to dwell upon it, as much when it escapes our perception as when it openly appears. Nor is our faith the worse for apprehending what is unknown, since we are not enjoined here to distinguish between the elect and the reprobate (this belongs not to us, but to God only), but to feel firmly assured in our minds, that all those who, by the mercy of God the Father, through the efficacy of the Holy Spirit, have become partakers with Christ, are set apart as the proper and peculiar possession of God, and that as we are of the number, we are also partakers of this great grace.

But as it is now our purpose to discourse of the visible church, let us learn, from her single title of mother, how useful, nay, how necessary the knowledge of her is, since there is no other means of entering into life unless she conceive us in the womb and give us birth, unless she nourish us at her breasts, and, in short, keep us under her charge and government, until, divested of mortal flesh, we become like the angels (*Matthew* 22:30). For our weakness does not permit us to leave the school until we have spent our whole lives as scholars. Moreover, beyond the pale of the church no forgiveness of sins, no salvation, can be hoped for, as Isaiah and Joel testify (*Isaiah* 37:32; *Joel* 2:32). To their testimony Ezekiel subscribes, when he declares "They shall not be in the assembly of my people, neither shall they be written in the writing of the house of Israel" (*Ezekiel* 13:9); as, on the other hand, those who turn to the cultivation of true piety are said to inscribe their names among the citizens of Jerusalem. For which reason it is said in the *Psalm*, "Remember me, O Lord, with the favor that you bear unto your people: O visit me with your salvation; that I may see the good of your chosen, that I may rejoice in the gladness of your nation, that I may glory with your inheritance" (*Psalm* 106:4, 5). By these words the paternal favor of God and the special evidence of spiritual life are confined to his peculiar people, and hence the abandonment of the church is always fatal.

But let us proceed to a full exposition of this view. Paul says that our Saviour "ascended far above all heavens, that he might fill all things. And he gave some, apostles; and some, prophets; and some, evangelists; and some, pastors and teachers; for the perfecting of the saints, for the work of the ministry, for the edifying of the body of Christ: till we all come in the unity of the faith, and of the knowledge of the Son of God, unto a perfect man, unto the measure of the stature of the fulness of Christ" (*Ephesians* 4:10-13). We see that God, who might perfect his people in a moment, chooses not to bring them to manhood in any other way than by the education of the church. We see the mode of doing it expressed; the preaching of celestial doctrine is committed to pastors. We see that all without exception are brought into the same order, that they may with meek and docile spirit allow themselves to be governed by teachers appointed for this purpose. Isaiah had long before given this as the characteristic of the kingdom of Christ, "My Spirit that is upon you, and my words which I have put in your mouth, shall not depart out of your mouth, nor out of the mouth of your seed, nor out of the mouth of your seed's seed, says the Lord, from henceforth and forever" (*Isaiah* 49:21). Hence it follows, that all who reject the spiritual food of the soul divinely offered to them by the hands of the church, deserve to perish of hunger and famine. God inspires us with faith, but it is by the instrumentality of his Gospel, as Paul reminds us, "Faith comes by hearing"

(*Romans* 10:17). God reserves to himself the power of maintaining it, but it is by the preaching of the Gospel, as Paul also declares, that he brings it forth and unfolds it. With this view, it pleased him in ancient times that sacred meetings should be held in the sanctuary, that consent in faith might be nourished by doctrine proceeding from the lips of the priest. Those magnificent titles, as when the temple is called God's rest, his sanctuary, his habitation, and when he is said to dwell between the cherubim (*Psalms* 132:13, 14; 80:1), are used for no other purpose than to procure respect, love, reverence, and dignity to the ministry of heavenly doctrine, to which otherwise the appearance of an insignificant human being might be in no slight degree derogatory. Therefore, to teach us that the treasure offered to us in earthen vessels is of inestimable value (2 *Corinthians* 4:7), God himself appears and, as the author of this ordinance, requires his presence to be recognized in his own institution. Accordingly, after forbidding his people to give heed to familiar spirits, wizards, and other superstitions (*Leviticus* 19:30, 31), he adds that he will give what ought to be sufficient for all – namely, that he will never leave them without prophets. For, as he did not commit his ancient people to angels, but raised up teachers on the Earth to perform a truly angelical office, so he is pleased to instruct us in the present day by human means. But as anciently he did not confine himself to the law merely, but added priests as interpreters, from whose lips the people might inquire after his true meaning, so in the present day he would not only have us to be attentive to reading, but has appointed masters to give us their assistance. In this there is a twofold advantage. For, on the one hand, he by an admirable test proves our obedience when we listen to his ministers just as we would to himself; while, on the other hand, he consults our weakness in being pleased to address us after the manner of men by means of interpreters, that he may thus allure us to himself, instead of driving us away by his thunder. How well this familiar mode of teaching is suited to us all the godly are aware, from the dread with which the divine majesty justly inspires them.

Those who think that the authority of the doctrine is impaired by the insignificance of the men who are called to teach, betray their ingratitude; for among the many noble endowments with which God has adorned the human race, one of the most remarkable is that he deigns to consecrate the mouths and tongues of men to his service, making his own voice to be heard in them. Wherefore, let us not on our part decline obediently to embrace the doctrine of salvation, delivered by his command and mouth; because, although the power of God is not confined to external means, he has, however, confined us to his ordinary method of teaching, which method, when fanatics refuse to observe, they entangle themselves in many fatal snares. Pride, or fastidiousness, or emulation, induces many to persuade themselves that they can profit sufficiently by reading and meditating in private, and thus to despise public meetings, and deem preaching superfluous. But since as much as in them lies they loose or burst the sacred bond of unity, none of them escapes the just punishment of this impious divorce, but become fascinated with pestiferous errors, and the foulest delusions. Wherefore, in order that the pure simplicity of the faith may flourish among us, let us not decline to use this exercise of piety, which God by his institution of it has shown to be necessary, and which he so highly recommends. None, even among the most petulant of men, would venture to say, that we are to shut our ears against God, but in all ages prophets and pious teachers have had a difficult contest to maintain with the ungodly, whose perverseness cannot submit to the yoke of being taught by the lips and ministry of men. This is just the same as if they were to destroy the impress of God as exhibited to us in doctrine. For no other reason were believers anciently enjoined to seek the face of God in the sanctuary (*Psalm* 105:4) (an injunction so often repeated in the Law), than because the doctrine of the Law, and the exhortations of the prophets, were to them a living image of God. Thus Paul declares, that in his preaching the glory of God shone in the face of Jesus Christ (*2 Corinthians* 4:6). The more detestable are the apostates who delight in producing schisms in churches, just as if they wished to drive the sheep from the fold, and throw them into the jaws of wolves. Let us hold, agreeably to the passage we quoted from Paul, that the church can only be edified by external preaching, and that there is no other bond by which the saints can be kept together than by uniting with one consent to observe the order which God has appointed in his church for learning and making progress. For this end, especially, as I have observed, believers were anciently enjoined under the Law to flock together to the sanctuary; for when Moses speaks of the habitation of God, he at the same time calls it the place of the name of God, the place where he will record his name (*Exodus* 20:24); thus plainly teaching that no use could be made of it without the doctrine of godliness. And there can be no doubt that, for the same reason,

David complains with great bitterness of soul, that by the tyrannical cruelty of his enemies he was prevented from entering the tabernacle (*Psalm* 84). To many the complaint seems childish, as if no great loss were sustained, not much pleasure lost, by exclusion from the temple, provided other amusements were enjoyed. David, however, laments this one deprivation, as filling him with anxiety and sadness, torment- ing, and almost destroying him. This he does because there is nothing on which believers set a higher value than on this aid, by which God gradually raises his people to Heaven. For it is to be observed, that he always exhibited himself to the holy patriarchs in the mirror of his doc- trine in such a way as to make their knowledge spiritual. Whence the Temple is not only styled his face, but also, for the purpose of removing all superstition, is termed his footstool (*Psalms* 132:7; 99:5). Herein is the unity of the faith happily realized, when all, from the highest to the lowest, aspire to the head. All the temples which the Gentiles built to God with a different intention were a mere profanation of his worship – a profanation into which the Jews also fell, though not with equal grossness. With this Stephen upbraids them in the words of Isaiah when he says, "Howbeit the Most High dwells not in temples made with hands, as says the Prophet, Heaven is my throne," etc. (*Acts* 7:48). For God only consecrates temples to their legitimate use by his Word. And when we rashly attempt anything without his order, immediately setting out from a bad principle, we introduce adventitious fictions, by which evil is propa- gated without measure. It was inconsiderate in Xerxes when, by the advice of the magicians, he burnt or pulled down all the temples of Greece, because he thought it absurd that God, to whom all things ought to be free and open, should be enclosed by walls and roofs, as if it were not in the power of God in a manner to descend to us, that he may be near to us, and yet neither change his place nor affect us by earthly means, but rather, by a kind of vehicles, raise us aloft to his own heav- enly glory, which, with its immensity, fills all things, and in height is above the heavens.

Moreover, as at this time there is a great dispute as to the efficacy of the ministry, some extravagantly overrating its dignity, and others erro- neously maintaining, that what is peculiar to the Spirit of God is trans- ferred to mortal man, when we suppose that ministers and teachers penetrate to the mind and heart, so as to correct the blindness of the one, and the hardness of the other; it is necessary to place this controversy on its proper footing. The arguments on both sides will be disposed of without trouble, by distinctly attending to the passages in which God, the author of preaching, connects his Spirit with it, and then promises a beneficial result; or, on the other hand, to the passages in which God, separating himself from external means, claims for himself alone both the commencement and the whole course of faith. The office of the second Elias was, as Malachi declares, to "turn the heart of the fathers to the children, and the heart of the children to their fathers" (*Malachi* 4:6). Christ declares that he sent the apostles to produce fruit from his labors (*John* 15:16). What this fruit is, Peter briefly defines, when he says that we are begotten again of incorruptible seed (*1 Peter* 1:23). Hence, Paul glories that by means of the Gospel he had begotten the Corinthians, who were the seals of his apostleship (*1 Corinthians* 4:15); moreover, that his was not a ministry of the letter, which only sounded in the ear, but that the effectual agency of the Spirit was given to him, in order that his doctrine might not be in vain (*1 Corinthians* 9:2; *2 Corinthians* 3:6). In this sense he elsewhere declares that his Gospel was not in word, but in power (*1 Thessalonians* 1:5). He also affirms that the Galatians received the Spirit by the hearing of faith (*Galatians* 3:2). In short, in several passages he not only makes himself a fellow-worker with God, but attributes to himself the province of bestowing salvation (*1 Corinthians* 3:9). All these things he certainly never uttered with the view of attributing to himself one iota apart from God, as he elsewhere briefly explains. "For this cause also thank we God without ceasing, because, when you received the Word of God which you heard of us, you received it not as the word of men, but (as it is in truth) the Word of God, which effectually works also in you that believe" (*1 Thessalonians* 2:13). Again, in another place, "He that wrought effectually in Peter to the apostleship of the circumcision, the same was mighty in me toward the Gentiles" (*Galatians* 2:8). And that he allows no more to ministers is obvious from other passages. " So then neither is he that plants anything, neither he that waters; but God that gives the increase" (*1 Corinthians* 3:7). Again, " I labored more abundantly than they all: yet not I, but the grace of God which was with me" (*1 Corinthians* 15:10). And it is indeed necessary to keep these sentences in view since God, in ascribing to himself the illumination of the mind and renewal of the heart, reminds us that it is sacrilege for man to claim any part of either to himself. Still everyone who listens with docility to the ministers whom

God appoints, will know by the beneficial result, that for good reason God is pleased with this method of teaching, and for good reason has laid believers under this modest yoke.

The judgment which ought to be formed concerning the visible church which comes under our observation, must, I think, be sufficiently clear from what has been said. I have observed that the Scriptures speak of the church in two ways. Sometimes when they speak of the church they mean the church as it really is before God – the church into which none is admitted but those who by the gift of adoption are sons of God, and by the sanctification of the Spirit true members of Christ. In this case it not only comprehends the saints who dwell on the Earth, but all the elect who have existed from the beginning of the world. Often, too, by the name of church is designated the whole body of mankind scattered throughout the world, who profess to worship one God and Christ, who by baptism are initiated into the faith; by partaking of the Lord's Supper profess unity in true doctrine and charity, agree in holding the Word of the Lord, and observe the ministry which Christ has appointed for the preaching of it. In this church there is a very large mixture of hypocrites, who have nothing of Christ but the name and outward appearance: of ambitious, avaricious, envious, evil-speaking men, some also of impurer lives, who are tolerated for a time, either because their guilt cannot be legally established, or because due strictness of discipline is not always observed. Hence, as it is necessary to believe the invisible church, which is manifest to the eye of God only, so we are also enjoined to regard this church which is so called with reference to man, and to cultivate its communion.

Accordingly, inasmuch as it was of importance to us to recognize it, the Lord has distinguished it by certain marks, and as it were symbols. It is, indeed, the special prerogative of God to know those who are his, as Paul declares in the passage already quoted (2 *Timothy* 2:19). And doubtless it has been so provided as a check on human rashness, the experience of every day reminding us how far his secret judgments surpass our apprehension. For even those who seemed most abandoned, and who had been completely despaired of, are by his goodness recalled to life, while those who seemed most stable often fall. Hence, as Augustine says, "In regard to the secret predestination of God, there are very many sheep without, and very many wolves within" (Augustine, *Hom. in Joan.* 45). For he knows, and has his mark on those who know neither him nor themselves. Of those again who openly bear his badge, his eyes alone see who of them are unfeignedly holy, and will persevere even to the end, which alone is the completion of salvation. On the other hand, foreseeing that it was in some degree expedient for us to know who are to be regarded by us as his sons, he has in this matter accommodated himself to our capacity. But as here full certainty was not necessary, he has in its place substituted the judgment of charity, by which we acknowledge all as members of the church who by confession of faith, regularity of conduct, and participation in the sacraments, unite with us in acknowledging the same God and Christ. The knowledge of his body, inasmuch as he knew it to be more necessary for our salvation, he has made known to us by surer marks.

Hence the form of the church appears and stands forth conspicuous to our view. Wherever we see the Word of God sincerely preached and heard, wherever we see the sacraments administered according to the institution of Christ, there we cannot have any doubt that the church of God has some existence, since his promise cannot fail, "Where two or three are gathered together in my name, there am I in the midst of them" (*Matthew* 18:20). But that we may have a clear summary of this subject, we must proceed by the following steps:

The church universal is the multitude collected out of all nations, who, though dispersed and far distant from each other, agree in one truth of divine doctrine, and are bound together by the tie of a common religion. In this way it comprehends single churches, which exist in different towns and villages, according to the wants of human society, so that each of them justly obtains the name and authority of the church; and also comprehends single individuals, who by a religions profession are accounted to belong to such churches, although they are in fact aliens from the church, but have not been cut off by a public decision. There is, however, a slight difference in the mode of judging of individuals and of churches. For it may happen in practice that those whom we deem not altogether worthy of the fellowship of believers, we yet ought to treat as brethren, and regard as believers, on account of the common consent of the church in tolerating and bearing with them in the body of Christ. Such persons we do not approve by our suffrage as members of the church, but we leave them the place which they hold among the people of God, until they are legitimately deprived of it. With regard to the general body we must feel differently; if they have

the ministry of the Word, and honor the administration of the sacraments, they are undoubtedly entitled to be ranked with the church,
because it is certain that these things are not without a beneficial result.
Thus we both maintain the church universal in its unity, which malignant minds have always been eager to dissever, and deny not due authority to lawful assemblies distributed as circumstances require.

We have said that the symbols by which the church is discerned are
the preaching of the Word and the observance of the sacraments, for
these cannot anywhere exist without producing fruit and by prospering
by the blessing of God. I say not that wherever the Word is preached
fruit immediately appears; but that in every place where it is received,
and has a fixed abode, it uniformly displays its efficacy. Be this as it may,
when the preaching of the Gospel is reverently heard, and the sacraments are not neglected, there for the time the face of the church appears without deception or ambiguity and no man may with impunity
spurn her authority, or reject her admonitions, or resist her counsels, or
make sport of her censures, far less revolt from her, and violate her
unity.... For such is the value which the Lord sets on the communion
of his church, that all who contumaciously alienate themselves from
any Christian society, in which the true ministry of his Word and sacraments is maintained, he regards as deserters of religion. So highly does
he recommend her authority, that when it is violated he considers that
his own authority is impaired. For there is no small weight in the designation given to her "the house of God," "the pillar and ground of the
truth" (1 Timothy 3:15). By these words Paul intimates, that to prevent
the truth from perishing in the world, the church is its faithful guardian,
because God has been pleased to preserve the pure preaching of his
Word by her instrumentality, and to exhibit himself to us as a parent
while he feeds us with spiritual nourishment, and provides whatever is
conducive to our salvation. Moreover, no mean praise is conferred on
the church when she is said to have been chosen and set apart by Christ
as his spouse, "not having spot or wrinkle, or any such thing" (Ephesians
5:27), as "his body, the fulness of him that fills all in all" (Ephesians 1:23).
Whence it follows, that revolt from the church is denial of God and
Christ. Wherefore there is the more necessity to beware of a dissent so
iniquitous; for seeing by it we aim as far as in us lies at the destruction
of God's truth, we deserve to be crushed by the full thunder of his
anger. No crime can be imagined more atrocious than that of sacrile-

giously and perfidiously violating the sacred marriage which the only begotten Son of God has condescended to contract with us.

Wherefore let these marks be carefully impressed upon our minds, and let us estimate them as in the sight of the Lord. There is nothing on which Satan is more intent than to destroy and efface one or both of them – at one time to delete and abolish these marks, and thereby destroy the true and genuine distinction of the church; at another, to bring them into contempt, and so hurry us into open revolt from the church. To his wiles it was owing that for several ages the pure preaching of the Word disappeared, and now, with the same dishonest aim, he labors to overthrow the ministry, which, however, Christ has so ordered in his church, that if it is removed the whole edifice must fall. How perilous, then, nay, how fatal the temptation, when we even entertain a thought of separating ourselves from that assembly in which are beheld the signs and badges which the Lord has deemed sufficient to characterize his church! We see how great caution should be employed in both respects. That we may not be imposed upon by the name of church, every congregation which claims the name must be brought to that test as to a Lydian stone. If it holds the order instituted by the Lord in Word and sacraments there will be no deception; we may safely pay it the honor due to a church: On the other hand, if it exhibit itself without Word and sacraments, we must in this case be no less careful to avoid the imposture than we were to shun pride and presumption in the other.

When we say that the pure ministry of the Word and pure celebration of the sacraments is a fit pledge and earnest, so that we may safely recognize a church in every society in which both exist, our meaning is that we are never to discard it so long as these remain though it may otherwise teem with numerous faults. Nay, even in the administration of Word and sacraments defects may creep in which ought not to alienate us from its communion. For all the heads of true doctrine are not in the same position. Some are so necessary to be known, that all must hold them to be fixed and undoubted as the proper essentials of religion: For instance, that God is one, that Christ is God, and the Son of God, that our salvation depends on the mercy of God and the like. Others, again, which are the subject of controversy among the churches, do not destroy the unity of the faith; for why should it be regarded as a ground of dissension between churches, if one, without any spirit of contention or perverseness in dogmatizing, hold that the soul on quitting the body flies to Heaven, and another without venturing to speak positively as to the abode, holds it for certain that it lives with the Lord? [2] The words of the apostle are, "Let us therefore, as many as be perfect, be thus minded: And if in anything you be otherwise minded, God shall reveal even this unto you" (*Philippians* 3:15). Does he not sufficiently intimate that a difference of opinion as to these matters which are not absolutely necessary, ought not to be ground of dissension among Christians? The best thing, indeed, is to be perfectly agreed, but seeing there is no man who is not involved in some mist of ignorance, we must either have no church at all, or pardon delusion in those things of which one may be ignorant, without violating the substance of religion and forfeiting salvation. Here, however, I have no wish to patronize even the minutest errors, as if I thought it right to foster them by flattery or connivance; what I say is, that we are not on account of every minute difference to abandon a church, provided it retain sound and unimpaired doctrine in which the safety of piety consists,[3] and keep the use of the sacraments instituted by the Lord. Meanwhile, if we strive to reform what is offensive, we act in the discharge of duty. To this effect are the words of Paul, "If anything be revealed to another that sits by, let the first hold his peace" (1 *Corinthians* 14:30). From this it is evident that to each member of the church, according to his measure of grace, the study of public edification has been assigned, provided it be done decently and in order. In other words, we must neither renounce the communion of the church, nor, continuing in it, disturb peace and discipline when duly arranged.[4]

Our indulgence ought to extend much further in tolerating imperfection of conduct. Here there is great danger of falling, and Satan employs all his machinations to ensnare us. For there always have been

2. French: "Pour donner exemple s'il advenoit qu'une Eglise tint que les ames etant separées des corps fussent transferés au ciel incontinent: une autre, sans oser determiner du lieu pensât semplement qu'elles vivent en Dieu; et que telle diversité fut sans contention et sans opiniatreté porquoi se diviseroient elles d'ensemble?" – To give an example, should one church happen to hold that the soul when separated from the body is forthwith transported to Heaven, and should another, without venturing to determine the place, simply think that it lives in God, and should such diversity be without contention and obstinacy, why should they be divided?

3. French: "La doctrine principale de nostre salut" – The fundamental doctrine of our salvation.

4. French: "Et aussi que demeurant en icelle nous ne troublions point la police, ni la discipline" – and also that, remaining in it, we disturb not its order and discipline.

persons who, imbued with a false persuasion of absolute holiness, as if they had already become a kind of aerial spirits,[5] spurn the society of all in whom they see that something human still remains. Such of old were the Cathari and the Donatists, who were similarly infatuated. Such in the present day are some of the Anabaptists, who would be thought to have made superior progress. Others, again, sin in this respect, not so much from that insane pride as from inconsiderate zeal. Seeing that among those to whom the Gospel is preached, the fruit produced is not in accordance with the doctrine, they forthwith conclude that there no church exists. The offence is indeed well founded, and it is one to which in this most unhappy age we give far too much occasion. It is impossible to excuse our accursed sluggishness, which the Lord will not leave unpunished, as he is already beginning sharply to chastise us. Woe then to us who, by our dissolute license of wickedness, cause weak consciences to be wounded! Still those of whom we have spoken sin in their turn, by not knowing how to set bounds to their offense. For where the Lord requires mercy they omit it, and give themselves up to immoderate severity. Thinking there is no church where there is not complete purity and integrity of conduct, they, through hatred of wickedness, withdraw from a genuine church, while they think they are shunning the company of the ungodly. They allege that the church of God is holy. But that they may at the same time understand that it contains a mixture of good and bad, let them hear from the lips of our Saviour that parable in which he compares the church to a net in which all kinds of fishes are taken, but not separated until they are brought ashore. Let them hear it compared to a field which, planted with good seed, is by the fraud of an enemy mingled with tares, and is not freed of them until the harvest is brought into the barn. Let them hear, in fine, that it is a thrashing floor in which the collected wheat lies concealed under the chaff, until, cleansed by the fanner's and the sieve, it is at length laid up in the granary. If the Lord declares that the church will labor under the defect of being burdened with a multitude of wicked until the Day of Judgment, it is in vain to look for a church altogether free from blemish (*Matthew* 13).

5. French: "Comme s'ils eussent ete quelques anges de Paradis" – as if they had been some angels of Paradise.

39

The Church Irrational

John W. Robbins

MANY OBSERVERS have lamented the lack of discernment among professing Christians, the disappearance of "antithesis" in the thinking of contemporary Christians, and the worldliness of the churches. Some writers have made livings decrying the lack of discernment, though their own claims to discernment are frequently exaggerated; other observers, more Biblical, have tried to analyze the problem and suggest how it might be solved. One of the most discerning among the latter group is Dr. Jay E. Adams, who wrote *A Call for Discernment: Distinguishing Truth from Error in Today's Church*. Dr. Adams cites four factors that he believes contribute to the present lack of discernment by Christians:

(1) disappearance of church discipline

(2) continuum thinking replacing antithesis

(3) de-emphasis of systematic theology

(4) liberation of the laity.

These four, he writes, "are sufficient to demonstrate that many closely-connected factors play a part."[1]

Now, Dr. Adams' many books are among the best written by a Christian in the past 30 years. He has attempted to apply the principle of *sola Scriptura* to psychology and counseling.[2] However, his analysis of the causes of the present lack of discernment by Christians and churches seems confused. Dr. Adams does not discuss the fundamental reason

---

1. Jay E. Adams, *A Call for Discernment*. Woodruff, South Carolina: Timeless Texts [1987] 1998, 40.

2. Martin and Deidre Bobgan have provided the most detailed and cogent criticisms of both secular psychology and counseling in the churches. One cannot discuss this subject intelligently without having studied their work.

for the worldliness of the churches; and at least one reader is baffled by the inclusion of factor 4, the "liberation of the laity," for it seems to have nothing to do with causing the contemporary lack of discernment. "Parachurch organizations," which Dr. Adams and many others decry, are no worse theologically than the churches. The name of every erring parachurch organization can be matched by the name of an erring church. More importantly, and more fundamentally, Christians ought not to endorse, or appear to endorse, a view of the church that implies ecclesiastical totalitarianism. The institutional church is only one institution among many in a free and Christian society: There are also families, schools and colleges, businesses, charities, clubs and social organizations, political parties, and governments. All of these are parachurch organizations, and all of them are legitimate. None of them requires permission from the institutional church to be organized or maintained.[3] Let us not advocate ecclesiastical totalitarianism in order to avoid what Dr. Adams calls "anarchy." Let us recall that just as Marxists find the free market "anarchic," and fascists find elections and parliaments anarchic, so ecclesiastical totalitarians, such as the Roman Church-State, find parachurch organizations anarchic.[4]

In the New Testament there are at least two passages that are relevant to any discussion of parachurch organizations:

3. When Christ said, "I will build my church, and the gates of Hell will not prevail against it," he was not speaking of any institutional church. The gates of Hell have prevailed against thousands of institutional churches in the past two millennia. They have become apostate and in most cases have disappeared. The churches to which Paul wrote his letters – Ephesus, Corinth, Thessalonica, Rome, Galatia, Philippi, Colosse – no longer exist as Christian churches. The gates of Hell prevailed against the Methodist Church, the Presbyterian Church, and the Lutheran Church. Christ's church is not to be confused with any visible organization.

4. By using the word *anarchy*, Dr. Adams falls into the trap of the Romanists. The alternatives are not anarchy or tyranny over the laity (and I am sure Dr. Adams was not advocating tyranny; he was simply decrying parachurch organizations); the Biblical model is education of the laity by their elected teachers, *whose teaching the laity always have the right and the duty to judge*. When there were no parachurch organizations, because the church was a totalitarian institution that not only constituted civil governments, congregations, and families, but claimed a monopoly on salvation as well, there was far less discernment in both church officials and church-goers than there is today. The institutional church justifies its hegemony by claiming that only it has discernment. See, for example, chapter 26, *War Against the Idols* by Carlos M. N. Eire. The Roman Church-State, of course, finds all non-Roman churches, as well as parachurch organizations, anarchic.

Now John answered him, saying, "Teacher, we saw someone who does not follow us casting out demons in your name, and we forbade him because he does not follow us."

But Jesus said, "Do not forbid him, for no one who works a miracle in my name can soon afterward speak evil of me. For he who is not against us is on our side."[5]

Most of the brethren in the Lord, having become confident by my chains, are much more bold to speak the Word without fear. Some indeed preach Christ even from envy and strife, and some also from good will: The former preach Christ from selfish ambition, not sincerely, supposing to add affliction to my chains; but the latter out of love, knowing that I am appointed for the defense of the Gospel. What then? Only that in every way, whether in pretense or in truth, Christ is preached; and in this I rejoice, yes, and will rejoice.[6]

In the first passage, taken from the *Gospel of Mark*, Christ makes it clear that institutional or organizational connections are relatively unimportant. What is important is in whose name the work is being done. He forbids the disciples from interfering with these parachurch activities. The second passage from *Philippians* informs us that the motivation for preaching the Gospel is relatively unimportant to Paul – even if the Gospel is preached out of selfish ambition, a sinful motivation, Paul rejoices. So neither organizational connections nor motivations are the central issue; the important consideration is the message preached. The matter of parachurch organizations is a red herring. If the churches do not proclaim the Gospel, God will make rocks preach. The important question is: What is being preached? Paul and Christ commanded that the Gospel be preached, and they rejoiced when it was preached, even by men who were not of the company of the disciples or by men who were acting out of sinful motives. Neither Jesus nor Paul criticized or made any effort to stop this incipient parachurch activity.[7] Instead they rejoiced. Their focus was on the doctrine and its dissemination.

5. *Mark* 9:38-40.
6. *Philippians* 1:14-18.
7. Of course, some may wish to argue that the institutional church during Christ's life on Earth was that governed by the Scribes and Pharisees. In that case, the ministry of Christ and the apostles is a parachurch activity – indeed the most important parachurch activity ever.

Luther understood the importance, to the well-being of both the church and the churches, of doctrine and of ordinary Christians' right to judge doctrine. He wrote:

> Once the right to judge doctrine is taken away from the hearers, what can or may a teacher not dare though (if that were possible) he were worse than Satan? Conversely, if judging doctrine is permitted, aye, commanded, what can or may a teacher dare though he were more than an angel from Heaven…? In fact, nothing would ever have come of the entire papacy if this judgment [by the hearers] had been in control. Therefore they [the popes and councils] consulted their own interests exceedingly well by claiming the sole right to this office.[8]

Let us not make the mistake of exalting the authority of church officers beyond the limited ministerial authority they are given in Scripture, simply because Christianity is perverted and distorted on every side. That is the mistake the institutional church made in the first millennium when it acceded first to episcopal arguments and then to papal Rome's claims to rule the churches.

The other three factors Dr. Adams discusses are quite relevant to the issue of the lack of discernment in today's churches, but rather than explaining our current predicament, they are effects that themselves need to be explained: Why has church discipline virtually disappeared? Why does everyone tend to think in a "continuum"? Why has systematic theology been de-emphasized in the seminaries and in the churches? If we answer those questions correctly, then we can explain the lack of discernment in the churches. In fact, one might turn Dr. Adams' whole analysis on its head and argue that it is the lack of discernment that explains the disappearance of church discipline and the contemporary de-emphasis on systematic theology. Dr. Adams has drawn our attention to many trends within the church, but he seems not to have explained the cause of any of them. And he is one of the best theologians among those who discuss the lack of discernment among churchgoers.

8. *What Luther Says*, Plass, editor, 1234.

The Definition of Discernment

Before we get too far into a discussion of discernment, it might be wise to define our terms.[9] According to the *Oxford English Dictionary*, "to discern" is

> to separate (things, or one thing from another); to distinguish and divide...to recognize as distinct, to distinguish or separate mentally (one thing from another)...to perceive the difference between...to distinguish or discriminate between...to distinguish (one thing or fact) by the intellect.

"Discernment" is "the act of discerning or perceiving by the intellect; intellectual perception or apprehension...discrimination, judgment, keenness of intellectual perception; penetration; insight...." The Hebrew words used in the Scriptures, *nakar* and *shama,* mean "to scrutinize" and "to know." The Greek words *anakrino* and *diakrino* mean "to separate thoroughly," "to discriminate." *Arndt and Gingrich* lists these meanings for judge (*krino*): "separate, distinguish, think, consider, decide, hale before a court, condemn, administer justice, see to it that justice is done, pass judgment upon, criticize, find fault with." These definitions show how closely related discernment and judging are, and thereby provide us a clue to the proximate causes of today's lack of discernment.

The First Cause of the Lack of Discernment

The Bible provides several answers to the question: Why do people lack discernment? The fundamental answer, the will of God, is an unpopular and an unpalatable answer, and modern men will not hear it. The pagan Greeks and Romans had several similar proverbs: "Whom the gods would destroy, they first make mad."[10] Publius Syrius (42 B.C.) wrote: "Whom Fortune wishes to destroy she first makes mad." Lycurgus (820 B.C.) wrote: "When falls on man the anger of the gods/

9. To show what lack of discernment currently prevails, this writer was recently reproached by a professed Christian who called his concern for the clear definition of terms the "Socratic fallacy." Well, gentlemen, if defining terms be fallacious, let us make the most of it.

10. These words are from Henry Wadsworth Longfellow's 1875 *The Masque of Pandora.* The anonymous Latin version is "Quos [or Quem] deus vult perdere prius dementat."

First from his mind they banish understanding." The seventeenth-century English poet John Dryden echoed these proverbs in *The Hind and the Panther* (1687): "For those whom God to ruin has designed / He fits for fate, and first destroys their mind." Removing the pagan meanings from the sayings, we arrive at some pretty sound theology: "Whom God wishes to destroy he first makes foolish." Or to put it another way, "Whom God wishes to destroy, he first makes undiscerning." That is exactly what passages such as *Romans* 1 teach:

> They are without excuse, because, although they knew God, they did not glorify him as God, nor were thankful, but became futile in their thoughts, and their foolish hearts were darkened. Professing to be wise, they became fools.... And even as they did not like to retain God in their knowledge, God gave them over to a debased mind...undiscerning....

The Apostle Paul, writing to the Thessalonians, warned:

> The coming of the lawless one is according to the working of Satan, with all power, signs and lying wonders, and all unrighteous deception among those who perish, because they did not receive the love of the truth, that they might be saved. And for this reason God will send them strong delusion, that they should believe the lie, that they all may be condemned who did not believe the truth but had pleasure in unrighteousness.[11]

The consistent message of the Bible is that God gives knowledge and wisdom to those who are to be saved; and withholds knowledge and wisdom from those who are to be destroyed. Consider these verses:

> Then you shall say to them "Thus says the Lord: 'Behold I will fill all the inhabitants of this land – even the kings who sit on David's throne, the priests, the prophets, and all the inhabitants of Jerusalem – with drunkenness! And I will dash them one against another, even the fathers and the sons together,' says the Lord. 'I will no more spare nor have mercy, but will destroy them.'"[12]
>
> With him are wisdom and strength; he has counsel and understanding. If he breaks a thing down, it cannot be rebuilt; if he imprisons a man, there can be no release. If he withholds the waters, they dry up; if he sends them out, they overwhelm the Earth. With him are strength

11. *2 Thessalonians* 1:9-12.
12. *Jeremiah* 13:13-14.

and prudence. The deceived and the deceiver are his. He leads counselors away plundered and makes fools of the judges. He loosens the bonds of kings, and binds their waist with a belt. He leads princes away plundered and overthrows the mighty. He deprives the trusted ones of speech and takes away the discernment of the elders. He pours contempt on princes and disarms the mighty.... He takes way the understanding of the chiefs of the people of the Earth, and makes them wander in a pathless wilderness. They grope in the dark without light, and he makes them stagger like a drunken man.[13]

You have hidden their heart from understanding....[14]

All this came upon King Nebuchadnezzar. At the end of the twelve months he was walking about the royal palace of Babylon. The King spoke, saying, "Is not this great Babylon, that I have built for a royal dwelling by my mighty power and for the honor of my majesty?"

While the word was still in the King's mouth, a voice fell from Heaven: "King Nebuchadnezzar, to you it is spoken: The kingdom has departed from you! And they shall drive you from men, and your dwelling shall be with the beasts of the field. They shall make you eat grass like oxen; and seven times shall pass over you, until you know that the Most High rules in the kingdom of men, and gives it to whomever he chooses."

That very hour the word was fulfilled concerning Nebuchadnezzar; he was driven from men and ate grass like oxen; his body was wet with the dew of heaven till his hair had grown like eagles' feathers and his nails like birds' claws.

And at the end of the time I, Nebuchadnezzar, lifted my eyes to Heaven, and my understanding returned to me, and I blessed the Most High and praised and honored him who lives forever: For his dominion is an everlasting dominion, and his kingdom is from generation to generation. All the inhabitants of the Earth are reputed as nothing; he does according to his will in the army of Heaven and among the inhabitants of the Earth. No one can restrain his hand or say to him, "What have you done?"

At the same time my reason returned to me....[15]

These passages clearly show that discernment is an intellectual function, and that God controls the minds of all men, giving understanding and discernment to those whom he favors, and withholding understanding and discernment from those whom he is punishing.

13. *Job* 12:13-25.
14. *Job* 17:4.
15. *Daniel* 4:28-36.

In *Proverbs*, it is the man who understands, the man who gets wisdom, that lives and prospers; it is the man who does not understand, the foolish man, who dies. God confuses their minds, makes them undiscerning, so that they cannot tell right from wrong, true from false. Discernment is the intellectual ability to judge correctly. To judge is to evaluate a particular (person, group, event, or idea) according to a general principle or standard. To those whom God wishes to save, he gives light; to those whom he wishes to punish, he sends confusion. A typical passage showing that intellectual light is from God is *Ephesians* 1:15-18:

> Therefore I also…do not cease to give thanks for you, making mention of you in my prayers, that the God of our Lord Jesus Christ, the Father of Glory, may give to you the spirit of wisdom and revelation in the knowledge of him, the eyes of your understanding being enlightened, that you may know....

Another is *Ephesians* 4:17-23:

> This I say, therefore, and testify in the Lord, that you should no longer walk as the rest of the Gentiles walk, in the futility of their mind, having their understanding darkened, being alienated from the life of God because of the ignorance that is in them, because of the hardening of their heart.... But you have not so learned Christ, if indeed you have heard him and have been taught by him, as the truth is in Jesus; that you...be renewed in the spirit of your mind....

This teaching – that knowledge, wisdom, discernment is from God – is repeated in many verses of Scripture. Here are just a few:

> But there is a spirit in man, and the breath of the Almighty gives him understanding.[16]
> Who has put wisdom in the mind? Or who has given understanding to the heart?[17]
> Therefore, give to your servant [Solomon] an understanding heart to judge your people, that I may discern between good and evil....
> Because you [Solomon] have asked this thing...understanding to discern justice, behold, I have done according to your words; see, I have given you a wise and understanding heart....[18]

16. *Job* 32:8.
17. *Job* 38:36.
18. *1 Kings* 3:9, 11-12.

My son, if you receive my words, and treasure my commands within you, so that you incline your ear to wisdom and apply your heart of understanding; yes, if you cry out for discernment, and lift up your voice for understanding; if you seek her as silver, and search for her as for hidden treasures; then you will understand the fear of the Lord, and find the knowledge of God. For the Lord gives wisdom; from his mouth come knowledge and understanding.[19]

These things we also speak, not in words which man's wisdom teaches but which the Holy Spirit teaches, comparing spiritual things with spiritual. But the natural man does not receive the things of the Spirit of God, for they are foolishness to him; nor can he know them, because they are spiritually discerned. But he who is spiritual judges all things, yet he himself is rightly judged by no one.[20]

It is clear from Scripture that all knowledge, wisdom, and discernment come from God alone. It is equally clear that it is God who withholds knowledge, wisdom, and discernment from people. God darkens the minds and hardens the hearts of men; he withholds his knowledge and wisdom and sends delusions and lying spirits to men; he diminishes the ability of some men to judge correctly, not merely of those he wishes to destroy eternally, but those whom he wishes to destroy temporally as well:

Then Micaiah said, "Therefore, hear the Word of the Lord: I saw the Lord sitting on his throne, and all the host of Heaven standing by, on his right hand and on his left.

"And the Lord said, 'Who will persuade [King] Ahab to go up, that he may fall at Ramoth Gilead?' So one spoke in this manner, and another spoke in another manner.

"Then a spirit came forward and stood before the Lord and said, 'I will persuade him.'

"The Lord said to him, 'In what way?'

"So he said, 'I will go out and be a lying spirit in the mouth of all his prophets.'

"And he said, 'You shall persuade him, and also prevail. Go out and do so.'

"Now, therefore, look! The Lord has put a lying spirit in the mouth of all these prophets of yours, and the Lord has declared disaster against you."[21]

19. *Proverbs* 2:1-6.
20. *1 Corinthians* 2:13-15.
21. *1 Kings* 22:19-23.

With some individuals, such as Nebuchadnezzar and the demoniacs, God's withholding of knowledge and wisdom and his restoration of understanding and discernment are sudden: "Then they came to Jesus and saw the one who had been demon-possessed and had the legion, sitting and clothed and in his right mind."[22] In these cases God acted suddenly, darkening and enlightening minds in an instant. But God's usual method of operation is gradually to darken the minds of those he intends to abase and destroy, and gradually (after the sudden change of regeneration / resurrection) enlightening the minds of those whom he intends to save. He darkens minds both objectively and subjectively. Objectively, he sends famines of the preaching and hearing of the Word of God:

> "Behold the days are coming," says the Lord God, "that I will send a famine on the land – not a famine of bread, nor a thirst for water, but of hearing the words of the Lord. They shall wander from sea to sea, and from north to east; they shall run to and fro, seeking the Word of the Lord, and they shall not find it."[23]

He gradually darkens minds, not only of isolated individuals, but also of whole societies; he hides his Word in dark sayings and parables,

> And the disciples came and said to him, "Why do you speak to them in parables?"
> He answered and said to them, "Because it has been given to you to know the mysteries[24] of the Kingdom of Heaven, but to them it has not been given. For whoever has, to him more will be given, and he will have abundance; but whoever does not have, even what he has will be taken away from him. Therefore, I speak to them in parables, because seeing they do not see, and hearing they do not hear, nor do they understand. And in them the prophecy of Isaiah is fulfilled, which says: 'Hearing you will hear and not understand, and seeing you will see and not perceive, for the heart of this people has grown dull, their ears are hard of hearing, and their eyes they have closed; lest they should see with their eyes and hear with their ears, lest they should understand with their heart and turn, so that I should heal them.' "[25]

22. *Mark* 5:15. *Luke* 8:35.
23. *Amos* 8:11-12.
24. The Greek word means secrets, not paradoxes or contradictions.
25. *Matthew* 13:10-15.

The lack of discernment is the lack of wisdom and knowledge. It is an intellectual deficiency. Professed churches and professed Christians lack discernment today because they do not know or believe the truth. They profess to, but they do not. Those who decry the lack of discernment in today's churches usually fail to attribute that lack to its first cause: the purpose, plan, and providence of God. Further, they fail to indicate how God carries out his plan, how he darkens minds, how he withholds his light and his face. Objectively this darkening is the dearth of preaching and publication of the Word; subjectively it is the rejection of revealed truth, including, at the present time, the revealed truth about logical thought.

Logic and His Enemies

It is on the latter cause that I wish to focus, for this rejection of logic – this misology – explains in large part the lack of discernment, the de-emphasis on systematic theology, the prevalence of what Dr. Adams calls "continuum thinking," and even the disappearance of church discipline. Another part of the explanation–the dearth of preaching of God's Word in today's churches – is discussed elsewhere in this volume. These two causes – the hatred of logic and the suppression of the Word – are the proximate causes of today's lack of discernment. The ultimate cause is, of course, the will of God.

Today, logic – usually denigrated as "mere human logic" – is suspect, not only in humanist circles, but also, perhaps even more so, in religious circles: It is despised and rejected in liberal, Roman Catholic, Orthodox, Arminian, Neo-evangelical, and charismatic churches, and in many professedly Reformed churches as well.[26] All contemporary churches have been influenced by the world on this point. In "The Church Effeminate" I traced some of the effects of anti-intellectualism in the nineteenth and early twentieth centuries, leading to the feminization of the churches in the twentieth century. But the effects of modern misology – the hatred of logic – have been far more extensive than

26. For a recent example of this misology, see Douglas Wilson, The Paideia of God, 1999, especially chapter 6: "The Great Logic Fraud." Wilson, a leader in the "Classical-Christian" school movement, is a disciple of medievalist Dorothy Sayers; medievalist C. S. Lewis; and a motley crew of rock groups of the 1960s and 1970s, whom he frequently quotes. It is not surprising that his writing demonstrates deep-seated hostility toward logic and rationality.

the feminization of the churches. It is because church officers and churchgoers disdain "mere human logic" that systematic theology is de-emphasized in both seminaries and churches, and unsystematic theology is preferred. It is because seminary professors and students detest "mere human logic" that "practical" books, and in seminaries and churches "practical" courses, are preferred to doctrinal courses. It is because church officers and churchgoers despise "mere human logic" that they prefer "continuum thinking" to making distinctions and judgments. They are religiously and piously opposed to precision and clarity.[27] It is because church officers and churchgoers decry "mere human logic" that church discipline has disappeared, for the exercise of just discipline requires the most rigorous application of our rational powers of definition, distinction, and judgment. Church discipline requires clarity and precision, two godly qualities decried by modern churchmen. Those things which modern churchgoers and church officers find offensive about Christianity – its claim to be an exclusive religion; its claim to have a systematic monopoly on truth and salvation; its insistence on clarity in written and oral expression; its demand for clear definition of terms; its demand that judgment be done righteously, according to defined and objective standards; its requirement that Christians discriminate between right and wrong, good and evil, godly and ungodly; its requirement that Christians be a distinct people, separate from the world – they find all these things offensive because of their deep-seated and sinful antipathy to logical thought.

This antipathy is itself due to their hostility to God, who is the *Logos*, the Logic who lights the mind of every man:

> In the beginning was the *Logos*, and the *Logos* was with God, and the *Logos* was God. He was in the beginning with God. All things were made through him [the *Logos*], and without him nothing was made that was made. In him was life, and the life was the light of men...the true light which gives light to every man who comes into the world.[28]

---

27. A defense of imprecisionism is Vern Poythress, *Philosophy, Science, and the Sovereignty of God*, who bizarrely apes precision by numbering his paragraphs to the third decimal place. Dr. Poythress is a student of Cornelius Van Til and a member of the faculty at Westminster Theological Seminary. See *Clark Speaks from the Grave* for Gordon Clark's discussion of the irrationalism of Dr. Poythress.

28. *John* 1:1-4, 9.

The world and the worldly church hate "mere human logic," because it is the image of God in man, and they hate God:

> There is none righteous, no not one; there is none who understands; there is none who seeks after God. They have all gone out of the way; they have together become unprofitable; there is none who does good, no, not one.[29]
>
> Because the carnal mind is enmity against God, for it is not subject to the law of God, nor indeed can be.[30]

God is a rational being, and man, his image, is also rational. God was not joking or waxing metaphorical when he invited sinners, through Isaiah, "Come, let us reason together." Because man is God's image, his logic is God's logic, and God and man can reason together. God's truth and man's truth are not two different truths; the concept of twofold truth, in which one thing can be true in theology and its contradictory true in philosophy, or in which two contradictories can both be true in theology, is medieval and modern Antichristian nonsense. God's logic and man's logic are not two different logics; the notion of polylogism – many logics – is nonsense. The divine *Logos* lights the mind of every man, John wrote. Since the *Logos* is not created, the light of the *Logos*, logic, is not created. Man's arithmetic and God's arithmetic are not two different arithmetics; the notion of many arithmetics is mathematical nonsense. There are many examples of addition, subtraction, division, and multiplication revealed in Scripture, and in every case, God's revealed answers are man's answers. Truth, logic, and arithmetic are one truth, one logic, and one arithmetic; they all are uncreated; they all originate with God, who is truth itself, for they are the way God himself thinks. Whatever man has of them, he has from God alone, because he is made in the image of God, and because God reveals himself to men. There is no such thing as "mere human logic," just as there is no such thing as "mere human arithmetic" or "mere human truth." Man is logical because he is the image of God – he has the capacity to think, to reason, as God thinks and reasons. John says that the divine *Logos* lights the mind of every man; Peter and Jude describe beasts as "without logic": *aloga*.[31] They are not the image of God.

29. *Romans* 3:10-12.
30. *Romans* 8:7.
31. See 2 *Peter* 2:12 and *Jude* 10.

"Postmodernism," which is merely a trendy name for the ancient idea of epistemological relativism – the idea of the Greek sophist Protagoras that "man is the measure of all things" – is also the view of those who assert epistemological relativism in their theology. Postmodernism in the churches – even many of the professedly Reformed churches – takes many forms:

Men cannot know God's truth, but only an analogy of God's truth.

Man, being finite, cannot understand the infinite.

God cannot be understood.

God is "Wholly Other."

Logic is created and is not the way God thinks.

There is an "infinite qualitative difference between man and God."

God's knowledge and man's knowledge do not coincide at any single point.

Truth is not propositional but personal.

God and the medium of conceptuality are mutually exclusive.

To *think* God is not to think *God*.

Life is deeper than logic.

Such pious platitudes are relativistic, agnostic, and Antichristian. They explicitly deny the central and fundamental idea of propositional revelation – "You shall know the truth." Christ did not say, "You shall know an analogy of the truth"; nor, "You shall encounter truth"; nor, "You shall know something approximating truth"; nor, "You shall know probable truth." The pious platitudes of the religious irrationalists implicitly deny the doctrines of the omnipotence of God and of man as the image of God; and they make nonsense of all of Christianity, for they make it all unknowable. It is this rejection of the ontological and epistemological status of logic, this pious theological agnosticism, that lies at the root of the lack of discernment, the lack of judgment, and the worldliness of today's churches.

The Creative Logos

God is a rational being, the architecture of whose mind is logic. How the *Logos* functions in creating the universe is made clear in *Genesis* 1: He speaks; he distinguishes and judges; he separates; and he names.

"In the beginning was the Word," and the Word, naturally, speaks: The statement "God said" appears nine times in *Genesis* 1 alone. In the act of speaking God reveals his rationality: The laws of speech are the laws of logic. The rules of grammar are derivative from the principles of logic. For a word – any word, human or divine – to mean something (and every word of God means something, for God does not talk nonsense), that word must also not-mean something else. When God says, "Let there be light," *light* does not mean *dark*; or *bees*, or *matter*; *let* does not mean *do not let, write,* or *rent*; *be* does not mean *buy, destroy,* or *eat. Bereshith,* the Hebrew word translated "in the beginning," does not mean in A.D. 2000 or even one second after the beginning. This is the logical law of contradiction: Not both A and not-A. If sounds and written symbols do not obey this fundamental rule of logic, they are mere noises in the air or mere scribbling on the paper; they are not words; they are not speech. God can and does speak because, as John tells us, God is Logic.

Second, the *Logos* distinguishes and judges: The statement "God saw" appears seven times in *Genesis* 1 alone. Of course, God's seeing has nothing to do with physical vision. God has no rods and cones, no retinas, no optic nerves or eyeballs. "Saw" is a figure of speech for "understood." We use the same metaphor in English when we exclaim, "Oh! I see." In the act of distinguishing, God reveals not only his rationality, but also the rationality of the creation, which is implied by John's statement that "All things were made through him [the *Logos*], and without him nothing was made that was made." The laws of logic are not merely the laws of God's own thinking and God's own speech, but of the entire creation as well. All creation is rational because the Word of God who created it is rational. Life is not deeper than logic, as the poets and romantics tell us; Logic is deeper than, and created, life. Those are pagan views that teach, as the German Romantic Goethe did, "in the beginning was the deed";[32] or as Democritus did, "in the beginning was matter and motion"; or as contemporary scientists do, "in the beginning was the Big Bang." It is those pagan views that make logic, not the designer and creator of the universe, but an effect, an evolutionary byproduct of blind, purposeless, and unintelligent events. It is the pagan view that makes the universe – and man in it – irrational. Those movements within the churches for the past two thousand years that have gloried in uttering gibberish, deceptively calling their gibberish "tongues," that is lan-

---

32. This is the "translation" of *John* 1 that Goethe offered in *Faust.*

guages, are merely imitating the gibberish uttered by pagan savages, who in their hatred for God and logic attempted to suppress the truth of God in them, by attempting to deny and destroy the human capacity for rational thought and speech, by asserting that gibberish is speech.

While all creation cannot and does not imitate God in thinking and speaking, all creation does obey the laws of logic. A dog is a dog, not a cat or a car. A thing is itself. This is the logical law of identity: A is A. It is first the name of God: "I Am that I Am." Those theologians and philosophers who assert that logic is an effect of creation (their counterparts, the evolutionists, make logic an effect of evolution; both agree that logic is an effect, not a cause), make God illogical. Logic is not an effect; Logic is the creator, John tells us, of the universe. Because the universe was created by the *Logos*, animals and plants reproduce after their own kinds. In distinguishing, the *Logos* reveals that the creation is not an amorphous, undefined, ineffable lump – indeed, *Genesis* 1 is the account of God transforming the formless void into a *cosmos*, an ordered universe.[33] The *cosmos* is the creation of the *Logos*. Logic is not an effect of the *cosmos*. In judging, the *Logos* reveals that one thing differs from another – that "good" differs from "bad," and that "very good" differs from "good." It is not the original formless void that God pronounced good, but the creation that had distinctions and separations made by the *Logos*. From this we ought to learn, *inter alia*, that there are several forms of unity, and not all of them are good. These acts of rational discrimination, in which one thing is distinguished from another, in which "good" is distinguished from "bad," and "very good" from "good," are acts of the *Logos*. These acts of distinguishing are acts of evaluation and judgment. They are acts of discernment.

The Bible is filled with such pairs of opposites. Here are just a few:
Light/darkness
Day/night
Seas/dry land
Good/evil
True/false
Right/wrong

33. The political philosopher Leo Strauss wrote: "Creation is the making of separated things, of things or groups of things that are separated from each other, which are distinguished from each other, which are distinguishable, which are discernible" ("On the Interpretation of Genesis," *L'Homme*, 1981, 10).

Obedience/disobedience
Christ/Belial
Righteousness/lawlessness
Life/death
Heaven/Hell
Election/reprobation
Blessing/cursing
Narrow way/broad way
Godly wisdom/ worldly wisdom
God's righteousness/self-righteousness
Grace/merit
Belief/works.

These opposites cannot be synthesized; they cannot be integrated; they are forever "either-or," not "both-and." There is no continuum; there are dichotomies; there are antitheses.

Third, the *Logos* in *Genesis* 1 separates: The statements, "God divided," "let it divide," "to divide," "God gathered," "be gathered," occur six times in *Genesis* 1 alone. God divides the light from the darkness; he divides the waters under the firmament from the waters above the firmament; he gathers the waters under the firmament together, thus dividing the seas from the dry land; he divides the day from the night. By separating one thing from another, God displays his rationality as well as the rationality of the creation. It is only such divisions that give form, structure, and unity to the creation; and each division that God makes, makes a more intricate structure, a more complex unity, possible. Separating the seas from the dry land makes possible the creation of sea creatures, plants, and land animals. Without these separations and divisions, there could be no structure in creation, and no plan, no cooperation of parts, no function. All would be a formless, meaningless mass. In creating, God is making the world conform to the patterns in his mind, as *Hebrews* says.

Finally, the *Logos* in *Genesis* 1 names: The statements "God called" and "God named" appear five times in *Genesis* 1, and God names all the creatures he makes – grass, herbs, seeds, trees, days, years. In giving names, God is not only revealing his rationality and the rationality of the creation – the fact that concepts and propositions can be used to refer accurately to particulars (an idea that some professing Christian philosophers deny) – God is also revealing his dominion over all things, including man, whom he names. Divine dominion is, first of all, intellectual mastery, for it is by the Word that the universe is created and by the Word that each part named. At other places in Scripture, God names individual men: Abram becomes *Abraham*; Sarai becomes *Sarah*; Jacob becomes *Israel*; Elizabeth's son becomes *John*; Mary's son becomes *Jesus*.

When we come to chapters 2 and 3 of *Genesis*, it is man, the image of God, who performs the functions that God performed in *Genesis* 1. Adam is commanded to speak and to understand, to distinguish between obedience and disobedience, to judge between good and evil, to name the animals, and to separate his children into families. Adam names his wife *Eve*. Adam and all men, as rational creatures, are commanded to exercise judgment. We are commanded to distinguish good from evil, to discriminate one thing from another, to discern what is true and what is false; to make judgments about all things. We are commanded to act as rational creatures, to use the gift of rationality that God has given us.

Judgment

Because we are creatures with the gift of rationality, made in the image of the rational God, the *Logos*, refusing to judge is impossible. All declarative statements – the cat is black, abortion is murder, chocolate is poison – are judgments. All our knowledge consists of such judgments. This is the sense in which Paul uses the term in *1 Corinthians* 1:10, where he writes:

> Now I plead with you, brethren, by the name of our Lord Jesus Christ, that you all speak the same thing, and that there be no divisions among you, but that you be perfectly joined together in the same mind and in the same judgment.

The word *judgment* is used in Scripture many times with this meaning:

> I will praise you with uprightness of heart when I learn your righteous judgments.[34]
> With my lips I have declared all the judgments of your mouth.[35]
> The judgments of the Lord are true and righteous altogether.[36]

34. *Psalm* 119:7.
35. *Psalm* 119:13.
36. *Psalm* 19:9.

Oh the depth of the riches both of the wisdom and knowledge of God! How unsearchable are his judgments and his ways past finding out![37]

The verb *to judge* has three meanings, one more fundamental than the others. The more fundamental meaning is *to distinguish*; the first derivative meaning is *to evaluate* according to a standard; and the second derivative meaning is *to condemn* or *to acquit*. The attack on judging must be seen, first and most importantly, as an attack on the faculty that understands, that distinguishes – an attack on the image of God in man. It is an attack on the rational faculty, and implicitly an attack on God, who is Truth himself. The Holy Spirit, writing through Paul, says that all Christians ought to be perfectly joined together "in the same mind and in the same judgment." They are to agree on the same propositions, to have the same beliefs, to hold the same faith, to believe the same doctrine. The Christian faith – sometimes called Christian doctrine or Christian theology – is a collection of judgments, a system of propositions such as "Jesus Christ is both God and man"; "Christ died according to the Scriptures and rose again after three days according to the Scriptures." Those are some of the judgments that all Christians are to believe. It is their agreement in these judgments that creates, or better, is, the unity of the church. Paul repeatedly exhorts us to be "likeminded," to "not be conformed to this world, but [to] be transformed by the renewing of your mind," to "be of the same mind toward one another," to "stand fast in one spirit, with one mind striving together for the faith of the Gospel." There is no command in Scripture to have one organization or one institution, but to have one mind, the mind of Christ. Christians are to be unified in their doctrine, in their judgments.

Moral judgments, which are condemned by many today, must be understood as a species of the genus "judgment." Some theologians, pathetically following the lead of the world, have attempted to separate "moral judgments" from "cognitive judgments," as if morality were not a matter of knowledge, but a matter of feeling, desire, or emotion. When we make a judgment, for instance, that "murder is sinful," we are stating a truth. It is as intellectual an act as solving a quadratic equation. When we make a judgment, "Joseph Stalin was a murderer," we are

---

37. *Romans* 11:33.

stating a truth. Moral judgments are a form of judgment, and as such they are either true or false. If moral judgments are made correctly, that is, according to the principles of God's Word, including a rigorous application of the laws of logic, then they are true judgments. Because we are rational creatures, we do not have the ability to avoid making judgments. Because we are rational creatures, we do not have the ability to avoid making moral judgments. The question is not whether we will make judgments or not, but whether the judgments we make will be righteous judgments or not. Rationality is the ability to judge. To be rational is to make judgments, including moral judgments. Therefore, to refuse to make moral judgments is impossible, for even those who misquote Christ's words, "Judge not," judge that those who make moral judgments are wrong. All moral judgments are judgments; that is, they are matters of true and false, right and wrong.

Because we are rational beings made in the image of God, we cannot avoid making moral judgments. Moral agnosticism, which says we cannot know what is right and wrong, what is true and false in matters of ethics and morality, is as self-contradictory and Antichristian as theological agnosticism. The Greek root of *agnostic* is *gnosis*, knowledge, and the word literally means "without knowledge." The Latin equivalent of *agnostic* is *ignoramus*. Agnosticism is not a position; it is a confession of ignorance; and ignorant people, particularly those who are proud of their ignorance, are not to be learned from; they need to be taught. Unfortunately agnostics – some of whom are arrogant, ignorant people – control both the churches and the schools. As we have seen, ignorance of the truth, in their view, is commendable, for it shows we are humble, finite creatures. When moral agnostics teach that one must never judge others or their actions, they are attacking knowledge and truth; when they teach that distinguishing good from evil is evil, they are making a moral judgment. It is impossible to avoid making intellectual and moral judgments; the only question is whether such judgments will be made correctly or not.

Judging ideas, men, and their actions is an extremely serious matter. Here is Christ's statement about judging that is so often misquoted by religious moral agnostics:

> Judge not, that you be not judged, for with what judgment you judge, you will be judged, and with the same measure you use, it will be measured back to you. And why do you look at the speck in your brother's

eye, but do not consider the plank in your own eye? Or how can you say to your brother, "Let me remove the speck out of your eye"; and look, a plank is in your own eye? Hypocrite! First remove the plank from your own eye, and then you will clearly see to remove the speck out of your brother's eye.

Do not give what is holy to the dogs, nor cast your pearls before swine, lest they trample them under their feet, and turn and tear you in pieces.[38]

It will be well worth our while to analyze Christ's statement, for Christ does not endorse moral agnosticism; he does not command us not to judge *simpliciter*; and his statement clearly shows both how we are to make moral judgments and the purpose for making them.

The first thing to note is that Christ concludes this statement by commanding us not to give what is holy to the dogs – expecting us to judge what is holy and what is not, and who are dogs and who are not. He repeats the idea: Do not cast your pearls before swine; and he expects us to judge which things are pearls and which are not, and who are swine and who are not. All this requires judgment, and moral judgment is an intellectual act. One cannot obey Christ's injunctions here without making moral judgments. The moral agnostic would have us believe that there are no dogs and there are no swine – "I'm OK; you're OK"; "There's no such thing as a bad boy" – and there are no pearls, nor anything that is holy. The moral agnostic cannot obey Christ.

Now Christ not only expects Christians to make moral judgments; he tells us how to make them: "Do not judge according to appearance, but judge with righteous judgment."[39] The sin of Adam and Eve in the Garden was to judge according to appearance; their sin was not the fact that they judged; nor was it the fact that they used their own human faculty of judgment in deciding whether to obey or disobey God. As rational beings, we all must constantly use our own judgments; that is included in the idea of rationality.[40] The sin of Adam and Eve was not in judging, but in using the wrong standard to make their judgment. Rather than judging by the standard of God's propositional revelation, they choose to judge by the evidence of their senses, "according to appearance":

38. *Matthew* 7:1-6.
39. *John* 7:24.
40. The Roman Church-State rants and rails against private judgment; what it really fears is rationality.

So when the woman saw that the tree was good for food, that it was pleasant to the eyes, and a tree desirable to make one wise, she took of its fruit and ate. She also gave to her husband with her, and he ate.[41]

The sin of Adam and Eve was not their use of private judgment, as some totalitarian theologians have suggested, but their abandonment of propositional revelation as the only standard by which to make all judgments. Adam and Eve did not believe the Word of God, and their unbelief separated them and all their children born by natural generation from God.[42] Judging by appearance was also the sin of the Jews in *John 7*, when Christ commanded them to "judge righteous judgment," not according to appearance. Making moral judgments is a serious affair. We must use the Word of God as our only standard in making such judgments, and we must labor to understand that Word, praying that God will give us wisdom in applying the principles of his Word to specific men, ideas, and events.

Unlike the first Adam, the second and last Adam, according to Isaiah, will not judge according to appearance:

> There shall come forth a rod from the stem of Jesse, and a branch shall grow out of his roots. The Spirit of the Lord shall rest upon him, the Spirit of wisdom and understanding, the Spirit of counsel and might, the Spirit of knowledge and of the fear of the Lord. His delight is in the fear of the Lord, and he shall not judge by the sight of his eyes, nor decide by the hearing of his ears, but with righteousness he shall judge the poor, and decide with equity for the meek of the Earth.[43]

Notice that in all these passages it is not judging *per se* that is condemned, but judging according to the wrong standard. That is also how we should understand Paul's words in *Romans 14*:

> Who are you to judge another's servant? To his own master he stands or falls.... But why do you judge your brother? Or why do you show contempt for your brother? For we shall all stand before the judgment seat of Christ.... So then each of us shall give account of himself to God. Therefore let us not judge one another any more, but rather resolve this, not to put a stumbling block or a cause to fall in our brother's way.

41. *Genesis* 3:6.
42. This, by the way, is why belief alone unites us to Christ.
43. *Isaiah* 11:1-4.

In this passage Paul is speaking of "doubtful things" – things about which brothers may differ. When there is no clear statement of Scripture, or no clear inference from Scripture, by which to judge, we must indeed not judge; we must recuse ourselves, for in those cases we would be making our own opinions our standard of judgment. It is that sort of judging that Paul condemns in this passage; he does not condemn judging according to the Word of God. Paul commands Christians – such as the Christians at Corinth – to judge church members for their scandals. It is not judging, but incorrect judging that Paul condemns. The misinterpretation of Paul's words has caused the virtual disappearance of church discipline.

James' warning against unlawful judging in the fourth chapter of his letter is the same:

> Do not speak evil of one another, brethren. He who speaks evil of a brother and judges his brother, speaks evil of the law and judges the law. But if you judge the law you are not a doer of the law but a judge. There is one Lawgiver, who is able to save and to destroy. Who are you to judge another?

James has in mind the judge who establishes his own opinion as his standard of judgment. By adopting a standard of judgment other than the Word of God, this sort of person judges the law itself. But James reminds us that there is only one Lawgiver, and no mere man (or group of men) has the competence to establish his own opinions as law.

Many commands are given to us to forsake our own imaginations and our own ideas, and instead to think God's thoughts, revealed to us in Scripture alone, and to bring all our thoughts into captivity to Christ. But nowhere in Scripture is there a command to forsake logic, to abandon the mind, or to spurn the gift of rationality.[44] In fact, in order to bring all our thoughts into captivity to Christ, we must become not less and less rational, but more and more rational, for Christ is the *Logos, the logic and wisdom of God.* Scripture in hundreds of passages praises knowledge, wisdom, and understanding, and urges – commands – all men to seek them ardently. The book of *Proverbs* and *Psalm* 119 show that clearly. The central concern of Scripture is epistemological: How can we know

---

44. The command in *Proverbs* 3:5 to "trust in the Lord with all your heart and lean not on your own understanding" is not a command to become irrational, but to accept truth as a gift from God, rather than relying on one's own observations and opinions.

God? But those who think that God (or the universe) is illogical or irrational think that men ought to be so as well. Such ideas are not only Antichristian, they are self-stultifying: No one can applaud the virtue of irrationality without using the very laws of logic he despises. To speak – even to think – the misologist must use the law of contradiction. He cannot win the war against logic and rationality; he cannot even declare it. As soon as he formulates a thought, he has lost the war, and the *Logos* has won. That is why the fellow who says silently in his heart, let alone out loud, that there is no God, is a fool: He must use the Logic that lights every man even to think that there is no Light.

Now this is a very important matter. The lack of discernment in today's churches, the reluctance to make distinctions, the antipathy to rendering moral judgments – all of this means that proper distinctions are not being made and righteous judgments are not being rendered. *It does not mean that distinctions and judgments are not being made at all.* Insofar as anyone thinks at all, he must make distinctions and render judgments. Just as the irrationalist is fatally ignorant of the fact that he must use rationality to propound irrationalism, so the moral agnostic – the man who is opposed to making judgments – is fatally ignorant of the fact that he must make moral judgments in order to state his position. The judgment the moral agnostic unwittingly makes is this: "Judging others is wrong." But the moral agnostic does not stop with that judgment; he eagerly adds another: "Those who judge others are wrong." And in these two moral judgments we can see clearly the self-stultifying, self-contradictory nature of the notion that one ought not to make moral judgments. If those who judge others are wrong, as the moral agnostic asserts, then moral agnostics are wrong, for they judge those who make judgments. That is why the Bible neither condemns nor commends those who make no judgments – for there are no such people – but instead condemns those who make false judgments, who call good, evil, and evil, good:

> Woe to those who call evil good, and good evil, who put darkness for light, and light for darkness, who put bitter for sweet, and sweet for bitter. Woe to those who are wise in their own eyes, and prudent in their own sight.[45]

45. *Isaiah* 5:20-21.

By refusing to distinguish good from evil, right from wrong, true from false – that is, by attempting to abandon logic and rationality – a person merely succeeds in making evil judgments. He calls good, evil, and evil, good. It is the man who makes perverse judgments that the Bible condemns. Ironically, the most censorious men are those who condemn anyone who makes a moral judgment.

Scripture repeatedly commands Christians to "test," to "try," to "judge," and to "prove" all things. For example, in 1 *Thessalonians* 5:21, Paul commands us to "test all things; hold fast what is good." Isaiah commands us in these words:

> And when they say to you, "Seek those who are mediums and wizards, who whisper and mutter," should not a people seek their God? Should they seek the dead on behalf of the living? To the Law and to the Testimony! If they do not speak according to this Word, it is because there is no light in them.[46]

John tells us, "Beloved, do not believe every spirit, but test the spirits, whether they are of God; because many false prophets have gone out into the world."[47] And in his *Gospel*, "Do not judge according to appearance, but judge with righteous judgment."[48] In *Proverbs* we are commanded: "Open you mouth, judge righteously, and plead the cause of the poor and needy."[49] Paul, giving instructions for church meetings, says, "Let two or three prophets speak, and let the others judge."[50] Scripture commands us to be skeptical of everything except the written Word of God, and to judge all things by that Word. The Bereans were commended for testing even an apostle's preaching by the written Word.

In all this, Christians are exercising their rationality. In his letters, Paul repeatedly makes moral judgments. For example, in *Romans* 1 Paul writes: "professing themselves to be wise, they became fools." In 1 *Corinthians* 5 he writes, "And you are puffed up." In verses 11 through 13 he gives further instructions:

> But now I have written to you not to keep company with anyone named a brother, who is a fornicator, or covetous, or an idolater, or a reviler, or a drunkard, or an extortioner – not even to eat with such a

46. *Isaiah* 8:19-20.
47. *1 John* 4:1.
48. *John* 7:24.
49. *Proverbs* 31:9.
50. *1 Corinthians* 14:29.

person. For what have I to do with judging those who are outside? Do you not judge those who are inside? But those who are outside God judges. Therefore, "put away from yourselves that wicked person."

Here Paul's command to judge – to distinguish and evaluate certain persons in the church as fornicators, covetous, idolaters, revilers, drunkards, and extortioners – is followed by a command to separate from such men. It is a command to exercise church discipline. But the moral agnostics in the churches, because they are opposed to rendering moral judgments, are opposed to discipline and to separation as well, a point to which we shall return shortly.

Paul continues his discussion of judging:

> Do you not know that the saints will judge the world? And if the world will be judged by you, are you unworthy to judge the smallest matters [now]? Do you not know that we shall judge angels? How much more [then], things that pertain to this life?[51]

Here Paul expects Christians to judge; he demands that they judge. Paul himself calls men "foolish,"[52] "dogs,"[53] and "evil workers,"[54] as well as "saints."

But what is the motivation of the moral agnostic who urges us not to judge others and who condemns us for doing so? It is not benevolence or tolerance. One motivation is quite clear: The moral agnostic wants to escape judgment himself. He thinks that if no one is permitted to judge others, then he himself will escape judgment. Paul explains in *Romans* 1 that sinful men suppress the truth (which they know innately) in unrighteousness, for they do not like to retain God in their knowledge, because the wrath of God is revealed from Heaven against all ungodliness and unrighteousness. Men, "knowing the righteous judgment of God, that they who practice such things are worthy of death, not only do the same but also approve of those who practice them." The proscription of moral judgment is a futile attempt by sinners to escape judgment. Paul says that moral agnosticism is futile, whether one condemns or approves the sinful practices of others:

51. *1 Corinthians* 6:2-3.
52. *Galatians* 3:1.
53. *Philippians* 3:2.
54. *Philippians* 3:2.

> Therefore, you are inexcusable, O man, whoever you are who judge, for in whatever you judge another you condemn yourself; for you who judge, practice the same things. But we know that the judgment of God is according to truth against those who practice such things. And do you think this, O man, you who judge those practicing such things, and doing the same, that you will escape the judgment of God?[55]

One motivation that lies behind moral agnosticism is the desire to escape the judgment of God for one's own beloved sins. Its purpose is to allow the unrepentant sinner to escape uncondemned and unpunished. When a moral agnostic argues that we must not judge between good and evil, his advice, when followed, benefits only the evil and harms only the good. To refuse to judge righteous judgment is not neutrality or tolerance; it is an attack on the good and a sanction to the evil.

There is a related but slightly different motivation as well: Whenever a person makes a judgment, that judgment discloses his own values, his own standard, and opens him to judgment by others. If a man would not judge, the moral agnostic believes, then he would not reveal his own values, and he would escape the judgment of others in this way as well. The Bible's statement of the principle that in judging one discloses one's own values is found in the *Gospel of Matthew*:

> A good man out of the good treasure of his heart brings forth good things, and an evil man out of the evil treasure brings forth evil things. But I say to you that for every idle word men may speak, they will give account of it in the Day of Judgment. For by your words you will be justified and by your words you will be condemned.[56]

Once again Scripture teaches that the moral agnostic cannot escape judgment by refusing to judge, for he cannot refuse to judge. Rational creatures must judge, and we will all be held accountable for the judgments we make, the words we speak, the thoughts we think. The moral agnostic condemns moral judgment because he hopes to avoid responsibility for his own sins. He does not want to be held accountable by God or by anyone else. He desires to be a law unto himself, a completely irresponsible, a completely lawless, being.

---

55. *Romans* 2:1-3.
56. *Matthew* 12:35-37.

Black, White, and Gray

One of the most common forms moral agnosticism takes is illustrated in the statements: "There are no blacks and whites, only shades of gray"; and "There are two sides to every issue." Moral grayness, we are told, applies to everything: persons, ideas, actions, events, principles, movements, and organizations – to every ethical issue. "There are no blacks and whites" is the ethical counterpart to the epistemological falsehood: "All truth is relative." The ethical statement, in fact, logically depends on the epistemological statement, for moral judgments are a species of the genus judgment. Both statements are hopelessly contradictory. The statement, "All truth is relative" is proclaimed as an absolute truth, true for all people at all times, thus contradicting itself. If it is true that "all truth is relative," then it must be false that "all truth is relative." On the other hand, if truth is absolute, then it is false that truth is relative. In either case, the statement "all truth is relative" is false. Similarly, if it is true that "there are no blacks and whites," then there can be no gray, for gray is nothing but a mixture of black and white. Those who parrot, "There are no blacks and whites" intend the statement to be understood as white, that is, as a correct statement, without any mixture of error or evil. If the statement itself were gray, then it would be partly wrong, and nobody would be required to believe it. Those who assert, "There are no blacks and whites, only shades of gray" do not intend the statement to be an evil statement or a false statement, or a mixture of right and wrong. They want us to take it as white, even while they deny the existence of white. Moving from metaphor to literal language, if there were no goods or evils, no rights or wrongs, nothing true and nothing false, there could literally be nothing at all – including the principle that "there are only shades of gray."

Before one can evaluate or judge (as we have already seen, judgment cannot be avoided; the only question is whether one will judge correctly or not) a person, an idea, or an action as "gray," that is, before one can legitimately conclude that it is a mixture of good and evil, one must have distinguished good and evil in the person, event, or action, and judged them to be so. But if one has already distinguished – discerned – the good and evil, there is no excuse for maintaining that there is only gray. That is as black a lie as one can imagine. Nor is there any excuse for choosing some evil along with the good – nor for denigrating the good by calling it gray, nor for condoning the evil by calling it gray.

If by saying, "There are two sides to every issue," one simply means that it is wise and prudent to hear all arguments before deciding a matter, that is quite true – but it is not what the users of the platitude usually mean. They mean that there are two sides to every issue, and both sides are right. There is no right or wrong; there are only "right" and "right." There is no true or false; there are "true" and "true." We ought not to judge anything good or bad, right or wrong, for there are two sides to every issue.

Moral agnostics, like their theological cousins, do not state their agnosticism tentatively; they do not humbly say, "I do not know," for that would be a candid admission of their ignorance. But it is not their ignorance that they are admitting. They are actually boasting of their omniscience. They are asserting that no one can know. They say (translating their words into their actual meaning), usually quite loudly and boldly, "No one knows, and no one can know." They are very dogmatic about their agnosticism. And they are very arrogant in accusing anyone who claims to know of arrogance and pride. Usually they interrupt by exclaiming, "You don't think in terms of black and white, do you?" And the victim of such an attack, if he is unsure of his own epistemological and moral principles, is frequently intimidated by the confident tone of the agnostics who are stating an objection so obvious, a principle so absolute – there are no blacks and whites – that only a fool would not know it. Rather than be intimidated, what the victim must do is translate the agnostic objection into literal language: "You don't think in terms of right and wrong, do you?" or "You don't think in terms of good and evil, do you?" or "You don't attempt to distinguish between good and evil, do you?" or "You don't dare to judge something good and something evil, do you?" or "You don't try to tell right from wrong, do you?" When the metaphorical objection is translated into clear, literal English, one can begin to understand how evil the idea of moral grayness – of moral agnosticism – is. It is not good men who use such ideas; it is those who cherish their sins and want to avoid their just condemnation. Moral agnosticism, like theological agnosticism, is not an independent position; it is disguised evil – unbelief masquerading as ignorance; sin masquerading as neutrality.[57]

57. The sin of the church at Laodicea seems to be of this sort: "And to the angel of the church of the Laodiceans write, 'These things says the Amen, the Faithful and true

The Sin of Silence

Since the Christian is commanded to test all things by the written Word of God, he must be prepared to do so. The fear of men, the doctrine of moral agnosticism, and the popular condemnation of judging must not induce him either to agree with the world or to remain silent. Whenever the Christian is confronted with any situation in which the Bible and its doctrines are attacked, he must speak up. How he speaks up will depend on the situation, but that he speaks up is his duty.

> Behold, I send you out as sheep in the midst of wolves. Therefore be wise as serpents and harmless as doves.... Whatever I tell you in the dark, speak in the light; and what you hear in the ear, preach on the housetops. And do not fear those who kill the body but cannot kill the soul. But rather fear him who is able to destroy both soul and body in Hell.... Therefore, whoever confesses me before men, him I will also confess before my Father in Heaven. But whoever denies me before men, him I will also deny before my Father who is in Heaven.[58]

In some situations, a simple objection, such as "That is not what the Bible says," or "That statement is not true," may suffice. Other situations will call for more extended responses, rebuttals, and refutations. But in all situations in which the faith is under attack in the presence of a Christian, the Christian must speak up. He cannot adopt a neutral position by remaining silent, expressing neither agreement nor disagreement, for to be silent when falsehood is taught and truth denied is not neutral – it is an alliance with falsehood and treason to truth. In such a situation, silence speaks loudly: "There is no difference between right and wrong; there is no difference between true and false." To fail to object when error is taught and truth denied is to condone error by treating error and truth as if they were the same. If Christ is under attack and a Christian keeps silent, he has not maintained his neutrality; he has denied Christ.

It is imperative not only to know, to discern, and to judge, but to speak as well; it is required not only to apply Biblical principles to all

---

Witness, the Beginning of the creation of God: "I know your works, that you are neither cold nor hot. I could wish you were cold or hot. So then because you are lukewarm, and neither cold nor hot, I will spew you out of my mouth" ' " (*Revelation* 3:14-16).

58. *Matthew* 10.

thoughts and actions, but also to express that judgment when Biblical ideas are being denied. And it is required not only to express our judgment, but to defend it as well. Luther wrote:

> Confessing Christ is the most important activity in Christian life; on it one must venture life and limb, goods and honor. The evil spirit does not so severely assail him who believes aright and lives a good life in seclusion and by himself. But to come out into the open and spread, confess, preach, and extol one's faith for the good of others also, that he cannot bear.[59]

In defending the faith a Christian must keep his focus on what is most important: doctrine and ideas. He must not allow himself to be distracted by personal attacks, either on himself or by him on others. Again Luther:

> I am not concerned with life but with doctrines. Evil life does no great harm except to itself. But evil teaching is the most pernicious thing on Earth, for it leads hosts of souls to Hell. Whether you are good or bad does not concern me, but I will attack your poisonous and lying teaching which contradicts God's Word, and with God's help I will oppose it vigorously.[60]

There is another reason why we must always discern and always speak: Keeping the lines sharply drawn between good and evil, white and black, truth and error, is vital, not only to the well-being of those who might hear us, but to our own well-being. If we fail to judge righteously, as natural-born sinners we slip back into the moral twilight in which all principles and actions are gray. "Solid food," the writer of *Hebrews* says, "belongs to those who are full of age, those who by reason of use have their senses exercised to discern both good and evil."[61] If we do not exercise our senses (that is, our rational faculties, not our nose and ears), then we will not be able to discern, to tell right from wrong, true from false, good from evil. By failing to judge righteously and to speak up, we not only deny Christ, we harm our neighbors and ourselves. By not exercising our rational faculties properly, we regress or fail to develop, to grow as Christians. We lose the ability to tell right from wrong.

59. *What Luther Says*, Plass, editor, 597.
60. *What Luther Says*, 1224.
61. *Hebrews* 5:14.

The Sin of Collaboration

As we have seen, one of the functions – the basic function – of ratio-nal minds is to know. Knowing requires one to distinguish and to sepa-rate things that are different. The laws of logic involve the discernment of A and not-A, where A represents any word and any thing. The law of identity, A is A – a thing is itself – requires that we identify a thing. The law of contradiction, not both A and not-A – a word, in order to mean something, must also not mean something – requires that we distin-guish between something and all other things. The law of the excluded middle, either A or not-A, eliminates "continuum thinking" and the morass of moral grayness. Logic is indispensable in knowing and dis-cerning.

All that we have said above about the lack of discernment, the dearth of knowledge, the condemnation of judging, and the moral grayness that are prevalent in church and society applies to very prac-tical problems: Which church should one attend and join, if any? Which charities should one support financially, if any? Which denomi-nation should a congregation join, if any? Whom should we cooper-ate with in evangelism, if anyone? In political action? Many people do not think about these questions at all. The notion that there are some Biblical, theoretical principles that help us make practical deci-sions is foreign to many people. They have adopted the pragmatic view: Do whatever works.

If it were true that there are no blacks and whites but only shades of gray, it really would not matter which church one joins. Sometimes those who are concerned about the doctrines their church is teaching are told, "There are no perfect churches, so you might as well stay here." Do you, dear reader, discern the "only shades of gray" dogma in this statement? It is as if one were to argue, "There are no perfect women (or men), so it doesn't matter whom you marry." Or "There are no pure foods, so it doesn't matter what you eat." The "no perfect churches" argument is a variation of the "only shades of gray" argument. It is designed and intended to prevent one from examining the doctrine of the church, to thwart discerning truth and error in the church's teach-ing. Many people buy that argument. People who would not think of acting so foolishly in hiring employees or eating food check their minds at the church door, along with their coats. We have been told for centuries that Christianity is a matter of heart, so many Christians do not use their heads.[62] We applaud foolishness and imprecision in religion as piety or true spirituality or theological profundity. It is nothing of the sort. Foolishness in religion is a sin greater than foolishness in business or family. The stakes are much higher in matters of theology than they are in matters of finance.

Now there are principles, Biblical principles, that answer the questions I raised above about cooperation and collaboration with others. The first principle is this: Do not collaborate with anyone, Christian or non-Christian, for a non-Christian purpose. What do I mean by "non-Christian purpose"? It is an aim or goal that is not explicitly Christian and stated as such by the organization. Providing relief to hurricane victims, for example, is a non-Christian purpose, if that relief is not given in the name of Jesus Christ, together with the Gospel. Christ did not say that it is the giving of a cup of cold water that is good, but the giving of a cup of cold water "in Christ's name."[63] The purpose must be explicitly Christian. Now as citizens we all must cooperate with governors; we are told even to go the extra mile if they make us go one mile.[64] Slaves are instructed to obey their masters.[65] Those are instances in which cooperation is compulsory. In the family, Christian spouses are not to leave non-Christian spouses, but to cooperate with them. The marriage contract is legally and morally binding. Children are to obey, that is, cooperate with, non-Christian parents. Employees are to obey their employers. But even in these situations cooperation extends only to purposes that are not sinful. If a governor, a spouse, an employer, or a parent commands one to do something sinful, one is to disobey – to refuse to cooperate.

In the economy, Christians are free to cooperate with anyone when they engage in trade; they are not required to trade only with other Christians. That is one of the implications of Paul's teaching about meat offered to idols. But cooperation and collaboration are two different things. In a market economy one cooperates daily with people one does

---

62. Of course, the Bible makes no distinction between the heart and the head. See "The Church Effeminate."

63. "For whoever gives you a cup of water to drink in my name, because you belong to Christ, assuredly, I say to you, he will by no means lose his reward" (*Mark* 9:41).

64. *Matthew* 5:41.

65. *Colossians* 3:2.

not even know. Cooperation does not require even acquaintance with others, let alone unity of purpose. The buyer intends to purchase the wares for his own good. The seller intends to sell the wares – for *his* own good. God has so structured the market economy that producers and consumers, unknown to each other, cooperate with each other, though their purposes might be as different as night and day. There is in the economy a division of labor such that each person benefits, though he may not even know most of the persons with whom he cooperates.

Collaboration, unlike cooperation, requires unity of purpose. One may collaborate with persons unknown, say in a large political or social organization, but only for a common purpose. The principle governing collaboration is: Do not collaborate in any purpose, project, or organization that has a non-Christian purpose. We are not to be unequally yoked together with unbelievers.

> Do not be unequally yoked together with unbelievers. For what fellowship has righteousness with lawlessness? And what communion has light with darkness? And what accord has Christ with Belial? Or what part has a believer with an unbeliever? And what agreement has the temple of God with idols? For you are the temple of the living God.... Therefore, Come out from among them and be separate, says the Lord.[66]

Notice that the reason that Christians are not to be unequally yoked with unbelievers is fundamental: Light and darkness, righteousness and lawlessness, Christ and Belial have nothing in common. The reason there is to be no collaboration is not to avoid personality conflicts, but because the systems of thought to which believers and unbelievers belong are antithetical to each other. Now both believers and unbelievers, because they are sometimes logically inconsistent with their most fundamental beliefs, may have some views in common; both may believe in God, for example. James tells us that the devils believe in one God, and they tremble. But Christians are not free to join organizations established for ecumenical purposes simply because the devils are monotheists, although some recent religious writers have advocated an alliance of all monotheists to oppose atheists.[67] It is not some incidental overlapping of views that is important, but the different thought systems to

---

66. *2 Corinthians* 6:14-17.
67. Two of these writers are John Paul II and Peter Kreeft.

which believers and unbelievers belong that require them to remain separate.

The principle of non-collaboration implies that Christians should not attend or join a church that does not believe and teach the whole counsel of God. Christians should not contribute either their time or their resources to any church or to any other organization that does not believe the Bible, especially the doctrine of justification by faith alone – and that includes charitable, educational, political, and social organizations. All that Christians do is to be done in the name of Christ. To offer their time or money for any purpose which is not explicitly Christian is a violation of the principle of non-collaboration.

The laws of the Old Testament tried to teach the idea of separation – non-collaboration – to the Hebrews in many ways: no hybrid seeds, no mixed fabric, no intermarriage with unbelievers, etc. The lessons frequently failed. Many Hebrews failed to see the theological reason for non-collaboration. Three thousand years later, many Gentiles still fail to understand the theological reason. God is separate from the creation; he is transcendent. God is holy, and he desires a holy – that is, a separated – people. In the Old Testament separation was political and physical; in the New it is neither: It is intellectual and institutional. Abram was called out from Ur of the Chaldees, away from his family, so that God could form a new people. God separates:

> You shall therefore distinguish between clean beast and unclean, between unclean birds and clean, and you shall not make yourselves abominable by beast or by bird, or by any kind of living thing that creeps on the ground, which I have separated from you as unclean. And you shall be holy to me, for I the Lord am holy, and have separated you from the peoples, that you should be mine.[68]

Christ today separates people, not geographically, but spiritually, one by one:

> Do you suppose that I came to give peace on Earth? I tell you, not at all, but rather division. For from now on five in one house will be divided: three against two and two against three. Father will be divided against son and son against father, mother against daughter and daughter against mother, mother-in-law against her daughter-in-law and daughter-in-law against her mother-in-law.[69]

68. *Leviticus* 20:25-26.
69. *Luke* 12:49-53.

It is not just Abram's family that is divided; in the New Covenant it is all families. Christ is building his church, and to build it, he must first separate the stones from the world and then assemble them into one building. The church cannot be assembled, it cannot be unified, unless many separations occur first.

At the Last Judgment, there will be a final separation:

> When the Son of Man comes in his glory, and all the holy angels with him, then he will sit on the throne of his glory. All the nations will be gathered before him, and he will separate them from one another, as a shepherd divides his sheep from the goats. And he will set the sheep on his right hand, but the goats on his left.[70]

There is another, related reason for the principle of non-collaboration: When Christians collaborate with non-Christians in non-Christian organizations, Christianity is diluted or denied, and the false opinions of non-Christians prevail. Continued collaboration between believers and unbelievers in non-Christian organizations always leads to a further denial of truth. If the common cause in which both Christians and non-Christians are engaged is not explicitly Christian, Christians are working to further a non-Christian cause. Those persons who hold views consonant with the purpose of the organization have the moral high ground and a psychological edge; it is the Christians who are out of step with the purpose of the organization. The Christian has nothing to gain by working for a non-Christian purpose; the non-Christian has much to gain by exploiting the time, resources, and reputations of Christians for non-Christian purposes. The Christians lend an aura of respectability and rationality to the non-Christian enterprise, and non-Christian ideas and purposes benefit. Worst of all, the ideas of Christianity themselves become muddled, distorted, and perverted by such collaboration. Only unbelief can benefit from such a situation.

The cause of Christ has nothing to gain by vagueness, distortion, indirection, or irrationality. Because Christianity is the only rational religion – the only religion that teaches the truth – it has nothing to hide. Unbelief needs obscurity; it requires vagueness; it demands grayness; it has everything to hide, because it is evil. The chief work of the devil is deception, and he must hide his purposes under the appearance

---

70. *Matthew* 25:31-33.

of genuine belief. It would do the devil no good candidly to admit that deception is his goal; people must be deceived, first of all, about deception. Paul prayed earnestly that his readers and listeners would not be deceived, and that he would teach the Gospel boldly and clearly. Boldness means no pulling of punches, no fear of men, but an intransigent allegiance to the truth of Scripture. We are also instructed to teach the whole counsel of God, not merely those parts that certain non-Christian organizations might tolerate for awhile. Christianity is a *system* of thought, a logical concatenation of premises and conclusions, not a collection of unrelated, disjointed, discrete facts. The Word of God is also to be handled accurately, rightly divided, and taught clearly. None of these requirements can be met by Christians who are collaborating with non-Christians for a non-Christian purpose. Still less can such collaborators present the Word of God clearly in such situations, for they have already compromised their positions by joining non-Christian organizations. Unbelief, irrationality, has everything to gain by obscuring the truth of Christianity, and by confusing Christians. When Christians collaborate with non-Christians for non-Christian purposes, it is only unbelief that can gain. That is why Christians should always strive to make their doctrines crystal clear, to define their terms, to explain the ideas in the Bible as unambiguously and as precisely as possible. Unbelief has everything to gain by the lack of definition, by confusion; Christianity has everything to lose.

There is, of course, another possibility: Suppose that Christians collaborate with non-Christians in Christian organizations for Christian purposes. Many churches are in this situation: The churches are confessionally committed to Christianity, but there are non-Christians among the Christians in the church. Does the principle of non-collaboration imply that Christians should leave such churches? Not at all. In such situations, where the purpose for which the organization exists is an explicitly Christian purpose, then Christians may not only attend and join, but support and lead. In such situations, since the purpose of the organization is explicitly Christian, it is the Christians who have the moral high ground and the psychological edge; it is the non-Christian who is out of step. In such situations, there ought to be no toning down of Christianity, no compromise with the world, and if anyone leaves, it ought to be the non-Christians. That is where church discipline comes in. Of course, if we have been misled by a misunderstanding of Christ's commands about judging, there will be no church discipline. Martyn Lloyd-Jones made some pertinent remarks on the subject:

> Discipline, to the Protestant fathers, was as much a mark of the church as the preaching of the Word and the administration of the sacraments. But we know very little about discipline [today]. It is the result of this flabby, sentimental notion that you must not judge, and which asks, "Who are you to express judgment?" But the Scripture exhorts us to do so.
>
> The question of judging applies also in the matter of doctrine. Here is this question of false prophets to which our Lord calls attention. We are supposed to detect them and to avoid them. But that is impossible without a knowledge of doctrine, and the exercise of that knowledge in judgment.... In writing to Titus he [Paul] says, "A man that is an heretic after the first and second admonition reject." How do you know whether a man is a heretic or not if your view is that, as long as a man calls himself a Christian, he must be a Christian, and you do not care what he believes? Then go on to John's epistles, John "the apostle of love." ...If a man come to you and does not hold the true doctrine, you must not receive him into your house, you must not bid him Godspeed and provide him with money to preach his false doctrine. But today it would be said that that is a lack of charity, that it is being over-punctilious and censorious. The modern idea, however, is a direct contradiction of the Scripture teaching with regard to judging.[71]

Unfortunately many American Christians have ignored the Bible's instructions on discipline and non-collaboration with non-Christians. One example of this disobedience to Scripture is the Neo-evangelical movement. It repudiated the separationist – derogatorily called isolationist – theology of the fundamentalists and began to collaborate with those who were not Reformed, were not Protestant, and were not Evangelical. The evangelist Billy Graham became one of the leading Neo-evangelicals of the century, inviting theological liberals, Roman Catholics, and churchmen of all sorts to cooperate with him in his "crusades." The results of this sin of collaboration surround us: *Christianity Today*, the leading publication of the Neo-evangelicals, is a hotbed of feminism, heterodoxy, Arminianism, Pentecostalism, and liberalism; there is widespread apostasy in the Evangelical churches; feminism and socialism reign in Neo-evangelical educational institutions; the Neo-

71. *Studies in the Sermon on the Mount*, 1960, II, 164-165.

evangelicals are promoting union with Rome through Evangelicals and Catholics Together; the Roman Church-State is by far the largest in America, and growing rapidly; and Evangelical pastors are defecting to Rome in significant numbers. The Neo-evangelicals thought they were smarter than God and could infiltrate liberal institutions in order to win them over. By collaboration with non-Christians, they lost their Christianity.

Conclusion

Today's churches and churchgoers lack discernment because they lack knowledge and wisdom. They lack knowledge and wisdom for two reasons: There is a famine of the preaching of God's Word in America, and churchmen and churchgoers despise logic, clarity, definition, and precision. There is a famine of preaching and hearing God's Word and a disdain for logic because God apparently intends to destroy us, either temporally or eternally or both. The only way in which to improve the situation is by repenting of the sin of unbelief, the sin of irrationalism, the sin of moral agnosticism, the sin of silence, and the sin of collaboration; by begging the forgiveness of God; and by asking God, who is truth himself, for wisdom:

> If any of you lacks wisdom, let him ask of God, who gives to all liberally and without reproach, and it will be given him. But let him ask in faith, with no doubting, for he who doubts is like a wave of the sea driven and tossed by the wind. For let not that man suppose that he will receive anything from the Lord; he is a double-minded man, unstable in all his ways.

Index

Scripture Index

The Crisis of Our Time

Historians have christened the thirteenth century the Age of Faith and termed the eighteenth century the Age of Reason. The twentieth century has been called many things: the Atomic Age, the Age of Inflation, the Age of the Tyrant, the Age of Aquarius; but it deserves one name more than the others: the Age of Irrationalism. Contemporary secular intellectuals are anti-intellectual. Contemporary philosophers are anti-philosophy. Contemporary theologians are anti-theology.

In past centuries, secular philosophers have generally believed that knowledge is possible to man. Consequently they expended a great deal of thought and effort trying to justify knowledge. In the twentieth century, however, the optimism of the secular philosophers all but disappeared. They despaired of knowledge.

Like their secular counterparts, the great theologians and doctors of the church taught that knowledge is possible to man. Yet the theologians of the twentieth century also repudiated that belief. They too despaired of knowledge. This radical skepticism has penetrated our entire culture, from television to music to literature. *The Christian at the beginning of the twenty-first century is confronted with an overwhelming cultural consensus – sometimes stated explicitly but most often implicitly: Man does not and cannot know anything truly.*

What does this have to do with Christianity? Simply this: If man can know nothing truly, man can truly know nothing. We cannot know that the Bible is the Word of God, that Christ died for his people, or that Christ is alive today at the right hand of the Father. Unless knowledge is possible, Christianity is nonsensical, for it claims to be knowledge. What is at stake at the beginning of the twenty-first century is not simply a single doctrine, such as the virgin birth, or the existence of Hell, as important as those doctrines may be, but the whole of Christianity itself. If knowledge is not possible to man, it is worse than silly to argue points of doctrine – it is insane.

The irrationalism of the present age is so thoroughgoing and pervasive that even the Remnant – the segment of the professing church that remains faithful – has accepted much of it, frequently without even being aware of what it is accepting. In some circles this irrationalism has become synonymous with piety and humility, and those who oppose it are denounced as rationalists, as though to be logical were a sin. Our contemporary anti-theologians make a contradiction and call it a Mystery. The faithful ask for truth and are given Paradox. If any balk at swallowing the absurdities of the anti-theologians, they are frequently marked as heretics or schismatics who seek to act independently of God.

There is no greater threat facing the true church of Christ at this moment than the irrationalism that now controls our entire culture. Totalitarianism, guilty of tens of millions of murders – including those of millions of Christians – is to be feared, but not nearly so much as the idea that we do not and cannot know the truth. Hedonism, the popular philosophy of America, is not to be feared so much as the belief that logic – that "mere human logic," to use the religious irrationalists' own phrase – is futile. The attacks on truth, on revelation, on the intellect, on words, and on logic are renewed daily. But note well: The misologists – the haters of logic – use logic to demonstrate the futility of using logic. The anti-intellectuals construct intricate intellectual arguments to prove the insufficiency of the intellect. Those who deny the competence of words to express thought use words in their denials. The proponents of poetry and myth do not inform us of their theories by using poetry and myth – they use literal prose, whose competence they deny. The anti-theologians use the revealed Word of God to show that there can be no revealed Word of God – or that if there could, it would remain impenetrable darkness and Mystery to our finite minds.

Nonsense Has Come

Is it any wonder that the world is grasping at straws – the straws of experientialism, mysticism, and drugs? After all, if people are told that the Bible contains insoluble mysteries, then is not a flight into mysticism to be expected? On what grounds can it be condemned? Certainly not on logical grounds or Biblical grounds, if logic is futile and the Bible unintelligible. Moreover, if it cannot be condemned on logical or Biblical grounds, it cannot be condemned at all. If people are going to have a religion of the mysterious, they will not adopt Christianity: They will have a genuine mystery religion. The popularity of Eastern mysticism, of drugs, and of religious experience is the logical consequence of the irrationalism of the twentieth century. There can and will be no Christian reformation – and no reconstruction of society – unless and until the irrationalism of the age is totally repudiated by Christians.

The Church Defenseless

Yet how shall they do it? The spokesmen for Christianity have been fatally infected with irrationalism. The seminaries, which annually train thousands of men to teach millions of Christians, are the finishing schools of irrationalism, completing the job begun by the government schools and colleges. Some of the pulpits of the most conservative churches (we are not speaking of the apostate churches) are occupied by graduates of the anti-theological schools. These products of modern anti-theological education, when asked to give a reason for the hope that is in them, can generally respond with only the intellectual analogue of a shrug – a mumble about Mystery. They have not grasped – and therefore cannot teach those for whom they are responsible – the first truth: "And you shall know the truth." Many, in fact, explicitly deny it, saying that, at best, we possess only "pointers" to the truth, or something "similar" to the truth, a mere analogy. Is the impotence of the Christian church a puzzle? Is the fascination with pentecostalism, faith healing, Eastern Orthodoxy, and Roman Catholicism – all sensate and anti-intellectual religions – among members of Christian churches an enigma? Not when one understands the studied nonsense that is purveyed in the name of God in the colleges and seminaries.

The Trinity Foundation

The creators of The Trinity Foundation firmly believe that theology is too important to be left to the licensed theologians – the graduates of the schools of theology. They have created The Trinity Foundation for the express purpose of teaching the faithful all that the Scriptures contain – not warmed over, baptized, secular philosophies. Each member of the board of directors of The Trinity Foundation has signed this oath: "I believe that the Bible alone and the Bible in its entirety is the Word of God and, therefore, inerrant in the autographs. I believe that the system of truth presented in the Bible is best summarized in the *Westminster Confession of Faith*. So help me God."

The ministry of The Trinity Foundation is the presentation of the system of truth taught in Scripture as clearly and as completely as possible. We do not regard obscurity as a virtue, nor confusion as a sign of spirituality. Confusion, like all error, is sin, and teaching that confusion is all that Christians can hope for is doubly sin.

The presentation of the truth of Scripture necessarily involves the rejection of error. The Foundation has exposed and will continue to expose the irrationalism of the twentieth century, whether its current spokesman be an existentialist philosopher or a professed Reformed theologian. We oppose anti-intellectualism, whether it be espoused by a neo-orthodox theologian or a fundamentalist evangelist. We reject misology, whether it be on the lips of a neo-evangelical or those of a Roman Catholic charismatic. To each error we bring the brilliant light of Scripture, proving all things, and holding fast to that which is true.

The Primacy of Theory

The ministry of The Trinity Foundation is not a "practical" ministry. If you are a pastor, we will not enlighten you on how to organize an ecumenical prayer meeting in your community or how to double church attendance in a year. If you are a homemaker, you will have to read elsewhere to find out how to become a total woman. If you are a businessman, we will not tell you how to develop a social conscience. The professing church is drowning in such "practical" advice.

The Trinity Foundation is unapologetically theoretical in its outlook, believing that theory without practice is dead, and that practice without theory is blind. The trouble with the professing church is not primarily in its practice, but in its theory. Churchgoers do not know, and many do not even care to know, the doctrines of Scripture. Doctrine is intellectual, and churchgoers are generally anti-intellectual. Doctrine is ivory tower philosophy, and they scorn ivory towers. The ivory tower, however, is the control tower of a civilization. It is a fundamental, theoretical mistake of the practical men to think that they can be merely practical, for practice is always the practice of some theory. The relationship between theory and practice is the relationship between cause and effect. If a person believes correct theory, his practice will tend to be correct. The practice of contemporary Christians is immoral because it is the practice of false theories. It is a major theoretical mistake of the practical men to think that they can ignore the ivory towers of the philosophers and theologians as irrelevant to their lives. Every action that the "practical" men take is governed by the thinking that has occurred in some ivory tower – whether that tower be the British Museum; the Academy; a home in Basel, Switzerland; or a tent in Israel.

In Understanding Be Men

It is the first duty of the Christian to understand correct theory – correct doctrine – and thereby implement correct practice. This order – first theory, then practice – is both logical and Biblical. It is, for example, exhibited in Paul's *Epistle to the Romans,* in which he spends the first eleven chapters expounding theory and the last five discussing practice. The contemporary teachers of Christians have not only reversed the order, they have inverted the Pauline emphasis on theory and practice. The virtually complete failure of the teachers of the professing church to instruct the faithful in correct doctrine is the cause of the misconduct and spiritual and cultural impotence of Christians. The church's lack of power is the result of its lack of truth. The *Gospel* is the power of God, not religious experience or personal relationship. The church has no power because it has abandoned the Gospel, the good news, for a religion of experientialism. Twentieth-first-century American Christians are children carried about by every wind of doctrine, not knowing what they believe, or even if they believe anything for certain.

The chief purpose of The Trinity Foundation is to counteract the irrationalism of the age and to expose the errors of the teachers of the church. Our emphasis – on the Bible as the sole source of truth, on the primacy of truth, on the supreme importance of correct doctrine, and on the necessity for systematic and logical thinking – is almost unique in Christendom. To the extent that the church survives – and she will survive and flourish – it will be because of her increasing acceptance of these basic ideas and their logical implications.

We believe that The Trinity Foundation is filling a vacuum in Christendom. We are saying that Christianity is intellectually defensible – that, in fact, it is the only intellectually defensible system of thought. We are saying that God has made the wisdom of this world – whether that wisdom be called science, religion, philosophy, or common sense – foolishness. We are appealing to all Christians who have not conceded defeat in the intellectual battle with the world to join us in our efforts to raise a standard to which all men of sound mind can repair.

The love of truth, of God's Word, has all but disappeared in our time. We are committed to and pray for a great instauration. But though we may not see this reformation in our lifetimes, we believe it is our duty to present the whole counsel of God because Christ has commanded it. The results of our teaching are in God's hands, not ours. Whatever those results, his Word is never taught in vain, but always accomplishes the result that he intended it to accomplish. Professor Gordon H. Clark has stated our view well:

> There have been times in the history of God's people, for example, in the days of Jeremiah, when refreshing grace and widespread revival were not to be expected: The time was one of chastisement. If this twentieth century is of a similar nature, individual Christians here and there can find comfort and strength in a study of God's Word. But if God has decreed happier days for us and if we may expect a world-shaking and genuine spiritual awakening, then it is the author's belief that a zeal for souls, however necessary, is not the sufficient condition. Have there not been devout saints in every age, numerous enough to carry on a revival? Twelve such persons are plenty. What distinguishes the arid ages from the period of the Reformation, when nations were moved as they had not been since Paul preached in Ephesus, Corinth, and Rome, is the latter's fullness of knowledge of God's Word. To echo an early Reformation thought, when the ploughman and the garage attendant know the Bible as well as the theologian does, and know it better than some contemporary theologians, then the desired awakening shall have already occurred.

In addition to publishing books, the Foundation publishes a monthly newsletter, *The Trinity Review.* Subscriptions to *The Review* are free to U.S. addresses; please write to the address on the order form to become a subscriber. If you would like further information or would like to join us in our work, please let us know.

The Trinity Foundation is a non-profit foundation, tax exempt under section 501 (c)(3) of the Internal Revenue Code of 1954. You can help us disseminate the Word of God through your tax-deductible contributions to the Foundation.

JOHN W. ROBBINS

Intellectual Ammunition

THE TRINITY Foundation is committed to the reformation of philosophy and theology along Biblical lines. We regard God's command to bring all our thoughts into conformity with Christ very seriously, and the books listed below are designed to accomplish that goal. They are written with two subordinate purposes: (1) to demolish all secular claims to knowledge; and (2) to build a system of truth based upon the Bible alone.

PHILOSOPHY

Ancient Philosophy
Gordon H. Clark   Trade paperback $24.95
    This book covers the thousand years from the Pre-Socratics to Plotinus. It represents some of the early work of Dr. Clark – the work that made his academic reputation. It is an excellent college text.

Behaviorism and Christianity
Gordon H. Clark   Trade paperback $5.95
    Behaviorism is a critique of both secular and religious behaviorists. It includes chapters on John Watson, Edgar S. Singer, Jr., Gilbert Ryle, B. F. Skinner, and Donald MacKay. Clark's refutation of behaviorism and his argument for a Christian doctrine of man are unanswerable.

A Christian Philosophy of Education   Hardback $18.95
Gordon H. Clark   Trade paperback $12.95
    The first edition of this book was published in 1946. It sparked the contemporary interest in Christian schools. In the 1970s, Dr. Clark thoroughly revised and updated it, and it is needed now more than ever. Its chapters include: The Need for a World-View; The Chris-

tian World-View; The Alternative to Christian Theism; Neutrality; Ethics; The Christian Philosophy of Education; Academic Matters; and Kindergarten to University. Three appendices are included: The Relationship of Public Education to Christianity; A Protestant World-View; and Art and the Gospel.

A Christian View of Men and Things   Hardback $29.95
Gordon H. Clark   Trade paperback $14.95
   No other book achieves what *A Christian View* does: the presentation of Christianity as it applies to history, politics, ethics, science, religion, and epistemology. Dr. Clark's command of both worldly philosophy and Scripture is evident on every page, and the result is a breathtaking and invigorating challenge to the wisdom of this world.

Clark Speaks from the Grave
Gordon H. Clark   Trade paperback $3.95
   Dr. Clark chides some of his critics for their failure to defend Christianity competently. *Clark Speaks* is a stimulating and illuminating discussion of the errors of contemporary apologists.

Ecclesiastical Megalomania:
The Economic and Political Thought
of the Roman Catholic Church   Hardback $29.95
John W. Robbins   Trade paperback $19.95
   This detailed and thorough analysis and critique of the social teaching of the Roman Church-State is the only such book available by a Christian economist and political philosopher. The book's conclusions reveal the Roman Church-State to be an advocate of its own brand of global religious Fascism. *Ecclesiastical Megalomania* includes the complete text of the *Donation of Constantine* and Lorenzo Valla's exposé of the hoax.

Education, Christianity, and the State
J. Gresham Machen   Trade paperback $9.95
   Machen was one of the foremost educators, theologians, and defenders of Christianity in the twentieth century. The author of sev-

eral scholarly books, Machen saw clearly that if Christianity is to survive and flourish, a system of Christian schools must be established. This collection of essays and speeches captures his thoughts on education over nearly three decades.

Essays on Ethics and Politics
Gordon H. Clark   Trade paperback $10.95
Dr. Clark's essays, written over the course of five decades, are a major statement of Christian ethics.

Gordon H. Clark: Personal Recollections
John W. Robbins, editor   Trade paperback $6.95
Friends of Dr. Clark have written their recollections of the man. Contributors include family members, colleagues, students, and friends such as Harold Lindsell, Carl Henry, Ronald Nash, and Anna Marie Hager.

Historiography: Secular and Religious
Gordon H. Clark   Trade paperback $13.95
In this masterful work, Dr. Clark applies his philosophy to the writing of history, examining all the major schools of historiography.

An Introduction to Christian Philosophy
Gordon H. Clark   Trade paperback $8.95
In 1966 Dr. Clark delivered three lectures on philosophy at Wheaton College. In these lectures he criticizes secular philosophy and launches a philosophical revolution in the name of Christ.

Language and Theology
Gordon H. Clark   Trade paperback $9.95
There are two main currents in twentieth-century philosophy – language philosophy and existentialism. Both are hostile to Christianity. Dr. Clark disposes of language philosophy in this brilliant critique of Bertrand Russell, Ludwig Wittgenstein, Rudolf Carnap, A. J. Ayer, Langdon Gilkey, and many others.

Logic   Hardback $16.95
Gordon H. Clark   Trade paperback $10.95
  Written as a textbook for Christian schools, *Logic* is another unique
  book from Dr. Clark's pen. His presentation of the laws of thought,
  which must be followed if Scripture is to be understood correctly,
  and which are found in Scripture itself, is both clear and thorough.
  Logic is an indispensable book for the thinking Christian.

Logic Workbook
Elihu Carranza   Oversize paperback $11.95
  Designed to be used in conjunction with Dr. Clark's textbook *Logic*,
  this *Workbook* contains hundreds of exercises and test questions on
  perforated pages for ease of use by students.

Lord God of Truth, Concerning the Teacher
Gordon H. Clark and Aurelius Augustine   Trade paperback $7.95
  This essay by Dr. Clark summarizes many of the most telling arguments against empiricism and defends the Biblical teaching that we
  know God and truth immediately. The dialogue by Augustine is a
  refutation of empirical language philosophy.

The Philosophy of Science and Belief in God
Gordon H. Clark   Trade paperback $8.95
  In opposing the contemporary idolatry of science, Dr. Clark analyzes three major aspects of science: the problem of motion,
  Newtonian science, and modern theories of physics. His conclusion is that science, while it may be useful, is always false; and he
  demonstrates its falsity in numerous ways. Since science is always
  false, it can offer no alternative to the Bible and Christianity.

Religion, Reason and Revelation
Gordon H. Clark   Trade paperback $10.95
  One of Dr. Clark's apologetical masterpieces, *Religion, Reason and
  Revelation* has been praised for the clarity of its thought and language. It includes these chapters: Is Christianity a Religion? Faith
  and Reason; Inspiration and Language; Revelation and Morality;
  and God and Evil. It is must reading for all serious Christians.

The Scripturalism of Gordon H. Clark
W. Gary Crampton   Trade paperback $9.95
  Dr. Crampton has written an introduction to the philosophy of
  Gordon H. Clark that is helpful to both beginners and advanced
  students of theology. This book includes a bibliography of Dr. Clark's
  works.

Thales to Dewey: A History of Philosophy   Hardback $29.95
Gordon H. Clark   Trade paperback $21.95
  This is the best one-volume history of philosophy in English.

Three Types of Religious Philosophy
Gordon H. Clark   Trade paperback $6.95
  In this book on apologetics, Dr. Clark examines empiricism, rationalism, dogmatism, and contemporary irrationalism, which does
  not rise to the level of philosophy. He offers an answer to the question, "How can Christianity be defended before the world?"

William James and John Dewey
Gordon H. Clark   Trade paperback $8.95
  William James and John Dewey are two of the most influential
  philosophers America has produced. Their philosophies of instru-
  mentalism and pragmatism are hostile to Christianity, and Dr. Clark
  demolishes their arguments.

Without a Prayer: Ayn Rand and the Close of Her System
John W. Robbins   Hardback $27.95
  Ayn Rand has been a best-selling author since 1957. *Without a Prayer*
  discusses Objectivism's epistemology, theology, ethics, and politics
  in detail. Appendices include analyses of books by Leonard Peikoff
  and David Kelley, as well as several essays on Christianity and philosophy.

THEOLOGY

Against the World: The Trinity Review 1978-1988
John W. Robbins, editor   Oversize hardback $34.95
  This is a clothbound collection of the essays published in *The Trinity Review* from 1978 to 1988, 70 in all. It is a valuable source of information and arguments for explaining and defending Christianity.

The Atonement
Gordon H. Clark   Trade paperback $8.95
  In *The Atonement,* Dr. Clark discusses the covenants, the virgin birth and incarnation, federal headship and representation, the relationship between God's sovereignty and justice, and much more. He analyzes traditional views of the atonement and criticizes them in the light of Scripture alone.

The Biblical Doctrine of Man
Gordon H. Clark   Trade paperback $6.95
  Is man soul and body or soul, spirit, and body? What is the image of God? Is Adam's sin imputed to his children? Is evolution true? Are men totally depraved? What is the heart? These are some of the questions discussed and answered from Scripture in this book.

The Church Effeminate
John W. Robbins, editor   Hardback $29.95
  This is a collection of 39 essays by the best theologians of the church on the doctrine of the church: Martin Luther, John Calvin, Benjamin Warfield, Gordon Clark, J. C. Ryle, and many more. The essays cover the structure, function, and purpose of the church.

The Clark-Van Til Controversy
Herman Hoeksema   Trade paperback $7.95
  This collection of essays by the founder of the Protestant Reformed Church — essays written at the time of the Clark-Van Til controversy — is one of the best commentaries on those events in print.

Cornelius Van Til: The Man and The Myth
John W. Robbins   Trade paperback $2.45
The actual teachings of this eminent Philadelphia theologian have been obscured by the myths that surround him. This book penetrates those myths and criticizes Van Til's surprisingly unorthodox views of God and the Bible.

The Everlasting Righteousness
Horatius Bonar   Trade paperback $8.95
Originally published in 1874, the language of Bonar's masterpiece on justification by faith alone has been updated and Americanized for easy reading and clear understanding. This is one of the best books ever written on justification.

Faith and Saving Faith
Gordon H. Clark   Trade paperback $6.95
The views of the Roman Catholic Church, John Calvin, Thomas Manton, John Owen, Charles Hodge, and B. B. Warfield are discussed in this book. Is the object of faith a person or a proposition? Is faith more than belief? Is belief thinking with assent, as Augustine said? In a world chaotic with differing views of faith, Dr. Clark clearly explains the Biblical view of faith and saving faith.

God and Evil: The Problem Solved
Gordon H. Clark   Trade paperback $4.95
This volume is Chapter 5 of Religion, Reason and Revelation, in which Dr. Clark presents his solution to the problem of evil.

God's Hammer: The Bible and Its Critics
Gordon H. Clark   Trade paperback $10.95
The starting point of Christianity, the doctrine on which all other doctrines depend, is "The Bible alone, and the Bible in its entirety, is the Word of God written, and, therefore, inerrant in the autographs." Over the centuries the opponents of Christianity, with Satanic shrewdness, have concentrated their attacks on the truthfulness and completeness of the Bible. In the twentieth century the attack was not so much in the fields of history and archaeology as

in philosophy. Dr. Clark's brilliant defense of the complete truthfulness of the Bible is captured in this collection of eleven major essays.

The Holy Spirit

Gordon H. Clark   Trade paperback $8.95

This discussion of the third person of the Trinity is both concise and
exact. Dr. Clark includes chapters on the work of the Spirit,
sanctification, and Pentecostalism. This book is part of his multi-
volume systematic theology that began appearing in print in 1985.

The Incarnation

Gordon H. Clark   Trade paperback $8.95

Who is Christ? The attack on the doctrine of the incarnation in the
nineteenth and twentieth centuries has been vigorous, but the orthodox response has been lame. Dr. Clark reconstructs the doctrine
of the incarnation, building and improving upon the Chalcedonian
definition.

The Johannine Logos

Gordon H. Clark   Trade paperback $5.95

Dr. Clark analyzes the relationship between Christ, who is the truth,
and the Bible. He explains why John used the same word to refer to
both Christ and his teaching. Chapters deal with the Prologue to
John's Gospel; *Logos* and *Rheemata;* Truth; and Saving Faith.

Justification by Faith Alone

Charles Hodge   Trade paperback $10.95

Charles Hodge of Princeton Seminary was the best American theologian of the nineteenth century. Here, for the first time, are his two
major essays on justification in one volume. This book is essential
in defending the faith.

Karl Barth's Theological Method

Gordon H. Clark   Trade paperback $18.95

Karl Barth's Theological Method is perhaps the best critique of the
neo-orthodox theologian Karl Barth ever written. Dr. Clark dis-

cusses Barth's view of revelation, language, and Scripture, focusing on his method of writing theology, rather than presenting a comprehensive analysis of the details of Barth's theology.

Logical Criticisms of Textual Criticism

Gordon H. Clark   Trade paperback $3.25

Dr. Clark's acute logic enables him to demonstrate the inconsistencies, assumptions, and flights of fancy that characterize the science of New Testament criticism.

New Testament Greek for Beginners   Hardback $16.95

J. Gresham Machen   Trade paperback $10.95

Long a standard text, New Testament Greek for Beginners is extremely helpful in the study of the New Testament in the original Greek. It may profitably be used by high school, college, and seminary students, either in a classroom setting or in self-study. Machen was Professor of New Testament Literature and Exegesis at Princeton Theological Seminary and the founder of Westminster Theological Seminary and the Orthodox Presbyterian Church.

Predestination

Gordon H. Clark   Trade paperback $10.95

Dr. Clark thoroughly discusses one of the most controversial and pervasive doctrines of the Bible: that God is, quite literally, Almighty. Free will, the origin of evil, God's omniscience, creation, and the new birth are all presented within a Scriptural framework. The objections of those who do not believe in Almighty God are considered and refuted. This edition also contains the text of the booklet, Predestination in the Old Testament.

Sanctification

Gordon H. Clark   Trade paperback $8.95

In this book, which is part of Dr. Clark's multi-volume systematic theology, he discusses historical theories of sanctification, the sacraments, and the Biblical doctrine of sanctification.

Study Guide to the Westminster Confession
W. Gary Crampton   Oversize paperback $10.95
  This *Study Guide* may be used by individuals or classes. It contains a
  paragraph-by-paragraph summary of the *Westminster Confession*,
  and questions for the student to answer. Space for answers is provided. The *Guide* will be most beneficial when used in conjunction
  with Dr. Clark's *What Do Presbyterians Believe?*

The Trinity
Gordon H. Clark   Trade paperback $8.95
  Apart from the doctrine of Scripture, no teaching of the Bible is
  more fundamental than the doctrine of God. Dr. Clark's defense of
  the orthodox doctrine of the Trinity is a principal portion of his
  systematic theology. There are chapters on the Deity of Christ;
  Augustine; the Incomprehensibility of God; Bavinck and Van Til;
  and the Holy Spirit; among others.

What Calvin Says
W. Gary Crampton   Trade paperback $7.95
  This is a clear, readable, and thorough introduction to the theology
  of John Calvin.

What Do Presbyterians Believe?
Gordon H. Clark   Trade paperback $10.95
  This classic is the best commentary on the *Westminster Confession of
  Faith* that has ever been written.

CLARK'S COMMENTARIES
ON THE NEW TESTAMENT

Colossians	Trade paperback	$6.95
Ephesians	Trade paperback	$8.95
First Corinthians	Trade paperback	$10.95
First John	Trade paperback	$10.95
First and Second Thessalonians	Trade paperback	$5.95
New Heavens, New Earth		
(*First* and *Second Peter*)	Trade paperback	$10.95

The Pastoral Epistles	Hardback	$29.95
(*1* and *2 Timothy* and *Titus*)	Trade paperback	$14.95
Philippians	Trade paperback	$9.95

All of Clark's commentaries are expository, not technical, and are written for the Christian layman. His purpose is to explain the text clearly and accurately so that the Word of God will be thoroughly known by every Christian.

The Trinity Library

We will send you one copy of each of the 53 books listed above for $450 (retail value over $600), postpaid to any address in the U.S. You may also order the books you want individually on the order form on the next page. Because some of the books are in short supply, we must reserve the right to substitute others of equal or greater value in The Trinity Library. This special offer expires October 31, 2004.

Order Form

NAME _____

ADDRESS _____

_____

TELEPHONE AND E-MAIL _____

Please: ❑ add my name to the mailing list for *The Trinity Review*. I understand that there is no charge for *The Review* sent to a U. S. address.

❑ accept my tax deductible contribution of $ _____ .

❑ send me ___ copies of *The Church Effeminate*. I enclose as payment $ _____.

❑ send me the Trinity Library of 53 books. I enclose US $450 as full payment.

❑ send me the following books. I enclose full payment in the amount of $ _____ for them.

The Trinity Foundation
Post Office Box 68, Unicoi, Tennessee 37692
Website: www.trinityfoundation.org
Email: Jrob1517@aol.com
United States of America

Please add $5.00 for postage. For foreign orders, please enclose 20 percent of the total value of the books ordered for shipping and handling.